Deedee
June 2003.

LEGACY

THE WEST AND THE WORLD

Senior Author

Garfield Newman
Curriculum Consultant
York Region District School Board

Authors

Usha James
Teacher
Milliken Mills High School
York Region District School Board

Jennifer Watt
Instruction Leader
Social, Canadian, and World Studies
Toronto District School Board

Tom Cohen
Associate Professor
Department of History
York University
Toronto, Ontario

Michael Butler
Head of History
Northern Secondary School
Toronto, Ontario

Contributors

Gilbert Allardyce   *University of New Brunswick*
David Higgs   *University of Toronto*
Doug Lorimer   *Wilfrid Laurier University*
Sonia Riddoch   Queen's University

McGraw-Hill Ryerson Limited

Toronto Montréal Burr Ridge, IL Dubuque, IA, Madison, WI New York San Francisco St. Louis
Bangkok Bogotá Caracas Kuala Lumpur Lisbon London Madrid Mexico City Milan New Delhi
Santiago Seoul Singapore Sydney Taipei

McGraw-Hill
Ryerson Limited

A Subsidiary of The McGraw·Hill Companies

Legacy: The West and the World

ISBN: 0-07-091453-2

http://www.mcgrawhill.ca

1 2 3 4 5 6 7 8 9 10   TRI   10 9 8 7 6 5 4 3 2

Printed and bound in Canada

National Library of Canada Cataloguing in Publication

Main entry under title:

   Legacy : the west and the world / authors, Garfield Newman ... [et al.].

Includes bibliographical references and index.
ISBN 0-07-091453-2

   1. History, Modern. 2. Civilization, Modern. I. Newman, Garfield.

D209.L43 2002   909.08   C2002-901666-5

PUBLISHER: Patty Pappas
EDITORIAL DIRECTOR: Melanie Myers
PROJECT MANAGER: Joseph Gladstone
DEVELOPMENTAL EDITOR: Ellen Munro
SUPERVISING EDITOR: Cathy Deak
COPY EDITOR: Sandra Otto
PRODUCTION CO-ORDINATOR: Sandra Deak
PERMISSIONS EDITORS: Maria DeCambra, Krista Alexander
EDITORIAL ASSISTANTS: Erin Parton, Joanne Murray
INTERIOR/COVER DESIGN: Dave Murphy/ArtPlus Limited
ELECTRONIC PAGE MAKE-UP: Barb Neri/ArtPlus Limited
ILLUSTRATIONS/MAPS: Sandy Sled, Joelle Cottle, Nancy Charbonneau, Corey Slone/ArtPlus Limited
COVER IMAGE: Austrian Archives/CORBIS/MAGMA

COPIES OF THIS BOOK
MAY BE OBTAINED BY
CONTACTING:

McGraw-Hill Ryerson Ltd.

WEBSITE:
http://www.mcgrawhill.ca

E-MAIL:
orders@mcgrawhill.ca

TOLL FREE FAX:
1-800-463-5885

TOLL FREE CALLS:
1-800-565-5758

OR BY MAILING YOUR ORDER TO:
McGraw-Hill Ryerson
Order Department
300 Water Street, Whitby
Ontario, L1N 9B6

Please quote the ISBN and
title when placing your order

Reviewers

Miriam Bardswich
(retired) Head of History,
Lorne Park Secondary School
Peel District School Board

Dan Bowyer
History Teacher,
Turner F. Fenton
Secondary School
Peel District School Board

Evelyn Clarke
Head of History,
Lorne Park Secondary School
Peel District School Board

James Ellesworth
(retired) Program Coordinator –
Assessment and Accountability,
Grand Erie District School Board

Paul Harkison
Senior Tutor,
University of Toronto School

Peter Harley
Head of Social Sciences,
Glenview Secondary School
Waterloo District School Board

Donna McIntyre
History Teacher (former head),
Southwood Secondary School
Waterloo District School Board

David Neelin
History Teacher (on leave),
East York Collegiate Institute
Toronto, Ontario

George Sherwood
(retired) Head of History,
North Albion Collegiate
Toronto, Ontario

Dominic Talarico
Head of History,
Earl of March Secondary School
Ottawa Catholic District
School Board

Student Reviewers

Sally Couto
Father Michael Goetz
Secondary School
Dufferin-Peel Separate
School Board

Jennifer Martinez
Father Michael Goetz
Secondary School
Dufferin-Peel Separate
School Board

Donnah Topacio
Father Michael Goetz
Secondary School
Dufferin-Peel Separate
School Board

Advisory Board

Jennifer Borda
Appleby College
Oakville, Ontario

Colleen Chandler
Mother Teresa Catholic
Secondary School
Toronto Catholic District
School Board

Ilan Danjoux
Markham District High School
York Region District School Board

Bruce Fink
Educational Consultant,
Ottawa-Carleton District
School Board

Nigel Lee
Cameron Heights
Collegiate Institute
Waterloo Region District
School Board

Jack MacFadden
President, OHASSTA
Bradford, Ontario

Dr. Constance McLeese
Lisgar Collegiate Institute
Ottawa-Carleton District
School Board

Darcy Mintz
Cameron Heights
Collegiate Institute
Waterloo Region District
School Board

Rick Olma
White Oaks Secondary School
Halton District School Board

Rachel Powell
Dr. Norman Bethune
Collegiate Institute
Toronto District School Board

Mary Anne Sodonis
Westside Secondary School
Upper Grand District
School Board

Paul Sydor
West Elgin Secondary School
Thames Valley District
School Board

Jim Terry
Wallaceburg District
Secondary School
Lambton-Kent District
School Board

Acknowledgements

Geographers measure the impact of individuals on the environment using what they call the "Ecological Footprint". As historians, we consider the lasting impact of individuals and groups on a community, a society, and sometimes, the world. Each of us leaves a lasting legacy, which could be described as an historical watermark—a luminescence that continues to shine after our relatively short time on Earth. Often our historical watermark is most evident in our children and those with whom we shared much of our lives. In some cases, the body of work produced, the ideas brought forth, or the even the destruction wrought by an individual on society, defines a person's historical watermark. *Legacy: The West and the World* is a journey around the world and through five centuries of often turbulent times. Through its pages, you will come to sense the legacy of both famous and nameless individuals who have shaped, directed, and endured the challenges posed by an ever changing world.

Putting together an engaging history of the West and the World over the past half millennium required the collective talents of many diverse people. It began with the assembling of an author team that blended scholarship, passion, and a keen understanding of the young learner. I was privileged to work with the authors of *Legacy*, who provided superb manuscript around which to build an engaging text. Throughout the project, Patty Pappas supplied endless support and encouragement, while Joseph Gladstone guided the project with tremendous insight, grace, and professionalism. The entire editorial staff at McGraw-Hill Ryerson was a delight to work with. Ellen Munro's ability to weave together disparate styles and infuse the text with stunning visuals is without equal. Cathy Deak transformed the book from the idea to reality, by guiding the process from manuscript into production thus helping the team to realize its vision for *Legacy*. Maria DeCambra and Krista Alexander had the mammoth task of tracking down permissions for images and sources that spanned the world, no small feat when considering the tight deadlines.

Children are my greatest source of inspiration; those I interact with on a daily basis, and those I kiss good night. In a year marred by terrorism and war, it is my children, Mathew, Geoffrey, and Nikita who constantly remind me of the beauty, and boundless potential of humanity.

The person I admire most in this world is my wife, Laura Gini-Newman. She is the personification of all that is good, beautiful, kind, and compassionate. Not only is she a superb educator, but she is also a loving mother, and she is my best friend. Thank you Laura for your limitless support and for the many ways you continually enrich my life.

Garfield Newman

Thank you Garfield for your friendship, your mentoring, your encouragement and your faith in me.

I am eternally grateful to my husband, Greg James, who is always supportive, understanding and forever willing to be a sounding board for ideas. His insights are always helpful and his comments always appreciated.

This project has seen the birth of my baby boy who has been an unimaginable source of joy to us both. Born a Canadian and with an ethnic heritage that is part Gujarati, part Sindhi, part British, and part mixture of Sicilian, French-Canadian, German and aboriginal Canadian (we think Cree), he is truly a product of "the West and the World". Thank you darling Nikhil for helping me keep things in perspective.

Usha James

To Barry for his love and support. To Matt and Sean for being wonderful and special boys whom I love very much. And to Bailey for not eating the manuscript or chewing the computer cord.

Jennifer Watt

To my wife, Rainie, whom I love very much. Thank you for all your support. And to my parents, Joan and Larry, and to Charlotte and Duncan. Finally, a special thank you to Patty for allowing me this opportunity .

Michael Butler

Students, may your eyes be sharp, your thoughts lively, your hearts warm, and your conclusions utterly your own.

Tom Cohen

Contents

A Tour of Your Textbook   x

Prologue: Making History in the West   2

Seeing the Future Through the Past   4

Hot Topic: Cultures of the Non-Western World   13

Hot Topic: Economic Structures   14

Hot Topic: Citizenship and Human Rights   15

Hot Topic: Interaction Among Communities   16

Hot Topic: Science and Technology   17

Hot Topic: Women at Work   18

Hot Topic: Can a Minority Co-Exist
   With a Majority?   19

Hot Topic: Does Western Mean Better?   21

Our Subject: What was Europe?   22

**UNIT ONE THE WORLD
   REINVENTED 1480-1715**   24

Unit Overview   25

**Chapter One *Renaissance
   and Reformation 1480-1600***   26

Time Line: Renaissance and Reformation   28

Early Modern European Society and Culture   29

Communities   34

A Revolution in the Military   39

Intellectual Life in the Renaissance   41

Renaissance Art   42

The Sense of History   43

Focus on Genius:

   Renaissance Man: Leonardo da Vinci   *44*

The High Renaissance in Rome   46

Intellectual Developments   47

The Reformation   50

Primary Sources: The Fourth Estate:

   Luther's 95 Theses   *52*

The Counter-Reformation   55

Primary Sources:

   The Act in Restraint of Appeals, 1533   *60*

Eastern Europe and the Ottoman Empire   64

Chapter Review   66

**Chapter Two *The Age of Absolutism
   1600-1715***   **68**

Time Line: The Age of Absolutism   70

Revolutions in Thought   71

Scientific Method and the Birth of
   Modern Philosophy   73

The Age of Absolutism   77

Louis XIV, The Sun King   78

Absolutism in Eastern Europe   83

England in the Seventeenth Century   86

Life in Seventeenth-Century England   88

Western Art in the Seventeenth Century   90

Music as History:

   King Arthur, by Henry Purcell   97

Chapter Review   100

**Chapter Three *Contact and
   Conflict 1450-1715***   **102**

Time Line: Contact and Conflict   104

History Reconsidered   105

The World in 1450   105

Fate, Fortune, and Faith   107

Exploring the Americas   113

West Meets East   115

Human Servitude   116

Primary Sources: Historiography:

   *Sir Walter Raleigh,
      The History of the World, 1614*   *117*

Trading Companies   119

Cross-Cultural Exchange   120

Chapter Review   126

Unit Review   128

UNIT TWO AN AGE OF
ENLIGHTENMENT
AND REVOLUTION   130
Unit Overview   **131**

Chapter Four *The Enlightenment*
1700-1789   **132**
Time Line: The Enlightenment   134
European Society in the Eighteenth Century   135
The Beginning of the Industrial Revolution   136
The Enlightenment   139
Enlightenment Ideas   141
Enlightened Despotism   151
Art in the Early Eighteenth Century   152
Music in the Eighteenth Century   156
Literature in the Eighteenth Century   157
Music as History:
   Music for the Royal Fireworks,
   by George Frideric Handel   *158*
Focus on Genius:
   Wolfgang Amadeus Mozart (1756–1791)   *160*
Primary Sources: The Fourth Estate:
   Jonathan Swift, Power to the Pamphlets *163*
Chapter Review   166

Chapter Five *Revolution to Restoration*
1789-1815   **168**
Time Line: Revolution to Restoration   170
Before the Revolution   171
Social History   174
On the Eve of the Revolution   179
The Year of Liberty in France   180
Primary Sources:
   The Declaration of the Rights of Man
   and of the Citizen   *182*
Political Organization: From
   Monarchy to Republic   187
Women and the Revolution   191

The Age of Napoléon   195
Redefining the State: Napoleonic Government   196
The End of Napoléon: A Search for Order   199
Social History: Living the Revolution   201
Two Revolutionary Artists: David
   and Beethoven   203
Chapter Review   206

Chapter Six *The World in the*
Eighteenth Century   **208**
Time Line: The World in the
   Eighteenth Century   210
The West and the World   211
Major Arenas of European Conflict in the
   Eighteenth Century   213
Africa in the Eighteenth Century   218
Islam and the West   224
India and the West   225
China and the West   228
Europeans on Non-Europeans   231
Changing Tastes   233
Primary Sources: Historiography:
   History of the Reign of Charles V
   by William Robertson   *234*
Chapter Review   236
Unit Review   238

UNIT THREE MODERN EUROPE   240
Unit Overview   **241**

Chapter Seven *The Birth of Modern*
Industrial Society: Europe 1815-1850   **242**
Time Line: The Birth of Modern
   Industrial Society   244
The Industrial Revolution   245
Evolution of the Family   253
The Role of Government in Society   256
Maintaining Political Order   259

Developments in Political Thought 266
Primary Sources: *The Communist Manifesto* 268
1848: The Year of Revolutions in Europe 270
Counteroffensive: June 1848 271
Nineteenth-Century Western Art 272
Music as History:
   Tchaikovsky's 1812 Overture 278
Literature of the Nineteenth Century 280
Chapter Review 286

Chapter Eight *Nations in Upheaval:*
   Europe 1850-1914 **288**
Time Line: Nations in Upheaval 290
The Rise of the Nation-State 291
France: The Role of Key Individuals 292
Italy: The Role of Key Individuals 294
Modern Germany: The Role of Key Individuals 295
The Franco-Prussian War (1870-1871) 297
Czarist Russia: Reform and Repression 299
Developments in Political Thought:
   The Advent of Democracy 300
Bismarck's Germany 1871-1890 302
Britain 1867-1894: Disraeli and Gladstone 303
Society in Modern Europe 305
Social Organization in the Nineteenth Century 306
The Evolving World of Women 308
Primary Sources: The Fourth Estate:
   Sarah Josepha Hale 310
Developments in Political Thought: Socialism 312
Developments in Scientific Thought 315
Philosophy and Society 315
Focus on Genius:
   Charles Darwin 316
Family Life in the Nineteenth Century 318
Western Art of the Nineteenth Century 319
Literature in the Nineteenth Century 325
Chapter Review 328

Chapter Nine *Imperialism,*
   Colonialism, and Resistance
   in the Nineteenth Century **330**
Time Line: Imperialism, Colonialism, 332
   and Resistance
Imperialism in the Nineteenth Century 333
Change and Continuity: Causes
   of Imperialism 337
Unco-operative Colonies 338
The Legacy of Imperialism 341
Agents of Human Rights Advancement 350
The Legacy of Emancipation 353
The Struggle for an Independent Latin America 356
War and Resistance to Colonization 358
Colonial Nationalist Movements 359
Primary Sources: Historiography:
   Leopold von Ranke on Objective History 365
Chapter Review 366
Unit Review 368

UNIT FOUR THE WORLD AT WAR
   1914-1945 370
Unit Overview **371**

Chapter Ten *The War to End War,* **372**
   World War I 1914-1918
Time Line: The War to End War 374
World War I 375
Primary Sources:
   Notes of a War Correspondent 382
Wartime Leadership 384
War and Revolution in Russia 386
The Social Impact of the War 392
Wartime Artists 395
The End of the War 396
Music as History:
   Igor Stravinsky's The Rite of Spring 397
The Treaty of Versailles, 1919 399

The Consequences of the War 401

Chapter Review 404

Chapter Eleven *Between the Wars:*
   An Anxious Generation **406**

Time Line: An Anxious Generation 408

A Challenge to Peace 409

Economic Ruin: The Great Depression 411

The Rise of Fascism 413

Primary Sources: The Fourth Estate:
   TIME Magazine *416*

The Rise of Stalin 418

The Great Purge, 1935-1938 422

Hitler and the Rise of National Socialism 424

Post War North America, 1920-1939 429

Daily Life in Europe, 1900-1939 433

Visual Art in the Early Twentieth Century 435

Focus on Genius:
   Sigmund Freud Frees the Unconscious *440*

Early Twentieth-Century Literature 442

Chapter Review 446

Chapter Twelve *World War II*
   1939-1945 **448**

Time Line: World War II 450

Conflict and War: Europe, 1939 451

War Again 454

The Fall of France 459

The Battle of Britain 461

Widening Aggression 463

War in the Pacific 466

Diplomacy and Coalition Warfare 468

Operation Overlord: The Normandy Invasion 473

Reorganizing Europe 477

The Holocaust: A War within the War 478

Primary Sources: Historiography:
   Inside the Third Reich, by Albert Speer *481*

Planning the Postwar Era 482

The Impact of War on Society 483

Victory in the Pacific 484

Chapter Review 486

Unit Review 488

UNIT FIVE THE NEW WORLD
   ORDER **490**

Unit Overview **491**

Chapter Thirteen *The Western*
   Experience, 1945 to Today **492**

Time Line: The Western Experience 494

European Recovery 495

Dealing with a Defeated Germany 497

The New Face of Europe 498

The Cold War 500

Korea and Vietnam 503

From Crisis to Détente 504

Postwar Europe 1950-1970 506

Education, Alienation, and Revolt 507

Primary Sources: *The Universal*
   Declaration of Human Rights *512*

The Americanization of Culture 514

Big Science 516

The Post-Stalin Soviet Union 519

Focus on Genius: *Rachel Carson* *520*

Europe: 1970s-1990s 525

Social Changes at the Turn of the Millennium 530

The Arts at the Turn of the Millennium 530

Chapter Review 536

Chapter Fourteen *Challenge and*
   Change in the Global Village **538**

Time Line: Challenge and Change
   in the Global Village 540

Forces of Change: The Collapse of Colonialism 541

The Process of Decolonization 543

Imperialism and its Legacy:

After Independence 546

Artistic Movements in the Non-Western World 547

International Efforts for a Peaceful Co-existence 552

Music as History: *Band Aid Treatments?* 554

Conflict and War: Neo-Colonialism
and Revolution 556

The Middle East 560

The Collapse of Communism 562

Terrorism and its Roots 565

In the Global Village, Who Owns
the Mass Media? 571

Primary Sources: The Fourth Estate:
Noam Chomsky and the Media,
Manufacturing Consent 572

A Corporate Agenda? 574

Proposing a Citizens' Agenda 576

Chapter Review 578

Unit Review 580

Epilogue: The Lessons of History 582

Notes 587

Skills Focus Appendix 591

Skills Focus One: *Laying the Foundation:*
Developing Inquiry Skills 591

Skills Focus Two: *Sleuthing Through the Ages:*
Bibliographies and Notes 592

Skills Focus Three: *Working with*
Primary Sources 594

Skills Focus Four: *Formulating a Thesis* 596

Skills Focus Five: *Organizing Your Essay:*
From Cue Cards to Outline 597

Skills Focus Six: *The Final Edit: Revising,*
Editing and Polishing Your Essay 599

Glossary 600

List of Maps 603

Index 605

Credits 620

A Tour of Your Textbook

Welcome to *Legacy: The West and the World*. This textbook provides you with a view of history from the 1600s up to the present day. The text is designed and written to make this history course understandable, relevant, and meaningful. The Prologue is both an introduction to the course and a set of ideas and insights into history and its relevance to you as a 21st century citizen. The Epilogue addresses the issues surrounding history, your involvement in the world, and history's strength in helping us understand the events of the day. To make better use of this text and more fully understand its structure, begin by taking the tour on the following pages.

Cover:

The art on the front cover is a reproduction of a socialist pamphlet that was distributed in the late nineteenth century. It is an allegory of Freedom (the woman in the centre) extending her welcome to all the peoples of the world. The words on the banner read, "Workers of the world unite." Each person depicted represents a different continent. Look at the type of person chosen to represent each continent. Why do you think the pamphleteer made these choices?

Unit Opener

o **Mini Table-of-Contents:** The chapters and their titles that make up the unit.

o **Thought-Provoking Visual**: This visual illustrates the character of the period under study in the unit.

o An **Overview** puts the entire unit into perspective as related to the course as a whole.

o **Unit Expectations:** These overall expectations indicate the goals of the unit as a whole and show the broad spectrum of material you will be studying.

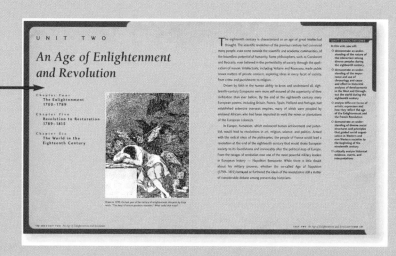

Chapter Opener

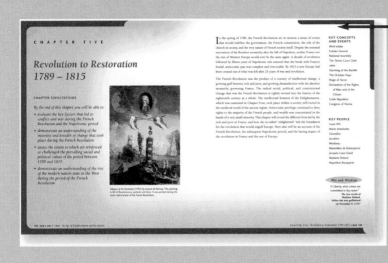

o **Title:** indicates the period of study

o **Chapter Expectations:** the goals of the chapter

o **Visual:** indicates a particularly relevant insight into the period covered

o **Wit and Wisdom:** quotes that provoke thought about the theme of the chapter

o **Key Concepts and Events:** major events that form the chapter's focus

o **Key People:** major figures introduced in the chapter

o **Opener:** an overview of the main topic of the chapter

o **Time Line** puts major events and people examined in the chapter in chronological perspective for you.

Special Features

Legacy: The West and the World has a set of special features providing interesting, challenging, and meaningful viewpoints from which you can scan the history developed in the text.

Focus on Genius

o This two-page feature examines individuals who have made key or pivotal contributions in any field or in connection with an important event or discovery. The focus is on the event, discovery, or contribution rather than biographical details.

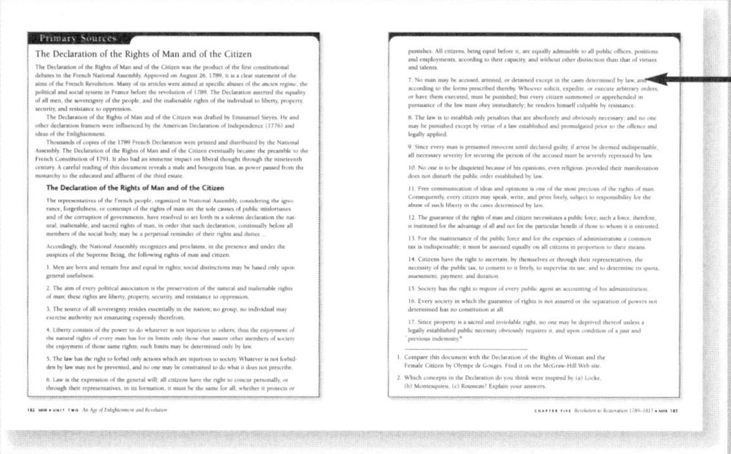

Primary Sources

The Declaration of the Rights of Man and of the Citizen

Primary Sources

- This two-page feature allows you to examine the text of key historical documents that have generated considerable debate and are important to the period being studied.

Primary Sources: The Fourth Estate

- The fourth estate is any medium that informs public opinion. This two-page feature includes material that demonstrates the importance of public opinion and how the media changed or affected public opinion about particular people, issues, or events.

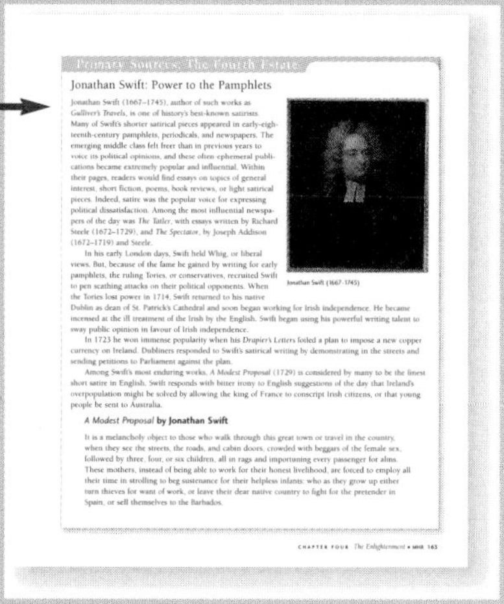

Primary Sources: The Fourth Estate

Jonathan Swift: Power to the Pamphlets

A Modest Proposal by Jonathan Swift

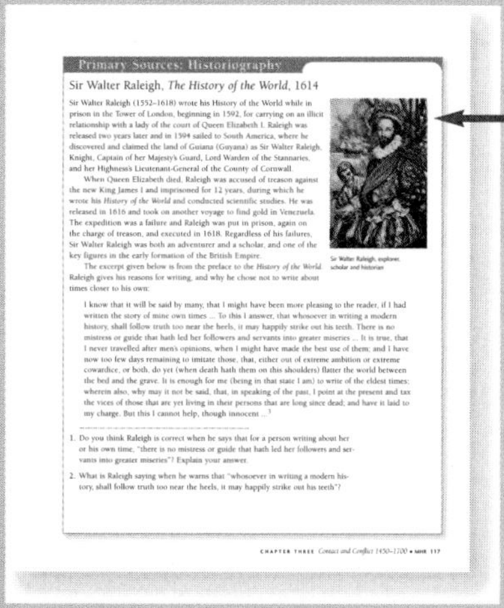

Primary Sources: Historiography

Sir Walter Raleigh, *The History of the World*, 1614

Primary Sources: Historiography

- There is an expression that says, "History is written by the winners." This one-page feature looks at historians of the past and examines how recorded history can change depending on the methods and views of its writer.

Music as History

o This feature examines specific musical compositions, performers, or performances and explores both their relationship to world events and how those events are reflected in the music.

Pleasures and Pastimes

o By describing popular pastimes, games, sports, and crazes, this feature provides an unusual insight into the social life of the times. The articles are historically interesting, lighthearted, and fun.

History Bytes

o This sidebar features interesting or strange historical phenomena including science and technology, inventions, and ideas.

Web Connections

o There are several Web Connections in every chapter. These provide an opportunity to explore more deeply various topics, issues, events, and people through the Internet. McGraw-Hill Ryerson monitors these sites and adds new ones on a regular basis.

Photos, maps, and diagrams

o Throughout the text there are many different types of visuals. They add greater meaning to the material being studied. Often there is a challenging question built in that invites you to pause and reflect.

Review, Reflect, Respond

o These questions appear three times in each chapter. They provide you with an opportunity to ensure that you understand the material you have just studied. They often give you a method of organizing the ideas and content of the preceding few pages.

Reflections

o At the end of each chapter, there is a short summary of the chapter tying the ideas, people, and events together in a way that reflects back to the introduction and foreshadows upcoming events.

Chapter Review

o At the end of each chapter there are two pages of chapter review. The data and activities on these pages are designed to help you reinforce the development of skills and understanding of history and its methods.

o **Chapter Summary**
This summary in point form reminds you of the major ideas developed in the chapter.

o **Chapter Review**
These activities and questions are designed to help you solidify your knowledge and understanding of the chapter, demonstrate your grasp of the material, and apply these insights through a variety of questions.

Unit Review

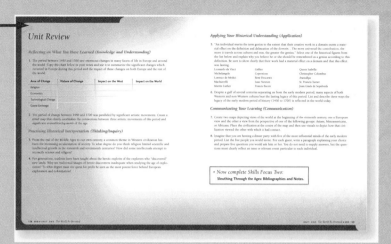

o At the end of each unit, there is a set of
questions and activities designed to give you
an opportunity to demonstrate your knowledge and understanding of the issues and
ideas developed in the unit as a whole by
reflecting upon, interpreting, and then communicating your learning.

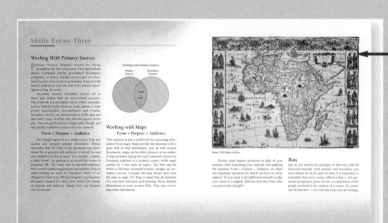

Skills Focus

o At the end of each unit, you are directed to a
specific skill in the Skills Appendix at the back
of the text. The skills are sequential and give
you a step-by-step guide to developing your
major history essay for the course.

Making History in the West

CHAPTER EXPECTATIONS

By the end of this chapter, you will be able to:

- demonstrate an understanding of the importance of chronology as a tool in analysing the history of events in the West and the rest of the world since the sixteenth century

- explain how and why an understanding of cause and effect relationships is an essential tool for historical analysis

- demonstrate an understanding of the consequences of global economic inter-relationships that developed in the twentieth century

- compare key interpretations of world history

Is this cultural colonialism?

"To know nothing of the past is to remain forever a child." These words of the ancient Roman orator and philosopher Cicero remind us of the importance of the study of history. Although it is false to suggest that history repeats itself, knowledge of the past nourishes our understanding of the present and helps to prepare us for the future. It is also important that we understand the processes by which history is written, for if we are not critical consumers of history, we can fall prey to manipulations and distortions of the past. History is much more than the simple recording of past events. Historians must work with the record of the past that has survived, select from the body of evidence, and then shape and mould the image of the past as they see it. Obviously, if history is about interpreting the past, it is fraught with potential dangers. Are the records from which we reconstruct the past truly representative of the people and societies we want to study? From which perspective does a given historian write? Is the interpretation a Marxist view, a feminist view, or a postmodern interpretation? Have the ravages of time denied us critical evidence needed to construct an accurate picture of the past? As we study history, we encounter these and many other questions.

After much thought and debate, the authors of Legacy: The West and the World have come to the conclusion that the history of the past 500 years can best be understood by raising the important issues of our time at the beginning rather than the end of the text. In this way, your journey through the past can focus on how to understand the world in which you live today. For history to have value in our lives, it must not only illuminate the past but also help us to prepare for the future.

Whether you are interested in mathematics and science, art and literature, folklore, economics, philosophy, or anthropology, the study of history can enrich your appreciation of the world around you. History involves more than economic wealth, political power, and military strength: It is concerned with the triumphs and failures of humanity, with its advances and setbacks, and with our continual search for an understanding of ourselves and our world.

Wit and Wisdom

The thing about short-term predictions is that they can only ever be true in the short term. If you want long-term predictions you have to look deep back into the past of human experience ...
Felipe Fernandez-Armesto, Author, *Millennium*

SEEING THE FUTURE THROUGH THE PAST

Designing with the End in Mind

This prologue has been designed as an introduction to the nature of historical inquiry, and to raise several of the big questions of our day. Throughout the second half of this chapter, topics for history research papers are suggested. These are meant to serve as a framework for understanding a current issue in light of the past. Pursuing such a topic will help you see the relevance of history to the world today and the issues that affect our lives.

Legacy concludes with a unit that brings the history of the West and the world up to the present, and an epilogue that asks you to reflect on what you have learned.

Having crossed paths with many of the West's foremost thinkers, artists, and political leaders, as well as those who toiled anonymously in the fields and factories, you will be challenged to reflect on what it all means.

Reconsidering the Modern Age

The modern age, which began with the Renaissance, was one of certainties about values and conventions; it placed tremendous faith in the potential of rational human thought. There was also a great deal of emphasis on the acquisition of knowledge and a belief that history meant progress. Generation after generation built on the discoveries and experiences of its forebears to nudge the world forward. The modern age

Finding historical data: This section of the Bayeux Tapestry, made in the late eleventh century, recorded the appearance of Halley's Comet at the time. Is this a primary or secondary source?

was an age dominated by the Western world and by capitalism, by a belief in the inevitable triumph of freedom, and by Christian values. A recent American textbook dealing with modern European history concluded this way:

> Perhaps our Western heritage may even inspire us with pride and measured self-confidence. We stand, momentarily, at the end of the long procession of Western civilization winding through the ages ... Through no effort of our own, we are the beneficiaries of those sacrifices and achievements. Now that it is our turn to carry the torch onward, we may remember these ties with our forebears.

Statements such as these are riddled with potential problems because they assume that we can apply a standard set of values to both the past and the future. Many people now question such assumptions, claiming that there is no irrefutable body of truth and that the assumed leadership of the Western world, with its ideals and sense of moral superiority, may no longer fit the world now unfolding. Furthermore, we are not the culmination of history, but rather a mere speck on the continuum of time. History has and will continue to unfold randomly: There are no set patterns, and we cannot predict the future.

What Is History?

In 1066 William the Conqueror seized control of England after King Harald died from an arrow wound to his eye; in 1434 the Italian city-states signed the Treaty of Lodi, beginning a period of peace that lasted over half a century; in 1517 a Catholic monk named Martin Luther posted his 95 Theses on a church door in Wittenberg; and in 1816 Mary Shelley published her famous novel *Frankenstein, or the Modern Prometheus*. A common misconception among students is that, by memorizing facts such as these, they will ace their history exams. They think that the sign of a good historian is an ability to recall important names, dates, and

events. Were this true, historians would be nothing more than clerks recording data. The study of history requires an ability to read and write critically, to carry out research, and, especially, to think analytically and creatively. Memorizing countless names, dates, and events is futile if in the process these facts are not used constructively to detect trends and understand the human experience.

Change and History

History is the study of change over time; without change there is no history. If Europeans dressed the same way, ate the same food, had the same culture as they did in the eighteenth century, there would be very little for historians to write about. Thus, the first lesson for the history student is that the foundation of history is the study of change over time, and that the primary question historians ask is "Why?" History is the attempt to understand the underlying causes and consequences of events. Using historical data in a meaningful way gives history purpose and relevance.

Continuity in History

Although historians are primarily interested in the process and agents of change, continuity also demands our attention. Throughout history, certain institutions have reinforced continuity. Since the Revolutionary War (1775–1783), the American constitution has provided political stability in the United States. Similarly, the British parliamentary system has been a vehicle for the evolution of democracy without the need for a radical break with the past. This stability has been passed on to Canada, where we have been able to bring about an effective and responsive democratic system of government without a violent revolution. In many societies, religious institutions provide a link with the past through a body of beliefs and traditions. In times of turmoil and change, many people turn to their religious faith for a sense of continuity. The family has also been a source of stability for countless generations. Customs and rites of passage, from baptism and marriage to funeral rituals, remain relatively unchanged despite rapid change around them over centuries. Sources of continuity such as government, religious institutions, and the family are important in the study of history, as they help us to remain connected to the past. They also help us comprehend why people faced with rapid and unpredictable change may seek solace in those institutions for a feeling of stability.

The Relevance of History

How can the study of history help enrich our lives? Imagine living in a society where none of us knew any history; where we knew nothing of our ancestors or the events that brought us to this time. English historian Arthur Marwick suggests that "a society without memory and self-knowledge would be a society adrift." We would suffer from a sort of cultural amnesia and be unable to understand who we were and where we were heading. French anthropologist Claude Lévi-Strauss argued that those who ignore history condemn themselves to knowing nothing about the present because historical development alone permits us to evaluate elements of the present.

Social, Economic, and Political Structures

Some people think that history is about those with power and wealth, and that preliterate societies have no history. A good understanding of history must encompass both people and society. To suggest that women have no history because until recently they had no power, or that Native Canadians had no history until Europeans began studying them is absurd. As historians have broadened their definition of history and historical developments, it has become increasingly evident that writing history requires drawing on a wide variety of sources, including art, music, folktales, dance, religious practices, food, and family relations.

By studying many aspects of the past — and not limiting history to written records — we can have a fuller sense of the present.

Methods of Historical Inquiry

When first introduced to the study of history, students often assume that what is written by historians is fact. Students are seldom asked to consider a historian's point of view or to understand the influence of the historian's culture. History is shaped by those who write it as well as those who live it. British historian E. H. Carr wrote, "When we attempt to answer the question 'What is History?' our answer, consciously or unconsciously, reflects our own position in time, and forms part of our answer to the broader question of what view we take of the society in which we live."

The Roman emperor Caracalla (below right) obliterated the image of Geta (below left), his younger brother in this family portrait. This was not the first time a ruler tried to rewrite history by eliminating all memory of his or her rivals or predecessors.

Historian or School of History	Theoretical Basis
Plutarch **1st century CE Greek historian**	Actions of great individuals determine the course of history; lays the foundation for the Great Man Theory of history
Historical Forces School of History	Ideas and forces shape the direction of history, e.g., Christianity undermined the vitality of the Roman Empire and led to its demise.
Georg Wilhelm Friedrich Hegel **19th-century German philosopher**	Introduced the concept of history as dialectic. For every old idea, there is a new one that conflicts with it. Out of the struggle, a new idea is created (thesis, antithesis, synthesis). History is the product of conflict.
Karl Marx **19th-century German philosopher**	Built on Hegel's concept of the dialectic but adds the idea of class struggle. Whenever a new method of production occurred, there was conflict between the older ruling class and a newer class using the newer and superior means of production. Marxist historians examine history in light of class struggle.
Radical School of History	History is written by the victors and is for the benefit of those who rule. History is little more than myth-making because it is written by those who won; it demonizes those who lost.
Frederick Jackson Turner **19th-century American historian**	Suggested that geography determined the nature of a people and gave them advantages or disadvantages. For example, the fact that England is an island predisposed the English to be good sailors and led them to dominate overseas trade. The frontier led Americans to be open to new ideas and prepared them to be world leaders in an age of rapidly changing technology.

In English, as in many European languages, though not all, the word "history" has a tricky double meaning. On the one hand, it denotes what really happened: the real past, in all its glorious complexity, more than the hand can write or the mind can comprehend. On the other hand, the word also means "the story of what happened." That double meaning points at puzzles: thinking carelessly, people can conflate the two and imagine that a credible tale has captured what really went on. Wiser heads know better. The past, especially the past long gone, has left few traces, mere scattered shards, elusive hints of what the dead thought, felt, and did. Careful readers, sharp-eyed students, and professional historians all agree that any history in the second sense — as story — is at best an approximation, an informed, intuitive reconstruction, a take on the past.

Interpretation and Analysis

The study of various schools of historical thought or the perspective from which different historians write is referred to as historiography. Historians drawing on the same body of information may reach completely different conclusions. Historiography increases the complexity of the study of history, but it helps to draw informed and reasoned conclusions about the past regardless of the varying schools of thought adopted by historians. The list below briefly outlines several schools of historical thought that dominated the writing of history through much of the twentieth century. In recent decades, there have been significant shifts in the schools of historical thought that dominate universities.

In recent decades, among historians, the idea that all scholarship, all narrative, is mere interpretation has taken a strong hold. Several intellectual movements have heightened our sense that, in "doing history," we are telling a story, not laying out the naked truth. It is good to know these movements, since they shape both this book, and much other historical writing. They also swirl through universities; students there encounter them at every hand.

One movement, "postmodernism," is fascinated by the power of language and other media to shape thought. We are all, it argues, prisoners of our modes of communicating; thus, our thoughts and works are not even half our own. If that is so, any history, as tale, belongs only partly to its historian; it belongs also to the culture that helped write or tell it. Postmodernism undercuts faith in objectivity; it also celebrates and liberates interpretation.

The defining features of the early modern and modern eras in European history were their search for truth, beauty, and goodness; the confidence that it was possible to understand everything; and the faith that, through the application of human knowledge and rational thought, we could perfect society. The very belief that society could achieve some kind of utopia implies a common set of goals and values. This assumption is no longer valid and the Western world must come to terms with the fact that it does not have a monopoly on what defines good government or the moral foundations of society. Irish author James Joyce described the postmodern cosmopolitan mind as "Europasianized Afferyank."

"Postmodern" is a difficult term to define and understand. Essentially, postmodernists reject the earlier premises that there are universal truths or standards of goodness and beauty, so they embrace plurality. They no longer accept that individuals are capable of understanding everything because they recognize that the realm of knowledge has become too vast for any one mind to grasp. Furthermore, postmodernists reject the West's centuries-old quest for common values and accept that in the present and future world there will be diverse moral codes, each equally valid. This attack on individualism and rationalism can be dangerous, as it reduces individuals to mere cogs in an incomprehensible machine and removes the foundation upon which Western societies have been built. But if we reject the pluralism of postmodernism, who will be the arbiter of what is best? By what standards will they judge? Historian Roland Stromberg points out that, "The encounter between the European West and Africa and Asia, begun long ago, has now reached the stage of a true syncretization of cultures ..."

Postmodernism presents us with many challenges as it forces us to rethink the ways in which we respond to the world around us. In the teaching of history, it becomes impossible to establish the "essentials" of a course, as there are, theoretically, no fundamental truths and therefore no events of universal significance. Rather, what have long been considered milestones of history must now be acknowledged as favourite topics of the teacher. Postmodernists could question the value and accuracy of much of the material covered in these pages: such is the nature of viewing history from an eclectic perspective.

A second movement is called "post-colonialism." It shares with postmodernism a lot of skepticism, but takes on the question, "whose story is it anyway?" Both intellectual movements agree that, most often, the masters have told the story. After all, they controlled the record-keeping, they took down what served their conscious and unconscious ends. When it came to telling stories, they fit the narrative to their pursuit of power. The post-colonial movement aims to liberate history from its customary masters: male, White Europeans or North Americans, and to allow the voices from the margins to catch our ears.

Together, postmodern and post-colonial thinkers urge historians to heed those at the margins: outsiders, the weak, and the poor. History, they say, needs to be "de-centred." Under their influence, historians have unearthed the experiences, voices, and stories of people often lost in the narratives of the master classes: women, adolescents, children, the poor, slaves, vagrants, deviants, and outsiders of every sort. This movement in historical writing has had its enemies, guardians of old standards who fret that too much pursuit of magic, witchcraft, low love, and lower life will neglect the works of genius and the sharp debates that shaped our culture and institutions.

There is a third movement as well: "the return to narrative." In the nineteenth century, history was a literary form, often read for pleasure. In the twentieth, however, history fell under the spell of the social sciences. Much historical writing, shedding good storytelling, opted instead for flat prose and heaps of data, astutely collected, tabulated, and graphed. In the past decades, however, many historians have yearned to win back the larger public by telling good stories, as gripping as the best movies and far more accurate. Historians are very aware of the appetite for history. Countless successful films and novels, not to mention flourishing biography channels, prove that the audience is huge. But more than envy or cash hunger underlies the return to narrative. Many historians now feel that past experience is often better caught by a complex story, with its odd tangles of freedom and necessity, than by a table's summed-up scraps of many lives.

What can the homeless tell us about the history of our society? Who will write their history?

Kinds of Historians

Historians come in many stripes. They divide themselves not only by the times and places that they study, but also by what they investigate. There are, in the main, political, economic, social, intellectual, and cultural historians. They have specialities; some study the family, women, children, or even men as men, ethnic groups, races, and sexual subcultures. There are historians of workers' movements, of coinage, of medicine, of ecosystems, to name a few. Institutions shape their output; associations, wide and narrow, and learned journals, conferences, listservs, and informal alliances all air and discuss discoveries and ponder routes to follow. And there are presses and information conglomerates, selling books, films, CDs, and access to the Web. These groups have the power to air and amplify ideas or to squelch them by turning a deaf ear. Historical inquiry, like knowledge of any sort, is never free of institutions and of their links to politics and markets. The stories we tell ourselves inevitably reflect the forces on us, the storytellers.

History, then, is not a fixed story, nor is it totally objective; it is an intellectual practice, lodged in institutions and buffeted by political, economic, social, and intellectual forces. It is a fluid discussion and argument, usually good-natured, but sometimes heated. This textbook, inevitably, is a product of such forces, and such discussions. It springs from a moment in the history of historical discourse. It invites, you, its readers, to join in the excitement and fun. You will join the great conversation that shapes our understanding of the past. That means you will join the process that eventually will render this book obsolete.

Chronology and Cause and Effect

Where should a course in modern Western and world history begin? Is the Enlightenment a logical starting point? How about the French Revolution? The difficulty with beginning with either of these eras is that the foundation for an understanding of the changes that occurred in Europe over the past 250 years lies before the eighteenth century. An awareness of Europe's medieval heritage is essential. That highly religious, agrarian society then contrasts sharply with the more humanistic, urban society of the Renaissance.

The Big Picture: Times and Places that Label History

One job of history, and of historians, is to label the big picture. Our intellectual culture likes to cut the world into segments of time or space. Journalism indulges this habit endlessly: "The Seventies," "The Jazz Age," "The West," "Latin America," "The Third World." This custom of labelling and schematizing time and space is

What made "The Seventies" so "Seventies?" What were the Middle Ages in the middle of? How do we recognize periods in history?

not unique to us today; historians and geographers long ago and far away sometimes did the same. But the obsession with periods of history is, as we like to say, both "European" and "modern." Medieval Europeans did not say, "Oh, that church is just so, so twelfth century! Let's try for a modern, thirteenth-century style!" For that matter, medieval people had little sense of their own time as medieval, or special, except insofar as it had declined from ancient Roman greatness or had drifted toward Christ's promised Second Coming at the end of time and history.

The Renaissance was a period of revolutionary changes in thought. Humanism, individualism, and the quest for knowledge allowed overseas exploration to occur, challenged the power of the Catholic Church, and produced the scientific revolution. When the reason and logic of the scientific revolution were applied to society, the foundations for the Enlightenment were laid and a revolution in politics, government, and economics was close at hand. It is this concept of a time continuum that is essential to perceiving the full picture of history. Also important is the realization that just as major developments of the past were the product of preceding events, the trends and events of today are presently shaping the developments of the future.

As students of history, we must understand that history is studied but not defined in time periods (such as the Renaissance, the Industrial Revolution, the Age of Romanticism); history does not unfold "in packages" and often the periods identified by historians overlap. The Renaissance, which was largely an Italian phenomenon, began to fade by the mid-sixteenth century, while the Reformation was transforming much of Europe north of the Alps. Similarly, while the French Revolution brought radical change to much of Europe, the Industrial Revolution was transforming England. Historical time periods are only organizers to help understand the past.

Is History Progressive?

Some historians assume that history is not a random series of events but is moving in some kind of ordered direction. According to ancient Greek and Roman scholars, history was an inevitable, cyclical progression descending from prosperity to adversity and eventually rising again from adversity to prosperity. Nineteenth-century scholars tended to regard history as progressive, while twentieth-century scholars tend to question the concept of continual forward progress in history. Being able to understand history in a broad context helps to establish a relevance to our present and future lives. Consider, for example, how important understanding history is in negotiating fair and equitable agreements with a nation's indigenous peoples.

Italian Renaissance writer Niccolò Machiavelli captured the essence of the classical view of history in his famous work *The Prince*. At the end of the fifteenth century, the Italian city-states were in decline after having experienced the glory of the Renaissance. Foreign powers were invading cities such as Florence, Rome, and Milan, leading to chaos. Machiavelli wrote *The Prince* as a guide to restoring the city's grandeur. He expressed the classical view of history when he wrote: "And if, as I said, the Israelites had to be enslaved in Egypt for Moses to emerge as their leader; if the Persians had to be oppressed by the Medes so that the greatness of Cyrus could be recognized; if the Athenians had to be scattered to demonstrate the excellence of Theseus, then, at the present time, in order to discover the worth of an Italian spirit, Italy had to be brought to her present extremity." Thus, Machiavelli viewed history as cyclical, holding out great hope for a return to prosperity for Florence. He did not, however, view history as necessarily progressive; he did not believe that each time a society returned to a golden age, it would have progressed further than the golden age that had preceded it. A progressive view of history did not emerge until the eighteenth-century period known as the Enlightenment.

Giambattista Vico, a renowned Italian philosopher of the eighteenth century, produced the most revolutionary theory of history in more than one thousand years. His *New Science*, first published in 1725, was a truly original historical work that contradicted the view of his contemporaries and helped establish a basis for the modern study of history. Vico argued that since we are ourselves the creators of history, we can know it with certainty. This idea is fundamental to modern historiography because it defines what historians study (past human actions) and states their aim (to recover human thinking).

The major aim of Vico's *New Science* was to discover the universal laws of history. The pursuit of this aim resulted in Vico's theory of an "ideal and eternal history," which is the "schematic account of the successive ages through which nations have run their course, and of the *ricorsi* [alternative courses] in which subsequent ages have repeated the patterns of those which came before." In other words, the "ideal" is the universal traits of all cultures and the "eternal" is the commonality and permanence of these traits through the rise and fall of all nations.

Vico's unique view of human history as progressing spirally developed from his theory of an ideal and eternal history. The idea that humanity could have been rational, virtuous, and wise from the beginning was totally rejected by Vico. He also rejected the idea of progress as a causal process, asserting instead that humanity moves forward slowly and painfully to reach maturity only after turmoil, oppression, and bitter conflict. Vico believed that human progress was based on building upon the ideas of past cultures.

Summarizing his view of the rise and fall of nations, Vico wrote: "Men first feel necessity, then look to utility, next attend to comfort, still later amuse themselves with pleasure, then grow dissolute in luxury, and finally go mad and waste their substance."

In the early eighteenth century, theories of human perfectibility and progress were shaping the writing of history. Many intellectuals wanted to see a pattern in the course of historical change because they were convinced that history was going somewhere and that the miseries suffered by humanity were not in vain but were part of the inevitable process of achieving some morally satisfactory goal. This view of history as progressive has survived into the twentieth century. E. H. Carr defines history as "progress through the transmission of acquired skills from one generation to another." In defence of his progressive view of history, Carr wrote: "Everything that happens has a cause or causes, and could not have happened differently unless something in the cause or causes had also been different."

For many students of history in the late twentieth century, the view of history as progress is quite appealing. North Americans have experienced unprecedented economic growth since the end of World War II; there have been countless medical and technological breakthroughs; and individual rights are being protected. It would be difficult not to perceive progress in the twentieth century.

And yet the contemporary historian Felipe Fernandez-Armesto rejects the very idea that history is unfolding in any rational and ultimately progressive manner. Rather than examining history from the narrow perspective of a colonial power such as England, France or the United States, Fernandez-Armesto challenges us

Where would Giambattista Vico say we, as Canadians, are in his cycle of history?

to consider the plight of both the victors and the victims of history. He suggests the idea of progressive history is "repugnant," as history "lurches between random crises, with no direction or pattern, no predictable end. "It is a genuinely chaotic system," he concludes.

Progressive or chaotic? Is it a matter of perspective? The obvious problem with believing that history is progressive is that the historian must place a value judgment on events. How many technological advances of the twentieth century have brought with them negative side effects (e.g., increased stress, pollution)? When reflecting on progress, we must first establish what we mean by progress and, secondly, we must acknowledge that others may not share our view. Thus, although historians may be able to discern trends and patterns in history, which help us respond to issues of the present and future, conclusions regarding the progress of humanity will forever remain subjective.

Considering the Present in Light of the Past

The insights into the past provided by history can act as our guide to the future. As you read about the people, places, events, and trends that constitute modern Western and world history, consider what history is teaching you about yourself and the society in which you live. History is about the spirit of the past; in the face of the Mona Lisa lives the essence of the Renaissance; in the writings of Voltaire lives the spirit of the Enlightenment; the scientific revolution lives in our understanding of the universe and the human body; and in the memory of those who died in senseless wars and at the hands of ruthless oppressors lives a constant reminder of our capacity for inhumanity. The study of history is the study of the triumphs and failures that have brought us to this point and helps us to make sense of the world in which we live. In the study of history lives the spirit of hope that someday the lessons to be learned from the past may enable us to live harmoniously in a truly global village.

The various schools of thought that define historical study provide us with many different views of the past and, consequently, myriad insights into how the past has brought us to this point. The balance of this chapter is devoted to raising questions regarding the dominant issues of our times. Use these questions to guide your examination of the past five hundred years. Considering the present in light of the past will bring relevance and meaning to your study of history.

HOT TOPIC: CULTURES OF THE NON-WESTERN WORLD

Aboriginal groups throughout North America have long struggled against the loss of their lands. Their struggles have included battles with the early European settlers, signing treaties with European and North American governments, and protesting when those treaty agreements have been ignored or dismissed by more recent governments. The ongoing conflicts between Aboriginal peoples and Western settlers are just some of the examples of key conflicts and controversies that have arisen as a result of resistance to Western expansion.

Is conflict inevitable when cultures encounter one another? At Oka, Québec, Native warriors met modern, western warriors.

Flashpoint: The Ipperwash Tragedy

In September 1995, Dudley George was shot and killed by an Ontario Provincial Police officer. What was the significance of his death? Dudley George was the first Aboriginal Canadian to be killed in a land claims dispute in over a hundred years. His death sparked a fire of angry protests and demands for an inquiry. In the fall of 1995, Dudley George was one of approximately 30 Aboriginal protesters occupying Ipperwash Provincial Park. They were protesting the destruction of their burial ground and were demanding the return of land that had been appropriated by the Department of National Defence during World War II to create a military training facility.

What began as a peaceful protest ended in violence and tragedy. The tragedy heightened as the courts found the police officer guilty of criminal negligence — a finding which, by law, should have led to an inquest into the circumstances of George's death. A public inquiry has still not been called by the provincial government despite several years of protests, pressure from various concerned citizens' groups, and ongoing court battles.

Potential Research Questions:

1. What key factors contributed to the failure (or success) of Aboriginal resistance to European settlement in North America (or Latin America)?
2. Compare and contrast the relative success of passive resistance (e.g., Gandhi's methods in India) against colonial rule versus violent uprising.
3. To what extent was the rise of communism in Latin America a form of resistance to neocolonial policies of the United States?
4. In the late twentieth century, what are the main vehicles for the spread of Western ideas (e.g., music, media), and what resistance are these vehicles encountering in the non-Western world?

HOT TOPIC: ECONOMIC STRUCTURES

Although the term "global village" was only coined in the 1960s, cultures around the world have been in contact with one another through trade, travel, and conflict for thousands of years. Recently, however, the economic interaction between nations has had a profound impact on both developed and developing nations.

Flashpoint: Distribution of Wealth around the World

- Europe, North America, and Asia possess over 90 percent of the world's wealth, while Africa, South America, and Oceania combined possess less than 10 percent.
- Many Third World countries have a debt service ratio of over 50 percent; this means that more than half of what the country earns from exports must be used to pay off international loans.
- Eight out of the 10 countries with the smallest GDP per capita (total earnings of the country divided by the population) are in Africa.
- Countries that have adopted the most vigorous free market policies — like New Zealand, the U.K. and the U.S. — are often the same ones in which inequality between the rich and poor is growing most rapidly.
- If the world were a village of 100 people, 80 would live in substandard housing, 50 would be malnourished, and 70 would be illiterate; six would own 59 percent of all the wealth and they would all be from the United States.

Potential Research Questions:

1. How have the policies of international institutions like the World Bank and International Monetary Fund (IMF) affected the social and economic status of developing nations?
2. Compare and contrast the economic policies of two former colonial societies. Examine one that has adopted communist or socialist ideology and one that has adopted the free enterprise model.
3. Examine the purpose of one or more global trade alliances (APEC, NAFTA, and so on). To what extent has it been successful in achieving its primary objectives?

4. Compare and contrast the nature of trade in the twentieth century with that of an earlier era (e.g., global trading relationships of the seventeenth century).

HOT TOPIC: CITIZENSHIP AND HUMAN RIGHTS

The responsibilities and rights of a citizen have been the subject of heated debate among thinkers from ancient times to the present. What are fundamental human rights? What does it mean for a state to be truly democratic? What consequences have been faced by totalitarian states or by those nations that claim to be democracies but whose actions are not democratic?

Flashpoint: "Fortress Québec" — negotiating the Free Trade of the Area of the Americas

Since the late 1990s, meetings of world leaders to negotiate trade agreements have been routinely met by tens of thousands of protesters who are opposed to various aspects of these deals — from their impact on the environment and human rights to the overwhelming power they seem to give multinational corporations. As protests increase in size and in their potential to erupt into moments of violence, authorities have gone to greater and greater lengths to beef up security and keep protesters from disrupting summit meetings.

Security measures reached new levels in Quebec City in April 2001 during the Summit talks on the proposed Free Trade Area of the Americas (FTAA). Dubbed by protesters "Fortress Québec," concrete barriers and a 10-foot security fence were erected to keep protesters at bay. The conference required the largest security mobilization in Canadian history. Protesters called the fence "the wall of shame" and said that it symbolized the refusal by leaders to allow public participation in the talks.

After the confrontations in Québec, many Canadians wondered what they revealed about the rights and responsibilities of citizens in Canada and other democratic countries.

Maude Barlow, Volunteer Chair of the Council of Canadians said,

> If the process were truly democratic, the federal government would have released the negotiating text months ago, engaged in genuine consultations with citizens, never erected a wall around the negotiators, nor permitted corporations to buy privileged access to them ... Given the profound impact the FTAA will have on democracies throughout the hemisphere, governments should allow the citizens of every country to vote directly on the proposed deal.

Having been excluded from the talks, protesters set up a parallel "People's Summit" aimed at voicing concerns about the proposed trade agreement and educating people about potential problems with the agreement. In addition to the extensive peaceful protests, however, the security wall became a target of some protesters whose objective was to bring down the wall. The ensuing confrontation involved riot police who used tear gas, rubber bullets, water cannon, and mass arrests to control protesters. Dozens of people were injured, including police officers and innocent bystanders.

Potential Research Questions:

1. Examine the evolution of democratic rights. How have citizens' demands for greater democracy changed during various time periods (e.g., the French Revolution, the Industrial Revolution, and the late twentieth century)?
2. Analyse the impact of the writings and ideas of a Western philosopher on a movement for reform (e.g., Hobbes versus Locke and the American Revolution; Marx and better working conditions during the Industrial Revolution, and so on).
3. To what extent has a recent political development (e.g., the growth of multinational corporations, anti-terrorism laws since September 11, 2001) compromised the democratic rights of citizens in Canada or the United States?
4. To what extent was a restriction of democratic rights in the past justifiable (e.g., the War Measures Act during the FLQ crisis in Canada, the internment of Japanese-Americans and -Canadians during World War II)?

HOT TOPIC: INTERACTION AMONG COMMUNITIES

For centuries, imperialism provided the framework for interaction between the Western and non-Western worlds. European imperialist nations interacted with their colonies or client states to obtain raw materials, access to trade routes, or to bolster their military status. In more recent years, as the process of decolonization has broken down the formal relationships of imperialism, a new force has been central in shaping present world relations: the growth and expanding influence of multinational corporations. Today, companies such as Nike, Wal-Mart, McDonalds, and so on, form the main bridges between the Western and non-Western world as they contract out their manufacturing to factories in countries like China, Indonesia, and Mexico. Critics say that, consequently, these companies must take responsibility for human rights abuses or poor living and working conditions they seem tacitly to support.

Flashpoint: Multinationals and Developing Nations

In the past, multinational companies often claimed that they played a pivotal role in the North American economy by providing thousands of jobs. But these "engines of economic growth" (as they called themselves) changed their role drastically in the 1990s as they changed strategy. They closed factories in which they once manufactured their own products — creating unprecedented mass layoffs — and contracted out their manufacturing to factories in developing countries. This increased their profit margins since they were no longer responsible for the physical assets and employment costs associated with manufacturing. This has resulted in some alarming numbers. For example, in 1998 — a year when the American economy was booming — hundreds of thousands of jobs were cut by American corporations. Where did the jobs go? Many jobs moved to developing countries where labour is cheap and regulations are minimal.

Potential Research Questions:

1. Compare and contrast the way in which the non-Western world was used by the Western world as a source of labour in an earlier period of history (e.g., seventeenth-century slave trade/indentured labour, and so on) to the labour relationship that exists between the West and non-West today.
2. To what extent did the philosophies of Western economists (Adam Smith, David Ricardo, and so on) influence the nature of trade between Western and non-Western nations?
3. Examine the impact of situations in which economic interaction between nations has been terminated (e.g., the American trade embargo on Cuba, economic sanctions on Iraq).
4. Analyse the nature of interaction between Western peoples and Aboriginal groups living in Western nations (e.g., First Nations in Canada, Maori in New Zealand, Aborigines in Australia). Examine their relative status and rights as citizens.

HOT TOPIC: SCIENCE AND TECHNOLOGY

The conflict between scientific discovery and ethics has roots reaching back many centuries. From Galileo's assertion that the Earth revolved around the Sun (and not vice versa) to modern-day questions about cloning and genetic engineering, the struggle between those who believe that scientific discovery should not be hindered and those who believe that science should be guided by ethical considerations continues to rage.

Flashpoint: "Frankenfoods?" — GM Foods and Our Right to Know

- Over 60 percent of all packaged foods in the U.S.A. contain genetically modified (GM) foods.
- The most common genetically modified crops are corn, canola, soybeans, and cotton.
- The purpose of genetically modifying foods is often to make crops more tolerant of herbicides so that fields can be sprayed with weed killers and the crops will not be harmed; or to make plants produce their own pesticide; or to build a resistance to viruses.
- Sometimes genetic engineering goes very wrong. For example, researchers who tried to modify petunias to make them twice as colourful ended up producing flowers with no pigment at all. Other scientists tried to raise pigs that had human growth hormone in an attempt to make their meat leaner. The experimental pigs turned out cross-eyed and could not stand up because their organ development and metabolism were not normal.
- Many people are concerned about genetically modified foods since potential health risks are still largely unknown. This has been the motivation for worldwide campaigns to have GM foods labelled. Thirty-five countries have mandatory labelling laws but the U.S. and Canada have resisted adopting mandatory labelling.
- Biotech companies like Monsanto, Novartis, and Pioneer are at the forefront of research on genetic engineering. A particularly controversial

This is Dolly, the first cloned sheep. Our government has said it will not allow human cloning. Do you agree with this decision?

development was Monsanto's design of a "terminator seed" — plants that grow from the terminator seed would not be able to produce their own seeds. Therefore, instead of saving seeds from year to year as farmers have done for millennia, they would be forced to buy new seeds every year from the supply company.

- Worldwide protests have included burning fields of GM crops in India, farmers marching across Thailand, and "tours" of GM foods in local Loblaws stores in Canada.

Potential Research Questions:

1. To what extent has religion or morality interfered with scientific discovery throughout history (e.g., Galileo, Darwin, and so on)?

2. Analyse the impact of a particular technological advancement on the social welfare of people it affected (e.g., the Green Revolution on farmers, assembly line production on factory workers, and so on).
3. To what extent was the Industrial Revolution a result of technological invention (e.g., the cotton gin, steam power, and so on)?
4. Examine protest movements that have emerged throughout history against technological development (e.g., the Luddites, modern-day movements against GM foods). What are the main issues surrounding their opposition?

HOT TOPIC: WOMEN AT WORK

Although, ideally, history tells the story of experiences of both sexes, women have often played a unique role and have undergone experiences unknown to men. Industrialization, urbanization, and modernization have had a striking impact on the lives of women in the West and the rest of the world.

Should women, simply because they are women, be subject to regulations at work that men are not expected to follow?

Flashpoint: Unfair Treatment of the "Fairer" Sex?

- According to a 1995 United Nations report, 1.3 billion people in the world live in poverty — 70 percent of them are women.
- 33.6 percent of women around the world are illiterate compared with 19.4 percent of the male population.
- On a worldwide average, women earn 40 percent of what men earn in the same jobs.
- Factories in developing countries — particularly in the export processing zones where products are manufactured for companies based in the West — tend to recruit young women from distant villages to work for them: They are far from home, often uneducated and, therefore, frightened and easily manipulated.
- Although hired as teenagers, many young women in developing countries face unemployment within a few years as factories attempt to avoid having mothers on the payroll — so they do not have to pay benefits. Some company tactics include: inspecting women's sanitary pads once a month to ensure workers have not become pregnant; requiring workers to undergo routine pregnancy tests; forcing pregnant women to work night shifts, overtime hours, or to physically strain themselves at work — all aimed at getting them to resign.
- In El Salvador and Honduras, factory owners have been known to hand out contraceptive pills or force workers to have abortions.
- In Sri Lanka, female employees have had to sign a contract that requires them to resign if they get married.
- Women employed in factories in developing countries also routinely face sexual harassment by their employers.
- Critics lay blame for many of the intolerable working conditions in developing countries on the Structural Adjustment Programmes that the World Bank requires them to adopt in return for loans. One of the requirements of these programs

focusses on opening up the country's economy to foreign trade — often resulting in the creation of export processing zones or free trade zones — where many of these abuses take place.

Potential Research Questions:

1. Compare and contrast the general living and working conditions of women in the West to those of women in the non-Western world. What are the main factors that seem to explain the difference (or similarity) in their relative status?

2. Compare and contrast the general living and working conditions of men to those of women in one (or a group of) nation(s) (e.g., Canada, Latin America). What are the main factors that seem to explain the difference (or similarity) in their relative status?

3. Examine the contribution of women to a major event in the history of the Western world (e.g., the French Revolution, World War I or World War II, the Enlightenment, and so on).

4. Examine the main objectives of one of the women's movements for increased rights in the West (e.g., the suffragette movement, the second wave of feminism). To what extent was it successful in achieving its objectives?

HOT TOPIC: CAN A MINORITY CO-EXIST WITH A MAJORITY?

All human beings have a basic desire to belong to a community. As social animals, we are all raised to share, protect and promote the beliefs, values, and norms of our community. History allows us to examine a vast range of communities. Often historians focus on the communities formed by the majority of a population, but it is equally important to consider those communities that "opt out" of the larger community and maintain their own, unique way of life. These smaller communities have often been labelled as "fringe," different from the more mainstream community in their beliefs and practices. Some of these communities are based on religious practices, ethnicity, and/or intellectual principles (as were the Jesuits, Loyalists, Creole and Jewish peoples historically). There are many other examples of such communities throughout history.

Flashpoint: Branch Davidians and Roma

Two recent examples of the clash of communities are the Branch Davidians in the United States and the Roma (incorrectly called gypsies) of Europe. The first was a violent confrontation between the Federal Bureau of Investigation (FBI) and a religious community called the Branch Davidians that occurred in 1993 near Waco, Texas. Four federal officers were killed while investigating alleged stockpiling of weapons by the religious group. After a 51-day standoff that attracted enormous media attention, the buildings inhabited by the Davidians burnt to the ground, leaving 80 people dead. Although an extreme example of the clash of communities, one based on religious principles and one based on more secular principles, there are countless other historic examples of minority communities that have refused to integrate with the mainstream community that represents the majority.

In Europe today, Roma people continue to face extreme forms of discrimination. Historically, the Roma have faced slavery, large-scale, state-sponsored persecutions, assimilation, or fragmentation. They are considered "outside" of the mainstream communities they inhabit and therefore are targets of scapegoating and racism.

The *Roma* and the Branch Davidians are contemporary examples of communities whose beliefs differ from those of the larger community in which they live. These smaller communities must struggle to maintain their own identities and culture, or risk being absorbed into the mainstream community around them. Some choose to live quietly alongside the mainstream culture while rejecting most of its beliefs and values. Some take a more political and/or even violent stand to protect

Roma people have been persecuted and rejected by larger communities throughout Europe. What makes them so different?

Flashpoint: The War on Terrorism

The September 11, 2001, attacks on the World Trade Center in New York and the Pentagon in Washington made terrorism a worldwide concern. We wondered what could motivate people to do such a thing. The sense of security among people in the Western world has been forever altered. Consequently, a number of governments are attempting to wipe out terrorism through military and political action.

The main aim of terrorists, regardless of when and where they live, is to destabilize or overthrow existing political institutions. Terrorism, however, is only one type of conflict: The key factors that have led to civil and international wars, the consequences of war, and the prevention of war are all critical areas of study for historians.

Potential Research Questions:

1. Examine the historical roots, contemporary actions, and responses to specific examples of terrorism throughout history. Compare two areas where terrorism has been used (e.g., Northern Ireland, Algeria versus France, Vietnam versus the United States or France, Palestinians versus Israelis, Iran, Nicaragua, El Salvador, the Soviet Union, Canada, Argentina, the Philippines, Indonesia).
2. "The modern media is the terrorist's number one weapon." Evaluate this statement by examining terrorist actions both before and after the invention of modern communications media.
3. "War promotes change." Assess both the positive and negative impacts of war (e.g., social, political, ethical, cultural, technological). Possible wars/conflicts to examine include the Napoleonic Wars, the American Civil War, the Mahdist Insurrections, World War I, the Spanish Civil War, the Cold War, or another of your choice.
4. Evaluate one approach to maintaining international order (e.g., the Westphalian nation-state system, Wilsonian internationalism, United Nations mandates and peace-keeping actions, movements to defend and promote universal human rights, the World Court at The Hague, and so on).

themselves from an outside threat. The co-operation and/or conflict of communities has at times been a major factor in historical change and/or continuity.

Potential Research Questions:

1. Choose two communities, one Western and one non-Western, that successfully shun the mainstream and maintain their own identity (e.g., Zen Buddhists, Mennonites, Sikhs, and so on).
2. Compare the causes of urbanization, the structures and infrastructures of the urban landscape, as well as the results of urbanization in nineteenth-century England, with the same structures in China or India (or other nations of your choice).
3. Evaluate the effect that Jesuit communities had on two Aboriginal communities (one North American, one South American).
4. Assess the interaction between the Sikh and Hindu communities in India.

HOT TOPIC: DOES WESTERN MEAN BETTER?

What does it mean when a nation becomes increasingly "Western"? There are many examples of nations whose cultures are being increasingly supplanted by Western culture. But "westernization" denotes more than eating hamburgers and watching Hollywood movies. Modern Western thought has helped shape the West and the rest of the world since the sixteenth century. Such thought includes the belief in positive progress and the spread of popular democracy. Western beliefs, philosophies, and ideologies ranging from Marxism to *laissez faire* economics have had both positive and negative impacts on scientific and religious thought, as well as on economic and political structures worldwide.

Potential Research Questions:

1. What was the impact of the Reformation and Calvinism on Western thought?
2. Compare communism in the former Soviet Union to communism in China, Cuba, or an African state.
3. Outline and assess the spread of liberal democracy in a non-Western state.
4. Evaluate the impact of modern Western economic and political thought on an indigenous group.
5. Has pessimism replaced the belief in positive progress? Comment from economic, environmental, and social perspectives.

Flashpoint: Social Structures and Social Organization

The September 2001 United Nations Conference on Racism, held in Durban, South Africa, was extremely controversial for a number of reasons. One major reason was the attempt to identify and condemn the historical social structures of some nations (e.g., caste systems in India, apartheid in South Africa, slavery in North America) and the suggestion that those nations pay reparations to compensate for the ills of slavery, colonization, and for perpetuating institutionalized discrimination and racism. Historians realize that the social structures (i.e., family, government, religion) of our time can either perpetuate racism and discrimination or aid positive social stability and/or change. The historical examination of how diverse social structures and principles have guided social organization is critical in understanding the challenges facing contemporary societies.

Potential Research Questions:

1. Has the West traditionally facilitated greater social mobility than did the rest of the world? Focus your research on two nations (one Western, one non-Western) throughout several centuries.
2. "Is God dead?" Compare and contrast worldwide changes in attitudes toward religion and religious observance in the Judeo-Christian tradition and in a non-Judeo-Christian religion (e.g., Islam, Buddhism).
3. Using a specific example, evaluate the role of religious fundamentalism in facilitating or preventing social, economic, and political change.
4. Analyse the causes and effects of historical changes in the structure of the family and the roles of members within the family (elders, children, gender differences).
5. Outline the role of technology in creating social change.

How might white South Africans have reacted to the removal of signs such as this?

OUR SUBJECT: WHAT WAS EUROPE?

Let us look at the meaning of a very familiar term: Europe. For the past half-millennium, Europe has been a major player. It took time for this to happen. In 1500 it was just one civilization among several scattered around the globe, some of them isolated, like the Aztec and the Inca, and others only sporadically in touch, like India and China. The next two hundred years saw an unprecedented spread of inter-zonal contact, commerce, and conquest, almost all of it at European hands. The results were profound, and sometimes catastrophic, as European men and microbes smashed or blighted whole civilizations and cultures. At the same time, vast new trade networks carried germs, plants, animals, captives, settlers, products, faiths, and cultures around the globe. Exchange was multilateral, and Europe received as well as gave; nevertheless, in balance, it exported. Deep into the twentieth century, the rest of the planet took on the coloration of both Europe and its ex-colonies in the Americas and elsewhere.

A planetary observer, with a wide-screen, bird's eye-view of the globe in 1500 would hardly have foretold Europe's imminent dominion. In Asia — Turkey, Persia, India, Java, China, Japan, Korea — were other civilizations, as rich, as complex, as gifted. Sub-Saharan Africa and the Americas, though with less technology, had well-built states, subtle cultures, and keen warriors. Furthermore, Europe was marginal, the western fringe of the great Eurasian super-continent. Not only that, it lacked unity; many states, many languages, many peoples jostling one another. It had no great emperor, no united military. Indeed, it even lacked a single faith. It did not even think of itself as "Europe" or the "West." That notion would come slowly, much later.

The Landscape

The story of how this divided continent invaded and colonized the planet comes in later chapters. What needs saying here is about the complexity and ambiguity of "Europe." The geographic boundaries were often blurred. From the west and north, there was no perceptual problem. From the wild Atlantic or the icy Arctic Ocean, one splashed or crunched ashore. The southern boundary was trickier; the western Mediterranean separated Muslim North Africa from Catholic Portugal, Spain, France and Italy. That was clear enough. But, further east, much of what we now call Europe was in Turkish hands: modern Hungary (after 1526), Romania, Bulgaria, Bosnia, Serbia, Montenegro, Macedonia, Albania, Greece, southern Ukraine. It is easy to forget how Turkish much of Europe was and how European much of Turkey was. The Turkish zone was richly mixed; peoples, languages, faiths and cultures lived side by side. As for the eastern boundary, Russia merged imperceptibly into the woods, grasslands and arid steppes of western Asia.

Physically, European geography was very complicated. From north to south, it had four major zones. At the top was a mini-Canada, ex-glacial, with the familiar rocks, trees, and lakes, and with the usual shaggy quadrupeds: bear, moose, beaver, otter, wolf, representatives of a circumpolar subarctic world. Further south was a well-watered zone, generally temperate, easily farmed, densely settled, and home to towns and cities. Yet further south was a belt of massive mountains: Pyrenees in Spain, Alps in France, Switzerland, northern Italy, southern Germany, Slovenia, and deeper in the Balkans. These mountains drew a sharp boundary, both physical and cultural, between the Mediterranean and the rest of Europe. They kept out the summer rains. The Mediterranean itself, therefore, had dry summers, scarce grass, and insufficient livestock. It was a region of striking contrasts: rough mountains, narrow, fertile valleys, rolling hills covered in olives, vines and fruit trees, and malarial flatlands. A zone of clashing tectonic plates, it had good scenery and far too many earthquakes.

United by Faith?

It takes more than geography to define a place. Europe is Europe because it plays host to a civilization. Civilizations are far easier to imagine than to define. As a rule, internally, they have common symbols, belief systems, institutions, and social patterns. In 1500 most Europeans were Christians — Catholic or Orthodox. Their religion furnished common values, rituals, and sacred art and architecture. It also offered identity and a label for it. Though there were Christians elsewhere — in Ethiopia, Armenia, southern India, and among Arabic speakers, for instance — in relationship to the world, Europeans often defined themselves as Christians, since most peoples they encountered were not. Europe also shared a heritage from the ancient Roman world. Not all the continent had been under the Caesars' rule, but classical Greek and Roman culture left a profound mark everywhere, on language, intellectual culture, literature, and all the visual arts. One great link to ancient Roman culture was Roman law. It lived on, in adapted form, in the canon law that governed the Latin Church. Its vocabulary, concepts, and procedures also infiltrated the law codes of states and cities, all the way from Portugal to Russia. Alongside religion and the classical heritage was a third common strand: Much of Europe, in the Middle Ages, had seen some form of feudalism, with its codes of knighthood and lordship. The feudal heritage shaped not only manners but also social relations and politics.

Who were the Europeans?

Ethnicity also made a difference. It was not wide nationhood, but local custom that mattered most. Since the nineteenth century, Europeans have come to think of themselves as distinct, often rival peoples defined by language: Poles, Germans, Italians, Basques, Welsh and so on, most of whom believe they deserve a state to call their own. That link between speech and political identity that now seems natural was, in 1500, still very foreign. Ethnicity then hinged not on language but on folkways — riddles, stories, songs, dress, cuisine, festivals, marriage customs and so on — held in common by townsfolk or inhabitants of a country district. Attachments and hostilities were often local: the Sienese sneered at the near-by Florentines; the Swiss in Bern battled the townsfolk of Zurich, a few miles down the road. Europeans, in 1500, had not yet homogenized their states. That centuries-long process, still alive today, had barely begun. Despite its unifying traits, Europe was extremely diverse. Religion mattered a good deal for group identity; there were religious minorities outside the Christian community. In many places there were sizable populations of Jews. Persecution made them mobile; it often banished them from cities and kingdoms, and encouraged them to form networks of distant allies. In the sixteenth century, western bigotry drove many Jews into the Turkish Empire, where they often prospered. There were also Muslims, pockets of them in Spain, where they had to pretend they had converted to Catholicism, and flourishing colonies in the Turkish Southeast. In Italy, Portugal, and Spain were Muslim slaves, bought or stolen, sometimes held in anticipation of a trade of prisoners, in exchange for Christian slaves in North Africa. There were also wandering bands of Roma people outside Christian churches and society.

---

* *Now complete Skills Focus One (p. 591):*

Laying the Foundation: Developing Inquiry Skills.

UNIT ONE

The World Re-Invented

Chapter One
Renaissance and Reformation
1450–1600

Chapter Two
The Age of Absolutism
1600–1715

Chapter Three
Contact and Conflict
1450–1700

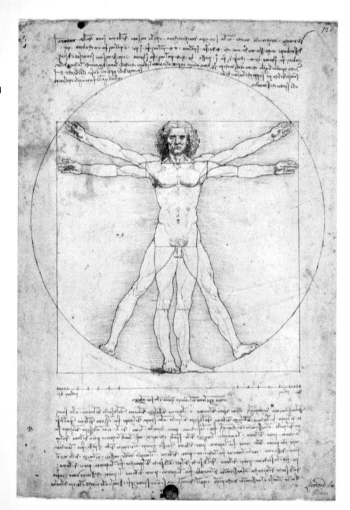

Leonardo da Vinci, *Vitruvian Man* (1485-90). The Renaissance was about the rebirth of antiquity. This drawing by Leonardo illustrates theories of proportion developed by the first-century BCE Roman architect Vitruvius.

In 1450 the world was on the brink of a dramatic change. In the Americas, the empires of the Inca and the Aztec would collapse within a century. The populations of indigenous peoples of the Americas would be decimated by European diseases and the swords of the conquistadors. The conquering Europeans would have to look elsewhere for a cheap source of labour to work their plantations and dig their mines. By the seventeenth century, the African diaspora (dispersion) was well under way as millions of young African slaves were shipped across the Atlantic. This contributed to the cultural transformation of the Americas and denied African society the vitality of much of its youth. With the vast and powerful Islamic Empire of the Near East acting as a barrier to overland trade with the Far East, the Europeans chose to set out in search of a sea passage to India and China. In the sixteenth century, Europeans succeeded in unlocking the secrets of the oceans' winds and currents, and beginning to make regular voyages to the Far East. As trade between Europe and the Far East expanded, it brought a vast assortment of goods to markets across Europe. Although Europeans traded extensively with India, China, and Japan, they would have much less success at dominating trading relationships.

While trade transformed the material culture of the world, the European Reformation would usher in a spiritual revolution. From the Spanish Inquisition to the wars of religion, Europeans would experience religious civil war lasting for nearly a century and a half. This religious turmoil was not limited to Europe alone. Indeed, one of the driving forces of European exploration and expansion in the sixteenth century was the search for souls. Catholics and Protestants alike sought new converts. The world of 1450 was thus re-invented over the succeeding two and half centuries as major forces drove change on a global scale.

Renaissance and Reformation 1450–1600

CHAPTER EXPECTATIONS

By the end of this chapter, you will be able to:

- *demonstrate an understanding of the roots and nature of a variety of communities and groups founded on religious, ethnic, and/or intellectual principles*

- *assess the influence of key individuals and groups who helped shape Western attitudes to change*

- *assess the extent to which art reinforces and/or challenges prevailing social and political values*

- *demonstrate an understanding of key developments in attitudes toward religion and religious observance since the sixteenth century*

This woodcut entitled *Religion Under Siege* (1520) is an allegorical representation of the Catholic Church in broken down condition being swarmed by Reformers. At the top of the house, the Pope and his bishops are trying to escape. What are they trying to escape?

Historians often label the period between 1500 and around 1750 as "early modern Europe." Imperfect and controversial, like most labels, this one is still useful. It points to a world no longer medieval, but still very unlike our own, a time of transitions, some swift, others slow. Early modern Europe played host to two more famous periods, and events: the Renaissance and the Reformation. The former was an intellectual and artistic flourishing that began in Italy around 1350. By 1500 the Renaissance had spread to much of Europe, from Spain and England to Hungary and Poland, but missing Russia and Turkish Europe.

Like the Renaissance, the Reformation was an intellectual movement. But its scope was narrower; only religion was at issue. The Reformation was a kind of revolution; it upended churches and drove states to riot, civil strife, and international war. Unlike the Renaissance, which came gradually, the Reformation exploded on the scene, in Germany, in 1517. But, like the Renaissance, it went more quietly, around 1650, when at last a century and more of religious wars came to an end. Both Renaissance and Reformation, as ingredients of European culture and its offshoots around the world, are still with us.

Before turning to these two dramatic movements, it helps to survey the whole early modern landscape. Historians of the Renaissance and Reformation today very often set these two developments against a larger background of demography, ecology, culture, and social and political structures. For, in many ways, Renaissance and Reformation shared in larger developments in Europe's evolution. In 1500 Europe was still very close to the Middle Ages. By 1650 or 1700, this was far from true, but change was slow and subtle. Moreover, the practical conditions of life — the economy, society, politics and the ecosystem seldom moved in phase with intellectual life.

KEY CONCEPTS AND EVENTS

Renaissance

Reformation

humanism

Utopia

indulgences

Diet of Worms

Protestantism

Anabaptists

Council of Trent

Inquisition

Counter-Reformation

Edict of Nantes

KEY PEOPLE

William Shakespeare

Leonardo da Vinci

Johann Gutenberg

Michelangelo

Niccolò Machiavelli

Desiderius Erasmus

Martin Luther

Jean Calvin

Henry VIII

Elizabeth I

Ivan the Terrible

Wit and Wisdom

Here I stand. I can do no other. God help me. Amen.

Martin Luther, at the Diet of Worms, April 18, 1521

TIME LINE: RENAISSANCE AND REFORMATION

Bubonic plague, the Black Death, kills as much as one-third of the population of Europe	1347	
	Ca. 1350	Renaissance begins in the northern Italian states
Johann Gutenberg invents movable type	Ca. 1445	
	1492	Spanish conquer Granada, the last Muslim state on the Iberian Peninsula
Leonardo da Vinci paints *The Last Supper*	Ca. 1595	
	1512	Michelangelo completes the painting of the ceiling of the Sistine Chapel in Rome 1514 Baldassare Castiglione writes *Book of the Courtier*; Niccolò Machiavelli writes *The Prince*
Thomas More, *Utopia*	1514	
	1517	Martin Luther posts his *95 Theses*, the Reformation begins
Peasants' War erupts in southern and central Germany	1524	
	1525	Anabaptist movement born in Switzerland
Rome sacked and vandalized by Germans and Spaniards	1527	
	1533	Henry VIII of England is excommunicated by the Roman Catholic Church over his marriage to Anne Boleyn
Jesuit order founded by former Spanish soldier and future saint Ignatius Loyola	1534	
	1572	Hundreds of Huguenot (Calvinist) nobles killed in Saint Bartholomew's Massacre
Spain annexes Portugal and its African-Asian trading empire	1580	
	1598	Edict of Nantes grants political and military privileges to French Huguenots

Not to scale.

EARLY MODERN EUROPEAN SOCIETY AND CULTURE

The Big Picture

In 1500 Europe was, by our standards, local, hierarchic, tradition-bound, slow-moving, poor, and dangerous. In the ensuing half-millennium, the world would move from local loyalties to national culture and identity. There would also be profound social shifts, as the Continent changed from rural to urban, from thinly to densely populated, from intimate to impersonal. Late medieval society was hierarchic: Status was often inherited rather than achieved. This would change, very gradually, as mobility and democratic ideals ate away at privilege.

The same localism that marked society and culture also affected early politics. Central institutions were still weak, unstable, and unambitious, while local power centres remained very influential. Real authority rested with informal bodies such as guilds, neighbourhoods, parishes, and especially families, which had many more tasks and powers than today. The economy also would change radically, as the household output of peasants, artisans, merchants, and officials gradually gave way to more complex, non-domestic forms of production. In the intellectual sphere, the old unity of knowledge would be shattered.

In 1500 to 1600, religion, philosophy, and natural science mingled in their picture of a God-filled universe. After 1650 or so, first science, and then social science, would break off, pursuing "facts" and leaving "values" to churches and philosophers. Traditions and revered, holy texts would be taken over in importance by the senses and systematic investigation. This intellectual shift would gradually shrink religion's sphere of influence. As for information, scarcity gave way to glut, as literacy, presses, and new media spread. As for danger, early modern Europe lacked the means to protect itself from famine, disease, accidents, and social violence. A pervasive sense of insecurity set the tone for feelings, the arts, and faith. In 1500 many of these great changes had already begun.

A Dangerous World

No world is completely safe. Our own times live in the shadows of ecological disaster and weapons of doom. The twentieth century has seen numerous catastrophes of human origin: colossal wars, and the expulsions and exterminations of whole peoples. There is no guarantee that the twenty-first century will prove wiser or more moderate. Nevertheless, seldom in history have humans enjoyed as much personal security as do those who, today, have the luck to live in a rich country like Canada or the United States. The average North American, European, Japanese, or Australian enjoys a sense of safety that, to a European in 1500, would have been utterly unthinkable, for many reasons.

The plague revisited Europe several times. This seventeenth-century woodcut shows Londoners fleeing their city because of plague.

First of all, there was disease. Our medicine works, whereas pre-modern cures did not. In 1500 antibiotics did not exist, surgery often killed the patient, and since germs were unheard of, antiseptic practices had no meaning. Add to the mixture poor diet, scarce clothing that was seldom washed, crowded housing, dirty streets and rivers, abundant rats, fleas and lice, and you had epidemics by the dozens. Early modern diseases were swift, like influenza, not slow like AIDS — they moved, and killed, quickly. Typhus, smallpox, typhoid, and many others, were deadly. Most famous, and worst of all, was bubonic plague. This catastrophic disease came back to medieval Europe in 1347 (there had been an earlier wave in the

One of a series of etchings dated 1633 by French artist Jacques Callot. The series was titled *The Miseries and Griefs of War*, and here we see mass executions by hanging.

sixth century). It raced across the Continent, killing in five brief years perhaps a third of the population. But it did not leave. Rather, down through the 1650s and 1660s, the plague came back again and again.

Plague is a disease of rats and other rodents, transmitted by their fleas. Humans are not the standard host. When the disease flares, the rats die off and their desperate fleas, even though they dislike our taste, grow so hungry that they start biting humans. The standard early modern practice, when plague broke out, was to seal the infected houses with all their people inside. For the inhabitants of a flea-ridden dwelling, this move often spelled doom. The disease produced egg-sized lumps, called buboes, in the groin and armpits — it was painful, swift, and almost always fatal.

Plague was not the only killer. All sorts of lesser dangers killed great numbers of people. Wounds, for instance, could fester, poisoning the blood. In the summer, diarrhea from bad water killed infants and small children. In the winter, respiratory infections killed both young and old. Therefore, life expectancy was short — in plague-times, few Europeans ever knew their grandparents. Of all children born, perhaps a quarter died by the age of one, and another quarter by the age of marriage. Many women, sooner or later, died in childbirth; perhaps one in seven. So much mortality destabilized the nuclear family. Parents lost children, children lost parents, husbands and wives replaced dead husbands and wives. Far more than now, death was a fact of life.

Disease was not the only danger. Famine was also a threat. Crop yields were low, and hail, drought, flood, and unseasonable heat or cold could doom harvests. Poor roads and weak governments made it hard to relieve a stricken area. In a crisis, desperate country folk migrated in search of food; sometimes, many died. Other natural disasters like floods and earthquakes also took their toll, but while these were no more common than today, they were harder to foresee or remedy. In northern Europe, where cities were built of wooden houses crowded peak to gable across narrow lanes, fire could lay waste whole neighbourhoods. All these risks combined to create unease; the world looked dangerous.

A reminder that death stalks everyone, any time. This etching is called *The Dance of Death* and dated to the mid-sixteenth century

In addition to natural disasters were the human dangers. Wars, like the states that waged them, were small-scale affairs. But they were chaotic. Early modern armies were ragged bands of hooligans who "borrowed" from foe and friend. They wrecked the landscape and spread diseases, venereal and other. When armies disbanded, loose soldiers fanned out, bullying and stealing their way home, or on the way to the next battle. Banditry was a common by-product of war, feud, famine, poverty and courts that exiled convicted men.

Violence of all sorts was common; most men carried knives, and many also wielded clubs, swords, guns or battle-axes. Social custom and codes of honour often fostered violence, among men and women. Early modern governments strove to curb such unofficial violence. The official violence of the state — the police and the courts — was their chief remedy. Their campaign would succeed, but very slowly.

Alongside disease, natural disasters, war and mayhem, all harmful to the body, was a second set of dangers — to the soul. To early modern Europeans, the devil and hell were both very real and powerful. God was stern, quick to punish, both on Earth and in the afterlife. The Last Judgement was no metaphor, but a looming truth — sooner or later it would arrive. Although religion offered remedies — prayer, confession, last rites — there was always the risk that, like Hamlet's murdered father, one might die a sudden death, unblessed by a priest, and therefore doomed. Against all these looming menaces, early modern Europeans had three shields: religion, community, and government.

Religion

Although for some people today, prayer, worship, and observance are part of everyday life, most of us have tucked whatever faith we have into a corner of our lives. Births, weddings, funerals, and other special occasions call forth religion, as do holidays, but most of life rolls on without much thought of holy things.

This early sixteenth-century painting by Giovanne Bellini shows a procession through St. Mark's Square in Venice. Public processions were a way for communities to court providence through their patron saint.

In this respect, in 1500, Europe was very different from today, since religion pervaded almost everything. The impact of the Reformation makes no sense unless we keep this crucial fact in mind. Religion had three crucial tasks: providence, salvation, and community.

Providence was God's justice, here on Earth. To early modern eyes, there were no pure accidents. If the chimney fell and broke your leg, it was your sins coming back on you. If the army lost the war, it was because the citizens had been scorning the Sabbath, gambling, swearing, and drinking in the wine shops when they should have been at prayer in church. If you gave birth to a lovely, healthy baby and came out alive it was not just the midwife's skill that saved you, it was her prayers, and yours, and your friends' prayers to Saint Margaret, patron saint of pregnant women. By this scheme of things, all the bad things — the hail, the storms, the clouds of hungry locusts, the plagues, the wars — in some sense came from God. He made them, or let them happen, to punish sin. And, of course, all good things, from bountiful harvests and successful voyages to luck in love and sport and war, were all God-given.

Although providence, and the whole divine scheme, came from God, he — as Father, Son and Holy Spirit — was not its only agent. The Virgin Mary was a potent source of providence, as were the countless saints. While God was universal, and a bit remote, Mary seemed more human, more likely to have favourite holy places, shrines famous for their special powers to cure and shelter, images with tremendous powers. The saints were even more local and specialized. Some saints were good for illnesses: St. Roch for plague, St. Lucy for sore eyes, Anthony for skin ailments. Other saints attached to professions: St. Ives for lawyers, Nicholas for sailors, Luke for painters. Others, as patrons, protected their favourite kingdoms, towns, guilds, families, or private persons. Saints were at once in heaven and on Earth, for their holy power was concentrated in their relics — their bones, their clothing, other objects they had touched or owned — and in their painted, carved, or moulded images. Churches and chapels, then, were great storehouses of holy objects venerated for their providential power.

There were several ways to invite providence. Be good, avoid sin, individually and collectively. Pray to God, to Mary, to the saints, asking them for help, or thanking them when it comes at last. There was private prayer, always helpful, but, when a community felt urgent need, it turned to public prayers, masses, processions with banners, statues and psalms. All sorts of self-punishment helped atone for sin: fasts, vigils, sexual abstinence, hard pilgrimages, alms, and social services. And one could also give God, Mary, and the saints fitting gifts. Much of the great religious art and architecture of the Renaissance were bargaining for providence.

This painting, *The Temptation of St. Anthony* was the altarpiece for a monastic hospital for skin diseases. It shows St. Anthony keeping his faith despite being tormented by devils.

If providence was God's justice in this world, salvation was his equity in the next. Original sin was a serious matter; through Adam and Eve, it had passed down to all mankind. Baptism washed off Adam's sin, but evil inclinations lived on. Without Christ's sacrifice on the cross, the doctrine went, all hope would have been in vain. But even with Christ, Christians were far from safe; inevitably, they would sin and sin again, and theologians agreed that without help, people lacked the power to save themselves. The necessary help was "grace," an undeserved gift dispensed by God alone, but channelled through his Church. Without it, Christians were doomed to an eternity in hell.

Before the Reformation, Christians prayed not only for themselves but also for their families and allies. Much of the church's massive edifice was paid for by prayer, for Christians, in the face of death and danger, paid the clergy to pray for them, and over the centuries, huge sums changed hands. Monasteries, churches, confraternities, and colleges of poor scholars heaped up lands and other wealth, donated in exchange for prayers and masses for the dead. Ever since the Middle Ages, the doctrine of purgatory had spurred and focussed prayer. Purgatory was a place of cleansing for imperfect souls. Though fiery and grim, it was no hell, but a stopover to paradise. Most souls went there first; only saints and the saintly went directly to heaven. In 1500 prayed that their dead loved ones would rise to paradise faster. Purgatory, then, was an excellent device for assuaging grief and cementing social community because it gave those who were grieving a useful task, and a focus for their feelings.

Prayers for the dead were only one of many ways in which religion served communities. It also provided a calendar of occasions for shared worship and celebration. Alongside the familiar great holidays — Christmas, Easter — there were countless others. Some were elaborations of the Nativity of Jesus, like the Feasts of Kings, of the Holy Innocents, and of the Circumcision. Others were related to Easter, like Ash Wednesday, Good Friday, the Ascension, and Pentecost. Other holidays celebrated the life of Mary or the lives and deaths of saints. Since saints had local ties, many communities, professions, and families celebrated their favourite patrons, not only with solemn prayers, but also with processions in the street, and perhaps with a market, feasting, games, or dancing.

Religion, as social glue, also marked the shape of time. Its holidays, great and small, signalled not only celebration, but also the rhythms of agriculture, commerce, politics, and the academic year. With its sacraments, it also observed and solemnized the life cycle: birth, the age of reason, marriage, parenthood, and death. And religion, with its vision of creation, Adam's fall, Christ's redemption, and the looming end of time, also gave a shape to history.

Religion also defined a social ethic, and, through preachers, teachers, censors, and church courts, supported social control. On the model of Jesus, Christianity preached sacrifice: "put others first" It praised self-denial: chastity, voluntary poverty and generous alms, humility, forgiveness. And, of course, it praised love of one's neighbours. Thus, religion, as inherited from medieval Europe, was a rich web of beliefs and practices draped over much of life. The Reformation, where it won, would rip out many beliefs, and modify almost all the rest. It was sudden, violent, and passionate, and it touched so much of life.

The Fair on St. George's Day (1559) by Peter Brueghel the Elder shows peasants celebrating the saint by feasting and dancing. The banner says "Let the peasants have their festival."

The Honour Code

Christian ethics, however, did not rule the moral scene alone. There was a second ethic, not inscribed in any holy text, and not defended by the church and clergy, but so potent that in much of Europe it often had more to do with real behaviour than all the sermons given. This was the honour code. Be proud, it said, not humble. Be rich, not poor. If thine enemy smite thee, smite him back. If not, he will steal thine honour. The honour code was a social ethic, rooted not in God, but in custom and in opinion, for one's honour was one's reputation; its opposite was shame. All sorts of social assets thus built honour: power, wealth, prestige, strength, courage, knowledge, intelligence, artistic skill, and social *savoir faire*. Men won honour, it was often said, by what they did, women by what they did not do, i.e., engage in sex outside the rules. This was imprecise, for women, by beauty, intelligence, industry, courage, discretion, taste, elegant dress, and social skill, could win honour for themselves, and for their families. Nevertheless, males often were guardians of the bodies, and the reputations, of dependent females. Fathers, husbands, brothers all suffered shame when a woman broke the rules; in some times and places, if the offending man would not or could not marry or offer a dowry for the woman, he, or she, or both might suffer death.

Religion fought the demands of honour. Against revenge, it argued mercy, against wealth and pride, it preached humble simplicity. Honour praised those who looked out for friends, allies and kin. Religion countered with universal brotherhood. Where honour stressed reputation and the view of peers, religion exalted conscience and the all-seeing eye of God. Still, the two ethics did have points in common; both praised generosity, courage, justice, and honesty. But the differences were stark. Nevertheless, European culture juggled these contradictory demands handily. No society has a single code; moral contradictions leave room for choice. [1]

The Renaissance, though often deeply Christian, was laced with honour too. For high culture, we shall

Eleanor de Toledo (1546), wife of the Duke of Tuscany by Bronzino. The elaborate dress of the Duchess is the story behind this picture. The moral is: clothing = image = the honour and splendour of the grand ducal house.

see, not only glorified the Virgin and the saints; it also gave polish to nobles, lords and princes, who wrapped themselves in prestigious art. The Reformation and its Catholic response, of course, worked hard to squelch honour's violence, pride, and love of luxury.

COMMUNITIES

Families and Friends

Against all the dangers, natural and human, early modern Europeans took shelter in communities. Honour reinforced group loyalties, since it praised all who stood up for their allies. Besides, honour was contagious; one basked in the glory of one's associates.

Also, by inciting competition and mayhem, honour encouraged men, especially, to stand by any coalition that would avenge their harm. Thus, the values of early modern Europe had much in common with the culture of today's street gangs. The more dangerous the world, the more willingly one makes sacrifices to groups. Coalitions not only shielded their members from violence; they also advanced their welfare in social life, business, and politics.

Of all premodern solidarities, family was the most important. By the standards of European history, the modern family has remarkably few functions. Our families still provide residence, love, nurturing, and socialization. But they have lost some crucial pre-modern jobs. No longer are they the main units of economic production, education, healthcare, social welfare, small-scale governance, and armed defence. Modern families are fragile, partly because they have lost so many functions. Other institutions have replaced them, liberating family members and loosening bonds of loyalty and costly obligation.

Property was a family's bedrock. In a slow-moving economy, a youngster's inheritance, far more than skills and determination, dictated his future place in life. The bulk of land and capital was in the hands of fathers or their surrogates. Under such rules, youthful rebellion was very hard. Some women did have some goods of their own, often passed down the female line. And widows could run the shop or farm. But, in general, the whole regime was male. In many zones, while sons inherited, their sisters had little more than a dowry, a sum handed by their fathers to their grooms. This belonged to a wife by law, but the husband invested and enjoyed it. Dowry was like female life-insurance; it reverted on the husband's death. But too bad for the adulteress; she forfeited title, whereas unfaithful husbands got off free and clear. This arrangement chained women to their husbands and divorce was barely possible. Assets held a family together, while the poor, with few or none, had weaker family ties and greater liberty.

The household, almost everywhere, was the basic unit not only of ownership, but also of most production. Most property — land, buildings, tools — was itself productive. Family was not just the reproductive group — husband, wife, and offspring — but also included all other persons under a single productive roof as well: more distant relatives, servants, apprentices, and other employees. All these persons, as workers, served the head of a household. Thus, the family was the smallest unit of the state. Heads answered for servants and apprentices who stole or brawled. By law, the head of the house could beat underlings, even his wife.

When it came to marriage, solid families thought strategically. Whether peasants, merchants, officeholders, or nobles, they scouted for good alliances. Young men and women should marry into money, land, and good connections. Marriages served the interests of parents and siblings. Love and happiness were seldom first in the minds of the elders who arranged a match. While, in theory, if repelled by the family's choice, a bride or groom could protest, resistance was often futile. Only the poor could enjoy the luxury of a love match.

The Renaissance Social Hierarchy

Pre-modern Europeans saw inequality as both natural and good. They had little of our ideal of democracy and equality. Like the Middle Ages, the Renaissance saw the whole cosmos as full of hierarchies. The four elements rose from base earth, up through water and air, to noble fire. The beasts went from worms and slugs to lions and eagles. The metals climbed from lead to gold. A whole cosmic chain of being rose to the throne of God. Accordingly, soul was better than body, ideas nobler than mere physical objects. Human beings, a combination of body and spirit, of sense and reason, of passion and intellect, lived in the borderlands between two realms. Above were angels, below were beasts. This broad pre-modern vision pervaded astronomy, physics, biology, political theory, rhetoric, ethics, theology, and all the Renaissance arts, and reinforced social distinctions of high and low.

From the Middle Ages, the Renaissance also inherited feudal attitudes. Feudalism was an arrangement that was economic, social, political, and legal. It had been a model of governing in which land was central. Lords — those who held fiefs (feudal lands) — had all sorts of powers: to judge, to tax, and to run the local market, wine press, mill and tavern. These powers were hereditary, since a lord's office was attached to his possessions. At the same time, feudal law and custom hitched most lords to higher lords, to whom they owed military help ("aid") and advice ("counsel"). In medieval times, when a lord needed support, he called on his dependent vassals, themselves noble lords. Lords constituted a hereditary fighting class; their dependent peasants did all the work and paid the rents that fed the ruling class. When the Middle Ages slowly shifted into early modernity, feudalism did not shrivel. Rather, it changed, adapting itself to new markets, new military roles in the armies of the state, and new political forms. Therefore, a vision of social inequality lived on, dividing the world into nobles and mere commoners and distinguishing the lesser titles (gentleman, knight) from the greater (count, duke, earl, prince). The mania for rank survived, and ran through Shakespeare and all other Renaissance literature.

At the same time, countless other divisions expressed hierarchy. Youth deferred to age, females to males, servants to masters, foot soldiers to their officers, the disenfranchised to citizens, and citizens to the officials of town or guild. Slaves bowed down to everybody. In general, ordinary citizens deferred to clergy, and low clergy yielded to prelates (bishops, archbishops, cardinals). At the top of the church sat the pope, while the emperor of Germany lorded it over even kings, who outranked all others. The world was full of ceremonies of precedence: taking the best seat at the central table, marching first in line, passing first through gates and doors, lifting second the hat in greeting, having the first hello, and so on, almost without end.

In the basement, and around the edges, of society, were the dispossessed. These poor folk had so few resources that at times they seemed almost to have fallen off the bottom rung of any ladder of prestige.

Pleasures
AND PASTIMES

During the Renaissance, dancing was a way for men and women to show themselves off, to demonstrate their awareness of the latest fashions, and to display their mastery of polite behaviour — qualities required for acceptance into society (much like today). Literally hundreds of dance manuals were published during this time. Three of the most important dance masters who wrote "how-to" papers on dancing were Thoinot Arbeau, Cesare Negri, and Fabritio Caroso. All three wrote detailed explanations of the different kinds of dances and how they were performed. To be a somebody at court, you had to be able to dance well. Just like among young people today, knowing about music and dance was critical to your social standing.

They included: peasants too poor in land to feed themselves, reduced to casual labour or begging; women who had lost their husbands and their health, doing odd jobs like washing or, again, begging at church doors; vagrants of all sorts, living off charity or theft. This was a fluid world, but with luck, some might escape into better times. Prostitutes are a case in point; in an economy with few good jobs for women, many, down on their luck, rented themselves out as part-time surrogate wives to multiple men, providing not only sex but, often, sewing, laundry, cooking, hospitality, and companionship. Some in a year or two scraped together a dowry and married back into the working class.

The Renaissance, a movement in high culture, had little impact outside of the elite classes. Some painters, carvers, and other artisans took part, producing for churches and their social betters. Most other artisans, wage labourers, and peasants, had no Renaissance at all. The Reformation, on the other hand, where it happened, touched the whole social hierarchy, since providence and salvation were the concern of all — even the very poor worshipped.

The Renaissance was a movement of high culture and had little impact on the lives of the poor and destitute, such as these beggars painted by a sixteenth-century artist.

Demography

Historians have invented a powerful technique for investigating past demography — the statistical study of pre-modern birth, reproduction, and death. Their method, "family reconstitution," is not content with aggregate figures, such as total births or deaths; rather, it studies individuals, one by one, *en masse*. It does so by examining parish registers, generally in villages where migration rates are low, to compile weddings, baptisms, and funerals. Reconstructing whole life histories, scholars learn how soon, how often, and how long, women had babies. They can also trace the seasonal, annual, and long-term movements in fertility and mortality. Their studies show us a society fascinatingly different from our own.

The pre-modern world was very close to what demographers call Malthusian equilibrium, named after Thomas Malthus (1766–1834) the famous eighteenth-century political economist. Think of a population as water in a giant bathtub, where birth gushes from the faucet and death goes gurgling down the drain. So long as fertility (F) exceeds mortality (M), the tub fills up — the population rises. But, where resources are finite and nature is already under stress, there are limits. The bigger the population, the scarcer are food, energy, shelter, and other necessities. And crowding spreads infections. So, as the tub grows fuller and population (P) keeps rising, mortality (drainage) accelerates. Meanwhile, in a pre-modern world, as P grows, fertility dries up. This is because marriage is, above all, an economic union, and young people will delay the wedding if they lack sufficient land or goods to sustain a household. Also, dire poverty can sap natural fertility by splitting families in search of work, cutting desire, and suppressing the menstrual cycle at times of extreme stress. Meanwhile, in many zones, down to 1700 or so, periodic famines and epidemics sparked death waves more readily when the population was already stressed. Under such conditions, population growth was slow at best. When, in the great tub of life, M equaled F, the water level held steady. [2]

Despite this simple model, the long-term curve of population had a complex shape. After the first shock of the Black Death (1347–1353), the population of Europe kept falling for several decades, due to epidemic aftershocks. Then, around 1400, it stabilized, near half its pre-plague level. The emptier, less crowded Europe lived better, ate more meat, and, in general enjoyed a better diet but, probably due to plague, could not begin to grow until perhaps 1480. Then, in the next 140 years, the Continent gradually filled up again. The natural environment degraded as land clearances stripped forests, drained wetlands, eroded hillsides, and clogged riverbeds with silt. As

WEB CONNECTION

www.mcgrawhill.ca/links/legacy

Go to the site above to find out more about the Renaissance.

this happened, living standards sank because agriculture could not improve as fast as numbers rose. By 1620, the European diet had regressed and wages had fallen. Under these pinched circumstances, population stagnated or shrank, almost everywhere, into the early eighteenth century.

Political Bodies

After the fall of the Roman Empire (ca. 500), for the next 500 years European political units fragmented more and more. Feudalism, the prime medieval political structure, was fundamentally local. The next half-millennium and more, from 1000 to 1500 and beyond, reversed the trend. Very gradually, political units reached out across the landscape and deepened their control. Many were kingdoms, but not all; there were independent city-states in Germany and Italy. And, eventually, there arose confederal states, like the Netherlands and Switzerland. No single model ruled. By 1500, in many places, there emerged kings more competent than their medieval predecessors; historians call these "Renaissance monarchies." In France, England, Spain, Hungary, Sweden, and some petty German and Italian states, kings and princes grew richer. They hired more officials, laid down more law, and surrounded themselves with more sumptuous courts.

As great lords, royalty had always kept a sumptuous household. Honour demanded hospitality and largesse. Easy eating, ready entertainment, and feudal counsel drew an entourage of hangers-on and advisers. As monarchs grew richer, ambitious men and women swarmed around them like bees around jampots, in hopes of receiving lands, gifts, pardons, titles, privileges, promotions, commissions, jobs, monopolies, secrets, and royal smiles. All courtiers were not equal; the stronger and better placed became patrons to the weaker, who patronized the weaker still. Courts thus were rife with jockeying and intrigue, as coalitions of courtiers manoeuvred for advantage. Courts, like Hollywood today, were envied for their luxury and power, and loathed as dens of intrigue, avarice,

hypocrisy, and loose sexual mores. At the same time, its very extravagance gave lustre to a regime, and honour liked nothing better than a pompous show. Splendid music, dance, theatre, tapestries, and furniture, and gorgeous banquets with sugar statues of Hercules and live birds or piglets in the pies, not to mention roast peacocks and herons with the feathers deftly re-attached — all these things elevated princes.

The pleasures of the Renaissance court are here in the rich furnishings, tapestries and elegant courtiers shown in this sixteenth-century painting.

Many surviving Renaissance treasures, now sitting lonely in museums, once graced palaces, where they made a proud claim for honour. In your imagination, refurnish a Renaissance court, setting the elegant bronze statues and gold tableware on dazzling inlaid marble tables before a brilliant tapestry, then add sweet music, the bustle of servants, and the smell of spiced pheasant in saffron-flavoured broth. (If you suspect poison in your food, just slip it to a dog under the table or make a servant take a taste.)

Although, from 1500 to 1700, European monarchies and other states gradually grew stronger, the process was far from smooth or simple. Some monarchs were checked by opposing forces, as in England and the Netherlands, where hybrid regimes emerged. The kings of Poland remained feeble; there, landed nobles were in charge. In Germany, the emperor, failing to consolidate his empire, left most power in the hands of landed princes. Moreover, even where regimes did flatten opposition, they rarely just laid down the law; rather, much more subtly, they compromised and co-opted. Early modern states thus were ramshackle affairs, full of holes and vague zones where local powers claimed ancestral privileges.

Review, Reflect, Respond

1. How was European society different from Western society today? Give three examples.

2. Explain why an understanding of the role of religion in daily life in early modern Europe is critical to understanding the Renaissance and Reformation periods.

3. Describe how the social organization of early modern Europe differed from that of the medieval period.

A REVOLUTION IN THE MILITARY

Fortresses and Firearms

The Middle Ages had perfected two key military devices: the armoured knights on horseback and the stone castle. The former ruled the battlefield. Their prowess had assured the power and precedence of a landed, noble class that alone could afford fine horses, expensive armour, and long adolescent training in mounted warfare. Yet the latter invention was the stronger — a well-stocked castle could face knights down, and just wait them out. In the Middle Ages, then, defence had the upper hand over offence. As a result, local lords, strong within their stone walls, could defy monarchs and hoard powers and privileges of governance.

The Fortress of Peter and Paul in St. Petersburg, Russia was built in the early eighteenth century but uses the star shape that was developed in Italy in the early sixteenth century.

Gunpowder changed all that. Yet early guns were slow to load, and wildly inaccurate; it took Europeans some 200 years to perfect marching drills and learn how to face down cavalry. The spread of firearms never unseated the noble class, but it did change both the nature of its fighting and the rhetoric of its claims to military command. For the balance of power, what mattered more than muskets was the mobile siege cannon. Stone castles were brittle structures, well suited to repelling arrows but, in the face of cannon, utterly helpless. Ten hits and down they went.

Around 1500, first in Italy, and then almost everywhere, Renaissance military engineers found a good answer to the cannon: the star-shaped, bastioned fortress. This model even spread to Louisbourg, Quebec, and Kingston in the New World. With its sloping walls of earth, clad in stone, and its protruding platforms, the new un-castle could absorb or deflect incoming cannon balls. Fairly quickly, then, defence once more beat offence. But these new forts were massive, and expensive to build or seize. Only states could afford or beat them. So the old nobility, by virtue of technology, lost its remote fortresses, its military self-sufficiency, and, eventually, the local loyalties that had resisted central power. Without their old impregnability, the Renaissance upper classes shifted from periphery to centre, and invested in court careers, royal offices, or military commands. [3]

Ambitions of the State

Early modern states inherited from their medieval predecessors their chief ambitions: raise money, make war, feed the court, and do justice. Most other political ambitions familiar today, were outside their scope: to foster trade, and promote health, education, and social welfare, were not central state concerns. Trade was for the towns. The other three aims concerned churches, guilds, and urban magistrates. Only gradually would central states take much interest in the prosperity and well-being of their subjects. Justice, on the other hand, did matter; it both elevated rulers and kept the peace, they hoped.

Early modern justice, however, was haphazard. There were no police forces of the modern sort, and no detectives to investigate crimes. The world was unruly; honour both caused and glorified violence, and poverty led to theft. In 1500, in many places, local powers sheltered and encouraged outlaws. Unable to catch many criminals, justice often made examples of the few it did, imposing horrid punishments to scare the masses. It was a rare city that lacked a gallows or execution wheel outside the walls, or its share of severed heads on pikes or at the gate, grim reminders of the terrible hand of justice. Between 1500 and 1650, and beyond, justice gradually became steadier, more ambitious, but hardly less cruel. Western European states gradually criminalized the violence traditionally sanctioned by honour and slowly tamed the Continent.

Every early modern European town had its own torture wheel and gallows.

INTELLECTUAL LIFE IN THE RENAISSANCE

Worldviews

In early modern Europe, high intellectual culture changed radically and rapidly. The fields of law, philosophy, political theory, history, literary theory, literature itself, language studies, medicine, theology, and the natural sciences grew, and changed. The worldview in the 1500s was still largely medieval. By comparison, the 1700s would look almost modern. Historians sum up this complex, momentous process with two terms, "Renaissance" and "scientific revolution."

What was the Renaissance? As its French name suggests, it was a rebirth. Sculpture, painting, architecture, and the lesser visual arts recaptured, with striking success, the skills and expressive habits of the ancient Greeks and Romans. The same happened in literature and in many intellectual disciplines: philosophy, political theory, mathematics, medicine, historical scholarship. Still, the Renaissance was not a simple revival of what the ancients had done; Renaissance artists and thinkers blended what they recovered with medieval traditions, and then added new knowledge. The result was a cultural effervescence that pushed Europe toward modernity.

The medieval intellectual heritage upon which the Renaissance built was itself rich and subtle. It was a braided ribbon with intertwining strands of Greek aesthetics, philosophy, mathematics, science, Roman law, Judeo-Christian ethics, and feudal attitudes to authority and justice. These ancient ingredients were potent, but often garbled in translation. They influenced intellectual life and the arts, giving rise to novel combinations unintended in antiquity. Medieval language, literature, law, and arts, despite their ancient ingredients, had a character of their own.

Aspects of the Medieval Worldview

Medieval civilization bequeathed to early modern Europe several habits of mind. Though none would still hold total sway by 1700, all remained influential. We have seen some of these already. The main ones were:

1. The notion of a divine plan: The world was the product of God's intelligence. Insofar as it was orderly, its arrangements testified to his benign power.

2. Closely related to the first: the idea of hierarchy, or "Great Chain of Being." One sign of God's design was the division of high from low. Ascending orders of elements, creatures, social classes, church dignitaries, postures, rhetorics, civic offices, and countless other things all bore witness to divine good order. This thinking traced back to Plato and his Greek followers.

3. Dualism: another Platonic idea, profoundly influential on Christianity. It divided the world into two natures: spirit on the one hand, matter on the other. Spirit, soul, intellect, and reason gave shape and nobility to unruly matter, which, by nature, inclined to chaos and decay. In Christian eyes, our physical bodies incited us to sin, slightly controlled by reason. Christian self-denial had roots in such ideas.

4. Allegory: originally a Greek literary device. An allegory reads a material thing, or story, to find the higher spiritual or moral meaning behind it. When joined to dualism and the notion of God's plan, allegory was more than a writer's trick. In the hands of preachers and poets, it coloured many sorts of thought. To give an example: in medieval folklore, when chased by enemies, the beaver (castor in Latin) turns around and bites off its testicles (castrates itself). The allegory, or higher moral truth was this: When pursued by the devil, be chaste (castus) and, like the beaver, cut off the sources of temptation. Notice that the allegory does not study the beaver for its material nature, but only looks "behind" it for immaterial wisdom.

5. Providence: Mere accidents seldom happen. God, who sees all, makes sure that the wicked suffer for their sins, and the just receive their rewards.

6. Teleology: from Aristotle, the Greek philosopher, medieval thought derived the notion that all things have a telos, an inherent purpose, or goal. In

physics, for instance, the goal of heavy objects is to fall downward. In politics, the telos of the ruler is justice. Such thinking sat well with notions of order and hierarchy.

The Renaissance Worldview

The profound cultural change we call the Renaissance did not start out as a rebellion against the medieval vision of the world. Rather, it adopted and adapted much of it. Instead, the Renaissance began as a linguistic campaign. Its prime target: medieval Latin. From 1350 on, first in Italy, then elsewhere, learned purists rebelled against the pragmatic Latin of the law courts and universities. In its place, they adopted the elegant language of the orators and poets of Augustan Rome.

A loose coalition of men we now call "humanists" undertook to restore lost eloquence. Some scoured monastic libraries, rooting up long-forgotten antique works, obscurely copied by dutiful monks. Treasures surfaced: the private letters of Cicero, the erotic love poems of Catullus, the architectural treatises of Vitruvius, the histories of Tacitus. Soon, the search extended to Greek works, sometimes salvaged as the Turks swallowed the last shreds of the eastern Roman Empire.

Humanists not only unearthed lost works; they also perfected a linguistic detective science called philology, the study of vocabulary and usage. It served for dating passages, and for sniffing out the many forgeries and mislabelled or garbled works in libraries. Humanism gave rise to school reforms that pushed eloquence in place of logic. It also published careful editions of the classics. Under humanism's influence, literature, both Latin and vernacular (the language of the common folk), sported more and more antique form and content. Without it, Shakespeare could never have written *Anthony and Cleopatra* or *Julius Caesar*.

The Renaissance was more than humanism. The taste for the antique extended to the visual and other arts. Very Roman domes, arches, columns, and cornices returned to architecture. The ancient practice of monumental inscriptions revived. Statues, nude or thinly clad, took on classic poses, as did painted figures. Painters added ancient themes — myths of Olympus, tales from Ovid. Dramatists modelled plays on Greek and Roman comedy, with tricky servants or amorous shepherds, while the set designers copied the ancient stages, whose ruins still survived. All this artistic imitation shared with humanism a taste for authenticity. It championed the harmony of form and content. Medievals knew of Mars, but dressed him as a knight. The Renaissance exchanged his medieval armour for Roman.

RENAISSANCE ART

The Invention of Linear Perspective: Seeing Far into Space

The realism that emerged in Renaissance painting went beyond mere fidelity to ancient costumes, architecture, and statuesque posture. It also extended to the portrayal of three-dimensional space. In the 1440s, Florentine theoreticians and working painters solved the problem of the vanishing point. Their pic-

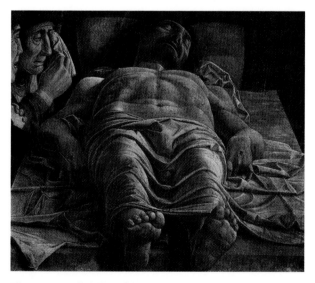

This painting called *The Dead Christ* (1500) by Mantegna is a striking example of foreshortening, a perspective technique rediscovered in the Renaissance.

tures acquired depth. Then, around 1500, scientist and artist Leonardo da Vinci (1452–1519), worked out how distance fades colours, how shadows modulate, and how surfaces pick up the reflected tints of nearby objects. By the early sixteenth century, brilliant painters like Raphael (1483–1520) had mastered all the new techniques and could paint works of astonishing naturalism. Medieval artists had not tried for naturalism; for them, in general, the divine truths mattered more. Images could serve as symbols. Renaissance artists were still Christian, but their art, when sacred, also evoked the world around them.

THE SENSE OF HISTORY
Seeing Far in Time

The Renaissance espoused a novel view of history. For medieval scholars, history, when it mattered, had been a story of providence and salvation, or of local precedents; cultural difference was beside the point. For the Renaissance, however, the cultural integrity of antiquity was what mattered. The ancients were to be admired and imitated. Though new, this Renaissance sense of history still looked backwards; the norm still lay in the past, presumed to be perfect. Nevertheless, two things helped swing the norm from past toward future. One was a growing awareness of the conflicts and contradictions in the ancient heritage. Another was a growing confidence: "We can sculpt, and paint, and build as well as they." It would take the scientific revolution to clinch the ideal, or myth, of "progress."

Print

With so much information available to them, people today cannot easily imagine an almost pageless world, where household lore, tavern talk, and the occasional sermon of a passing friar delivered the important news. Medieval information had been scarce, often private and tightly held. Books, handmade, had been a costly rarity, and when elegantly inscribed and painted

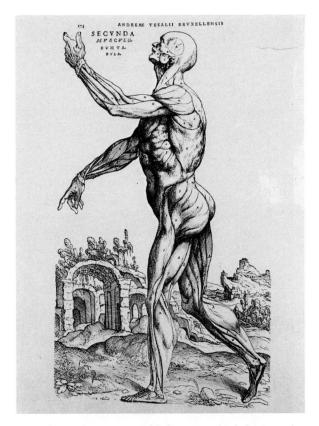

A page from *De humani corporis fabrica,* anatomy books by sixteenth-century artist-anatomist Andrea Vesalius. The poses of the figures are borrowed from antique sculpture.

on supple calfskin pages (called vellum), were treasures for churches or rich collectors. University "lectures" had been what their Latin name implied, readings: students copied down an excerpt, dictated from the teacher's precious text, with all the attached comments, plus his own remarks.

Under these conditions, the invention of movable type by Johann Gutenberg (1397–1468), in Mainz, in the 1440s, set off a revolution. Books went from rare to common, from expensive to often cheap. The inaccuracy of scribal copies waned, and the range of content grew ever wider. Print promoted vernacular languages: English, French, Spanish, German, Czech, and others. It fostered news and propaganda. It encouraged scholarship and literacy, lowered the barriers between cultures low and high, and served both repression and rebellion. Still, only a minority, largely male, could read and write. [4]

The Renaissance Man

You might know Leonardo da Vinci (1452–1519) primarily as the painter of *The Last Supper* and *The Mona Lisa*. He was also renowned as a sculptor, architect, musician, engineer, anatomist, mathematician, inventor, and scientist, to name only some of the many roles in which he excelled.

Da Vinci lived during a time when faith and tradition gave way to learning and curiosity.

> *It seems to me that those sciences are vain and full of error which do not spring from experiment, the source of all certainty.*

From the time he was about 30, da Vinci kept a notebook in which he recorded observations and ideas. All entries were written in a peculiar backward script, sloping from left to right and requiring a mirror to read.

Many notebook pages reveal that he made startling connections between ideas. For da Vinci, everything he did reminded him of something else. Da Vinci's notebook pages provide rare insights into the workings of an amazingly inventive mind.

During the Renaissance, artists tried to achieve greater realism, which led to richer detail in their works but required anatomical research. Over a period of 25 years, da Vinci dissected about 30 corpses to create almost two hundred drawings of the human anatomy. He developed a way of drawing that medical artists still follow today.

Indeed, he saw the human body as a model for many of his inventions and wrote in his notebook, "Man is the model of the world."

Da Vinci observed birds closely, studying the anatomy of their wings, and the function and arrangement of their feathers. He became fascinated with the possibility of human flight. In one notebook entry, he wrote: "Be sure to draw the anatomy of a bird wing ... I feel like making miracles!" Da Vinci's initial ideas about

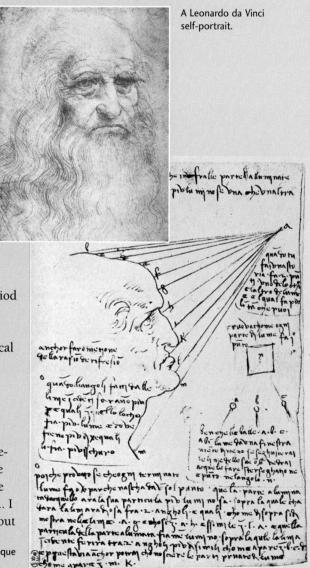

A Leonardo da Vinci self-portrait.

A page from Leonardo's notebook showing his unique technique of writing that could only be read with the help of a mirror.

human flight involved constructing a large flapping pair of wings that simulated those of birds. He later abandoned the idea after observing how birds of prey are lifted up by air currents. From this insight, he concluded the best prospect for human flight lay in fixed-wing gliding. It is amazing to think that it was not until hundreds of years later, in 1903, that the Wright brothers first achieved powered flight.

Da Vinci also designed several types of weapons. He invented models of machine guns, grenades, and a very modern-looking bomb. He improved an old idea to create an armoured car that had a complex motor and cannons. More than four hundred years later, with the addition of a modern engine and caterpillar treads, this device was called a tank, and became an important weapon in twentieth-century wars.

However, Da Vinci was not a war-loving person. He wrote in his notebook, "War! What barbaric madness!" and explained why he created instruments of war: "I do it to preserve nature's most precious gift — and that gift is our freedom."

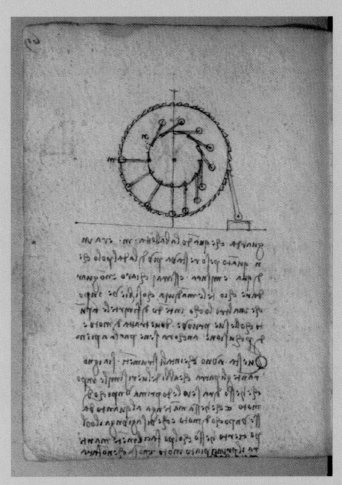

This is a drawing of a weapon invented by da Vinci, apparently for firing multiple projectiles.

---

1. The term "Renaissance Man" was invented to describe people like da Vinci, people with multiple capabilities, including artistic talent. Think of someone you know, or know of today who deserves the title "Renaissance Man" or "Renaissance Woman" and briefly describe their talents and skills.

2. Can a "Renaissance Person" be successful today? Explain.

THE HIGH RENAISSANCE IN ROME

Patronage

In the fourteenth century, the principal residence of the Renaissance was Florence, a prosperous city dominated by bankers and great wool merchants. For almost 60 years, the Medici, a dynasty of merchant princes, dominated politics and patronized the arts. In 1494, however, the family fell; the city had four revolutionary years as a holy republic under the influence of a puritanical prophet-friar named Savonarola (1452–1498), who encouraged bonfires made of paintings of such things as naked Roman goddesses. The Florentine Renaissance never recovered its old sparkle.

At about the same time, a number of popes used their wealth and power to draw the best artists and intellectuals to their Roman court. The most famous of these are Julius II (1503–1513) and Leo X (1513–1521). Julius "*il papa terribile*" — the fearsome pope — was an ambitious warrior who used papal armies to expand his state. He brought Michelangelo, Raphael, and Leonardo da Vinci to his court. He had Michelangelo paint the ceiling of the Sistine Chapel, while Raphael and his team of talented helpers decorated the *Stanze*, the official rooms of the Vatican palace, with frescoes. Julius had the audacity to level the old church of Saint Peter's, a venerable building that went back 1200 years to the time of Emperor Constantine. He commissioned architects to work out a radical, circular design for its replacement. Their work, and their successors', created the enormous church we have today. Though decades later, Michelangelo himself would eventually design the dome.

After Julius II came Leo X, a Medici, who was as plump and luxurious as Julius had been lean and stern. Leo loved food and hunting. He loved all the arts as well. His Rome swarmed with sculptors, goldsmiths, painters, poets, and philosophers. Under Leo's successor, Clement VII, however, the Roman Renaissance died a sudden death. Clement, another Medici, bungled foreign affairs, and in 1527, a ragged, mutinous army of Germans and Spaniards in imperial service stormed Rome. The sacking went on for months, killing, raping, stealing, torturing cardinals and other Romans for their treasures, and leaving the city a physical and cultural wreck. Most artists who survived scattered to other cities. The Roman Renaissance never recovered.

Castiglione: The Courtier As Idealist

In 1514 Baldassare Castiglione (1478–1529), a diplomat and courtier who had served assorted princes, wrote his *Book of the Courtier*. This work on the skills and values of a good courtier, was set not as a dry treatise but as a series of polite but spirited conversations and debates. The conversations were among real persons who had lived in the grand palace of the dukes of Urbino. The palace is still there, though the furniture is gone. If you visit the palace, you will have to imagine the courtiers, the servants, the dogs, the horses, and the conversations, if they really happened. Castiglione's courtiers were models of discretion, masters and mistresses of the well-chosen act or word. They admired women and heeded their requests. The key to the courtly life was *sprezzatura*, an untranslatable Italian term for an artful and artificial naturalness, a sort of Renaissance cool. The book caught on, not only in Italy; translations carried it across Europe and inspired aristocrats in many countries, validating their wealth and show, but preaching the self-control that gives one high style.

Machiavelli: The Courtier As Cynic

Just when Castiglione was writing his *Book of the Courtier*, a Florentine civil servant, Niccolò Machiavelli (1469–1527) was losing his job, with literary results. Machiavelli had been busy secretary to the Florentine Republic until, in 1512, the Medici retook the city. He was worse than just out of work; he suffered arrest, judicial torture, and exile. Like many accidental authors

Portrait of Baldassare Castiglione, author of *The Book of the Courtier,* here painted by the High Renaissance master Raphael (1483-1502)

INTELLECTUAL DEVELOPMENTS

The Renaissance Spreads Through Europe

After 1500 the Renaissance spread across those parts of Europe that then belonged to the Church of Rome. Orthodox Christian zones like Russia and the Balkans, which were under Turkish rule, were little affected. Several mechanisms helped the Renaissance to spread. One was a great diaspora of Italian merchants, artists, and artisans who brought with them tastes and skills. Another was the movement of other Europeans in and out of Italy. Many Germans and French studied at Italian universities. Many Spaniards did military service or governed in the Italian peninsula.

The new tourist trade brought wealthy visitors in search of sites, sights, and pleasures. The French invaders carried Italian treasures and Italian artists back home with them. Their royal court was full of Italians of great talent; Leonardo da Vinci, for example, died in the Loire Valley, a guest of king François I. At the same time, thanks to the printing press, more and more northerners picked up the humanist scholarship of the Italians, infusing it as they did with their own

(such as Dante, Marco Polo, Chaucer, Cervantes, and Solzhenytsin), he took to thinking, and writing. One product was his famous pamphlet, *The Prince*, dedicated to the Medici pope, Leo X, in vain hopes of a job with his old enemies. The work is puzzling, crystal clear and elusive at the same time, profoundly amoral and passionately patriotic. Machiavelli jettisoned all the usual restrictions of honour and religion. He asks: Is it better that a prince be loved or feared? (He votes for fear). Should a prince keep his word? (Only when it works). Should he be generous? (Why waste funds!) Should he pardon his enemies? (Guess the answer.) Other Europeans loved to deplore it, and when Renaissance Englishmen called the devil "Old Nick," they had Machiavelli's name in mind. Legend has it that the great Holy Roman Emperor Charles V kept three books by his bedside: Castiglione's *Courtier*, Machiavelli's *Prince*, and his Bible. Even if the tale is a mere fable, it points out the moral complexities and ambiguities of Renaissance culture, for Charles, and for everyone.

History
BYTES

Unless you were headed for the church, or high public office, you probably had little schooling, in snatches. If you were a peasant, or a poor city-dweller, you could easily have none. Most women and many men could neither read nor write. Most schools were simple affairs, mixed pupils on mixed levels in a single room with the school's sole teacher, hired by the town, village or parish, or paid by parents. No frills, just rote instructions, reading from scripture, and ample beatings. Nobles, meanwhile, often studied at home with tutors, and learned to ride, hunt, dance and fence.

religious energies. Northern humanism, as we call it, had a strong streak of piety, and even of mysticism. It would help launch the Reformation.

Desiderius Erasmus and Thomas More

Of all Renaissance northerners, by far the most influential was a Dutch man, Desiderius Erasmus of Rotterdam (1469–1536). Of modest birth, young Erasmus found the monkish life confining but kept a streak of mystical piety that coloured his whole scholarly career. He learned Latin, Greek and humanist philology, and sharpened his editorial skills in Venice, in the employ of a great humanist publisher. Erasmus applied his scholarship to a new translation, from Greek to Latin, of the New Testament, correcting many philological errors of the official Bible. He also wrote *Colloquies*, model Latin conversations for schoolchildren, nicely spiced with wry and funny editorial comments on religion, morality, war, politics, education, and courtship. His most famous book, *The Praise of Folly* (1508), satirized fools of every type and criticized princes for their violent wars.

Thanks to the new force of print, Erasmus became Europe's first public intellectual, and his vast correspondence with just about everybody educated, everywhere, helped knit together the whole world of scholarship. Erasmianism, as a movement, had a moral core; it blended humanism with piety. Though Erasmus was to remain a Catholic, as did many of his admirers, his influential ideas helped start the Protestant Reformation.

Thomas More (1478–1535), a brilliant, witty English lawyer, was so close a friend of Erasmus that the Latin title of *The Praise of Folly* (*Moriae Encomium*) was a pun on his name. More himself, like many humanists, also punned in the title of his most famous book, *Utopia* (1516). The Latin title plays upon two Greek words — *eutopia* (good place) and *outopia* (no place) — with the ironic subtext: no place this good could ever exist. More's utopia was the first of many

dozens ever written; it gave the name and model for all the rest — an imaginary world that, by its good order acts as a foil for our own imperfect institutions and habits. More, a deeply moral man with an austere streak, intended his book as a meditation on the dangers of wealth, pride, and political power. He opened with a passage on the moral risks of serving monarchs, but failed to heed his own advice. After rising high in the service of Henry VIII, he would be destroyed by his sovereign when his conscience would not allow him to join Henry in the break with Rome. In 1935 the pope honoured his martyrdom with sainthood.

Writing in the Vernacular

There was, however, more to the non-Italian Renaissance than Latin scholarship. Spain, France, Germany, England, and other countries acquired a rich literature in the vernacular: poetry, plays, histories, short stories, travel tales, and a wealth of how-to books on manners, magic, fishing, medicine, metallurgy, war, and many other subjects. For a sense of the richness of the Renaissance imagination, think for a moment of Shakespeare's extraordinary variety: *Julius Caesar*, *Antony and Cleopatra*, *Hamlet*, *Macbeth*, and *Romeo and Juliet*, and *Othello*, to name a few. Add to this the fantastical *Midsummer Night's Dream* fairies, and the *Tempest*'s sprites, monsters, and wizard king.

Shakespeare was not the only writer to scan the world; his rival, Christopher Marlowe (1564–1593), brought on stage the Mongol warlord *Tamberlaine*, and the German *Dr. Faustus*. Faustus, after selling his soul, met the pope, Helen of Troy, and his master, Mephistopheles. Meanwhile, northern painting also flourished, especially in the Netherlands and Germany. Northerners invented oil paint; it gave lustre and, in a master's hand, gem-like detail. They also pioneered the landscape. A lively transalpine exchange of Italian and northern European painters enriched both schools but never merged them. Northern art had an eye for the everyday details of life less prominent in Italian art. Dürer's hare is a fine

In 1502, German artist Albrecht Dürer painted this watercolour study of a *Hare*, a fine example of the naturalistic eye of Northern Renaissance artists.

example. The northeners were also less attracted to Roman gods and goddesses. In composition, they were less poised and gracious than the Italians, less classical, and far more willing to paint grotesque devils and quirky monsters. Grünewald's swarming tormentors of Saint Anthony are northern to their core. Northern too is the painting's religious intensity.

Skepticism

The Renaissance, as time went on, gave birth to several intellectual movements that eroded the legacy of medieval thought. One was formal skepticism, an ancient school of thought, lately revived. Its most effective proponent was Michel de Montaigne (1533–1592), inventor of the essay. His short pieces,

playful, thoughtful, and introspective, won him an enthusiastic readership in France and elsewhere. Montaigne also boosted a second movement with ancient origins — materialist philosophy, which held that the world was only stuff, not spirit. Such notions would lend themselves easily to physics and, eventually, to a cosmos with little room for either God or values. The brilliant French mathematician, and passionate mystic, Blaise Pascal (1623–1662), youthful inventor of an ancestral calculator and reader of Montaigne, was well aware of the dangers of pure scientism: no anchor left for right and wrong. His *Pensées* point out a widening schism between "is" and "ought" that still haunts the twenty-first century.

The Growth of Science

Science grew ever faster. In the Middle Ages, much of the best work was done by Arabs, who had a firmer grasp of the classical Greek heritage. Europeans translated their work, and experimented too. But the sixteenth century sped matters up; more and better translations of Greek mathematics, astronomy, geography, medicine, and natural sciences helped, as did print, with its wood-block illustrations of anatomy, botanical specimens, instruments, and celestial bodies. Scientific academies — sometimes with wealthy sponsors — sprang up, as did a growing mania for collecting not only ancient cameos, gems and statues, but also stuffed crocodiles or live monkeys from the Antilles.

The intellectual developments of early modern science contributed to a process the great German sociologist Max Weber (1864–1920) once called "the demystification of the world." As the old dualism gave way to materialism, magic drained away. So did providence, and allegory. Hail, from now on, would just be falling balls of ice, not poetry or punishment. Angels and devils, fairies and witches, spells and amulets, gradually would fade from view as the scientific revolution came forward. But that was a slow process. From 1500 to 1650, and even beyond, nothing gripped Western Europeans more than religion.

THE REFORMATION

A Matter of Perspective

To say, as many do, that the Reformation or Catholic Reform corrected "problems" in religion is too absolute, for problems reside in the eyes of the believer. The problems of the late medieval church, accordingly, stemmed from the shifting tastes and needs of Christian believers, and from the evolving habits and imperatives of Christian institutions. The Reformation's various solutions, likewise, were rooted in the culture and politics of their time.

By 1500 the papacy had taken on the trappings of the early modern state. Reunited after a confusing schism (1378–1418), it returned to Rome. Between 1440 and 1510, a series of energetic popes retook control of the band of central Italy over which Rome had sovereignty. Like other princes, they had a fleet, an army, governors, customs services, tax men, courts, and grain reserves. And, like other princes, they connived and dickered, waged war, broke treaties. The papal court, like other courts, attracted courtiers, and with them, intrigue. Like any monarch, the pope put his assets into play, using the wealth of the church to reward his clients and to advance his kin. But the pope had an ambiguous double personality, at once local prince and father of all believers.

The Pre-Reformation

The Reformation grew in the fertile ground of religious feeling. It took more than worldly papal trends to set it off. One ingredient, almost a constant in medieval history, was anticlericalism. Europeans had a long, sporadic history of accusing the clergy of idleness, wealth, officious meddling, and hypocritical self-indulgence in food and sex. This feeling might emerge in jokes and bawdy stories, usually by committed Christians. Or it might spill over into movements that were banned as heresies (unorthodox beliefs).

A second Reformation ingredient was an appetite for spiritual experiences, among clerics and educated people. In many parts of Europe, the fifteenth century had seen a trend toward a religion less of ceremonies and practices, more of meditation, understanding, and feeling. In mysticism, the believer reaches up for grace; no need to go through clerical channels. Its greatest exponent was Erasmus, whose influential books rejected pilgrimages, relics, vows to saints, and other "empty" ceremonies. He praised a pious, informed reading of the sacred text. In Erasmus, religion focussed on individual experience and largely overlooked the collective uses of cult — celebration and community. His faith was all salvation, no providence.

Erasmus, and his admirers, were symptomatic in another way as well. Like the Italian humanists, Erasmus wanted to "go back to the sources." Like them, he aimed to use scholarship to recover and clarify ancient texts. He too was anti-medieval, but his texts were both pagan and Christian. Applied to religion, humanist principles undercut anything invented after the year 400 CE. When the Reformation broke out, Erasmus, like many other humanists, stayed with Rome; his ideas inspired reformers on both sides of the widening religious divide. Not all reform rebelled, but as a principle, "back to the sources" was easily subversive.

Martin Luther and the Start of the Reformation

Without the conditions of the times, Martin Luther would never have broken the Church of Rome. Without Luther, another could easily have started the fire. Nevertheless, Luther himself was an imposing figure, earnest, energetic, eloquent, pugnacious. His knack for language, surfacing in his Bible translation, helped found modern German prose. A miner's son, well educated, he gave up an intended law career for monastic orders, becoming an Augustinian. But he was an unquiet monk, afraid that nothing he did, no fast or vigil, would ever save his soul. His confessor, to soothe his soul, sent him to teach at the University of Wittenberg, in Saxony. Lecturing on St. Paul, he found a passage in Romans, to the effect that we are saved "by faith alone." To Luther, St. Paul's words were soothing. They told him that all his "works" had been beside the point. It was not the outward actions, but the inward spirit that brought salvation. Taken literally, Paul's words drained the institutional church, built as it was on the donations and pious acts of the faithful.

While Luther lectured on Paul, Pope Leo launched a sale of indulgences, aimed at funding the new Saint Peter's Cathedral and defraying political expenses. Indulgences had begun as a donation to underwrite thirteenth-century crusades. He who could not go, could still find grace through cash. Outliving the crusades, the lucrative device acquired a theology; the spare good works of saints heaped up in heaven. Purchase an indulgence and tap that store for yourself, or transfer it to your beneficiary of choice, exempting a fellow Christian from grim days or years in purgatory. Indulgences typified the medieval church: grace passed through channels. In the quest for salvation, the faithful both funded the Church and bolstered the community of the living and the dead. But to Luther, indulgences were neither biblical, nor efficacious. They were works, not faith.

WEB CONNECTION

www.mcgrawhill.ca/links/legacy

Go to the site above to find out more about the Reformation

The indulgences set off the Reformation. In 1517, as the chief seller of indulgences neared Saxony, Luther posted on the door of Wittenberg's castle church his famous 95 theses against the practice. Posting theses — debating points — was a university custom, an invitation to scholarly discussion. But print broadcast Luther's points all over Germany, arousing interest and stirring debate. Luther himself, thanks to print a celebrity, debated famous theologians, in front of crowds. The pressure of controversy pushed him into ever more radical positions. By June 1520, the pope issued a bull (papal order), excommunicating

Luther if he would not submit. In December, surrounded by supporters, Luther burned the bull.

Charles V, the young Emperor of Germany, eager to keep the peace, had Luther summoned to the assembly (Diet) of the German Empire. Before the monarch, Luther refused to submit and recant: "Here I stand. I cannot do otherwise." These famous words at the Diet of Worms (pronounced Vormss), whether or not he really said them, sum up his stubborn determination. Fearing for Luther's safety, his protector, the Elector (Prince) of Saxony kidnapped Luther, hiding him in the castle, where he translated the New Testament into German.

What Luther started was more than anyone could control. His basic principles uncorked a genie of dissent and innovation, giving rise not to a single Protestantism, but to a number of new styles of faith. Luther's basic points, *sola fide* (by faith alone) and *sola scriptura* (by scripture alone) offered a starting point, but no blueprint for a church. Most forms of Protestantism, like Luther's, desacralized the priesthood, furnishing the faithful with a more direct line to God and grace. Holy scripture was to be the great authority, interpreted not by experts, but by lay readers, whose consciences would dictate doctrine and inform them if they had grace. Accordingly, Protestants of every stripe translated the Bible, and preached abundantly. Their clergy, no longer intermediaries between God and humans, became teachers, "ministers," servants of the congregation.

Protestantism stripped away the medieval heritage: monks, nuns, pilgrimages, relics, patron saints and their holidays, Easter plays, amulets and special prayers, purgatory, indulgences, canon law, and papal governance. In much of Europe, zealots staged a massacre of art, smashing stained glass and statues, burning altar pieces, melting golden reliquaries and slapping whitewash on frescoes. In its iconoclastic austerity, the new religion wrought havoc with high culture. Meanwhile, in Germany and elsewhere, in a frenzy of secularization, princes laid greedy hands on the accumulated riches of the church. This booty confirmed them in their attachment to the new religious order.

Luther's 95 *Theses*

The 95 Theses were the propositions for debate posted on the door of the Castle Church in Wittenberg on October 31, 1517, by the German monk Martin Luther. This event is considered the start of the Protestant Reformation.

Luther's key reason for posting the theses was to protest the sale and abuse of indulgences by the Roman Catholic Church. Indulgences commuted part of an individual's temporal penalty for sin — in exchange for money. They were granted by papal authority and made available through accredited agents. During the Middle Ages, as papal financial difficulties grew, the Church frequently resorted to the sale of indulgences and abuses were common.

The cause of a 1517 German indulgence scandal was the issue of an indulgence for the rebuilding of St. Peter's in Rome. Johann Tetzel, an agent, made extravagant claims for the indulgences he sold. Wittenberg church members showed Luther pardons they had received for their sins. Luther became outraged at what he considered a grave theological error and wrote the *95 Theses* in protest.

Portrait of *Martin Luther* (1520) by Northern Renaissance artist Lucas Cranach.

Luther's theses were soon translated into German and printed. They found sympathy among those who deplored the draining of German funds to Rome. The Church made several unsuccessful attempts at reconciliation with Luther, but instead he broadened his position to include calls for more comprehensive reforms.

By 1530, Luther's initial attack on the Catholic Church had spread to many areas throughout Europe. So, what had begun as a manifesto protesting an indulgence scandal turned into the greatest crisis in the history of the Western Church. Below are Excerpts from the *95 Theses*.

Disputation of Doctor Martin Luther on the Power and Efficacy of Indulgences (1517)

Out of love and concern for the truth, and with the object of eliciting it, the following heads will be the subject of a public discussion at Wittenberg under the presidency of the reverend father, Martin Luther, Augustinian, Master of Arts and Sacred Theology, and duly appointed Lecturer on these subjects in that place. He requests that whoever cannot be present personally to debate the matter orally will do so in absence in writing.

1. When our Lord and Master, Jesus Christ, said "Repent," He called for the entire life of believers to be one of penitence.

2. The word cannot be properly understood as referring to the sacrament of penance, i.e., confession and satisfaction, as administered by the clergy.

4. As long as hatred of self abides (i.e., true inward penitence) the penalty of sin abides, viz., until we enter the kingdom of heaven.

5. The pope has neither the will nor the power to remit any penalties beyond those imposed either at his own discretion or by canon law.

6. The pope himself cannot remit guilt, but only declare and confirm that it has been remitted by God; or, at most, he can remit it in cases reserved to his discretion. Except for these cases, the guilt remains untouched.

8. The penitential canons apply only to men who are still alive, and, according to the canons themselves, none applies to the dead.

10. It is a wrongful act, due to ignorance, when priests retain the canonical penalties on the dead in purgatory.

12. In former days, the canonical penalties were imposed, not after, but before absolution was pronounced; and were intended to be tests of true contrition.

13. Death puts and end to all the claims of the Church; even the dying are already dead to the canon laws, and are no longer bound by them.

16. There seems to be the same difference between hell, purgatory, and heaven as between despair, uncertainty, and assurance.

17. Of a truth, the pains of souls in purgatory ought to be abated, and charity ought to be proportionately increased.

20. Therefore the pope, in speaking of the plenary remission of all penalties, does not mean "all" in the strict sense, but only those imposed by himself.

21. Hence those who preach indulgences are in error when they say that a man is absolved and saved from every penalty by the pope's indulgences.

22. Indeed, he cannot remit to souls in purgatory any penalty which canon law declares should be suffered in the present life.

24. It must therefore be the case that the major part of the people are deceived by that indiscriminate and high-sounding promise of relief from penalty.

25. The same power as the pope exercises in general over purgatory is exercised in particular by every single bishop in his bishopric and priest in his parish.

26. The pope does excellently when he grants remission to the souls in purgatory on account of intercessions made on their behalf, and not by the power of the keys (which he cannot exercise for them).

27. There is no divine authority for preaching that the soul flies out of purgatory immediately [after] the money clinks in the bottom of the chest.

28. It is certainly possible that when the money clinks in the bottom of the chest avarice and greed increase; but when the church offers intercession, all depends on the will of God. [5]

---

1. Write a brief explanation of how indulgences differ from money given to support a local, church, synagogue or temple today.

2. What do you think happened to the money collected for indulgences by the "agent"?

For all its variety, the Reformation had several standard forms. Germany, wherever it took hold, and Scandinavia, moved to a Lutheran model of state churches under the protection of local rulers. Ministers became civil servants; authority remained top-down. This model did not export very easily. In Geneva, Jean Calvin (1509–1564) founded a church, and a theology that spread. Calvinist churches took over in Scotland and the Netherlands. They came close to winning France and England, and put colonies in Poland, Hungary, South Africa, and New England. In Canada today, the Presbyterians and the United Church have Calvinist roots.

Calvinist theology pushed Luther to his logical consequences; if works are nothing, all is in the hands of God. We are thus predestined, from the moment of God's creation, to heaven or to hell. But God's ways are secret; try for faith. If it comes, it is a sign; you are of the elect. And be good, very, very good. As forbidding as it sounds, this grim doctrine found enthusiastic adherents. Calvinist churches were less hierarchic than Lutheran ones. The congregation ran itself. A council of elders (male, prosperous, no longer young) governed it and, sitting as a morals court, tried to force the majority, however damned, to behave as if they were not. English detractors called their Calvinists "Puritans." The word and sense live on.

Passing from Rome to Wittenberg, from Wittenberg to Geneva, one can line up churches from more hierarchic to less (and from strict to stricter). Beyond Geneva came the "gathered churches," which returned to the earliest sect, the Pentecostal gathering of true believers. The gathered churches of the Radical Reformation scared the rest; they had little hierarchy, few ceremonies, much trust in mutual love and little care for sacraments, except baptism, for adults only. To rival eyes, they looked like anarchists. Since the gathered churches refused to baptize ignorant babies, their enemies taunted them as "Anabaptists" (rebaptizers). Some gathered churches had so little regard for hierarchy that they undermined the usual social deference that assured the wealth and power of elites. Unprotected by most rulers, such churches — Mennonites, Baptists, Quakers — lay low or fled to distant regions. But many groups survived; the Hutterites of Canada, and the Mennonites, Quakers, and Moravians of North America descend from the radical Reformation, as do the many Baptist churches. "Born again" has a sixteenth-century origin.

Within a few years of Luther's sudden fame, the peasantry of southern and central Germany took his teaching, and his more radical followers to heart. Luther's assault on tradition and on ecclesiastical authority translated easily into rebellion against lords and heavy feudal obligations. A great rebellion, the Peasants War (1524–1525) broke out. Peasants and their urban allies rioted, looted, and murdered. They formed vast armies, led by visionaries. Alarmed, the upper classes, both Catholic and Lutheran, gathered forces and smashed the insurgency, killing the rebel forces and putting captured leaders to death. Luther himself denounced the rebels in a pamphlet. The debacle cost his Reformation much popular support.

In 1534 a sect of ultra-Anabaptists took over Münster, in western Germany. There they set up a radical utopia, with community of goods and women. Alarmed, the ruling princes united to besiege and crush them. Until the Second World War, their leaders' bones hung from the cathedral steeple.

Review, Reflect, Respond

1. How did the Renaissance worldview differ from the Medieval worldview?

2. Despite their very different tones and content, do the writings of both Machiavelli and Castiglione reflect Renaissance culture? Explain your answer.

3. List and explain in order of importance the top three causes of the Reformation.

THE COUNTER-REFORMATION

The Church Responds

At first, the Catholic response to Luther seemed slow to come. There were reasons; reformers, both inside and outside the Church, sought changes in both doctrine and practice not easily absorbed. The absenteeism of bishops, and the careerism that encouraged ambitious courtiers to stockpile the incomes of many church positions, while leaving local administration to hired substitutes, were patterns hard to break. These customs fed the patronage networks of the Roman court. The popes also hesitated to call a general council of the Church, as Emperor Charles and many others wanted. This was because popes recalled how, in the early fifteenth century, general councils had tried to trim papal authority.

By the 1540s, some two decades into the Reformation, a Catholic response gathered steam. Under Paul III, a general council finally met at Trent, an Italian-speaking alpine town just inside the boundaries of Charles's empire. Meeting off and on for 18 years, the Council of Trent produced a papal victory. In matters of doctrine, it gave Rome the conservative result desired. Against the Protestant "scripture only" it reaffirmed the whole corpus of medieval church law. Against translations of scripture, it clung to Latin and, despite Erasmus and philology, to the fourth-century Latin Bible. Against "faith only," it reasserted "works." It reaffirmed the old definitions of the sacraments, kept purgatory and all the saints, and proclaimed the priesthood as men with holy power, not mere ministers. On the other hand, when it came to practice, Trent did make changes. It pushed bishops into their cities and strengthened their authority. To improve the

This illusionistic ceiling painting by Gaulli is called *The Triumph of the Name of Jesus* (1674-79). It is in the church called Il Gesú, the main Jesuit church in Rome. It shows the dazzling baroque style typical of the Counter-Reformation churches. Looking up at this painting how might you feel?

clergy, it stipulated that each diocese (a bishop's district) erect a seminary to train priests. Gradually, these measures had effect. By the seventeenth century, the clergy was better schooled, better supervised, and more often celibate.

Not all Catholic countermeasures came from Trent. Three stand out. One was the Roman Inquisition, a tribunal of medieval origin designed to root out heretics (those who held unorthodox beliefs) and revived in 1542 to police Italian orthodoxy. Another measure was the Roman Index of Prohibited Books (1559) and the machinery of review, revision, and censorship that went with it. Both these institutions were quite successful at suppressing dissent and enforcing conformity. The third Catholic countermeasure of note was the founding of religious orders given to teaching, propaganda, and social services. Of these, the most famous and influential were the Jesuits, or Society of Jesus, founded in 1534, but finally chartered in 1540 by the Spanish mystic (and future saint) Ignatius Loyola (1491–1556). The Jesuits stood out for their efficiency, skill, effective propaganda, and highly regarded schools, tuition-free and open to all, including Protestants. The Jesuits fanned out across Europe, Asia and the Americas, winning new converts and bringing back families of Protestants, often the grateful parents of pupils at their schools. The survival and vitality of Catholicism in Poland, Czechoslovakia, Austria, Hungary, Belgium, and parts of Germany owes much to the Jesuits.

The Catholic counteroffensive, or Counter-Reformation, was often quite successful. It could thank the energetic policies of the militant popes of the later sixteenth and early seventeenth centuries, who invested funds and diplomatic efforts in a campaign to gain the upper hand. The popes' best allies were the Hapsburg kings of Spain, sometimes seconded by the Austrian ducal (dukes) and imperial cousins, all related to Charles V. Trent helped, as did the splintering of Protestantism. Catholics could point to the advantages of an undisputed head and doctrine. Against Protestantism, a religion largely of the written and spoken word, Catholics deployed almost all the arts: architecture, sculpture,

painting, music, stagecraft, as well as preaching and pamphlets. They developed the Baroque style: splendid buildings, sumptuous furnishings, elaborate ceremonies, dramatic images of heroic saints and of souls in celestial bliss. A touch of Catholic Reformation style made its way to Canada and survives in the splendid altars of old Quebec churches.

Social Control

Despite hostility, Catholicism and Protestantism still had things in common. More than medieval religion, both stressed individual experience, and conscience. Both strove to mobilize believers' feelings, and both attended more to salvation, and less to providence, than before. Moreover, both churches, in league with states, supported moral reform, policing manners and waging ceaseless war on the impulses and values of lay society. What Reformation churches and their modern historians call a campaign for virtue against vice, we might better label a fairly successful attempt to tilt the balance among competing moral codes and rhetorics.

Sixteenth-Century Politics

Spain

Between 1517 and 1660, religion was the focus of state politics. It was not the only factor; monarchs still lusted after land and glory, and still wrestled to tame their territories. And almost all of Europe, down to 1600, felt pressure from the Turks, by far the strongest, most compact empire. On the European stage itself, there were two great powers, France and Spain, the latter linked by dynastic blood and politics to Germany. Until 1559 the two tussled for first place, and then bad luck and religious strife weakened France, leaving the continent under partial Spanish hegemony until the early seventeenth century. Then, slowly, France rebounded, until, by 1660, it dominated Western Europe. Founding New France, the future Canada, on nominal Spanish ground was both symptom and part of the French bid for leadership. Religious conflicts, dynastic ambition, and skirmishes with Islam all made for warfare, which was increasingly expensive in an age of siege artillery and massive fortresses.

As a great power, Spain was an unlikely candidate. Its population was thin, its economy mediocre. It had been a divided place — several kingdoms, some facing the Mediterranean, others the Atlantic or the dry interior. In the Middle Ages, the South was held by Muslim states; these sparred intermittently with the Christian North. The country also held a substantial Jewish minority. The late fifteenth century changed this picture radically. A dynastic union, the marriage of Ferdinand and Isabella (1478), joined Mediterranean Aragon with inland Castile. This monarchy then, in 1492, took Granada, the last Muslim state. Having expelled or converted the Muslims, the victorious monarchs then turned upon the Jews. One-third fled, carrying their Spanish language with them as they scattered across the Mediterranean. The others converted, under duress, leaving Spain apparently united, but with many unwilling, insincere Christians. As the century went on, the *conversos*, descendants of these converts, faced increasing suspicion, exclusion from good jobs, and intermittent persecution by the Inquisition.

Two strokes of fortune thrust Spain onto the world stage. One was the voyages of Christopher Columbus (1451–1508), an Italian aboard Spanish ships. Though he himself found little treasure, his discoveries gave Spain a legal claim to the Americas, and to their vast reserves of silver, Mexican and Peruvian. By 1525, treasure ships were funding royal armies and buoying the prosperity of Seville. For some hundred years, the silver kept coming. The second stroke of fortune was an accident of inheritance that, in 1516, left the throne to the man we call Charles V (Rey Carlos I in Spain). When, in 1519, Charles became the fifth Karl on the German throne, Spain was tied to the fortunes of a sprawling dynastic union, more coalition than solid state, that stretched from Holland to Vienna and to Naples and that was swiftly acquiring American acreage and treasure.

Until Charles retired, tired and frustrated, in 1556, his fortunes and Spain's intertwined. Beset by Turks to the south and east, and by restless Protestants within, Charles had to contend as well with the Valois kings of France, François I and Henri II. To get at Charles, the French even allied with what seemed the very devil, the Sultan, the Lutherans. The favourite theatre of combat was Italy, where the two rivals vied for Naples and Milan. We call this almost incessant conflict the "Hapsburg-Valois wars."

In 1559 a peace called Cateau-Cambrésis ended these wars, leaving Spain with the upper hand. What might have been just one more truce lasted, thanks to luck, as king Henri, jousting to fete the settlement, died of a lance splinter through the eye. His untimely death unhinged the monarchy and sidelined France for the next four decades.

When Charles abdicated, he divided his empire; it had proved too much for one man to run. He gave Spain to his son, Philip II, a man as Spanish in style and culture as his father had been international. Philip had Castilian reserve and dignity, and ferocious loyalty to the Roman Church. Unfortunately, in parcelling out his lands, Charles attached the Netherlands to Spain. Old economic ties between northern cloth-production and Spanish wool argued for the link, but it proved disastrous. Philip governed from afar, through underlings, and bungled everything. He alienated the Netherlands nobility and, when Calvinism made headway, espoused oppressive measures that turned the populace against him. The Netherlands rebelled in the early 1570s; Spain waged incessant war to get the Low Countries back, not giving up until 1648. In the end, it held on to the southern half and, with Jesuit help, kept it safely Catholic. This was to become Belgium. The northern Netherlands, what we call "Holland," held out, and remained largely Protestant. As for Spain itself, the long, costly wars slowly ground the kingdom down. In 1580, Spain annexed Portugal, with its African-Asian trading empire, and so girdled planet Earth until, in 1640, the Portuguese seceded.

France

Compact and influential, France in 1559 was in ghastly trouble. The death of Henri II left the monarchy to his three incompetent sons, who ruled, one after the other, under the eye and hand of their Italian mother, Catherine de Médicis (1519–1589). The swift spread of Calvinism and the ambition of noble factions threw France into almost forty years of the civil "Wars of Religion." Though neighbours of rival faith often managed to co-exist, the wars were marred by savage acts, most famously by the "Saint Bartholomew's" massacre of 1572, when, at Queen Catherine's and the king's behest, Parisian mobs wiped out hundreds of Huguenot (Calvinist) nobles, in town for a royal wedding, and a host of local Protestants. As the news spread across the realm, there was more slaughter. In 1589 an assassin killed Henri III, the last Valois king. Still, it took his rival, Henri IV of Bourbon, almost a decade more to win the kingdom over. He had to convert: "Paris is worth a mass," he is said to have declared. Henri, in the Edict of Nantes of 1598, granted the Huguenots wide political and military privileges; this helped settle the kingdom.

Under Henri IV, France began to recover from the mayhem. But, in 1610, an assassin, ultra-Catholic, cut him down, tipping the kingdom once more into a minority. Louis XIII (1610–1643), of lesser talents, relied on the skilled Cardinal de Richelieu, his canny first minister, to steer the kingdom. Richelieu first squelched the Huguenots (1628), and then turned upon the Spaniards and their Austrian allies, in Italy and Germany. Though a cardinal, for reasons of state, he was content to back the Protestants in the Thirty Years War.

England

In 1500 England was a middling power, with a middling, extractive economy, geared to exporting wool. By 1700 it had built a global trading empire with colonies and trading posts on several continents, and London had become a swollen metropolis. England's political history was tumultuous, largely thanks to the odd Reformation there. In most states, the Reformation came from below, where it had popular support. In England, it came from above, a matter of royal convenience when Henry VIII (1491–1547), besotted with Ann Boleyn and still without sons, petitioned the pope

for a divorce. Henry's Spanish wife, Catherine of Aragon, was an aunt of Charles V, and the pope, after the Sack of 1527, squirmed under Charles's thumb.

Thwarted in Rome, Henry cut all his church's papal ties and took over the newly autonomous Church of England. There followed a very partial Reformation; the Bible went English, the monasteries succumbed, their wealth cascading into royal coffers. But the old structure — archbishops, bishops — lived on and much of the feel of the old religion lingered. But not for long. When Henry died, under his teenaged heir, Edward VI, the Church became more Protestant. But Edward died young, succeeded in 1555 by his Catholic older sister, Mary, daughter of Henry's divorced Spanish queen. A trenchant foe of heresy, Mary married her cousin Philip, King of Spain, and burned chief Protestants; many fled to the Continent, often to the Netherlands, and there absorbed Calvinist ideas. After four years of Catholic restoration, Mary died, childless. The crown passed to Elizabeth I (1533–1606), the daughter of Ann, the second of Henry's six wives.

Elizabeth reigned long (1558–1603) and skilfully. She faced threats from many quarters. Her refusal to marry clouded the succession and stirred up plots. In Catholic eyes, her mother had never married Henry; so as a bastard, Elizabeth could be deposed. Foreign powers allied with Rome plotted her overthrow, hoping to install Mary of Scotland instead. In the late 1580s, Elizabeth let Mary to be beheaded, and sent men and subsidies to stiffen the Dutch revolt. In response, Philip II mustered a fleet, one of Europe's largest seen, in hopes of invading England. In a series of dramatic battles in the Channel and North Sea, the English, with Dutch help, held them off, weakening them so badly that Atlantic storms on the way home sunk many ships. The dramatic Spanish Armada campaign of 1588 became a moral legend for both sides, enhancing Elizabeth's reputation, then and later.

Elizabeth died with religion and constitution still unsettled. But her kingdom passed smoothly to James I, son of her old enemy, Mary of Scotland. James, and his son Charles, were less skilled at reconciling com-

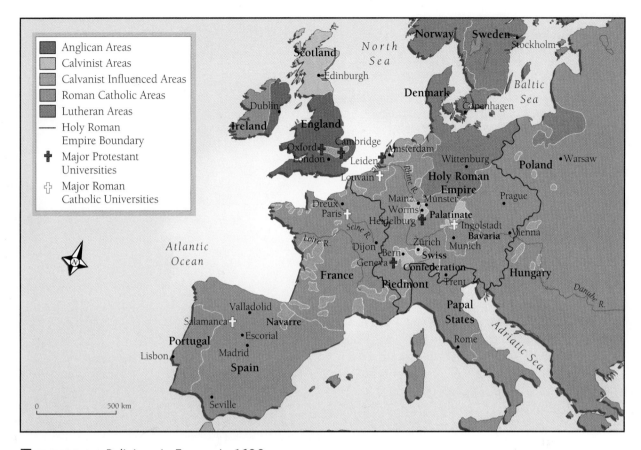

■ FIGURE 1.1 Religions in Europe in 1600

Why did the Protestant religion gain footholds where it did? In which areas do you think the Protestant minority would face persecution?

peting interests in politics and religion. Both strove to consolidate royal power at the expense of the law courts, and Parliament, two medieval institutions that had held onto influence. This struggle between ambitious monarchs and traditional bodies was not unique to England. On the Continent, the monarchs usually won; slowly, they pared back old privileges. But not in England. Charles II, having lost a war with Scotland, to buy off the invaders had to summon at long last his neglected Parliament. Bad relations led to rupture, and, in 1642, to a Civil War that in the end unseated and beheaded Charles (1649). England became a wobbly Calvinist republic (or Commonwealth). Though kings sometimes died in battle, or at an assassin's hand, it was almost unheard of for a people to behead its monarch. In the midst of this instability, England

prospered; its merchants and pirates (sometimes hard to tell apart) encroached on the overseas empires of Spain and Portugal, and then on Dutch trading zones, and penetrated the Mediterranean. London grew, not only as a capital, but also as a port, and a centre of manufacture, the arts, literature, and intellectual life.

Italy

Italy was not a single state. It would not become one until 1870. Rather, it was a hodgepodge of middling and small states of varied constitution. There were city-states, princely regimes, and domains ruled by foreign dynasties. In the centre a broad swath, the State of the Church, was ruled by the pope himself. Despite the hodgepodge, geopolitics gave the peninsula a common fate and history. In the fifteenth century, thanks to

The Act in Restraint of Appeals, 1533

The later part of the reign of Henry VIII was dominated by two closely related issues: the King's desire for an heir and the English Reformation, which led to the separation of the Church of England from the Roman Catholic Church.

King Henry had married his brother's widow, Catherine of Aragon, in 1509. Catherine produced only one surviving child — a girl. By the end of the 1520s, Henry's wife was in her forties and the king was desperate for a son. The Tudor dynasty had been established in 1485, and Henry was only its second monarch. He felt the dynasty was not secure enough to risk handing the crown to a woman, which could lead to disputes over succession or domination of a foreign power through marriage.

Henry had fallen in love with Anne Boleyn and tried to persuade Pope Clement VII to grant an annulment of his marriage to Catherine, but all efforts by Henry and his advisers failed. In spite of this, he secretly married Anne Boleyn in January of 1533. A few months later, the Archbishop of Canterbury declared Henry's marriage to Catherine invalid, and Anne Boleyn was soon crowned queen. The Pope in Rome responded by excommunicating King Henry.

Portrait of Henry VIII (1539-40) by Hans Holbein the Younger.

Thomas Cromwell, the King's chief adviser, then used the powers of Parliament to decide the issue. Cromwell orchestrated a series of acts that cut back papal power and influence in England and eventually brought about the English Reformation, the Church of England and the faith called Anglicanism. The Act in Restraint of Appeals is one of the acts that took judgments regarding issues such as marriage and divorce out of the hands of the Pope in Rome and into the hands of the English monarch.

> Where, by divers sundry old authentic histories and chronicles, it is manifestly declared and expressed that this realm of England is an empire, and so hath been accepted in the world, governed by one supreme head and king having the dignity and royal estate of the imperial crown of the same, unto whom a body politic, compact of all sorts and degrees of people divided in terms and by names of spirituality and temporality, be bounden and owe to bear next to God a natural and humble obedience, and whereas the king his most noble progenitors, and the nobility and commons of this said realm, at divers and sundry parliaments as well in the time of King Edward I, Edward III, Richard II, Henry IV, and other noble kings of this realm, made sundry ordinances,

laws, statutes, and provisions for the entire and sure conservation of the prerogatives, liberties, and pre-eminences of the said imperial crown of this realm, and of the jurisdictions spiritual and temporal of the same, to keep it from the annoyance as well of the see of Rome as from the authority of other foreign potentates attempting the diminution or violation thereof, as often and from time to time as any such annoyance or attempt might be known or espied; and [whereas] notwithstanding the said good statutes and ordinances ... divers and sundry inconveniences and dangers not provided for plainly by the said former acts ... have risen and sprung by reason of appeals sued out of this realm to the see of Rome, in causes testamentary, causes of matrimony and divorces, right of tithes, oblations, and obventions ... in consideration whereof, the king's highness, his nobles, and commons, considering the great enormities, dangers, long delays, and hurts that as well to his highness as to his said nobles, subjects, commons, and residents of this his realm in the said causes ... do daily ensue, doth therefore by his royal assent, and by the assent of the lords spiritual and temporal and the commons in this present parliament assembled and by authority o the same, enact, establish, and ordain that all causes testamentary, causes of matrimony and divorces, rights of tithes, oblations, and obventions ... whether they concern the king our sovereign lord, his heirs, or successors, or any other subjects or residents within the same of what degree soever they be, shall be from henceforth heard ... and definitively adjudged and determined within the king's jurisdiction and authority and not elsewhere.

The Act in Restraint of Appeals forbade appeals to Rome, stating that England was an empire, governed by one supreme head and king who possessed "whole and entire" authority within the realm, and that no judgments or excommunications from Rome were valid. Later, the Act of Supremacy (1534) established a separate Church of England and recognized the king as its head.

---

1. Find the passage in this act that you think is most important and significant to the reign of Henry the VIII and future kings of England. Explain your choice.

2. Draw diagrams illustrating the hierarchies of the Roman and Anglican churches. Research the information on the Internet or in your school or local library.

disarray in Germany and France, Italian powers of middling rank had managed on their own, making and breaking alliances and perfecting diplomatic art. The ambassador, with his immunities, secretary, and secret codes, his prying and conniving, and his astute dispatches home, is a largely Italian invention. On the peninsula, besides the pope, the strongest powers were Venice, Milan, Florence, all city-states with subject territories, and the Kingdom of Naples. These five were nimble enough to keep any one from lording over all the others. Toward 1490, the rise of stronger kingdoms outside Italy subverted the cozy equilibrium; France, Spain, and the German Empire all waded in. A French invasion, in 1494, was the first of many by rival powers. A low point was the catastrophic Sack of Rome (1527) that wrecked the local Renaissance. By 1559, the Hapsburg-Valois wars had reduced the peninsula to a semi-satellite of Spain. Viceroys in Palermo, Naples, and Milan ruled for Philip II; Tuscany was under Hapsburg protection and the pope was a frequent ally. Venice was the least dependent. So long as France was down, Spanish power brought relative tranquillity; the next 60 years were generally prosperous and unusually plague-free. Italian cities continued to churn out the best cloth, arms, glass, and art. As population rose, however, living standards slipped; in the 1580s, there were famines, eased by Baltic grain. Nevertheless, Italy remained the most urban, most sophisticated place in Europe.

All of this changed after 1620. France's recovery revived its Italian ambitions and its clash with Spain. Richelieu's Hapsburg rivalry brought debilitating wars. Thirty years of war in Germany hurt trade, as did the exhaustion of Italian forests, fatal to shipbuilders; increasingly, Dutch and English sailors horned in on traditional Italian markets in Turkey, Syria, and Egypt. The northern goods they carried displaced the more expensive Italian manufactures. Then, from 1630 to 1656, plagues swept the peninsula, cutting down city dwellers. Under these dismal conditions, the old trading elites increasingly shunned commerce, investing instead in agriculture. All these changes sapped urban life, trade, and culture. Italy, long Europe's centre, drifted toward the margins.

Germany

Like Italy, Germany was a nation modern only in retrospect. It too was a political quilt. It had a curious constitution. The Holy Roman Emperor ("neither holy, nor Roman, nor an emperor," as Lord Acton said) — alias the Kaiser (Caesar) — was an elected monarch, chosen by seven electors. He was a feudal lord, not a sovereign. Under him, loosely hitched, were a mix of middling princes with assorted titles: duke, count, margrave, elector. Under him, too, were ample lands ruled by archbishops and bishops, and even by independent abbots. Add the "imperial free cities," most of them with territories two-dozen kilometres or so across, some with less. To make things more feudal still, include a swarm of "imperial free knights," lords of a castle, and a few square miles of dependent peasantry. All these subjects of the emperor convened at periodic parliaments, called (in Latin) "diets" (as with Luther's, at Worms).

In theory elective, the empire, in fact, had become hereditary, in Hapsburg hands. But election still curbed Kaisers. Power's fragmentation hobbled Charles V in his campaign to curb the Protestants, as did, of course, the menace of the Turks, who swallowed Hungary (1526) and besieged Vienna (1529), and relentless pressure from France. Charles fought two wars against a Protestant Schmalkalkic League, the first glorious, the second decidedly inglorious. The latter defeat hastened his retirement and pushed him into a reluctant treaty, the Peace of Augsburg (1555). In that pact, a famous formula tried to settle for once and all the question of religion: "*cuius regio, eius religio*" (he who holds the power determines the religion). For 63 years, it worked, sort of, and Germany knew general peace. But it proved impossible to freeze the hearts of rulers and their subjects; militant Catholicism and assertive Calvinism kept clashing. Finally, in 1618, Germany slipped into a complicated, dismal war, called — in retrospect — The Thirty Years War.

The cause of the war was the Bohemian crown. Under the tolerant Hapsburg emperor, Rudolf II (1576–1612), who lived in Prague, Bohemia (now in the Czech Republic) had been pluralistic. When the succession, six years past his death, passed to a zealous Catholic, Ferdinand II, the Bohemian elite tried to slip their crown instead to a Protestant, Frederick, the brief Winter King. The Austrians crushed the Bohemian revolt at the battle of White Mountain (Bela Hora) in 1620, but the Catholic victory drew in other German states, and outside powers, among them Denmark, Sweden, France, and Spain. Such were the stakes, both territorial and confessional, that it took 30 years of misery to make the peace of Westphalia (1648) that, in most ways, reaffirmed the religious settlement of 1555 and the territorial status quo. The war and peace replaced the Czech elite, exhausted Spain, entrenched the independent Netherlands and the German princes, strengthened France and Sweden, gave the Hapsburgs a free hand in Austria and, above all, made hash of much of Germany. It also helped discredit religious war. But war itself, of course, stayed alive and well.

The Netherlands

Belgium and the "Dutch" Netherlands are called "low" countries because they straddle a triple delta of two mid-sized rivers, the Scheldt and the Maas (Meuse in French, upstream), and of one great one, the Rhine, the chief source of silt. It is a fertile zone, much of it reclaimed marsh and peat bog. The famous windmills of Holland, aligned on dikes, pumped water to canals well above the fields. Most of the zone is slightly higher and drier, but gently rolling, temperate and well suited to agriculture. A friendly landscape and one reason why the Netherlands, in medieval, early modern and later times, was unusually urban and rich. Good farms feed cities. But there were other reasons, also geographic. In the pre-modern world, when roads were poor, rivers made superb routes, as did seas. The Rhine, draining much of western Germany and the Alps, and the Meuse, from eastern France, brought goods, even from northern Italy. Turn right at the river's mouth, and sail into the North Sea, a herring fishery, or trade for timber and dried fish in Norway, or enter the Baltic, to load Polish grain or Swedish copper. Turn left, and sail to France and Spain for wine and salt. Keep sailing, through the Straits of Gibraltar, and tap the Mediterranean for all its refined and exotic goods. Or just go straight ahead, slip up the Thames, and dock in London for the fine wool of England. All those routes invited trade and traders, and trade stimulated industry.

So, in the Netherlands, the traders of many nations met and haggled. They exchanged the goods of the subarctic, temperate, Alpine, and Mediterranean regions. They also picked up manufactured goods of the local cities. These were above all textiles, spun, dyed, and woven from English and Spanish wool. From the fourteenth century on, there was always a chief city, the site of warehouses awaiting merchants. Until 1500, until its river silted, Bruges served. Down to 1585, Antwerp did the job. Then war and politics threw the role to Amsterdam, the city that, deep into the seventeenth century, dominated Europe's commerce, until London shouldered it aside.

What hurt Antwerp and exalted Amsterdam was the rebellion against Philip II's distant, rigid, pro-Catholic rule. Seventeen provinces, some long associated, others recently acquired, made up Philip's Netherlandish inheritance. Each province had its government, with privileges and customs; central institutions were weak. In the late 1560s, harsh pro-Catholic policies by the Spanish Duke of Alva and his army sparked a wide rebellion, and a civil war. In the 1580s, under the brilliant Alessandro Farnese, the Spanish army retook the south, seizing Antwerp in 1585 and driving thousands of refugees, many of them highly skilled, into the still independent northern provinces. The odd geography of the seven northern provinces helped defend them; big rivers, dikes easily breached to flood the fields, and fleets of shallow draft fighting boats frustrated the Spaniards. Decades of warfare (there was a 1609–1621 truce) proved only that the frontier was fairly stable.

Despite the fighting, the Dutch northerners prospered. Their fleet closed the mouth of the Scheldt, choking Antwerp and letting Amsterdam grab its trade. Dutch ships entered the Mediterranean and cruised the outer reaches of the Spanish/Portuguese empires, trading, plundering, and taking forts and markets. Meanwhile, Dutch ships and capitalists colonized the economy of the Baltic, pulling copper, good for bronze cannons, out of Sweden, and floating tons of wheat and rye from Poland. The grain fed their cities, and, when Mediterranean crops fell short, supplied Italy as well. The Netherlands, though Calvinist, were, for the times, quite tolerant of faiths and ideas. Amsterdam welcomed Jews; many forced converts from Spain and Portugal arrived, returned to their ancestral religion, and often flourished in long-distance trade.

Review, Reflect, Respond

1. List and describe three actions taken by the Catholic Church during the Counter-Reformation.

2. Why was the emergence of Spain as a dominant power in the sixteenth century somewhat surprising? What were two key factors that contributed to Spain's emergence as a world power?

3. Explain, using examples, why conflict and disunity rather than unity and stability best describe early modern Europe.

EASTERN EUROPE AND THE OTTOMAN EMPIRE

The Gradual Rise of Muscovy

The nucleus of the future Russian empire was Moscow, and its zone. The local ruler, after the fall of Constantinople to the Turks, in 1453, had gradually taken on the grand but undeserved title of Caesar, "tsar'" in Russian. Despite the claim to be a "third Rome," Muscovy was a mediocre principality, landlocked, poor, and boxed in by a sprawling Poland, by Turkey, and by the Tartars of the Black Sea. An ambitious, erratic monarch, Ivan IV (1533–1584), "the Terrible" in English ("the Grim" in Russian), undercut the power of the old boyar nobility, grabbing their lands and installing his faithful in their place and, warring on the Tartars, pushed his borders down the Volga to the Caspian. He also exhausted Muscovy with unsuccessful Baltic wars. Worthy of his nickname, Ivan also killed his son and heir. His own death threw Muscovy first to a regent, Boris Godunov, and then to a Time of Troubles (1606–1613). At least 20 pretenders vied for the throne, and Poles and Swedes invaded. Under the new Romanov dynasty, Muscovy would stabilize and grow, but only slowly.

The Turkish Empire

Throughout the sixteenth century, European states feared Turkey. They had good reason. Down to the death of Suleiman the Magnificent (1520–1566), the empire grew and grew. In 1517 it took Egypt, and then spread across almost the entire North African coast. In 1526, at Mohacs, it crushed the Hungarians, killed their king, and swallowed most of their country. In 1529 its armies camped at the walls of Vienna, and throughout most of the century, its annual war fleets cruised the Mediterranean.

Turkey had traits in common with Europe: prosperous cities, guilds, skilled craftsmen, pious corporations that used assets to run charities. Like Europe, it had a class of feudal land holders who raised fighting men when summoned. And, like Europe, it had a clergy with judicial functions. At the same time, there were some striking differences. One was a kind of high slavery. The civil service was made up of slaves, children of Christian mothers conscripted, converted to Islam, and schooled to run the country. And the best soldiers, the famous Janissaries, companies of musketeers, were also privileged slaves. A second difference was the practice of tolerance of other faiths, of Christian churches and Jews, who paid a special tax but ran and judged themselves, under their own officers, as did colonies of foreign merchants, under licence from the government. A third, and striking difference, was the manner of choosing a sultan. Since the reigning sultan had many wives and concubines, there was no clear succession. Instead, talented princes went to the provinces, learned politics, gathered support, and, at their fathers' demise, fought one another to the death. Though disruptive, this method assured a talented successor. The European method of succession, though more tranquil, could install a dud. In the early seventeenth century, the Turks abandoned their bracing, if drastic, method, and took to raising princes in the Topkapi palace harem. Future sultans would be untested, and less than worldly.

Citizens of the modern successor states of the Balkans, built on the bones of the Turkish Empire, and their historians liked to think of the Turkish period as a time of backwardness. Down to 1600 or so, Turkish Europe did not do badly, except in frontier districts like Hungary where border raiding did much damage. On the other hand, Turkey, like other empires on the globe, could not keep pace with Europe's restless scientific and technological experiments. There was no Renaissance or scientific revolution. Forms of commerce changed slowly; joint stock companies did not appear. The star-shaped fort, a geometer's delight, never arrived to stiffen the defences. The printing press came slowly; there were no printed books in Turkish until the eighteenth century. Newspapers were unknown; news of novelty moved slowly. Gradually, the balance of power tilted against Turkey.

Reflections

Early modern politics had some common themes. One was eternal: states tried to aggrandize themselves at their neighbours' expense. They fought for land, and sometimes for markets and commercial privileges. But religious ideology, less eternal, also entered in. Wars between Turks and Christians could take on the characteristics of holy war — crusade or *jihad*. So, the Catholics celebrating their bloody naval victory of Lepanto (1571) just forgot to note that most of the drowned enemy sailors were Greek Christians. States also made internal war to put down rebels: lords, cities, peasants. Rebellion was the extension of political resistance by other means, not so much an irrational explosion as a canny, if risky move in a high-stakes game. The seventeenth century, more pinched than the sixteenth, was a great age for spectacular revolts; the path to absolutism was far from smooth.

Chapter Review

Chapter Summary

In this chapter, you have seen:

- that certain key factors led to conflict and war during the sixteenth and seventeenth centuries
- that forces such as humanism facilitated the process of change, while traditional customs tended to impede change
- that the sixteenth century was an age during which important developments in a variety of modes of artistic expression took place
- the role of and restrictions faced by women in sixteenth-century European societies

Reviewing the Significance of Key People, Concepts, and Events (Knowledge and Understanding)

1. Understanding the history of Renaissance and Reformation periods requires a knowledge of the following concepts, events, and people and an understanding of their significance in the shaping of the history of modern world. Select and explain three from each column.

Concepts	Events	People
Reformation	Peasants' War	Leonardo da Vinci
Utopia	Council of Trent	Johann Gutenberg
anticlericalism	Roman Inquisition	Niccolò Machiavelli
Indulgences	Counter-Reformation	Desiderius Erasmus
Sola fide/sola scriptura	Saint Bartholomew's Massacre	Martin Luther
Protestantism	Edict of Nantes	Jesuits
Roman Index of Prohibited Books		Henry VIII
		Elizabeth I

2. Copy and complete a chart like the one below and use it to explain how the essence of the Renaissance was reflected in the various aspects of society.

Aspect of Society	Renaissance Reflections
Politics	
Science	
Religion	
Art	

Doing History: Thinking About the Past (Thinking/Inquiry)

3. Below are additional excerpts from the *95 Theses* posted by Martin Luther on the church doors in Wittenberg. In your own words, explain what each statement means. Then, considering the statements together, write two paragraphs that explain why the Roman Catholic Church excommunicated Luther after he refused to recant.

   32. Vain is the hope of salvation through letters of pardon, even if a commissary — nay, the Pope himself — were to pledge his own soul for them.

   86. Again: why does not the Pope, whose riches are at this day more ample than those of the wealthiest of the wealthy, build the one Basilica of St. Peter with his own money, rather than with that of poor believers?

4. Revolution can be defined as a dramatic change. Should the Renaissance be considered an artistic and intellectual revolution given the nature of change that occurred during the fifteenth and sixteenth centuries? Respond to this question with a clear thesis statement and at least three well-articulated and historically supported arguments.

Applying Your Learning (Application)

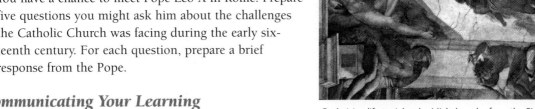

5. What aspects of this image tell you it is not a medieval painting? What aspects of the painting (theme, content) suggest the legacy of the medieval period continued to influence the art of Michelangelo?

6. You have a chance to meet Pope Leo X in Rome. Prepare five questions you might ask him about the challenges the Catholic Church was facing during the early sixteenth century. For each question, prepare a brief response from the Pope.

Communicating Your Learning (Communication)

God giving life to Adam by Michelangelo, from the Sistine chapel.

7. As an entrepreneurial person of the Renaissance, you decide to sell a guide for young social climbers. Prepare a poster listing five to seven ways to become part of the "in-crowd." Use appropriate Renaissance images and icons in the design of your poster.

8. Imagine you have been hired as a spin doctor by the Catholic Church. You are to write a concise summary of the roles to be played by the following during the Counter-Reformation: the Jesuits, the Roman Inquisition, the Index of Prohibited Books, and the Council of Trent. Remember your audience and purpose as you write your summary.

CHAPTER TWO

The Age of Absolutism 1600–1715

CHAPTER EXPECTATIONS

By the end of this chapter, you will be able to:

- *assess the reasons for the failure or success of various approaches to maintaining international order*

- *demonstrate an understanding of the importance of chronology as a tool in analysing the history of events in Europe during the seventeenth century*

- *assess the impact of modern Western thought on economic, social, scientific, and political developments in the West*

- *describe how family structures have changed since the seventeenth century*

The Sun King, Louis XIV was the centre of the universe, at least during the seventeenth century.

The end of the Thirty Years' War brought about a profound change in how European countries dealt with one another. For over a century, bloody battles had been waged between warring religious factions throughout Europe. The Treaty of Westphalia, which marked the end of the war in 1648, was accompanied by an acceptance of national sovereignties. The recognition of a country's sovereignty meant that other countries would not interfere in the internal affairs of that country. How a government treated people within its own borders would be no business of any other government. This paradigm shift in European international relations had far-reaching consequences. It helped to restore a degree of stability in Europe as issues between governments and religious groups now became an internal matter in any country. For nearly three hundred years following, the principle of national sovereignty seemed to serve Europe well.

By the mid-seventeenth century, England and France had emerged as the two dominant powers in Western Europe. While Spain, the Netherlands, Russia, and Sweden were also important military and economic powers, it was England and France that led the revolutions in science, philosophy, and political theory. The same two countries also provided us with the clearest expressions of two antithetical political philosophies: absolutism and constitutionalism. This chapter will focus on England and France for an in-depth examination of the forces and trends that shaped the seventeenth century.

KEY CONCEPTS AND EVENTS

Thirty Years' War
Treaty of Westphalia
scientific revolution
absolutism
Fronde
Palace of Versailles
mercantilism
War of the Spanish Succession
Restoration
constitutionalism
Glorious Revolution

KEY PEOPLE

Galileo Galilei
Isaac Newton
William Harvey
René Descartes
Thomas Hobbes
John Locke
Louis XIV
Peter the Great
Charles I
Gianlorenzo Bernini
Molière

Wit and Wisdom

Eppur, si muove
(But it does move)
Galileo Galilei. Wispered after his trial in 1633.

This sun-centred conception of the universe, by Nicolaus Copernicus, was banned by the Roman Catholic Church in 1616. Why?

TIME LINE: THE AGE OF ABSOLUTISM

Cardinal Richelieu becomes Louis XIII's first minister	1628	
	1629	William Harvey, *On the Motion of the Heart and Blood in Animals;* Charles I suspends Parliament
Galileo Galilei, *Dialogues on the Two Chief Systems of the World*	1632	
	1633	Before the Inquisition, Galileo recants his belief that the Sun is the centre of the universe
René Descartes, *Discourse on Method*	1637	
	1642	Charles I storms Parliament; the beginning of the English Civil War
Beginning of the reign of Louis XIV	1643	
	1648	The Thirty Years' War ends
Charles I is beheaded by order of Parliament	1649	
	1660	Charles II rules England as a Constitutional Monarchy
Louis XIV declares the papacy has no power in France	1682	
	1685	James II ascends the throne of England
	1688	The Glorious Revolution; William of Orange seizes the English throne
The Treaty of Utrecht	1713	

Not to scale.

REVOLUTIONS IN THOUGHT

The Trial of Galileo

On June 22, 1633, a scene that underscored the widening gulf between religious authority and the search for scientific truth unfolded in a Roman convent. As an aged Galileo Galilei (1564–1642) knelt before cardinals of the Roman Catholic Church who had been selected as his judges, he was informed that he was suspected of heresy. Galileo was then ordered to renounce "the false opinion that the Sun is the centre of the universe and immovable, and that the Earth is not the centre of the same ..." The Church had already placed *On the Revolutions of the Celestial Spheres*, by Nicolaus Copernicus (1473–1543), a book that held a theory similar to Galileo's, on its index of banned books in 1616.

The Church had earlier declared the idea of a heliocentric universe "absurd in philosophy and formally heretical," and Pope Paul V had ordered Galileo not to teach or defend these theories. In defiance of the Church, Galileo had published his findings in 1632, in a book entitled *Dialogue on the Two Chief Systems of the World*. It was this that brought Galileo to the Holy Inquisition, where with the instruments of torture used to extract confessions laid before him, and the threat of being burned as a heretic, the scientist agreed to recant his views. Although Galileo's life was spared, he was sentenced to house arrest in Florence for the rest of his life and ordered not to publish on the subject again. It was not until 1992 that the Catholic Church acknowledged its error and accepted Galileo's findings. What might Galileo have accomplished, had he not been silenced?

THE SCIENTIFIC REVOLUTION

Astronomy and Physics

The trial of Galileo was a symptom of the growing rift between the authority of the Church and scientific thought. From the middle of the sixteenth century to the beginning of the eighteenth century, a revolution in science would challenge how Europeans perceived themselves and the universe, and would radically alter the course of European history.

Scientific thought was not new to the sixteenth century. What was new were the methods and questions that scientists were asking. The scientific mind of the Middle Ages sought answers that would fit preconceived notions about the universe. For example, it was assumed that a planet follows a circular orbit because the circle was a perfect pattern created by God. Similarly, medieval scientists held firmly to the view that the Earth was the centre of the universe and that the reason objects fell toward the Earth when dropped was because objects sought the place of greatest heaviness in the universe: the Earth. Such notions held scientific progress in check for centuries. But just as the Renaissance revolutionized art and religion through a rebirth of classicism and humanism, changes in scientific method would ultimately revolutionize science. Central to this revolution would be the use of experimentation to develop new scientific theories.

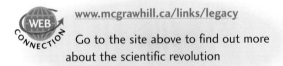

www.mcgrawhill.ca/links/legacy

Go to the site above to find out more about the scientific revolution

Nicolaus Copernicus

Among the first to challenge traditional views of the universe was a Polish scientist named Nicolaus Copernicus (1473–1543). His great work *On the Revolutions of the Celestial Spheres*, published in 1543, created quite a stir among educated Europeans. Drawing inspiration from the work of Aristarchus of Samos (a Greek philosopher of the third century BCE), Copernicus put forward the idea of a heliocentric universe, a Sun-centred universe in which the planets revolved around the Sun, not the Earth, as previously thought. Copernicus's theory further suggested that

Earth rotated on its own axis every 24 hours and that the Moon revolved around Earth. As revolutionary as Copernicus's ideas were, he was in many ways a conservative thinker who based his conclusions on philosophical deductions rather than astronomical observations.

Galileo Galilei

Galileo Galilei, a Florentine astronomer, gathered important astronomical and mathematical evidence to support the ideas of Copernicus. Performing controlled experiments such as rolling balls down slopes and measuring their speeds, Galileo showed that motion could be described mathematically. Based on these findings Galileo formulated the principle of inertia, showing that bodies, once set in motion tend to stay in motion. Galileo also gathered astronomical evidence using a telescope he built in 1609. Through direct observation, Galileo showed that the Moon was not a perfectly smooth heavenly body, but rather had a rough surface, covered in craters and mountains. His telescope also revealed that Jupiter had moons and the Sun had spots. These and other findings reinforced Galileo's belief in the validity of Copernicus's theory of a heliocentric universe. He proclaimed, "in discussions of physical problems we ought to begin not from the authority of scriptural passages, but from sense-experiences and necessary demonstrations." When Galileo published his *Dialogue on the Two Chief Systems of the World*, he openly supported a Copernican view of the universe and described those who opposed this view (such as the Jesuits) as simple-minded. His public support for the idea of a heliocentric universe brought Galileo up against the conservative forces within the Catholic Church.

Tycho Brahe

Tycho Brahe (1546–1601), a Danish aristocrat, was another important astronomer of the sixteenth century. Despite his rejection of Copernicus's idea of a heliocentric universe, Brahe made important contributions to astronomy. Working from his well-equipped (by the king of Denmark) laboratory, Brahe recorded thousands of accurate and detailed observations about planets and stars over a 20-year period. His discovery of a new star in 1572 and a comet in 1577 disproved Aristotle's belief in a universe of fixed, unalterable stars.

Johannes Kepler

It required the genius of Johannes Kepler (1571–1630) and Isaac Newton (see below), building upon the ideas of Copernicus and Galileo to arrive at a better understanding of how the universe works. Kepler was a German contemporary of Galileo and had at one point served as Tycho Brahe's assistant. Convinced that Copernicus was right, Kepler observed planetary motion and formulated the mathematical laws that govern the solar system. Kepler eventually arrived at three universal laws of planetary motion.

- Kepler's first law states that planets move in elliptical orbits, with the Sun at one focus of the ellipses. This law disproved Galileo's concept of circular orbits.
- Kepler's second law, expressed in simple language, states that as a planet draws closer to the Sun, it moves faster in its orbit; as it moves farther from the Sun, it moves more slowly. This law challenged the traditional notion that heavenly motion is steady and unchanging.

Johannes Kepler (left) gave us the universal laws of planetary motion. Why was this important?

- Kepler's third law states the relationship among the movements of all planets as opposed to the motion of any individual planet. This law states that the square of the ratio of the time it takes any two planets to complete their orbit equals the cube of the ratio of these planets' average distance from the Sun. This simply means that the size of a planet's orbit is proportional to the time required for one revolution around the Sun.

Isaac Newton

Isaac Newton (1642–1727), an English scientist, was to provide the great synthesis that would draw together the discoveries made during the preceding century. Incorporating into one coherent system the concepts of Copernicus, Galileo, and Kepler, Newton formulated his famous Three Laws of Motion:

- If no force acts on an object, it will remain at rest or maintain its constant motion in a straight line.
- Every change of motion or acceleration of a body is directly proportional to the force that caused the change and inversely proportional to the object's mass.
- For every action force, there is an equal reaction force in the opposite direction.

Thus, the work begun in Poland by Copernicus, continued in Italy by Galileo, and in Germany by Kepler, had been completed in England by Newton during the last two decades of the seventeenth century. All of Europe had witnessed a quiet revolution in ideas that would have a lasting and profound impact.

The Revolution in Anatomy

William Harvey

Unlike his predecessor Vesalius, William Harvey (1578–1657), an English physician, was not satisfied with divine power as an explanation for the workings of the heart. Harvey's work on the heart was a synthesis of many of the ideas about human anatomy, which he published in *On the Motion of the Heart and Blood in Animals* in 1628. Harvey described the heart as a pump rather than as a filtration plant, as it had been traditionally described.

Harvey also discovered that in a single hour the heart pumps out more than a person's mass in blood; therefore, the veins would burst if the blood were not somehow circulating. Harvey wrote: "I began to think whether there might not be a motion, as it were a circle." Despite its obvious logic, his discovery of the circulation of the blood would take almost half a century to win acceptance. Harvey's work nevertheless opened up a whole new set of questions and problems regarding blood and human anatomy.

SCIENTIFIC METHOD AND THE BIRTH OF MODERN PHILOSOPHY

Scientific Method

The underpinning of the scientific revolution was a new approach to determining "truth." For centuries, it was believed that one arrived at truisms by relying on long-trusted authorities such as the Bible or classical scholars, and making deductions from their propositions. The major revelations in science during the seventeenth century were arrived at through systematic skepticism, experimentation, and reasoning based on observed facts and mathematical laws. The two key figures in outlining the new scientific methods were the English politician, Francis Bacon, and the French philosopher, René Descartes.

Francis Bacon

Francis Bacon (1561–1626) was clearly a product of the English Renaissance. Well versed in politics, literature, and philosophy, Bacon earned a lasting reputation for his work in science. Rejecting the deductive methods of the Middle Ages, Bacon stressed the importance of direct observation in ascertaining truth. His *Novum Organum*, which was published in 1620, was an attempt at replacing Aristotle's *Organon*. Bacon's work explored

This dedication to the English Royal Society shows Francis Bacon (right) and his king, Charles II.

René Descartes

René Descartes (1596–1650) laid the foundations for modern philosophy, though he remained a devout Catholic throughout his life. Descartes' greatest contribution to the intellectual revolution of the seventeenth century was his application of methods and reasoning used in mathematics to the field of philosophy.

Unlike Bacon, Descartes did not believe that we can rely solely on our senses in the search for truth. Descartes argued that the empiricist faith in our senses was naive, because our senses can be tricked. He maintained that all things can be doubted. Our senses can be deceived and information can be false. Therefore, we can be absolutely certain of only one thing — that we exist. To doubt requires that we exist. Therefore, proof of our existence comes from the fact that we think. Descartes said: "I think, therefore I am" (*Cogito ergo sum*). All other truths are based on our mental perceptions. The mind is essential, while that which we experience is secondary. How each of us interprets experiences determines our truths. For Descartes, the route to truth lay in the detached reasoning of the individual mind.

The thinking of Descartes led to a conception of the universe as purely mechanical and physical. He was able to rationalize God's existence only through reason because God cannot be physically experienced. Descartes believed that much of our knowledge is innate and either already within us, or deduced by totally rational means, without the help of our senses. For example, Descartes argued that knowledge of God and God's perfection could never be arrived at through the senses, but rather results from the use of the intellect and reason. Descartes' views were certainly influenced by his interest in mathematics, usually seen as a purely rational field of study.

Questioning Political Legitimacy Hobbes versus Locke?

The Reformation openly challenged the authority of the papacy and the Roman Catholic Church. The scientific revolution challenged long-held beliefs

the faulty traditional methods of science and proposed a method of inquiry that is still used in scientific study today. Bacon outlined an inductive method based on the direct observation of nature. Francis Bacon also believed that knowledge is the basis of power, and allows human control of nature. He wrote:

> Knowledge and human power are synonymous, since the ignorance of the cause frustrates the effect; for nature is only subdued by submission, and that which in contemplative philosophy corresponds with the cause in practical science becomes the rule.

> There is another powerful and great cause of the little advancement of the sciences, which is this: It is impossible to advance properly in the course when the goal is not properly fixed. But the real and legitimate goal of the sciences, is the endowment of human life with new inventions and riches.

about the universe, ourselves, and the basis of all knowledge. It is perhaps not surprising that a challenge to political legitimacy also occurred during the seventeenth century.

Claiming to govern by divine right was losing credibility in a century when challenges to traditional forms of knowledge were becoming routine. During the seventeenth century, political philosophy began to tackle the thorny question of who had the right to govern, and on what basis. Two prominent English philosophers, Thomas Hobbes and John Locke, each wrote a discourse that began with imagining life in the state of nature, but from there they diverged dramatically.

Thomas Hobbes

Since Thomas Hobbes (1588–1679) was witness to the conflict and violence of the English revolution of the 1640s, his political philosophy was shaped by the chaos after the execution of King Charles I. In his famous work *Leviathan*, Hobbes explained what he believed was the justification for any government.

Hobbes, like John Locke (see below) and later, Jean Jacques Rousseau, began his arguments on government with an imagined "state of nature." This expression refers to a period of human history prior to the development of societies and prior to any form of social organization, such as governments or laws. In

Philosophers John Locke and Thomas Hobbes held different views of what human beings were like in a "state of nature." Here we see a portrait of Locke and the frontispiece for *Leviathan*, the best-known work of Hobbes.

the state of nature, people were free; they could do anything they wanted with no restrictions or repercussions. But in the state of nature, each individual had to fend for himself or herself, and survival was entirely dependent on one's own ability to acquire food, build a shelter, and protect oneself from danger; however, Hobbes also believed that human beings were by nature selfish and aggressive, and left to their own resources would be in a constant state of conflict and chaos. Hobbes described life in the state of nature as "short, nasty, and brutish."

Since the state of nature, in which people have complete freedom but are in a constant state of conflict, is one in which there are no laws, it must follow that a state of peace must be one in which there are laws. Hobbes believed that only the establishment of an absolute sovereign could bring peace out of the chaos. The people must agree, as in a contract, to submit to the sovereign and her or his laws in return for the peace that would result. If people wanted to avoid a return to the state of nature, they must obey the laws and follow their sovereign.

John Locke

Like Hobbes, John Locke (1632–1704) used the idea of a "state of nature" as the beginning of his political philosophy. But unlike Hobbes, who believed that people were basically selfish and had to be controlled by a ruler, Locke thought that over time, people willingly began to join together in societies to benefit from co-operation. With co-operation and living together emerged rules, laws to govern peoples' actions, and governments to create the laws. People surrendered some of their freedoms in exchange for the benefits they received from living in a society. This is often referred to as a "social contract."

Locke argued that once people chose to leave the state of nature and enter into a social contract, sovereignty (power) remained in their hands. According to Locke, the only justification for government comes from a people's willingness to surrender some of their freedoms and be governed in a society.

There were certain rights, however, such as the right to life, liberty, and property that were inalienable and not to be surrendered. Since people enter into a social contract and agree to the rule of law, power remains with the people, and governments act on their behalf.

If Locke's argument that power should remain in the hands of the people is accepted, then it follows that the people retain the right to remove the government if it is not acting on their behalf. For Locke, this argument applied to kings and queens, and elected officials. People enter into society to preserve their property and they submit to the authority of government and laws as a means to safeguard what is theirs. Locke wrote:

> Whenever the legislators endeavour to take away and destroy the property of the people, or to reduce them to slavery under arbitrary power, they put themselves into a state of war with the people who are thereupon absolved from any further obedience ...

When a controversy exists between the government and the people, Locke was insistent that it is the people who must be heard, since the government's power derives only from the people.

Both Thomas Hobbes and John Locke made important contributions to modern political thought. One need look no farther than our own country and our neighbour to the south to see the lasting impact of these two political philosophers. Canada's first constitution, the British North America Act, included the phrase "peace, order, and good government." The United States Constitution guarantees the right to "life, liberty, and the pursuit of happiness." Canada has embraced a Hobbesian view in which the primary function of government is to ensure stability and order in society even if at the expense of individual liberties. The American Constitution was, in contrast, a more Lockeian document, designed to ensure the liberties of individual citizens.

The scientific revolution during the sixteenth and seventeenth centuries coincided with an equally important revolution in politics. The central issue of the age would be the basis of a monarchy's authority. In countries such as Russia, Spain and France, where the concept of absolutism flourished, monarchs ruled unopposed by parliament. Despite their best efforts, the attempts of the English monarchy to establish an absolute state led to civil war and the beheading of the king. Politics in seventeenth-century Europe saw a clear division between absolutism and constitutionalism — both of which would eventually change the face of politics in Europe.

Review, Reflect, Respond

1. How did the Treaty of Westphalia affect relations among the European states?

2. In a chart, list the major contributions to the scientific revolution made by Galileo, Kepler, Newton, and Harvey, and explain how each challenged long-held assumptions.

3. If you had a chance to meet Francis Bacon, René Descartes, Thomas Hobbes or John Locke, whom would you choose? Explain your choice and compose two questions you would ask during your meeting.

THE AGE OF ABSOLUTISM

Absolutism Defined

Before studying the reign of Louis XIV (1638–1715), it is important to have a clear understanding of the concept of absolutism. In the absolutist states, monarchs claimed to rule by divine right. In 1610 England's King James I insisted before the English Parliament: "Kings have power of ... life and death; [they are] judges over all their subjects and in all causes, and yet accountable to none but God." Absolutist monarchs were not limited in their actions by parliaments or representative bodies; they controlled all competing interest groups and regulated all religious sects. Crucial to the success

of an absolute monarch was his or her ability to gain control of the nobility, which posed the greatest threat to the Crown.

Prior to the seventeenth century, European monarchs fought wars using temporary armies raised by feudal lords. Once the war was over, these soldiers would return to their occupations. Relying on the nobility for military support was always risky for medieval monarchs: it could lead to internal strife should the nobility withhold its support or challenge the monarchy. Absolute monarchs avoided such problems by creating permanent, standing armies recruited, paid, and trained by the state. They also employed secret police to watch over potentially troublesome subjects.

A long and widely held myth about Louis XIV of France is that he proclaimed "I am the state" ("L'état, c'est moi"). What Louis did say was: "The interests of the state come first. When one gives these priority, one labours for one's own good. The advantage to the state redounds to one's glory." These two phrases cast different lights on the reign of Louis XIV. The former suggests a king who put his personal interests and glory ahead of those of France. The latter reflects a king whose primary goal is to ensure the vitality of France, and who believes that this can best be accomplished through the unity and stability provided by a strong monarch. Louis XIV did indeed exemplify the absolutist belief that the monarchy personifies the state. France during the second half of the seventeenth century epitomized absolutism in that Louis reined in competing factions and centralized all authority in himself. As historian Jacques Barzun noted, Louis XIV brought unity to France by making "etiquette serve as an anti-revolutionary force."

Foundations of Absolutism in France

Louis XIV did not create absolutism; he inherited it. During the reign of his father, Louis XIII, the powerful statesman and cleric Cardinal Richelieu (1585–1642) was appointed to the council of ministers. By 1628 he had risen to be first minister of the French Crown. Richelieu reflected the increasing secularization of the seventeenth century, in that although he was a Roman Catholic bishop, his first loyalty was to the French state. Richelieu used his appointment and influence over the young king Louis XIII to promote the French monarchy as the embodiment of the French state. During his tenure as first minister, Richelieu laid the basis for French absolutism, and paved the way for French cultural dominance throughout Europe in the late seventeenth century.

In an attempt to subordinate all groups to the king, Richelieu repeatedly challenged and alienated the nobility, levelling their castles and crushing aristocratic conspiracies with summary executions. To centralize control under the crown, Richelieu divided the country into 32 districts, each of which had a royal *intendant* with extensive powers over justice, the police, and finances. These *intendants*, drawn largely from the upper middle class or the minor nobility, were appointed directly by the monarch to ensure that royal orders were enforced and that the power of the regional nobility was weakened.

Cardinal Richelieu died in 1642, and Louis XIII in 1643. Richelieu was succeeded by Jules Mazarin (1602–1661) and the child-king Louis XIV (1638–1715) replaced his father. Mazarin's attempt to deal with the increasing financial problems of the crown by raising taxes in 1648 led to the civil wars known as the *Fronde* ("slingshot" or "catapult" in French, but came to mean "revolt"). The bitter civil war that broke out between the monarchy and the *frondeurs* (nobility and upper middle class) continued intermittently for 12 years.

Perhaps the most important and lasting impact of the *Fronde* was the political education it provided the young Louis XIV. Louis never forgot the trauma he suffered as a young boy when he and his mother were threatened and at times treated as prisoners by rebel aristocrats. The 12 years of the *Fronde* convinced Louis that the only alternative to chaos and anarchy was absolute power.

LOUIS XIV, THE SUN KING

During his long reign (1643–1715), Louis XIV was able to take France to the pinnacle of its power, creating the most centralized nation-state in Europe. This gave birth to a new sense of French nationhood. Feudal regionalism and dominance of the Church were replaced with national pride. Louis XIV came to symbolize this new spirit of French culture and became the embodiment of the French state. The title "Sun King" was appropriate: Louis was seen as the brilliant star that provided light, warmth, and sustenance at least to his court, if not his people. From the time he was a child, Louis was seen as a young Apollo, the radiant Greek god who personified the Sun and embodied beautiful young men and the arts of poetry and music. Allusions to the Sun and Apollo featured in all aspects of the Court at Versailles, from paintings and statues to ballet costumes and fountains.

The power and influence of Cardinal Richelieu inspired this official portrait by French court painter Philippe de Champaigne.

Louis loved all the fine arts and even participated in ballet performances. Here he is seen in costume as the god Apollo. Why Apollo?

Consolidating Power

When Louis XIV reached the age of 23, he began to centralize power under his control. He created a standing army maintained in peacetime. In 1666 Louis appointed François-Michel Le Tellier his secretary of war; Le Tellier created the first modern army. Louis took personal command of the army and directly supervised all aspects and details of military affairs. The army was modern not only in the sense that it was permanent and professional but also in its training and administration. Gone was the ancient practice of soldiers living off the countryside. This was replaced by a *commissariat*, responsible for feeding the troops. An ambulance corps was designed to look after the wounded; uniforms and weapons were standardized; and a rational system of recruitment, training, discipline, and promotion was put into place. This new military machine would allow France to dominate European politics for decades.

Louis XIV also moved quickly to centralize government. The day-to-day governing of France in the seventeenth century was largely carried out by three councils: the Court of State, the Court of Finances, and the Court of Dispatches, which was responsible for the administration of law. By presiding over all the councils and meeting with all high government officials at least once a week, Louis XIV retained absolute control over the government.

To ensure loyalty to the king at all levels of government, Louis XIV used bribery to guarantee that provincial governors sympathetic to him were elected. He also kept their term to three years so that any governors who were not loyal could not remain in power long enough to undermine his authority. Furthermore, Louis insisted that all laws receive his approval before being passed. The bureaucracy was staffed largely by the upper middle class, depriving the nobility of their traditional role in government. The modern bureaucratic state was born, dominated by middle-class professionals who were paid a salary by the government and whose loyalty was to the state.

Pleasures
AND PASTIMES

Every couple of years, Louis XIV put on grand spectacles to showcase the wealth of his kingdom and the glory of his reign. The grandest of these extravagant displays was the fete of the *Pleasure of the Enchanted Isle*, which took place at Versailles in May 1664. The week-long extravaganza, to which more than 600 members of the nobility were invited, included games, masques, receptions, theatrical performances, ballets, and fireworks. To plan and carry out the fairytale conceived by the king, many of the greatest artists and entertainers of the age were brought together. Jean-Baptiste Lully was put in charge of the music for the affair while the theatrical events were under the direction of Molière. *The Pleasures of the Enchanted Isle* was a perfect example of how Louis XIV used culture and entertainment rather than brute force to subdue and control the nobility.

Louis XIV's efforts to centralize power under him challenged the authority of the Catholic Church in France and a power struggle ensued, with the papacy maintaining its ascendancy. In 1682 Louis produced four articles that essentially stripped the papacy of its power in France. Eventually, the articles were annulled: Louis, having made his point was now willing to return the power. The papacy would never again issue church laws pertaining to French social, political, or economic issues. Louis XIV had won control over the Catholic Church in France. Louis's next centralizing move, in 1685, was to revoke the Edict of Nantes (1598), in which Henri IV had granted religious freedom to the Huguenots (French Protestants). More than religious intolerance, this was a manoeuvre to unite church and state under the leadership of the king.

Colbert's Economic Reforms

French absolutism owed much to the financial genius of Jean-Baptiste Colbert (1619–1683), who was appointed controller-general by Louis XIV. Colbert operated on the central principle of mercantilism, a system is which the government regulates economic activity based on the premise that international power is a product of its wealth. Colbert believed that France's economic success depended on self-suffi-ciency. He encouraged the creation of new domestic industries (such as silk, cotton, and tapestries) and discouraged imports of goods in an attempt to limit the export of money.

One of Colbert's most important achievements was the creation of a powerful merchant marine, which was crucial to ensure France's positive balance of trade. In 1661 France had only eighteen seaworthy vessels, but within 20 years it had 276 frigates, galleys, and ships. Many of these vessels, were used to develop trade between France and its colonies in the Caribbean and North America. The Caribbean islands supplied resources, such as sugar cane, while Canada was rich in minerals, fish, furs, and prime agricultural land.

Under Colbert, the colonization of New France was encouraged. In 1684 the French explorer Robert Cavelier de La Salle claimed the territories along the Mississippi and its delta for France; the territory was appropriately called Louisiana. Overseas colonies not only provided vital natural resources, they also were potential markets for manufactured French goods. When Jean Talon, the first *intendant* of New France (French possessions in the St. Lawrence, Great Lakes, and Mississippi Valley during Colbert's time), suggested ways to help make the colony more self-suffi-cient by encouraging the establishment of local industry, he was rebuked by the crown for failing to understand the role the colony was to play in the French empire.

The primary goal of Colbert's domestic taxation policy was to provide more money for the royal treasury. By reducing income tax (paid by the rich) and increasing indirect taxes such as road tolls, milling, and shipping taxes, Colbert shifted the tax burden to the poor, believing if the rich had more money left in their pockets, they would spend it on productive goods, thereby benefiting the French economy.

The Palace of Versailles

Louis XIV wanted to establish a new court that would reflect his power and prestige. He decided to build a new palace on the outskirts of the small town of Versailles, about 30 km from Paris. No expense was spared during the construction of Versailles, which took nearly 20 years to complete.

Before Versailles, European palaces had been dec-orated largely with exquisite wood carvings. Versailles was to be different: Wood was replaced with marble and gold, and a new French Provincial style was intro-duced, with white walls trimmed with gold ornament. Elaborate tapestries were to adorn so many of the walls that a factory in Gobelins, near Paris, was created specifically to meet the needs of the new palace.

The most famous room in the palace is the Hall of Mirrors (*Salle des glaces*). This brilliant room, with mirrors covering one long wall, huge windows looking out on the famous gardens along the other wall, and dozens of chandeliers, became a symbol of French

The Palace at Versailles was not only the royal residence but also the place where foreign dignitaries came for audiences with Louis. To that end, Versailles was meant to dazzle the eye and overwhelm with its sheer size and extravagance. Drawing by seventeenth-century artist Patel.

power. The palace also contained an ornate two-storey chapel decorated with paintings, able to accommodate 900 members of the nobility.

The palace had to function not only as a residence for Louis and his court, but also as the setting for the many official duties and activities of a seventeenth-century absolute monarch. Hallways, staircases, reception rooms, banquet rooms, and ballrooms were designed to hold elaborate court spectacles. These were explicitly theatrical and designed to enhance the image of the king as the central authority and focus of all activity at court. Ambassadors, nobility, statesmen, and dignitaries from other countries were to be awed by their experience at the palace of Louis XIV.

The 365 hectares of gardens at Versailles, like the palace, reflected and enhanced the majesty of the king. The endless, manicured gardens, with their perfectly trimmed hedges and carefully sculpted fountains, created a seemingly perfect landscape: a reflection of the perfectibility of nature possible under the rule of the Sun King. At Versailles, order and reason reigned supreme alongside opulence and splendour.

Versailles became the envy of every European monarch. Louis and his palace staff succeeded in making it one of the most important tools in gaining control of the French nobility — it was the goal of every nobleman or noblewoman to be invited to live at Versailles. By granting pensions and extending invitations to live at Versailles, the French aristocracy surrendered its power and accepted the absolute rule of the king. Versailles also welcomed French intellectuals, artists, musicians, and writers as visitors or to live. The magnificent palace thus helped Louis XIV to further enhance his role as the embodiment of the French state.

Life at Versailles

Life at the palace of Versailles came to resemble a carefully staged theatrical production, with the nobility competing for roles. Louis XIV used Versailles and the vanity of the nobility to disarm potential threats to the throne by carefully exploiting a fusion of revelry and rivalry. Previous to his reign, monarchs had had to contend with competing factions among the nobility by employing spies throughout France and putting down rebellions as they flared up. Louis XIV, like a brilliant director and choreographer, orchestrated events at Versailles so that there were always grand balls, ballets, plays, banquets, and other such festivities to keep the nobility occupied. And those who were not at Versailles, channeled their energies into earning an invitation to live at the palace rather than toward overthrowing the king.

Even the daily routines of the king came to be ritualized so that the nobility would compete for the king's favour and an opportunity to hand him his shirt, assist him in bathroom rituals, or sit across from him during a meal. Article 21 of Louis' House Rules (1681) included these directions for the serving of his meals:

> His Majesty's meals shall be brought in thus: Two of the guards will walk in first, then the door-keeper, the maître d'hôtel carrying his staff, the gentleman who serves bread, the controller-general, the controller's clerk, the squire of the kitchen, and the keeper of table settings.

Louis surrendered virtually all of his privacy in the interest of the state, but no one among the nobility was ever allowed to see the king without his wig. Louis had lumps on his head (sebaceous cysts), the sight of which would have undermined his image.

The Wars of Louis XIV

Driven by unlimited ambition, Louis XIV would embark on no fewer than four major wars of aggression during the last four decades of his reign. Although he already governed the most powerful European state (militarily, economically, and culturally) and had managed to gain control over the nobility and the church, Louis' desire for wealth, land, and glory proved to be insatiable. Beginning in 1667, Louis XIV took France into wars against virtually all of the powers of Western Europe. In the War of Devolution (1667–1668), France realized only minor gains against the Spanish in their efforts to lay claim to parts of the Spanish Netherlands (today Belgium).

In 1672 Louis' armies invaded the Netherlands but were turned back when the Dutch opened the dikes and flooded the land. When the Dutch allied with Spain, Sweden, Brandenburg and the Holy Roman Empire against France, Louis' armies were held to a standstill, although some valuable territories were gained through the Peace of Nijmegen (1679). Ten years after the signing of the Peace of Nijmegen, France was once again embroiled in a war, this time against a coalition of European powers called the Grand Alliance. After eight years of bloodshed and misery, the war ended with few gains for France.

The final war of Louis' reign was the War of the Spanish Succession, but Louis' efforts to enforce French claims to the Spanish throne ended in disaster. After 11 years of war (1702–1713) the Grand Alliance defeated the French and Louis XIV was forced to accept the Peace of Utrecht. Decades of war had left France defeated and impoverished with little territorial gains to show for its sacrifices. The grandeur of the French state was in tatters and the people were threatening to revolt, frustrated by years of war and increasing taxes. Archbishop Fenelon, a critic of Louis XIV, summarized the final decades of Louis' reign with these words:

> for 30 years, your principal ministers have ... overthrown all the ancient maxims of the state in order to increase your authority beyond all bounds ... For the sake of getting and keeping vain conquests abroad, you have destroyed half the real strength of your own state.

The Legacy of Louis XIV

As absolute ruler of France, Louis XIV created the grandest court Europe had ever seen. His long, 73-year reign left an unparalleled political and cultural legacy. Feudal lords and the Catholic Church had surrendered much of their power to the king. France had gained the stature of Europe's leading cultural and military power and a strong sense of nationhood had developed — people now saw themselves as French rather than from a particular region. By 1715, France had established an extensive overseas empire that provided the resources and markets to make France an economic power as well.

At the same time, Louis' vast expenditures and costly wars created unprecedented misery for the majority of the French population. Financing numerous wars, paying a professional army and pensions to the nobility, and maintaining the elaborate court at Versailles put a strain on the royal treasury. The increasing tax burden of the lower classes would create a crisis in the eighteenth century that the monarchy could not survive. As the procession carrying the body of the deceased Sun King wound its way through the streets of Paris in 1715, people could be heard cursing his name.

ABSOLUTISM IN EASTERN EUROPE:

Peter the Great

It is said that history is largely created by those who write it. This certainly seems to be the case when one reads the many and varied accounts of the reign of Peter I of Russia, called Peter the Great (1672–1725). Some see him as a superhuman hero who transformed Russia into a modern state; others maintain that the human costs were far too high. We do know that, during the seventeenth and eighteenth centuries, Peter was instrumental in turning Russia away from its feudal past and down the road to westernization.

Peter the Great's reign began in 1682, when, at the age of 10, he was proclaimed the first czar of Russia. By 1696, with his mother and older half-brother both dead, Peter was able to establish himself as the absolute sovereign of Russia. Peter set to work reforming Russia despite staunch opposition from his family, court circles, and government officials. Finding little support among the Russian elite, the czar chose to fill important posts based on merit rather than lineage or rank.

Peter the Great created strong ties with Eastern Europe and brought hundreds of foreign scholars to lecture at his court. Why would he do this?

The Westernization of Russia

Peter the Great believed firmly that the key to Russia's progress was the development of closer ties with Western Europe. In March 1697, he sent a group of 250 Russians to visit numerous European countries where it was hoped they would learn a great deal about everything from shipbuilding and navigation, to crafts and technical skills, and Western manners. His interest in the West was so great that Peter himself travelled abroad incognito as Peter Mikhailov. As a result of their 18 months spent abroad, the Russian emissaries not only learned a great deal but also managed to recruit over 750 foreigners to serve in Russia. Isaac Newton was among those who took up the czar's invitation. Peter also realized the value in maintaining and developing ties with Eastern Europe and Asian countries. Young men were encouraged to learn Turkish, Persian, and even Japanese, and emissaries were sent to Mongolia and China.

Like other European monarchs, Peter the Great tried to make his palace at St. Petersburg in the image of Versailles.

Peter's desire to westernize Russia can most clearly be seen in the educational and cultural reforms he implemented. Schools such as the School of Mathematics and Navigation, were created to train specialists; the Academy of Sciences was created for the most learned in Russia. A minimum education was required for service in the czar's government, and education became compulsory for the gentry. Peter also brought Western culture to Russia by encouraging Western dress and manners, often meeting with stiff resistance from the people. A clear sign of Peter's intent to westernize Russia was his demand that men shave their beards "for the glory and comeliness of the state and the military profession." Peter also changed his own title from czar to emperor.

Securing Power

Like all other absolute monarchs, Peter the Great faced the constant challenge of raising enough revenue to meet his needs. And, like all other absolute monarchs, he never found an effective method to do this. Peter's only recourse was to raise taxes on the Russian masses, already heavily overburdened. By adding new taxes or increasing existing taxes, 550 percent more was wrung from the Russian people in 1724 than in 1680. This was done by taxing almost everything, including beehives, mills, fisheries, bathhouses, beards, and even the number of corners in a house.

Peter the Great was ruthless with those who opposed him. Prior to his journey to the West, a group known as the *streltsy* (musketeer regiment in Moscow), plotted to depose Peter and put his more conservative elder half-sister, Sophia, on the throne. Although the conspiracy was uncovered and defused, Peter had over one thousand *streltsy* tortured and executed, and their bodies put on display as a lesson to the public. His wife, Eudoxia, and his half-sister, both of whom had sympathized with the rebels' defense of tradition and religion, were forced to become nuns.

The Legacy of Peter the Great

A good summary of the changes brought to Russia by Peter the Great was written by the Russian historian Mikhail Pogodin (1800–1875), who wrote:

Yes, Peter the Great did much for Russia ... We cannot open our eyes, cannot make a move, cannot turn in any direction without encountering him everywhere ... We wake up. What day is today? January 1, 1841 — Peter the Great ordered us to count years from the birth of Christ ... [Peter changed the Russian calendar]

It is time to dress — our clothing is made according to the fashion established by Peter the First, our uniform according to his model. The cloth is woven in a factory which he created; the wool is shorn from the sheep which he started to raise.

A book strikes our eyes — Peter the Great introduced this script and himself cut out the letters. You begin to read it — this language became a written language, a literary language, at the time of Peter the First, superseding the earlier church language. Newspapers are brought in — Peter the Great introduced them.

At dinner, all the courses, from salted herring, through potatoes which he ordered grown, to wine made from grapes which he began to cultivate, will speak to you of Peter the Great.

Let us go to the university — the first secular school was founded by Peter the Great.

You decide to travel abroad — following the example of Peter the Great; you will be received well — Peter the Great placed Russia among the European states and began to instill respect for her ...[1]

Review, Reflect, Respond

1. List and explain what you believe were the three most important factors that allowed Louis XIV to centralize power and establish a strong absolute state under his control.

2. If you were asked to write a biography of Louis XIV, would you portray his reign as a success or a failure? Explain your views.

3. List and describe what you believe was Peter the Great's greatest success or failure.

ENGLAND IN THE SEVENTEENTH CENTURY

The Triumph of Constitutionalism

In sharp contrast to the absolute monarchy of France and other European states, England, by 1688, was governed by a constitutional monarchy — Parliament ruled over the Crown. Many blame the Crown's loss of power on the incompetence of the Stuart kings who ruled for the first half of the seventeenth century, but the Tudor monarchs of the sixteenth century were also responsible.

As early as 1529, Henry VIII was forced to appeal to Parliament for support in his struggle against the papacy over his divorce. This elevated the power of Parliament and set a precedent in English government. Henry's daughter, Elizabeth I, failed to deal with the rise of Puritanism (which challenged the state religion, Anglicanism), thus failing to establish the type of religious unity that Louis XIV had managed to secure in France. Elizabeth was forced repeatedly to ask Parliament for tax increases to finance Britain's ongoing war with Spain, and Parliament was becoming increasingly reluctant to comply.

Finally, the absence of a standing army left the monarchy dependent on the questionable loyalty of the militia, which was controlled by the nobility. Consequently, when James I came to the throne in 1603, England was essentially an absolute state governed by a constitutional monarchy. The struggle between the Crown and Parliament for supremacy would dominate English politics for most of the seventeenth century.

The Reign of James I

James I (also James VI of Scotland), son of Mary Queen of Scots, inherited the English throne when his cousin Elizabeth died childless in 1603. The financial problems he inherited as well as his lavish spending habits soon led to a crisis, and James was forced to appeal to Parliament for an increase in taxes of one million pounds. When Parliament granted an increase of only £200 000, James was forced to look for other methods to increase revenues. James I renewed long-forgotten dues that people had been required to pay the Crown for their children to marry, and this angered the common folk. The king also sold titles (such as baron, earl, and duke), angering the nobility. He sold monopolies, thus angering the merchants. James also devised a plan to force people to lend money to the Crown or face a fine.

James I also projected a negative image among the people. He was known to be very bright, but fascinated by witches (he wrote a book entitled *Demonology*); he was known to be lazy, and it was said that he lavished money on court favourites. The king's reputation earned him the title "the wisest fool in Christendom." During his 22-year reign, James was in constant conflict with Parliament over his policies, and under his son Charles, the conflict would escalate.

Charles I and the English Civil War

When Charles I came to the throne in 1625, his stubborn nature and refusal to compromise quickly earned him Parliament's dislike and led to a debate on the constitutional powers of the Crown and Parliament. Parliament's refusal to grant the tax increases requested by Charles led to what is known as the Eleven Years of Tyranny. In 1629 Charles I suspended Parliament and brought England as close as it would ever come to absolutism. The ongoing war in Ireland, however, had drained the treasury to the point where Charles, in 1640, had to recall Parliament for its support to finance the war.

Once Parliament was recalled, Charles I was forced to deal with hostile and rebellious parliamentarians who tried to thwart the king's attempts to raise money. After two years of continual conflict, Charles I stormed Parliament with fifteen hundred horsemen in an attempt to arrest his major opponents in the House of Commons. Most of the parliamentarians managed to escape through the windows and then gather support for the civil war that soon erupted. From 1643 to 1649, Royalists (supporters of the monarchy) and Roundheads (supporters of Parliament) battled for control of the government. In 1646 Charles I was captured by the parliamentarians, who attempted to negotiate with him, but he stubbornly refused to compromise. Feeling they had no alternative, the parliamentarians charged Charles I with treason. On January 30, 1649, the English king Charles I was beheaded.

Following the execution of Charles I, England was governed as a parliamentary republic from 1649 to 1658, under the leadership of Oliver Cromwell (1599–1658). The government put in place in 1649 was not radically different from the previous one except for the absence of a monarch. Divisions among parliamentarians over issues such as control of the army and religious tolerance left England a divided nation. Cromwell refused the crown when it was offered to him and his death in 1658 left England without a ruler, despite the efforts of his son, Richard,

After storming Parliament and losing to the Roundheads, Charles I was beheaded. Who gave the order?

whose lack of experience failed to earn him the respect and following of the English people.

Finally, frustrated by disunity, Charles II, son of the beheaded Charles I, who sought refuge in France, was invited back to the throne eleven years after his father's execution. But the terms of the invitation made it impossible for him or any English monarch to pass laws or raise revenues without Parliament's approval. After accepting his role as a constitutional monarch, Charles II ruled effectively despite his known pro-French and pro-Catholic feelings. The historical period that began with the return of the monarch to the throne of England is usually referred to as the Restoration.

The Glorious Revolution

James II came to the throne on 1685 following the death of his brother, Charles II. He immediately made it known that he intended to restore the Roman Catholic faith and revive the power of the English monarch. This confrontational act alienated the English people and prompted a group of prominent citizens to oppose the king. The Dutch monarch, William of Orange, who had a claim to the throne through marriage to his wife, Mary, was asked by the parliamentarians to invade England and seize the throne. William entered England at the head of 15 000 troops and James II fled to Europe without offering any resistance. This event, during which not a single shot was fired, came to be known ironically as the Glorious Revolution.

WEB CONNECTION

www.mcgrawhill.ca/links/legacy

Go to the site above to find out more about the rule of William of Orange.

William and Mary accepted the crown of England as constitutional monarchs and governed jointly. To ensure that no future monarch would attempt to govern

Dutch monarch, William of the House of Orange, and his wife Mary ruled England, Scotland and Ireland from 1689-1702.

without Parliament, the English passed the Bill of Rights in 1689, which outlined the powers and rights of Parliament: "That the pretended power of suspending of laws, or the execution of laws, by regal [royal] authority, without consent of Parliament, is illegal."

Economic Change in Seventeenth-Century England

The English economy underwent significant changes during the seventeenth century, as it grew out of evolving local and global economies. At the beginning of the seventeenth century, England was still comprised of a series of local economies, each independently striving for self-sufficiency. Market towns with populations ranging from a few hundred to several thousand inhabitants were primarily places where stall-holders or retailers would sell their surplus produce or goods made with local raw materials.

During the seventeenth century, numerous projects had improved river navigation so that by 1690, no point in England was more than 120 kilometres from the sea or 35 kilometres from a navigable river. Improved transportation routes facilitated the development of trade between regions. Regional specialization could now occur and take full advantage of local soil and climatic conditions. By producing the goods best suited to the area and trading for surplus goods from elsewhere, most regions of England improved their material well-being.

Another effect of improved transportation and the emergence of a national economy was a revolution in retailing. By 1690, most market towns in England had shops in the sense we know them today. Shops sold produce and goods from across England and around the world. For example, a man named William Stout owned one such shop in Lancaster. Beginning in the 1680s, Stout rented a shop for five pounds per year. He then visited London and Sheffield where he purchased over 200 pounds in goods, half of which he paid for in cash and half of which he financed. Realizing a healthy return on his investment, Stout was soon purchasing goods from far and wide. Among many other goods, his shop offered his customers West Indian sugar, American tobacco, and iron works from West Riding in England.

Once towns became distribution centres for the world's goods, people began to bypass smaller towns with limited selection in favour of larger market towns. Over time, large towns experienced rapid growth and prosperity while smaller towns began to fade away. The shifting nature of urban economies saw the transformation of many English cities. When prosperous farmers and members of the gentry came to town to do business or to visit the shops, they would also visit doctors, seek advice from lawyers, or take their families to enjoy the newly developing theatres or recreational facilities offered by the city. By the end of the seventeenth century, regional economies had given way to a national economy, and urban centres had reinvented themselves to become centres of retail, services, and entertainment.

LIFE IN SEVENTEENTH-CENTURY ENGLAND

Social Classes and Cultural Units

One of the great challenges in the study of social history is the constant need to remind ourselves that people in the past did not think the way we do today. Not only that, to look only at the daily life of the upper or ruling class is to forget that the past involved all people in the societies we study. The impact of rural communities and the contributions made by men and women of all classes must also be understood.

English society, like all European societies in the seventeenth century, was composed of many distinct social classes. These included the aristocracy, the landowning gentry, wealthy merchants and professionals, small property owners, wage-earning peasants, urban wage earners, and the destitute. Each of these social classes made up a cultural unit with unique values, codes of behaviour, and ways of communicating.

Acts considered acceptable by one class would be frowned upon by another. For example, among the peasantry and the poor, there was a rapid increase in the number of births outside of marriage during the seventeenth century; such an increase did not occur among the upper middle class. Similarly, the shift to a more child-oriented society that began in the Renaissance among the upper and middle classes and continued in the seventeenth century did not occur among lower class families until the late nineteenth and early twentieth centuries. The discoveries of the scientific revolution would also take some time to reach the less literate, lower classes. Throughout the seventeenth century beliefs in magic and witchcraft remained deeply embedded in the minds of the majority of the population in England and Europe.

Family Life

The study of daily life during the seventeenth century poses unique problems and challenges to the historian, especially when reconstructing the lives of the illiterate or the poor people, about whom written records are scarce. Important sources of data for the social historian include diaries, letters, and legal papers such as wills, birth and death certificates, baptism records, and contracts. Other important sources include newspapers, broadsides, almanacs, popular novels, poems, plays, architectural plans, folk customs and folktales, and popular art such as caricatures.

When speaking of the family in the seventeenth century, it is important to remember that the small, nuclear family (mother, father, children) was not yet the norm. A seventeenth-century family included all people living under the same roof. Thus the family unit could include parents and children, possibly grandparents, aunts and uncles, as well as servants, boarders, apprentices, or anyone else living in the home. All members of the family unit were legally and morally subordinate to the male head of the household and were not considered free persons. During the seventeenth century, live-in servants were the norm in almost all households except for the poorest families. In an age in which police were virtually non-existent, the family unit was an important agent of social control at the village level. The father typically kept tight control over the potentially unruly young people in the family.

Marriage Trends

Marriage in the seventeenth century had three purposes. The primary purpose was the continuity of the male line. The other two considerations were the preservation intact of the family property and the acquisition of additional property or beneficial alliances through marriage. Because the continuance of the male line was of vital importance, couples had as many children as possible in hopes that one male child would survive to adulthood.

For daughters and second-born sons, the seventeenth century brought challenges. When Henry VIII dismantled nunneries across England during the English Reformation, he also removed one of the common options for young women. The seventeenth century saw a flood of marriageable young women, many of whom would have spent their adult life in a nunnery. As a result, the number of English women who never married rose from 10 percent in the sixteenth century to 25 percent by the end of the seventeenth century. Similarly, about one-fifth of the younger sons of the elite classes remained bachelors throughout their lives. Fortunately, for many second-born sons and daughters, colonies in the Caribbean and the Americas opened up new lands and new opportunities.

Perhaps surprisingly, a convincing argument can be made that the family unit in the 1990s was actually more stable than the seventeenth-century family unit. Considering that the average age of marriage in the seventeenth century was between 22 and 25, and that often one spouse died by his or her early forties, the median length of a marriage in England was about 17 years. This is considerably less than the median length of marriage in Western societies in the 1990s. Social historian Lawrence Stone suggested that rising divorce rates in the late twentieth century might have been a functional substitute for death. He noted that in the history of the family, it is only since the late twentieth century that declining mortality rates have meant that married couples live together for 20 to 30 years after their children have left home. In the seventeenth century, there was only a 50 percent chance that both mother and father would survive more than two years after their children had left home.

Death: Life's Constant Companion

Perhaps the most striking difference between the family of the seventeenth century and the family of today is the fact of death. Today, Western families are fortunate in that they have limited experience with death; usually it is the elderly who die. In the seventeenth century, however, death was at the centre of life; it threatened every member of the family.

Aside from diseases such as smallpox, young children faced many other dangers early in life. They died from intestinal worms, diarrhea, insufficient milk from

The higher classes commonly employed wet nurses (lactating women who had their own children) to breastfeed their babies.

wet nurses, and lead poisoning from pewter dishes and nipple shields. The middle- and upper-class practice of hiring wet nurses (from the lower classes) to breast-feed their children continued throughout the seventeenth and eighteenth centuries. Upper-class women regarded breast-feeding as crude and beneath their station in life.

Both personal and public hygiene were of little concern to people of the seventeenth century. Often city ditches were used as toilets; butchers threw the offal (guts) of the carcasses they butchered into the streets, and dead animals were often left to rot and decay where they died. Many people never took baths. These practices led to contaminated water and food, and the spread of disease. The fact that the cemetery was often in the centre of town attests to all the filth, disease, contamination, food shortages, poor medical practices, and wars that made death a central part of life in the seventeenth century.

WESTERN ART IN THE SEVENTEENTH CENTURY

Patrons and Patronage

Artistic expression reflects both the values and aspirations of a people and the intellectual climate in which they live. Human beings have always expressed their innermost thoughts, desires, fears, triumphs and defeats through the arts. At the same time, artists have been constrained and inspired by the demands of their patrons. Funding for artistic endeavours has always been in the hands of those with wealth and power; artists who chose to ignore the wishes of patrons often toiled in obscurity and poverty. Understanding the arts of the seventeenth century requires an exploration of the works produced by painters, sculptors, writers and musicians, as well as the patronage and politics behind the works.

Flemish artist Peter Paul Rubens (1577–1640) was one of the most successful artists in the baroque style. This painting of the *Martyrdom of St. Ursula* (1615–20) was the altarpiece of a Catholic church. It shows the saint and her followers being killed by the Huns.

The baroque style, which dominated the arts of the seventeenth century, reflected continuing religious fervour as a result of the Counter-Reformation and the political uncertainty of the age. Unlike the ordered, restrained and classical style of the Renaissance, the baroque style tended to be asymmetrical and dynamic, reflecting a taste for the dramatic and emotional. Often violent narrative scenes were popular subjects for baroque painters and sculptors. At the same time, the scientific revolution had spawned an interest in naturalism, helping to elevate landscape and still-life painting to new heights in the artistic world. Allegory took on new themes and ideas in baroque art, extending beyond the biblical and into popular classical and historic subjects.

Baroque art originated in Rome, but found perhaps its greatest expression in France, at the court of Louis XIV. In this sense, the development of the baroque style paralleled the political developments of the seventeenth century as the focus in European politics shifted northward from the Italian peninsula to France. Patrons, who could be clergy of the Catholic Church, absolute monarchs or wealthy merchants, influenced the themes and functions of the art produced. The artists described below represent a cross-section of painters, sculptors, writers, and musicians who contributed to the tremendous artistic outpouring of the seventeenth century. Each artist relied on the patronage of wealthy and powerful people or institutions. It was largely patronage that shaped the artistic legacy of the seventeenth century.

Gianlorenzo Bernini

Gianlorenzo Bernini (1598–1680) was the most admired and successful sculptor of the baroque era. Unlike his Renaissance predecessors, who favoured ordered restraint and passive reflection, Bernini's sculptures capture figures in the throes of intense action or emotion. Consider, for example, the contrast between Michelangelo's *David* (see Chapter One) and Bernini's *David*. Michelangelo depicts David deep in thought, contemplating the action he is about to take

Bernini's *David* (1623) is a life size marble statue of an active and dynamic young man with a look of determination on his face.

(killing the giant Goliath). The upright, calm, reflective pose and expression of David suggests that it is the decision to act rather than the act itself that is truly heroic. By contrast, Bernini's David is in a typically baroque twisting pose from the head across and down to the left foot. Rather than showing David deep in thought, Bernini captures the biblical hero in motion, releasing his slingshot. The work assumes the presence of Goliath, psychologically expanding the space to involve the viewer in the action.

One of Bernini's most striking works is *The Ecstasy of Saint Teresa*. In this sculpture, Bernini blends the baroque interest in emotional experience with the Counter-Reformation's emphasis on religious mysticism. This composition captures a visionary moment, as an angel pierces Saint Teresa with a golden spear. Saint Teresa's face suggests a moment of extreme ecstasy, her body in a state of collapse and floating on a cloud. Saint Teresa was a Carmelite nun who described in her writings the mystical experience captured by Bernini's sculpture. She wrote about how an angel from heaven pierced her heart with a flaming golden spear. At the moment her heart was pierced, she claimed to have felt a merging of pleasure and pain, as if God were "caressing her soul."

Recognized throughout Europe as the greatest sculptor of his age, Bernini quickly became a much sought after artist. Louis XIV, intent on establishing France as the leading cultural centre of Europe, invested huge sums of money in the arts to glorify Versailles and reflect the grandeur of the French Crown. Bernini executed a number of sculptures for Versailles at Louis' request, including a monumental bust and an equestrian statue of Louis. Bernini was in such demand that he had to operate a large workshop to look after all the projects for his patrons. This constituted a small industry in which many of the works attributed to Bernini were actually designed by him but executed by his assistants, with only finishing touches left to the master.

Michelangelo Merisi da Caravaggio

Michelangelo Merisi (1571–1610) was born in the northern Italian town of Caravaggio in the late sixteenth century. After moving to Rome in about 1590, Merisi bore the name of the town he came from rather than his family name. As a young man, Caravaggio was known for both his artistic talent and his violent temper, which repeatedly led him into problems with the law. Karel van Mander (1548–1606), a seventeenth-century Flemish biographer of artists described the effect of Caravaggio's lifestyle on his art this way:

> He does not study his art constantly, so that after two weeks of work he will sally forth for two months together with his rapier at his side and his servant-boy after him, going from one tennis court to another, always ready to argue or fight, so that he is impossible to get along with. This is totally foreign to art; for Mars [god of war] and Minerva [goddess of the arts] have never been good friends.[2]

The Ecstasy of St. Teresa (1645-52) by Bernini shows the saint in a moment of mystical union with God. This 3m marble sculpture is in the chapel of a church in Rome.

Doubting Thomas (1601) by Caravaggio shows an episode from the life of Jesus Christ. We see Thomas and others examining the wounds of Jesus to see if they are real.

Caravaggio made innovations in painting and influenced artists in Italy, Spain, and northern Europe. Unlike most artists of the period, he made no preliminary drawings. Instead, he also chose to paint directly on the canvas. He introduced a type of naturalism, or realism, that had not been seen before in Italian painting. Some critics were repelled by the dirty fingernails and unkempt appearance of Caravaggio's figures of common people. Others thought his dramatic use of light and shade (*chiaroscuro*) made his paintings too dark and sombre.

Caravaggio painted this screaming monster Medusa from classical Greek mythology in the form of a shield.

Despite his short life, Caravaggio produced a body of work as diverse in subject matter as the patrons who commissioned him. *Medusa*, reputed to have been commissioned by Cardinal del Monte as a wedding present for the Grand Duke of Tuscany, depicts the decapitated head of Medusa on a round tournament shield. This painting, in a graphically realistic style, reflects the artist's fascination with violence and captures the mythological figure in a state somewhere between life and death. By highlighting the distorted face, surrounded by the monster's writhing snaky hair, Caravaggio draws the viewer's attention to an image that is at once fascinating and repulsive. The face may actually be a self-portrait.

Artemisia Gentileschi

Caravaggio's style, while admired by many, was controversial and not to everyone's taste. Nevertheless, his techniques and style were copied by numerous artists. One of Caravaggio's more remarkable and faithful followers (known as the *Caravaggisti*) was Artemisia Gentileschi (1593–1652), a woman born in Rome but who spent much of her life in Florence.

One of Gentileschi's best-known works is *Judith Slaying Holophernes* (dated between 1614 and 1627), painted during a time when the artist was involved in a very public rape trial. In a novel approach to this often-done biblical story, Gentileschi employs the deep

What do you think motivated Gentileschi to paint this scene?

shadows and spot lighting of Caravaggio combined with typically baroque violent, twisting motion. Judith's expression shows not only her revulsion at the act but also her determination to rid the Jews of an oppressor, Holophernes, a general of King Nebuchadnezzar of Babylon. With her much-admired work, Gentileschi was one of the first woman artists to make her mark in the history of Western art.

Rembrandt van Rijn

Rembrandt van Rijn (1606–1669), or Rembrandt of the Rhine, was born in Leiden, 25 miles south of Amsterdam, on July 15, 1606. His father, a miller, and his mother, the daughter of a baker, both encouraged Rembrandt's religious education. His father converted from Catholicism to Calvinism when Rembrandt was a young boy. As a consequence, Rembrandt's education was in the Calvinist schools, which stressed the study of the Bible. The influence of his strong Calvinist upbringing could be seen in many of Rembrandt's paintings, which are often described as the most profound Christian images produced by a Protestant artist in the seventeenth century.

Shortly after embarking on his artistic career, Rembrandt realized that to earn a decent living he would have to move from his native Leiden into Amsterdam, where he could get portrait commissions from wealthy patrons. Unlike most other European countries where most commissions came from the church, the monarch, or the aristocracy, patronage in the Netherlands came from either institutions such as guilds or wealthy middle class merchants.

One of the most significant commissions Rembrandt completed was *The Anatomy Lesson of Dr. Nicolaes Tulp*. This portrait of a doctor giving an anatomy lesson was a commemorative work and considered one of the most prestigious commissions granted in the Netherlands at the time. The anatomy lesson was the high point of the academic year and so the presiding professor of anatomy selected the best artist to do the work. Prior to Rembrandt's painting, the portraits tended to be stiff and unrealistic. Rembrandt chose instead to capture a moment of

The Prodigal Son (1665), by Rembrandt, illustrates the biblical story of a son who went astray but was welcomed home by his forgiving father.

action. He grouped the people in the painting around the cadavre and painted their reactions the instant after Professor Tulp exposed the muscles and tendons of the arm and hand. Rembrandt here turned a portrait into a history painting and highlighted science in the Netherlands of the mid-seventeenth century.

The most famous of all of Rembrandt's paintings is also a group portrait. *The Nightwatch* (1642) is actually titled *The Company of Captain Frans Banning Cocq and Lieutenant Willem van Ruytenburch*. Rembrandt chose to represent the militia company just after its marching orders have arrived, as the soldiers are in a state of confused preparation — spears raised and muskets being loaded. It is quite likely that the painting shows the soldiers before a festive visit of Marie de Medici, the Queen of France, to Amsterdam in 1637. In this monumental work (3.7 x 4.37m),

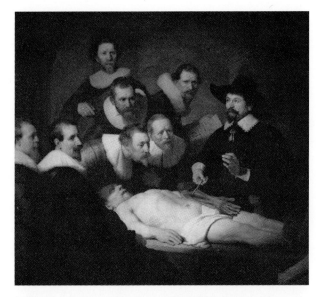

In *The Anatomy Lesson of Dr. Nicolaus Tulp* (1632) Rembrandt captured a moment in the history of science in the Netherlands.

Rembrandt again rejected the traditional arrangements for such portraits, which gave equal prominence to each member of the group, and again turned a portrait into a painting of a moment in history.

Baroque Music

Jean-Baptiste Lully

Jean-Baptiste Lully (1632–1687), the inventor of French opera and widely regarded as the greatest French composer of the seventeenth century, was actually Italian by birth. Born Giovanni Battista Lulli in Florence, Lully travelled to France in 1646 to serve as a *garçon de chambre* for Mademoiselle de Montpensier, a noted French aristocrat. During his six years as a servant of Mlle. de Montpensier, Lully established a

Though he executed many religious paintings, it was commissions for portrait paintings such as *The Nightwatch* (1632) that Rembrandt depended on for his livelihood. Where might a painting so large be displayed?

reputation as a superb dancer in court ballets and polished his skills as a musician and composer. Lully suddenly found his comfortable existence in the employ of Mlle. Montpensier disrupted by the civil conflict in France. As a leading supporter of the *Fronde*, Montpensier was exiled to her chateau at St. Fargeau in 1652. Lully asked to be released from Mlle. Montpensier's service and returned to Paris.

Just three months after leaving Mlle. Montpensier, Lully had the good fortune to dance several parts in a ballet performed for the young King Louis XIV. The king, obviously impressed by Lully's talents, had him appointed composer of instrumental music a few weeks later. Initially, Lully's service to the king was in the form of writing the instrumental music for *ballets de cour* (court ballets); however, over time, as he gained more influence at the court, he took on responsibility for entire ballets.

After receiving his French citizenship in 1661, Lully was appointed composer of chamber music for the king and saw his influence steadily grow. Between 1664 and 1670, Lully collaborated with the playwright Molière to produce a series of comedic ballets that combined humorous dialogue with singing and dancing. These performances were in the early form of French opera. In 1672 Lully was granted the exclusive right to produce operas in Paris. His first full opera, *Cadmus et Hermione*, was performed in April 1673. Between 1673 and 1686, Lully composed another 13 operas. In 1681 Lully achieved a social milestone when he was able to purchase the office of "secretary to the king," granting him noble rank.

Lully's life came to a sudden and tragic end in 1687, when an injury to his toe, suffered during the performance of a work to celebrate the king's recovery from surgery, developed an abscess. Once gangrene set in, Lully quickly became ill and died within a couple of months.

Literature in the Seventeenth Century

John Dryden

The period of the Restoration in England is also called the Augustan Age, after Augustus, first emperor of the Roman Empire. In the arts, architecture and literature, this marks a return to classicism, called neoclassicism, characterized by more ordered, rational, and simple forms. John Dryden (1631–1700) developed a lucid, clear prose that became the model for all writing of the period and beyond. In the spirit of the neoclassical age, Dryden's prose was plain and practical: Anyone could read it. Below is a stanza from Dryden's *A Song for St. Cecilia's Day*, written in 1687. St. Cecilia is the patron saint of music and a popular subject for artists and poets. Her feast day is November 22.

Song for St. Cecilia's Day

From harmony, from Heav'nly harmony
This universal frame began.
When Nature underneath a heap
Of jarring atoms lay,
And could not heave her head,
The tuneful voice was heard from high,
Arise ye more than dead.
Then cold, and hot, and moist, and dry,
In order to their stations leap,
And music's pow'r obey.
From harmony, from Heav'nly harmony
This universal frame began:
From harmony to harmony
Through all the compass of the notes it ran,
The diapason closing full in man.[3]

Dryden created a large body of poetry, prose and plays, many of which took classical themes. As noted above, his play *King Arthur* provided the libretto for his friend Henry Purcell's opera of the same name. Along with Dryden, other noted seventeenth-century British writers include Elizabeth Cary, John Donne, Richard Lovelace, Margaret Cavendish, Ben Jonson, and William Wycherley

King Arthur, by Henry Purcell, story by John Dryden

The English counterpart to Lully was Henry Purcell (1659-1695). Purcell became a chorister in the Chapel Royal as a young boy and was already writing music by the age of eight. During the English Restoration period (1660–1688), the French opera pioneered by Lully became popular in Britain. Purcell, influenced by Lully, quickly became known as a brilliant composer and at the young age of 20 was appointed organist at Westminster Abbey. Within a year of his appointment, Purcell had established a solid reputation and was in great demand. In 1682 Purcell was appointed organist of the Chapel Royal, and over the next 13 years Purcell composed many works that became classics of English music. His theatre pieces such as as *Dioclesian*, *King Arthur*, *The Fairy Queen*, and *The Indian Queen* are considered masterpieces of English opera.

Henry Purcell (1659-1695)

Over his brief but prolific career, Purcell composed much music for reigning monarchs. In June 1683, he published *Sonata of Three Parts*, which he dedicated to Charles II, and he provided music for the coronations of James II and William III. The last piece of music he provided for a royal occasion was for the funeral of Queen Mary in 1694. Purcell died of pneumonia, which he is likely to have developed after spending a night locked out of his home by his angry wife.

Purcell's opera *King Arthur* was devised to involve music, dancing, spectacular scenery, and elaborate costumes. It is enveloped in myth and fantasy and observes the Restoration convention of making the main characters speak but not sing. This is left to the spirits named Philidel and Grimald, who both sing and dance. These two spirits put into action the spells created by the rival wizards, Merlin and Osmond. It all has little to do with the Camelot legends and there is no Round Table.

The written work used as the libretto (the lyrics or words for an opera) is a version of the myth, or history, of King Arthur and the Knights of the Round Table as they inhabit the kingdom of Camelot. The text is based on the version of the story of Arthur by John Dryden (1631–1700), another key figure in English Restoration literature.

1. Find and briefly describe two other works that tell the story of King Arthur and the Knights of the Round Table. These could be books, movies, plays, musicals, or songs.

2. If Purcell were writing today, what form of musical presentation do you think he would favour? Consider rock concerts, mega-musicals, opera, or other forms. Explain your choice.

Two characters from the plays of Moliere, Crispin and Scapin. Such personages have a long history in traditional French comedy. This painting is by Honoré Daumier, a renowned French artist of the late nineteenth century.

Molière

France's most celebrated playwright of the seventeenth century was also one of the most controversial figures of the age. Molière, whose name at birth was Jean-Baptiste Poquelin, so angered the aristocrats he made fun of in his plays, that he found himself the target of threats on his life and person.

Molière was the son of an upholsterer who served King Louis XIII as the *valet tapissier de chambre du roi* (decorator of the king's room). He was born in Paris in 1622. Although he had some experience in upholstery and had the opportunity to succeed his father as *valet tapissier*, Molière's true passion was the stage. As a young man, Molière developed an intense interest in philosophy, which would provide inspiration for many of his plays.

In 1643 Molière received a substantial sum of money from his deceased mother's estate. His inheritance provided him with the means to surrender his claim to succeed his father as *valet tapissier de chambre du roi*, and to embark on a theatrical career. Initially, Molière traveled with a group of amateur comedians who earned a living performing in small towns. Late in 1643, Molière and a group of other writers founded a company called *L'Illustre Théâtre* and rented an indoor tennis court, which they outfitted for theatrical performances.

Molière's first performance before King Louis XIV was nearly a disaster. After a highly disappointing performance of *Nicomede*, Molière came forward and asked the king's permission to perform a short piece that had often been used to entertain rural audiences. The performance of *Docteur amoureux* was received so favourably by the king that Molière and his troupe were asked to establish themselves permanently in Paris.

During the 1650s, Molière and his company of actors entertained Parisian audiences with such hit plays as *L'Etourdi*, and *Depit amoureux*. By the end of the decade, Molière's success was such that he no longer had to rely on the patronage of princes, and his work became increasingly satirical. His philosophical training led Molière to despise hypocrisy, a feeling clearly evident in his most famous play, *Tartuffe*.

Tartuffe, a satire about a manipulative priest who makes sexual advances toward the wife of a man who has befriended him, led to charges of blasphemy, calls for the suppression of the play, and for the prosecution of Molière. Fortunately, Louis XIV was in the midst of his own battles with the Catholic Church, so he sympathized with the actors. As a result, the king not only endorsed the play, but also made Molière's troupe servants of the Crown, and gave it the title *troupe du roi*.

The personal attacks against Molière continued throughout his life. At one point, a jealous actor named Montfleury claimed that Molière had married his own daughter. King Louis XIV responded to these accusations by becoming the godfather of Molière's child. And when Molière was accused of impiety after the production of *Don Juan* (1665), the king responded by providing him with a pension. Fortunately for Molière and for the history of theatre, King Louis XIV's patronage helped to keep the playwright alive.

Review, Reflect, Respond

1. Create a time line that traces and explains the development of constitutionalism in England between 1603 and 1688. Try to use graphics, pictures, or symbols in your time line.

2. If you were transported back to seventeenth-century England to spend time in the towns and homes of various families, describe three ways their home life would be different from your own.

3. Select any three of the artists (painters, sculptors, poets, playwrights, composers) discussed in this chapter. For each, explain how their works reflect major trends or developments in seventeenth-century art.

Reflections

The revolutionary changes in science, politics, religion, and culture that had rocked European society between 1400 and 1648 had thrust Europe from a warring feudal society into a series of modern nations. The full impact of these dramatic changes would begin to be realized during the second half of the seventeenth century. The renewed emphasis on humankind and human achievement allowed tremendous intellectual and artistic growth, challenging the individual's relationship to God, place in the universe, and loyalty to the Crown. By the early eighteenth century, Europe's interaction with cultures around the world, and its revolutions at home, had laid the foundations for radical changes that would reshape the Western world.

Chapter Review

Chapter Summary

In this chapter, you have seen:

- how pre-industrial economies in Europe functioned
- that artists such as Molière, Bernini, and Lully reflected prevailing social and political values in their works
- how the seventeenth century was an age of intense and wide-ranging change
- several of the factors that led to war and conflict during the seventeenth century

Reviewing the Significance of Key People, Concepts, and Events (Knowledge and Understanding)

1. Understanding the history of the seventeenth century requires a knowledge of the following concepts, events and people, and an understanding of their significance in the shaping of the history of the modern world. Select and explain two from each column.

Concepts	*Events*	*People*
Treaty of Westphalia	Thirty Years' War	Galileo Galilei
scientific revolution	War of Spanish Succession	Louis XIV
absolutism	Glorious Revolution	Isaac Newton
Versailles		William Harvey
Fronde		Francis Bacon
mercantilism		René Descartes
constitutionalism		Catherine the Great

2. From the end of the Middle Ages through our own century, there has been a trend toward increased secularization of Western society. Many of the great minds of the seventeenth century directly or indirectly contributed to this trend. Complete the following chart in your notes.

Individual	Key Aspects of their Works/Ideas	How their work contributed to secularization
Galileo		
Newton		
Hobbes		
Bacon		
Locke		
Molière		

Doing History: Thinking About the Past (Thinking/Inquiry)

3. By the beginning of the twentieth century, virtually all of Europe's monarchs had fallen. Britain today is one of the few remaining monarchies. Has the longevity of the British monarchy been the result of limits placed on it by the constitution? Do you think the British monarchy would also have fallen had the kings of the seventeenth century been able to establish absolute rule?

4. The scientific revolution brought science into conflict with religion as answers to riddles of the physical world once explained through biblical sources became the subject of scientific investigation. The trial of Galileo highlighted the growing discomfort of the church with new scientific discoveries and theories. Below is an excerpt from Isaac Netwon's *Optics*, published in 1704. How does Newton attempt to reconcile God in a scientific universe?

> All these things being consider'd, it seems probable to me, that God in the Beginning form'd Matter in solid, massy, hard, impenetrable moveable Particles, of such Sizes and Figures, and with such other Properties, and in such Proportion to Space, as most conduced to the End for which he form'd them ...
>
> Now by the help of these Principles, all material Things seem to have been composed of the hard and solid Particles above-mention'd, variously associated in the first Creation by the Counsel of an intelligent Agent. For it became him who created them to set them in order. And if he did so, it's unphilosophical to seek for any other Origin of the World, or to pretend that it might arise out of a Chaos by mere Laws of Nature; though being once form'd, it may continue by those Laws for many Ages.

Applying Your Learning (Application)

5. What is your initial reaction to the painting by Artemesia Gentileschi shown in this chapter (page 93)? How does it reflect the baroque themes discussed? Gentileschi was raped by a man who had been hired to teach her drawing and perspective. When the rapist was sued by her father, Gentileschi was tortured to test the truth of her story. She was found to be telling the truth and the rapist was convicted. Does this information affect how you view this painting? Explain your answer.

6. Imagine you have the opportunity to travel back to Louis XIV's France to interview various members of society. To get a comprehensive picture of life in court, you are to prepare questions for each of these individuals: an artist; a minister in Louis' government; a member of the nobility not living at Versailles; a member of the nobility living at Versailles; a member of the clergy; a peasant; a merchant; and a foreign diplomat who has visited the court of Louis XIV. For each, prepare two relevant questions that will provide insights about France under Louis XIV.

Communicating Your Learning (Communication)

7. Create a poster that clearly captures essential differences between absolutism and constitutionalism. Include on your poster pictures of monarchs and philosophers who represent each, key words and phrases that define aspects of each, and icons and symbols which have been or could be used to reflect the role of the monarchy and parliament in each of the systems.

8. Write a poem or draw a political cartoon that either celebrates or mocks the monarchy in one of: France, England, or Russia. Be sure to make reference to specific individuals and/or historical events that support the view of the monarchy expressed by the poem.

CHAPTER THREE

Contact and Conflict 1450–1700

CHAPTER EXPECTATIONS

By the end of this chapter, you will be able to:

- *describe factors that prompted and facilitated increasing interaction between peoples during the sixteenth and seventeenth centuries*

- *explain how and why cause and effect relationships are essential tools for historical analysis*

- *describe key conflicts and controversies that arose as a result of resistance to the assertive spread of modern Western ideas*

- *describe key social developments that have occurred as a result of Western technological innovations*

The coat of arms of the family of Christopher Columbus: What could the various elements signify?

The year 1992 marked the 500th anniversary of the discovery of North America by Christopher Columbus (*Cristobal Colon*). The voyage of Columbus was one of many European voyages of discovery that occurred between 1487 and 1780. During these three centuries of exploration and colonization, Europe underwent profound economic changes as it altered the histories of native peoples all over the world. The driving force behind European expansion was a hunger for new markets and sources of raw materials to feed the emerging capitalist economy.

For nearly six hundred years, from the fall of the Roman Empire to the beginnings of the first crusade, Europeans knew little of the world beyond theirs. This included only minimal interaction with the civilizations of the East. The spread of Islam, which began in the mid-seventh century and reached its zenith by about 1500, was considered a constant threat to Christendom. Until they were driven out in the mid-fifteenth century, the Islamic Moors had ruled Spain for seven hundred years. During the early Middle Ages, few people in their lifetime travelled more than 50 kilometres from where they were born, and trade was primarily limited to local exchanges of goods and services. For the most part, Medieval Europe was self-sufficient.

Given the history of the past five hundred years, it is easy to get caught in the trap of historical determinism. In the centuries following Columbus's voyage, European civilization spread through trade, imperialism, and colonialism. Was this inevitable? Was the spread of European culture a result of Western superiority over other cultures? Did history unfold as if by some preordained plan to lead the world forward progressively? Some would suggest that if we were to examine the world of the fifteenth century through the eyes of the fifteenth century and not in hindsight, we would arrive at a very different interpretation of history — one that might suggest that history is not progressive but chaotic.

With the launch of the First Crusade in 1096, Europeans unwittingly began a venture that would lead them to the four corners of the Earth. Although the Crusades were largely a failure, in that Europeans failed to recapture the Holy Land from the Ottoman Turks, the residual effects were profound. Many crusaders returned home with their saddlebags laden with spices and rich cloths, which were sold for handsome profits. The Crusades may have failed to recapture the Holy Land but they led to an insatiable demand for goods from the Middle and Far East. This was the impetus for European exploration as entrepreneurs sought safe routes to Asia.

KEY CONCEPTS AND EVENTS

Crusades

capitalism

Terrestrial Paradise

caravels

Christian Century in Japan

Asiento

Treaty of Tordesillas

Encomienda

KEY PEOPLE

Christopher Columbus

Ptolemy

Marco Polo

Vasco da Gama

John Cabot

Jacques Cartier

Mehmed II

Sulieman I the Magnificent

Hernán Cortés

Atawallpa

Francisco Pizarro

St. Francis Xavier

Tokugawa Ieyasu

Immanuel Wallerstein

André Gunder Frank

Juan Ginés de Sepúlveda

Wit and Wisdom

In vain God in his wisdom planned
The ocean separate from the land
If ships, defying his intent,
Cross the forbidden element…

Horace, Odes, I, 3
Translation by James Michie

TIME LINE: CONTACT AND CONFLICT

Age of European exploration begins when the Portuguese capture the Muslim port of Ceuta on the African side of the Straits of Gibraltar	1414	
	1453	Ottoman Turks capture Constantinople (now Istanbul) and bring about the demise of the Byzantine Empire
Columbus arrives in the Americas during his attempt to reach Asia by sailing west	1492	
	1494	Treaty of Tordesillas divides up the exploration in South America between Spain and Portugal
Vasco da Gama's voyage around the Cape of Good Hope opens sailing route to India	1497	
	1518	Transoceanic slave trade begins with the first cargo of African captives arriving in the Caribbean
Sugar cane first cultivated in the Americas	1506	
	1533	Spanish execute the Inca emperor Atawallpa
Jacques Cartier sails up the St. Lawrence, claiming lands in North America for the French	1534	
	1550	Famous debate begins between Bartolome de Las Casas and Juan Ginés de Sepúlveda over the nature of Amerindians
Potatoes from South America first used in Spain to feed prisoners	1573	
	1600	Tokugawa Ieyasu unites Japan and moves the seat of government to Edo (Tokyo)
France enters the slave trade with the building of the fort of Saint Louis in Senegal	1626	

This seventeenth-century plate illustrates the arrival of Columbus to America. What did the artist think was most important?

[HISTORY RECONSIDERED

Generations of schoolchildren have learned of the heroic exploits of European explorers who bravely set out to explore the far reaches of the world in search of fame or fortune. Unfortunately, these heroic tales have often left the impression that Europeans discovered wild, untamed lands and brought superior civilization to the people they encountered. In a popular high school history text published in 1969, the author commented: "He [Columbus] had found for Europe two new continents that someday would far exceed in wealth, power, and achievements the ancient civilizations of Asia.[1]" Yet, could it have been Columbus who was discovered by the people living on the islands where he turned up, lost and confused?

This interpretation of history suggests that lands inhabited for thousands of years by millions of people

were discovered for the Europeans by European explorers. This view, while much less prevalent today, does persist. One historian, referring to the importance of Columbus's voyage of 1492, stated: "It is witness to the tremendous vitality and verve of late medieval and early modern Europe — which was on the verge of acquiring a world hegemony."

[THE WORLD IN 1450
A Medieval View

Prior to the fifteenth century, European ideas about foreign lands were limited to the few reports recorded by travellers such as Marco Polo. It was during the fifteenth century that a revolution in geographic knowledge occurred with the reappearance of *Geography*, a guide written by the ancient Greek scholar, Ptolemy (100-178 CE). Ptolemy's guide, with his famous map of the world, was one of the ancient works that resurfaced in Europe during the Renaissance. Translated from Greek and printed by the new printing presses, Ptolemy's *Geography* came to be widely circulated and was accepted by early explorers as the most reliable source to guide them in their journeys to the East.

Ptolemy portrayed the world as a globe, which he divided into 360 degrees of longitude. He assumed the world was made up of three continents — Asia, Africa, and Europe — and two oceans — the Indian Ocean and the Western (Atlantic) Ocean. Aside from his errors in the number of oceans and continents, Ptolemy underestimated the ratio of land to water. His portrayal of the world showed that land covered three-quarters of the Earth's surface. He also miscalculated the size of the Earth, showing it to be one-sixth smaller than its actual size. With no other sources to guide them, it is no wonder the early explorers underestimated the time it would take to cross the Western (Atlantic) Ocean.

Throughout the centuries, tales of exotic and bizarre creatures and peoples inhabiting far-away lands circulated through Europe. When the first explorers

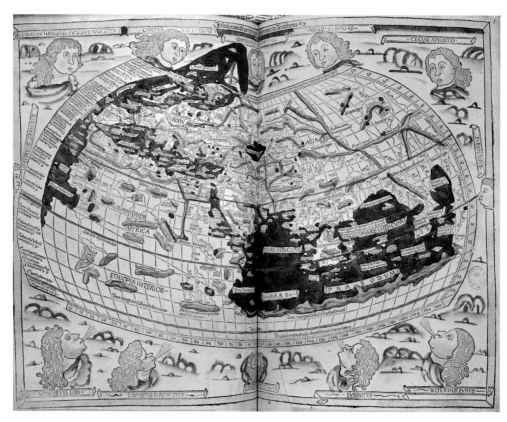

The conception of the world devised by Ptolemy in the second century was the best map available to explorers setting out in the fifteenth century.

set out in search of riches, they fully expected to encounter the beasts of classical mythology, as well as dragons and unicorns. They also imagined dog-headed humans, one-legged "sciopods", and "antipods" (people whose feet faced backwards), south of the equator. In a fifteenth-century manuscript about the travels of Marco Polo, pictures of a "blemmyae", a headless man whose face was on his chest, and a one-eyed cyclops, further encouraged the mythology of far-off places.

The Wider World in 1450

The world in the mid-fifteenth century was not as the Europeans imagined it, nor as the historical writings of later centuries described it. The world was not populated by mythical beasts and bizarre people nor by inferior societies destined to be subjugated by European colonizers. Not only that, were we able to look at Europeans of the fifteenth century, we probably would not imagine they were capable of dominating anybody. The civilization that was clearly the most dominant for the first half of the last millennium was not Europe, but China.

China was the most populous, most technologically advanced, and most powerful military force for much of the period between 1000 and 1500. By the fifteenth century, several other societies were also thriving. Both the Ottoman and Muscovite states were rapidly expanding in wealth, power, and territory. In Mesoamerica, the Aztecs had rapidly conquered much of what is today central Mexico, and the Inca had established a far-flung empire stretching from the area of modern-day Columbia to the tip of South America. Africa, too, had its powerful civilizations including the Songhay, Mali, and Mwene Mutapa empires.

Some explorers fully expected to find cannibals in the New World. This seventeenth century print shows cannibals capturing and butchering sailors.

Why was it the Europeans who set out to explore the world? Why did other societies not also engage in transoceanic exploration? Why were the Europeans able to conquer and colonize vast areas of the world? What resistance did they encounter and how did European colonization affect both the colonized and the colonizers?

FATE, FORTUNE, AND FAITH

The Rise of Capitalism

By the early 1500s, the feudal economy of medieval Europe had been largely replaced by a capitalist economy that had redefined wealth. In the pre-capitalist era, usury — profiting from lending money by charging interest — was not only frowned upon in society, but also violated church law. Land was considered the only form of secure wealth, while capital (money) was seen as liquid and volatile. The emergence during the fifteenth century of powerful banking families, such as the Medicis of Florence and the Fuggers of Augsberg, changed this view of wealth.

The elements of the economy that developed at this time are familiar to us today, since they remain the underpinnings of our capitalist economic system. Of primary importance was using money to make money. Capitalism, which relies on the organization of capital, labour, and raw materials to produce surplus wealth, provided the impetus for powerful merchants to sponsor voyages of exploration and colonization. This brought about a radical change in the nature of long-distance trade. Rather than trading for luxury goods, merchants began to look for raw, unprocessed materials that could be refined by European manufacturers.

Searching for Wealth

By the late Middle Ages, trade with India and the Orient was supplying Europe with spices for flavouring and preserving foods, silks for fine clothing, and herbs essential for medicine. The exotic nature of the goods imported from Africa and the Orient led many to imagine that a Terrestrial Paradise existed. This land of splendour was thought to be enclosed by a high wall of crystal or diamonds. It was also believed to be the source of all the great rivers of the world. Over the rivers hung branches of balsam, cinnamon, myrrh, cardamom, and benzoin (a fragrant resin).

While the Terrestrial Paradise was a mythical land, it was a reflection of how people thought of the East and the increasing importance of trade between Europe and the Orient. The Turkish conquest of Constantinople in 1453 had created a serious problem for European merchants who imported goods from the East. Although the Ottomans did not intend to close trade between the East and West, they did attempt to regulate it by imposing duties on goods. The result was that trade goods from the Orient were either not available or became too expensive, and this caused Western merchants to look elsewhere for their supplies.

Geography

While the search for secure access to the riches of the East provided the impetus for European exploration, geographic fate provided the opportunity. All European powers engaged in overseas exploration and colonization shared one thing in common: an Atlantic seacoast. Perhaps the greatest maritime discovery of the fifteenth century was the cracking of the codes of the Atlantic wind systems. The wind systems of the

Atlantic Ocean provided European sailing ships with a highway to the Americas and ultimately to the Far East. The Westerlies of the south Atlantic, discovered at the end of the fifteenth century, led European explorers to the Indian Ocean. The central Atlantic trade winds discovered by Columbus provided the Spanish with relatively easy passage to Mexico, from which the shortest and only viable trans-Pacific routes could be navigated.

By comparison, both China and Japan faced the vast and treacherous Pacific Ocean. Although curiosity had led the Chinese into earlier voyages of exploration, they had not discovered riches worth risking the crossing of the Pacific on a regular basis. Similarly, the Indian subcontinent faced the monsoon rains. While Indian navigators braved the waters to trade with Asian neighbours, they had no need or desire to embark on long-distance sea travel.

Both a desire for goods and favourable sailing conditions provided Europeans with the impetus and opportunity to engage in transoceanic travel. Their counterparts in Asia shared neither the insatiable demand for goods nor the favourable winds necessary for sea travel. Due to the often low demand for European goods, many became brokers, trading Indian tea for Chinese silk in order to engage in trade with the Orient.

Technological Developments

Advances in maritime technology played a significant role in enabling European explorers to navigate the world's oceans. During the Middle Ages, devices such as the quadrant and the astrolabe allowed sailors to venture far out to sea, without needing to be within sight of land to navigate. Mapmaking had also made great strides, allowing for the graphic documenting of long-distance travels. The galleys that had plied the waters of the Mediterranean for centuries, relied primarily on slaves who rowed the big ships. Given that the slaves occupied much of the space below deck, these ships were ill-suited to long-distance travel, as there was little space to store the provisions needed for a lengthy voyage.

Astrolabes, such as these sixteenth-century examples, were vital for long-distance travel. How does this navigational aid work?

During the fifteenth century, the Portuguese developed a new type of sailing ship. The caravels — small sailing ships about 25 metres long — became the first European ships to conquer the vast oceans. Large square sails allowed the ships to travel in the direction of the wind, and a new triangular, movable sail called a lateen not only allowed ships to travel faster but also could be set at a right angle to the wind, and allow travel upwind. This was a crucial factor in cracking the wind codes of the Atlantic. The new ships, powered exclusively by wind, allowed long-distance travel and the transportation of valuable cargo back to Europe.

The Search for Souls

Although the search for untold wealth was the driving force behind European exploration, religion was also a major motivator during the fifteenth and sixteenth centuries. The rapid expansion of the Islamic empire of the Ottoman Turks had led to great unease among Europeans, as they felt their eastern borders were under threat. Some voyages were undertaken in hopes of finding Christian allies. Portugal's Prince Henry the Navigator sponsored voyages down the coast of Africa in search of the mythical "Prester John," believed to be a rich and powerful king ruling in the heart of Africa.

The Reformation, beginning with the posting of Martin Luther's *95 Theses* in 1517, led to the splitting of Christendom into Catholic, Protestant, and Anabaptist faiths. Through much of Europe, religious division followed political lines as kingdoms and principalities either adopted a Protestant faith or defended the Catholic Church. Rivalries between European powers also became battles for souls. The quest for souls provided added incentive for both exploration and colonization as Protestants and Catholics engaged in a race to win converts. Overseas colonies became home for people of Protestant and Anabaptist faiths including Quakers, Mennonites, and Puritans. In these new lands, they could practise their religions free from persecution.

Discoveries

The age of European exploration and expansion began in 1414 when the Portuguese captured the Muslim port of Ceuta on the African side of the Straits of Gibraltar. While the primary objective of the Portuguese had been only to secure access to the Mediterranean, their presence on the North African coast opened the door to European exploration of the southern Atlantic. The need for raw materials to fuel the emerging capitalist economy of Europe, and the blockade of the overland routes by the Ottoman Turks, prompted Europeans to search for a

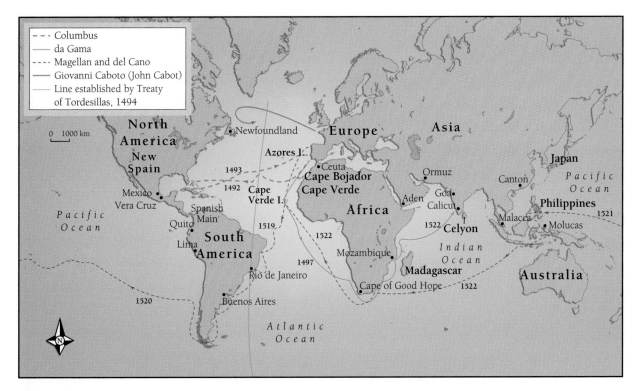

■ **FIGURE 3.1** World Wide Exploration in the Fifteenth and Sixteenth Centuries
There was for a period of time an explosion of exploration by European countries. Why were some countries better positioned to take advantage of the new opportunities of the age?

sea route to the riches of Asia. By 1487 the Portuguese had established settlements at Madeira and on Arguin Island, they had explored the mouth of the Congo River, and rounded the Cape of Good Hope. With the voyage of Vasco da Gama (1469–1524) around the Cape to East Africa and the Indian Malabar coast in 1497, the Portuguese had opened the route to India.

The Portuguese were not alone in their quest for new sources of wealth. In 1492 Columbus (sailing west in search of a route to the East) came upon the islands of the Caribbean. The Spanish followed up on Columbus's discovery by exploring the mainland of South and Central America. In 1513 Vasco Nuñez de Balboa (1475–1519) reached the Pacific Ocean by crossing the Isthmus of Panama; in 1519 Hernán Cortés (1485–1547) began the conquest of Mexico; and in 1530 the Spanish, under Francisco Pizarro (1471–1541), set out to conquer Peru.

Despite their fortuitous discovery of the Americas, the Spanish continued with the original quest to discover a western route to Asia. This route was discovered by Ferdinand Magellan (1480–1521), who, between 1519 and 1521, completed the first circumnavigation of the globe. In his journey around the world, Magellan found a route around the southern tip of South America, through what is now called the Straits of Magellan, and thereby crossed the Pacific and reached the Philippines and Moluccas Islands.

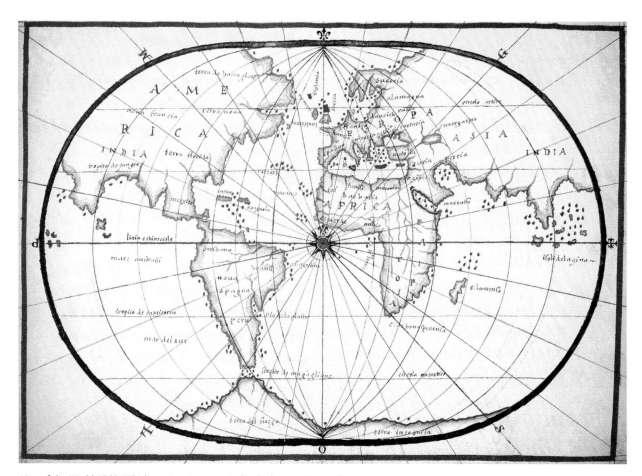

Map of the World 1560. Which continent appears to be the least understood?

The Portuguese voyages around the Cape of Good Hope (Africa) and the Spanish voyages westward around the southern tip of South America proved that the oceans of the southern hemisphere were connected, and thus opened up sea routes to the East. Throughout the sixteenth century the Spanish and Portuguese zealously guarded the passages to the East, using force to maintain their monopoly on the spice trade. Anxious to participate in the lucrative trade with Asia, other countries (including England, France, and the Netherlands) sought alternative routes. This search led men such as John Sebastian Cabot (1497), Jacques Cartier (1534 and 1535), Martin Frobisher (1574), and Henry Hudson (1610) to explore the coastline of North America. While they were unsuccessful in finding a passage to the East, their voyages did reveal the extent of the North American landmass and opened up the exploration and settlement of eastern North America.

The Trial of Columbus

In the years following his encounter with the Americas, Christopher Columbus was made Viceroy of Espanola (modern Haiti and the Dominican Republic). His efforts at establishing Spanish colonies and spreading Christianity among the Amerindians came under such severe criticism that King Ferdinand of Spain dispatched Francisco de Bobadilla to investigate in 1500. Upon his arrival in Espanola, Bobadilla has Columbus arrested and sent back to Spain in chains. Over the next two years, Bobadilla governed the island colonies and carried out an exhaustive investigation into the charges against Columbus.

In his novel *Caribbean*, author James Michener recreates this investigation, exploring the paradoxical nature of Columbus. The explorer's skills as a navigator contrast sharply with his incompetence as a governor. The fictional character Señora Pimental testified:

Colon [Columbus] filled it [their home] with his extraordinary vitality, his imagination, his quest always for something new and challenging, and I came to admire him as a genius, difficult but standing at the edge of the known world. To hear him explain his dreams in his accented Spanish was to witness greatness in action, and I was awed by his volcanic power.

But my husband and I also saw his flaws, and they were montrous, almost disqualifying. He rarely followed through on what he started. He could not govern for the simple reason that he could not keep his eyes on the task at hand ... always looking to the future. He was a brutal man at times, arbitrary to the point of hanging anyone who disagreed with him, and he was certainly avaricious, mean, untruthful and petty, even when dealing with his own men. And his greatest fault was his almost insane nepotism and favouritism.[2]

It took a great deal of persuasion for Queen Isabella of Spain to agree to sponsor the voyages of Columbus.

Indeed, Columbus's governance of Espanola was brutal affair. Several of the Spanish colonizers under his command were hanged for a variety of offences. But it was the Tainos, the indigenous inhabitants, who fared the worst under Columbus and the Spanish. The Tainos were a peaceful people who arrived on Espanola in the 1300s after fleeing attacks by the Carib people. When Columbus arrived on Espanola in 1492, the Tainos population was estimated to be approximately three hundred thousand. By 1496 the population had declined by at least one hundred thousand. Many of the Tainos had been slaughtered by the Spanish under the orders of Columbus. When they reacted against Spanish abuse of Tainos women or their theft of food, the Tainos were brutalized. The Spanish also slaughtered the Tainos who did not immediately and completely convert to Christianity. A census of the Tainos in 1508 showed their number had further been reduced to a scant 490. By the end of the sixteenth century the Tainos on Espanola, as well as indigenous peoples on neighbouring islands were extinct; wiped out by disease and senseless slaughter.

Bobadillo never made it back to Spain to present his findings; he was drowned in 1502 when his ship sank as it set sail for the return voyage. Columbus was eventually exonerated by the Spanish monarchy, and sailed on a final voyage in 1502. He died in 1506 having never achieved the wealth promised by the Spanish crown, and never having reached Asia.

The Clash of Empires

As European explorers embarked on voyages in search of routes to Asia and new sources of wealth, they encountered complex and highly developed societies on every continent they reached. From the Aztec and Incas in the Americas to the Japanese in the Far East, European civilization would be forever changed by its interaction with these diverse cultures. Although trade often began as a mutually beneficial exchange of goods, the European thirst for conquest and control led to clashes of empires in nearly every part of the world.

The Ottoman Empire

The initial impetus for European overseas exploration resulted from the expansion of the Ottoman Empire in the fifteenth and early sixteenth centuries. The Ottoman Empire consisted of groups of Asiatic nomads who had migrated westward from the Asian steppes during the thirteenth century. As they moved west, they converted to Islam and soon became the driving force behind a renewed Muslim expansion. By the mid-fourteenth century, the Ottoman Turks had surrounded the Byzantine Empire which had, for centuries, acted as a buffer between the West and the Islamic Middle East. When Mehmed II (d. 1481) came to power in 1451, he set out to expand the boundaries of the Ottoman Empire. The death of the last emperor of the east, Constantine XI Palaeologus, and the fall of Constantinople in 1453, marked the end of the Byzantine Empire.

WEB CONNECTION

www.mcgrawhill.ca/links/legacy

Go to the site above to find out more about the Ottoman Empire.

Nearly a century later, the Ottoman Empire would reach the peak of its power under the leadership of Suleiman I, known as the Magnificent. By 1529, Sulieman had extended the Ottoman Empire throughout the Middle East, into North Africa, through the Balkans, and he nearly captured Vienna, the heart of the Austro-Hungarian Empire. From the mid-sixteenth century on, European monarchs would have to consider the ever-present Ottoman Turks when planning their diplomatic and military affairs.

With the Ottoman Empire expanding westward and European powers seeking to protect their eastern boundaries and secure trade routes to Asia, a relationship developed, which historian Albert Hourani described as "crusade on the one side and *jihad* on the other." Despite the enmity that existed between the

Ottoman Turks and the West, there were individual alliances between Muslim sultans and European kings when mutual interests brought them together. For example, in the 1560s, France and the Ottomans allied against the Hapsburgs in Spain.

Prior to the eighteenth century, the Ottoman Empire and its Western adversaries were equal powers. The disciplined Ottoman army, skilled in the use of firearms, was a match for any European power of the fifteenth or sixteenth century. By the eighteenth century the Ottomans had fallen behind the major European states in military might and technical skills. Indeed, during the reign of the Ottoman Turks there had been few advances in technology and a decline in the level of scientific knowledge. Advances in Western science and medicine were only slowly making their way to the Middle East by the eighteenth century. With population growth stifled by plague and famine, and limited expansion of wealth, the Ottomans were unable to expand and improve their military. Meanwhile, these challenges had largely subsided in Europe thanks to better medical practices and the introduction of new foods such as maize. By exploiting the mines and fields of their new overseas colonies, Europeans were able to acquire the wealth and growth in population that allowed the expansion and maintenance of armies and navies. Hence, the ascendancy of the West grew steadily beginning in the eighteenth century.

Review, Reflect, Respond

1. Briefly describe the world as imagined by Europeans prior to the fifteenth century.

2. How did geography contribute to the age of European exploration?

3. Describe the relationship between European powers and the Ottoman Turks during the fifteenth and sixteenth centuries.

EXPLORING THE AMERICAS
The Conquest of the Aztecs

When the Europeans arrived at the Aztec capital of Tenochtitlán in central Mexico, and the Inca capital of Cuzco on the west coast of South America, they found cities as wealthy and complex as their own.

During the first encounters, the Europeans held Aztec achievements in awe. The conquistadors married Aztec women, the priests were pleased by the Indians' adoption of Christianity, and there was optimism about the creation of a New World culture that would surpass the Old. But it did not take long for prejudice to take over and for greed to develop, as Spaniards poured into Mexico bent on making fortunes by exploiting Indian labour, and taking Indian land.

The *Codex Mendoza,* a seventeenth-century collection of drawings created by Aztec artists, is an invaluable source of information about Aztec life and customs.

The most devastating consequence of conquest was the radical depopulation that took place as the result of introduced diseases, forced labour, slavery, and demoralization. Not least important was also the introduction of cattle, sheep and goats, whose demands for grass and leaves had to be met; this transformed the relationship between people and the land forever. Estimates vary as to what the population of central Mexico was before the Spaniards arrived; a figure of roughly 25 million just before the conquest is reasonable, with a decline of perhaps 95 percent by the end of the sixteenth century. The New World had not been free of disease prior to the conquest, but it was free of major epidemics and chronic endemic ailments. Invading Europeans brought with them diseases such as tuberculosis, measles and the deadly smallpox, against all of which they had developed immunity over thousands of years. When the first waves of disease washed over the Native Americans, people died by the hundreds and then thousands, and neither the Native Americans nor the Europeans understood why. Eventually, some gained immunity and populations recovered, but it has taken until modern times in some areas for this to happen.

Hemán Cortés, in one of his letters to the Spanish king, demonstrates the conflicting emotions the conquerors felt about the people they were to overcome and the culture they were to destroy:

> Yet so as not to tire Your Highness with the description of the things of this city ... I will say only that these people live almost like those in Spain, and in as much harmony and order as there, and considering that they are barbarous and so far from the knowledge of God and cut off from all civilized nations, it is truly remarkable to see what they have achieved in all things.

In the end it was neither superior morale nor superior technology that allowed the Spanish to defeat the Aztecs. The Aztecs were starved and plagued into defeat. Their empire had been built on the tribute paid by conquered neighbouring peoples. According to surviving tribute lists, Tenochtitlán, the Aztec capital, annually received 140 000 bushels of maize, 105 000 bushels of beans, 4 000 loaves of salt, and 980 loads of cacao among many other foodstuffs. Tribute was the basis of Aztec wealth and their greatest weakness. When the Spanish were unable to capture the city of Tenochtitlán, they laid siege, cutting off the supply of tribute. Weakened by disease and denied access to the tribute upon which their empire had been built, the Aztecs could not hold out against the Spanish *conquistadors*.

The Conquest of the Incas

Building on civilizations of the past, in a period of about 90 years, just three generations, the Inca were able to forge an empire that exceeded anything that had ever been seen in the Andes, or the New World. Their military accomplishments have been compared to the conquests of Alexander the Great. Administratively, they have been compared to the Romans. It is therefore all the more remarkable that this sophisticated and powerful empire was brought down by a single, shattering event, a clash of cultures that changed the New World forever.

The event was the first encounter between the Inca emperor Atawallpa (d.1533) and Francisco Pizarro, the leader of a small Spanish force of about 60 horsemen and 100 foot soldiers. The circumstances of this meeting were described by several eyewitnesses, retold by Spanish historians who drew on the eyewitness testimony, and later re-interpreted by Native chroniclers. The accounts note that when the Spanish attacked Atawallpa's retinue and army, no Inca offered armed resistance. At the end of the day, 7 000 Indians lay dead. Eventually, after extracting a huge ransom — more than 13 000 pounds of gold and 26 000 pounds of silver — the Spanish executed Atawallpa on July 26, 1533.

Following the death of Atawallpa, the Inca quickly succumbed to the Spanish invaders. Like the Aztecs, the Incas were decimated, not by superior weapons, but by disease. The encounter between the Inca and the Spanish turned out to be a biological disaster that allowed the Europeans to conquer the formidable Inca Empire.

WEST MEETS EAST
China

The entry of European powers into the Far East trade circle was markedly different from that of Africa or the Americas. By attempting to establish trade relations with China and Japan, Europeans found themselves involved with a highly developed Asian world system in which they had to adapt to an existing economy.

China in the sixteenth century was a highly centralized and bureaucratized state that strictly followed the directives of Beijing. This was the cause of much frustration for the Dutch because they repeatedly tried to establish a base in China but were unable to play any other role than transporter of goods within an established trade circle. At no point were they able to make themselves essential to trade. Once the Manchu dynasty (1644–1911) was firmly established and the threat of Japanese piracy lessened, the Chinese decided to limit contact with foreigners to commercial relations only, and only on selected coastal sites. Furthermore, no European power ever managed to establish a monopoly in trade with the Chinese. Rather, the English and the Portuguese became very competitive with the Dutch by the 1690s, illustrating that the Dutch had never played an essential role in the Asian world economy.

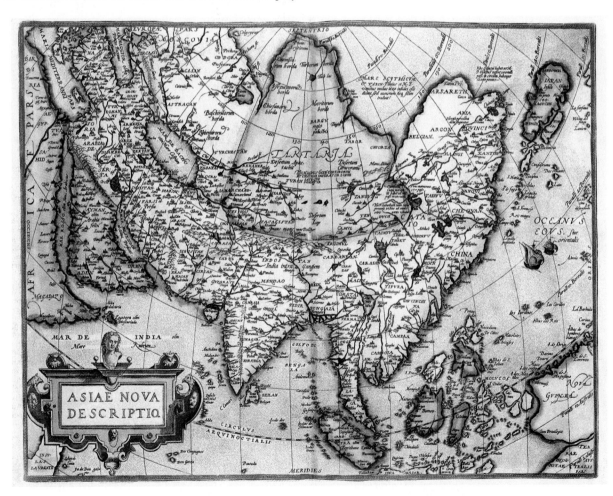

A sixteenth-century map of Asia by Ortelius. Note the relative sizes of countries and the ratio of land to ocean.

Japan

Japan, unlike China, was unstable at the time of its first contact with Europeans. This instability made it much easier for the Europeans to penetrate but also meant they held a somewhat tenuous position in Japanese society. Leading Europe's entry into sixteenth-century Japan were Portuguese Jesuit and Spanish Franciscan missionaries from Manila, South America, and India.

Both the Jesuits and the Franciscans chose different methods and a different focus in their efforts to Christianize the Japanese. The Jesuits focussed on the leaders of society, the *daimyo* and the *samurai*, believing that converting the lower classes would be a wasted effort should an anti-Christian authority be installed. The Franciscans, conversely, focussed their attention on the lower classes and rejected Japanese culture, choosing instead to expose the Japanese to their monastic habits, rosaries, crosses, and other outward expressions of their faith.

The first Europeans to arrive in Japan found the Japanese friendly, civilized and eager to acquire European knowledge of firearms and ships. The Japanese paid generously, in silver, to acquire Portuguese clothes and guns, as well as the silks and other luxury goods the explorers had acquired in China. One sea captain, Jorge Alvares, visited Kagoshima in southern Kyushu in 1547 and wrote with enthusiasm about all things Japanese, describing the beauty of the country and the abundance of exotic fruits and flowers. Alvares took some Japanese to Goa (in India) to meet the missionary St. Francis Xavier, and there they became the first converts to Christianity. Xavier, intrigued by accounts of Japan, travelled there in 1549 and in his first year, succeeded in baptizing 150 converts. Soon, however, everywhere Xavier went, he encountered proud *daimyo*, who were more interested in having Portuguese ships protect their valuable cargoes from the China trade than in hearing about God.

Following the crucial Battle of Sekigahara in 1600, the *shogun* Tokugawa Ieyasu united Japan and moved the seat of government to Edo (now Tokyo). Ieyasu and his successors brought the country an era of complete peace and order. They soon expelled all foreigners from the land and crucified thousands of Native Christian converts who had rebelled in 1638. Thereafter, no foreigner would be allowed to live on Japanese soil. This was the beginning of Japan's seclusion policy. Japan would remain isolated from the rest of the world for the next 250 years.

HUMAN SERVITUDE

Origins of Slavery in Africa

Slavery was practised in traditional African society long before the Europeans arrived. Arabs from North Africa had slaves, and the earliest market was the line of the Sahel and Sub-Saharan peoples exchanging slaves for gold. Coastal tribes were predatory, venturing inland to capture people from smaller settlements. The principal sources of slaves were criminals who were sold as punishment, individuals sold by families at a time of famine and need, those kidnapped by slaving bands of merchants, and prisoners of war.

European slavers in the early days felt no urge to apologize for their occupation. Indeed, slavers could invoke religion as a reason for what they were doing: baptizing whole shiploads of puzzled Africans, and declaring that they should be grateful for slavery because it led them to Jesus, their saviour. The earliest coastal stations were places where business was done with traders coming from the interior. Europeans quickly learned that the most efficient way to obtain slaves was to trade on the coast with Africans who specialized in selling their neighbours in exchange for trade goods and metals.

As the Spanish need for slaves grew, so too did the maritime trade in human beings, especially from the coast of Guinea. The *Asiento* (monopoly on the supply of cargoes) was first given in 1595 to supply 38 000 slaves in nine years. The Spanish and the Portuguese dominated the slave trade across the Atlantic in the sixteenth century, but in the seventeenth century it was the Dutch. British and Danish ships also began participating in the

Sir Walter Raleigh, *The History of the World*, 1614

Sir Walter Raleigh (1552–1618) wrote his History of the World while in prison in the Tower of London, beginning in 1592, for carrying on an illicit relationship with a lady of the court of Queen Elizabeth I. Raleigh was released two years later and in 1594 sailed to South America, where he discovered and claimed the land of Guiana (Guyana) as Sir Walter Raleigh, Knight, Captain of her Majesty's Guard, Lord Warden of the Stannaries, and her Highness's Lieutenant-General of the County of Cornwall.

When Queen Elizabeth died, Raleigh was accused of treason against the new King James I and imprisoned for 12 years, during which he wrote his *History of the World* and conducted scientific studies. He was released in 1616 and took on another voyage to find gold in Venezuela. The expedition was a failure and Raleigh was put in prison, again on the charge of treason, and executed in 1618. Regardless of his failures, Sir Walter Raleigh was both an adventurer and a scholar, and one of the key figures in the early formation of the British Empire.

Sir Walter Raleigh, explorer, scholar and historian

The excerpt given below is from the preface to the *History of the World*. Raleigh gives his reasons for writing, and why he chose not to write about times closer to his own:

> I know that it will be said by many, that I might have been more pleasing to the reader, if I had written the story of mine own times ... To this I answer, that whosoever in writing a modern history, shall follow truth too near the heels, it may happily strike out his teeth. There is no mistress or guide that hath led her followers and servants into greater miseries ... It is true, that I never travelled after men's opinions, when I might have made the best use of them; and I have now too few days remaining to imitate those, that, either out of extreme ambition or extreme cowardice, or both, do yet (when death hath them on this shoulders) flatter the world between the bed and the grave. It is enough for me (being in that state I am) to write of the eldest times; wherein also, why may it not be said, that, in speaking of the past, I point at the present and tax the vices of those that are yet living in their persons that are long since dead; and have it laid to my charge. But this I cannot help, though innocent ...[3]

1. Do you think Raleigh is correct when he says that for a person writing about her or his own time, "there is no mistress or guide that hath led her followers and servants into greater miseries"? Explain your answer.

2. What is Raleigh saying when he warns that "whosoever in writing a modern history, shall follow truth too near the heels, it may happily strike out his teeth"?

eighteenth century. The trade in captives was gradually abolished in the nineteenth century, as was slavery itself. The last great emancipation of slaves took place in Brazil in 1888. The East European equivalent, the freeing of Romanian serfs, was a little earlier, in 1864.

As early as 1501, there were Africans on Hispaniola, but only in 1518 did the slave trade proper begin with the landing of the first cargo of African captives. It took between 35 and 50 days to cross from the west coast of Africa to Brazil—somewhat less to Cuba. The Dutch joined the slave trade after their independence from Spain. In 1626 the French built the fort of Saint Louis in Senegal, marking its entry into the slave trade, to supply its sugar islands with labour. The English took a Portuguese castle on the coast and began to supply Barbados with slaves. In 1663 the commercial association called Royal Adventurers of England was formed, with its slaves branded on the chest with "dy," for Duke of York. Using the coins made from the Guinea coast, gold advertised the company: a gold coin worth 21 shillings (1£+1s) was called a guinea. In 1672 the adventurers were replaced by the Royal African Company, a sign of the state approval of this line of endeavour.

Europeans introduced chattel slavery (slaves as property) and they provided an insatiable market for slaves. Moreover, Europeans also encouraged a century of civil wars between African kingdoms, in order to produce prisoners to be sold into slavery. The net result of the exploitation of Africans as slaves was widespread depopulation, particularly of young males, and the consequent underdevelopment of Africa. No contribution to Africa's infrastructure was made, only cheap manufactured goods were exchanged for slaves. All this contributed to the continued status of African countries as developing nations today.

The Evolving European World System

In his 1974 book, *The Modern World-System*, Immanuel Wallerstein suggested that sixteenth-century Europe responded to a "crisis in feudalism" through the expansion of the geographic world and the development of a capitalist world economy made possible by "a new form of surplus appropriation." Like a world war, a world economy does not include all countries of the world but is called a world economy because it is larger than any recognized political unit. Indeed, there were at least two other world economies coexisting with Europe: Asia and Russia. The European world economy alone chose the path of capitalist development, which thrust it into the markets and resources of the world.

Fuelling this new world economy were various kinds of workers throughout the world. Slaves taken from Angola to work the sugar plantations and mines of the Caribbean; serfs working the large farms and woodlands of Eastern Europe; "tenant" farmers and "yeomen" farmers of western and northwestern Europe respectively; and finally, the ruling classes who, although existing throughout Europe, were disproportionately from Western Europe.

Early Contact

Within 30 years of the landfall of Christopher Columbus, the Spanish discovered the largest concentrations of precious metals in the Americas — the Aztec Empire with its capital in what is now Mexico City, and the Inca Empire of Peru. These were highly developed Amerindian societies with sophisticated knowledge of astronomy, masonry construction, and agriculture. Both civilizations were doomed to military defeat accompanied by a population collapse induced by epidemic disease and intermarriage with their conquerors.

The rivalry between Spain and Portugal over the control of newly discovered lands caused tensions that the papacy tried to forestall with the Treaty of Tordesillas (1494), which divided the respective areas of exploration according to a line of longitude west of the Azores. The idea was that the Portuguese would continue to move southward along the Atlantic Coast of Africa, where they might encounter new islands, and the Spanish would do the same in the Americas.

The treaty was drawn before the shape of South America was completely known, however, leaving Brazil (which protrudes into the Atlantic) on the Portuguese side. The first export from Brazil was a kind of wood that produced a red dye. Only later did Brazil become the largest exporter of coffee.

Central America was crucial for access from the Atlantic to the Pacific coast of South America before the construction of the Panama Canal (1881–1914). The first expedition to the Panama-Colombia border took place between 1509 and 1513. Great mule trains carried goods from one ocean to the other. Fortresses such as El Moro in San Juan de Puerto Rico provided protected anchorage for the Spanish fleet, and the fortress at Acapulco on the Pacific Coast of Mexico protected the fleets that crossed to Manila and the Philippine Islands. The protection was needed against pirates from the northern European powers who had realized that the easiest way to get bullion was to steal it after the Spanish had collected it for shipment to the royal treasury.

The Spanish concentrated more on settlement than trade. They started to enslave the Native peoples wherever they landed. The Taino of Puerto Rico became extinct within 100 years of the Spanish conquest. The abuses of slavery helped decimate the Amerindian populations. Places like the silver mines of Potosí in what is now Bolivia (discovered in 1545) effectively functioned as death camps. Priests and royal officials tried to prevent the worst abuses, but the greed of the settlers and the complicity of many royal governors were too strong for them to protect the Native peoples successfully.

Review, Reflect, Respond

1. Explain any similarities there were between the conquest of the Aztecs and the Incas?

2. Why were the Europeans less successful at dominating trade relationships in China and Japan?

3. How did the slave trade have an impact on African states and communities?

Pleasures AND PASTIMES

Polo has often been referred to as the sport of kings. Today, it is a popular sport in many countries of the world but is still largely the preserve of the wealthy. Polo's origins lie in Persia where it first developed as a form of training for the cavalry. By the sixteenth century, polo had developed as a popular pastime among the Persian nobility and had begun to spread throughout the Middle East and India. The first Mogul ruler of India, Babur (1494–1530), was an avid polo player and the game was soon adopted by *nawabs* and *maharajahs* (nobles and princes). In the sixteenth century, the Englishman George Mainwaring reported on a polo game: "Having in their hands long rods of wood about the bigness of a man's finger, and on the end of the rods a piece of wood is nailed on like onto a hammer. After these were divided and turned face to face, there came into the middle, and did throw a wooden ball between both companies and, having goals made at either end, they began their sport, striking the ball with their rod from one end to the other ..." In time the sport of polo would become a favourite sport among the nobility of Europe; one of many examples of cross-cultural influences of the early modern period.

TRADING COMPANIES

The northern countries of Europe had a well-developed commercial system in which certain cities financed and organized long-distance enterprises. The family capitalism that had been typical of the Hansa traders in the Baltic or the Italian merchant republics could not marshal enough money to mount the new endeavours, so they formed companies:

- The East India Company (1600) in England to trade for spices with the Indian Malabar Coast
- The United East India Company (1602) in the Netherlands, which was set up as a trading post at the Cape of Good Hope to trade with Indonesia and Malaya

- The French East India Company (1604) in north-western France (port of Lorient)
- The Dutch United West India Company (1621) in the Netherlands, which dealt in furs and slaves. This was the company that sent Henry Hudson to explore northern Canada.

Set up by government initiatives, these companies formed the cutting edge of economic exploitation overseas. These great joint-stock companies underwent unprecedented development after 1600. In many cases, they were awarded monopoly rights, exemptions from taxation, the right to own land, and more.

No country better exemplified this phenomenon than the Netherlands. The ambassador of Louis XIV to The Hague from 1672 to 1679 compared the modest but comfortable existence of the merchants of Amsterdam with the rituals of the French court at Versailles:

> It must be granted that this little republic can now be numbered among the mightiest powers of Europe. In this we have reason to admire the fruits of industry, shipping, and trade for these are the sources from which all their wealth flows with an abundance which is all the more remarkable because, until now, the skill and ability of Holland have kept this flow almost completely away from the other nations of Europe.

In 1594 the Far East Company was formed in Amsterdam. It was composed of nine merchant members. Although not a big commercial success, it had an enormous impact on European expansionism. It linked maritime exploration, trading posts, and large-scale rather than individual capitalism. The Far East Company decided that the Portuguese, despite the king's claims they were "lords of the conquest, navigation, and commerce of Ethiopia, India, Arabia, and Persia," were actually strained to the limits in maintaining their trading network in the Indian Ocean. To celebrate the dawn of a new century and a new contender, the Dutch fleet engaged

Portuguese ships off Java and won. From then on, the Dutch would carry on the war against the Spanish Crown (at the time linked with that of Portugal) not only in the Netherlands but also far away across the ocean.

The Dutch began to absorb products from the colonial territories into their economy: Delft porcelain patterns owed much to models brought from the Orient; the Dutch specialization in tobacco was a result of the colonies, as was the start of the chocolate and liqueur businesses. These products, brought from overseas and processed at home (giving work to Dutch people), were then re-exported. When sailing outward-bound, the Dutch carried salt herring from the North Sea, as well as woollen goods and other European products to be used in their holdings in the West Indies, Java, South Africa, and Ceylon (Sri Lanka). The Dutch had snatched these centres from the Portuguese; they would be snatched from the Dutch by the English.

CROSS-CULTURAL EXCHANGE

Europe Abroad

The passing of knowledge between Europe and the wider world was always a two-way process. In many parts of the world, other societies were getting used to the arrival of exotic individuals. On screens painted in Japan, which are a source of information about the first contacts with the Portuguese, we see Blacks represented, perhaps the first Africans ever seen in that part of the world. On the beach in Acapulco, Mexico, stands a monument to a Japanese envoy who crossed there on his way to Europe at the start of the seventeenth century. Several years later, he would again cross Mexico on his return voyage to Japan with news about European societies. A hundred years earlier, Montezuma, the Aztec ruler of Mexico who was captured by Hernán Cortés, liked to ask his Spanish page-boy questions about Spain.

Euro-American Societies

The colonial societies that developed in the Americas, best labelled "Euro-American," were blends of European and American cultures. In South America, the Spanish adapted the Inca tribute system, which came to be known by its Spanish name of *encomienda*. The Inca tribute system was designed to ensure the fair distribution of resources in society. Land was allocated under a tripartite division with one part going to the state, one for the Cult of the Sun, and one for the *ayllu* or communities (by far the largest part). The land of the *ayllu* was divided among its members in variable sizes according to the size of the family. The tribute took the form of labour on state land. The land and other resources appropriated to the Inca state provided for the members of the royal family and others in government, and created a reserve of food in case of famine. Thus the tribute system was very much a reciprocal arrangement designed to ensure the well-being of all members of society, in both good and bad times. The Spanish found the tribute system ready-made for their capitalist exploitation of Peru.

The means by which the Spanish adapted the tribute system to their needs reflects both their insensitivity to Inca tradition and their greed. The Spanish, immediately upon conquest, seized the lands formerly set aside for the Inca state and the Cult of the Sun. The tribute crops required from the Indians therefore had to be taken from their own land. Furthermore, the tribute crops supplied by the Indians no longer were held in reserve in case of famine. The Spanish did not redistribute the wealth for the benefit of all.

New Foods

The greatest impact Columbus made on the world was not his initial contact in 1492, but his return visit in 1493. From Spain Columbus brought horses, pigs, wheat, chickpeas, vegetable seeds, and fruit trees to America. Later Europeans would bring chickens, barley, oats, and rye as well as coffee and sugar from Africa. The flow of foodstuffs was equally great from North and South America to Europe, Africa, and China.

Maize (corn) entered the peasant food chain in northern Spain, Portugal, and Italy as animal food. It was also ground into flour. Tomatoes, first encountered by Spaniards in the valley of Mexico, became a staple of the peasant diet in northern Spain, Portugal, and Italy. In Cuba Columbus found that corn was also tasty either boiled, roasted, or ground into flour. The Spaniards took corn to the Philippines in the sixteenth century, and Chinese merchants there brought it to China. The Portuguese took it to Africa, where it was widely cultivated and used as food on the slave ships.

Another New World crop that made a big impact on the European diet was the potato. Potatoes were used to provision ships returning to Europe and to feed poorhouse inmates in Spain. Knowledge of the potato travelled to Spain's Italian possessions and spread to France, Germany, and Britain. Potatoes were nutritious, grew on land not suitable for other crops, and took pressure off the demand for wheat, which was more expensive to cultivate.

Other New World foods to enter the European diet were chocolate, peanuts, vanilla, pineapple, lima beans, and peppers sweet and hot. "Retransmission" by Europeans from one area of the world to another was rapid: pineapples, papaya, and sweet potatoes had been taken across the Pacific to Asia within a century. Manioc, rice, yams, cowpeas, and a variety of citrus fruits not previously known in Africa were taken there before 1700. Coffee, a plant that originated in Arabia, was taken to South America, and the second Spanish governor of Colombia took the first cows to the New World to provide both milk and meat. By the sixteenth century, the turkey, native to North and Central America, was also well domesticated in Western Europe.

Sugar cane was planted in the New World as early as 1506. Arabs had cultivated sugar in the Mediterranean area from as early as 750 in Palestine, and then in Egypt and Sicily. In 1550 there were at least five sugar plantations in Brazil, and by 1623 the number had jumped to more than 350. By 1580, the sugar plantations of northeastern Brazil were the major source of revenue there. Europe was avid for a sweetener other than the traditional honey. When the

Dutch attacked the Portuguese colony of Pernambuco during the seventeenth century, their motivation was to take over the valuable sugar plantations. Coffee, tea, sugar, and spices were all soon generating revenues. These crops also provided new sources of taxation for governments. The diet of the average European was now healthier and more varied than it had been a few centuries earlier.

The Rise of Colonial Empires

The first European references to Native American peoples were when the Norse sagas spoke of the Skraelings, a derogatory term. Columbus informed Spanish monarchs Ferdinand and Isabella that he had found people in the new lands who were "very well built, of handsome bodies and faces." He actually thought that he had arrived in India, so he and his Spanish sailors called them Indians.

In 1534 Jacques Cartier (1491–1557) came to Canada from Saint-Malo in Normandy. Upon his return to France, he took some Amerindians with him who, after amusing the French court, became sick and died. When Cartier returned to Canada, he claimed that these Amerindians were alive and well, and so happy in France that they had no desire to return to their families. The Native people likely were not convinced of this. They also were not happy when the French established a fort where a number of men remained for the winter: They were attacked and wiped out. The following winter, another group tried to survive, but this time it was scurvy that killed them. (They did not know about stewing the bark and needles of white cedar to get vitamin C, as the Native people did.) Later, French renegades and *coureurs de bois* (fur traders) who had learned such survival skills, extended their knowledge of Native customs to the immigrants from France. Samuel de Champlain

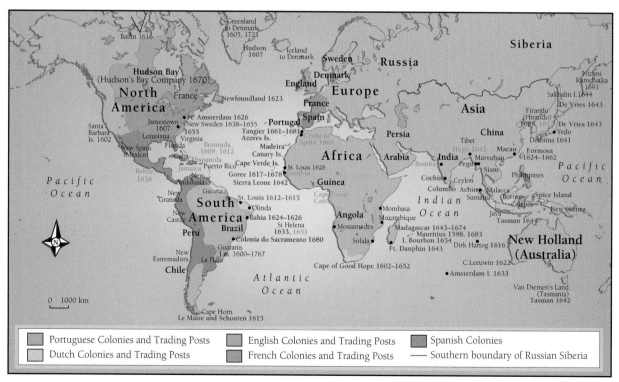

■ **FIGURE 3.2** European Expansion to 1700
Consider the ways that trade controlled by the colonial powers helped the colonizer and hurt the colonized.

(1567–1635), as commander of a Spanish vessel, explored the West Indies, Mexico, Colombia, and Panama. He then explored the St. Lawrence River and founded Montréal for France while systematically collecting information about the Indians.

Seventeenth-century missionaries observing a North American Indian village. What could the Europeans teach the native people about living in North America?

The religion of the newcomers was, of course, Christianity. In his *City of God* (411 CE), Saint Augustine, an early Christian philosopher (354–430 CE) who had lived in North Africa, preached that all people, regardless of colour, were God's creation:

> Whoever is born anywhere as a human being, that is, as a rational mortal creature, however strange he may appear to our senses in bodily form or colour or motion or utterance, or in any faculty, part or quality of his nature whatsoever, let no true believer have any doubt that such an individual is descended from the one man who was first created.

Unfortunately, the egalitarianism that had characterized early Christianity was not extended to Africans or Amerindians as their conquerors converted them to the new faith. Arguments over whether Amerindians were either rational or capable of understanding Christianity went on even before a famous debate

(1550–1551) between Bartolomé de Las Casas and Juan Ginés de Sepúlveda. Las Casas (1474–1566) was a native of Seville who, at age 40, became a missionary priest known as Fray Bartolomé de Las Casas and devoted his life to fighting for justice for Amerindian people, and condemning the "robbery, evil, and injustice perpetrated against them." Las Casas was opposed by Sepúlveda (1490–1573), who was a learned humanist and Aristotelian thinker. The ancient Greek philosopher Aristotle had said that some individuals are slaves by nature, and Sepúlveda believed that just as children are inferior to adults, women to men, or monkeys to humans, so Indians are "naturally" inferior to Spaniards. These issues were referred to theologians in 1550, but no final decision was made. Consequently, the Church did not call for an end to Amerindian slavery.

The Las Casas-Sepúlveda debate, and others, drew support from different factions of Spanish society. The *conquistadors*, or Spanish conquerors, wanted to enslave and exploit the Amerindians as agricultural labourers and miners. The clergy defended the Indians from cruelty and set up schools to educate them according to Christian values. In 1511 a Dominican priest, Antonio de Montesinos, warned the Spanish settlers of Hispaniola that they were in mortal sin, "for the cruelty and tyranny you use in dealing with these innocent people." He went on to ask them: "Tell me, by what right or justice do you keep these Indians in such cruel and horrible servitude? On what authority have you waged a detestable war against these people, who dwelt quietly and peacefully on their own land?"

Pope Paul III, in 1537, ordered members of the clergy to "Go ye and teach all nations. All, without exception, for all are capable of receiving the doctrines of the faith." Echoing St. Augustine, Paul III denounced as satanic any effort to hinder the preaching of salvation by attempting to "publish abroad that the Indians of the west and the south, and other peoples of whom we have recent knowledge, should be treated as dumb brutes created for our service, pretending that they are incapable of receiving the Catholic Faith. The Indians are truly men."

Spanish settlers viewed the world through medieval eyes. They believed that God stood above the saints, who were above the believers. Below these were the unbelievers, such as Hindus, Jews, Muslims, Buddhists, animists — but who were, however, clearly humans. These minds also believed in a world between humans and beasts — the hermaphrodites and witches — among whom they included the Amerindians. The latter could be enslaved because, as argued by Aristotle, the inferior were destined to serve the higher orders.

This view of the world is called a Mercator projection, after the Flemish geographer and cartographer Gerardus Mercator who developed it in 1569. This projection remained in use for a long time due to its suitability for navigation. In this 1608 rendering, are the continents and oceans represented realistically?

Review, Reflect, Respond

1. What role did trading companies play in the world capitalist economy?

2. Does the term "Euro-American" accurately describe early colonial societies in North America? Explain your answer.

3. Explain how the Las Casas-Sepúlveda debate defined the relationship between Europeans and Amerindians.

There was no certainty among Europeans about the origin of Amerindians, although it was obvious from their appearance that they were more like Asians than Africans. French writer Pierre d'Avity, in the 1630s, gave the following composite account of Amerindians drawn from various visitors:

> They are as handsome young men and beautiful young women as may be seen in France. They are great runners and swimmers, and the women too have a marvellous disposition ... not at all malicious but literal, have a good mind and clear one so far as discerning common and sensible matters, deducing their reasons with gracefulness, always employing some pleasing comparison. They have a very good memory for material matters, such as having seen you, the qualities of a place where they have been, or what one did in their presence some 20 or 30 years ago.

Franciscans and Jesuits were active missionaries among Amerindians in the seventeenth century. They observed that the Indians thought Frenchmen were weaker, and that the heavy body hair of Europeans was ugly. Clerics called for "suitable" holy pictures for missionary work that represented Christ and the Saints without beards or curly hair.

The accounts of Amerindians by those who had met them, or those who read about them, were not always consistent. We can see that both good and bad characteristics were assigned to them over the centuries. In time, the view of Amerindians as inferior subhuman beings was repudiated and they came to be regarded as fully human, although of a younger civilization. Unfortunately, by the time this view was accepted, the Amerindian population had been decimated by disease and European atrocities. Racism continues to plague the survivors as they struggle to maintain their culture and heritage in a European world system. Guatemalan activist Rigoberta Manchú won the Nobel Peace Prize in 1992 for her heroism in defending the Maya of Guatemala against genocide by the government.

Reflections

Felipe Fernandez-Armesto admits in the prologue to his provocative book *Millennium* that "Western supremacy is presented as imperfect, precarious and short-lived." He goes on to suggest that the dominance of Atlantic civilization (Western Europe and European colonies along the eastern seaboard of the Americas) is over "and that the initiative has shifted again, this time to some highly developed technically proficient communities of the Pacific seaboard, typified by California and Japan." While some may dispute Fernandez-Armesto's assertions, he does force us to think about European imperialism and colonialism from a more detached perspective. Looking at the world in 1450, it becomes apparent that it was not the destiny of Europeans to dominate the world, and that cultural superiority was not the key to the victories Europeans enjoyed in other parts of the world. European hegemony can no longer be viewed as a permanent fixture in world history. Although Europeans did manage to establish colonies around the world and came to dominate trade through their capitalist world economy, the period of European dominance was actually only about three hundred years and much less in some parts of the world.

Chapter Review

Chapter Summary

In this chapter, you have seen:

- the impact of Western colonization on both the colonizer and the colonized
- how certain forces have facilitated the process of change and others have tended to impede it
- how non-Western ideas and cultures influenced developments in indigenous societies
- key elements of pre-industrial economies throughout the world

Reviewing the Significance of Key People, Concepts, and Events (Knowledge and Understanding)

1. Understanding the history of the interaction between the West and the world during the sixteenth and seventeenth centuries requires a knowledge of the following concepts, events and people, and an understanding of their significance in the shaping of the history of modern world. Select and explain two from each column.

Concepts	Events	People
capitalism	Crusades	Mehmed II
caravels	Treaty of Tordesillas	Atawallpa
Asiento		Francisco Pizarro
Encomienda		St. Francis Xavier

2. For each of the following regions, list the role it played in the capitalist economy, the European view of the people, and the nature of their trading relationship with Europeans: Africa, the Americas, and Asia.

Doing History: Thinking About the Past (Thinking/Inquiry)

3. In his book *The Fall of Natural Man: The American Indian and the Origins of Comparative Ethnology* (1982), Anthony Pagden offers the following advice to those studying early contact between Europeans and Amerindians:

> The early chroniclers ... were not committed to an accurate description of the world "out there." They were attempting to bring within their intellectual grasp phenomena which they recognized as new and which they could only make familiar, and hence intelligible, in the terms of an anthropology made authoritative precisely by the fact that its sources ran back to the Greeks.[3]

Considering Pagden's words of advice, how might we make sense of the following quote from the log maintained by Captain John Locke on a voyage to Guinea in 1554?

> The elephant (which some call an oliphant) is the biggest of all four-footed beasts, his forelegs are longer than his hinder, he hath ankles in the lower part of his hinder legs, and five toes on his feet undivided, his snout or trunk is so long, and in such form, that it is to him in the stead of a hand ... They love rivers, and will often

go into them up to the snout, wherewith they blow and snuff and play in the water. They have continual war against dragons, which desire their blood because it is very cold: and therefore the dragon lieth in wait as the elephant passeth by.[4]

4. Europeans became the dominant economic and military force in the world after the sixteenth century. How can we explain this domination of such well-organized, advanced civilizations as those in Mexico, Peru, and India?

Applying Your Learning (Application)

5. The sixteenth-century painting (on the right) depicts the peoples of the Americas. How does this painting reflect the European worldview at the time? Can you suggest why depictions such as this would have been popular in Europe during the sixteenth century?

North American Indians Collecting Gold, by Theodore de Bry (1564)

6. Imagine you are Francisco Bobidalla and that you have been sent to investigate complaints against Columbus. Prepare a list of four questions you would ask each of the following:

   a)   Amerindians

   b)   Europeans under Columbus's command

   c)   Columbus

   For each of the questions, provide a brief answer that might have been possible, given the historical evidence available.

Communicating Your Learning (Communication)

7. Prepare a map of the world based on our current knowledge of the continents and oceans but using symbols and icons reflective of the sixteenth century. Clearly indicate the flow of trade, and use visuals or labels to show the civilizations with which Europeans came into contact, and major areas of European expansion.

8. Prepare a script for the opening segment of a documentary exploring the period of first contact between Europeans and other civilizations, ca. 1450 to 1650. Your script must clearly reflect a thesis relating to the period and address the following questions: What factors drove European exploration and expansion? How did the relationship that Europeans had with the peoples of Asia differ from the one it had with the people of the Americas? What allowed Europeans to dominate trade relationships with various cultures?

Unit Review

Reflecting on What You Have Learned (Knowledge and Understanding)

1. The period between 1450 and 1700 saw enormous changes in many facets of life in Europe and around the world. Copy the chart below in your notes and use it to summarize the significant changes which occurred in Europe during this period and the impact of these changes on both Europe and the rest of the world.

Area of Change	Nature of Change	Impact on the West	Impact on the World
Religion			
Economics			
Technological Change			
Grand Exchange			

2. The period of change between 1450 and 1700 was paralleled by significant artistic movements. Create a mind map that clearly establishes the connections between three artistic movements of this period and significant events/developments of the age.

Practising Historical Interpretation (Thinking/Inquiry)

3. From the end of the Middle Ages to our own century, a common theme in Western civilization has been the increasing secularization of society. To what degree do you think religion limited scientific and intellectual growth in the sixteenth and seventeenth centuries? How did some intellectuals attempt to reconcile science and religion?

4. For generations, students have been taught about the heroic exploits of the explorers who "discovered" new lands. Why are traditional images of heroic discoverers inadequate when studying the age of exploration? To what degree must the quest for profit be seen as the most potent force behind European exploration and colonization?

Applying Your Historical Understanding (Application)

5. "An individual merits the term genius to the extent that their creative work in a domain exerts a material effect on the definition and delineation of the domain... The more universal the contribution, the more it travels across cultures and eras, the greater the genius." Select one of the historical figures from the list below and explain why you believe he or she should be remembered as a genius according to this definition. Be sure to show clearly that their work had a material effect on a domain and that this effect was lasting.

Leonardo da Vinci	Galileo	Queen Isabella
Michelangelo	Copernicus	Christopher Columbus
Lorenzo de Medici	René Descartes	Atawallpa
Machiavelli	Isaac Newton	St. Francis Xavier
Martin Luther	Francis Bacon	Juan Ginés de Sepúlveda

6. Despite a gulf of several centuries separating us from the early modern period, many aspects of both Western and non-Western cultures bear the lasting legacy of this period. List and describe three ways the legacy of the early modern period of history (1450 to 1700) is reflected in the world today.

Communicating Your Learning (Communication)

7. Create two maps depicting views of the world at the beginning of the sixteenth century, one a European view and the other a view from the perspective of one of the following groups: Asians, Mesoamericans, or Africans. Place the civilization at the centre of the map and then use visuals to depict how that civilization viewed the other with which it had contact.

8. Imagine that you are hosting a dinner party with five of the most influential minds of the early modern period. List the five people you would invite. For each guest, write a paragraph explaining your choice and prepare five questions you would ask him or her. You do not need to supply answers, but the questions must clearly reflect an issue or relevant event particular to each individual.

---

* Now complete Skills Focus Two (p. 592):

Sleuthing Through the Ages: Bibliographies and Notes.

UNIT TWO

An Age of Enlightenment and Revolution

Chapter Four
**The Enlightenment
1700–1789**

Chapter Five
**Revolution to Restoration
1789–1815**

Chapter Six
**The World in the
Eighteenth Century**

Drawn in 1799, the last year of the century of enlightenment, this print by Goya reads, "The sleep of reason produces monsters." What could that mean?

The eighteenth century is characterized as an age of great intellectual thought. The scientific revolution of the previous century had convinced many people, even some outside the scientific and academic communities, of the boundless potential of humanity. Some philosophers, such as Condorcet and Beccaria, even believed in the perfectibility of society through the application of reason. Intellectuals, including Voltaire and Rousseau, made public issues matters of private concern, exploring ideas in every facet of society, from crime and punishment to religion.

Driven by faith in the human ability to know and understand all, eighteenth-century Europeans were more self-assured of the superiority of their civilization than ever before. By the end of the eighteenth century, many European powers, including Britain, France, Spain, Holland and Portugal, had established extensive overseas empires, many of which were peopled by enslaved Africans who had been imported to work the mines or plantations of the European colonists.

In Europe, humanism, which embraced human achievement and potential, would lead to revolutions in art, religion, science, and politics. Armed with the radical ideas of the *philosophes*, the people of France would lead a revolution at the end of the eighteenth century that would shake European society to its foundations and irrevocably alter the political map of Europe. From the ravages of revolution rose one of the most powerful military leaders in European history — Napoléon Bonaparte. While there is little doubt about his military prowess, whether the so-called Age of Napoléon (1799–1815) betrayed or furthered the ideals of the revolution is still a matter of considerable debate among present-day historians.

UNIT EXPECTATIONS

In this unit, you will:

O demonstrate an understanding of the nature of the interaction among diverse peoples during the eighteenth century

O demonstrate an understanding of the importance and use of chronology and cause and effect in historical analyses of developments in the West and throughout the world during the eighteenth century

O analyse different forms of artistic expression and how they reflect the age of the Enlightenment and the French Revolution

O demonstrate an understanding of diverse social structures and principles that guided social organization in Western and non-Western societies to the beginning of the nineteenth century

O critically analyse historical evidence, events, and interpretations

CHAPTER FOUR

The Enlightenment 1700–1789

CHAPTER EXPECTATIONS

By the end of this chapter, you will be able to:

- *describe the main tenets of key Enlightenment philosophies and explain how they have shaped Western thought*

- *assess the impact of modern Western thought on economic and political developments in the West during the eighteenth century*

- *demonstrate an understanding of key developments in attitudes towards religion and religious observance during the eighteenth century*

- *assess the influence of key individuals and groups whose ideas during the Enlightenment helped to shape Western attitudes*

The decorative style known as *chinoiserie*, was popular among the wealthy and middle class, especially in France and England. It copied and combined artistic features seen in objects brought back from China by merchants and traders, with traditional European forms.

The conservative outlook of pre-revolutionary European society was challenged by intellectuals in what was coined the new "Age of Reason" or "Age of Enlightenment." Politically, the eighteenth century was a time of government by absolute monarchies supported by armies led by aristocrats. Socially, a rigid class hierarchy existed that was dominated by a nobility with hereditary privileges. Economically, the urban labour force was organized into guilds, while the agricultural activities of peasants continued to be subject to a variety of heavy feudal dues, such as the *banalités*, fees for the use of the lord's facilities (windmills, wine press), or the *péages*, for the use of particular roads or rivers. The *ancien régime* (former pre-revolutionary governments) in Europe, and especially France, relied on colonies to enrich state treasuries. Scarcity of food, a low level of iron production, and rudimentary financial institutions marked the period. But there were forces at work that would bring sweeping and dramatic changes by the end of the century. In Britain, France, and Holland a growing middle class would emerge as an agent of political and economic change. An increasing population would put enormous pressure on food supplies, jobs and available land, all leading to heightened tensions among the classes. Leading "enlightened" intellectuals were laying the foundations of gradual political, economic, and social change that would characterize the modern age in Europe. Artists such as David and Fragonard, literary personalities such as Swift and Pope, musicians such as Mozart and Handel, would all reflect and record changes through new forms of artistic expression.

In this chapter, we will examine the forces that set the stage for the French Revolution of 1789, one of the most significant events in European history. By the end of the eighteenth century, Western Europe had broken with much of its past and was leading the Continent into a period of tumultuous social, political, and economic changes that were instrumental in the development of the modern age.

KEY CONCEPTS AND EVENTS

humanism

agricultural revolution

enclosure

Enlightenment

philosophes

Freemasonry

Encyclopedia

deism

neoclassicism

KEY PEOPLE

François-Marie Arouet de Voltaire

Denis Diderot

John Locke

Baron de Montesquieu

Cesare Beccaria

Jean-Jacques Rousseau

Adam Smith

Marquis de Condorcet

Catherine the Great

Madame de Graffigny

Wit and Wisdom

Superstition sets the whole world in flames; philosophy quenches them.

Voltaire, *Dictionnaire philosophique*, 1764

TIMELINE: THE ENLIGHTENMENT

The "Glorious Revolution" in England	1688–89	
	1690	John Locke, *Essay Concerning Human Understanding*
Jethro Tull of England invents the seeding drill	1701	
	1713	The Board of Longitude is established in England to promote the discovery of a means of determining the longitude of ships at sea
Rule of Louis XV in France	1715–1774	
	1717	Alexander Pope revises his epic poem *The Rape of the Lock*
Montesquieu, *The Persian Letters*	1721	
	1726	Jonathan Swift, *Gulliver's Travels*
Voltaire, *Philosophic Letters to the English*	1733	
	1740–1772	Rule of Frederick the Great of Prussia
Denis Diderot, *Encyclopedia*	1751–65	
	1759	Voltaire, *Candide*
Rousseau, *The Social Contract* and *Émile*	1762	
	1762–1796	Rule of Catherine the Great of Russia
Cesare Beccaria, *On Crimes and Punishments*	1764	
	1776	Adam Smith publishes his economic theories in *An Inquiry into the Nature and Causes of the Wealth of Nations;* The American Revolution begins; Thomas Jefferson drafts the Declaration of Independence
Edmund Cartwright invents the power loom	1785	
	1789	The French Revolution begins
The Reign of Terror in France	1793	

Not to scale.

EUROPEAN SOCIETY IN THE EIGHTEENTH CENTURY

Population Growth

An important feature of eighteenth-century Europe was a steady rise in population. A decline in the number of deaths due to fewer wars, fewer epidemics such as typhus and bubonic plague, and improved hygiene and sanitation all led to a decrease in mortality rates and an increase in the number of people of all ages. It is estimated that Europe's population stood at approximately 100 million in 1700. A century later, the population is estimated to have grown to 190 million, and by 1850, it had reached 260 million. There was also an improved food supply brought about by changes in methods of agricultural production. Increased grain production and the introduction of corn and the potato from the New World also provided a more stable food supply. As a result of these improvements, people were able to have and sustain larger families.

The rise in population led to increased demands for food, jobs, goods, and services. More people now lived in the countryside than the countryside could sustain, and this led to a migration into towns and cities. The population explosion also produced an increasing number of socially disadvantaged and politically discontented people, as food production and the manufacture of goods strained to keep up.

Land Use and Agriculture

In eighteenth-century Europe, most of the population lived in small villages and worked the land; however, the scale and type of agriculture differed depending on the climate. For example, in southern Europe it tended to be dry, with sparse rain for several months of the year. On the other hand, coastal areas of northern Europe had a much higher annual rainfall and hence more intensive agriculture.

Agriculture was also affected by the managerial skills of landowners. Natural fertilizers were used and

These women are gleaning, or collecting, grains of wheat left behind after the harvest. For many poor rural folk of the early eighteenth century this was all the grain they would get. Jean-François Millet, *The Gleaners* (1857)

the rotation of crops to replenish the soil was practised, but yields were still low. Many estates belonged to aristocrats who spent much of their time at court. They appointed agents to manage their estates and were often uninterested in the details of daily agricultural practice. Farms owned by resident farmers were generally better managed. Poorer peasants held small farms or mere scraps of land that often did not provide even for one family. There were also labourers who owned no land or who were permitted only to grow a few crops for their own consumption, on the condition that they finish their work for the landowner first.

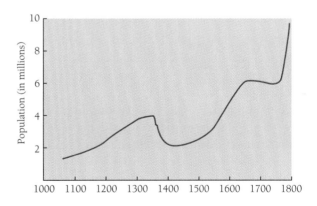

Population growth in England 1000–1800. How do historians account for the pattern of fluctuations revealed in this graph?

Over the course of the eighteenth century, agriculture was also becoming increasingly commercialized, especially on large estates as landlords sought ways to make more profits from their land. Most of the agricultural innovations had their origins in England, northern Italy and the Netherlands, where large tracts of land were being reclaimed using dikes and drainage canals, and where landlords were willing to finance more experiments. English agriculturalist Jethro Tull (1674–1741), for example, introduced the steel plow, which turned over the soil more effectively, and the seed drill, which improved planting. Charles Townsend, also from England, learned from the Dutch how to gain yields from sandy soils by applying fertilizers. He also instituted a new system of crop rotation using turnips, barley, wheat, and clover. When this method was used, no field was left fallow; crops that both produced feed for livestock and replenished the soil were rotated. As a result of this innovation, there was more food available for both animals and human beings. These and several other agricultural innovations in animal husbandry and crop production created what has become known as the agricultural revolution. The impact of this revolution would gradually extend throughout Europe.

Innovations in agriculture led to radical changes in land distribution. For example, in areas where poor peasants held only small strips of land, it was virtually impossible to co-ordinate the kind of crop rotation Townsend introduced. In some areas of Europe and especially Britain, landlords intent on earning higher profits from their land abandoned the centuries-old system of land division. Exercising their right to control land previously rented out to peasants, many British landlords by the mid-eighteenth century began reclaiming common land and renting out strips in large, fenced-in block fields. This movement by landlords to consolidate their land is known as "enclosure," and Parliament passed acts of enclosure in the interests of the landlords. The fields were then farmed using more efficient and profitable methods of agriculture, with the aim of producing a surplus to be sold on the open market. Enclosure often resulted in riots led by displaced peasants and caused much economic and social conflict in the countryside. Many farmers would be forced to seek employment as factory workers in manufacturing cities such as Manchester and Glasgow.

The agricultural revolution and the enclosure movement were most prevalent in Europe west of the Elbe River. Britain and the Netherlands led the way in agricultural reform, while France and northern Italy led the way in agricultural improvement, but practised limited enclosure. Under the more autocratic governments of Prussia, Austria, Poland and Russia, the great landlords did little to improve agricultural production, choosing to demand more labour from the serfs rather than more productivity from the soil.

THE BEGINNING OF THE INDUSTRIAL REVOLUTION

In previous centuries, cottage industries and guilds had been the economic norm for the production of goods. The genesis of what was to be a worldwide industrial revolution came in the 1750s. However, the term "industrial revolution" can be misleading, in that it implies a rapid change that happened in a specific period. Actually, the Industrial Revolution was a gradual series of changes in agriculture, trade, and industry

Inventions that improved productivity in cotton manufacturing were introduced in 1733 by British weaver John Kay. Kay invented a device called the flying shuttle, which cut weaving time in half. Both the spinning jenny and water-powered frame, invented by Richard Arkwright, also quickened the production of textiles. These early steps in industrialization increased productivity (at the expense of labour), facilitated urbanization, and increased consumerism.

Luxury and Consumerism in the Eighteenth Century

When the influential philosopher Voltaire (1694–1778) observed that "the superfluous is necessary," he meant that consumerism created jobs and stimulated commerce.

Research and commentary on the effects of economic activity increased substantially in the eighteenth century. Dr. François Quesnay (1694–1774) and other writers known as physiocrats believed that the rural economy was the root of national wealth. Quesnay coined the phrase *laissez faire* (no interference) in recommending a more open marketplace. An article on luxury in the *Encyclopedia*, a set of volumes published in France throughout the second half of the eighteenth century, reads:

> Without luxury, there is less exchange of goods and less commerce; without commerce, nations cannot be as populous. A nation whose work force consists only of agricultural labourers will have a smaller population than that which supports also sailors and textile workers ... Every government, unless it is founded on equality and property in common, has and must have as one of its mainsprings the citizen's desire to accumulate wealth. [Source?]

Among the more important economic changes that also began in the eighteenth century was the spread of commercial capitalism throughout Western Europe. Joint-stock companies such as the Dutch East India Company, as well as family businesses, increased the volume of trade, and merchant banking became more widespread. As a result, money increasingly flowed into the hands of a new middle, or merchant class, and out of the hands of the monarchs and nobles.

The Weakening of the Nobility

Much of the land on the European continent was owned by nobles, members of privileged families who claimed to be descended from warriors. They saw themselves as superior to farmers and merchants. Nobles enjoyed profits from the crops and other products of the land, and demanded obedience from those who worked on their property. While some peasant farmers owned their land, many others paid rent to a noble, or worked for wages on land owned by the church or a middle-class landowner. In much of Central and Eastern Europe, peasants could not legally negotiate the price of their labour: they were serfs and they were not free to move away from designated areas without the permission of the landlord. Serfs were obliged by law to provide labour — sometimes as much as four or five days per week — to the landowner.

The eighteenth century saw a broad weakening of the social authority of the nobility in many parts of Europe, especially France. When the French king Louis XIV died in 1715, most of Europe was governed by monarchs who presided over empires or kingdoms in which nobles enjoyed privileged positions as landowners, judges, officials, and military officers. Although kings and emperors bestowed titles, they were often unhappy with the greed of the nobility and its demands for protection of its privileges.

Government in the Eighteenth Century

European politics in the eighteenth century were still largely dictated by the dynastic ambitions of powerful ruling families served by nobles. Much attention was given to military strength and the funds to pay for it. Not much attention was given to public opinion, except in Britain and Holland, where there were effective representative assemblies under constitutional monarchies.

The royal court was the place where the nobility could get power and rewards. Rulers were human and therefore fallible; a favourite of the court today could be disgraced tomorrow. Rulers could be children with limited authority; they could become sick, or even insane, like George III of England (who ruled from 1760 to 1792) or Queen Maria I of Portugal (who ruled from 1777 to 1792). The royal courts of the eighteenth century were full of personal intrigue and scandal where nobles jockeyed for position with an eye on the heir to the throne. Monarchies were neither public nor accountable institutions; they were constrained by tradition, religion and, to some extent, obedience to legal precedents.

The death of the "Sun King," Louis XIV of France (1643–1715), had marked the end of an era. Hardly any of his subjects were old enough to remember conditions before his reign. A regent had ruled from 1715 to 1722 in place of the infant great-grandson who was to be the next king, Louis the XV (1723–1774). During the time when Louis was too young to rule, the Regency became a time of novelty and change in French culture.

Europe after Louis XIV

At the death of Louis XIV, the families struggling to increase territory and wealth were the Spanish Bourbons, the French Bourbons, the Hanoverians in Britain, the Hapsburgs in Central Europe, with their capital in Vienna, and the Romanovs in Russia, with their capital in Moscow (later moved to St. Petersburg). One of the newest contending families was the Hohenzollern of Prussia, whose king had only recently (1701) been recognized by the Holy Roman Emperor.

At this time, the whole of southeastern Europe was particularly conscious of the Ottomans, a great Islamic power with its capital in Constantinople. The Ottomans were overlords of much of the Balkans and also the Middle East and North Africa. There were smaller European dynasties, like the Braganza family in Portugal, the House of Savoy in northern Italy, the Bourbons of Naples, the Orange family in the Netherlands, the Wasa in Stockholm, and the families who ruled in the smaller German states. These smaller dynasties could not provoke the major families without danger to themselves. They constantly sought alliances with the major states and often profited from unforeseen events, victories, or defeats.

Conflicts were based on expanding territories and commercial advantage, not on religious or philosophical

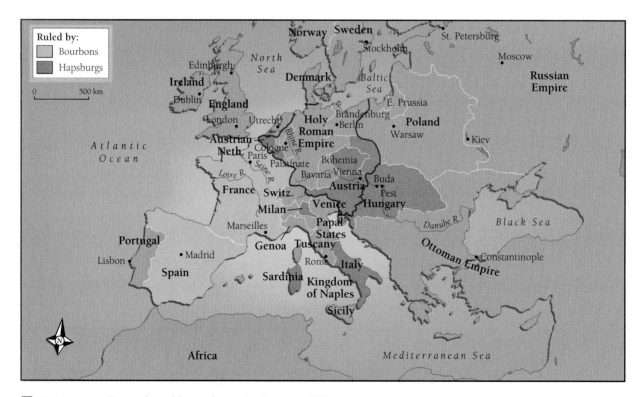

■ **FIGURE 4.1** Geopolitical boundaries in Europe, 1715
Compare this map to a current map of the region. What names appear on this map that do not appear on the more current one?

differences. Military glory was a focus for the most powerful groups, and peace was considered necessary only to prepare for the next war. During the wars of the eighteenth century, non-combatants continued to travel unimpeded through enemy territory. Officers in opposing armies dined with each other and frequently played chess before battle. More soldiers died from malaria and typhoid than from combat. Military commissions (of officers) were bought and sold, and regiments were often owned by their colonels. Military campaigns (i.e., wars) occurred only in the summer months and never far from supplies. Whenever possible, battles were avoided. Foreign policy decisions were made in England, France and Holland, with the opinions of influential groups kept in mind. In other areas, monarchs and aristocrats continued to decide when and how to wage war and cared little for the wishes of the local populations involved. Maintaining a balance of power in Europe and crippling the trade abilities of other countries were the primary military objectives.

THE ENLIGHTENMENT

Most people in the eighteenth century (and today) thought only of their own needs and those of their loved ones. There were some, however, who also thought about the welfare of society as a whole. In medieval times, only the clergy transmitted the message of compassion and morality. During the Renaissance and Reformation, increasing numbers of educated individuals thought about the problems of society in ways that were not exclusively related to Christian teachings. They were what we now call intellectuals, a nineteenth-century word for people who make public issues matters of private concern. Thinkers of the Enlightenment in France were called *philosophes* (philosophers).

The Enlightenment was a period that exalted freedom of thought and debate over obedience to tradition and belief. In the economic realm, enlightened thinkers praised the action of the free market and advocated an end to medieval guilds that restrained membership in professions. Enlightened thinkers promoted rationalism (faith in human reason) and encouraged cultural optimism, the understanding that once reason and knowledge became widespread, humanity would make inevitable progress. Many advocated a return to nature, since in a state of nature humans were believed to have natural reason which civilization would ruin. Some thinkers also promoted what was called "natural religion," a rejection of traditional religion in favour of a belief that it was irrational to imagine a world without God (deism). Finally, enlightened thinkers espoused the need for human rights through public education, freedom of thought, speech and the press, the abolition of slavery, and the more humane treatment of criminals. This change in thinking was fundamental to modern secular thought about the relationship between the individual and society.

The ideas of the Enlightenment were expressed in the writings of French, English, Italian, and German writers. Books were translated and read in all European languages. While Britain and France were home to several of the most illustrious minds of the eighteenth century, other areas of Europe took on the ideas of the Enlightenment, sometimes reformulating the issues in their own terms.

Literacy and Book Production

Many absolutist monarchs were ambivalent about widespread literacy. Social theorists hostile to change said that a population needed only education sufficient to do its job. Some argued that book learning would only breed dissatisfaction with rural life. During the eighteenth century, however, government advisers became convinced that a literate population was an advantage. In Portugal, for example, the establishment of primary schools was ordered in every jurisdiction by 1759. By 1800 there were 850 such schools for boys and 24 for girls in the two largest cities. Children in *bourgeois* (middle class) families were encouraged to read extensively.

Before 1456 (when the first books were printed using movable type), literate Europeans copied texts and records by hand on parchment or paper, on slate, and on stone monuments. Ownership of individual handwritten scrolls or books was limited to a small minority. With the invention of movable type, it became possible to produce many copies of the same text. In Western Europe after 1500, there was an increase in the number of writers and readers of the new books, thus facilitating the spread of ideas of exceptional thinkers to a broad public.

During the Enlightenment, information was typically transmitted on printed pages in leather-bound books with few, if any, illustrations. There were also newspapers, called *gazettes* (from the Italian word for the small coin used to pay for them), and pamphlets. By the end of the eighteenth century, gazettes were published from Lisbon to Moscow. Wealthy, enlightened individuals also held literary and philosophical discussion groups called *salons* in their homes, where writers and intellectuals could present and exchange ideas and opinions.

The Encyclopedia

Perhaps the single most important publishing venture of the Enlightenment was the *Encyclopédie*, or the *Encyclopedia*, published in France starting in 1751. Some 300 writers wrote 72 000 articles by the time all the volumes were completed in 1765. The chief editors were the mathematician Jean d'Alembert (1717–1783) and the writer and critic Denis Diderot (1713–1784). The contributors included virtually every leading French intellectual of the time and included Montesquieu, Voltaire, Rousseau, and many others. The *Encyclopedia* covered a great variety of subjects including government, the social system, and religion. It summarized and praised advances in biology, chemistry, medicine, and engineering. It also used scientific knowledge to support its contributors' scorn of Christianity, and therefore was condemned by the Pope. In its attempt to encapsulate human knowledge and to elevate the triumphs of the human mind, the *Encyclopedia*, more than any other work of the eighteenth century, embodied the ideals of the Enlightenment. The government of France forbade further production of the *Encyclopedia* at the beginning

of the Seven Years' War in 1756, but various individuals protected its contents until finally, when the war was over in 1765, the remaining volumes were published.

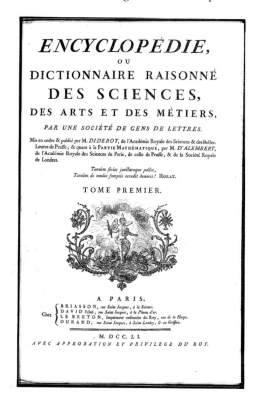

The *Encyclopedia* provides information on all aspects of life in eighteenth-century France. Many of the most important intellectuals of the time contributed articles and insights on everything from manufacturing to the fine arts. Would such a project be undertaken today?

Freemasons and the Enlightenment

The origins of Freemasonry have always been shrouded in mystery. Freemasons were members of a fraternal order of free thinkers who were particularly influential in eighteenth-century Europe. According to legend, the founders of this secret society, called "the Craft," were the builders of the ancient Jewish Temple in Jerusalem, built long before the Common Era, and destroyed during the Roman period. Modern historians associate the origin of Freemasonry with the Templars, a military order of Catholic monks sent to Jerusalem during the Crusades in the twelfth century.

The historical record of Freemasonry, however, started in the rooms of a London public bar near the Anglican Cathedral of Saint Paul in June of 1717. In addition to supporting an open market, Freemasons promoted freedom of speech, thought, and belief. They helped spread the leading ideas of the Enlightenment. By the end of the *ancien régime* in 1789 (with the French Revolution), almost every medium-sized town in Europe had at least one Masonic lodge.

Review, Reflect, Respond

1. List three factors that contributed to change in the eighteenth century, and for each explain the nature of the change.

2. In a paragraph, explain how developments in technology contributed to a rise in population in Europe during the eighteenth century.

3. How important do you believe the rise of literacy in the eighteenth century was to challenging the rule of the *ancien régime*? Explain your answer.

[ENLIGHTENMENT IDEAS

Enlightenment ideas were not accepted to the same degree in all parts of Europe. In Portugal, Spain and Italy, Enlightenment thinkers had to confront religious censorship and the ever-vigilant Inquisition, a court set up by the Catholic Church to purge society of heretics and their books. In the German states and the Austrian Empire, there were also barriers to the publication of criticism of the state, and open discussions of new philosophical notions were frowned upon.

Britain, France, Holland, and Denmark had fewer constraints on debates about religious authority, or theological explanations of the universe that countered the new scientific revelations. East of the Elbe River there were fewer towns, lower levels of literacy, and a scant tradition of resistance to authority. In European areas under Ottoman rule, there was almost no possibility of encountering the major works of the Enlightenment. In other words, the Enlightenment did not take root everywhere in Europe at the same time; even within different countries, there were often gaps in knowledge and different ideas among men and women, peasants, priests, and intellectuals.

Enlightened calls for change and improvements met with resistance among those who were satisfied with traditional ways, and the status quo. Many nobles would see the Enlightenment as an attack on them, and many Christians, particularly members of the Catholic Church, saw it as an attack on their beliefs as well. Voltaire, the French poet, playwright, historian and writer of the mid-eighteenth century, was particularly disliked by conservatives because of his anticlerical sarcasm.

The Enlightenment effectively criticized unquestioned obedience to authority, whether royal or religious. Above all, it praised the merits of free inquiry and debate as the best way to reach the truth. But, perhaps Enlightenment thinkers were too optimistic about the applicability of strict rationality to human affairs. Their arguments did leave little or no room for the emotions and moral convictions of individuals. There was a certain arrogance in the unflinching commitment of the leading Enlightenment thinkers to the notion of progress. This rational optimism, expressed in its extreme in Voltaire's satirical novel *Candide,* was a hallmark of the Enlightenment.

Deism, a term derived from the Latin word for god (*deus*), was a philosophical trend during the Enlightenment that advocated, among other things, the simplification of religious rituals. Deists believed that God did not participate directly in human affairs, but rather that God created the universe and then let it run (like a clockmaker and a clock). Deism had many followers in the eighteenth century, including revolutionaries like Robespierre (1758–1794), since it permitted criticism of particular rituals but retained the idea of a supreme, divine moral power in the universe. Eighteenth-century thinkers also renewed interest in the moral, religious, and artistic systems of the "Golden Age" of the ancient Greeks and Romans. The

Roman philosopher Lucretius (98–55BCE), for example, postulated ethical values that were foreign to Judaism, Christianity, and Islam.

Eighteenth-century intellectuals, especially Voltaire, promoted religious tolerance and rejected miracles and superstitions that seemed ridiculous in an age of reason. A phrase often heard during the Enlightenment was "My mind is my church," an expression of belief in God without the intolerance of earlier centuries. In response to the rational religion of intellectuals, counter-movements did arise, like the one led by John Wesley (1703–1791). Wesleyans, also known as Methodists, emphasized emotion over reason. They found their greatest appeal among the poor and the lower middle class, which drew emotional support from the highly charged religious meetings of the Methodists.

The Constitution of the United States, written in 1787, was inspirational to the writers of the Declaration of the Rights of Man and of the Citizen, in 1789 France.

WEB CONNECTION www.mcgrawhill.ca/links/legacy
Go to the site above to find out more about the Enlightenment.

Foremost Enlightenment Thinkers

John Locke

In his *Essay Concerning Human Understanding* (1690), English philosopher John Locke (1632–1704) dealt with the relationship of what he called "innate ideas" to human thought, language, and the limits of human understanding. He called for clarity of language to combat "those who will not take care about the meaning of their own words and will not suffer the significance of their expressions to be inquired into." Once the meaning of words was established, Locke discussed those experiences that lead to the elaboration of simple and complex ideas. While *Essay* is theoretical, its purpose was to make the reader critical of all that is believed by virtue of external authority rather than rational, empirical evidence.

Locke defended the right to own property as fundamental to a well-ordered society. He defended the need for elected governments in order to uphold freedom and tolerance. For him, the decision to leave the "state of nature" was based on the assumption that one would enjoy a better life by entering into a well-ordered society in which good government looked after its people. If this did not happen, the people had the right to overthrow the government and elect new leaders. Locke's ideas are most clearly articulated in the constitution of the United States, which guarantees its citizens the "right to life, liberty, and the pursuit of happiness." In contrast, the British North America Act, Canada's only constitution from 1867 to 1982, guaranteed Canadians "peace, order, and good government."

Baron de Montesquieu

The Baron de Montesquieu (1689–1755) was a judge in the Court of Appeal of Bordeaux, France. He was also a writer and amateur scientist. In *The Persian Letters* (1721) he commented satirically on Western institutions as described by Muslim Persian visitors to France writing home. Montesquieu had never been to Persia (today Iran) and he made factually incorrect statements about Islam. Nevertheless, his aim was to make French readers look at their own country with the same detachment that a foreigner with a different religion and different attitudes toward freedom and sexuality might have in a newly encountered land. Montesquieu's book conveys the idea that laws and social customs are products of the different conditions that exist in each society.

Montesquieu's *Spirit of the Laws* (1748) was probably the most influential work on social policy during the first half of the eighteenth century. It set out to prove that law derives from differing circumstances and social systems; that laws are "the necessary relationships deriving from the nature of things." The nature of things was largely a consequence of politics, whether in a small republic (as illustrated in classical writing) where virtue was found, in an aristocracy where a defence of honour by the nobility guided public activity, or in a monarchy in which authority was concentrated in an individual. Montesquieu's ideas were drawn from classical writings and from Asia, notably China and the Islamic world. His arguments tended to show that France was too large for a republic to be feasible there. He also thought that an overly strong monarch could become despotic and arbitrary. He implied that a monarchy, held in check by an aristocracy — of which Montesquieu was a member — was the best form of government.

The novelty of Montesquieu's thought was its wide scope over space and time. He showed the good and the bad in all political systems; he pondered the effects of climate, of social and sexual customs (such as monogamy or polygamy); he referred to skilled economic minorities and provided an excellent summary of the knowledge of his time.

François-Marie Arouet de Voltaire

Though contemporaries of Voltaire (1694–1778) enjoyed his plays, prose and poetry, we know him best for his political commentary, satirical writing, and challenges to religious authority. Voltaire's genius was sharp and witty; he constantly defended tolerance and attacked religious piety.

Voltaire resisted his father's plans to make him study law. Instead he travelled to Holland, where he completed *Oedipus*, a play based on the Greek myth.

What kind of character is revealed in this sculpture of Voltaire done in 1781 by Jean-Antoine Houdon?

This after already having been in the state prison in Paris for satirical verses about the Duke of Orléans, regent for the child king Louis XV. As a young man of 25, Voltaire had quarrelled with an aristocrat whose servants then gave him a beating. By the age of 40, Voltaire was an established public figure. By his early fifties, he had a personal grievance against capricious government and the arrogance of rich aristocrats. Voltaire then went to England to avoid stirring up more trouble and perhaps to avoid further prosecution.

During his time in England, Voltaire met a number of famous writers and intellectuals, such as Jonathan Swift (1667–1745), Alexander Pope (1688–1744), and Lord Henry Bolingbroke (1678–1751). He subsequently wrote a book entitled *Philosophical Letters on the English* (1733), in which he praised English law, science, philosophy, and religious tolerance. Much of this was exaggerated and meant as a deliberate critique of France, and the Paris Court of Appeal condemned the book. He continued to read widely and began publication of a history entitled *The Century of Louis XIV*, which was a success.

In 1750 Voltaire was invited to Germany by the Prussian king Frederick the Great (1712–1786), who wanted to foster a society of advanced thinkers in Berlin. Voltaire had been in correspondence with the king for 14 years and this journey to Berlin was the beginning of a long exile from Paris, where he was afraid of being punished for his writing. Voltaire's stay with Frederick the Great lasted for two years but ended when the *philosophe* clashed with the Prussian's despotic temperament.

During the 1750s and 1760s, Voltaire became increasingly involved in crusades on behalf of victims of injustice. The most notable was Jean Calas, a Protestant from Toulouse who was put to death in a horrific, drawn-out public execution (1762) for the alleged murder of his own son, a crime he had supposedly committed to prevent the boy from converting to Catholicism. In response, Voltaire wrote a famous treatise on tolerance. Calas was found guilty by the local Catholic judiciary, but three years after the execution a court edict recognized that the case against Calas had in fact been unproven.

WEB CONNECTION

www.mcgrawhill.ca/links/legacy

Go to the site above to find out more about the works of Voltaire.

In the year following this court action, Voltaire was appalled by the July 1768 execution of the Chevalier de la Barre, a 19-year-old noble accused of mocking the Procession of the Sacrament and using obscene words while miming other religious rituals. The punishment was to apologize, bareheaded, and wear a coarse hair shirt while holding a heavy torch of "ardent wax" (that would sputter and scald) at the main door of Saint Wulfran Church. The Chevalier would then be taken to the place of execution in a cart while wearing a placard on his chest and back reading "impious." There, on his knees, he would confess his crime of blasphemy in a loud voice. The executioner would then cut out the young man's tongue and cut off his right hand. Finally, the young man was to be burned alive. During the execution there was a slight change of sentence: The Chevalier's head was cut off before he was burned. A copy of Voltaire's *Philosophical Dictionary* went into the flames as well. The judiciary's attitude toward blasphemy and Enlightenment ideas was evident in the ritualism and savagery of the sentence, and in the book burning. Voltaire campaigned against the cruelty of such punishments and used a famous sign-off in all his letters, *Écrasez l'infâme*" (Crush infamy), until the end of his life.

The second half of the eighteenth century has been described as a historical revolution, in that more objective sources and accounts of the past began to emerge. Instead of myths and legends, readers asked for evidence of what had taken place in previous centuries. In his *Essay on the Manners and Spirit of Nations* and other discourses written between 1753 and 1756, Voltaire would show how:

> ... A historian must limit himself and select from these immense collections which serve only to confuse. They constitute a vast storehouse from which you take what is necessary for your own purposes ... There is more writing in the archives of a single convent than in the annals of the Roman Empire ... Woe to details! Posterity neglects them all; they are a kind of vermin that undermines large works.

Voltaire was resolutely against looking at the past as a better time. Although well versed in the classics, he believed that it was more important to study the recent past, which is "essential for us to know," than to investigate a remote antiquity, which "only serves to satisfy our curiosity." Voltaire died in Paris, after returning from the triumphant staging of his last play. Few writers have had as profound an impact on their time and contemporaries as did Voltaire.

Cesare Beccaria

Cesare Beccaria (1738–1794), a nobleman from Milan, Italy, had strong views on the need to change the way the criminal justice system treated the accused. He associated with a group of writers who believed that harsh punishment did nothing to reform the individual. Beccaria especially enjoyed discussions generated by the intellectual periodical called *Le Café*. The *café* was a new sort of place where people could drink coffee, the new beverage from Africa, and discuss ideas. Unlike the *salon*, the *café* did not require a special invitation and the atmosphere was more casual.

Discussions with other lawyers and officials led Beccaria to write *On Crimes and Punishments*, published in 1764. It called for an end to the judicial torture of suspects and of capital punishment, and it met with huge international success. Many of the so-called

The oldest coffeehouse, or *café*, in Paris is *Le Procope*, founded in 1686. Notables such as Voltaire, Ben Franklin, young Thomas Jefferson, and actors from *le comédie française* sipped the new drink from Africa.

"enlightened" rulers, such as Frederick the Great of Prussia, Maria Theresa and Joseph II of the Hapsburg Empire, and the Grand Duke Leopold of Tuscany, expressed admiration for and a desire to follow the wise suggestions in Beccaria's book. Catherine the Great of Russia (1729–1796) invited Beccaria to take up residence at her court. English utilitarian philosopher Jeremy Bentham (1748–1832), who sought the greatest good for the greatest number, described Beccaria in glowing terms: "Oh my master! First evangelist of reason!" Bentham admired the moral earnestness, or what he called the censoriousness, of Beccaria's book.

Though Beccaria was lavishly praised by enlightened foreigners, a monk named Facchini published a book denouncing him as an enemy of religion. The Venetian Inquisition also attacked Beccaria's book, mistakenly attributing it to another author. The Spanish translation of the book was forbidden by the Council for Civil Censure, even for readers with a special licence to read "dangerous" books. Many in Europe remained in favour of torturing and executing criminals.

Jean-Jacques Rousseau

Jean-Jacques Rousseau (1712–1778) is considered one of the foremost European minds of the eighteenth century. He was most concerned with the moral reform of society. Personally, he was an eccentric loner who detested the *salons*. Often described as a harbinger of modernity, Rousseau was the man of the Enlightenment closest to the Jacobins, the most radical element of the French Revolution.

Rousseau could not accept the Enlightenment notion that the world was improving. In his famous treatise *The Social Contract* he would write: "Man was born free, and everywhere he is in chains." His moral indignation and sense of spiritual superiority echoed the Calvinism of his Swiss childhood in Geneva. His father had abandoned him when he was 10, so Rousseau had been apprenticed to an engraver who also treated him badly. At 16, Jean-Jacques began to travel, leaving behind the Protestant city of Geneva.

Rousseau had various love affairs, the most important of which was with a woman 10 years his senior, Madame de Warens, a Catholic Swiss baroness who helped perfect his education. In 1741 he went to Paris and took up with a chambermaid with whom he had five children, all of whom were abandoned to an orphanage. Rousseau had converted to Catholicism as a teenager but his worldview still had an obvious Protestant influence — he looked down on luxury and had a strong sense of individual responsibility. He thought that French life was too artificial, *salon* conversation too glib, manners too elaborate, the theatre too frivolous, and religion too concerned with ritual and appearance. Rousseau was also a music teacher, and wrote articles about music for the *Encyclopedia*, including one on a new system of musical notation.

In 1749 Rousseau submitted his *Discourse on the Arts and Sciences* to a competition at the Dijon Academy. This essay was about the effects of the progress of civilization upon morals. Rousseau argued that " ... our minds have been corrupted in proportion as our arts and sciences have made advances toward their perfection." Rousseau confronted the Enlightenment idea of progress head-on, praising the superiority of the natural "savage" state over the civilized one. The Academy awarded him the prize, printed his essay, and made him famous. Rousseau's second discourse, published in 1755, is concerned with the contrast between egotistical self-love, or *amour propre*, and the love of oneself, or *amour de soi-même*, which is a healthy instinct for self-preservation. He thus contrasted biological drives with those produced by society.

Early in the 1760s, Rousseau published *The Social Contract*, and a book on education called *Émile*. These met with immediate success but both were condemned in 1762 by the Paris parliament as contrary to the government and religion. Rousseau put forward new concepts of political authority, which he called the "general will" and "the common good."

Rousseau fled to Switzerland and three years later travelled to England, where the Scottish philosopher David Hume (1711–1776) helped him. Jean-Jacques began to write his autobiography, *Confessions*, a title that seems to be a reference to the classic work of St. Augustine (fifth century CE). By 1767 Rousseau had broken with Hume and returned to Paris. By 1777 his obvious mental instability made city life unbearable to him. Friends found him a country cottage near Ermonville, which he moved into in 1778 and where he died soon after.

Rousseau acknowledged that his introspection and self-analysis fuelled much of his work. He was attracted by the idea of childhood innocence corrupted by adulthood and sexuality. This contrast between innocence and experience was for him a paradigm of human life. Earlier humans seemed purer, less corrupt, and closer to nature, whereas the "adult" present was urban, brittle, and artificial. Contemporary conservatives instantly perceived the threat in this notion. The Irish-born politician and philosopher Edmund Burke (1729–1797) wrote that Rousseau was "a ferocious, low-minded, hard-hearted father, devoid of fine general feelings." Young Napoléon Bonaparte submitted an essay to the Lyon Academy in which he asked, "Oh Rousseau, why did you live for only 60 years! In the interests of virtue, you should have lived forever!" Yet, when Napoléon declared himself First Consul in a coup in 1799, he said to the nobleman who had provided Rousseau's last refuge: "Your Rousseau is a fool — he has led us to this pretty pass!"

Radical contemporaries of Rousseau were interested in his ideas. In the provincial city of Arras, a young man who was 20 when Rousseau died, avidly read *The Social Contract*. He was Maximilien de Robespierre (1758–1794), future leader of the Jacobins during the French Revolution. Another man who read Rousseau was Brissot de Warville, a leading figure of another revolutionary faction, the Girondins. Still another was Jean-Paul Marat, an army doctor and revolutionary who, like Rousseau, grew up in a Protestant environment, and who would become an advocate for the poor.

Adam Smith

Theoretical analysis of economies was on the increase in the eighteenth century. Perhaps the most famous economist of the time was Adam Smith (1723–1790), a Scot with a remarkable intellect. He was a proponent of free trade whose work was translated into many European languages before 1800. Smith's writings clearly reflect the intellectual, social, and economic conditions of the time. They not only contained a powerful message, but also prophesied a new order that would reshape the world in economic and social terms. His *Inquiry into the Nature and Causes of the Wealth of Nations* (1776) emphasized the need for free trade and argued that the invisible hand of competition should regulate the economy through supply and demand. Smith was thus against the existing mercantile system and in favour of greater, more competitive trade. Smith wrote: "Consumption is the sole end and purpose of all production; and the interest of the producer ought to be attended to, only so far as it may be necessary for promoting that of the consumer ... the mercantile system ... seems to consider production, and not consumption, as the ultimate end and object of all industry and commerce."

Unlike many of his contemporaries, whose fame came posthumously, Smith's work earned him fame during his own lifetime. In *The Wealth of Nations*, Smith advanced ideas that appealed to his contemporaries by seeming to justify their self-interested pursuit of wealth, and arguing that this activity was beneficial to society as a whole. Smith described a type of capitalist economy and tried to explain the laws that governed its operation. Ultimately, Smith was an optimist, but industrialists later used his theories to legitimize their exploitation of the working classes.

Immanuel Kant

An admirer of Rousseau, German philosopher Immanuel Kant (1723–1804) made systematic studies of ethics, logic, metaphysics, and aesthetics that influenced all later philosophy. The book considered his masterpiece is entitled *Critique of Pure Reason*. In this, and in his many other works, Kant patiently worked out the most comprehensive and influential philosophical program of the modern era. In Germany,

lively discussion went on during the 1780s about the meaning of the word *Aufklärung*, the German word for enlightenment. In his essay of 1784 entitled *What is Enlightenment?* Kant wrote:

> It is now asked whether we at present live in an enlightened age, the answer is: no, but we do live in an age of enlightenment. As things are at present, we still have a long way to go before men can be in a position (or can even be put into a position) of using their own understanding confidently and well in religious matters, without outside guidance. But we do have distinct indications that the way is now being cleared for them to work freely in this direction, and that the obstacles to universal enlightenment, to man's emergence from his self-incurred immaturity, are gradually becoming fewer.[1]

Like Voltaire, Kant saw "religious matters" — and freedom from bigotry and superstition — at the heart of enlightenment.

Edmund Burke

The Anglo-Irish philosopher Edmund Burke (1729–1797) presented the conservative view of the political situation in the eighteenth century in a clear and eloquent voice. Burke expressed grave concerns about the French Revolution and the consequences of rapid, widespread reforms in his work of 1790 entitled *Reflections on the Revolution in France*:

> The science of government being therefore so practical in itself and intended for such practical purposes — a matter which requires experience, and even more experience than any person can gain in his whole life, however sagacious and observing he may be — it is with infinite caution that any man ought to venture upon pulling down an edifice which has answered in any tolerable degree for ages the common purposes of society, or on building it up again without having models and patterns of approved utility before his eyes.

Burke believed in the importance to society of established institutions and traditions, and that throwing these out in favour of a new set of "natural" rights and abstract principles would lead to chaos and anarchy. According to Burke, society was a contract, a partnership not only between the living but also between the dead and the as yet unborn. Clearly articulating the essence of conservatism, Burke stated, "A spirit of innovation is generally the result of a selfish temper and confined views. People will not look forward to posterity, who never look backward to their ancestors."

Johann Gottfried von Herder

Johann Gottfried von Herder (1744–1803) was an exponent of the different characteristics of peoples, or, as some say, of national character. He attended university in northeastern Prussia at Königsberg. Between 1764 and 1769, the young von Herder lived in Riga, capital of Latvia. Riga was for von Herder what Geneva had been to Rousseau: a small, idealized city-state where he did not live, but which remained with him as a model of morality and patriotic spirit. He had gone to Latvia in order to avoid rigidly enforced military service in the Prussian army. He next moved to France in 1769, where he hoped to draft a constitution for Russia. In his multi-volumed work *Ideas on the Philosophy of the History of Mankind* (1784–1791), von Herder said that the future of humanity lay with what he characterized as "the tireless, peaceful Slavs." Von Herder, unlike most of the East European intelligentsia, did not admire French culture. When the opportunity presented itself, he left Paris for Strasbourg.

Working as a librarian in the German-speaking duchy of Weimar, von Herder wrote down his ideas on national character — today we would say ethnic identity. He became conscious of his German culture while living in cities where another language predominated. He thought of his "Germanness" not in terms of loyalty to a particular ruler or dynasty, or as a citizen of a state, but rather to a language and culture.

Von Herder was actually opposed to the individual, liberal contract theory of society advocated by the *philosophes*. He was influenced by Rousseau and emphasized feelings, emotions, and the need for shared sentiments. Von Herder believed that "essential force" (*Kraft* in German) was the cultural glue that bonded together individuals in a community, and that the core of this bond was language. He wrote: "Each nation speaks in the manner it thinks, and thinks in the manner it speaks." To him, a people without a common language was an absurdity. Von Herder thought that cultures could and should remain pure, that a people removed from its original habitat was weakened and degenerated. He studied folk poetry, which sprang from the creativity of working people and responded directly to the eternal questions of human existence. Some of von Herder's ideas would be echoed in the nationalism of the nineteenth century, and cause great suffering to ethnic minorities in countries where one, or more than one, language was spoken.

Marquis de Condorcet

The Marquis de Condorcet (1743–1794) is often referred to as the last of the *philosophes*. He marked the end of the universalizing, rationalistic Enlightenment and died in prison, probably by suicide, while awaiting execution by the new "rational" decapitating machine called the guillotine. He had been a critic of the *ancien régime* and welcomed the 1789 revolution enthusiastically. He was a distinguished mathematician who believed that the calm application of reason would bring about a better world. Condorcet was forced into hiding by his political enemies and it was during the Reign of Terror in France (1793–1794) that he wrote what is sometimes called the testament of the Enlightenment: *Sketch for a Historical Picture of the Progress of the Human Mind*, an intellectual history of humanity divided into 10 epochs. The enemies of clear thinking, Condorcet wrote, were priests of the various religions who kept their own power and wealth through the ignorance and subservience of the masses. In the tenth and last epoch, he hailed the triumph of enlightenment. Condorcet was also helpful in founding the Society of the Friends of the Blacks (1788), an anti-slavery group.

The Marquise du Châtelet

The ideals of the Enlightenment did little to free women of the eighteenth century from the constraints of a male-dominated society. Although *salons* allowed some women to engage in intellectual discourse, women were not given the same respect as men. The intellectual and artistic works of even the most influential women were denied a public and remained highly personal efforts. One woman whose work defied the odds and became public was the Marquise du Châtelet (1706–1749).

The Marquise du Châtelet had been married at a young age to one of the most prominent and powerful generals in the French army. A wide gulf in years and lack of similar interests may have been factors that prevented a loving relationship. What developed instead was an understanding that allowed the Marquise to pursue her interests in mathematics and science, and to carry on a lengthy romance with Voltaire.

Very few women in the early eighteenth century had the opportunities to express their intelligence and ideas as did the Marquise du Châtelet, a respected intellectual and long-time companion of Voltaire.

The Marquise du Châtelet had many talents and a nearly inexhaustible energy. In 1739 she and Voltaire made a trip to the Netherlands in order to resolve an outstanding lawsuit over one of her husband's estates. While on this trip, the Marquise spent three hours each day taking instruction in algebra from a tutor, another three hours a day working on algebraic equations by herself, and also took a crash course in law from two university professors so she would be able to understand the lawsuit. Despite this rigorous schedule, she found the time to begin translating Sophocles' play *Oedipus Rex*, which, when published, would become a classic in French theatre for over a century. While in the Netherlands, the Marquise hired a tutor to teach her Flemish, a language she could read and understand after only a month's instruction.

After four months, the Marquise du Châtelet won the lawsuit and she and Voltaire returned to France. The Marquise returned to her usual pattern of attending balls, fetes, galas, dinner parties and banquets in the evening, sleeping for two or three hours at sunrise, clearing her head by working through complex mathematical equations before breakfast, and devoting her days to the serious study of science.

In 1735 du Châtelet translated Bernard Mandeville's *Fable of the Bees*. Mandeville's work was a collection of essays including *An Enquiry into the Origin of Moral Virtue*. In the preface, du Châtelet states her observations about the status of women in her time:

> I feel the full weight of the prejudice which so universally excludes us from the sciences; it is one of the contradictions in life that has always amazed me, seeing that the law allows us to determine the fate of great nations, but that there is no place where we are trained to think. Let the reader ponder why, at no time in the course of so many centuries, a good tragedy, a good poem, a respected tale, a fine painting, a good book on physics has ever been produced by women. Why these creatures whose understanding appears in every way similar to that of men, seem to be

stopped by some irresistible force, this side of a barrier ... If I were king ... I would redress an abuse which cuts back, as it were, one half of humankind. I would have women participate in all human rights, especially those of the mind.[2]

In the fall of 1739, du Châtelet began a study of the philosophy and scientific theories of the famous German scientist Gottfried von Leibniz (1646–1716). By April 1740, she had finished writing *Institutions de Physique*, a book that explained the theories of Leibniz with brilliance, clarity, and precision. Du Châtelet's *Institutions* was greeted with much excitement among the intellectuals of France and helped to solidify her growing reputation as one of the leading intellectuals of her day.

History

BYTES

Throughout history and in all cultures the desecration of human remains has been reviled. Eighteenth-century surgeons, doctors and anatomists, however, needed cadavers to conduct scientific research. Often these scientists were provided with the bodies of criminals who had been executed for murder. The possibility of being dissected after death was more of a deterrent to crime than the actual execution. At public hangings, fights would break out between the loved ones of the deceased and the surgeons who were waiting to claim the bodies. A shortage of bodies through legal means led to the ghoulish (from the Arabic word *ghul*, a mythological creature that robbed graves and ate bodies) practice of grave robbing. Surgeons hired body snatchers in what was to become a thriving illegal business in eighteenth-century England. Despite the fact that grave robbing was a punishable crime, some anatomists kept their expensive secrets hidden for future study. This practice of storing human remains entered the vernacular of the time in the expression "skeleton in your closet." Mary Shelley's famous novel *Frankenstein* (1816) in part reflected society's abhorrence of grave robbing.

Review, Reflect, Respond

1. In a chart, summarize what you believe to be the most significant developments in political, economic, and social thought in the eighteenth century.

2. List two groups who opposed the Enlightenment and explain the basis of their opposition.

3. Underlying much of the work of Enlightenment philosophers was a belief in the perfectibility of society. Can we still learn from these ideas or were they just naive assumptions destined to fail?

The Enlightenment Embraced and Resisted

The Enlightenment was as much a general attitude as it was a set of programs. In some parts of Europe, it was most apparent as a demand for more rational government, standardization of weights and measures, free markets in grain and other commodities, better training for officials, more open justice, and an end to judicial torture; however, in Catholic countries, the Enlightenment was often seen as an enemy of faith.

The opposition was never simple or clear-cut. Eighteenth-century clerics were influenced by the prevailing intellectual climate of rationalism, deductive thinking, and a mistrust of emotionalism. Thus many archbishops, bishops, and parish priests began to look down on traditional activities such as the veneration of relics, the adoration of particular statues of saints or the Virgin Mary, the burning of candles at altars, ostentatious forms of piety such as vigils, self-flagellation, or attending numerous masses.

The Enlightenment had an indirect effect in weakening some traditional forms of belief. The archbishop of a small town in southern Italy, when asked by his bishop about the condition of faith in Francavilla in 1783, replied:

In this town, foolish credulity in demoniacal manifestations and in the superstitions to undo their effects prevails quite strongly. That ignorant people believe in them is not surprising, but that a few ecclesiastics, and especially monks, encourage these false beliefs and superstitions — whether out of ignorance or out of malice — is displeasing to all good people.

ENLIGHTENED DESPOTISM

The political literature, philosophical ideas, and artistic expressions of the French Enlightenment influenced a new breed of monarchs that included Frederick II of Prussia, Joseph II of Austria, and Catherine II of Russia. These rulers were students of a new science of good government designed to mobilize human and material resources in the interests of the welfare of the people and the power of the state.

Frederick the Great

Frederick the Great (1740–1786), the Prussian ruler from 1740–1786, defined a new type of monarch of the eighteenth century: the enlightened despot. He granted religious tolerance and freedom of the press. He established a law code and enforced general educational reforms. His military successes and domestic reforms made Prussia a powerful European nation, and his personal beliefs have been described as humanist rather than Christian. Frederick's humanist beliefs were articulated in his *Political Testament* of 1752: "It is no concern in politics whether the ruler has a religion or whether he has none. All religions, if one examines them, are founded on superstitious systems, more or less absurd.[3]" In the same testament, Frederick stated his basic theory of politics and the role of the sovereign: to maintain the peace and preserve the nobility, and to have a well-conducted government whose actions are well reasoned and whose purpose it is to strengthen the state and further its power. Frederick clearly defined the new breed of monarch as one who is an absolute ruler but acts with reason.

Catherine the Great

Catherine the Great (1762–1796) was a minor Germanic princess who became Empress of Russia after her eccentric and ineffectual Russian husband, Peter, was assassinated. She is considered one of the most successful European monarchs, but historical debate continues over the extent of Catherine's success at implementing enlightened ideals.

WEB CONNECTION

www.mcgrawhill.ca/links/legacy

Go to the site above to find out more about Catherine the Great of Russia.

Nevertheless, Catherine's many accomplishments on behalf of her people do reflect an enlightened personality at the helm of the ship of state. For example:

- Catherine excelled at empire building and added an additional 518 000 square kilometres to Russian territory.
- She established the first college of medicine to train doctors and surgeons, and decreed in 1775 that each Russian province have a hospital.
- In 1783 she appointed an educated and able woman, Princess Dashova, as the Director of the Academy of Science.
- In 1786 Catherine passed the Statute for Schools and this began a free public education system in Russia that included the education of girls and serfs (with the permission of their masters).
- She doubled the number of civil servants in Russia: firefighters, mapmakers, builders, and managers of orphanages and prisons.

As a patron of the arts, Catherine amassed artwork by the world's masters, commissioned the building of palaces and a theatre, wrote several operas, and corresponded with Voltaire and Diderot. She bought Diderot's library and Voltaire's books after both men had died, and donated them to the Imperial Library. Catherine was well educated in Enlightenment literature and philosophy.

Though Catherine the Great embraced several aspects of enlightenment thinking, she remained a despotic and ruthless monarch.

In terms of agricultural and industrial reforms, Catherine spearheaded important changes. She provided money to farmers to buy machinery and learn new agricultural techniques. She encouraged immigration into Russia, notably from her native Germany, to increase the rural population. Experts from England were brought to Russia to help build factories, warships, dockyards, and to facilitate agricultural reform. The number of factories in Russia increased from 984 at the beginning of her reign to 3 161 at its end. She focussed on silver mining and fur trading as two important exports that would enrich the Russian economy.

Despite all these dramatic changes, Catherine never liberated the millions of serfs in Russia. Ironically, though the Empress liked to converse with philosophers about liberal and enlightened ideas, she ruled Russia as a traditional monarch. An excerpt from her *Decree on Serfs* (1767) illustrates this point:

The Governing Senate ... has deemed it necessary to make known that the landlords' serfs and peasants owe their landlords proper submission and absolute obedience in all matters, according to the laws that have been enacted from time immemorial by the autocratic forefathers of Her Imperial Majesty and which have not been repealed, and which provide that all persons who dare to incite serfs and peasants to disobey landlords shall be arrested and taken to the nearest government office, there to be punished forthwith as disturbers of the public tranquillity, according to the laws and without leniency. And should it so happen that even after the publication of the present decree of Her Imperial Majesty any serfs and peasants should cease to give proper obedience to their landlords ... and should make bold to submit unlawful petitions complaining of their landlords, and especially to petition Her Imperial Majesty personally, then both those who make the complaints and those who write up the petitions shall be punished by the knout [whip] and forthwith deported to Nerchinsk to penal servitude for life and shall be counted as part of the quota of recruits which their landlords must furnish to the army.[4]

Despite her refusal to liberate the largest percentage of her population — perhaps due to threats, fear of alienating the nobility, or weakening the economy — Catherine's 34-year reign elevated Russia to the status of a major world power.

ART IN THE EARLY EIGHTEENTH CENTURY

To understand the art of the early eighteenth century, it helps to go back to the seventeenth century and look at the styles of that era: the baroque, and its counterpart, classicism. Baroque art can be seen as a reaction to the art and architecture of the Italian Renaissance. Whereas Renaissance art is static and appeals to the intellect, baroque art is dynamic, grandiose, and appeals to the emotions. Classicism in the seventeenth century was a reaction to the baroque style and a reworking of the Renaissance style on a grander scale. Classicists felt that baroque art was too emotional, too "real"; they preferred the ideal world of classical Greece and Rome.

Two seventeenth-century paintings that illustrate the conflict between these two styles are the *Descent from the Cross* by Flemish painter Peter Paul Rubens (1577–1640) and *Landscape with Polyphemus* by French painter Nicolas Poussin (1593–1665). The Rubens painting is a dramatic, physically graphic depiction of a dead body being brought down from the cross on which it had been hanging moments earlier. Death and the memory of pain and psychological anguish confront the

viewer. This is a dynamic, passionate work with a powerful interplay of light and shadow enhancing the drama.

The Poussin painting, on the other hand, has captured a moment in time; it is an ideal, tranquil image that follows strictly geometric forms. It is useful to compare the work of these two masters because many European painters in the seventeenth and eighteenth centuries, particularly the French, did just that. Artists saw their vocation divided into two schools: those who followed Rubens, the Rubenists, and those who followed Poussin, the Poussinists.

The early eighteenth century was very much a continuation of the style and aesthetics of the seventeenth century, which was strongly influenced by Louis XIV, a monarch whose tight political control extended to the arts. Louis established the Royal Academy of Painting and Sculpture in l648, a regulatory and academic institution meant to ensure that all "official" art met with the standards set by the state.

The standards of the state were further strengthened by the construction of the Palace of Versailles, designed to be a monument to the glory and power of the Sun King, Louis XIV. It became the model for many other European architectural projects in the seventeenth and eighteenth centuries. Versailles was to be a microcosm of Louis' absolute monarchy.

These two seventeenth-century paintings express the baroque and classical styles handed down to artists of the eighteenth century. *The Descent from the Cross* (1611) by Flemish artist Peter-Paul Rubens is a highly emotional work that uses dramatic light and shade and realistic detail to express the sorrow of the people removing Christ from the cross. *The Landscape with Polyphemus* (1648) by French artist Nicolas Poussin is classical in its geometrical forms, even lighting and balanced composition.

Although there is a baroque character to this enormous building, Louis favoured classicism. He felt it was more serious and better suited to his taste for displaying his power and influence.

Louis believed he could control not only his subjects, his country and much of Europe, but also nature itself. Versailles is the supreme example of the eighteenth-century desire to subordinate nature to the power of the human intellect. The huge formal gardens of Versailles tame nature and manipulate both it and the viewer, who strolls along the avenues encountering gushing fountains, sculptural tableaux, and colourful mazes of trees and flowers.

All over Europe, many royal and aristocratic families tried to emulate this enormous architectural achievement. Some of the resulting buildings were even designed to commemorate political victories over Louis XIV himself. In England, the Duke of Marlborough was given Blenheim Palace as a gift to commemorate his victory over the French at Blenheim, Belgium, during the War of the Spanish Succession. Some find this baroque palace too ponderous and theatrical, but like Versailles, it was built to celebrate power. Soon critics would begin to deplore this extravagance of the few at the expense of the many.

Rococo

When Louis XIV died in 1715, there was a period of relative calm. The formality and opulence of Versailles was countered by the more sensuous and ornate style called rococo. The word comes from the French word *rocaille*, which literally means "loose stones" and refers to the small shells that became a principal design element in

The Palace at Blenheim was built from 1705-1722 for the Duke of Marborough, ancestor of Sir Winston Churchill. These buildings show an English version of the baroque style: colossal, dramatic, awe-inspiring, here meant more as a monument to victory than a place to live.

rococo interiors. Unlike the interiors of Versailles, where enormous rooms and mirrored galleries overwhelmed, rococo interiors were smaller, lighter, and made people feel more at ease. This style was meant to serve the new, smaller, and elegant *appartements* being built in Paris.

Because its more intimate spaces gave the people a setting for conversation, the rococo *salon* became an extremely important part of eighteenth-century society. Influential women became the dominant figures in these *salons* as they brought together many of the greatest minds of the age. People conversed and exchanged ideas, many of which foreshadowed the social and political upheaval to come near the end of the century.

Painting in the later eighteenth century also took two paths that strongly reflected social and political trends. The painting of Antoine Watteau, a Rubenist

The rococo is more an interior design style than a painting style. All the decor, including furniture, wall coverings and paintings were meant to blend together into a light and intimate atmosphere.

In his short life, Antoine Watteau created few paintings, and the *Pilgrimage to Cythera* (1718-19) is perhaps his best-known. The society that these elegantly-dressed young people knew would be shattered by the end of the century. To what level of society do you think these people belong?

painter, illustrates the rococo aesthetic perfectly. His works may be compared to delicate pieces of chamber music, as consciously contrived as a rococo *salon*. However, there is a serious note — these paintings show a doomed society. The pleasure-seeking individuals in Watteau's paintings seem conscious of the fact that pleasure is fleeting, that the golden moment of European aristocracy is almost over. Watteau's *Pilgrimage to Cythera* depicts a group of visitors to the island of Cythera, the mythical birthplace of Venus, goddess of love, in search of pleasure. What should be a carefree outing is tinged with sadness at the realization that such pleasures are only momentary.

Compared to Watteau, Jean-Baptiste-Siméon Chardin (1699–1779) gives a very different view of French society in the eighteenth century. Chardin's paintings pay homage to the life of the French middle class. His simple interiors explore domestic life as people quietly go about their daily routines, untouched by extravagance or wealth. Chardin's paintings reveal a shifting of attention away from the aristocracy and onto the growing middle class. His paintings record *bourgeois* reality in intimate scenes of people attending to their lives and the objects with which they are surrounded.

In this painting, called *The Benediction* (1740), Chardin gives us a glimpse of middle-class life in eighteenth-century France. The young governess is teaching a little girl how to say her prayers. Both patrons and art critics of the time admired Chardin's art for its realism and quiet intimacy.

Paintings such as this, titled *The Stolen Kiss* (1775), fit well into a rococo decor. The artist, Fragonard, developed a unique style and used it in hundreds if paintings, most of which were romantic or erotic subjects.

MUSIC IN THE EIGHTEENTH CENTURY

Like the art and architecture of the eighteenth century, the music of the period may be divided into two styles. The first half of the century was dominated by the baroque (which had begun in the early seventeenth century) and the second half saw the emergence of classicism.

Like painters, sculptors and architects, musicians continued to be patronized by the rich courts of Europe. Like the monumental buildings erected to the glory of kings and aristocrats, their music, whether religious or secular, reflected the wealth and power of those who commissioned it. Nevertheless, baroque masters such as Johann Sebastian Bach (1685–1750) and George Frideric Handel (1685–1759) were still able to experiment and make lasting achievements in music within the existing forms of the time. The baroque style itself was meant to arouse emotions and was characterized by an often complex logic, along with unifying themes and variations. Typical baroque forms include the fugue, the prelude, and the cantata.

Handel was a master of the opera, a form of drama or comedy that blends instrumental and vocal music. Since opera usually involves many participants — soloists, a chorus, actors, and sometimes dancers — it is a difficult art form to produce successfully. The plot of the opera is carried forward by a musical narration called a recitative. The aria, perhaps the equivalent to a soliloquy or monologue in a play, is usually a long song revealing the emotions or thoughts of a character. In the eighteenth century, opera, like film today, became the most popular entertainment for aristocrats and common people alike.

Handel was a German composer who spent most of his adult life in England, where he enjoyed being a part of the royal court and prospered as one of the directors of the Royal Academy of Music. He was a prolific opera writer, composing 40 in only 30 years. Among Handel's religious "operas," called oratorios, are *The Messiah* (with the famous *Hallelujah* chorus), *Israel in Egypt*, and *Solomon*. Several other Handel works, such as *Dido and Aeneas, The Clemency of Titus*, and *Xerxes* were on classical themes. Handel's operas strongly influenced composers such as Wolfgang Amadeus Mozart later in the eighteenth century.

The development of the classical style in music is consistent with the classicism in painting and architecture at this time. The four masters of this period were three Austrians — Franz Joseph Haydn (1732–1809), Wolfgang Amadeus Mozart (1756–1791), and Franz Peter Schubert (1797–1828) — and one German, Ludwig van Beethoven (1770–1827). It was during the classical period that the orchestra as we know it today was fully developed, and some of the best-loved symphonies composed. Concerts were given in large halls so composers had an opportunity to perform their works before a far wider public than ever before. Classical music is noted for its recognizable structure, melodies, and multiple, varied themes. Classical composers often incorporated folk and traditional elements into their music, making it even more appealing to their new middle-class audiences.

While large orchestras performed symphonies, smaller groups of musicians continued to perform what is called chamber music. In its elegance, intimacy and lyricism, chamber music reflected the more private atmosphere of the *salons*. Favourite forms of chamber music are string quartets (four musicians), and other groupings of instruments such as woodwind octets (eight musicians) and the concerto, a composition in movements for a solo instrument accompanied by an orchestra.

LITERATURE IN THE EIGHTEENTH CENTURY

England tended to dominate the literary scene in the eighteenth century, as it had done for centuries before. The literature of the eighteenth century comprised a period that began in the mid-seventeenth century with the Restoration of the English monarchy after the Puritan Revolution of 1649, and ended with the French Revolution in 1789. During these turbulent political times, English writers were still very much at the whim of those who financed their art. Charles II, for example, was a staunch patron of the arts and, when he became king, brought musicians and painters from the European continent to enliven his court. He also encouraged the theatre.

In the late seventeenth century, England was recovering from puritanical austerity and the people were hungry for pleasure and luxury. But, by the late eighteenth century, England under George II was being run by the practical and powerful prime minister Robert Walpole. Since Walpole had no interest in literature, writers had to look to publishers (rather than the court) to make a living. Writers had to appeal to a broad literate public in order to support themselves. As with painting and music, literature began to focus on the affairs of the middle class and came to protest the political and moral corruption of the ruling bodies of church and state. Satire was born and literature became a powerful social tool.

Music for the Royal Fireworks by George Frideric Handel

George Frideric Handel (1685–1759), though born in Germany, was a favourite in the court of England's George I (probably because George I, though King of England, spoke only German). It therefore came as no surprise to the court and to other working musicians that His Majesty King George I repeatedly asked Handel to compose pieces for special occasions. The *Music for the Royal Fireworks* is one of those pieces.

The *Music for the Royal Fireworks* was commissioned to celebrate the end of the War of the Austrian Succession in 1748. On April 23, 1749, the public was invited to a grand celebration in Green Park, London, where fireworks of unsurpassed magnificence were to be displayed both on land and on barges floating on the Thames River in London. Giovanni Servandoni, the then famous Italian pyrotechnical genius, was brought in by the Duke of Richmond especially for the occasion. Servandoni erected a gigantic arch and prepared all the rockets and missiles. The stage was set for a truly grand spectacle. The planning had been perfect except for one detail — the weather. It rained (this was England, after all) and only a fraction of the fireworks went off as planned. Also, in the middle of it all the grand arch and all the scaffolding caught fire. Although only the overture to the *Music for the Royal Fireworks* was actually performed before the fire and the rain sent everyone running for cover, the full piece had been given a wonderful public rehearsal before a crowd of 12 000 several days earlier. The music was a hit.

This painting shows the first, official performance of Handel's *Music for the Royal Fireworks*. Note the barges in front carrying the musicians, some of the fireworks, and the members of the court as spectators.

Besides the fiasco on the night of the grand celebration, Handel had had other troubles with King George I. The king had insisted that the piece be purely military music, using winds and drums — no strings allowed. Handel, being a great and honoured composer, knew that the piece had to have a string section. He played it the king's way for the huge public rehearsal and for the celebration night, but then rewrote it to include strings for all future performances. Whatever George I and the excited crowd heard in 1749 compared to what we hear today (in symphony halls, shopping malls, and elevators), there is no doubt that Handel's *Music for the Royal Fireworks* is a work of art that has remained popular for nearly 300 years.

1. Handel wrote for other royal occasions and composed many operas. Do some research on Handel's most famous works and the occasions they celebrated.

2. Think about a major occasion of recent times. What music was composed for it and by whom?

Literary Theory

The Restoration period in England, starting in 1660, signalled the start of the neoclassical movement in literature, a reaction to the extravagance of the European literature of the late Renaissance and early seventeenth century — and the violent politics that accompanied it. Writers of the late seventeenth century tried to express their ideas through the classical ideals of order, simplicity, and reason. French literature under Louis XIV, as well as French fashions and manners imported by Charles II, had a great influence on English society; however, English writers felt that English literature should stay true to the tradition of Chaucer and Shakespeare and tried to remain wholly English in character by resisting these influences.

English writers called this period of neoclassical literature the Augustan Age because its literature was strongly influenced by the Roman writers Virgil and Horace. These two writers had celebrated the peace and order brought to Rome when the Emperor Augustus ended the civil war that broke out when Julius Caesar died. Writers now applied classical standards to poetry, just as classical standards were being applied to painting. A poet had to be a genius endowed with imagination, but these gifts had to be tamed by order, form, and wit.

The poetry of the Augustan age was strictly formal. A particularly disciplined form of poetic expression was the heroic couplet. Each couplet contained a pithy or witty pronouncement on some aspect of nature, society, or humanity in general. The master of this form was Alexander Pope (1688–1744). Here is a famous line from his *Essay on Man*: "Know then thyself, presume not God to scan. The proper study of mankind is Man." Later, blank verse, or unrhymed iambic pentameter, became a popular form that gave slightly more freedom to poets.

Restoration and eighteenth-century literature expressed moral truths through a variety of genres. One reaction to Puritanism resulted in a genre known as Restoration Comedy. These comedies, meant to encourage moral reform, were inspired by the corruption in court and in the political arena. They were full of satire and sexual intrigue and humour, very much like Roman comedy.

This was also a heyday for newspapers. Ideas and opinions were expressed through newspapers such as the famous *Tatler*. Just as eighteenth-century France created the *salon* as a place to exchange ideas, eighteenth-century England created the coffeehouse, where people gathered to drink coffee, read the paper, converse, and criticize the government.

Pleasures
AND PASTIMES

The culinary invention of John Montague, the fourth Earl of Sandwich, is a testament to the prevalence of gambling as a popular pastime of eighteenth-century society. Not wanting to interrupt his game of chance, Montague ordered roast beef on toast to be served to him directly at the gaming table instead of at the traditional dining table. Gambling was popular among rich and poor, male and female, young and old alike. Games of chance with dice and cards were played as well as bets taken on cockfights and bear baiting. Gambling dens were often the targets of police raids. One employee would be in charge of swallowing the dice during such raids. Wealthy travellers would form gambling parties to pass the time during their European trips. Coffee houses were frequented by those who wanted both to play a game of chance and buy legitimate stocks in companies.

The two masters of social criticism in eighteenth-century England were Alexander Pope and Jonathan Swift. As England was becoming a world power to rival France, so the corruption in the court and government became more and more apparent. Alexander Pope wrote brilliant essays on social problems but his most famous work is his mock epic, *The Rape of the Lock*, where he satirizes the shallow behaviour and values of the court. The plot is simple: A young dandy interferes with the coiffure of a beautiful society woman. He cuts off a lock of hair and the result is a battle of the sexes of epic proportions. Pope includes all features of the traditional epic form: invocation to the muse, epic battles, epic heroes, and heroines. The poem is a brilliant satire

Wolfgang Amadeus Mozart (1756–1791)

Mozart is a genius unparallelled in the history of music. He was a key figure in modernizing music of the late eighteenth century to create a revolutionary new classical style. The musical feats of Mozart's youth provide the standard by which we measure prodigies today. By age seven he had performed for Empress Maria Theresa of Austria. Soon his audiences were the kings and queens of Europe, who marvelled at the precocious youngster's otherworldly talent.

Mozart's father, Leopold, a music teacher in the court of the Archbishop of Strasbourg, had ambitions for his son and guided the young musician's career by organizing exhausting performance tours of Europe's cultural capitals, all the while supervising his musical education.

During the 1760s and 1770s, while travelling to the royal courts of Europe, Mozart received an unrivalled musical education — he heard new music, met composers, and absorbed different musical ideas and styles. At the same time, he was developing his astounding talent for composing music. As an adolescent, Mozart was named concertmaster in the court of the Archbishop of Salzburg. Like many musicians of his day, he was employed under a system of patronage, which meant he could perform only with the permission of his patron, the Archbishop.

Mozart as a young man by an unknown, eighteenth-century artist.

Mozart, who had a playful, irreverent and rebellious personality, chafed at the creative restrictions imposed on him. He had a strained relationship with the Archbishop until the composer moved to Vienna in 1781.

In the late eighteenth century, Vienna was the musical capital of Europe, and Mozart's move there began the most creatively productive period of his life, a time when he produced much of the music for which he is remembered. In Vienna, Mozart became one of the world's first freelance musicians, teaching music and composing works on commission. At this time, it was unheard of for a musician to work independently of the direct support and control of an aristocratic patron. With his great talent, Mozart initially prospered. But, although he flourished creatively, he increasingly fell from favour among the nobles who had once commissioned work from him. The last 10 years of his life were spent in a day-to-day struggle for financial survival.

Tension on a social level was also pervasive in Mozart's lifetime. He lived during the period when the European feudal era was coming to an end, and many people were championing freedom and individual rights. Mozart was 20 when the Declaration of Independence of the United States was written, and 33 when the Parisian mob stormed the Bastille at the beginning of the French Revolution. The forces liberating eighteenth-century society were reflected in the arts, and Mozart was a major catalyst in revolutionizing music as well. The prevailing musical style had been baroque, which was very much associated with the aristocracy and reflected a grand world of social stability. Mozart, influenced by his close musical contemporary Franz Joseph Haydn (1732–1809), forged a new classical style that emphasized balance, symmetry, and emotional expression. This style would also appeal to the emerging middle class.

Artistic change is seldom easily accepted, and Mozart's audience in Vienna, still mainly composed of nobility, was slow to appreciate his more democratized music. Mozart's best-known works, such as the opera *The Marriage of Figaro* (1786), in which the plot centres on class conflict, met with a lukewarm response in Vienna, but became a sensation in Paris.

In the final year of his life, desperate financial circumstances could not stifle Mozart's irrepressible creativity as he produced unforgettable works displaying the versatility of his genius. One, a joyous work for the masses that incorporated ideas related to the Freemasons (Mozart was a Mason), was the fantastic fairy-tale opera *The Magic Flute*. The other, his final masterpiece, the *Requiem*, was commissioned by a mysterious count in memory of his late wife. Mozart became obsessed with completing this work, seeing it as his own requiem. He did not live to finish the composition, which had to be completed by one of his pupils. Mozart became seriously ill and died on December 5, 1791, at only 35 years of age. His family was so deeply in debt that his wife chose the cheapest funeral arrangements possible. The man who was perhaps the greatest musical genius of all time was buried in a common, unmarked grave.

Mozart's Musical Legacy

Some comments about Mozart from fellow musicians:
- Johannes Brahms (1833–1887) on Mozart's *Marriage of Figaro*: "In my opinion, each number in *Figaro* is a miracle; it is totally beyond me how anyone could create anything so perfect."
- Ludwig von Beethoven (1770–1827) commented to a student on Mozart's String Quartet in A major, "That's where Mozart said to the world: 'Behold what I might have done for you if the time were right!'"

A Masterful Musical Legacy

In 1862 an Austrian musicologist Ludwig von Kochel listed Mozart's works, which totaled 626 pieces. The range of his great talent includes:

- 18 operas plus stage works and ballets
- 8 oratorios and cantatas
- 20 Masses
- about 80 vocal and instrumental compositions
- 40 Lieder for song and pianos
- 40 canons for voices
- more than 50 symphonies
- almost 30 piano and orchestra concertos
- about 7 violin and orchestra concertos
- around 20 divertimentos
- 10 serenades
- 3 cassations
- more than 15 church sonatas
- 30 trios, quartets, and quintets for strings and piano
- 15 wind compositions
- 20 violin and piano sonatas

---

1. Even today there are musical prodigies in the public view, though most are musicians rather than composers. Do some research for information about a musical prodigy known today, and write a one-page biography of her or him.

on the hypocrisies and foibles of eighteenth-century court society; it also points to a certain charm and beauty within the shallowness.

Review, Reflect, Respond

1. Historical personalities such as Catherine the Great and Jean-Baptiste Chardin represent the ideals of the Enlightenment in action. Define the enlightened personality.

2. Compare and contrast baroque and neoclassical art and music. How did artistic changes between the early and late eighteenth century reflect intellectual changes of the time?

3. How important was the literature of the Enlightenment as a form of social commentary? Explain your answer.

The Letters of Madame de Graffigny

Madame de Graffigny (1695–17?) was an extraordinary mind of the eighteenth century. Her vast body of work, which included a novel, plays and over 2 500 letters, is a window into the daily life of women during the Age of Enlightenment. Born Françoise d'Happoncourt in 1695, Madame de Graffigny married François Huguet de Graffigny, an abusive man who drank heavily and gambled. When her husband died at a relatively young age, he left her with virtually no money. Using her ingenuity and the generosity of others, Madame de Graffigny was able not only to survive but also to establish herself as a major writer. After staying with Voltaire and Madame du Châtelet at Cirey for a couple of months, she moved to Paris, where she pursued a literary career.

In 1747 Madame de Graffigny published her highly successful novel *Letters of a Peruvian Woman*, which became a bestseller and was reprinted 46 times over the next 30 years. Although *Letters of a Peruvian Woman* fell out of favour with the reading public during the nineteenth century, it is currently enjoying renewed success as required reading in some university courses.

The novel tells the story of Inca princess Zilia, who is taken to France. What makes this novel compelling reading is de Graffigny's brilliant use of the main character to create a new type of heroine, a model for the Age of Enlightenment. When she learns she is to be brought to France, Zilia announces, "I seek enlightenment with an urgency that consumes me." Once in France and accustomed to the language, Zilia becomes de Graffigny's voice of social satire. Through her main character, de Graffigny is critical of the superficiality of women's education and of the institution of marriage, into which women are thrust when they are too young and without proper preparation.

The greatest insights into life in the eighteenth century are contained in the 2 500 letters Madame de Graffigny wrote to her close friend François Antoine Devaux over a 25-year period. In these letters, de Graffigny and Devaux shared their thoughts on everything, pushing their platonic friendship to the limit. In one letter de Graffigny pleaded, "Tell me what you've drunk, eaten, peed. I'll be glad to know everything." Through the vast body of correspondence, we learn a great deal about life in the eighteenth century, from problems related to travel (how far one can go before changing horses, when it is advisable to travel with a friend) to how it felt to be cold, ill, poorly housed, and lacking money. Letters written upon her arrival in Paris give detailed impressions of the city, including bridges, palaces, and monuments.

The Eighteenth-Century Novel

The eighteenth century saw a rebirth of the novel, a genre that appealed to a wide audience and provided a means to teach a moral lesson or satirize a social situation. Daniel Defoe's novel *Robinson Crusoe* (1719) was an adventure story with serious undertones. Defoe also wrote the comic novel *Moll Flanders* (1723), defying convention by creating a female protagonist who enjoys many adventures by using her intelligence and sexual

Jonathan Swift: Power to the Pamphlets

Jonathan Swift (1667–1745), author of such works as *Gulliver's Travels*, is one of history's best-known satirists. Many of Swift's shorter satirical pieces appeared in early-eighteenth-century pamphlets, periodicals, and newspapers. The emerging middle class felt freer than in previous years to voice its political opinions, and these often-ephemeral publications became extremely popular and influential. Within their pages, readers would find essays on topics of general interest, short fiction, poems, book reviews, or light satirical pieces. Indeed, satire was the popular voice for expressing political dissatisfaction. Among the most influential newspapers of the day was *The Tatler*, with essays written by Richard Steele (1672–1729), and *The Spectator*, by Joseph Addison (1672–1719) and Steele.

In his early London days, Swift held Whig, or liberal views. But, because of the fame he gained by writing for early pamphlets, the ruling Tories, or conservatives, recruited Swift to pen scathing attacks on their political opponents. When the Tories lost power in 1714, Swift returned to his native Dublin as dean of St. Patrick's Cathedral and soon began working for Irish independence. He became incensed at the ill treatment of the Irish by the English. Swift began using his powerful writing talent to sway public opinion in favour of Irish independence.

Jonathan Swift (1667-1745)

In 1723 he won immense popularity when his *Drapier's Letters* foiled a plan to impose a new copper currency on Ireland. Dubliners responded to Swift's satirical writing by demonstrating in the streets and sending petitions to Parliament against the plan.

Among Swift's most enduring works, *A Modest Proposal* (1729) is considered by many to be the finest short satire in English. Swift responds with bitter irony to English suggestions of the day that Ireland's overpopulation might be solved by allowing the king of France to conscript Irish citizens, or that young people be sent to Australia.

A Modest Proposal by Jonathan Swift

It is a melancholy object to those who walk through this great town or travel in the country, when they see the streets, the roads, and cabin doors, crowded with beggars of the female sex, followed by three, four, or six children, all in rags and importuning every passenger for alms. These mothers, instead of being able to work for their honest livelihood, are forced to employ all their time in strolling to beg sustenance for their helpless infants: who as they grow up either turn thieves for want of work, or leave their dear native country to fight for the pretender in Spain, or sell themselves to the Barbados.

I think it is agreed by all parties that this prodigious number of children in the arms, or on the backs, or at the heels of their mothers, and frequently of their fathers, is in the present deplorable state of the kingdom a very great additional grievance; and, therefore, whoever could find out a fair, cheap, and easy method of making these children sound, useful members of the commonwealth, would deserve so well of the public as to have his statue set up for a preserver of the nation ...

I shall now therefore humbly propose my own thoughts, which I hope will not be liable to the least objection. I have been assured by a very knowing American of my acquaintance in London, that a young healthy child well nursed is at a year old a most delicious, nourishing, and whole-some food, whether stewed, roasted, baked, or boiled; and I make no doubt that it will equally serve in a fricassee or a ragout. I do therefore humbly offer it to public consideration that of the 120 000 children already computed, 20 000 may be reserved from breed, whereof only one-fourth part to be males; which is more than we allow to sheep, black cattle, or swine; and my reason is, that these children are seldom the fruits of marriage, a circumstance not much regarded by our savages, therefore one male will be sufficient to serve four females. That the remaining 100 000 may, at a year old, be offered in sale to the persons of quality and fortune throughout the kingdom; always advising the mother to let them suck plentifully in the last month, so as to render them plump and fat for a good table.

A child will make two dishes at an entertainment of friends; and when the family dines alone, the fore or hind quarter will make a reasonable dish, and seasoned with a little pepper or salt will be very good boiled on the fourth day especially in winter.

1. Political satire like this can be found in newspapers, magazines, and on television. Find a contemporary piece of political satire and comment on its effectiveness.

2. What kind of reaction do you think Swift's satire received from the upper class and from the lower classes?

charms. It was Samuel Richardson whom many believe was the master of the novel form in his book *Pamela*. *Pamela* is the story of a housemaid in an aristocratic domain. Her virtue is constantly under attack by the lecherous master, and the novel is a series of letters describing her situation in a serious tone. Richardson was attempting to expose the immorality of his society through his novel. Henry Fielding did a parody of Richardson's *Pamela* in his work *Joseph Andrews*, where a young man encounters problems similar to Pamela's. Fielding also took the comic novel to greater extremes in *Tom Jones*.

No discussion of the eighteenth century would be complete without reference to Samuel Johnson (1709–1784), an archetypal eighteenth-century man. He was a neoclassical humanist who defended the ideals of the Augustan Age and deplored the rising tide of sentimentality that foreshadowed romanticism. Johnson's *Dictionary of the English Language* gives a wonderful sense of eighteenth-century humour, wit, and sensibility. He gathered around him a literary circle that worshipped him and his work. Johnson's death in 1784 signalled the end of the Augustan Age and the beginning of the romantic period in English literature.

Reflections

As in every age, era or century, one is always aware of tensions between opposing bodies of thought. Born of the rigid, academic world of Louis XIV, the character of the early eighteenth century reflected the order the French king imposed on European society. History has taught us that human beings cannot stay under such control for long without reacting in some way. People in the eighteenth century slowly came to regard freedom of thought and spirit as something to strive for, and, at the end of the century, something to die for. The arts during the century, within the confines of order and structure, show a gradual movement toward the acceptance of emotion and sensation as legitimate subjects for art. We appreciate the eighteenth century for its reaffirmation of the beauty and forms of the classical period, and its recognition of people from all walks of life. By the end of the eighteenth century, the romantic period signalled the movement from a world that celebrated order and reason to a world that rejoiced in freedom and feelings.

Chapter Review

Chapter Summary

In this chapter, we have seen:

- how an increase in literacy and developments in science and technology contributed to significant change during the eighteenth century
- how the arts reinforced and reflected the prevailing social and political values of the eighteenth century
- that various intellectuals of the Enlightenment contributed to the advancement of individual and collective human rights
- how the growing middle class became a force for economic and political change

Reviewing the Significance of Key People, Concepts, and Events (Knowledge and Understanding)

1. Understanding the history of Europe in the eighteenth century requires a knowledge of the following concepts and people and an understanding of their significance to the Enlightenment. Select and briefly explain three from each column below.

Concepts	People
agricultural revolution	Voltaire
enclosure	Louis XIV
Enlightenment	John Locke
intellectuals	Baron de Montesquieu
Freemasonry	Cesare Beccaria
deism	Jean-Jacques Rousseau
rococo	Adam Smith

2. This chapter describes the essence of the Enlightenment. Create a mind map that explains how this essence is reflected in each of the following areas: art, music, literature, politics, crime and punishment.

Doing History: Thinking About the Past (Thinking/Inquiry)

3. Frank Manuel, a historian of ideas, argued that the *philosophes* of the eighteenth century introduced a new moral outlook that was particularly modern. In *The Age of Reason*, Manuel summarized:

> Although the *philosophes* did not solve the problem of the existence of evil and suffering in the world, they did manage to establish in European society a general consensus about conduct which is evil, a moral attitude which still sustains us ... the eighteenth-century men of letters did formulate a set of moral principles which to this day remain basic to any discussion of human rights.

> Considering the values of our society, do you think that Manuel gives a plausible view of the Enlightenment? Has he accurately described the importance of the *philosophes* in shaping the morality of the modern world?

4. When studying the ideas of the Enlightenment, we see a theme that has been common in European history since the Renaissance: a growing faith in human progress and achievement. Is there a cause-and-effect relationship between Renaissance humanism and the ideals of the Enlightenment? Explain your view.

Applying Your Learning (Application)

5. Compare the paintings by Chardin and Fragonard in this chapter (page 156). Which of these paintings would you purchase for your living room, and why? How are the theme, style, and content of the Chardin different from the Fragonard?

6. Imagine that you are a journalist of the eighteenth century and have the opportunity to interview one of the following people: Adam Smith, Jean-Jacques Rousseau, Voltaire, Cesare Beccaria, the Marquise du Châtelet. Prepare a list of five questions that would help assess the impact of their ideas in the eighteenth century. Your questions must be accompanied by answers you might have received. Base your questions and answers on research you can gather about the person and the time period.

Communicating Your Learning (Communication)

7. Prepare a biographical sketch of one of the monarchs of the eighteenth century for inclusion in Diderot's *Encyclopedia*. Be sure to evaluate his or her role in bringing about change or maintaining continuity. Your biographical sketch should be between 500 and 750 words.

8. Prepare a real estate flyer that lists at least three homes from the eighteenth century for sale. Your listings must include at least one home from a rural community, one from an urban community, the home of an intellectual, and the home of a member of the aristocracy. Include a picture or a sketch with a description of the home highlighting its key features.

CHAPTER FIVE

Revolution to Restoration 1789 – 1815

CHAPTER EXPECTATIONS

By the end of this chapter, you will be able to:

- *evaluate the key factors that led to conflict and war during the French Revolution and the Napoleonic period*

- *demonstrate an understanding of the intensity and breadth of change that took place during the French Revolution*

- *assess the extent to which art reinforced or challenged the prevailing social and political values of the period between 1789 and 1815*

- *demonstrate an understanding of the rise of the modern nation-state in the West during the period of the French Revolution*

Allegory of the Revolution (1794) by Jeaurat de Bertray. This painting is full of Revolutionary symbols and ideas. It was painted during the most radical phase of the French Revolution.

In the spring of 1789, the French Revolution set in motion a series of events that would redefine the government, the French constitution, the role of the church in society, and the very nature of French society itself. Despite the eventual restoration of the Bourbon monarchy after the fall of Napoléon, neither France nor the rest of Western Europe would ever be the same again. A decade of revolution followed by fifteen years of Napoleonic rule ensured that the break with France's feudal, aristocratic past was complete and irrevocable. By 1815 a new Europe had been created out of what was left after 25 years of war and revolution.

The French Revolution was the product of a century of intellectual change, a growing gulf between rich and poor, and growing dissatisfaction with the absolute monarchy governing France. The radical social, political, and constitutional change that was the French Revolution is tightly wound into the history of the eighteenth century as a whole. The intellectual ferment of the Enlightenment, which was examined in Chapter Four, took place within a society still rooted in the medieval world of the *ancient régime*. Aristocratic privilege continued to deny rights to the majority of the French people, and wealth was concentrated in the hands of a very small minority. This chapter will reveal the different lives led by the rich and poor in France, and how the so-called "enlightened" laid the foundation for the revolution that would engulf Europe. Here also will be an account of the French Revolution, the subsequent Napoleonic period, and the lasting impact of the revolution in France and the rest of Europe.

KEY CONCEPTS AND EVENTS

third estate
Estates-General
National Assembly
The Tennis Court Oath
salon
Storming of the Bastille
The October Days
Reign of Terror
Declaration of the Rights
    of Man and of the
    Citizen
Code Napoléon
Congress of Vienna

KEY PEOPLE

Louis XVI
Marie Antoinette
Girondins
Jacobins
Mirabeau
Maximilien de Robespierre
Jacques-Louis David
Madame Roland
Napoléon Bonaparte

Wit and Wisdom

O Liberty, what crimes are committed in thy name! [1]
The last words of Madame Roland, before she was guillotined on November 9, 1793

TIME LINE: REVOLUTION TO RESTORATION

Jacques-Louis David completes the painting *Oath of the Horatii*	1784	
	1789 (May)	King Louis XVI recalls the Estates-General for the first time in 175 years
Tennis Court Oath; The French Revolution begins	1789 (June)	
	1789 (July)	The fall of the Bastille
Slavery abolished in France	1791	
	1792	Establishment of the French Republic
Attempted constitutional monarchy ends with the execution of Louis XVI	1793	
	1794	The Reign of Terror reaches its height; Robespierre falls from power (July)
Oligarchy known as the Directory fails to restore order in France	1794–1799	
	1799	Napoléon seizes power in a *coup d'état*
Code Napoléon declared the new constitution of France and Napoléon crowns himself emperor	1804	
	1805	Napoléon's victory at Austerlitz
Beethoven completes his *Symphony Number Five*	1808	
	1814	Napoléon attempts the conquest of Europe; he is defeated after a failed invasion of Russia
Napoléon defeated at the Battle of Waterloo	1815 (June)	
	1815 (June)	Congress of Vienna brings the revolution to an end and restores European monarchies, including the Bourbons in France with Louis XVIII
Second exile of Napoléon	1815	

Not to scale.

BEFORE THE REVOLUTION

Europe in Transition

The eighteenth century was an important transitional period in the history of modern Europe. Prior to the eighteenth century, few talked of social or political equality or the inherent rights of all people. By contrast, the twentieth century was undoubtedly a democratic age in which all human beings were believed by most to have equal and inalienable rights. It is to the eighteenth century that we must look for seeds of the change that would come in the nineteenth and twentieth centuries. Eighteenth-century intellectuals, such as Voltaire, Rousseau and Diderot, talked of a new age, an age born with the ideals and promises of the French Revolution. By the end of the eighteenth century, Europe was on the road to revolutionary change, which could be seen in all aspects of life. Perceptions of class would be radically altered by Enlightenment ideals, as would views regarding children, family, and even crime and punishment.

Communities

As with many societies, France in the eighteenth century was comprised of many distinct communities, each with its own issues, concerns, and view of the world. Although enlightened thinkers such as Rousseau and Voltaire concerned themselves with the plight of the poor, they were isolated from the rural population. Similarly, other than the widespread anger and opposition to the rule of Louis XVI, Parisians had little in common with the country folk and peasants living in towns and villages throughout France. In the end, all these disparate communities would unite either in support of or in opposition to the revolution that was about to tear apart the fabric of society.

Rural Communities

A poor woodcutter lived with his wife and two children on the edge of a large forest. The boy was called Hansel and the girl Gretel. The woodcutter did not have much food around the house and, when a great famine devastated the entire country, he could no longer provide enough for his family's daily meal. One night, as he was lying in bed thinking about his worries, he began tossing and turning. He sighed and said to his wife: "What's to become of us? How can we feed our poor children when we don't even have enough for ourselves?" "I'll tell you what," answered his wife. "Early tomorrow morning, we'll take the children out into the forest where it is most dense. We'll build a fire and give them each a piece of bread. Then we'll go about our work and leave them alone. They won't be able to find their way back home and we'll be rid of them ..." [2]

What do folktales and fairy tales such as *Hansel and Gretel* and other stories by the Brothers Grimm, reveal about aspects of the society that created them?

The story goes on to describe how the hungry children wandered through the forest and found a house made of cake and candy. Inhabiting this house was a "wicked old witch" (an old woman who was probably starving herself) who was in the habit of cooking and eating young children. In the end, the children trick the old woman and throw her into the oven to be burned alive.

This well-known fairy tale can give insight into the peasant world of the eighteenth century. *Hansel and Gretel* is one of the more than two hundred such stories compiled by the Grimm brothers, Jacob and Wilhelm. These fairy tales have not only preserved the rich oral tradition of the European peasantry, but also illuminated aspects of life among the poorest classes prior to the Industrial Revolution. It is evident from this story that hunger was a constant threat for the rural poor, and that witchcraft and superstition were a part of daily life for lower-class folk in the eighteenth century, a life that had changed little for centuries. Among the educated middle and upper classes, however, the eighteenth century was an Age of Reason.

Poverty and Politics

One reason for a general unease during the eighteenth century was the increase in the number of poor people in Europe. The number of people available to work exceeded jobs available for them. Agriculture did not employ the excess rural population and there were not enough alternative types of work. Taxation and other feudal duties were heavy, but different groups in society, especially priests and nobles, were exempt. The church and nobility together numbered no more than three percent of the population. The bourgeoisie, townspeople who did not work with their hands, constituted about six percent, artisans another 10 percent, while 80 percent of the population was peasants.

French peasants had to pay the taxes that were levied by royalty either directly on each family or in indirect ways, as in parts of the country where a special tax was paid on salt (the government held the monopoly on salt). Peasants often had to pay the *seigneur* (landowner) for the right to cultivate his land, either in cash or with a share of the crops. The Catholic parish priest also expected a tenth part of the crop (called a tithe). This left little for peasant families to live on. Even in the most productive agricultural areas of Europe, in England and the Netherlands, the same kind of modest farming family was under pressure, as small farmers were forced out of less profitable small holdings by richer landowners with larger farms, who introduced new and more efficient methods of agriculture.

The Urban Community

Since the development of the world's first cities in Mesopotamia several thousand years ago, there has been a marked difference between rural and urban communities. While a symbiotic relationship has always existed — cities need the produce of the countryside to survive, and the countryside needs the markets of the cities to sell its produce — these two communities have always been quite distinct. Up to the nineteenth century, urban centres relied on rural communities for their growth. If a city hoped to grow and expand, it had to draw in the poor and unemployed from rural communities. This provided an important supply of cheap unskilled labour, which would drive both the pre-industrial and new industrial economies.

A market scene from the early eighteenth century. What does this picture reveal about urban life in European cities at the time?

Cities were generally unhealthy places to live, with high mortality rates. Consequently, it was rare that the number of births would exceed the number of deaths. Of the roughly 20 000 people who died each year in Paris in the late eighteenth century, 4 000 had been barely subsisting in the poorhouse. And for many, life began as it would end — as a struggle for survival. Abandoned children were so common that it became a full-time job to deliver the abandoned infants to the poorhouse. L. S. Mercier described the delivery of the babies to the poorhouse in his *Tableau de Paris* published in 1782. Mercier wrote:

> ... the man carried the babies on his back in a padded box which can hold three [babies]. They are held upright in their swaddling clothes, breathing through the top ... When [the carrier] opens his box, he often finds one of them dead; he completes his journey with the other two, impatient to be rid of the load ... He immediately sets off once more to start the same task, which is his livelihood.[3]

In an age before rapid transit that allows people to move relatively quickly, the suburbs of the eighteenth and nineteenth centuries were very different from the suburbs of the twentieth and twenty-first centuries. Eighteenth-century suburbs housed the poor, cheap inns, and the noisy or offensive trades such as tanning. The city core reflected the hierarchy of early modern cities. The urban elite, professionals, and leading business figures built elegant apartments in the city where they carried out their business.

While feudalism largely determined the social structure of rural communities, urban communities in Europe, such as Amsterdam, Paris and London, were dominated by wealthy merchants who sought the ways and means to establish autonomy for their city. As a result of these efforts, towns began to organize taxation and invented the concept of public loans to help finance city projects. In many ways, cities were the nesting grounds of much that would signify the modern age, as the wealthy merchants and industrialists sought the same power and influence as the nobility.

The symbiotic relationship between rural and urban communities became most evident during the 1780s. Repeated poor grain crops, a looming national bankruptcy (in part due to support given the 13 colonies during the American Revolutionary War, 1775–1783), and rapidly rising food costs led to hunger and discontent in the cities and countryside of France. Under these circumstances, the urban and rural poor shared the basic drive to survive, leading them eventually to unite in their frustration with the absolutist government of Louis XVI.

The Intellectual Community

Among the intelligentsia (the educated elite) toward the end of the eighteenth century, there was growing criticism of absolutist governments. Although events in France made the most dramatic break with the past at the end of the eighteenth century, the same atmosphere of conflict was to be found in much of Europe. Reactions against older forms of monarchy were not confined to France or even Europe. The American Revolution was initiated by a colonial elite dissatisfied with the government in London. In the mining areas of the Portuguese colony of Brazil, the local elite conspired unsuccessfully against the royal government of Lisbon in 1789. Revolts or disturbances broke out in Holland against the *Stadholder* (viceroy), as well as in Switzerland and the Austrian Netherlands where urban radicals rejected the authority of the enlightened Emperor Joseph II in Vienna. In 1784 a supplement to the *Moscow Gazette* praised American General George Washington for founding a republic that "without doubt will be the refuge of liberty forbidden in Europe by luxury and corruption." This kind of political commentary was becoming much more frequent in the *gazettes* and pamphlets published at the end of the eighteenth century.

The Salon

A *salon* was a room very like what today would be called a living room. During the eighteenth century, the *salons* in the homes of *philosophes* and intellectually inclined hostesses became places where men and women of the intelligentsia came together to exchange views on politics, literature, and a wide range of other subjects. *Salons* in the eighteenth-century sense actually began in early seventeenth-century France with the Marquise de Rambouillet, a sophisticated woman whose ill health prevented her from venturing far from her famous *chambre bleue* (blue room). The *salon* grew in popularity and reached its zenith in the second half of the eighteenth century. Smaller than the traditional, large formal halls for entertainment, the *salon* offered guests a casual atmosphere in which they could mingle and converse freely. Intellectually, the *salon* provided a sheltered outlet for views that were condemned by the courts of Europe. The renowned philosopher Voltaire, shunned by Louis XV for his critical views of the church and the monarchy, received numerous invitations to Parisian *salons*.

Pre-revolutionary France was a rigidly hierarchical society in which class determined who held important posts. *Salons* allowed both men and women some degree of social mobility, since they involved mixed elements of the nobility, bourgeoisie, and intelligentsia. The social equality promoted by the *philosophes* of the eighteenth century was embraced in the *salons*, as they were open to all who were well mannered, famous, talented, rich, or important in some way. Class and origins were less important than ideas.

The *philosophes* argued for ideas such as expanded women's rights (including better educational opportunities), claiming that prejudice against women was the sign of a barbaric society. In the *salons*, women participated equally with men, offering their works and opinions. Some met and married men of superior rank or wealth, while others used the *salon* as a base from which to influence kings, ministers, politicians, and literary and artistic personages. The *salon* of a woman named Madame Geoffrin, for example, counted writers and critics such as Diderot and Montesquieu

among its many famous guests. Yet another famous *salon* was held by the Marquise du Deffand and her niece Julie de Lespinasse. Historians Bonnie Anderson and Judith Zinsser described this *salon* as follows:

> ... from 1754 to 1764, these women maintained one of the most brilliant *salons* in Europe. Part of the attraction was the contrast between the two: aunt and illegitimate niece; one in her sixties, the other in her twenties; one known for her love affairs, the other a virgin; blind patroness and sighted protegée; the cynic and the romantic. Their *salon* became one of the ornaments of Enlightenment culture, and an invitation to the famous yellow drawing room was prized.[4]

Despite the decline of the *salon* by the nineteenth century, it was an important element in the transition from the dominance of upper-class culture of previous centuries to the more middle-class culture of the nineteenth and twentieth centuries.

[SOCIAL HISTORY
Good Taste and Good Manners

The *salons* of the eighteenth century drew a wide variety of people from different backgrounds and social classes. Wealth and brilliance began to join lineage as determinants of distinction in middle- and upper-class society. Having good taste (*le bon ton*) became a new and important requirement of eighteenth-century culture. The Middle Ages had placed courtliness above all other qualities, while the Renaissance had added conversation and civility as important qualities. The Enlightenment elevated good taste to an essential social virtue. Rather than being merely a superficial trait, taste defined who a person truly was. At least among the upper class, the most coveted sign of distinction in the eighteenth century was good taste — in art, in fashion, and particularly in food and manners.

During the eighteenth century, rules of etiquette and the nature of banqueting among the privileged classes underwent significant changes. Previously, many dishes were placed on the table at once, as we would do today in a buffet. In 1742 the book of recipes and etiquette *Nouveau cuisinier royal et bourgeois* suggested that for a dinner party of six to eight people, at least three courses should be served, each with at least seven dishes per course. The same source suggested that for a dinner party of 25 people, 27 dishes per course should be served, making a total of 81. The idea was to cater to a diversity of tastes.

The older practice of seating men at one end of the table and women at the other gave way to an alternating pattern. As a result, the boisterous toasts of the men became more refined. Other changes at the dinner table reflected a growing sense of individualism. During the Middle Ages, two or three people took sips from the same soup bowl, ate meat from a single platter, dipped their bread and meat in the same sauceboats, and drank from a single cup passed around the table. By the eighteenth century, upper-class diners had their own bowl, plate, fork, knife, and spoon. No longer was it acceptable for people to share utensils or eat from the same plate. John Trusler's book *The Honours of the Table*, published in 1788, outlined proper table manners:

> It is vulgar to eat your soup with your nose in the plate. You must avoid smelling the meat while it is on the fork ... It is exceedingly rude to scratch any part of your body, to spit, or blow your nose ... to lean your elbows on the table, to sit too far from it, to pick your teeth before the dishes are removed.[5]

Trusler went on to suggest that if you needed to go to the toilet during the meal, you should slip away unobserved and return without announcing where you had been. The earlier practice of keeping a chamber pot in or just outside the dining room was discontinued because it was now considered vulgar.

Science, Technology, and Society

The scientific and technological changes of the seventeenth century had affected nearly every aspect of life, including food quality and preparation. At the beginning of the eighteenth century, the way people lived and ate was still quite similar to that of their medieval predecessors. By the end of the century, however, some kitchens would have a wider array of equipment available, including tools, pots, dishes, and glasses. As is often the case, technological developments in one area brought changes in others. For example, improvements in the rolling of sheet iron led to better kitchen utensils and allowed the production of finer flour. This in turn improved the quality of bread.

This painting by Chardin takes us into an eighteenth-century kitchen. The servant shown here is bringing in food from the market to the pantry. In the background is a cistern for drinking water.

Advances in agriculture brought great improvements to people's diets. Up to the beginning of the eighteenth century, cattle had to be killed before winter, since winter feeding practices had not yet been developed. Consequently, salted meat was a major part of the diet. With the development of winter feeding practices that originated in Holland, cattle could be kept year-round, putting fresh meat on the table throughout the year and lessening the chance of improper preservation and spoiled meat.

With fresh meat, many of the old spices and flavourings common in previous centuries fell out of fashion. So too did the emphasis on appearance over taste. People of the Middle Ages placed a great deal of importance on the visual aspects of food: They served large birds complete with all their feathers. Gradually, birds such as swan, stork, peacock, and cormorant, more renowned for their visual splendour than their flavour, disappeared from eighteenth-century cookbooks. Medieval cookbooks had advised cooks to add saffron or other ingredients to enhance colour, whereas eighteenth-century cooks and gourmets

History
BYTES

During the late eighteenth century, Friedrich Anton Mesmer, an Austrian scientist and doctor, although considered by many to be a quack, developed a practice called "animal magnetism" (a forerunner to hypnotism). Mesmer (1733–1815) claimed the existence of a power, similar to magnetism, that exercised an extraordinary influence on the human body. In 1775 he published an account of his discovery, claiming it had medical value. Mesmer's pseudo-scientific theories received limited support among members of the medical profession, yet in 1785, Marie Antoinette, wife of the king, decided to offer Mesmer a sizeable pension to create an Institute of Animal Magnetism in France. The overthrow of the French monarchy marked an end to Mesmer's pension and therefore his research at the institute. Having lost his financial backer and finding little support in the scientific community, Mesmer fell into disrepute and spent the rest of his life in obscurity.

learned to appreciate the natural colour of foods properly cooked. Emphasis was now on the quality of the food rather than merely its appearance.

The Pre-revolutionary Family

Despite the prominent role some women played in hosting the *salons* of Europe, the Enlightenment did little to change the traditional role of women in society. Enlightenment thinkers advocated the inalienable rights of men — be they slaves, Indians, Jews, or the poor — but not women. Although some argued against the prejudices shown toward women, it was more common for men of the eighteenth century to defend the church-inspired view that women were inferior to men, lacking the crucial faculties of reason and ethics. Contrary to the logic, rationality and egalitarianism of the age, the ideal woman of the eighteenth century was no different from the ideal woman of the past: silent, obedient, subservient, modest, and chaste. Rousseau wrote about intelligent women in his popular novel *Emile* (1762):

> I would a thousand times rather have a homely girl, simply brought up, than a learned lady and a wit who make a literary circle of my house and install herself as its president. A female wit is a scourge to her husband, her children, her friends, her servants, to everybody. From the lofty height of her genius, she scorns every womanly duty, and she is always trying to make a man of herself.[6]

Voltaire had little to say about the subject of women's education or role in society, although he did write to a friend concerning the intellect of his mistress, the Marquise du Châtelet: "Emilie, in truth, is the divine mistress, endowed with beauty, wit, compassion and all of the other womanly virtues. Yet I frequently wish she were less learned and her mind less sharp."

Women of the lower classes were often sent away to work as servants in wealthy households. For their extensive duties, which included cleaning, cooking, shopping, and caring for children, women received little if any pay, their wages often sent directly to their parents. A young woman also had to endure frequent beatings from her ungrateful mistress or unwanted sexual advances from the master, his sons, or his friends. Sexual abuse of servant girls and women was widespread throughout Europe. The upper classes exploited them and the women had no legal protection. When a girl became pregnant as a result of abuse, she would quickly be fired and forced to fend for herself through petty thievery or prostitution.

Feminine values and consciousness were upheld by Catholicism: Convents were among the rare, large organizations with economic resources where women could hold positions of power, albeit at the cost of being a bride of Christ and confined. In 1789 no society in Europe had a better nursing service than that of the French Sisters of Charity. In pre-revolutionary France, some 2 000 hospitals were run by women whose only remuneration was their keep: From peasant woman to hospital nurse, women's work was poorly rewarded.

Marriage and Children

During the early eighteenth century, people tended to marry relatively late: The average age of marriage for both men and women was 27. Infant mortality, high even among the upper classes, was disturbingly common among the lower classes. Prey to cold and hunger, and diseases such as typhus, cholera, influenza and dysentery (diarrhea), surviving infancy was a challenge many babies did not meet. Those who did survive often succumbed later to childhood illnesses (measles, mumps, rheumatic fever) or accidents. In Europe prior to the twentieth century, the chances that a child would die were so high that it was common for parents to give successive sons the same name so that at least one would survive to adulthood carrying his father's name. The famous English historian Edward Gibbon (author of *The Decline and Fall of the Roman Empire*) was the first of six boys to be named after his father; none of the others survived the perils of childhood.

Prior to the eighteenth century, children were born into a world of constraints. Swaddling, an ancient practice, involved wrapping and immobilizing the infant. Babies were easier to care for using this method and probably more subdued and less prone to crying; often infants were strapped onto a board so mother could go about her business. Tight bonnets were used to help shape the child's head in conformity with an ideal. By the eighteenth century, both these practices were condemned as harmful to the development of the child. The practice of hiring a wet nurse to breast-feed one's children continued among the middle and upper classes throughout the century. Upper-class women regarded breast-feeding as crude and demeaning.

The care given infants is indicative of the general attitude toward children in the eighteenth century. Although it was important to have children so they could carry on the family line, children of all classes were treated with indifference by their parents. Outward signs of love and affection were uncommon, often creating a vast psychological gulf between parent and child. Unfortunately for many children, this indifference led to physical abuse, as the only attention received from their parents was discipline.

Education

During the eighteenth century, there was a significant rise in formal education. Compulsory education for children aged seven to 12 arose during the late seventeenth century, and both England and France established schools to teach basic literacy and religion to the children of the poor. In 1717, Prussia, under Frederick William I (ruling 1713–1740), was the first European state to institute compulsory education. Although this was intended to help improve the efficiency of the state, it marked an important development in universal education. Despite these advances in the eighteenth century, many children failed to receive any formal education; their education came from their parents beginning at the age of seven or eight, when young boys would accompany their fathers into the fields and young girls would begin learning the essentials of housekeeping. By the age of 12, young boys might be apprenticed to a master, from whom they would learn a trade, or find employment with a neighbour working in the fields. At the same age, young girls would be sent out as servants.

Review, Reflect, Respond

1. Compare and contrast rural and urban communities in the eighteenth century and explain their symbiotic relationship.

2. What role did the *salons and* the rising middle class play in bringing on the French Revolution?

3. Create a chart outlining the roles of men, women and children in eighteenth-century European society.

Popular Culture in the Eighteenth Century

Culture during the eighteenth century among the middle and upper classes was characterized by a flood of new ideas about politics, economics, morals, religion, and the nature of humanity. Intellectuals proposed radical new ideas that often challenged European society. Above all, Enlightenment thinkers were skeptical of miracles and superstitions that made religion seem ridiculous in an age of reason. This emphasis on reason and attack on superstition clearly distinguished the enlightened middle and upper classes from the unenlightened masses. When a child of the lower class was baptized, for example, parents often resorted to magic to ensure its health. Once the priest had left the church, the child was rolled on the altar to strengthen its muscles and protect it from rickets; godparents

This detail from a print, entitled *Gin Lane*, shows life in London, England around the middle of the eighteenth century. While beer was considered healthy, even for breakfast, gin was the refuge of the poor because it was much cheaper. What effects of poverty are shown?

were expected to kiss under the belfry to help prevent the godchild from developing a stammer or muteness.

Members of the middle and upper classes spent much of their leisure time in *cafés* and *salons* listening to music and poetry, and discussing ideas. The lower classes did the same in pubs, where they drank, gossiped, and perhaps discussed the latest pamphlet (if there was someone there who could read). By the eighteenth century, wine — usually adulterated or watered down — was fast becoming the favourite drink in Europe, while in England, gin had become the drink of the poor. The pamphlets and brochures read aloud in the pubs were generally of three types: religious material, consisting of Bible stories and lives of the saints; almanacs, which included guides on cleanliness, nourishment, and potions for illness; and entertainment literature, comprising stories, fables, and satires — hunger, sex, and oppression were the favourite themes.

The year was filled with holidays that allowed for merrymaking, eating, drinking, dressing up, and playing games. The festivities provided a time for the young to meet and for adults to enjoy a break from the daily grind in the fields. The highlights of the year's holidays occurred between the spring sowing and summer harvest, or in the early autumn once the harvest was in.

Entertainment among the lower classes included numerous blood sports, such as baiting, where a pack of dogs was set loose on a tied-up bear, bull or badger, and cock-fighting. The torture of animals, especially cats, which were associated with witchcraft, was also a popular amusement throughout Europe. The torture of cats was so common that expressions such as "as patient as a cat whose claws are being pulled out" were commonplace. By the end of the eighteenth century, enlightened reformers and moralists were denouncing such cruelties, although nothing was said about the blood sports of the gentry, such as fox hunting.

WEB CONNECTION
www.mcgrawhill.ca/links/legacy

Go to the site above to find out more about eighteenth-century culture.

ON THE EVE OF THE REVOLUTION

Government in Society

Wars (plus the loss of valuable colonies) and support for the American Revolutionary War combined with a weak economy, left the French monarchy on the verge of bankruptcy by 1788. Desperate to raise money, King Louis XVI recalled his former finance minister, Jacques Necker (previously dismissed for suggesting reforms), and decided to recall the Estates-General. This was the legislative body of the *ancien régime*, made up of representatives of the three estates, or levels of society:

The First Estate	the clergy
The Second Estate	the nobility
The Third Estate	the commons
The Fourth Estate	the press

Although limited in power, the Estates-General did have the right to approve or veto any new taxes or increases in taxes. For the previous 175 years, the absolute monarchs of France had been able to avoid calling the Estates-General by extracting money from overseas colonies and other sources. Now, faced with an economic crisis, the king was forced to take this radical step in the hope that the Estates-General would agree to increase taxes in exchange for some minor political and constitutional reforms. His desperate gamble would prove to be the death of the French monarchy.

French Public Opinion on the Eve of the Revolution

Nobody in France in 1789 could have imagined where the nation was going. What many hoped for was a reformed constitutional monarchy; however, even before the Estates-General were recalled by Louis XVI on May 5, 1789, reactionaries were alarmed. The king's brother said in 1788: "Sire, the state is in peril ... a revolution in the principles of government is under way ... the authority of the throne and the rights of the privileged order is in question. Soon property rights will be attacked."

In using the word "revolution," the prince showed how it had come to mean a wholesale upheaval in society. The prince's outburst reminds us that from the beginning of the revolutionary process, many in France opposed any basic changes to the government. Censorship of publications had been relaxed and many pamphlets that expressed opinions were printed. The most famous of all was *What Is the Third Estate?* by the abbé (a priest in minor orders) Emmanuel Joseph Sieyès. His answer, at the expense of the first estate (the clergy) and the second estate (the nobility), was that the third estate (the middle and lower classes) was "everything." And yet, Sieyès also believed that national unity was more important than the estates and local interests.

The Crown, seeking to consult the French people directly, called for statements of grievance to be drawn up by various entities. These notebooks of complaints, or *cahiers de doléances*, are one of the great primary sources of information for historians on France at the time of the Revolution. They were not necessarily radical, as we see from the canons of the cathedral chapter of Auxerre (a district in France):

> The conservation of monarchical government is the first wish of the Auxerre chapter. This government is the only one which is suitable to the vast expanse of the kingdom, and the happiness which the nation has tasted for so many centuries makes it feel the need to belong to its kings, its only true legislators.

Others, like the inhabitants of a small village in the Pyrenees Mountains, which separate France from Spain, railed against the tax collector: "The one and only tyrant [is] the financial administration, which night and day is busy to take gold from the crown, silver from the crozier, steel from swords, ermine from robes, the copper from the counters, iron from the plows and other tools and even the bronze of the bells.[7]" The desire to express opinion led to the establishment of discussion clubs in major French cities. Elections of deputies to the Estates-General were held in March and April of 1789.

THE YEAR OF LIBERTY IN FRANCE

The Estates-General: A Social Revolution

The meeting of the Estates-General at Versailles soon produced a deadlock among the three orders of the National Assembly. The first and second estates combined (with two votes) could outvote the third estate (one vote) despite the fact that the third estate represented the vast majority of the nation. Deputies of the third estate decided to meet and protest against this situation. Louis XVI, considering the actions of the third estate both intolerable and in defiance of his authority, had the meeting hall locked and guarded by soldiers. When the members of the third estate found themselves locked out of the palace, they feared the king was going to break up their assembly by force. With rain falling, they took cover in the nearest vacant building they could find, an indoor tennis court a short walk away. There, on June 20, 1789, the deputies of the third estate, along with sympathetic members of the other estates, swore an oath, known as the Tennis Court Oath, stating that they were the National Assembly of France — and that they would not dissolve until they had a constitution. The assembly also swore that it would not separate, but would reassemble whenever necessary, until a constitution was established and consolidated on firm foundations.

On June 23, 1789, the king sent a courtier to tell the deputies of the third estate to disperse and that voting would continue. In response, the comte de Mirabeau, a leading elected member, announced that they would only yield to force. The court's messenger turned to the president of the Assembly, the astronomer Sylvain Bailly, who backed Mirabeau by saying, "The nation is assembled here, and receives no orders." This legalistic exchange between the king's messenger and parliamentarians has been seen as the effective end of the legal authority of the old monarchical order; the national will was set above the orders of the king.

The people shown in the painting *The Tennis Court Oath* swore they would not leave this place until they had drafted a new constitution for the people of France. This was painted by David in 1791.

Urban Violence: The Storming of the Bastille

On July 14, 1789, several weeks after the proclamation of the National Assembly, a crowd attacked the Bastille (the Paris state prison). The Bastille was the symbol of the oppressive order of the *ancien régime* because it held special prisoners who were sent there without trial and solely at the whim of the authorities. The crowd believed the Bastille was full of wretched prisoners being kept in subhuman conditions. It was also thought that the building held arms and ammunition that might be used by those loyal to the king. In fact, the Bastille held only seven prisoners (one of whom was insane), who were treated much better than common criminals. The Bastille did not fall to ravening, famished, lower-class attackers but to craftsmen, journeymen, shopkeepers and some higher-placed leaders, representing a cross section of the now politicized Paris population. Political power was now in the streets of Paris and future Republican governments of France later proclaimed July 14 a national holiday, signifying approval of popular participation in politics.

When the Paris mob stormed the Bastille, long a symbol of the repressive governing of France, they found only a few prisoners, whom they set free.

The Declaration of the Rights of Man and of the Citizen

The Declaration of the Rights of Man and of the Citizen was the product of the first constitutional debates in the French National Assembly. Approved on August 26, 1789, it is a clear statement of the aims of the French Revolution. Many of its articles were aimed at specific abuses of the *ancien régime*, the political and social system in France before the revolution of 1789. The Declaration asserted the equality of all men, the sovereignty of the people, and the inalienable rights of the individual to liberty, property, security, and resistance to oppression.

The Declaration of the Rights of Man and of the Citizen was drafted by Emmanuel Sieyès. He and other declaration framers were influenced by the American Declaration of Independence (1776) and ideas of the Enlightenment.

Thousands of copies of the 1789 French Declaration were printed and distributed by the National Assembly. The Declaration of the Rights of Man and of the Citizen eventually became the preamble to the French Constitution of 1791. It also had an immense impact on liberal thought through the nineteenth century. A careful reading of this document reveals a male and bourgeois bias, as power passed from the monarchy to the educated and affluent of the third estate.

The Declaration of the Rights of Man and of the Citizen

The representatives of the French people, organized in National Assembly, considering the ignorance, forgetfulness, or contempt of the rights of man are the sole causes of public misfortunes and of the corruption of governments, have resolved to set forth in a solemn declaration the natural, inalienable, and sacred rights of man, in order that such declaration, continually before all members of the social body, may be a perpetual reminder of their rights and duties ...

Accordingly, the National Assembly recognizes and proclaims, in the presence and under the auspices of the Supreme Being, the following rights of man and citizen.

1. Men are born and remain free and equal in rights; social distinctions may be based only upon general usefulness.

2. The aim of every political association is the preservation of the natural and inalienable rights of man; these rights are liberty, property, security, and resistance to oppression.

3. The source of all sovereignty resides essentially in the nation; no group, no individual may exercise authority not emanating expressly therefrom.

4. Liberty consists of the power to do whatever is not injurious to others; thus the enjoyment of the natural rights of every man has for its limits only those that assure other members of society the enjoyment of those same rights; such limits may be determined only by law.

5. The law has the right to forbid only actions which are injurious to society. Whatever is not forbidden by law may not be prevented, and no one may be constrained to do what it does not prescribe.

6. Law is the expression of the general will; all citizens have the right to concur personally, or through their representatives, in its formation, it must be the same for all, whether it protects or

punishes. All citizens, being equal before it, are equally admissible to all public offices, positions and employments, according to their capacity, and without other distinction than that of virtues and talents.

7. No man may be accused, arrested, or detained except in the cases determined by law, and according to the forms prescribed thereby. Whoever solicit, expedite, or execute arbitrary orders, or have them executed, must be punished; but every citizen summoned or apprehended in pursuance of the law must obey immediately; he renders himself culpable by resistance.

8. The law is to establish only penalties that are absolutely and obviously necessary; and no one may be punished except by virtue of a law established and promulgated prior to the offence and legally applied.

9. Since every man is presumed innocent until declared guilty, if arrest be deemed indispensable, all necessary severity for securing the person of the accused must be severely repressed by law.

10. No one is to be disquieted because of his opinions, even religious, provided their manifestation does not disturb the public order established by law.

11. Free communication of ideas and opinions is one of the most precious of the rights of man. Consequently, every citizen may speak, write, and print freely, subject to responsibility for the abuse of such liberty in the cases determined by law.

12. The guarantee of the rights of man and citizen necessitates a public force; such a force, therefore, is instituted for the advantage of all and not for the particular benefit of those to whom it is entrusted.

13. For the maintenance of the public force and for the expenses of administration a common tax is indispensable; it must be assessed equally on all citizens in proportion to their means.

14. Citizens have the right to ascertain, by themselves or through their representatives, the necessity of the public tax, to consent to it freely, to supervise its use, and to determine its quota, assessment, payment, and duration.

15. Society has the right to require of every public agent an accounting of his administration.

16. Every society in which the guarantee of rights is not assured or the separation of powers not determined has no constitution at all.

17. Since property is a sacred and inviolable right, no one may be deprived thereof unless a legally established public necessity obviously requires it, and upon condition of a just and previous indemnity.

---

1. Compare this document with the Declaration of the Rights of Woman and the Female Citizen by Olympe de Gouges. Find it on the McGraw-Hill Web site. www.mcgrawhill.ca/links/legacy

2. Which concepts in the Declaration do you think were inspired by (a) Locke, (b) Montesquieu, (c) Rousseau? Explain your answers.

Country Protest: The Great Fear

During the summer of 1789, news of peasant dissatisfaction with the payments and services exacted by landowners was coming in from the countryside. Country folk wanted an end to extortion based on medieval systems of feudal landownership, in which all economic rights were in the hands of the *seigneurs*, or feudal lords. These included various kinds of quit-rents (rent paid in money rather than in services) and having to submit to the judgment of the feudal lord in all aspects of life. Peasants started to attack castles and tried to burn records of feudal dues, rents payable, and taxation.

At Versailles, on the unusually hot night of August 4, 1789, the Assembly stayed in session and abolished many feudal rights. The abolition of the specific terms of feudalism in 1789 (completed in 1793) was seen as an important aspect of making the rural economy more efficient; however, commoners held the perception that nobles who profited from the work of others were enemies of social change. This view continued to dominate the events of the summer. In June 1790, titles of nobility were also abolished, reflecting the strong desire for equality among French citizens.

Government Moves from Versailles to Paris

As long as the king, the court, and the Assembly remained in Versailles, the people of the largest city in the kingdom felt uneasy about the fate of the Revolution. On October 5, the so-called "October Days" began, when there was a great demonstration by Parisians motivated by fear of bread shortages. Women from the central markets led the march to Versailles to protest against high food prices. When they arrived, they burst into the royal apartments determined to take the good king from what they thought to be the bad company of Queen Marie Antoinette and the courtiers. The demonstration returned to Paris in triumph, with carts carrying sacks of flour, and the royal family in the royal carriage being led back to the old and long-vacant Tuileries Palace in the centre of Paris.

It was because of the price of bread, an almost sacred commodity in France, that the women marched on Versailles, demanding action by the king and effectively starting the Revolution. Popular legend has it that when the queen, Marie Antoinette, was told that the people had no bread, she replied "No bread? Let them eat cake." Explain the insult in her comment.

Now the court and the Assembly were under the watchful eye of the revolutionaries in the French capital. Once again, the power of the mob was apparent.

By the end of 1789, important changes had taken place in France: The Estates-General had become the National Assembly, also known as the Constituent Assembly, and was charged with writing a constitution. The king was no longer the central authority, but in a constitutional monarchy his approval of what the Assembly decided was needed for the state's authority to be fully legal.

Many nobles were anxious about events and began to emigrate; the clergy was aware that its property and internal organization were at risk; the population at large was apprehensive about the level of violence. Toward the end of 1789, the *philosophe* Condorcet complained in a pamphlet about what he called the false notion that the people had taken their rights, imagining that the "tumultuous will" of the inhabitants of a city, town, or village held the same authority as the will of a legal assembly.

A Constitutional Revolution: The Constituent Assembly 1789–1791

Once the Assembly had made clear its authority, it turned to implementing the reforms necessary to restore order. The government renewed the French legal system and wrote a constitution that would influence every subsequent constitution in France. It reorganized France into 83 new units called departments, confiscated church estates (releasing land to more productive management), and set up the so-called Civil Constitution of the Clergy, which by July 1790 provided for the election of bishops and priests by the people. Perhaps the change that caused the greatest conflict was the abolition of the obligation of the French Church to obey the Pope.

Mirabeau

The pre-eminent figure of the early revolution was Honoré Gabriel Riqueti, comte de Mirabeau (1749–1791), known simply as Mirabeau, eldest son of a noble family from Provence. His father was a noted writer on economics and a proponent of tax reforms who sided with the physiocrats, those who insisted on the primacy of an agricultural economy (unlike the *philosophes*, who were more interested in encouraging urban manufacturing). As a young man, Mirabeau defied the authority of his father, despite the fact that legally, males in the *ancien régime* were minors until age 25. He was imprisoned at the request of his father, on a warrant written by a local official. Mirabeau responded by writing the first of a series of pamphlets (1782) denouncing arbitrary arrest and putting forward his own views on justice and constitutional government. He was also vehement in his criticism of financial speculation.

Mirabeau's pamphlets showed his skill at making complicated issues understandable to the public. He was elected a member of the Assembly in 1789 and was in the forefront of the resistance to direction by the royal ministers, though he made himself the spokesman for a parliamentary monarchy. He urged the royal family to accommodate the Revolution. He also filled his pockets with gifts of money from the royal family. At the same time, he hurled barbs at the Jacobins, the left wing of the Assembly, consistently speaking against those he thought were dangerous to social harmony. Mirabeau's death in April 1791 was considered a national catastrophe by those who believed in a compromise between the court and the Assembly. His death also marked a transition from what might be described as conservative radicalism, which failed because there was no agreement about the direction the Revolution should follow among the "political class," the reformist-minded aristocrats, in mid-1791.

Three months later, new deputies met in a new Legislative Assembly. Those men who had sat in the National Assembly were disqualified from seeking re-election. As a result, experienced politicians such as Maximilien de Robespierre sought a power base in the discussion clubs. The inexperienced newcomers to the Legislative Assembly had to face a difficult situation. In the following spring, they took France into war.

Maximilien de Robespierre

If Mirabeau symbolized the attempt to set up a liberal constitutional monarchy in France, he is naturally compared with a younger man, Maximilien de Robespierre (1758–1794), a leading revolutionary radical elected to the Estates-General in 1789, who aimed

The young Robespierre, idealist and leader of the radical element of the Revolution, the Jacobins. It is said that revolutions feed on themselves. How is Robespierre an example of that?

to establish a republic. Robespierre was a small-town lawyer from northern France who expressed the ideas of Rousseau and the general culture of the Enlightenment. His intellectual honesty and revolutionary zeal for a new "Republic of Virtue" made him immune to attempts to divert him from his path.

As the revolution began to take shape, two dominant political groups emerged to direct the course of events. The Girondins, a moderate group, came largely from the Bordeaux region in southern France, which did not support extending political rights to the working class, known as the *sans-culottes*, meaning literally "without breeches" (the well-to-do wore knee breeches; the lower classes adopted trousers). These urban workers found support among the more radical Jacobins. The Jacobins, who took their name from the former Jacobin convent in which they met, were a Parisian club that advocated radical reform and harsh measures to bring about the change they desired. The French Revolution in its early stage marked a legalistic desire for an end to social privilege and it was carried out with the respect for law one might expect of an Assembly primarily composed of lawyers; however, after September 1792, legalism increasingly broke down into state terrorism by the Committee of Public Safety. Those who disagreed with policies were brought before the revolutionary tribunal and were either forced into submission or executed.

Change and Continuity in Revolutionary Times

Prior to 1789, politics was the exclusive domain of the monarchy and the aristocracy and took place in the remote and secretive world of the king's court at Versailles. With the outbreak of the Revolution, ordinary people began to take part in the political process by first electing representatives to the Estates-General and ultimately establishing universal male suffrage in the election for the National Assembly in 1792. The dramatic changes brought about by the French Revolution extended well beyond the political arena, reaching into the daily lives of the French people. The period between 1789 and 1794 witnessed one of the greatest assaults on individual privacy by an interventionist state in the history of Western civilization. During the early years of the Revolution, privacy became equated with secrecy and anti-revolutionary activities. Anyone expressing private interests was seen to be attempting to work against the "general will" of the Republic of Virtue (i.e., Rousseau's concept) and the nation, and therefore seen as an enemy of the French state.

The Revolutionary Wars

During the first years of the French Revolution, the other great powers of Europe were not particularly upset by what seemed a series of major domestic reforms in France, though there was unease in Britain. Concern did begin to mount, however, when the Alsatians declared themselves French and no longer subject to historical feudal rights of German *seigneurs*. Then Avignon, a papal enclave in Provence, was annexed in September 1791 at the request of the inhabitants who wanted to be part of France. Foreign absolutist governments were increasingly apprehensive that the Revolution was out of control. On August 27, 1791, a declaration by the Austrian emperor and the Prussian king threatening retribution if any ill befell the French royal family. In fact, this only increased the unpopularity of the monarchy. The Austrian emperor Leopold II died in March 1792 and was replaced by his son, the impetuous Francis II. An Austrian ultimatum to France was rejected and France declared war on Austria on April 20, 1792.

The declaration of war against Austria resulted from factional infighting among French politicians and from the provocative language used by Vienna about the feudal rights of German princes in Alsace. Some, like Brissot, favoured war and others, like Robespierre, were against it. Louis XVI had hoped for a foreign military intervention so that he would become the mediator between the invaders and the Assembly. He hoped to avoid bloodshed by accepting limits on his own constitutional authority and by outmanoeuvring radicals inside France and reactionary *émigrés* outside.

The struggle with Austria brought about the War of the First Coalition (Britain, Holland, Spain, Sardinia, and Naples) from 1792 to 1797. The fiercely nationalistic response it elicited can be gauged from the words of the *Marseillaise*, which Claude Rouget de Lisle modified from a popular war song for the Army of the Rhine in 1792, and which would become the national anthem of France on July 14, 1795:

> Come Children of the Fatherland
> The Day of glory has arrived
> Against us tyranny
> Raises its bloody standards
> Do you hear in the fields
> The bellowing of these ferocious soldiers
> Who have come to our arms
> To slaughter our sons and spouses ...
> Let impure blood
> Irrigate our ditches

From 1792 onward, there followed a devastating series of wars. By March 1793, the French were at war with Austria, Prussia, Britain, Holland, and Spain. France revealed itself as aggressively expansionist, in search of territorial gain just like the continental monarchies. Apart from a brief pause in 1802–1803, the series of wars would not end until 1815, with the defeat of Napoléon in the Battle of Waterloo.

The dramatic events that unfolded in France seemed to have no direction. Paris was the epicentre of a great upheaval that would grip most of continental Western Europe. The war against Queen Marie Antoinette's brother, the Austrian king, and the suspicion of treason that surrounded the royal family caused a steady decline in their popularity after their flight was foiled at Varennes. As a result, the Tuileries Palace was invaded by a mob of *sans-culottes* in June 1792; they insulted the king but the intruders then left. On August 10, 1792, there was an armed insurrection by Jacobins on the palace when the royal family was taken into custody and the king was suspended from his duties. During the following month, there was no clear focus of political power. Authority was claimed by the municipality of Paris, especially by the Jacobins, where Robespierre was prominent.

The September Massacres

With the coming to power of the Jacobins came one of the most infamous events of the Revolution: the September Massacres. During this series of attacks on the prisons in Paris, beginning on September 2, 1792, and lasting five days, more than 1 200 people were killed and mutilated by the mob. At one prison, 43 of the 162 prisoners massacred were less than 18 years old. A particularly grisly attack was on a young aristocratic woman, the Princesse Mme de Lamballe, who was stripped and raped. When she was dead, one member of the mob cut out her heart and ate it. One man who survived reported that one of the strangest things about the massacres was the silence with which the killers carried out their work. Most of the murders were preceded by what the assassins considered a "trial," but better known as "mob courts." The "judges" were the killers themselves.

POLITICAL ORGANIZATION: FROM MONARCHY TO REPUBLIC

Another turning point was reached on September 20, 1792, when the Legislative Assembly dissolved and the Convention convened. Its first act was the abolition of the monarchy, making September 21, 1792, the first day of the French Republic. On the same day, the Prussian invasion under the elderly Duke of Brunswick was halted at Valmy when an ill-trained citizen army stopped the Prussian regulars.

The Convention received news of the victory on September 21 with tremendous exultation. The membership of the Convention consisted of 750 men, including 189 deputies from previous assemblies. They were mostly lawyers, although there were two workers, a peasant, and even 23 former nobles. There was a black deputy who lived in France, but who represented

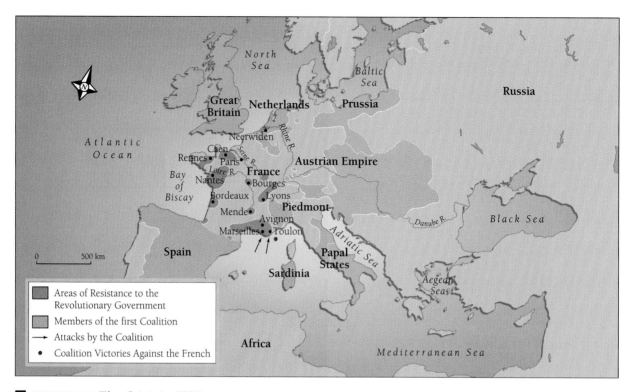

■ FIGURE 5.1 The Crisis in 1793
Are there connections among the areas that resisted the revolutionary government?

the sugar colony that is Haiti today. They sat in a semi-circle facing the president, with the radicals on the left and their more conservative opponents on the right, while the majority seated themselves in the middle. From this chance arrangement comes the modern terminology of the political left, right, and centre.

It is worth noting that of the seven million eligible voters, only 700 000 cast their ballots. Why this happened may have to do with reluctance on the part of the royalists as a result of the September Massacres. Or perhaps it was Jacobin watchdogs interfering with the balloting.

The Convention 1792
(the political spectrum)

The Convention of September, 1792 defined the political spectrum we know today: radicals on the left, conservatives on the right, and the moderate majority at the centre.

The Execution of Louis XVI

The French were ecstatic with the news of victory at Valmy, which spread at the same time as the news of the proclamation of the new republic by the Convention on the next day, September 21. Documents were henceforth to be dated "Year One of the Republic." Former king Louis XVI went on trial and was sentenced to death in a close vote, despite the efforts of the Girondins to save his life. He was decapitated in public on January 21, 1793, by the new "humane" killing machine called the guillotine.

By executing Louis rather than putting him in prison, the Jacobins signalled their determination to defy Europe and break with the past. Once the king was dead, there were struggles between groups of deputies in the Convention. Between 1793 and 1794, France was again threatened by foreign armies, by political struggles in which the losers were executed, and by the threat of civil war. From 1792 onward, French foreign relations took on a highly ideological tone not unlike that of the Cold War (1945–1990) between capitalist and communist states.

Each faction in the Convention reviled their enemies as either extremists or moderates. On June 2, 1793, twenty-nine Girondin deputies were arrested for treason. Most of them were condemned to death. The fate of these Girondins showed that being a revolutionary deputy was dangerous. Their elimination left the Jacobins as the ruling force in the capital.

WEB CONNECTION www.mcgrawhill.ca/links/legacy
Go to the site above to find out more about the French Revolution.

Revolutionary Names and Symbols

Further efforts to eradicate all signs of the *ancien régime* and to impose a rational, natural order on the world were reflected in everyday life. Throughout Paris 1 400 streets with names associated with the monarchy or saints were renamed. Place Louis XV, where most of the guillotining took place, became Place de la Revolution and later took its present name, Place de la Concorde. Churches were also given new names to reflect the secularization of society. The Church of Saint-Laurent became the Temple of Marriage and Fidelity, while the famous Notre Dame was renamed the Temple of Reason. Many of the revolutionaries even renamed themselves. Those with names such as Louis took on new names such as Brutus or Spartacus in imitation of Roman heroes. And those with last names such as Le Roy or Leveque adopted names such as *La Loi* or *Liberté*.

To reflect a new rationalism, changes in the measurement of space and time were also made. The introduction of the metric system was an attempt to impose a rational and natural organization on measurement. By decree in 1795, the metre was defined as

An English political cartoon satirizing the French Revolution. It reads: "The Zenith of French Glory: The Pinnacle of Liberty." What is the subject matter?

This allegorical figure represents the month called *Pluviose* (the rain month, February). All the months of the year were renamed and the years recorded according to a new, Revolutionary calendar. As propaganda tools, how might changes like this have affected the daily lives of most people?

"the unit of length equal to one-millionth part of the arc of the terrestrial meridian between the North Pole and the Equator."

The measurement of time was also divided into units that were seen to be more rational and natural. The revolutionary calendar was comprised of 12 months each with three 10-day weeks. The five days left over at the end of the year became patriotic holidays celebrating Virtue, Genius, Labour, Opinions, and Rewards. The names of the days of the week were changed to reflect mathematical regularity. The days were called; *primidi, duodi, tridi,* and so on, up to *decadi.* The 12 months were renamed to reflect the natural rhythm of the seasons. January became *Nivose* (the month of snow) and followed the months of *Brumaire* (fog) and *Frimaire* (cold). The fall of the monarchy, September 22, 1792, was used as the reference point for the start of time, and was referred to as Year One. The rational thought and belief in order that

characterized the scientific revolution and the Enlightenment were put into practice on a daily basis during the period of the French Revolution.

The Reign of Terror

The leaders in Paris instituted a reign of violence, which became known simply as the "Terror," against the enemies of the Revolution. A revolutionary tribunal summarily tried individuals accused of political crimes and sentenced many of them to death. From March 1793 to June 1794, there were 1 251 executions. At its peak, from June 10 to July 27, 1794, the Terror took a further 1 376, guillotined in Paris (about 30 per day). In November, Jean Sylvain Bailly, who had presided at the Tennis Court Oath of 1789 and served as mayor of Paris, was just one more revolutionary to die on the scaffold. Some 40 000 people died a violent death during the Terror (6.5 percent were priests, 8.5 percent nobles, and the rest commoners).

The Terror was a result of a revolutionary system of government with two powerful executive committees: the Committee of Public Safety (which fought against food shortages, foreign enemies, and political subversion) and the Committee of General Security. Both used drastic methods to achieve their goals.

In August 1793 a mass levy of men to fight (or conscription) was decreed. This became famous as an example of one of the elements of the modern concept of total war, in which the whole population had a part to play. The edict defined the roles for each group in the population:

Young men shall go to fight; married men shall forge arms and transport food supplies; women shall make tents, clothes, and serve the hospitals; children shall make bandages from old linen; elderly men shall sit in the public squares to excite the courage of warriors, preach hatred of kings, and the unity of the Republic. Bachelors shall fight with banners inscribed: "The French people stands against tyrants!"

Robespierre's ideas on democracy did not include accommodation or compromise: He wanted no constitutional checks and balances by judiciary and second chambers. He wanted males previously excluded from voting to participate in politics: Actors, Jews, and Blacks were now part of the nation. He proclaimed that "each man ... should take part in public affairs." No mention was made of "each woman."

History
BYTES

The perpetual symbol of the French Revolution is the guillotine. This device for decapitating people was invented in order to make executions more humane. The popular legend is that this effective and efficient killing machine was invented by a Doctor Guillotine in 1789, but this is not true. Whoever did invent the guillotine, it served its purpose well. The victim was placed on a bench with his or her head between the upright beams. The steel blade, which weighed about 40 kilos, dropped from a height of 2.3 metres at a speed of 7 metres per second. It took about two one-hundredths of a second to sever the head, which then fell into a basket below. Though the beheading was swift and clean, some doctors at the time said it could take as much as 30 seconds for the victim (the head only, presumably) to lose consciousness. Prior to the Revolution, decapitation was exclusively used to execute members of the aristocracy; with the Revolution, this privilege was granted to everyone.

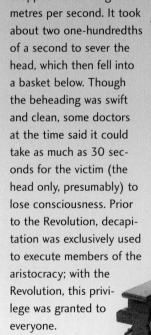

Review, Reflect, Respond

1. What evidence suggests that King Louis XVI misread the mood of the French people prior to the Revolution?

2. Explain why 1789 has been described as the "Year of Liberty."

3. Was the Reign of Terror a necessary evil for the long-term success of the Revolution or merely fanatics trying to take charge?

WOMEN AND THE REVOLUTION

Many male voters did not approve of women who took an interest in revolutionary politics. Yet, the *philosophe* Condorcet argued that women ought to vote as well as men: "Why should beings who have pregnancies and passing indispositions [menstrual periods] not be able to exercise rights which nobody has suggested taking from men with gout or who catch cold easily?" In 1788 Condorcet made it clear that all property owners of sufficient status should vote, irrespective of sex. A woman who paid property tax and was not a minor or mentally handicapped should vote. It was property that gave the right to vote. Condorcet's views, however, were not widely shared.

During the French Revolution, a number of radical women tried to make speeches and establish women's clubs. Most famous is the Belgian Théroigne de Méricourt (1762–1817). She was avidly interested in the debates at the Estates-General, but later became mentally ill and died in an insane asylum. Some of her enemies claimed that her madness was a result of her unnatural, unfeminine interest in politics. There were lower-class, highly politicized women of the French Revolution, and a gang of Jacobin women once attacked Méricourt. Women's clubs for political discussion were closed down by the autumn of 1793 and leading women were executed.

The Final Thoughts of Madame Roland

As France attempted to rebuild its society after the collapse of the *ancien régime*, individuals of widely divergent views clashed. Often these clashes had deadly results. Madame Roland (1754–1793), the wife of an inspector of manufactures in Lyon, was an ardent supporter of the cause of liberty. In the years leading up to the Revolution, Madame Roland had surrounded herself with idealists and radical thinkers who shared her vision for the future. Herself an intelligent, energetic, and self-educated philosopher — well read in English and Italian and well versed in the theories of Rousseau — Madame Roland welcomed the French Revolution. "Friends of humanity, lovers of liberty," she wrote, "we believed that it would regenerate the race … We welcomed it with rapture."

As one of those who fervently welcomed the Revolution, Madame Roland was also bitterly disappointed when events took a bloody turn during the Terror. An outspoken woman and defender of freedom, Roland was to be among the thousands killed by the Jacobins. Moments before she was decapitated on the guillotine, she is reported to have declared: "O Liberty, what crimes are committed in thy name!" Her enemies described Roland as "a petty philosopher and small-time intellectual." They accused her of being disdainful of the people and the judges, and of being arrogant and opinionated. According to her enemies, her greatest crime resulted from her failure to accept the limitations of her sex. They wrote, "… and yet she was a mother but she sacrificed nature in her wish to rise above it; her desire to be an intellectual led her to forget the virtues of her sex and this forgetfulness, always dangerous, finally led her to the scaffold." When Madame Roland's husband, who was away from Paris, heard of her execution, he committed suicide.

During her final months, when she had decided to starve herself to death, Madame Roland penned these thoughts, in which she pours out her disdain for those who destroyed the Revolution:

Marie Antoinette, Queen of France, was executed by guillotine after months of imprisonment. During that time, a campaign of character assassination went on, accusing her of sexual excesses. She is seen here in the last moments of her life.

Is life a blessing which is bestowed upon us? I believe it is. But I also believe that there are conditions attached which we must observe. We are born to seek happiness and to serve the happiness of our fellow mortals. The social order merely extends the range of this objective and indeed of all our faculties; it adds nothing new …

The Terror triumphs; all opposition is crushed. Insolence and crime rage furiously together and the people bow down in mindless homage. A vast city, gorged with blood and rotten with lies, wildly applauds the foul murders which are supposed to be necessary for its safety.

I know that the empire of evil never lasts long. Sooner or later the wicked get their desserts. If I was unknown, tucked away in some silent corner, I might find it possible to ignore the horrors that are tearing France apart and to wait patiently for better times, keeping virtue alive in private. But here in prison, a proclaimed victim, every hour that I remain alive gives tyranny new scope for boasting. I cannot beat them, but I can at least defraud them.[7]

WEB CONNECTION

www.mcgrawhill.ca/links/legacy

Go to the site above to find out more about revolutionary women

Madame Roland (1754–1793)

The Revolution of 1789 ended the political supremacy of the old court culture — where women were often highly influential — and replaced it with an Assembly of middle-aged men who would discuss male rights in The Declaration of the Rights of Man and of the Citizen. Even the most radical revolutionaries could not accept the idea of women participating in politics. They also suspected that women were too influenced by priests and counter-revolutionaries. In fact, the assumption that women were strongly influenced by Roman Catholicism was used as an excuse to deny them the vote during the nineteenth century. The following excerpt from an article in the *Moniteur* of November 19, 1793, expresses the male attitude: "Women, do you wish to be true Republicans? Then love, follow, and teach the laws that guide your husbands and sons in the exercise of their rights ... Be diligent in your housework; never attend political meetings with the intention of speaking there." The Revolution not only brought no change to the patriarchal attitudes of traditional European society, but also dispelled any hopes of women advancing into political life.

Robespierre's Demise

In 1793 and 1794 there were food shortages due to a poor grain harvest. Many people complained of rising food costs and in February 1793 a deputation in Paris called on the Convention to legislate lower bread prices. Robespierre struck at economic radicals who wanted price controls. He also turned on his compatriot Georges Jacques Danton, whom Robespierre thought was too moderate. Danton was sent to the guillotine in April 1794, and in the summer of that year Robespierre unwittingly caused many at the Convention to unite against him. He announced that another purge of enemies of the Revolution was coming — without giving any names. Almost everyone in the Convention feared that he might be on this list. The normally docile deputies had the motion removed and voted to have Robespierre and his associates arrested. Robespierre, his brother Augustin, the young radical Saint-Just, and others were sent to the guillotine on July 27, 1794 (9 *Thermidor* in the revolutionary calendar).

After Thermidor

Robespierre's death on 9 *Thermidor* marked the end of the most radical phase of revolutionary government. Henceforth, struggles within the political class would establish a more stable and conservative regime, the so-called "Thermidorian reaction." Gradually, the committees for Public Safety and Security were remodelled. The revolutionary tribunal, which had sentenced so many to death, now acquitted the accused. The so-called "gilded youth," or rich young people, would harass those they suspected of being radical sympathizers. Especially in the south of France there were attacks on those who had been militants during Robespierre's Terror. This is sometimes called the "White Terror," in contrast to the "Red Terror" of the revolutionaries. In reaction to Robespierre's austere Republic of Virtue, during this period many churches reopened, as well as many *cafés* and theatres. Generally, in the aftermath of Robespierre's government, there was a relaxation of revolutionary fervour.

The winter of 1794–1795 was the harshest in 100 years. Food was scarce and very expensive. Furthermore, paper money of the Revolution (called *assignats* because its value was assigned to national assets) was rapidly losing its value and sellers often refused to accept it. On April 1, 1795, revolutionary militants surged into the Convention, demanding bread and the 1793 constitution. They held the Assembly captive for several hours. There were more violent demonstrations in Paris during May. These demonstrations, known as *Germinal–Prairial* (from the names of the months in the revolutionary calendar) were the last spontaneous popular uprisings in Paris during the Revolution. In the aftermath of the backlash against extremism, radical activists such as François Emile "Gracchus" Babeuf (the name Gracchus comes from the days of the Roman

Republic), who dreamed of an egalitarian society, were arrested and executed.

With the demise of the Jacobin radicals came a more conservative and middle-class regime known as the Directory, the name given the new government executive. The Directory was a time of economic inflation and speculation; and the new government failed to reconcile revolutionary ideas of liberty with the need for order. In general, the Directory resisted both royalists and leftist radicals but did not govern effectively. It did, however, undertake military activities in Italy that would favour a bright young general who would have an immense impact on France and all of Europe.

Pleasures
AND PASTIMES

The reputation of Paris as one of the world's great culinary cities was firmly established during the Revolution. The popular dish lobster thermidor is one reminder of the Revolution. The establishment of many high-quality restaurants in Paris was directly tied to the decline of the old aristocracy and the rise of a new middle class. Many of the leading chefs who helped build Paris's culinary reputation had learned their trade in the kitchens of aristocrats who had either fled France or been executed during the Terror. In the new, supposedly egalitarian age, it became fashionable for representatives staying in Paris to dine in the new restaurants. While a chef in an aristocratic household sought to please a small number of wealthy employers, the chefs of the new restaurants competed for the business of a wider clientele. This led to the development of exciting new dishes to entice the new diners. Despite the claims of egalitarianism by the leading revolutionaries, a hierarchy of cuisine clearly developed. Often the conditions for the masses were appalling; leftovers from the finer restaurants were sold to lesser eating establishments until the food was nearly unfit for human consumption, at which time it was given to the poor.

THE AGE OF NAPOLÉON

Napoléon Bonaparte

To his contemporaries as well as to posterity, Napoléon Bonaparte (1769–1821) was almost superhuman in his military and governmental achievements. He came to symbolize order after the chaos and excesses of the revolutionary decade, with its civil strife, confiscations and arbitrariness.

Charles Maurice de Talleyrand-Périgord (1754–1838) was a bishop of the *ancien régime* and a revolutionary politician who served as Minister of Foreign Affairs under Napoléon.[8] *Talleyrand once observed*: "He [Napoléon] was clearly the most extraordinary man I ever saw, and I believe the most extraordinary man that has lived in our age, or in many ages."

Napoléon Bonaparte was born into an impoverished family of Corsican nobles in 1769, one year after the French foreign minister purchased the Mediterranean island for France from Genoa. In 1778 Napoléon arrived at Marseilles unable to speak French (Corsicans spoke Italian). He had enrolled in several military colleges and showed a special interest in artillery. As a young officer, he was given his first garrison posting in the south of France. At the outbreak of the Revolution, he joined the local revolutionary club in the town of Valence. In general, Napoléon welcomed — or at least did not resist — the Revolution, unlike some of his wealthier aristocratic companions at the military college. He no longer felt sympathy for those who wanted Corsican independence. He was grateful for the French connection that had provided him with a good education, and so decided to pursue his future in France. At the time of the Terror in 1793, Napoléon was involved in the attack on the Mediterranean port of Toulon, which had gone royalist and supported the English. The young Corsican's success won him praise and recognition, and revealed the first glimpse of his brilliance.

An opportunity presented itself to Napoléon in the aftermath of Jacobinism. The Thermidorians (winners in the political crisis of 9 *Thermidor*) did not want a return to a monarchy; but, they were exhausted by revolutionary government and political purges. They wanted to consolidate the internal changes in France but were under the constant pressure of the ongoing European wars involving Austria, Prussia, Britain, and Italy. In 1795, two years after the fall of the monarchy, the royalists had begun to agitate. The Thermidorians were now as apprehensive of vengeful royalists as they were of fanatical Jacobins.

In this tenuous situation, Napoléon, now a bright young general who had returned to Paris, grasped an opportunity to show his decisiveness. When the army came up against a mob of rightist demonstrators, Napoléon subdued the uprising by having his soldiers fire into the mob. This incident near a downtown Paris church was known as the "whiff of grapeshot." A leading Thermidorian politician, Paul de Barras, then decided to use his influence to advance Napoléon's career. At Toulon, Napoléon had shown his military skill, and in Paris he showed that he could be ruthless as well. At age 26, in March of 1796, he was appointed Commander-in-Chief of the French Army invading Italy. It was extraordinary to entrust such an important position to such a young officer.

Conflict and War: Italy and the Revolution

The French invasion of Italy in 1796, with 41 000 troops, recalled the *furia francese* (French fury) of earlier centuries, when the rich cities of the Italian peninsula were looted by French invaders. The Italian intelligentsia was soon drawn to the notion that these armies might carry the message of the Revolution, purify the corrupt feudalism of the Italian states, and perhaps even establish unity. In parts of Italy, there were people sympathetic to the reforms of the Revolution who hoped for the same changes in their own society.

With a few more military successes (e.g., Rivoli, Milan, Mantua), Napoléon proclaimed the Cisalpine Republic in northern Italy on December 27, 1796. This

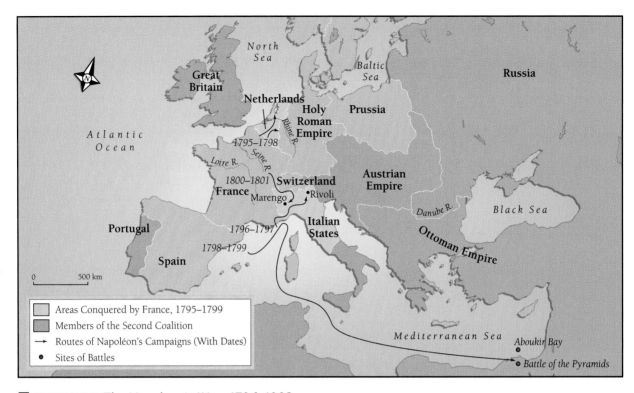

FIGURE 5.2 The Napoleonic Wars 1796-1802
Compare this map to the one on page 197. Note the shifting boundaries.

guaranteed the Italians freedom of the press, the right to petition, the right to education, and equality before the law. The French fought the Austrian armies vigorously and, by October 1797, the Austrians conceded a humiliating defeat and agreed to the Treaty of Campo Formio. Later, the French pushed southward, captured Rome, and went on to establish a Neapolitan republic.

Many Italians welcomed the French as friends, but still more hated the pillaging foreigners. In 1799 anti-French revolts broke out in northern Italy and Naples. In June 1799 the Army of the Holy Faith entered Naples and massacred more than 100 Italian republicans. In the same month, the ghetto of Siena was sacked and three Jews were burnt alive with a Tree of Liberty (a symbol to mark the acceptance of civil equality as taught by revolutionary codes). In Tuscany and Umbria, peasants attacked French sympathizers (mostly landowners) in the name of Catholicism. Various images of the Virgin

and Christ in Italy were reported to have wept in revulsion at the Godless French. By March the French had been expelled from Italy.

REDEFINING THE STATE: NAPOLEONIC GOVERNMENT

Napoléon took power in France in 1799 by the *coup d'état* known as 18 *Brumaire* (9–10 November), one month after his return to France from the important though militarily unsuccessful Egyptian campaign. The campaign was important in part because, while in Egypt, the soldiers and scholars Napoléon had taken with him documented ancient monuments, brought many other pillaged treasures back to France, and discovered the famous Rosetta Stone. It was the Rosetta Stone that finally allowed scholars to decipher Egyptian hieroglyphics.

■ **FIGURE 5.3** Europe Under Napoléon, 1810
How do you think Napoleon's conquests help shape the modern map of Europe?

In the constitution of the Year VIII, published in December 1799, Napoléon strengthened the centralization of government in France: There were to be three consuls as executives; the first would serve for 10 years. There were new assemblies — the Tribunate and the Legislative Body — and a complicated electoral system for men over 21. Despite the organizational formalities, in practice Napoléon dominated the government as First Consul.

The Concordat

Gradually, Napoléon took a number of important initiatives to bring stability and order back to France. In 1801 he concluded an accord with Pope Pius VII, intended to assuage the resentment of Catholics over the treatment of the Church and the clergy. The Concordat of July 1801 recognized Roman Catholicism as the religion of the majority of the French and agreed to pay the parish clergy. The Pope could, however, refuse government nominees for the clergy. The freedom to practise other religions was upheld. In 1807 Napoléon called a meeting of Jewish rabbis to discuss the relationship of their congregations to the French state. His general aim in matters of faith was to remove the main causes of friction between government and religion.

Napoléon also reorganized the higher educational system, setting up a system of *lycées* (secondary schools) under military discipline. There were also municipal colleges. Graduation from this system was a requirement for entry to the so-called Big Schools in Paris, which trained engineers and teachers. Other institutions reinforced an educational system based on opportunities for those with the best results in examinations.

In May 1804, Napoléon was proclaimed the "hereditary emperor of the French." In a referendum, 3.5 million voted yes and only 2 500 voted no to a proposal that "the government of the Republic is confided to an emperor who will carry the title of the Emperor of the French." Napoléon was crowned in the presence of Pope Pius VII, and swore to uphold the integrity of the territory of the Republic, the Concordat with the Church, freedom of religion, equality of rights, political and civil liberties, and the irreversibility of the sale of confiscated properties. No tax was to be levied without a law and the Emperor was to "govern with the sole aim of the interest, happiness, and glory of the French People."

The Code Napoléon

The 1799 constitution had set up the prefectoral system, with its parallels to the earlier system of nominees by the king (*intendants*) seen during the *ancien régime*. Napoléon also set up the State Council, described by French novelist M. H. B. Stendhal (1783–1842) as "the 50 least stupid Frenchmen," which drafted legislation. It also reorganized the civil law code, which came to be known as the *Code Napoléon* (1804), on the basis of equality before the law, and in taxation. Even if a couple had married in a religious ceremony, they had to go through a civil ceremony to register their union with the state. The criminal code specified jury trial for major cases. Napoléon worked with the state council on other legal reforms and insisted that they derive from general principles rather than local conditions. Napoleonic laws, although revised and expanded subsequently, remained the basic law of France and are still used in other parts of the world, including the province of Québec.

The Napoleonic Wars

In 1789 the French army had 228 000 men under the command of aristocratic officers. Proof of four noble forebears was required for admission to the officer corps. The decree of August 23, 1793, had requisitioned all the male inhabitants of the nation: "From this moment until the enemy shall have been ejected from the territory of the Republic, all of the French are requisitioned for the service of the armies." This opened the army to all. Later, under the Directory, a conscription law of September 23, 1798, made all French men between the ages of 20 and 25 subject to military service. This produced an annual levy of 200 000 young soldiers who were not particularly well trained but were full of youthful enthusiasm. Later, Napoléon also developed a special elite force of 80 000 men, called the Imperial Guard. The French casualties of the Napoleonic wars — more than 600 000 by a recent estimate — did not shake the loyalty of his soldiers.

In 1800 Napoléon crossed the St. Bernard Pass, defeated the Austrians at Marengo, and conquered Italy; and in 1801, the Treaty of Lunéville ended the war between France and Austria. Though the French fleet had been defeated by Britain in 1798 at the Battle of the Nile in Egypt, Napoléon resumed war with Britain in 1803. The French fleet (with the Spanish)

Napoléon Crossing the Alps (1800) by Jacques-Louis David. On the bottom left, what has David written?

would again be destroyed two years later by Admiral Lord Nelson (1758–1805) and the British fleet at the Battle of Trafalgar.

The battle usually considered Napoléon's greatest triumph was at Austerlitz, Austria, in 1805. Here, he defeated the combined forces of Austria under Francis II (1768–1835), and Russia, under Czar Alexander I (1768–1825). Using clever deception and manoeuvres, Napoléon crushed the coalition, forcing Austria to grant territorial concessions in Germany and Italy and sign the Treaty of Pressburg. Russia also recalled its forces from the war.

Napoléon defeated the Prussians at Jena in 1806, smashed the Austrian armies, and burned Moscow in 1812. He slept as a conqueror in many of the capitals of the Continent. With his military adventures, the map of Europe was permanently redrawn. After the Battle at Jena, and Napoléon's drive to Berlin, the Holy Roman Empire was eradicated, creating the Confederation of the Rhine and speeding the unification of Germany in 1870. The presence of French institutions in parts of Italy prepared the way for the later Italian unification under the house of Piedmont. The disruption that the Napoleonic invasion caused in Spain stimulated Latin American independence movements. The invasion of Portugal caused the Braganza

dynasty to cross over to Brazil and introduce policies that would lead to Brazilian independence in 1822. Although warfare in the Napoleonic period had major repercussions in Europe and overseas, his attempt to subjugate the entire continent of Europe through his dream of a "continental system" in the end failed, just as Louis XIV's bid for European hegemony had failed a century earlier.

THE END OF NAPOLÉON: A SEARCH FOR ORDER

Although Napoléon had successfully fought wars in many areas of Europe, it was the disastrous Russian campaign of 1812 that fatally weakened his forces. In October 1813, the Russian, Prussian, and Austrian armies combined to defeat Napoléon at the "Battle of the Nations." Allied armies invaded southwestern France from Spain and also from Germany. By the end of March, foreign armies had entered Paris. On April 11, 1814, Napoléon abdicated, and was exiled to the small island of Elba in the Mediterranean — without his empress, who had gone home to the Hapsburg court in Vienna, taking with her Napoléon's son, now the king of Rome.

Marshal Ney Retreats from Moscow in 1812, by Adolph Ivon. Though Napoléon's army burned Moscow, the campaign took a disastrous toll on the French forces. What went wrong?

Review, Reflect, Respond

1. Assess the role women played in the French Revolution. Explain their importance to its success.

2. What impact did the French Revolution have on religion and family life in France? In your opinion were these positive or negative results?

3. Create a time line tracing Napoleon's rise and decline. As his advisor, would you have encouraged the Russian campaign? Would you have supported his return from exile in Elba?

Exiled

Napoléon Bonaparte, who had risen from his humble Corsican roots to be the master of Europe, finally faced defeat in 1814. Under the Treaty of Fontainebleau, he agreed to abdicate, in exchange for which he was given the tiny kingdom of Elba, a small island in the Mediterranean Sea. When Napoléon arrived on Elba on May 3, 1814, he brought with him ambitious plans to reform government and stimulate the economy. To improve communications between the island's strategic points, Napoléon encouraged road construction. He also helped to modernize agriculture and improve fishing. He worked hard to win the support of the island's bourgeoisie by flattering them with honorary titles and invitations to his court. Beyond these measures, however, Napoléon accomplished little on the island. His efforts to revitalize the mining industry were thwarted by his own greed, as he pocketed much of the money from the mines and increased land taxes.

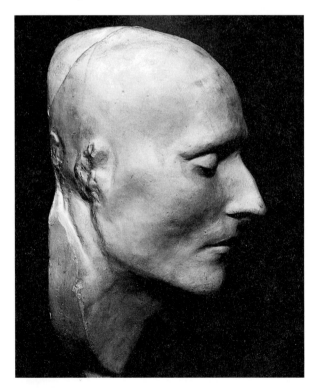

The death mask of Napoléon.

These measures led to revolts, which were suppressed under the threat of arms.

On the evening of February 26, 1815, Napoléon took advantage of the temporary absence of his English custodian, Colonel Campbell. Under the cover of night, he silently slipped away from Elba, returning to the mainland, where loyal supporters joined him. During this so-called "Flight of the Eagle," Napoléon travelled through areas where he knew he had support. About 500 000 partisan volunteers, called *fédérés*, welcomed him throughout the country.

Restoring International Order: The Congress of Vienna

The Congress of Vienna ended the dazzling Napoleonic adventure. Assembled in September 1814, the Congress was clearly dominated by the powers that had defeated Napoléon: Russia, Great Britain, Prussia, and Austria. Louis XVI's brother meanwhile had been recalled to the French throne, for lack of a more suitable candidate. Many of his advisers were out of touch with the new France. The Restoration (of the previous order) soon lost popular support and this helped Napoléon in his attempt to mount a comeback.

The Congress of Vienna failed to deal with liberalism or nationalism in Europe. But, after nine months of wearisome negotiations in Vienna, the treaty was signed in Paris on June 19, 1815, the day after the final defeat of Napoléon by Arthur Wellesley, Duke of Wellington, at the Battle of Waterloo. Always portraying himself as a man of the Revolution, Napoléon had created the idea of a grand nation, a European federation of different peoples linked by The Declaration of the Rights of Man and of the Citizen.

The great powers accepted the Vienna Treaty: Britain, Austria, Prussia, Russia, and France in the name of the restored Bourbon king, Louis XVIII. Sweden, Spain and Portugal also signed, and so did many smaller powers. Only the Pope and the Turkish sultan withheld assent to the new arrangements. Belgium was incorporated into the kingdom of the Netherlands (a union that broke down in 1830); Prussia was strengthened, and so was the House of Savoy in Italy. By 1870 Germany and Italy had both become unified, modern nations. The losers were Poland (which was partitioned), the Italian nationalists, whose hopes for a country in 1815 were dashed, and Saxony, which lost two-fifths of its territory to Prussia.

Napoléon was exiled again, this time to the tiny island of St. Helena, where he died in 1821. Over the years, there have been several theories on how Napoléon met his death. The theory today is that he was poisoned. This may well be true, but the one-time emperor of France was not poisoned by some crazed Jacobin or grudging royalist — it was the wallpaper that finally got him. Tests have shown that Napoléon died as a result of exposure to arsenic compounds in the wallpaper of his home in St. Helena.

German philosopher Friedrich Hegel, trying to encapsulate the impact of the French Revolution on Europe, wrote of the "fury of disappearance" and the "universal freedom" that resulted from an upheaval that could only destroy and not build. Napoléon's legacy has been seen more positively because of his administrative, educational and legal innovations, which endured despite the change of dynasties and forms of government. The Congress of Vienna established how international meetings should be conducted, and defined diplomatic relationships. In broad terms, it was a settlement that prevented a general European war for almost a century — until the summer of 1914.

SOCIAL HISTORY: LIVING THE REVOLUTION

Private Life and the Revolution

The effects of the invasion of public privacy during the Revolution were most evident in everyday family life. Clothing came to have political significance, and the old aristocratic style was seen as counter-revolutionary. Some argued that if private character was to be revolutionized, then dress too had to be entirely renovated.

How could true equality of French citizens be achieved if class distinctions continued to be expressed through dress? By April 1793, all French citizens, regardless of gender, were required to wear the tricolour cockade (a badge made of white, red, and blue ribbon).

Prior to the Revolution, women of the aristocracy wore exotic hairstyles, sometimes rising to a height of half a metre above the head, and adorned with various props, such as a bowl of fruit or a zoo. One woman's hair featured a pastoral scene complete with a pond, a duck hunter, a windmill that turned, and a miller riding on a mule while a monk seduced his wife. After the Revolution, fashion reflected the virtues of the common people, with flattened hair, skirts less flared, and lower heels. In general, clothing during the revolution was looser and lighter and, for women, showed more bare skin. This led one journalist to comment: "Several goddesses appeared in dresses so light and so transparent that they denied desire the sole pleasure on which it thrives: the pleasure of guessing."

A fashionably-dressed woman from the time of the Revolution, 1790. Note the patriotic blue, white and red skirt.

Clothing was not the only outward display of revolutionary spirit. Letters ended with "farewell and fraternity" rather than the usual "your obedient and humble servant." Inside the home, there were "revolution beds," as well as snuffboxes, shaving mugs, chests and even chamber pots decorated with revolutionary or allegorical scenes representing the revolution's motto, "Liberty, equality, and fraternity." Even chess pieces and playing cards were adapted to fit the Revolution. Chess pieces were renamed, because a good revolutionary would never play with kings, queens, bishops, and knights. The kings, queens, and jacks in playing cards were also replaced by liberties, equalities, and fraternities.

Even the family unit faced dramatic changes as a result of the Revolution. Inspired by the work of Rousseau, the revolutionaries stressed the importance of childbearing and motherhood. Slogans and banners encouraged people to have children, proclaiming "Citizenesses! Give the Fatherland Children" and "Now is the time to make a baby." Mothers were encouraged to breast-feed and reject the practice of paying wet nurses to feed their babies.

The National Convention also adopted several measures aimed at ensuring the equality of all children. The abolition of primogeniture (inheritance by the first-born) helped to end "paternal despotism" by ensuring that all children were given an equal share of the family inheritance, and that illegitimate children were granted full legal status. The National Convention attempted to establish a national system of education based on the principle that children "belong to the Republic before they belong to their parents." Saint-Just, a journalist and member of the Committee of Public Safety, wrote in his notebook: "The child, the citizen, belong to the fatherland. Common instruction is necessary. Children belong to their mother until the age of five, if she has [breast-] fed them, and to the Republic afterwards ... until death."

Marriage was taken out of the hands of the Catholic Church and secularized. After 1792 the state controlled marriage, establishing the requirements for marriage and charging a fee for a civil ceremony. It was the state that sanctioned marriages and granted rights to illegitimate children and orphans. In 1792 France also adopted the most liberal divorce laws in the world. Men and women could seek a divorce on several grounds, including insanity, brutality and abandonment for two or more years. A couple could also agree to divorce by mutual consent. The liberal divorce laws adopted during the Revolution would be significantly curtailed later, as would the rights of women.

Religion and the Revolution

The Revolution affected private thoughts as well as private lives. By 1794 religion in France had changed a great deal. Church lands were confiscated, bishops were elected like other public officials, and the clergy were required to swear oaths of allegiance to the state. During the Terror, Robespierre even tried to create a new civil religion, the Cult of the Supreme Being, with a special day designated for its celebration. Despite this, many people simply worshipped in clandestine groups.

The Abbé Sieyés, a religious man, neverless supported the Revolution and drafted the Declaration of the Rights of Man in 1789.

Someone calling herself or himself "Suzanne *sans peur*" expressed the frustration many felt when she or he wrote: "There is no governmental despotism anywhere that equals ours. They tell us, you are free and sovereign, while we are regimented to the point that we are forbidden to sing or play in our Sunday best, not even allowed to kneel to give homage to the Supreme Being." In the end, the attempts to reduce the role of the Catholic Church in French society failed largely due to the tenacious efforts of women who kept the faith alive during the Revolution and led the restoration of the faith when restrictions on religious practice were lifted.

TWO REVOLUTIONARY ARTISTS: DAVID AND BEETHOVEN

Jacques-Louis David

The artist whose work is most closely associated with the French Revolution is Jacques-Louis David (1748–1825). David rejected the rococo for more academic, classical subjects and styles. He felt strongly that his art should teach a lesson or reflect a moral. He was active in the Revolution and friendly with

The *Oath of the Horatii* by David (1785). This huge painting (3m by 3.5 m) was commissioned for Louis XVI, before the Revolution, yet it carries a revolutionary, republican theme. The three patriotic brothers are swearing an oath to put their country before their lives. David's extreme classicism is evident in the geometric composition, straight lines and blocks of pure, unshaded colour. Where else can one see figures posed in this way?.

revolutionaries such as Jean Marat and Robespierre, and was even one of the signatories of the order to execute Louis XVI. After the Revolution, David would become the official painter for the Emperor Napoléon.

David often chose stories and themes from the history of ancient Greece and the Roman Republic to illustrate virtuous and patriotic heroes. The *Oath of the Horatii*, for example, tells a story from the early history of Rome about three brothers who placed the state above their family and vowed to give (and gave) their lives for Rome. The strong gestures of the men as they take their oath contrast with the softer colours and curving forms of the weeping women on the opposite side of the tableau. Rendered in clear, simple lines and colours, both subject and style are as far from the rococo style as one can imagine. Determination and love of country above all are the ideas expressed forcefully in this work; it helped that the canvas measured 4.27 by 3.35 metres. Although painted before the Revolution, the *Oath of the Horatii* carried ideas that appealed to both the monarchy and its future political antagonists.

David's *Death of Marat* is at once a political painting and a revealing psychological study of one of the heroes of the Revolution. The revolutionary writer Jean-Paul Marat was murdered in his bath by a political enemy named Charlotte Corday in July 1793. David both commemorates and pays homage to his patriotic friend. *Death of Marat* depicts the murder scene in clear, sharp detail and also reveals the character of the dead man, his pen and paper still in hand. This emphasis on the individual, some would say, foreshadows the romanticism to come in the early nineteenth century. David signed the painting "À MARAT, DAVID" and dated it "L'AN DEUX," meaning "To Marat, from David. Year Two [of the Revolution]."

David was such a highly successful and influential painter that his works had a great effect on the artists of the nineteenth century. He was a classicist, but his devotion to truth, virtue, and morality is romantic as well. The classical and romantic styles continued through the end of the eighteenth century. They would co-exist as Europe lived through the revolutionary turmoil that characterized the late eighteenth century,

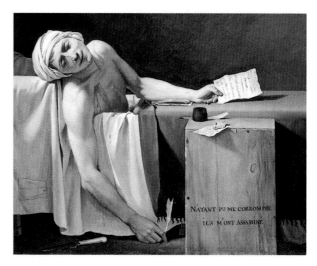

In this painting, called the *Death of Marat* (1793), David pays homage to his friend, Jean Marat, a Revolutionary writer. Marat had a painful skin disease that was relieved by soaking in a bath tub.

and the romanticism that began to dominate painting by the first decades of the nineteenth century.

Ludwig von Beethoven

Like David, Ludwig von Beethoven (1770–1827) was caught up in the French Revolution and closely followed the Napoleonic adventure. Like Michelangelo in the sixteenth century, Beethoven struggled to achieve his artistic vision, overcoming family problems, as he was obliged to support his mother and sisters from an early age. His musical virtuosity made him beloved by the aristocratic houses of Vienna. Unlike Mozart, Beethoven was never a court musician, but there were many people willing to help him financially with money or gifts. In an age that was starting to celebrate the individual, he considered himself a nonconformist and it suited him to work on his own, with no desire to entertain or glorify others.

In his twenties, just as his career was blossoming, Beethoven began to lose his hearing and eventually became profoundly deaf. After a heroic struggle within himself, he decided to pursue his art as a way to overcome his affliction. This decision reflected a purely romantic sensibility. Beethoven's musical themes centred around humanity's triumph over despair and conflict. His music went through various stages, but it is through his symphonies, nine in all, that he was and is able to reach many listeners, then and now. One of the most interesting of his symphonies is the third, called the "Eroica" (from the Italian word for hero).

Beethoven's brooding, romantic temperament is evident in this portrait. What does romantic mean today?

This work was dedicated to Napoléon. Beethoven worshipped the patriotic hero and the republican ideals of the Revolution, until he received word that Napoléon had proclaimed himself Emperor. It is said that Beethoven then wanted to tear up the score.

His fifth symphony is probably Beethoven's best-known work, with its famous opening four notes; many have interpreted these notes as the sound of fate knocking at the composer's door. His ninth symphony is most evocative of Beethoven's ultimate triumph over his deafness. He ends the symphony with a sweeping choral movement that uses the words of *Ode to Joy* by German poet Johann von Schiller (1759–1805). This is the archetypal romantic work of art: the romantic hero triumphing over pain and despair to rejoice in life.

Beethoven wrote one opera, *Fidelio*, which tells the story of a group of people struggling to gain their freedom from unjust imprisonment. Again, this theme mirrors Beethoven's personal obsession and the obsession of the time: freedom from oppression. Beethoven's works provide the bridge between the structured, intellectual music of the eighteenth century and the dynamic, passionate music of nineteenth-century romanticism. By the end of his career, the romantic movement had taken over all aspects of the Western arts.

Reflections

The quarter-century between the outbreak of the French Revolution and the end of Napoléon's reign brought drastic change to Europe. The *ancien régime* had fallen and ideas of the Enlightenment had taken root. Although there would be efforts by conservative forces in Europe to turn back the clock and restore the old order, Europe had entered a new age. No longer would the nobility be able to lay claim to the privileges it had held for centuries. Nor did the Roman Catholic Church remain the unquestionable authority it had been in previous centuries. The French Revolution had brought a new social and political order to France and the Napoleonic Wars had spread this change through much of Europe. As the nineteenth century dawned, so too did a new era.

Chapter Review

Chapter Summary

In this chapter, we have seen:

- that Europe on the eve of the French Revolution was comprised of a variety of communities — urban, rural, and intellectual
- the influence of key individuals — such as Abbé Sieyès and Napoléon Bonaparte — who helped shape Western attitudes
- the impact of Western thought on social and political developments in the world
- how the Revolution led to significant challenges to traditional attitudes towards religion and religious observance in France

Reviewing the Significance of Key People, Concepts, and Events (Knowledge and Understanding)

1. Understanding the era of the French Revolution requires a knowledge of the following concepts and people and an understanding of their significance to the events that reshaped Europe and the world. Select and explain two items from each column.

Concepts	Events	People
third estate	Storming of the Bastille	Louis XVI
Estates-General	The October Days	Marie Antoinette
National Assembly	National Convention	Mirabeau
Tennis Court Oath	Reign of Terror	Robespierre
salon	Coronation of Napoléon	Jacques-Louis David
Battle of Waterloo	Congress of Vienna	Beethoven
Code Napoléon	Madame Roland	Napoléon Bonaparte

2. The French Revolution swept out the *ancien régime* with promises of *liberté*, *égalité*, and *fraternité* for all French citizens. Over the following quarter-century, events and reforms transformed life in French society; but not always as initially imagined. Complete a Future Wheel showing the outcomes of the French Revolution. Your teacher will provide a guide to this activity.

Doing History: Thinking About the Past (Thinking/Inquiry)

3. Abbé Sieyès (Emmanuel Joseph Sieyès) published an influential pamphlet entitled *What is the Third Estate?* in January 1789. Carefully read the passage from it on the BLM you will be given. Then write two or three paragraphs on why this pamphlet was revolutionary and why it is considered one of the most significant documents of its time.

4. The rallying cry of the French Revolution was "Liberty, Equality, Fraternity." Did the revolution succeed at any point in achieving these goals with respect to women? Explain your answer.

Applying Your Learning (Application)

5. Carefully study the painting *Allegory of the Revolution* by Jeaurat de Bertray shown at the beginning of this chapter (page 168). This painting was completed in 1794 during the most radical phase of the Revolution and is full of revolutionary symbols and signs. What was the intended audience for this painting? Was Bertray a supporter or a critic of the Revolution? What evidence in the painting supports your answer? How effective is *Allegory of the Revolution* at conveying its message to its intended audience?

6. Imagine you are an adviser to King Louis XVI and have obtained a copy of Abbé Sieyès' *What is the Third Estate?* Create an imaginary dialogue between yourself and the king in which you discuss ideas on the financial crisis, while attempting to avoid further aggravating the members of the third estate.

Communicating Your Learning (Communication)

7. Imagine you are a member of the fourth estate. Write three editorials explaining the following events and their ramifications for France and Europe:
   i) The storming of the Bastille
   ii) The execution of Louis XVI
   iii) The coronation of Napoléon

8. Create a time line of significant events from 1789 to 1804 using only symbols, images, and key words or phrases to illustrate the events. Do not label the events; try to capture their essence pictorially.

CHAPTER SIX

The World in the Eighteenth Century

CHAPTER EXPECTATIONS

By the end of this chapter, you will be able to:

- *demonstrate an understanding of concepts and processes associated with imperialism, and their role in shaping developing nations.*

- *describe factors that prompted and facilitated increasing interaction between peoples in the eighteenth century*

- *analyse various forms of human servitude in Africa before, during and after the slave trade, and demonstrate an understanding of factors that constructed barriers to human-rights advancement*

- *demonstrate an understanding of how European imperialism affected the non-Western world, especially Africa, India, and China*

This sculpture from Benin, in west Africa was carved in the sixteenth century. Does it show any signs of western influence?

In the eighteenth century, Western Europe continued on the path it had begun to follow two centuries earlier, exploring the world and expanding Western influence, power, and wealth. Both the European and non-Western worlds were irrevocably changed as a result. Transformations occurred around the world as most of the world's cultures were drawn into global trading relationships, which ultimately favoured European interests rather than their own. The West's unceasing search for riches decimated indigenous cultures, created enduring dependence on the West, and enslaved millions. The European imagination ran wild with images of non-Western peoples depicted alternately as ruthless cannibals or enlightened, mystical beings. Artistic movements around the world reflected the impact of this contact as traditional elements of indigenous art combined with symbols, icons and ideals of conquerors, invaders and traders.

Europeans on the Atlantic Coast were gradually becoming accustomed to constant contact with great empires beyond the seas. Sometimes they even encountered cultures more sophisticated and ancient than European ones. All of these peoples were at some level being absorbed into a global trading system in which Europeans bought and sold goods all over the world: cotton, pepper and opium from India to China; Chinese porcelain and tea to Europe; European brandy and reshipped tobacco from Latin America for furs from Amerindians in North America, and so on. Europeans pressed forward everywhere, convinced of their notions on progress and the superiority of their religion.

Why study the history of contact between Western Europe and the rest of the world? Because the global trading system that emerged in the eighteenth century established the roots and patterns that govern connections between nations today. Some even argue that in order to understand why developing nations today are plagued with instability and poverty, we must understand the nature and importance of the contact these countries had with European countries at this time.

KEY CONCEPTS AND EVENTS

modernization theory

dependency theory

asiento

War of Austrian Succession

Peace of Aix-la-Chapelle

Seven Years' War

Abolitionist Movement

Ottoman Empire

Grand Exchange

KEY PEOPLE

Walt Whitman Rostow

East India Company

Jesuits

Daniel Defoe

Jonathan Swift

Engelbert Kaempfer

Wit and Wisdom

The first and greatest defect I observed in the English is their want of faith in religion ... The second defect ... is pride ... Their third defect is a passion for acquiring money and their attachment to worldly affairs.[1]
The Travels of Mirza Abu Taleb Khan (2:128-31)

TIME LINE: THE WORLD IN THE EIGHTEENTH CENTURY

Dutch land at Cape of Good Hope, Africa	1652	
	1713	Treaty of Utrecht
Jonathan Swift, *Gulliver's Travels*	1726	
	1727	Engelbert Kaempfer, *The History of Japan*
Peace of Aix-la-Chapelle	1748	
	1756	Seven Years' War begins
British gain control of East Indian state of Bengal at the Battle of Plassey	1757	
	1763	Seven Years' War ends; Treaty of Paris
England begins shipping convicts to the penal colony of Australia	1788	
	1775	American Revolution begins
Declaration of Independence drafted by Thomas Jefferson	1775	
	1791	Abolition of slavery in France

Not to scale.

THE WEST
AND THE WORLD

What does it mean to be a developing nation today? What do developing nations have in common? Some point to economic indicators — Gross Domestic Product (GDP), average wages, rate of industrialization — to explain why various countries share developing nation status. It is true that the average income in the developing world is approximately five percent of the average income in the developed world. Manufacturing output is also often low. In the 1970s, for instance, the total manufacturing output of Latin America was equal to the manufacturing output of Britain and France 100 years earlier. The number of cars produced in Peru per year equalled the number of cars produced in Canada per week. But, these economic indicators do not tell the whole story. There are many exceptions to the rule. The manufacturing out-

put of Taiwan, for example, certainly does not fit this explanation and yet this country is still considered a developing nation.

Some may point to the political structure of developing nations to explain why they do not progress at the same rate as Western nations. This explanation, though, seems flawed, since the political structures of these countries vary greatly: Cuba is a socialist state; Iran is a theocracy; Myanmar is a military dictatorship; Morocco is a monarchy; and China is a people's republic.

Others focus on literacy, claiming that developing nations have not progressed due to low rates of literacy. It is true that some countries, like Iran, have literacy rates that hover around 20 percent, but Cuba's literacy rate is 99 percent and it is still considered a developing nation.

Obviously, not all factors apply to all countries considered developing nations, and indeed there are some of

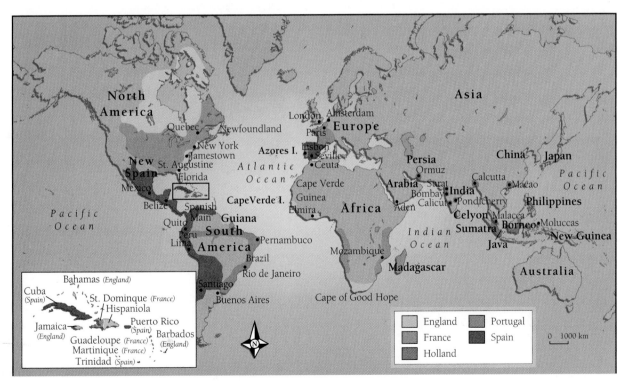

■ **FIGURE 6.1** European Possessions Overseas, ca. 1713
Consider the changes that have occurred around the region labelled Arabia in this map. Review a modern map of the region to see the new countries that have emerged. Are their boundaries geographical or geopolitical?

these characteristics in developed countries as well. The only common denominator seems to be that all present-day developing nations lived through a similar historical experience: *They all had to endure the expansion of Europe as it embraced capitalism, beginning in the eighteenth century*. There are two main theories that attempt to explain why some countries are developing nations today: modernization theory and dependency theory.

Modernization Theory

Modernization theory suggests that all societies were originally traditional. It defines "traditional" as "stagnant" and "unchanging" — societies in which daily work is simply for subsistence. Such cultures experienced little change, little progress, and little innovation. According to proponents of this theory, scientific discovery was happening in various parts of the world but for various reasons, they say, only in Europe did these discoveries lead to important technological change. Another force that fuelled change was the advent of capitalism as an economic system. In previous centuries, wealth had been used primarily for conspicuous consumption — to buy luxury items. Capitalism, however, includes the idea that wealth can be used to make more wealth. This ideological shift would ultimately power the Industrial Revolution in the nineteenth century.

Modernization theorists maintain that the reason some countries are developing nations today is because they failed to move from traditional societies to modern societies. They did not focus on science, technology, innovation, capitalism, or democracy. One of the main proponents of this theory was Walt Whitman Rostow, who wrote in the 1960s about the "stages of economic growth." He used the image of an airplane to help readers understand his theory that there were five stages of economic growth. Developing nations, Rostow believes, are stuck in one of the earlier stages, while since the eighteenth century, Europe has moved steadily through all five stages.

Rostow's Stages of Economic Growth

- **Stage 1**: The Traditional Society. People in a traditional society are simply living at a subsistence level. They do not focus on innovation, change, or progress. The airplane is immobile on the runway.
- **Stage 2**: The Preconditions for Takeoff. Something happens to stir up the traditional society. This may be an influence from the outside world, a scientific invention, or a discovery. At this point, the society might seize the opportunity to change and progress or, conversely, might reject the new idea and revert back to its traditional status. The airplane is warming up and getting ready to take off, but it might just stop dead in its tracks if the opportunity is not taken.
- **Stage 3**: The Takeoff. The country's political leaders seize the opportunity provided by the upset of traditional society and make progress, science, and technology their priorities. The airplane has left the runway and has started its journey.
- **Stage 4**: The Drive to Maturity. Economic growth begins and spreads to various sectors of society. The country gets involved in international trade, produces new goods for use at home and for export, and continues to use and develop modern technology. The airplane is steadily gaining altitude (although it may take two generations or more to reach the next stage).
- **Stage 5**: The Age of High Mass Consumption. The masses finally benefit from economic growth through increased standards of living. The airplane is flying high, at high speeds, and for a prolonged period of time.

Dependency Theory

Dependency theory is in direct opposition to modernization theory. In general, dependency theory states that the reason some countries are developing nations today is that, since the eighteenth century, growing European nations deliberately created poverty and dependency in these areas, in order to fuel and support their own growth. Dependency theorists such as F. H. Cardoso and S. J. Stein argue that none of these countries have remained "traditional." Rather, both European and non-European countries were transformed by European capitalist expansion, but while the former grew to new-found prosperity and power, the latter were held back, controlled, and impoverished. How did this happen? European capitalists were looking for profits and to make profits in manufacturing they required cheap labour and cheap inputs (natural resources and other goods). For cheap labour, they looked to indentured labour and slavery, and in order to maintain a cheap supply of inputs, they colonized and controlled areas with abundant natural resources or desired goods.

Dependency theorists focus on various important definitions to clarify their points. "Development" is the increase in capacity to produce goods. For example, countries that once used hand implements to farm later use tractors and combines. This shows an increase in productive capacity. A country that is "undeveloped" has simply not experienced these increases in productive capacity. On the other hand, a society that is "underdeveloped" lacks the autonomous capacity for change and growth. It is in a situation of dependency. It lacks control over its own development. Dependency theorists maintain that the developing world is where it is today as a result of its deliberate underdevelopment by European powers during and since the eighteenth century.

This having been said, however, writings by André Gunder Frank, one of the main proponents of dependency theory, caution that this can easily cause us to fall into the trap of Eurocentrism. It may lead us to believe that Europe had some sort of advantage in terms of ability, ethnic background, or inherent characteristics of its population. This is not true. In fact, the world economy until about 1800 was not Europe-centred; it was actually an Asian-based world economy that the Europeans were eager to exploit. The following quote by economist Adam Smith shows his view of Asia compared to Europe in the eighteenth century:

The improvements in agriculture and manufacture seem likewise to have been of very great antiquity in the provinces of Bengal in the East Indies, and in some of the eastern provinces of China ... Even those three countries (China, Egypt, and India), the wealthiest, according to all accounts, that ever were in the world, are chiefly renowned for their superiority in agriculture and manufactures ... [Now, in 1776] China is a much richer country than any part of Europe.[2]

Dependency theorists point out that these cultures were far from traditional if they were receiving such praise for improvements in agriculture and manufactures; however, Frank states that it was not necessarily Europe alone that caused certain parts of the world to become underdeveloped. We must also look at the structures and systems inherent in societies like India and China, which were already in decline by the time European expansion became a force to be reckoned with.

As you read through this chapter, keep these opposing theories in mind and think about how each might be relevant to an explanation of the status of developing nations today.

MAJOR ARENAS OF EUROPEAN CONFLICT IN THE EIGHTEENTH CENTURY

Within the emerging world system of the eighteenth century lay the seeds of conflict between European nations. Western Europe is a relatively small part of the world, but it contains a rich variety of rival states with a great diversity of social customs and systems of government.

By 1800 it was evident that Spain and Portugal had failed to take full control of the world they had pioneered. The Iberian (Spanish and Portuguese) legacy was in place in America with the predominance of Catholicism and the use of the Spanish and Portuguese languages. But Spain and Portugal did not have much of an influence in the realm of economics. The Dutch had

FIGURE 6.2 Geopolitical Boundaries in Europe, 1714
What is the difference between a geopolitical and geographical boundary?

also slowed down their activities in Africa, Indonesia, and Malaya after 1700. They lost some of their overseas markets to newcomers, and political infighting caused a certain decline in their vitality. With the dawn of the nineteenth century, the British were beginning a period of global authority that would not end until well after World War I.

The years 1715 to 1815 saw the emergence of a cluster of great powers that would dominate nineteenth-century Europe. Above all, Russia became a major power in Eastern Europe and German-speaking Prussia grew in importance in Central Europe. Britain and France fought a global duel for control of the seas, which Britain won. Although overextended, Austria remained influential in Central European politics. The southern European monarchies of Spain, Portugal, and the Italian states carried little weight. The Dutch, Danes, and Swedes were also now secondary powers. A number of smaller states disappeared as they were absorbed into larger units, such

as Weimar in the German states. The great powers were too closely matched in resources and strength, however, to be able to ignore the lesser states and they made frequent overtures for collaboration.

French Hegemony Thwarted

Louis XIV wanted to extend his authority in Europe. In response to his attempts to expand, an alliance among Britain, the Netherlands and others was formed, leading to battles in northwestern Europe. In 1704 the Duke of Marlborough, commander of an Anglo-Dutch army, won a great victory over French and Bavarian opponents at Blenheim. In the same year, the British navy fighting in the Mediterranean captured Gibraltar and, in 1708, the island of Menorca. Although the French and Spanish fleets had been outclassed by their Anglo-Dutch adversaries at sea, the maritime allies could not prevail on land against France.

After prolonged negotiations, the Peace of Utrecht was signed in April 1713. Under this treaty, the Bourbon King of Spain, Philip V (who ruled from 1700 to 1746), kept his throne and the Spanish Empire, but he ceded both Gibraltar and Menorca to Britain. He also renounced any claim to the French throne from himself or his descendants.

The Treaty of Utrecht had implications beyond Europe: Louis XIV of France returned Hudson Bay to Britain and gave up Acadia (Nova Scotia), as well as claims to Newfoundland and the Caribbean island of Saint Kitts. The British received an annual contract, the Asiento, to provide the Spanish Empire with slaves, an agreement later extended to the Austrian emperor.

Austria

Austria was now a power balanced between its interests, which stretched as far as the frontier lands held by the Turkish Ottoman Empire, and those in Central and Western Europe, especially Italy and the German states. With the Treaty of Karlowitz (1699), the Turks had already given up most of Hungary and Transylvania to Austria. The war of 1716–1718 led the Turks to surrender northern Serbia to Austria. Some Austrian gains were lost in the 1730s, but its authority over new possessions made Austria one of the foremost European powers on land, a position it would enjoy until World War I.

By the early decades of the eighteenth century, three powers dominated Europe: Great Britain had become the dominant naval power, Austria had become a formidable land force, and France had acquired considerable strength both on land and at sea. The British navy, after achieving supremacy over all maritime rivals in the Atlantic by the mid-1700s, was being challenged by the French, who were trying to rebuild their war fleet. By 1739 France had 50 major warships and Britain had 80. Despite the rivalry, there were no serious conflicts in the 1720s and 1730s between the two countries. Conflict between Britain and France did loom overseas in their trading and colonial interests, so in an effort to protect its overseas interests, Britain allied itself with France's continental adversary, Austria.

Meanwhile, France found support in the other dominant Germanic power, Prussia. Although there was no open conflict, the first half of the eighteenth century was a period of uneasy peace in Europe.

War of the Austrian Succession

The European calm of the early eighteenth century was broken when Maria Theresa became the new Austrian Empress in 1740. The young king of Prussia Frederick II — better known as Frederick the Great — reacted to her ascension to the throne by overrunning the valuable Austrian province of Silesia. Despite various efforts, the Austrians were never able to force Frederick to give up his conquest. This act of aggression was the first in a series of major European conflicts in the eighteenth century. The ensuing war, which pitted the Anglo-Austrian troops against Franco-Bavarian and Prussian troops, is known as the War of the Austrian Succession.

Peace of Aix-la-Chapelle

The 1748 Peace of Aix-la-Chapelle confirmed the state of affairs in much of Europe. Abroad, the British exchanged Madras in India to get the Louisbourg fortress in Canada from the French. There would be an undeclared war in North America as the French and British tried to map out their boundaries and zones of authority. Also at this time, both France and Britain entered into agreements with Amerindian groups in North America to fight their enemies. Britain, egged on by greedy American colonists, seized many French ships and was aggressive in its response to French diplomacy. This ongoing hostility erupted into open war in 1756.

The Seven Years' War: A World War

Meanwhile, in Europe, old alliances changed in response to new rulers and ambitions. In early 1756, Britain and Prussia signed an agreement not to attack each other;

then France and Austria signed a defensive alliance. In June of that year, France seized the Mediterranean island of Menorca from the British. In August, Prussian troops of Frederick the Great achieved great military success by invading Saxony but failed diplomatically, since it united the Austrians and Russians against him. Frederick did not give up Silesia, however, which he had snatched from Austria. Despite a desperate series of battles, the Prussian state survived undefeated. Europe's major naval and land-based powers were pitted against each other in a war that would have worldwide repercussions, especially for North America.

The Seven Years' War was caused by Britain's efforts to strengthen its global naval supremacy and by Russia's expansion in Eastern Europe. In this war, conflicts between two European powers — the French and the British — were fought outside the Continent: in North America, West Africa, the Caribbean, and India. In India, Robert Clive (known as "Clive of India") and his forces prevailed over the French at Plassey (northwest India) in 1757. The result was a steady buildup of British influence over the fractious Indian rulers in the centre of the Indian subcontinent. In Canada, many strategic points were captured by the British between 1758 and 1762: Louisbourg, Québec City, and Montréal among them.

The global nature of the Seven Years' War is evident in the events leading up to the fall of New France. In September 1759, while generals James Wolfe and Louis Joseph de Montcalm were locked in battle on the Plains of Abraham near Québec City, two other major battles were taking place far away. One battle was near

This famous painting by Benjamin West is entitled *The Death of Wolfe (1771)*. Wolfe died at the Battle of Québec in 1759, winning Canada for the British. The painting is in the National Gallery of Canada. How does this battle still reverberate in modern Canada?

Lagos (in Portugal) and the other at Quiberon Bay (in France), which decimated the French fleet on the Atlantic and established the clear supremacy of the British fleet. The removal of the French from the Atlantic cut off the supply line of French troops to New France, thus sealing its fate.

WEB CONNECTION

www.mcgrawhill.ca/links/legacy

Go to the site above to find out more about the Seven Years' War.

As a result of the loss of their strong navy, the French also lost coastal trading posts in West Africa, which disrupted the shipment of African slaves to the West Indian sugar islands. Following the French naval losses at Lagos and Quiberon Bay, the British seized Guadeloupe, Martinique, and other West Indian islands.

The Treaty of Paris

A peace agreement was reached in February 1763 at Paris. While at the diplomatic table, France showed little interest in reclaiming New France, choosing instead to retain only the small islands of St. Pierre and Miquelon, off Newfoundland, and secure the return of Guadeloupe. The French *philosophe* Voltaire scoffed at the English for relinquishing rich Guadeloupe to keep the vast but non-productive New France, claiming that they had won nothing more than a land of ice and snow. French colonists who remained in New France after the Treaty of Paris would have to rely on themselves to preserve their culture and heritage. This struggle for cultural preservation continues to this day in the form of Québec nationalism and the sovereignty movement. In India, France retained only a few coastal trading posts in a zone of clear British influence. France did manage to keep the valuable West Indian sugar islands. From a global perspective then, the Seven Years' War marked the undisputed maritime supremacy of the British navy,

which was firmly established with its defeat of the Spanish-French fleet at the Battle of Trafalgar in 1805.

Turks and Poles

From 1763 until the French Revolution in 1789, the major international concerns of France, Spain, and Britain had little to do with Eastern Europe. Britain, in particular, had its attention fixed on its American colonies, which were in open rebellion; the colonists would ultimately succeed in securing their independence after the American Revolution (1776–1783).

In Eastern Europe, Russia, Prussia and Austria were intent on grabbing land from their weaker neighbours. Poland lost a third of its territory at the time of the first partition (1772–1773). Russia was expanding into Siberia and Central Asia. With the treaty of Kutchuk-Kainardji of 1774, Turkey also lost land and influence to Russia in the Black Sea. That treaty ended a Russo-Turkish war that had raged from 1768. Russia kept steady pressure on the "sublime porte," as the Turkish Ottoman government was called. Catherine II of Russia annexed the Crimean peninsula in 1783, giving Russia a powerful naval base on the Black Sea from which to menace the Ottoman capital of Constantinople.

The Russo-Turkish War of 1787–1792 was an unsuccessful attempt by the Turks to strike back against relentless Russian expansionism into southeastern Europe. With the Treaty of Jassy (1792), Russia further secured its position (at Ottoman expense) on the northern shore of the Black Sea.

By the 1780s, the balance of power within continental Europe was not significantly altered from that of 20 years earlier. Russia and Austria now looked toward Poland and the Balkans for their territorial expansion. Despite several major conflicts, little change in European boundaries had occurred. But significant changes had occurred on the high seas, where Britain had clearly established itself as the dominant power, a position it would capitalize on during the next century, when nearly 25 percent of the globe's surface would come under British control.

AFRICA IN THE EIGHTEENTH CENTURY
Communities and Systems

Africa was incorporated into the world trading system in the eighteenth century, but it was not colonized, settled, or controlled as tightly as other parts of the world during this time period. Generally, Europeans maintained contact through coastal slave-trading posts and did not venture far into the interior.

What were African societies like before Europe widened its influence on the continent? In 1500 the population of West Africa was approximately 11 million, and West Central Africa about eight million. The population

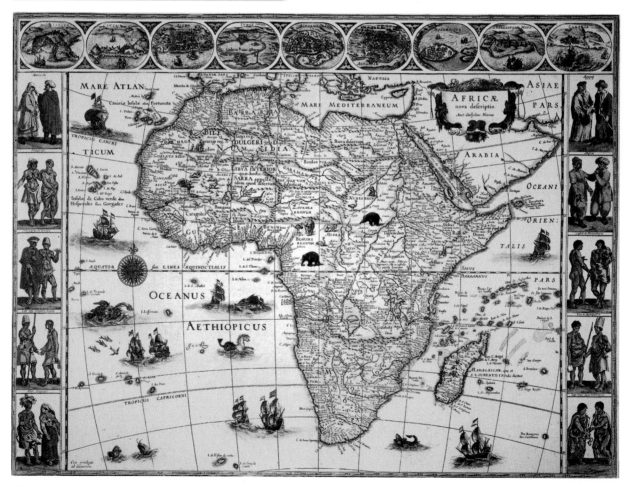

Blaeu's 1630 Map of Africa. Around the border are images of the peoples found in various regions of Africa. Why do you think this was done?

of these areas grew steadily through to the eighteenth century, due largely to the introduction of American food crops such as corn (maize). In addition to cultivation and raising livestock, there was a significant population of people who sustained themselves by working as iron-workers and by trading in craft products and resources such as iron ore, copper, salt, and palm products.

A complex hierarchical system governed African societies. At a local level, family lineage controlled access to land and resources. Alliances were formed between local lineages through marriage and the giving of "bridewealth" (opposite to dowries). These local lineages in turn were managed by elders who controlled the resources and the bridewealth. Ruling over several family lineages at times was a "divine king" — "divine" because people saw his political

powers as connected to various supernatural powers. In kingdoms of West Africa such as Mali, Ghana and Songhay, the king and royalty generally maintained control over warfare and trade.

Initially, trade with Europeans fit in quite easily with this system. African goods such as pepper, gold, and alum were originally traded for European goods such as firearms, metal, textiles, rum, and tobacco. These foreign goods carried with them a certain prestige and so were used as part of the bridewealth allocated through local families; however, when Europeans wanted to trade for slaves, the nature of West African societies changed. The allocation of labour and power was affected and this led African kings to form new states where none had existed before, so they could find a greater supply of potential slaves.

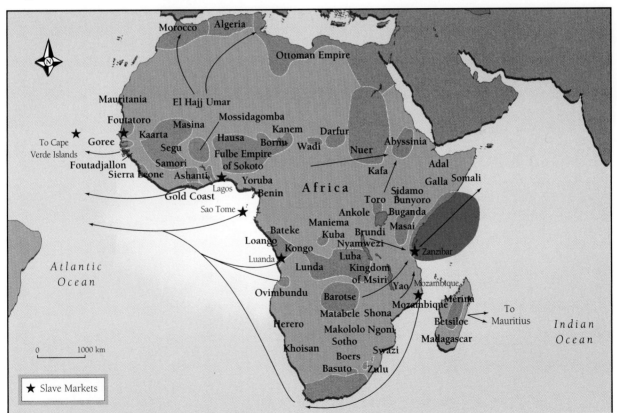

■ FIGURE 6.3 African and Overseas Slave Trade

Many groups around the world are demanding reparations for the damage done to them by the slave trade. What responsibility do you think citizens of today have toward events of the past?

Human Servitude

By the beginning of the eighteenth century, slaves had become the primary export from Africa. Slavery favoured the growth of European nations by solving the acute labour shortage in America. The production of sugar, cotton, and tobacco enabled enormous wealth to be made but required human labour on an industrial scale. Millions of Africans were enslaved for the benefit of manufacturing and commercial interests in Europe and America.

Africans Shipped to Slavery

Between 1701 and 1810, two million slaves were exported from Africa by England alone. The other two major powers, France and Portugal, exported approximately 600 000 slaves each in the same time period. Conservative estimates of Africans shipped to slavery range between 2.5 and 3 million; higher estimates range between nine and 14 million. The imprecision results from the high death rates and the poor record-keeping of slavers. In 1967 American scholar Philip D. Curtin of the University of Wisconsin calculated the grand total of Africans taken by sea for the whole period of the slave trade as 9.5 million, of which one percent went to Europe, 6.8 percent to Canada and the United States, 42.2 percent to the Caribbean, and 49.1 percent to Latin America.[3]

By the time slavery was abolished by all European powers, much of the world had been irrevocably altered. Heavy depopulation, particularly of young males, had weakened African communities and states. Meanwhile, indigenous peoples in the Caribbean who had been decimated by exploitation and disease were replaced by African slaves. In Latin America and the Caribbean, present-day populations reflect the blending of European settlers with indigenous peoples and African slaves.

Becoming a Slave

Slavery existed in African societies long before European contact and trade. There were three main mechanisms by which a person could become a slave. The first method was "pawnship." A person could sell another person or even pawn him or herself in order to settle a debt. Sometimes, in times of famine, people even pawned themselves in return for access to food. The bargain included the rights to the slave's labour and children. The second method of enslavement was as a result of the judicial process. If one committed a crime against one's own lineage, one was cut off from the support of kin. The person would be declared "at odds with the supernatural order," since by offending kin he or she had also offended his or her ancestors. When this happened, he or she could be sold as a slave. Finally, a person could become a slave if he or she were captured in war.

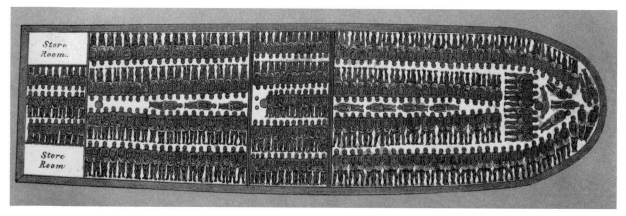

Slaves were arranged like this in the hold of a ship. They were crammed together, given little food or water and left to lie in their own filth during the month-long voyage across the ocean.

If a person were enslaved in Africa, it was still possible for him or her to become a functioning member of his or her owner's family. He or she would lack the rights of lineage of the owner's family, but the treatment received was generally far better than the brutal and inhumane treatment he or she would receive abroad after being bought and sold by European slave traders.

Profit from the Slave Trade

For some, the profits of the slave trade were enormous. An individual entrepreneur might make a 300-percent profit, while many others went bankrupt seeking their fortunes. Costs for European slave traders included fees and taxes that had to be paid to African authorities, and financial losses due to losses of ships and crew at sea. They also had to hire people in Africa to load slaves onto ships. It is estimated that the overall annual profit of slaving in the eighteenth century was as much as 24 percent, but that by the end of the eighteenth century (1769–1800) traders were only making eight to 13 percent annually.

The Colony at Cape of Good Hope

Although Europeans did not generally colonize or settle in Africa, there was one important exception to this rule: the colony at the Cape of Good Hope. The Cape of Good Hope at the southernmost tip of Africa was inhabited by approximately 50 000 Khoikhoi, San, and Bantu people when the Dutch first landed there in 1652. The Khoikhoi had been the first to establish relations with the Europeans. Initially, these were hostile relations, but they later developed into a relationship based on trade. British settlers from the East India Company tried to settle at the Cape of Good Hope but were driven out by the Khoikhoi in conflicts that ultimately weakened the Khoikhoi people. The Dutch moved in at this point and the Khoikhoi population eventually disintegrated as a result of military conflicts followed by smallpox epidemics.

The Dutch settled into colonial life at the Cape of Good Hope and began importing slaves by the middle of the seventeenth century. By 1711 there were 1 771 privately owned slaves in the colony, and by 1793, the number of slaves had reached 14 747. Originally, these slaves had come from India and Indonesia, but by the eighteenth century, they were coming primarily from nearby Mozambique and Madagascar.

Magnitude of the Slave Trade	
The following figures represent the best current estimate of the number of persons removed from Africa and transported as slaves to the New World during the entire period of the Atlantic slave trade.	
British Caribbean	1,665,000
British North America (to 1786)	275,000
United States (after 1786)	124,000
French Caribbean	1, 600,000
Dutch Caribbean	500,000
Brazil	3,646,000
Spanish America	1,552,000
Source: Philip D. Curtin, *The Atlantic Slave Trade: A Census*, 1969.	

This table shows the magnitude of the slave trade. Total these figures. What impact would removing this number of people have on Canada?

The Cape of Good Hope has been called one of the most rigid and oppressive slave societies that ever existed. The slaves had very little family life (if any) due to the low ratio of women to men. The Dutch made little or no effort to educate the slaves or convert them to Christianity but relied heavily on coercion as a means of control. There were also strong racial divisions between Indonesian and African slaves and even among Africans themselves, with the worst jobs going to the slaves from Mozambique. Curiously, the Cape of Good Hope colony did not experience any significant slave revolts until the nineteenth century. This may have been because the slaves formed a heterogeneous group. It was also relatively easy to escape the colony but very difficult to stay away from it since the remaining Khoikhoi living on the fringes of the colony often returned escaped slaves.

The Abolition of Slavery

Despite the widespread acceptance of slavery prior to the eighteenth century, not all people were completely indifferent to the cruelty, exploitation, and death that came with the slave trade. The long-term problems of slave life, including the use of flogging and other physical punishments to keep slaves from rebelling or running away, followed on the heels of the conditions on the slave ships. The horrors of the crossing from Africa to the Americas lasted a few weeks, but the spiritual and physical mutilation of slavery could last for a lifetime.

With the Enlightenment came calls for an end to slavery. The European movement for an end to African slavery and the slave trade in the eighteenth century coincided with efforts to ensure better treatment of Amerindians, Asians, and Pacific Islanders. Although settlers often disobeyed governments and churches, by the eighteenth century it was understood that indigenous peoples were not legally open to exploitation. Blacks were the exception; the history of slavery reveals that during the eighteenth century the numbers of Africans shipped rose to higher annual levels than ever, despite many calls for an end to slavery.

Barriers to Human Rights

As the scale of the slave trade grew, churches increasingly offered support for the practice of slavery. The French bishop Jacques-Bénigue Bossuet (1627–1704) in 1690 wrote that trading slaves was permissible under the laws of man and God, quoting works of Saint Paul for support (e.g., Ephesians 6:5-8: "Slaves, obey your earthly masters with respect and fear, and with sincerity of heart, just as you would obey Christ."). Protestant leaders in the Dutch Church, as well as the bishops of the Anglican Church, were just as ready to justify slavery. There were also many who defended slavery on the basis of a belief that Blacks were stronger and more resistant to the climatic and working conditions of the colonial plantations. Others argued that if the slave trade were to be legally terminated, it would continue illegally because it was so profitable.

Agents of Human Rights: The Abolitionists

During the eighteenth century, the abolitionist movement (the movement to abolish slavery) gained momentum, especially among Quakers in the United States and in humanitarian circles in England and France. The most famous European work written against slavery in the eighteenth century was by Abbé Guillaume-Thomas-François Raynal (1713–1796). Raynal never left Europe and composed his survey of world conditions of slavery entirely from books. The fact that his *Philosophical and Political History of the Commercial Establishments of Europeans in the Two Indies* (1770–1781) appeared in three editions and had 50 printings in a variety of languages is indicative of the worldwide interest in the issue of slavery.

Raynal, who had already published several books on Dutch and English history and one political commentary was influenced by Rousseau's ideas on freedom. Raynal's famous book was essentially a compilation of other works. It gave a negative overview of the European world system but was not uniformly hostile to what Europeans had done. Raynal also thought that commerce had brought arts and sciences to formerly barbarian lands, an idea he shared with Montesquieu. The abbé believed that the colonization of uninhabited places was acceptable, but that if a local population occupied a foreign territory, colonists could request only hospitality. He said that the Chinese were quite justified in trying to exclude the Europeans, who were such dangerous guests. European settlers who lived in the colonies, he went on, were vicious and quite likely to disobey their rulers in the homeland. Raynal believed in intermarriage as a means to end competition between groups of different racial origins. He discussed the Iberians (Spanish), the English, the Dutch, the French, and the North Americans. His book had 48 maps and numerous statistics, of perhaps questionable accuracy but which attempted to put issues into quantifiable form. Raynal generally espoused the notion that the discovery of the East and West Indies had been a catastrophe for much of humanity.

Leading physiocrats (those who believed the inherent order of society was based on nature) were vocal in their support of Raynal's book. So too were other intellectuals. As a result of the interest and support garnered by his ideas, organizations to end slavery sprang up. For example, political reformer Jacques Pierre Brissot founded (February 5, 1790) a club in Paris, the Society of Friends of the Blacks, in imitation of one in England, to bring together people interested in working to end slavery. The club attracted leading intellectuals (and revolutionaries) such as Condorcet, the abbé Sieyès, and others. It aimed to win over influential and powerful people.

Slavery was abolished in France on September 27, 1791. Decrees issued between 1792 and 1794 abolished slavery in the French colonies, with the opposition of the colonists. In 1793 the Assembly of the newly formed province of Upper Canada passed an act "to prevent the further introduction of slaves, and to limit the term of contracts for servitude." But, slavery for those who were already slaves persisted in Upper Canada into the first decades of the nineteenth century. There were very few, if any, slaves in Upper Canada by the time emancipation was enacted in England in 1834.

Unlike in Canada, there were big economic interests involved in plantation agriculture in the French tropical colonies. Toussaint L'Ouverture, a former slave who had read Raynal and had an understanding of the imperial expansion and trade of Europe, led an insurrection in Haiti. L'Ouverture was captured by the French in 1802 and taken to France, where he died in prison the following year. Bitter fighting continued, leading to the independence of the country with a Black majority in 1804.

In North America, slavery was abolished in Mexico in 1829 but persisted in the southern United States and was a major cause of the American Civil War. The war raged from 1861 to 1866 before slavery was put to an end. In some European colonies in Africa during the nineteenth century, however, working conditions on plantations were indistinguishable from those of slavery. In the twentieth century, the enslavement of Africans began to be universally regarded as a crime against humanity.

TOUSSAINT L'OUVERTURE.

Toussaint l'Ouverture, leader of the slave revolt in Haiti, 1802. Do you think this is a positive, or negative portrait? Why?

Art from the Non-Western World: African Carving

It was not just the trade and lifestyles of non-European cultures that were affected by European contact. A fundamental part of any culture is the way ideas, ideals, and values are expressed through art. The cultures with which the Europeans made contact often had rich and flourishing indigenous art movements. Like all other aspects of life, outside influences also affected indigenous art.

Interestingly, the simple image of a cross had been a symbol in the Congo long before the Europeans arrived; however, with the arrival of Christianity and European missionaries, the cross became a powerful symbol. It lingered as a religious icon even after the people of the Congo had abandoned Christianity as a faith and returned to their own religions. Similarly, artists had been skilled in carving ivory long before the arrival of the Europeans. After initial contact, wealthy

European patrons began commissioning ivory art from the African subcontinent. These pieces would often contain European symbols, such as the cross, knights on horseback and coats of arms, but still retained their distinctively African character.

An ivory carving from Benin, dated 1500-1800. These are Portuguese soldiers as seen by Africans.

ISLAM AND THE WEST

Communities and Systems

Islam, which in Arabic means literally "to surrender to the will of God," is a major world religion founded in Arabia by the Prophet Muhammad in the seventh century of the Common Era. Those who practise Islam, who accept God's commandments as revealed to the Prophet Muhammad in the Qur'an, are called Muslims. Islam flourished and expanded over the centuries so that by about 1500 much of North Africa and the Middle East was Muslim territory. In 1453 the city of Constantinople (today Istanbul) fell to the army of Sultan Mohammed II, and marked the new western border of the Empire of the Ottoman Turks. Constantinople had been a Christian stronghold for the previous 1 000 years; its fall to Islam was a severe shock to the Christian world.

One of the important consequences of the Muslim victory at Constantinople was the transfer of classical (Greek and Roman) manuscripts to the West (mainly to Italy), a significant factor in the development of the Renaissance. Muslim control also shifted the legal succession of the Byzantine Emperor and the leadership of the Orthodox Church to Moscow and the Russian Caesar, or czar. Yet another consequence was the loss of access to the Black Sea, depriving Europe of a land route to India. As a result, interest in the maritime route around Africa was increased and led to numerous voyages of exploration beginning in the late fifteenth century.

The Ottoman Empire, ruled by the Turks, was the dominant power of the eastern Mediterranean from the sixteenth to the nineteenth century. The Muslim Ottoman Empire was a very real threat to Eastern Europe. The Turks were at the walls of Vienna in 1529,

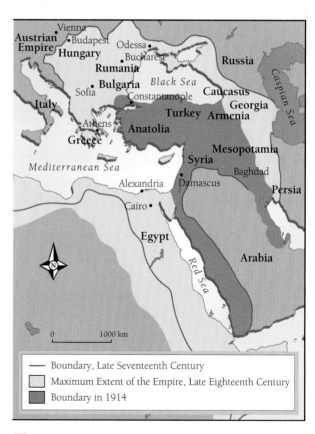

■ **FIGURE 6.4** The Ottoman Empire 1500 — 1900.
Research maps of this region from the time of Alexander the Great. Compare earlier countries and boundaries with those on this map

This seventeenth-century Turkish pulpit tile shows the plan of the Islamic *Kaaba* (shrine) in the holy city of Makkah (Mecca).

the state at the end of a tenure, rather than being inherited by relatives, as in the West. In true Islamic tradition, new appointments were given on the grounds of ability, not birth. Ottoman bureaucracy was thus open to talented people of diverse origin, and not restricted to those of Turkish descent. This led to a more competently and efficiently administered state.

The fatal flaw of the Ottoman Empire was its excessive exploitation of its peasantry. This prevented improvement in agriculture and the accumulation of surplus capital to stimulate demand, purchasing power, and the growth of a business class. Excessive taxation kept the artisan and commercial classes weak. The Ottoman decline was also due to its failure to develop artillery and ships that carried naval gunnery. The armed strength of the Muslim rulers lay in land armies. Over time, there was also a decline in the quality of leadership, and so the once-feared Ottoman Empire gradually weakened. By 1800 Europeans were calling the Ottoman Empire "the Sick Man of Europe."

INDIA AND THE WEST
Communities and Systems

The Indian subcontinent was another area of the world that was significantly affected by contact with Europeans, particularly the British, during the eighteenth century. Indians had experienced contact, trade and invasions from the "outside world" for hundreds of years, but experiences with the British altered their economy, lifestyle, and culture forever.

Just as it is incorrect to speak of Africa as a single political or cultural entity, India too cannot be considered a unified country but rather a collection of disparate states under local rulers. Although India did become unified as a political entity under Moghul (Mongol) rule, by the end of the seventeenth century the Moghul Empire was in decline. The first half of the eighteenth century saw the continuing deterioration of Moghul rule for a number of reasons. These included infighting between the sons of the emperor after his death, challenges to Moghul rule by the Sikhs, increased power of

and again in 1682. By the sixteenth century, the West was aware of three major Muslim empires: the Ottoman Empire, which had replaced Christian Byzantium; the Safavid Empire, which had replaced Zoroastrianism in Persia (today Iran); and the Moghul Empire, which had taken over Hindu India.

Western observers wanted to find the weak points of these dangerous adversaries with a long history of conflict with Christendom. The answer, in part, was the superiority of their military, which performed better in the field than the more undisciplined feudal armies of the Europeans. The Ottomans also had a more efficient bureaucracy than the West in the seventeenth century — especially because offices and property reverted to the Marathas (local Hindu powers), attacks by Persians, inter-regional religious wars, court incompetence, and general greed in the Moghul ranks.

Under the Moghul system, government had been structured around semi-independent Moghul provincial governors called *navabs*. The *navabs* controlled local landowners who were known as *zamindars*. These two figures seemed to be in constant conflict because the *zamindars* were supposed to pay revenue to their *navab* but often expanded their own territory without paying the required tribute.

The declining power of the Moghuls proved to be a boon for the British. British commercial enterprises flourished as Moghul influence declined in India. The establishment of a British settlement in Calcutta (in the eastern state of Bengal) in 1690 corresponded directly to the decline of Moghul rule.

An unprecedented event took place in the middle of the eighteenth century when the British East India Company, funded by local bankers, sided with the *zamindars* in their conflict with the *navabs*. This conflict was behind the story of the infamous "Black Hole" of Calcutta, the name given the place where 146 people of the East India Company supposedly were held prisoner. This was said to have occurred when the *navab* of Bengal seized the posts at Fort William and Calcutta, which were occupied by the Company. Early accounts said that 123 of the 146 people had died in this prison. But Indian scholars later showed that this incident had likely been greatly exaggerated; the *navab* had never been involved, and no more than 69 people had been held. Nevertheless, for many years this story was used to justify the British view that the Indians were a base and cruel people. The conflict ended in battle in 1757, and the British won. The consequences represented the dawn of a new era in Indian history.

Until this time, the British had exerted influence through trade and alliances. Now a new structure emerged with the British in direct control of import and export trade, price-setting, and the ability to force exclusive contracts with local craftspeople. They also had access to the considerable treasury of Bengal. By 1765 the East India Company had official control of civil administration and, therefore, control over the tax system. They increased taxes, often leading to bankruptcy for Bengali farmers, which resulted in the famines of 1770 and 1783. The Company's control of Bengal expanded to other parts of India through warfare and intervention. Sometimes the Company maintained direct rule over areas it conquered; sometimes it installed and supported puppet rulers.

After 1765 the British East India Company changed from a simple trading company to an official arm of the British government. As traders, they had maintained a relationship of relative equality with their Indian counterparts. As rulers, however, they often used their political power to suppress and oppress their subjects. The British felt that they were inherently superior to the Indians. Many were committed to reforming what they thought of as the "un-English" habits of the Indian people.

Economically, conquest led to the reform of the land tax system, which meant that Indians ended up paying for the costs of British-initiated warfare. This power was also used to shift agricultural production to more profitable goods, which could be used for export to England, to its colonies abroad, and to trade with other countries. These goods included cotton, opium, and salt. The British established a monopoly over the sale of salt in particular. Salt was a very important source of revenue for the British and they were hated as a result of the oppressive salt tax, which fell on the shoulders of poor Indian peasants. Ultimately, this would become a major issue in Gandhi's non-violent resistance to the British, 150 years later.

Art of the Non-Western World: Rajasthani Painting

The influence of the Moghuls in India had been far-reaching and perhaps most evident in the art and architecture of the time. Moghul art itself had been influenced by Indian art. It had lost many of its original

A Rajasthani painting of a foreign, Western dignitary being escorted by soldiers. How can you recognize him?

Iranian characteristics and adopted some of the characteristics of Indian art through the ages. With the decline of the Moghul Empire in the seventeenth century, however, Moghul art persisted only in terms of the influence it had on emerging Indian styles of the time. This influence can be seen most vividly in the art of Rajasthan (a northwestern Indian state). The emerging Rajasthani style emphasized romantic scenes between princely heroes and beautiful and alluring heroines. Often the hero and heroine depicted were popular Hindu gods and goddesses shown in a particularly well-known scene of their lives. The enduring Moghul influence shows a focus on concepts rather than realistic depictions, and an appeal to the emotions through brilliant colours on large areas.

Review, Reflect, Respond

1. Describe the impact of the European slave trade on West African societies.

2. How important were the ideals of the Enlightenment to the eventual ending of the slave trade? Explain your answer.

3. Explain why the year 1757 can be considered a pivotal point in the history of India.

The Pacific Northwest and the West

During the last decades of the eighteenth century, Europeans explored and mapped the Pacific Northwest. Russian expeditions searched the shores of the Pacific and Arctic oceans for furs that could be sold, and in the 1780s, Russians began to settle in Alaska. English vessels under Captain George Vancouver (1758–1798) and others explored the west coast of Canada in the years 1791 to 1795. The Spanish sailed north from California (then part of Mexico) and a detachment of soldiers wintered on the west coast of Vancouver Island. More elaborate expeditions, intended to make scientific and ethnographic observations for the Spanish Crown, sailed up the American coast, commanded by Alejandro Malaspina and Dionisio Alcalá Galiano (as in Galiano Island, British Columbia). This Russian, British, and Spanish naval activity led to a more accurate knowledge of the contours of Pacific North America. By 1800 the configurations of five continents were known. Artifacts from the inhabitants, as well as descriptions of family life and activities of the inhabitants, were taken back to Europe and given much attention.

North American Indians as seen by eighteenth-century artists. Do you think the artist was there at the time?

History

European travel over the high seas in the eighteenth century was particularly perilous. There are numerous accounts of ships and crew lost at sea and of the high risks associated with ocean crossings. Little did these sailors know that it was only a matter of time — literally — before voyages would become safer. Until the eighteenth century, there was no accurate way to calculate longitude — ships often ran ashore on a foreign island when calculations showed they were in the middle of the ocean. In order to determine longitude, sailors needed a clock that could determine exactly the right time anywhere in the world. This was such a major problem that the British government offered a reward of £20 000 to the person who invented such a timepiece. The prize went to John Harrison in 1763 for his invention of the marine chronometer, an instrument which finally allowed ships to land closer to their destinations. Harrison's invention was first tested on a transatlantic crossing made by Captain James Cook (1728–1789).

European artists had painted non-Europeans from the earliest days of overseas explorations. These were used to make prints or engravings to accompany travel accounts and often were highly subjective. Images could include depictions of cannibalism, or jewels and rich fabrics that suggested an exotic land of pleasures.

CHINA AND THE WEST

Communities and Systems

No one foreign society affected the eighteenth-century European consciousness more than China's. Accounts by Jesuit missionaries provided the first favourable descriptions of China since those of Italian merchant Marco Polo in the thirteenth century. Italian Jesuits such as Matteo Ricci were allowed into Beijing at the start of the seventeenth century (1601). They gained Chinese acceptance as a result of the help they provided with calendar reform, improvements in artillery, and advice on negotiations with the Russians; this would lead to the Sino-Russian treaty of 1689. Christianity was officially tolerated in China at the end of the seventeenth century, but in 1724 the Chinese Emperor, like the Japanese a century earlier, forbade the teaching of European religion.

Jesuits stayed on as technical assistants in Beijing until the dissolution of their order in 1773. Serious books about China were published, of which the most successful was one by the French writer Jean-Baptiste du Halde, which gave a positive view of China. He described the Chinese emperors as wise monarchs who took advice from knowledgeable officials. Indeed, supporters of the Enlightenment held China as an "empire of benevolent reason." The scientist Gottfried von Leibniz (1646–1716) hoped there would be a true communication of enlightenment between China and Europe.

Europeans were impressed by the fact that, aside from the Imperial dynasty and the descendants of the revered Chinese philosopher Confucius (551–479 BCE), there was no hereditary nobility in China. Voltaire was quite well informed about China and Japan from travellers' accounts, and went so far as to say that the Chinese Empire was the best in the world. He said of Confucius, whose ethical precepts were deeply rooted in Chinese culture, "I have read his books attentively and made extracts from them: I found they spoke only of the purest morality... he appeals only to virtue, he preaches no miracles; there is nothing in them of religious allegory."

French economist and physician François Quesnay (1694–1774), founder of the physiocratic school of political economy, published a book entitled *Chinese Despotism* (1767), wherein he maintained that despotism is the domination of natural law, which he believed had led the Chinese to be more dependent on agriculture than any other nation. Quesnay knew from the writings of visitors to China that the tithe (similar to a tax) on crops was the principal tax base, and that the Chinese Emperor performed solemn rites to mark the phases of the agricultural year. Quesnay even prevailed on Louis XV to guide the plow as a symbolic act to begin the 1756 spring tilling, just as the Chinese Emperor did each year. For the physiocrats, a powerful Chinese Emperor was the ideal, enlightened, paternalistic ruler.

Western Europeans were also fascinated by other systems of writing: Egyptian hieroglyphs, Babylonian and Assyrian cuneiform, and early Greek script, which had not yet been deciphered. They marvelled at Chinese, an ancient script that was still in use. Some Europeans even learned some spoken Chinese for use in trading but without any knowledge of script or grammar. Again, the Jesuits were the forerunners in making the language accessible to Westerners through books. Etienne Fourmont, who studied with a young Chinese man sent to Europe by the Jesuits, published the first book on the 214 radicals in the Chinese language (1719), and this was followed by *Grammatica Sinaica*, a book on Chinese grammar, in 1742. Baron Melchior Grimm (1723–1807), a German-born writer and critic who produced a French literary review, wrote in 1776 about this passion for China:

> The Chinese Empire has become in our time the object of special attention and of special study: The missionaries first fascinated public opinion by rose-coloured reports from that distant land, too distant to be able to contradict their falsehoods. Then the philosophers took it up and drew from them whatever could be of use in denouncing and removing the evils they observed in their own country. Thus, this country became in a short time the home of wisdom, virtue, and good faith; its government the best possible, and the longest established, its morality the loftiest and the most beautiful in the known world; its laws, its policy, its arts, and its industry were likewise such as to serve as a model for all nations of the earth.[4]

Global Economic Relations with China

British expansion in India was tied to expansion in China. Some scholars argue that China was the lion of the Asian economic markets in the eighteenth century and that the British needed the wealth and goods of India to gain access to the markets of China. The Chinese had considered Europeans "red-haired barbarians" and refused to trade with them. Ultimately, as power within China shifted, trade was opened up to Europeans and the main beneficiary was, again, the British East India Company.

The English bought silk, porcelain, and medicine from the Chinese and tried to sell them a number of things in return. They tried to sell woollens, but the Chinese had no interest. They tried to trade in lead, tin and rattan from the Malay Straits, and pepper and rice from Java. The Chinese were not interested in English wares — they wanted silver. The demand for silver soon created a huge drain on British resources, especially when the English began buying tea from China in the middle of the eighteenth century.

Tea had been introduced in England in 1664, when the tiny amount of two pounds, two ounces was imported. By 1783 six million pounds of tea were being imported annually by the English East India Company, and, by 1785, this figure had risen to 15 million pounds annually. These figures only represented officially declared imports; it is estimated that perhaps twice that amount was smuggled illegally every year. All this tea had to be paid for with silver, since the Chinese would not accept payment in anything else.

Scottish economist Adam Smith (1723–1790) noted that:

> ... the East Indies [Asia] is another market for the produce of the silver mines of America, and a market which, from the time of the discovery of those mines, has been continually taking off a greater and greater quantity of silver ... Upon all these accounts, the precious metals are a commodity which it always has been, and still continues to be, extremely advantageous to carry from Europe to India. There is scarce any commodity which brings a better price there [and it is even more advantageous to carry silver to China]

Where did the silver come from? The British relied heavily on the silver they procured from the Americas to pay for Chinese tea and other goods. Although the English sold large amounts of Indian cotton to China (27 million pounds between 1785 and 1833), which was also to pay for the tea, it was still not enough to buy all the tea that the English market demanded. Britain's financial problems were compounded by the fact that China began producing its own cotton at a lower price than India and, therefore, drastically reduced its need for Indian cotton. The British found the solution to this problem in opium. The British grew opium in India and sold it to the Chinese. Addiction to opium soon became a serious social problem in China — by the end of the nineteenth century, one in ten Chinese people were addicted to opium. Thus, the British had been able to create and assure themselves of a lucrative market for a drug that was highly addictive and the basis for the pain medication called morphine.

Art of the Non-Western World: Chinese Painting

Interest in China went as far as influencing interior decoration in Europe. *Chinoiserie* is the name of the European style of objects and decor that imitated the Chinese. As artisans attempted to re-create a version of an imperfectly understood original, *chinoiserie* became a style in its own right. One example is the willow-pattern motif of a popular English porcelain. Rooms were decorated in palaces and châteaux, such as the famous Chantilly near Paris, the equally famous porcelain rooms at the Palace of Queluz near Lisbon, Portugal, the Palace of Aranjuez in Spain, and of Capodimonte in Naples. French rococo painter Antoine Watteau appears to have produced the earliest *chinoiserie* when he decorated a royal residence in that style. Music by François Couperin called *Les Chinois* accompanied these paintings of priests and pagodas, ornately dressed mandarins, parasols, and rouged maidens. French painter François Boucher designed *chinoiserie* tapestries that were woven at the royal factory at Beauvais around 1742. This piece depicts a bizarre

Chinoiserie, Chinese subjects in European forms and styles became popular as a result of trade in Chinese porcelain wares.

marriage ceremony, a royal breakfast, and courtly ladies playing with parakeets. Curiously, a set of these tapestries was sent by Louis XV to the Chinese Emperor Kang H'si, and a panel was still hanging in the Imperial Palace in Beijing when it was looted by European troops in 1860.

The heyday of *chinoiserie* is illustrated in Voltaire's 1755 play entitled *The Chinese Orphan*, based on a Chinese play. This play caused a public sensation because it supposedly dramatized the morals of Confucius and was performed in elaborate versions of Chinese costumes.

Trade in "China"

When Portuguese navigator Vasco da Gama rounded the Cape of Good Hope and reached the Orient in 1498, he ushered in a new age of trade between Europe and the East. Direct access by ship, rather than reliance on overland traders, brought a wide array of items to the European marketplace including silk, spices, tea, and porcelain (fine pottery made of a special white clay). In response to the vast, new European market for porcelain, the Chinese began making porcelain to order for the Portuguese market and later for Europeans in general.

The Chinese porcelain room at the Charlottenburg palace in Germany. Chinese porcelain became so popular that factories in both France and England began to manufacture copies and reworkings of Chinese themes and designs.

By the seventeenth century, such large quantities of porcelain were being imported to Europe that some have referred to the onset of "china-mania" at this time. The increasing popularity of porcelain was reflected in its progression in European homes, from the cabinet of curiosities to the dinner table and then from the dinner table to the walls. Porcelain as a decorative accessory reached its peak in the late seventeenth and early eighteenth centuries in decorated rooms where the walls were covered in Chinese and Japanese porcelain panels.

By the eighteenth century, Europeans had learned the sophisticated Oriental techniques of making porcelain. With the establishment of porcelain production at locations such as Meissen, Germany, and the passing fad of porcelain rooms, the trade in Chinese porcelain declined. While fine china and porcelain remains popular in Europe and North America, the leading names are no longer Japanese or Chinese, but European: Delft, Wedgewood, or Royal Doulton. Nevertheless, Europeans and North Americans still call any fine porcelain (and sometimes other pottery) "china."

EUROPEANS ON NON-EUROPEANS

Idyllic Islands in the Pacific Ocean

Much can be learned about Europeans and the world they were exploring by reading travellers' accounts written at the time. The maritime explorations of Europeans continued throughout the eighteenth century. French officer and navigator Louis Antoine de Bougainville (1729–1811), who had been an *aide-de-camp* to General Montcalm at the battle of the Plains of Abraham in Québec in 1759, subsequently sailed the Pacific and published *Account of a Voyage Around the World*. Like the reports of Captain Cook (who explored Hawaii, Australia, New Guinea, New Zealand, and other Pacific islands), Bougainville described people with different moral and political systems in idyllic tropical settings such as Tahiti and the Sandwich Islands.

The chronicles by Cook and Bougainville added to the picture of tropical life on Pacific islands already spread by Daniel Defoe's book *The Life and Strange Surprising Adventures of Robinson Crusoe* (1719). This was based on the true story of Selkirk, an unpopular Scottish sailor who was marooned by his shipmates on an uninhabited island off the coast of Chile in 1704. He survived for four years before being picked up by a passing ship. Defoe changes the story by having Robinson Crusoe not abandoned, but shipwrecked, though able to hold on to European civilization from the wreckage. He has a dog, a set of carpenter's tools (products of European technology), some ink to write with (to record his thoughts), some rum to enjoy, and a Bible to study. As he looks at the island, he contemplates the wonders of God's creation. He also has a human companion whom he names Friday (the day on which he saved Crusoe from cannibals). Friday becomes the non-White, compliant servant who accepts as natural the authority of the European.

Mutiny on H.M.S. Bounty

Perhaps the most famous, or infamous, story of eighteenth-century Europeans in the South Seas, concerns the voyage of a British trading vessel, the *Bounty*. This

French nineteenth-century artist Paul Gauguin left his family to live among the Tahitians in the South Seas. Do his paintings of Tahitians seem more true to life than those done in the seventeenth and eighteenth centuries?

ship set sail from England in December 1787 with orders to reach the island of Tahiti and there collect young breadfruit plants. These plants were to be brought in pots to the West Indies and grown there as a cheap food for slaves working on plantations. The *Bounty* reached Tahiti almost a year later, in October 1788, having taken the longer route, around the Cape of Good Hope at the tip of Africa. The return voyage was delayed for various reasons, and, while on the island, many of the crew had taken "wives" and set up households with the Tahitians during their five months ashore.

For whatever reason, the mutiny on the *Bounty* took place 24 days after the ship left Tahiti for the West Indies. Captain William Bligh (1754–1817), the commander of the ship, and 18 loyal crewmembers were set adrift in a small boat and miraculously survived long enough to reach the Dutch East Indies, some 3 500 miles from Tahiti.

Meanwhile, the remaining crew of the *Bounty* returned to Tahiti and eventually separated into smaller groups, with some mutineers remaining on Tahiti (later caught and returned to England for trial) and the others setting out to find another island where they and their Polynesian companions could settle.

The descendants of the mutineers live to this day on the tiny island of Pitcairn, about 1 300 miles east of Tahiti. The story of the mutiny on the *Bounty* has inspired many books and at least three movies, featuring big-name stars such as Clark Gable, Marlon Brando and Mel Gibson. The lure of the South Seas remains strong and thousands of vacationers visit these "tropical paradises" every year. In the nineteenth century, the French artist Paul Gauguin (1808–1903) chose to abandon his wife and family to live with the Tahitians. He would create his own Western vision of these non-Western people.

WEB CONNECTION

www.mcgrawhill.ca/links/legacy

Go to the site above to find out more about the art of Paul Gauguin.

Engelbert Kaempfer, The History of Japan

Englebert Kaempfer (1651–1715) was a writer who travelled extensively in the late seventeenth century. His impressions of Japan's history and culture were published in England as *The History of Japan* in 1727. He describes the Japanese emperor in detail, particularly the taboos that seemed to apply to him.

Kaempfer notes that the emperor was so holy that he had to be carried everywhere on the shoulders of his servants so his feet would not touch the ground. Kaempfer said that the emperor could not cut his hair, beard or nails, since these parts of his body were particularly holy. If he had to be "cleaned," it was to be done while he was sleeping "because they say that what is taken from his body at that time hath been stolen from him, and that such a theft does not prejudice his holiness or dignity.[4]"

Scholars since the eighteenth century have both praised and criticized Kaempfer's accounts of Japanese customs. For example, an English scholar who wrote around the turn of the nineteenth century wrote that Kaempfer's statements about the emperor "... seem to consist of a good deal of ignorant gossip mixed with perhaps a few grains of truth." Some Japanese sources, however, seem to confirm some of Kaempfer's reports. For example, one Japanese writer, Tsamura Soan, writing in the late eighteenth century, claimed that when the "emperor's beard or nails grew long, a lady-in-waiting must bite them off to the required length with her teeth." Obviously, European descriptions of non-Europeans are complex sources that require rigorous analysis in order to understand what it is they teach us about both the subjects and the writers.

Review, Reflect, Respond

1. Why were many Europeans of the eighteenth century fascinated and impressed with Chinese culture and society?

2. Is it accurate to describe the economy of the eighteenth century as "global"? Explain your answer.

3. How do tales such as *Robinson Crusoe* and the story of the *Bounty* provide us with valuable insights into the minds of Europeans in the eighteenth century?

CHANGING TASTES

The Grand Exchange

When Columbus set sail on his return visit to the Americas in 1493, he could not have known the profound implications this voyage would have on the world. To begin with, certain items aboard his ships would begin a revolution that would change the diet of the world forever. Aboard the 17 ships were seeds, fruit trees, and livestock. This was only the beginning of the foods that would eventually be exchanged between the Old World and the New World.

Over the next few centuries, the variety of foods eaten by people the world over would increase through what has been called the Grand Exchange. Sunflowers, native to the Great Plains of North America, were exported to Europe, where they thrived in cold northern Europe and provided Russians with a welcome new cooking oil. In return, wheat, barley, and oats from Europe and the Middle East arrived in North America, eventually making the Great Plains the "breadbasket of the world."

Other crops of the Grand Exchange imported to Europe included coffee from Africa, which became one of the most important crops to the Caribbean and Brazil. Also exchanged was nutritious cacao, the primary ingredient of chocolate, exported from tropical America to Europe. Tomatoes from Mexico, known to Europeans as the "apples of love," became a favourite of Italian chefs. Peanuts, potatos, vanilla, corn (or maize), hot peppers, and tobacco are only a few of the many other crops that arrived in Europe, and eventually Asia, and enriched the diet of all classes. The grains mentioned earlier, along with cattle, horses, poultry and pigs, were all exported from Europe to the New World and became staples in the diet of Americans.

Developing a Sweet Tooth

Crusaders returning from the Middle East introduced sugar to Europe. Europeans began to import sugar first as a medicine and, in very wealthy households, as an expensive additive to food and drink. At this time, sugar was so highly prized that it was considered a suitable gift for princes to exchange with each other. Prior to Columbus's return voyage in 1493, sugar cane was unknown in the Americas and produced in only limited quantities in the Old World. Until the seventeenth century, sugar remained a luxury, affordable only by the European elite. After 1700, Europeans established colonies in the Caribbean and South America, where vast quantities of sugar cane could be grown. Eventually the price declined enough for sugar to become a regular part of the average European's diet. In England, the per-capita consumption of sugar increased 20 times between 1663 and 1775, an indication of its popularity

History of the Reign of Charles V by William Robertson

William Robertson (1721–1793) was born in Midlothian, Scotland, studied at Edinburgh, and at age 22 was ordained minister of Gladsmuir. Robertson enjoyed a successful military and political career, eventually becoming a royal chaplain in 1761 and principal of Edinburgh University in 1762. After the success of his *History of Scotland 1542–1603* (1759), William went on to become King's Historiographer in 1764. Robertson's most respected work was his *History of Charles V* (1769), excerpted here, which was praised by both Voltaire and Edward Gibbon, author of *The Decline and Fall of the Roman Empire*. Later works by Robertson included *History of America* (1777) and *The Knowledge which the Ancients had of India* (1791). The excerpt below is from Robertson's explanation of his historical method. Obviously very thorough, he felt it necessary to explain why he included certain pieces of information and excluded others. Note Robertson's scholarly generosity, evident in the "minute exactness" with which he says he has cited his sources. Robertson has tried to make it as easy as possible for his readers not only to find the sources he has used, but also to use his own work as a source for future research. Robertson wrote:

> I have carefully pointed out the sources from which I have derived information, and have cited the writers on whose authority I rely with a minute exactness, which might appear to border upon ostentation, if it were possible to be vain of having read books, many of which nothing but the duty of examining with accuracy whenever I laid before the public, could have induced me to open. As my inquiries conducted me often into paths which were obscure or little frequented, such constant recourse to the authors who have been my guides was not only necessary for authenticating the facts which are the foundations of my reasonings, but may be useful in pointing out the way to such as shall hereafter hold the same course, and in enabling them to carry on their researches with greater facility and success.

> Every intelligent reader will observe one omission in my work, the reason of which it is necessary to explain. I have given no account of the conquests of Mexico and Peru, or of the establishment of the Spanish colonies in the continent and islands of America. The history of these events I originally intended to have related at considerable length. But upon a nearer and more attentive consideration of this part of my plan, I found that the discovery of the new world; the state of society among its ancient inhabitants; their character, manners, and arts; the genius of the European settlements in its various provinces, together with the influence of these upon the systems of policy or commerce in Europe, were subjects so splendid and important, that a superficial view of them could afford little satisfaction; to treat of them as extensively as they merited, must produce an episode, disproportionate to the principal work. I have therefore reserved these for a separate history;[6]

---

1. Comment on the importance of citing sources of information and ideas for both the writer and the reader of history. What does Robertson say about this?

2. Why did Robertson decide not to write about the discoveries in South America? Explain why you agree or disagree with his decision.

and its increased use (along with consumption of coffee, tea, and chocolate). The great appeal of sugar lies in the fact that it is a powerful sweetener and does not leave an aftertaste as do maple syrup and honey. Sugar is also a better preservative than honey and can be more easily transported and stored.

Only in the late twentieth century, with its emphasis on health, weight and appearance, and scientific confirmation of the ill-effects of a sugar-heavy diet, have North Americans and Europeans begun to moderate their love affair with sugar. After three centuries, the decline in the price of sugar is no longer met with a rise in consumption; in fact, recent studies show that in the Western world, the per-capita consumption of sugar has begun to decline.

Pleasures
AND PASTIMES

During the eighteenth century, the British quickly developed a taste for what would become the nation's favourite beverage — tea. In 1711 the British newspaper the *Spectator* noted that a "good" household served tea in the morning. Tea had replaced the popular morning drink of breakfast beer. Even the lower classes in England were switching over to tea by the mid-eighteenth century, especially when the British government sharply increased the tax on gin. By the end of the eighteenth century, people from the working classes were spending five percent of their annual income on tea alone.

Reflections

Between 1450 and 1750, Europeans explored virtually the whole earth, leaving their mark everywhere they went through exploitation and acculturation. Diseases carried by Europeans, such as measles, mumps and smallpox, decimated the populations of America; the transatlantic slave trade depopulated Central Africa. Above all, the plantation economies of the New World had caused a demand for forced labour by African slaves. Europeans stripped millions of people of their basic human rights and dignity. From the outset, Europeans had gone in search of new riches, from fur and gold to slaves. The common thread one finds when studying the age of European exploration and colonization is the primacy of profit. Whether studying the French, English, Dutch, Spanish, Portuguese, or any European contact in America, Africa or Asia, one quickly recognizes that economic gain (usually accompanied by a religious zeal to convert the indigenous people) was the driving force behind three centuries of exploration. The establishment of a global economy was not a gentle or peaceful affair: Europeans fought each other for the control of markets and territory. This very struggle between European powers stimulated advances in military technology and nobody in the world had better weapons than the Western Europeans. Although Europeans liked to imagine that their religion and culture were attractive or even necessary to the wider world, in fact it was their technology — especially their guns — that allowed their success in establishing economic dominance.

Chapter Review

Chapter Summary

In this chapter, you have seen:

- key factors that led to conflict and war
- individuals and forces which advanced human rights through the development and success of the abolitionist movement
- the impact of the non-Western world on European imagination and art
- both change and continuity in trading patterns, lifestyles, and art forms of the world's peoples during the eighteenth century

Reviewing the Significance of Key People, Concepts, and Events (Knowledge and Understanding)

1. Understanding world history in the eighteenth century requires a knowledge of the following concepts and people and an understanding of their significance in the re-shaping of cultures and societies as a result of interaction. Select and explain two from each column.

Concepts	Events	People
modernization theory	War of Austrian Succession	Walt Whitman Rostow
dependency theory	Peace of Aix-la-Chapelle	East India Company
Ottoman Empire	Seven Years' War	Jesuits
Grand Exchange	Abolitionist Movement	Robinson Crusoe
		Jonathan Swift
		Engelbert Kaempfer

2. The development of a global economy during the eighteenth century had different effects in various parts of the world. Briefly describe how the emerging global economy had an impact on each of the following areas: Africa, China, the Americas, Europe.

Doing History: Thinking About the Past (Thinking/Inquiry)

3. To what degree can it be argued that the eighteenth century was the crucial bridge between Europe's aristocratic past and its democratic future? To answer this question you will need to draw on what you have learned in this unit and what you know about contemporary Western society.

4. During the eighteenth century, Europeans came to see the mistreatment of Amerindians, Asians, and Pacific Islanders as morally wrong. Why was the same view not extended to Africans? What factors inhibited the extension of protection for basic human rights to all people? Was the continued abuse of Africans through slavery a result of racist assumptions, economic pressures, or other factors?

Applying Your Learning (Application)

5. Carefully study the map of Africa from the mid-seventeenth century, shown in this chapter. What impressions of Africa does it give you? Why do you think its creator, Willem Blaeu, used animals such as elephants and lions to fill empty spaces? See if the following lines of poetry by Jonathan Swift give you any hints.

> So Geographers in
> Afric-maps,
> With Savage-Pictures
> fill their Gaps;
> And o'er unhabitable
> Downs
> Place elephants for
> want of Towns

6. Create a dialogue set in the late 1790s that may have taken place between a grandparent and a grand-child from Africa, China, India, or the Americas. In the dialogue, reflect on the impact of contact between Europe and your society. Your dialogue should show an understanding of the variety, intensity and breadth of change that took place, as well as how key social institutions have helped to maintain continuity.

Communicating Your Learning (Communication)

7. Analyse the impact of Western colonization on both the colonizer and the colonized by depicting the effects of the Grand Exchange through a poem, short story, or a script for a dramatic skit. Be sure to comment on all forms of exchange: food, ideas, slaves, etc.

8. Create a collage in the shape of one of the following areas of the world: China, India, Japan, Africa, Europe, North America, South America. Your collage should comprised pictures, symbols, and images or phrases that reflect the nature of change that occurred during the eighteenth century.

Unit Review

Reflecting on What You Have Learned (Knowledge and Understanding)

1. Although it was the financial crisis and the poor harvests of the 1780s which triggered the French Revolution, it was the ideas expressed by the *philosophes* that ensured that the period between 1789 and 1815 would truly be revolutionary. Select any three intellectuals of the eighteenth century and show how their ideas are reflected in the events and changes between 1789 and 1815.

2. While the French Revolution could be argued to be the ideas of the *philosophes* put into action, colonialism stands in stark contrast to the ideals of the Enlightenment. Describe how the treatment of colonized people represents the antithesis of the Enlightenment.

Practicing Historical Interpretation (Thinking/Inquiry)

3. In studying the relationships between European powers and their colonies, it is important that we realize that the foundations of the developed world and the developing nations were laid in the seventeenth and eighteenth centuries. Metropolis-satellite relations allowed the metropolis to dominate and exploit its satellites. In his provocative essay "The Development of Underdevelopment," André Gunder Frank argues that most developing nations have been intentionally underdeveloped to serve the capitalist needs of the West. Gunder Frank wrote:

   > When we examine this metropolis-satellite structure, we find that each of the satellites ... serves as an instrument to suck capital or economic surplus out of its own satellites and to channel part of this surplus to the world metropolis of which all are satellites. Moreover, each national and local metropolis serves to impose and maintain the monopolistic structure and exploitative relationship of this system ... as long as it serves the interests of the metropolis ...[7]

   Based on evidence in this chapter, develop an argument in two or three paragraphs to support Gunder Frank's theory. Are there moral obligations that arise out of European imperialism?

4. When studying the ideas of the Enlightenment, we see a theme that has been common in European history since the Renaissance: a secular move toward faith in progress and human achievement. To what degree is the Enlightenment an extension of humanism and to what degree were reason and logic applied to society during the eighteenth century?

Applying Your Historical Understanding (Application)

5. Select an individual from the eighteenth century whom you believe merits the title of genius. Review the definition of genius given in the Unit One Review to guide you. Prepare a biographical sketch that explains your choice. Be sure to show clearly how their work had a material effect on a domain and that this effect was lasting.

6. Enlightenment thinkers embraced a belief in progress. They were confident that through the application of reason, society could be improved and perfected. Giambattisto Vico, an Italian philosopher of the eighteenth century, saw history as a spiral, progressing through time with setbacks which help to propel society forward. In light of the slave trade, colonialism and imperialism, is this progressive view rooted in a eurocentric bias of the world?

Communicating Your Learning (Communication)

7. Write a short story set in a salon in the late 1780s that captures the essence of the intellectual community on the eve of the revolution. Write from the perspective of a woman hosting the salon, a participant, or a servant who quietly observes the behaviours of the philosophes.

8. Art of the eighteenth century reflected the rising tensions between the state (dominated by the aristocracy) and the emerging middle class. Select one piece of art which is representative of the following styles: baroque, rococo, neo-classicism, and romanticism. Arrange the paintings chronologically. Identify each and explain what the paintings tell us about the age. Also, provide a broad overall statement which explains the four distinct styles of art which emerged in the eighteenth century

---

> * *Now complete Skills Focus Three (p. 594):*
> **Working with Primary Sources.**

UNIT THREE

Modern Europe

Chapter Seven
The Birth of Modern Industrial Society: Europe 1815–1850

Chapter Eight
Nations in Upheaval: Europe 1850–1914

Chapter Nine
Imperialism, Colonialism, and Resistance in the Nineteenth Century

Artist Camille Corot was interested in the new technology of photography as some of his landscape paintings suggest. This view of the French countryside was done ca. 1860–65.

The nineteenth century was a period of dramatic transition throughout the Western world. Myriad forces came together in the nineteenth century to bring about radical changes in nearly every facet of life in Europe. In the decades following the French Revolution, Europeans struggled to find their way through a maze of political reform, while the Industrial Revolution brought about profound changes in economics and society. The advent of mass production transformed the societies of Europe as well as Europe's relationship with overseas colonies. At the same time, the rise of a mass electorate, an expanded press, and a growing middle class radically changed the nature of European politics and society.

During the nineteenth century, Western powers sought to extend their control and expand their colonial empires. Efforts to extend economic and cultural influence were met with various forms of resistance, to which Western powers responded with increasing force. From the Slave Revolt in Jamaica, to the Indian Mutiny, to the Boxer Rebellion at the end of the century, resistance to Western imperialism was common. The legacy of Western imperialist expansion in the nineteenth century continues to shape the relationship between the West and the world to this day.

The nineteenth century was also a period of revolutionary change in scientific discovery and intellectual thought. Whether it was the political ideology of communism, the new scientific theory of Darwinism, the provocative ideas of Nietzsche or Freud, or viewing the art of the Impressionists, no aspect of life in the nineteenth century remained untouched. By the end of the century, imperialism, nationalism and racism were travelling with Europeans around the world, setting the stage for the global warfare that would play out during the first half of the twentieth century.

UNIT EXPECTATIONS

In this unit, you will:

O demonstrate an understanding of the interaction among diverse peoples during the nineteenth century

O demonstrate an understanding of how the historical concept of change is used to analyse developments in the West and throughout the world during the nineteenth century

O demonstrate an understanding of the diversity of concepts of citizenship and human rights that developed during the nineteenth century

O demonstrate an understanding of women's economic, social, and political lives in Western and non-Western societies during the nineteenth century

O communicate opinions and ideas clearly and concisely, based on effective research

CHAPTER SEVEN

The Birth of Modern Industrial Society: Europe 1815–1850

CHAPTER EXPECTATIONS

By the end of this chapter, you will be able to:

- *describe the development of modern urbanization*

- *assess the influence of people such as Marx and Bentham, and groups such as the Luddites who helped shape Western attitudes*

- *assess the extent to which art reinforced or challenged prevailing social and political values in the early nineteenth century*

- *explain how the first Industrial Revolution affected the economy of the Western world*

Liberty Leading the People (2.5m x 3.2m) by Delacroix commemorates the July 1830 uprising that drove out King Charles X, and placed Louis-Philippe on the throne of France.

Following the tumult of the French Revolution and the Napoleonic Wars, Europe entered yet another period of rapid and dramatic change. The victors at Waterloo reached a new understanding about relations between states, but domestically these same oppressive aristocratic rulers confronted unprecedented economic change and ongoing social and political unrest. Consequently, the period from 1815 to 1850 is characterized by peace between states but conflict within states — again, it was revolution, not war, that arrived on the winds of change.

The forces of change came in the form of what contemporary British economic historian E. J. Hobsbawm has aptly called a "dual revolution." On the one hand, there was the political revolution, which tried to turn the ideas and hopes of the French Revolution into a living reality. On the other hand, remarkable economic and social changes had come about in England, where the Industrial Revolution would in turn transform the economies and societies of Western Europe. These were not two separate revolutions but one "dual" or two-track revolution. Economic changes and social conflict undermined customary authority and demanded new political solutions. Conservative forces tried to preserve tradition and find sources of stability in the midst of unprecedented change; reformers and radicals found church and state tied to outmoded aristocratic privilege and sought emancipation by political and social reform. Transformations and conflicts of such magnitude forced men and women to reconsider the received wisdom of tradition, and to re-examine the intellectual foundations of their government, society, and culture.

KEY CONCEPTS AND EVENTS

dual revolution

moral economy

multiplier effect

cash nexus

Poor Law Amendment Act of 1834

Factory Act of 1833

liberalism

July Monarchy

communism

romanticism

KEY PEOPLE

Friedrich Engels

John Stuart Mill

Klemens von Metternich

Jeremy Bentham

Luddites

Robert Owen

Karl Marx

Francisco de Goya

Eugène Delacroix

William Wordsworth

Wit and Wisdom

The only difference between the old-fashioned slavery and the new is that while the former was openly acknowledged the latter is disguised. The worker appears to be free, because he is not bought and sold outright. He is sold piecemeal by the day, the week, or the year.[1]
Friedrich Engels, *The Condition of the Working Class in England*, 1844

TIME LINE: THE BIRTH OF MODERN INDUSTRIAL SOCIETY

Frédéric Chopin born	1810	
	1814	Francisco de Goya, *The Third of May*, 1808; first exile of Napoléon
Congress of Vienna; second exile of Napoléon	1815	
	1817	David Ricardo, *The Principles of Political Economy*
Peterloo Massacre; Jean-Auguste Ingres, *La Grande Odalisque*	1819	
	1830	Fall of the Bourbon Monarchy in France; Eugène Delacroix, *Liberty Leading the People*
Reform Bill extends the vote in England	1832	
	1833	Factory Act passed in England
New Poor Law passed in England	1834	
	1840	Pyotr Ilich Tchaikovsky born
Friedrich Engels, *The Condition of the Working Class in England*	1844	
	1847	Charlotte Brontë, *Jane Eyre*; Emily Brontë, *Wuthering Heights*
Revolution sweeps through Europe; Karl Marx, *The Communist Manifesto*	1848	

Not to scale.

THE INDUSTRIAL REVOLUTION

With the Industrial Revolution, the production of goods by machine took on an altogether new dimension. Indeed, the word "manufacture" itself acquired a new meaning. Formerly, it had meant "to make by hand"; with industrialization, it began to mean "to make by machine." Moreover, earlier forms of production had been limited by the sources of power available: muscles, wind, and water.

The first Industrial Revolution harnessed steam, a new source of power. The application of this new power source involved much more than boiling water; it involved harnessing the expansive power of steam to run a wide range of machinery. Today, we tend to associate steam power with railway locomotives or ships, but these uses came relatively late. Early innovation used steam power to move stationary engines such as steam pumps in mines, steam bellows and hammers in iron foundries, steam engines for spinning and weaving machines in textile mills, and steam-threshing machines to harvest grain in the fields. All these applications, and countless others, involved technological innovation of considerable ingenuity, but the history of the Industrial Revolution is more than the history of mechanical invention.

Industrialization also brought an economic revolution. Over the course of two or three decades, industrial innovations significantly increased the production of goods, the scope of domestic and international trade, and the wealth generated as a result. This increase in production came from the new steam technology and required new ways of organizing production and human labour. In his economic classic, *The Wealth of Nations* (1776), Adam Smith said little about new machines, but he elaborated on how more specialized forms of production and labour, together with more

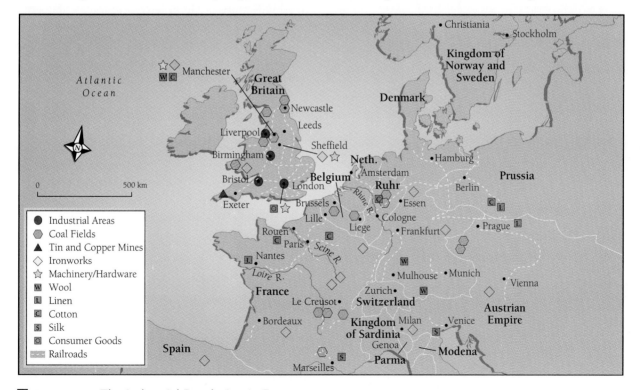

■ FIGURE 7.1 The Industrial Revolution in Europe
Consider why the industrial areas shown on this map came to be where they are.

efficient systems of trade, greatly enhance productivity. The Industrial Revolution led to changes in the form and supply of money, the provision of credit, and in forms of investment. It changed financial institutions such as banks and stock exchanges; it altered the role of the state in relation to the economy; and it brought about a new understanding of economics.

Yet, the Industrial Revolution was more than a technological and economic revolution. It was also a social and cultural revolution because it transformed the way human beings went about making a living. It created a new middle class as well as a new working class, living under new urban conditions and new patterns of work, family life, and leisure. Cities such as London and Paris became new centres of both wealth and poverty.

Industrial entrepreneurs became municipal leaders, setting the tone for the conspicuous consumption of the new middle class, which began to include industrialists,

clergy, doctors, lawyers, bankers and merchants. The new industries created new forms of labour, most notably at factories, where new machinery and new concentrations of workers were brought together. These changes were so dramatic that people began to think of themselves as living in a new era.

The term "industrial revolution" came into use in England in the 1830s to express how extensively society had changed within the living memories of that generation.

The "first" Industrial Revolution began there in the 1750s and progressed rapidly during the French Revolution and the Napoleonic Wars, from the 1790s to 1815. This transformed Great Britain into the "workshop of the world."

Industrialization in continental Europe followed the British lead after the Napoleonic Wars were over. What is now Belgium (then the Austrian Netherlands) led the way, beginning around 1810. In France, industrial innovations began to have a noticeable influence in the 1830s and in Germany, in the 1840s and 1850s. Other countries experienced their own industrial revolutions in the second half of the nineteenth century. Italy and Spain began later, in the 1870s, and Russia after 1890. Some historians see the timing of the industrial revolutions as having had profound consequences for the twentieth century. Countries with later industrialization proved more prone to totalitarianism after 1914. We need to keep this chronological difference in mind because it affects not only the character of political movements and social conflict, but also their resolution in different countries in the period from 1815 to 1850.

The First Industrial Revolution: England 1750–1851

With no earlier models to follow — and no blueprint or plan — the first Industrial Revolution was an example of "spontaneous combustion," so to speak. Between 1800 and 1850, the national income rose by 125 percent, while the share of national income

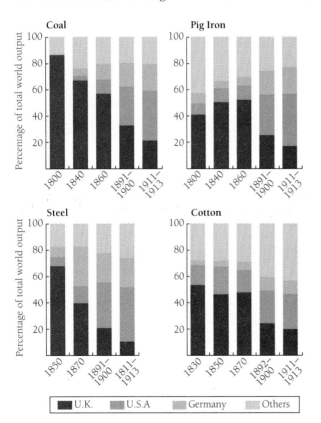

Britain in World Industry: The Nineteenth Century

derived from industrial production rose by 230 percent. To borrow Walt Whitman Rostow's phrase (from his *Theory of Modernization*), this "take-off" in the economy that occurred around 1780 was due to a number of preconditions peculiar to Great Britain.

There already existed a capitalist system in agriculture, in which land was privately owned and income derived chiefly from marketing produce rather than simply collecting rent. The pre-industrial economy had addressed the needs of the community through what was referred to as the "moral economy" — the belief that the first fruits of the soil belong to the community. The moral economy meant that farmers were expected to bring their produce to the village market and sell it at a fair price. If there was a surplus after the market, the farmer could sell his produce outside of the village. The concept of the moral economy prevented farmers from profiting from the hunger of the community. When a farmer attempted to sell at inflated prices, or to ship goods out of the area, riots could ensue, often led by the women of the community. The goods would be seized and brought to market, where they would be sold at a fair market price.

Although 80 percent of the land was owned by the English aristocracy and gentry, it — unlike the European nobility — was not composed of feudal landlords collecting dues from dependent peasants. Instead, the cultivators of the soil were independent landowners, tenants, or landless wage-earning labourers. Remember too, that, in the eighteenth-century Europe, the weather was warm, the harvests were reliable, and farming was prosperous for the most part.

Aside from farming, the landed aristocracy developed other sources of income from the land: it financed the mining of coal and iron and built roads, charging a toll on what came to be known as turnpikes. Aristocrats also constructed an elaborate network of canals. Heavy, bulky, or fragile cargo such as coal, iron, grain, pottery, raw wool, or cotton could not be hauled in horse-drawn wagons over rough roads. The solution lay in building canals to float the heavy cargo on barges. These canals served as a transportation network for the first 50 years of the Industrial Revolution, until the new railroads began replacing canals in the 1830s and 1840s.

WEB CONNECTION www.mcgrawhill.ca/links/legacy
Go to the site above to find out more about the first Industrial Revolution.

The prosperity of market agriculture and the building of a transportation network of canals were evidence of a thriving national economy. In fact, unlike in France or Germany, there were no internal tariff barriers restricting the flow of goods within Great Britain. Furthermore, there were well-established financial institutions, such as the Bank of England (established in 1694), both in London and in leading provincial towns. This well-established and thriving commercial sector, trading in agricultural produce and in handicraft products such as woollen textiles, also had an important international dimension, reaching out not simply across the English Channel to Europe, but across the oceans to Africa, Asia, and the Americas.

By the end of the eighteenth century, Britain had established itself as the world's leading maritime nation, and it had ousted France from Canada and India. British ships were the main carriers of the profitable trade in slaves from Africa to the Americas, and the West Indies were the jewels of the British Empire, supplying slave-grown sugar to the British Isles and Europe. Despite the setback of the American Revolution, trade with the newly independent United States continued to grow. Expanding trade with Asia created a demand for new products. It was no accident that the development of a national taste for an exotic drink from the East — tea sweetened with West Indian sugar — should be consumed in cups and saucers called "china."

In addition to fine porcelain from Japan and China, cotton textiles were imported from India. Soon, pottery and cotton textile production would become important new industries in England. Raw cotton was first imported from India and Egypt, but, by the 1790s, the main supply came from slave plantations in the United States. British foreign trade grew steadily, expanding over 70 percent between 1700 and 1750; it then underwent an upsurge just at the beginning of the Industrial Revolution, increasing 80 percent between 1750 and 1770.

All these signs of economic vitality meant that England had the best-fed and best-housed population in Europe. Furthermore, a relatively high proportion of the population, roughly 30 percent, was no longer directly dependent on agriculture for its livelihood. England was also exceptional in the size of its "middling sort": middle-class bankers, merchants, professionals, traders, shopkeepers, and self-employed artisans. Below the tiny elite of landowners, this group constituted some 40 percent of the population and was outnumbered only by the labouring poor, who accounted for just over half of the population. This cluster of economic and social preconditions came together in the 1780s to ignite the Industrial Revolution. The spark that set off this spontaneous combustion was consumer demand.

Consumer Demand and the Multiplier Effect

The existing system of domestic manufacture under the cottage system (workers working out of their homes) could not keep pace with the demand for goods. More consumers had sufficient income to afford exotic new groceries, such as tea and sugar, and manufactured goods such as cotton cloth and china. Those who benefited the most from this new situation were called the "middlemen." These traders purchased raw materials such as cotton or wool, let it out to the craftworkers in their homes to finish into cloth for piecework payment, and sold the finished product. In the second half of the eighteenth century, such traders realized that if they could produce goods in greater quantity at a cheaper price, they could find more consumers and make a higher profit.

It was out of the limitations of the domestic system and the demands of consumers that the industrial entrepreneurs were born. Traders, with limited funds and credit from existing trade, invested small amounts of capital in new properties and machines. Innovations were not without risk and not all were successful; those entrepreneurs who increased their profits would re-invest in further innovations. Consequently, once set in motion, the process of industrialization gained momentum. Self-sustained growth was intensified by the impact of new technologies. Mechanical inventions, which had parallels in many industries, stimulated the quest for new machines to solve technological bottlenecks. This pattern, called the multiplier effect, explains why once industrial innovation started, it became an ongoing process.

Technology and Society

The introduction of new machines solved problems, but also created new ones. For example, one of the key industries transformed by the Industrial Revolution was the textile industry. Raw wool or cotton would first be spun into thread. Then, handloom weavers would weave the thread into cloth. James Kay's flying shuttle (invented in 1733) greatly increased the capacity of handloom weavers to produce cloth, but it put great pressure on the spinners who made thread from raw wool or cotton. Consequently, the spinning process was the first to be industrialized, with the spinning jenny invented in 1764 by James Hargreaves and the introduction of water power to factories and spinning mills.

The productivity of spinning mills was further increased with the application of steam power in place of water. These innovations, in turn, created pressure on the weaving process. The mechanization of spinning introduced factory labour and, surprisingly, increased employment for handloom weavers working under the old domestic system. But, weaving was a far more difficult process to mechanize than spinning, and even Samuel Compton's power loom (1779), a cumbersome machine, required many modifications to be effective. There was a gap of as much as 30 or 40 years between the industrialization of spinning and that of weaving. Textile factories with steam-powered looms did not become common until the second decade of the nineteenth century.

The cotton industry used to be considered the industry with the greatest multiplier effect during the first Industrial Revolution; it was one of the first industries to mechanize and use steam power. This pioneering use of factory labour transformed the city of Manchester and the surrounding county of Lancashire. The cotton industry became the largest single employer of industrial labour, and cotton cloth became the most valued commodity in Britain's export trade. Recent historians, however, stress that developments in coal mining, iron production, and machine design had a more significant impact on the economy. Both in the realm of technical innovation and in the numbers of people employed, the combination of coal, iron, and steam had an even greater multiplier effect than the cotton industry. This impact would become most visible in the 1830s and 1840s, with the introduction of steam locomotion and the boom in railroad construction, also key to the later industrialization of continental Europe after 1830.

By 1830 Britain had established itself as the world's leading industrial power. With a population of 21 million — less than 10 percent of the total population of Europe in 1850 — Britain was producing two-thirds of the world's coal, one-half of its iron, and one-half of its cotton cloth.

Industrialization on the Continent

Two or three generations after its commencement in Great Britain, industrial change began to have an effect on the European continent. This delay was a reflection of political and social differences between Britain and Europe. There were important consequences for the disparities in the patterns of continental industrialization. The social conflicts and political movements of continental Europe in the first half of the nineteenth century also stemmed from these differences.

The key to industrial change was the emergence of consumer demand for manufactured goods. Britain and continental Europe both experienced a population boom in the period. The European population grew from 188 million in 1800 to 266 million in 1850. The British population grew at an even faster pace: from about 10 million in 1800 to 21 million in 1850. During the same period, the growth of the British economy surpassed that of the population. In contrast, population growth in Europe in the early nineteenth century outstripped the growth of the economy. Consequently, labour in Europe was abundant and cheap, but peasants and workers experienced a decline in living standards and often could not afford manufactured goods. As a consequence, industrialization on continental Europe significantly lagged behind Britain.

There were many other factors to affect Europe's later industrialization. The lengthy period of war with the French Republic, under Napoléon, disrupted trade and commerce, absorbed the resources of European states, and led to the conscription of potential workers into military service. Political divisions, especially in the numerous small states and principalities of Germany, hampered trade. The *Zollverein*, a customs union led by Prussia and formed by several German states in 1834, facilitated the flow of goods, which opened up the Rhine River as a major transportation artery. Transport over land remained difficult, though, and in many areas coal and iron resources could not readily be exploited.

Even by the time of Napoléon's defeat at Waterloo in 1815, early industrial initiatives in textile, coal mining, and iron production had begun in northern France and what is now Belgium. These initiatives copied British techniques and inventions. Anxious to protect its industrial lead and to prevent industrial espionage, the British government prohibited the export of machinery and the emigration of engineers and machine workers; however, this did not stop British entrepreneurs from taking their capital, their inventions, and their knowledge across the Channel.

Continental manufacturers also sent their agents to observe developments in Britain. It is well known that

Friedrich Engels (1820–1895), one of the fathers of communism, was sent to live in Manchester by his father, a German textile manufacturer. There, Engels had a vision of the new industrial future, and his classic, *The Condition of the Working Class in England* (1844), had a profound influence on Karl Marx (1818–1883) and other socialist thinkers. On the Continent, the new industries — with their steam engines and factories — did not take hold as quickly as British entrepreneurs or Friedrich Engels had imagined.

The real boom in the continental Industrial Revolution occurred with the construction of railroads. Here the Continent followed quickly on Britain's introduction of steam locomotion in 1830. In France, railway construction led industrial development in the 1830s and 1840s. In Germany, railways essential for the transport of raw materials and finished goods were built in the 1840s and 1850s. Railway construction acted as a "multiplier" because it required increased production of coal, iron, steam locomotives, railway carriages, and a host of related machines and mechanical devices. The railway boom laid the foundations for continental heavy industries, and as a labour-intensive industry, railroads created whole new categories of industrial employment.

The Social Impact of the Industrial Revolution

The early years of the Industrial Revolution, from 1780 to 1850, came with intense social unrest. Despite these signs of dramatic social change, the pace of the impact of new industries should not be exaggerated. For example, new industrial conditions such as factory labour were still exceptional rather than typical. Even in Great Britain in 1850, more people were employed in agriculture than in manufacturing. Similarly, cotton textile mills employed 272 000 women, whereas 905 000 worked as domestic servants. The new demands of industry stimulated not only new forms of employment, but also traditional handicraft production. For example, construction materials such as bricks and

iron nails were still hand-produced by women and children doing piecework. Women and children, regardless of where they worked, had the most exploitative working conditions and the lowest rates of pay.

Conservative moralists such as Thomas Carlyle (1795–1881) and artist William Hogarth (1697–1764), and political radicals such as Friedrich Engels (1820–1895), were shocked by conditions in the expanding industrial cities and dismayed by the new social relationships between employers and their workers. On the other hand, economists and engineers stressed the unprecedented growth of wealth, the labour-saving efficiency of the new machines, and the improvement of the living standards of both factory owners and factory workers. These contradictory observations set in motion a long-standing debate over the impact of the Industrial Revolution.

The Standard of Living

By today's standards, 1850s working conditions and urban environments were appalling, but extreme poverty and city squalor were no innovation of the Industrial Revolution. No one disputes that the landed aristocracy and the new middle class (industrial entrepreneurs, merchants, professionals) benefited as owners, investors, and consumers. The debate is over the living standard of the wage-dependent, labouring population, which, in Britain, constituted over two-thirds of the population. No one disputes that after 1850, the Industrial Revolution in Britain created greater material abundance for all social ranks in the long term. A major debate over the short-term impact of the Industrial Revolution is still ongoing.

The Urban Community: Conditions of City Life

If one looks at the entire nineteenth century, two striking developments are apparent: a remarkable increase in the total European population (from 188 million in 1800 to 401 million in 1900) and an increase in urban population as the century advanced. With the exception of Great Britain, most countries' populations continued to live in the country, even in the second half of the nineteenth century, but larger cities came to dominate the social and political landscape. This was particularly true of large capital cities, in the process of becoming the enormous metropolitan centres they are today.

With industrialization, what had been small centres of handicraft manufacture and commerce also became large modern cities. More people lived in cities and a larger proportion of them lived in cities of more than 100 000 inhabitants. In 1800 Europe had 22 cities of more than 100 000 people; by 1895 there were 120 cities of more than 100 000 and their residents comprised 10 percent of the population. At the beginning of the nineteenth century, only two German cities (Berlin and Hamburg) had more than 60 000 people; by 1871 there were eight German cities with more than 100 000 inhabitants.

The growth of cities was remarkable in the sense that until the 1860s, cities did not grow by natural increase but were dependent upon migration from the countryside. Given the total lack of any sort of urban planning, it is not surprising that overcrowding, poor housing, scarcity of fresh water, and poor or non-existent sanitation made cities an ideal environment for the spread of disease. The death rate exceeded the birth rate.

In the period from 1780 to 1850, the most outstanding examples of urban growth were in the industrial areas of the British Isles. Signs of such urban growth were evident in Belgium and France from the 1830s, but the pace of urbanization intensified there and in the German states from the 1840s onward. British municipalities were symbolic of a new and frightening age, with unplanned and unregulated explosion from the 1820s onward. Seventeen percent of the British population lived in towns of more than 20 000 people; by 1851, about 35 percent; and by 1891 more than 50 percent. In the crisis decades of the 1830s and 1840s, the leading industrial cities grew at a phenomenal pace.

Growth of British Industrial Cities

People flooded into cities from the countryside in search of jobs in the new industries. Beyond employment, their first need was housing. Prior to the French Revolution, buildings that housed both rich and poor on different floors were common in European cities. The nineteenth century, with its dominant middle class and expanding proletariat (the lowest, poorest class), saw an end to such social intermingling. In every European city of the nineteenth century, exclusive neighbourhoods were built for the wealthy bourgeoisie, while the proletariat was relegated to ghettos into which the bourgeoisie was sure never to set foot.

The homes of the urban poor were quite different from those of the middle class. Best described as living in filthy hovels, the poor were forced to tolerate intrusions even at the most intimate times. The apartments of the urban poor were barren except for mattresses, kitchen utensils, a table, a few chairs, and occasionally a family chest. Entire families lived in one or two rooms. Rarely would one find even a symbol of pleasure, such as a bird in a cage, or of privacy, such as curtains. Sometimes the apartment walls were decorated with a colour print cut from a weekly magazine. The floors were poorly tiled and the ceiling was supported

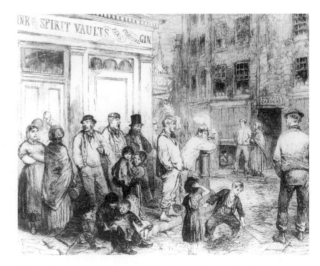

This poverty-stricken section of London was known, ironically, as "Paradise Gardens." Living conditions for the urban poor in the early nineteenth century were appalling.

by roughly hewn black wooden beams. As cities grew, housing shortages became acute, and overcrowding in filthy apartments increased dramatically, making privacy virtually impossible.

Workers needed to live close to their place of work since there was no public transit, and rural customs persisted. People were used to work and home being in the same place and it was normal for parents and children to work together. They also ate at home — the main meal was at noon — and so needed to walk to and from work several times during a working day ranging from 12 to 16 hours. Employers and builders constructed housing cheaply and quickly with a mind to profit rather than living requirements.

It was common for families to have two rooms, one for cooking and sitting, and the other for sleeping, with all family members often sharing a common bed. In the worst conditions of overcrowding, in which as many as eight or 10 people shared one room, families and single people of both sexes would sleep together, much to the dismay of contemporary moralists. Houses were built in rows or in squares with a common courtyard, in which there might be a water tap and a common toilet. In these crowded conditions, there was little access to fresh air and little provision for clean water or the removal of refuse, including human waste. In a parliamentary report for 1845, James Smith (1779–1849) reported on conditions in Leeds:

> But by far the most unhealthy localities of Leeds are close squares of houses, or yards, as they are called, which have been erected for the accommodation of working people. Some of these, though situated in comparatively high ground, are airless from the enclosed structure, and being wholly unprovided with any form of underdrainage, or convenience, or arrangements for cleansing, are one mass of damp and filth ... The ashes, garbage, and filth of all kinds are thrown from the doors and windows of the houses upon the surface of streets and courts ... The privies [toilets] are few in proportion to the number of inhabitants. They are open to view both in front

and rear, are invariably in a filthy condition, and often remain without the removal of any portion of the filth for six months. The feelings of the people are blunted to all seeming decency, and from the constantly contaminated state of the atmosphere, a vast amount of ill health prevails, leading to listlessness, and inducing a desire for spirits and opiates; the combined influence of the whole condition causing much loss of time, increasing poverty, and terminating the existence of many in premature death.

Skilled artisans and other more highly paid mechanics lived in better conditions, but many workers in the textile mills of Leeds and elsewhere lived in the crowded and unhealthy conditions described by James Smith.

Rural Homes

Along with the advent of the Industrial Revolution came the rise of the rural myth. This myth, which persists to this day, makes out that life in the country is more wholesome; that fresh air abounds and children live a happier, healthier life. The homes of the rural poor of the nineteenth century certainly would not have suggested an easy or healthy life. One description of the small farms that predominated throughout France noted that a home consisted of a room that served as kitchen, dining room, and bedroom for the whole family (as well as sometimes serving as stable and barnyard too). This description went on to say: "Occasionally a smoky oil lamp is used for light, but usually the only light comes from the fire. The floor is of rough, damp earth, with puddles here and there. One steps in them, and young children wade in the mud." Another description, found in a medical thesis of the mid-nineteenth century, provides vivid details of life in the homes of the rural poor:

> The same hovel is used for preparing food, storing leftovers used for feeding the animals, and storing small farm implements. The sink is in one

corner and beds are in another. Clothes are hung on one side, salted meats on the other. Milk is made into cheese and dough into bread. Even pets share the same room, in which they eat their meals and satisfy their physical needs. The chimney, which is too short and too large in diameter, allows a cold wind to enter, forcing the smoke back into this wretched dwelling, which is home to the farmer and his family.[2]

Conditions of Work

In addition to the new urban environment, labourers faced new conditions of work. Under the pre-industrial handicraft or domestic system, the family worked as a unit and had some measure of control over the pace of work. When their product was in demand, they worked extremely hard for long hours; at other times, especially when the market was slow, they worked at a more leisurely pace. Under the mechanized and specialized system of production in the factory, the work was boring and repetitive, and the pace was set by the steady and uninterrupted motion of the machine. Since the workplace was the factory and not the home, the employer could dictate the work and leisure times.

Early factories had clocks above the entrance, so workers would arrive at a specified time. Employers had a great deal of difficulty imposing this new time-related discipline. Labourers persisted in the pre-industrial habit of "Saint Monday," in which they took a day off to recuperate from the excesses of Saturday night and Sunday. Employers imposed fines and penalties for lateness, for interruptions in work, and for absenteeism. Many of the disciplinary features associated with strict nineteenth-century schools — penalties for lateness, permission to leave the room, quietness in corridors, and corporal punishment for misdemeanours — were originally factory practices.

Beyond the new intensity of machine-paced work and time-related discipline, there was the simple question of the hours of work. The workweek followed the

Pleasures AND PASTIMES

Holidays for the working class were few and far between in the nineteenth century. Although the Factory Act of 1833 legislated that workers were entitled to certain holidays throughout the year, employers were reluctant to comply. When the people of the working class did have some time off, though, they naturally enjoyed escaping the dirt, congestion and bustle of city life for the relative quiet, cleanliness and natural beauty of the countryside. Seaside resorts such as Blackpool and Brighton became the favourite haunts of the masses, who would escape the city by steamer or railroad, only to find their accommodations no better than home. Often, during peak season, the food was bad, and a half-dozen or more might be crammed into a single bed.

biblical precept of six full working days and one day of rest on Sunday. Saturday was payday, and Saturday evening was a time for dressing up, shopping, and parties. Some of the longest hours were put in by shop assistants, a respectable but poorly paid job for girls and young women who worked up to 90 hours a week. The factory day began at five or six in the morning, with a breakfast break at eight. Although actual working time was from 12 to 14 hours, the working day lasted 14 to 16 hours when meal times were included, and concluded at eight or nine in the evening. Working conditions were unsafe and work-related injuries and illness were common.

EVOLUTION OF THE FAMILY

Work and Private Life

One of the most contentious issues in the Industrial Revolution was child labour. In the early 1830s, at the height of the abolitionist movement against West Indian slavery, industrial reformer and moralist Richard Oastler led an effective campaign against what he termed "Yorkshire slavery." Oastler (who also campaigned for a 10-hour workday) argued that child labour in woollen textile mills was comparable to the chattel slavery of Africans on the plantations in the Americas.

The Industrial Revolution did not invent child labour. Children in the pre-industrial domestic system had been expected to contribute to the family income. Both boys and girls of nine or 10 years of age were sent to live and work with a farmer, master crafter, or merchant. The first generation of factory workers attempted to preserve the practice of working as a unit, and whole families were employed to tend spinning machines. As machines grew larger, employers had less need for adult males and employed larger numbers of women and children. Yet the division of

LETTING CHILDREN
DOWN A COAL MINE
From a Plate in the *Westminster Review*

Since children are smaller than adults, they were ideal for working in narrow mine shafts and tunnels. How do you think this affected the children?

occupations by gender perpetuated the distinction that the primary breadwinner was the male, and consequently, females, as secondary breadwinners, were paid lower wages.

Males became work-centred, and even leisure time was spent with workmates at pubs or fraternal lodges. Women divided their time between work and home, and the neighbourhood court or street was often a female domain. The preferred practice was for married women, especially with the arrival of the first child, to leave paid employment. For many women, widowed or abandoned with young children, or with husbands unemployed or in poor health, paid work was a necessity. The textile industry was almost entirely populated by women and children. Infants were cared for by grandmothers. Many women now faced the double shift of paid employment and domestic chores. Nonetheless, middle-class reformers still blamed them for neglecting their domestic and maternal duties; they also blamed their husbands for failing to provide sufficient income, attributing to them an inveterate laziness and excessive alcohol consumption. Without the provision of state or private pensions, and with the expectation that one worked until death, old age brought the years of greatest poverty. Of course, at any age, ill health, an industrial accident or unemployment could mean economic disaster.

Marriage and Divorce

Despite the efforts of the middle class to encourage respectable, moral behaviour, change came slowly in Europe. During the first three decades of the nineteenth century, the traditional pattern of males marrying late and of fairly widespread celibacy among women was replaced with more and earlier marriages, leading to a significant increase in the birth rate. By the latter half of the century, declining infant mortality and other factors led women to have significantly fewer children in many Western European countries. Increased sexual activity among the unmarried produced high illegitimacy rates. In many areas, local parish priests and ministers often attempted to arrange marriages, in order to avoid illegitimate births. Despite these efforts, it was estimated that up to 50 percent of the population of Paris in the early nineteenth century had been born out of wedlock.

Another challenge to the emerging nineteenth-century sense of morality was the number of people who opted not to bother with the formality of marriage, choosing instead to live together out of wedlock. This practice was so widespread in England in the eighteenth century, that the Marriage Act of 1753 was passed in an attempt to end irregular unions by making legal marriages easier. Still, in the early nineteenth century, it was quite common in rural areas for couples to evade formal weddings. For those who did choose to marry, elopement was fairly common. Although living together was considered bigamous, colonies such as South Africa and Australia did not enforce England's marriage laws.

When marriages broke down, the consequences varied for people of different classes. Until the Marriage Act was revised in England in 1857, only the wealthy and influential could afford to pursue a legal parliamentary divorce. Among the lower classes, divorces, albeit illegal, did take place. A woman who was deserted or beaten would often "return the ring" in front of witnesses, signalling the end of the marriage. In time, most poor couples did not bother with the ceremony. If the marriage broke down, they simply moved apart and perhaps remarried in the future, despite the absence of a formal divorce.

Family Violence

The nature and level of family violence varied according to class. Among working-class people, wife-beating was a male prerogative. Husbands, perhaps drunk or frustrated by a long day at work, often vented their anger by beating their wives. A man's excuse for beating his wife might be, "Dinner wasn't ready and the fire had gone out." Although children also faced the wrath of their father, regardless of class, women were the primary victims of family violence in the nineteenth century. Family violence became a favourite theme for crime stories appearing in major newspapers. These stories vividly illustrate the problems of private life in the nineteenth century.

Changing Roles of Men and Women

The *Code Napoléon*, which laid the foundation of laws throughout much of continental Europe, granted the husband absolute superiority in the family. Wives and mothers were legally stripped of all legal capacity by Article 213 of the civil code, which stated: "The husband is obliged to protect his wife, the wife to obey her husband." Because married women had no legal rights, they could not be part of family councils, where key decisions might be made, nor were they allowed to serve as the guardian for an underage child: This role would fall to a male relative. Furthermore, adulterous men faced no risks, whereas adulterous women could face a penalty as severe as death, since their crime struck at the very heart of the family: a legitimate male heir to carry on the family name. Finally, men had complete control of all family property, including any wages earned by the wife. Only in wealthy marriages, where women's property was protected by a marriage contract, could an equitable settlement be expected in case of divorce. A common practice in the nineteenth century was for the wife's wages to be paid directly to the husband, who then granted her an allowance to buy food and other necessities. The husband's control over the spending of a couple's wages remained the norm in France until a change in the laws in 1907.

The father also had absolute authority over his children. Any decisions regarding education or marriage were made by the father. It was often believed that mothers would be guided by emotions rather than reason and logic in making decisions concerning the children. Until 1896, children under the age of 26 in France could not marry without parental consent. In cases where the children were disobedient or obstinate, the father could request that the child be arrested and held in a state prison. Until the age of 16, children could be held in prison for up to one month; those between 16 and the age of majority could be held for up to six months. If, at the end of the sentence, the father refused to take back the child, the child could be held in prison until he or she reached the age of majority.

John Stuart Mill and Women's Role

While women had begun to agitate for changes that would significantly alter their participation in society, their domestic lives during the nineteenth century remained, at best, restricted and, at worst, harsh and brutal. During the 1820s, the well-known philosopher and economist John Stuart Mill (1806–1873) began his campaign against wife-beating and the failure of the courts to take appropriate action. His long struggle culminated in 1869 with the publishing of the powerful and influential book *The Subjection of Women*. Mill argued beyond the need to bring an end to the physical abuse of women, insisting that women as well as men required freedom to achieve happiness. Mill was not alone in his crusade for the rights of women. In the mid-nineteenth century, William Thomson (Lord Kelvin, 1824–1907) wrote a tract entitled *An Appeal of One Half of the Human Race, Women, Against the Pretensions of the Other Half, Men, to Retain Them in Political, and Thence in Civil and Domestic Slavery*. In this publication, Thompson claimed that the home was not "the abode of calm bliss," but "the eternal prison-house of the wife ... The house is his house, with everything in it; and of all the fixtures the most abjectly is his breeding-machine, the wife."

The nineteenth century would be a transitional period for European women, a time of continued exploitation and yet a time when female literacy improved rapidly and women began the crusade that would eventually win them full rights in the twentieth century.

THE ROLE OF GOVERNMENT IN SOCIETY

Changes in living standards, patterns of work, family life, and experience created stress and required significant adaptation by individuals and by the community. The cycles of expansion and contraction in the economy had a direct bearing on the individual's and the community's sense of well-being. In its early stages, the Industrial Revolution was subject to a series of radical booms and slumps. In boom times, with fuller employment, living conditions were better; but, during economic depressions, widespread unemployment in large urban populations such as Manchester, England, posed much more than a serious social problem.

Fluctuations between times of prosperity and times of hardship changed people's expectations. Having experienced improvement in good times, they were less tolerant of hard times, and so demanded action by employers and politicians. The experience of industrialization created a sense of common identity among working people, and this class consciousness expressed itself through political demands for the vote and for social change.

Working-class political activists, middle-class radicals, and conservative moralists interpreted the misery of the urban environment and the harshness of industrial work conditions as a new state of human relations. Scottish historian Thomas Carlyle (1795–1881), who believed in the need for leaders (such as "captains" of industry) and in the duty of workers to work, thought that human relations had been reduced to what he called a "cash nexus." By this he meant that the employer's interest was solely in profit and that workers were no longer human beings, but simply a cost factor in production.

Rejecting the inevitability of the cash nexus, trade unionists and other working-class activists asserted the values of community and co-operation, and sought a remedy in an egalitarian democracy. Thomas Carlyle and other conservative moralists, such as politician Benjamin Disraeli (1804–1881) and writer Charles Dickens (1812–1870), defended the social hierarchy in works such as *Oliver Twist* and *Great Expectations*. They hoped to restore a kind of paternalism in which employers and the state had a moral obligation toward their less fortunate social inferiors.

Laissez Faire: No Government Intervention

Manufacturers thought they had a good understanding of how economies functioned, free from old-fashioned morality. After all, the new science of political economy advised that freedom from government or other restrictions, referred to as *laissez faire*, optimized economic growth. In the early nineteenth century, these advocates of *laissez faire* — or of a free market — held a very pessimistic view of the possibilities for improvement in the living standards of the poor.

Thomas Malthus (1766–1834), an Anglican clergyman and pioneer of demography (the science of the dynamics of population), studied the growth of population and increases in poverty in rural England. In his *Essay on Population* (1798), he concluded that population grows more quickly than food supply. Even if living standards improved, the poor would simply have more children and breed themselves back into poverty. British economist David Ricardo, in *The Principles of Political Economy* (1817), linked Adam Smith's ideas about the free pursuit of individual self-interest with Malthus's theory of population. Ricardo concluded that population growth and diminishing levels of profit created an ironclad law limiting the level of wages. Consequently, little could be done to raise living standards.

The ideas expressed above gave powerful support to the liberal policy of *laissez faire* and of resistance to regulation of trade and industry. They also confirmed the entrepreneurs' vision of their own success through the virtuous practice of self-discipline, diligence, thrift, and independence. The difficulty was that liberal theory and social reality were in conflict.

Christian moralists, shocked by conditions in the new industries and the expanding cities, felt compelled to intervene. Tory paternalists, tired of liberal criticism of the status quo, readily pointed to the human suffering in the manufacturers' domain. An even greater urgency was created by the riots, strikes, and political protests of farm labourers and industrial workers, who demanded redress of their social and economic grievances. Following a policy of *laissez faire*, the government did nothing, while social realities called for political action.

Utilitarianism: Government Intervention and Regulation

Jeremy Bentham (1748–1832), an original and influential liberal philosopher and moralist, pointed a way out of the social impasse of the early nineteenth century. He accepted Adam Smith's argument that it was best to free individuals to pursue their own self-interest. Smith had argued that in the competition between individuals, conflicts were reconciled by an "unseen hand" that would automatically restore balance in the marketplace. Bentham, more realistically, accepted that conflicts were real and that there could be clear winners and losers.

Believing that all human responses were either pleasurable or painful, Bentham thought that the impact of legislation could be calculated by a simple formula called the "principle of utility." This principle stated that laws should be designed to create "the greatest happiness of the greatest number." If real conflicts arose, the government could intervene and create an artificial measure of societal utility. According to Bentham, though, Adam Smith's principle of free competition served to eliminate the need for such a measure — usually applied during conflict — making interventions unnecessary or exceptional. Nonetheless, his utilitarian philosophy made government action more acceptable. After his death in 1832, Bentham's influence manifested itself through his followers, who investigated social conditions and had a hand in shaping the new social legislation of the 1830s and 1840s. Ironically, partly due to the influence of Bentham, this age of *laissez faire* saw an expansion of the role of the state and the creation of a modern civil service.

Social Legislation

The social legislation of the times addressed issues such as the provision of relief for the poor, conditions in factories and mines, and the regulation of public health. A growing and more impoverished rural population, and the abuse of parish relief (a system of limited financial assistance for the poor), led taxpayers to protest against the old Poor Law Act (which had been put in place under Queen Elizabeth I in 1597). In drafting a revised law, the government conducted for the first time a survey of the existing system, and from this survey, members of the Royal Commission, some of whom were Benthamites, drafted the New Poor Law Amendment Act of 1834, which was based upon a pleasure–pain calculation called the "less eligibility principle." In order to receive poor relief, an individual had to enter a workhouse and, in order to discourage people from going on relief, conditions in the workhouse were designed to be worse than conditions outside. The idea was to make the conditions of relief "less eligible" than the lowest-paid and least-attractive jobs on the market, in an effort to push the rural poor into the free-market factory system. The new law also introduced the Benthamite idea of a central board overseeing local administration.

The New Poor Law was successful in addressing abuses of the system in rural areas, but was unsuited to industrial areas subject to periods of mass unemployment. Consequently, there were extensive protests against the new law. The protesters saw workhouses as prisons and named them "Bastilles." Nonetheless, the Poor Law of 1834 remained the basic provision of social welfare until 1909. During its 75-year history, about five percent of the population was dependent on the New Poor Law's provisions.

Bentham's ideas also influenced other pieces of social legislation. Evangelicals such as Richard Oastler and Michael Sadler, shocked by conditions in textile factories, demanded regulation of the employment of women and children. The Factory Act of 1833 prohibited the employment of children under nine and placed limits on the working hours of those between the ages of nine and 18. Unlike its predecessors, this act proved effective because it adopted the Benthamite principle of a central authority with an inspectorate. From the experience of these inspectors and further pressure from evangelical reformers and trade unionists, the new Factory Act of 1847 limited children to a 10-hour day. This limit became the standard working day for adults in textile mills.

Another royal commission investigating conditions in coal mines revealed shocking underground conditions of work for women, girls, and boys. In mining communities, children were stunted in growth and reached puberty at an older age; adults aged prematurely. Women, who worked underground hauling coal wagons to the surface even while pregnant, suffered miscarriages and internal injuries. The Mines Act of 1842 prohibited the employment of women, and of children under 10 years of age, in underground mines.

In the 1840s, Edwin Chadwick, a physician who had been Bentham's secretary as well as commissioner for the Poor Laws and Mines Act, reported on the high rates of mortality in cities. With public pressure mounting, an outbreak of cholera — a killer disease with a tendency to spread from inner cities to middle-class suburbs — prompted the government to act. Once more, Edwin Chadwick, serving on an investigative commission, helped draft the Public Health Act of 1848, which included a General Board of Health to oversee conditions.

History

Taken as a whole, the social legislation passed in the age of *laissez faire* redefined the government's role in social policy. It established new ways of investigating social problems and created a body of professional civil servants who would become a new source of influence on future legislation.

MAINTAINING POLITICAL ORDER

By 1815 revolutionary changes had begun in British society, with reverberations spreading to the Continent. As monarchs and princes gathered to determine the shape of Europe after Napoléon, the ascendant forces appeared not to be those of reform, but of reaction. Apart from France with its legacy of the Revolution, the old social order of the landed nobility and its dependent peasantry still dominated the social landscape of Europe.

With Napoléon and his revolutionary legions defeated, Europe's statesmen undertook the task of restoration — of restoring monarchs defeated by Napoléon to their thrones. The clock could not be turned back, however. The French Revolution had created new political visions and unleashed the forces of popular insurrection. Whether moderate or radical, political reform was to have only one certain outcome: the weakening of the authority and privileges of kings and nobles.

The Napoleonic Wars had exposed another danger: In a restored Europe, no single power could be allowed to dominate the Continent. Diplomats were quite successful at drawing up a peace settlement. In fact, no single power became dominant and there would be no general European war for almost a century, until 1914.

The task of restoration within states proved far more difficult. Population growth and economic change undermined the basis of the restored order, and social discontent gave new meaning to the famous French revolutionary call for "liberty, equality, and fraternity." The forces of conservative reaction were no match for the demands for change articulated in the competing claims of liberalism, democracy, nationalism, and socialism.

Metternich and the Congress of Vienna

With Austrian and Prussian soldiers occupying Paris and Napoléon temporarily exiled on the Italian island of Elba, the victorious Allied Powers restored the French monarchy under the legitimate Bourbon claimant, Louis XVIII. The terms of this First Treaty of Paris, concluded in May 1814, generously and realistically recognized France's continued status as one of the great powers.

When the Allied Powers reconvened in Vienna in October 1814 as the Congress of Vienna, the crowned heads of Europe brought with them their aristocratic courtiers and retainers. As host, the Austrian emperor had to provide accommodation, lavish banquets, and entertainment for 14 000 visitors. Much to the annoyance of the princes of lesser states, the real work of the Congress of Vienna was accomplished by the private meetings of representatives of the principal powers: Austria, Russia, Prussia, Great Britain, and France. These proceedings were unexpectedly interrupted in March of 1815 with news of Napoléon's triumphant return from Elba. The ensuing 100 days ended with Napoléon's defeat at Waterloo in June (in what is now Belgium) and his exile to the British island of St. Helena in the south Atlantic. The episode weakened the negotiating position of Prince Talleyrand, the French delegate, but did little to alter the objectives of the Congress.

Prince Klemens von Metternich (1773–1859), the Austrian foreign secretary, was the leading figure at the Congress. An aristocrat, self-confident to the point of vanity about his appearance and intelligence, Metternich sought to preserve and protect the position of Austria in the redrafted European order. Less of a visionary than a political realist, he recognized that Austria's interests were best served by the preservation of the conservative principles and institutions he cherished and by the establishment of stable diplomatic relations.

The Concert of Europe: Maintaining Political Stability

In addition to the territorial settlement, the Congress initiated the practice of leading statesmen consulting with one another in order to resolve potential disputes. This idea of a "concert" of Europe worked best with respect to France. The four victorious powers, Russia, Prussia, Austria and Great Britain, formed the Quadruple Alliance, in which they agreed to act in concert should France show signs of expansionist revival.

A far more contentious idea was proposed by Czar Alexander I of Russia (1777–1825), who was fervently attached to absolutism and wished to unite his diplomacy with his personal Christian mysticism. The czar believed that harmony in Europe depended upon states adopting the divinely sanctioned order of rule by legitimate monarchs. The principle of legitimacy asserted that God chose rulers through hereditary succession, not by representative assemblies or elections. The Congress had followed this principle in restoring the legitimate Bourbon monarchs to the thrones of France, Spain, and Naples. To protect such legitimate rulers, the czar proposed that, under the Holy Alliance, member states would agree to intervene in the internal affairs of other states, should their monarchs be challenged by the evils of the French Revolution: liberalism, popular insurrection, and the use of nationalism. Fearful of the forces of reform and anxious not to offend the czar, Austria and Prussia joined the Holy Alliance.

Metternich had little time for the czar's mysticism, but he fiercely opposed any form of liberalism. Until the revolution of 1848 proved his undoing, Metternich resisted the destabilizing tide of liberal reform. Consequently, he was prepared to use the Austrian army and support the actions of his partners in the

Austrian Foreign Secretary, Klemens von Metternich (1773–1859)

Holy Alliance to intervene in the internal politics of lesser states. Lord Castlereagh, the British foreign secretary who had supported Metternich in the construction of a new balance of power, forthrightly refused to join this alliance. In Great Britain, a constitutional monarch, George III (and then George IV), ruled through a powerful and elected parliament. Castlereagh rejected the idea that a Holy Alliance of powerful states could intervene in the internal affairs of other states in order to impose some divinely inspired political order.

In 1820, in view of the Spanish and Italian uprisings, Austria, Prussia and Russia signed the Troppau Protocol, agreeing to intervene against any sign of revolutionary upheaval. Castlereagh refused to sign the Protocol because he thought that such interventions simply created greater conflict. But Britain also had its own self-interested motives for not signing. The Spanish-American colonies were in revolt, and their independence would offer Britain new commercial prospects, so Castlereagh wanted no part in a European alliance seeking to re-impose Spanish legitimacy in South America.

The divisions over the Holy Alliance were indicative of troubles to come. The restoration had established a new equilibrium among the great powers, but it had done so at a price: The lands and peoples of lesser states were placed under the authority of larger states. In the restoration of governments, restoring the authority of legitimate monarchs had been the primary objective; little attention had been given to the rights of their subjects. Wanting to undo the impact of the French Revolution, Metternich and his allies inadvertently helped to revive the revolutionary forces they had sought to overcome, by ignoring the will and the needs of the people.

Reaction and Reform: 1815–1830

Napoléon and his armies had claimed to be liberating Europe from royal absolutism and aristocratic privilege. Conquered peoples often saw these claims as French propaganda, but nonetheless they contained a germ of truth. With Napoléon came constitutions and laws bearing the stamp of the Enlightenment and the Revolution. In the Low Countries, the Rhineland, Spain and Italy, segments of the middle class had benefited from the Napoleonic reforms; therefore, they did not necessarily welcome the restoration of absolutism in 1815. On the other hand, in Central and Eastern Europe — with the notable exception of Poland — these reforms made little headway, and absolutism remained secure in Russia, Prussia and the Austrian Empire. Out of self-interest, the two great powers, Britain and France, co-operated in the restoration of legitimate rule and, as a result, paved the way for future conflicts.

Liberalism, Democracy, and Nationalism

Liberalism, a political philosophy attuned to the interests of the middle class, stressed the liberty of the individual both in relation to the state and in the pursuit of economic self-interest. Liberals feared that under democracy, and with universal suffrage, the will of the majority might overcome the interests of the individual; consequently, they tied the full rights of citizenship, including the vote, to the possession of property. Radical democrats, who included middle-class, lesser property owners (such as shopkeepers, salary-earning professionals, and small peasant landholders) as well as working-class artisans and labourers, sought equality of citizenship with universal suffrage.

Until 1848, liberalism challenged the authority of absolute monarchy while rejecting the claims of popular democracy. The re-invigorated conservatism, defending the restored order of 1815, rejected the claims of liberalism and radical democracy. Consequently, liberals and radicals were often political allies against absolutism, but their differences quickly became apparent when the reforming alliance proved victorious. Inevitably, they disagreed over the key questions of who had the vote and were full citizens and whose economic interests the state should protect and advance. A growing population and a developing economy pressed these issues to the forefront of the political agenda.

As the forces of reform advanced against the tide of conservative reaction, the main struggle was the one between liberalism and democracy. With the rise of the urban population and the growth of industry, advocates of democracy among middle-class radicals, artisans, and labourers redefined their political and social objectives with the new ideology of socialism.

Another legacy of the French Revolution, linked to the competing claims of liberalism and democracy, was the idea of nationalism. The new sense of identity derived from citizenship in a nation-state rested upon the idea of popular sovereignty. This idea that the state belonged to the "people," and that the government derived its authority from the people, was given particular intensity by the experience of the French Revolution and Napoleonic armies. Soldiers saw themselves as armed citizens first, defending and advancing the cause of popular liberation against the forces of reactionary aristocrats. The French conquest of other peoples created the opposite reaction; peoples, especially in the German states, defined themselves in opposition to the occupying forces of France.

There were few, if any, examples of mass nationalism prior to 1848. Older forms of identity with the locality, of deference to local notables, and of a vague allegiance to the distant figure of the monarch persisted. Nationalism, with its sense of citizenship and popular sovereignty, was both new and radical. The post-1815 settlement imposed by the Congress of Vienna created conditions for a fusion of the more limited demands of liberalism with the first stirrings of nationalism.

The Defence of Absolutism

In 1819 Metternich, the Austrian foreign secretary, wary of any sign of reforming liberalism, persuaded the leading German states to issue the Carlsbad Decrees, which curtailed political meetings, censored the press and universities, and further limited the powers of legislative assemblies. This intervention was a significant setback for the development of liberalism in the German states: It spread police surveillance as established in Austria and strengthened the aristocratic authority of the Prussian state.

In 1820–1821, Metternich also faced liberal and nationalist upheavals in several Italian states (which were not under Austrian domination). He used the Austrian army in a quick intervention to quell the revolts. The ensuing protests in Naples and Piedmont, inspired by a small revolutionary organization, the *Carbonari*, laid the foundation of the Italian nationalist movement.

In Spain, an uprising against the restored Bourbon monarchy of Ferdinand VII had greater, if only temporary, success. The Spanish constitution of 1812, proclaimed during Napoléon's invasion, included the radical principle of universal male suffrage, but the Bourbon restoration abolished this democratic measure. In 1820 a faction of the middle class, led by officers in the army, successfully overthrew the monarchy and restored the constitution of 1812. In 1823, France, with the backing of its allies, intervened with 100 000 troops to restore the monarchy and absolutism.

Greek Independence: 1821–1830

The Greek struggle for independence from the Ottoman Empire from 1821 to 1830 was one of the nationalist movements that aroused the greatest sympathy in Europe. An evocative mix of history, culture, and religion gave the Greek struggle the mythic proportions of a battle between David and Goliath. From the biased perspective of Europe, the Ottoman Turks represented the decadent, exotic, and infidel culture of the Islamic Orient. The struggle, in which both sides committed savage atrocities, took place in the mountainous terrain and Aegean islands made familiar by the tales of Homer and the history of Classical Greece. The Greek struggle aroused the political passions and imaginative fancy of leading poets and writers of the

Western romantic movement. In Athens, the ancient Acropolis and its Parthenon provided a dramatic setting for the struggle between Greek and Turkish battalions. The English poet, Lord Byron (1788–1824), as romantic in his life as in his poetry, sped to Greece to assist in the cause and there met an early death from infection.

The outcome of the Greek struggle was determined by far less romantic influences. The great powers had conflicting interests in the decline of the Ottoman Empire. In jockeying for influence in the Balkans, Austria feared a Russian appeal to the Greeks and other peoples on the basis of their common religion, Orthodox Christianity. Britain also had a strategic interest in the area, which included the route from the eastern Mediterranean to the Persian Gulf, vital for trade to India. These conflicting interests arising from the decline of the Ottoman Empire led to a long diplomatic struggle known as the "Eastern question," a source of tension and conflict lasting until 1914. The one asset of the Ottoman Turks was the superiority of their navy. The European powers joined their naval forces and defeated the Turks at the Greek port of Navarino in 1827. This intervention turned the struggle in favour of the Greeks, whose independence was recognized in 1830.

Restoration and Reform : France and England, 1815–1848

In France, the unrealized dreams and fearful memories of the Revolution continued to shape political struggles. At the same time, a growing population and the beginnings of industrial change created new demands on the state and its political masters. These tensions led to revolutionary crises in 1830 and 1848.
When the Bourbon monarchy was restored after the defeat of Napoleon, Louis XVIII took power as a constitutional monarch and not as an absolute monarch. The king still claimed rule by divine right, but a Constitutional Charter, which remained in effect until 1848, placed limits on royal powers, thus securing some of the reforms effected by the revolution. The

Charter provided for equality before the law, including the right to due process. Unlike in the pre-1789 *ancien régime*, important state offices were not reserved for the nobility; careers were instead "open to the talents." Freedom of conscience, religion and expression was guaranteed, but the place of the Roman Catholic Church in the restored order remained uncertain. Security of private property was also guaranteed in order to prevent returning aristocrats from claiming ancient titles and estates and to secure the revolutionary gains of landowners from the middle class and wealthy peasantry. In addition to these Charter guarantees, there would be a legislature, with a hereditary upper house or Chamber of Peers and an elected Chamber of Deputies. This elected assembly had a very small electorate of wealthy property owners, numbering about 100 000 voters in a population of 28 million.

Although he retained the pomp and ritual of an absolute monarch, Louis XVIII was a pragmatic politician who accepted many of the rationalizing and centralizing administrative reforms installed by Napoléon. He also recognized that under Napoléon, wealthier segments of the bourgeoisie had acquired more wealth, social status and positions in the state, and that he was best advised to accept these new sources of influence and power rather than attempt a full restoration of 1789 conditions. Unfortunately, many of Louis' relations, friends, and advisers were not so pragmatic. Full of romantic and conservative fantasies of their years in exile, the ultraroyalists (known as the "Ultras") pressed the king to restore absolutism.

Opportunity for the Ultras came with the death of Louis in 1824. At age 62, Charles X, his brother, more conservative and less astute, came to the throne. The new king favoured his aristocratic friends among the ultraroyalists, and, eventually, his extreme measures alienated influential members of the bourgeoisie who had originally supported him. After the election of 1830, Charles X refused to convene the legislature and imposed more restrictive controls on the press. He called for a new election with a revised and limited electorate sure to exclude opposition deputies. In effect, the king had staged a *coup d'état* on his own state. A ruler with a better sense of history could have predicted the result. In July 1830, students, workers and liberal politicians called for a popular uprising. Revolutionary barricades 15 metres or more in height appeared on the streets of Paris, and the troops proved ineffective during three days of riots and demonstrations. Charles X, without the means to enforce his authority, fled the country. Louis Philippe, his cousin, upon the invitation of moderate liberal monarchists in the Chamber of Deputies and supported by the army, assumed the throne. His reign is referred to as the "July Monarchy" or the bourgeois monarchy.

The July Monarchy: 1830–1848

The coronation installing this new July Monarchy displayed a liberal constitutional character. Louis Philippe was not proclaimed "King of France" but "King of the French People," and the Revolution's tricolour, with its red, white and blue symbolizing liberty, equality and fraternity, was restored as the national flag.

The constitutional reforms that followed also reflected the liberalism of the new regime. Reforms on age and property qualifications to vote enlarged the electorate to 200 000 in a population of 32 million. In addition, laws censoring the press were abolished, and church and state were declared separate. The July Monarchy was neither a republic nor a democracy, but a liberal oligarchy of property owners. It removed the political influence of clerical and ultraroyalist factions, but failed to satisfy the political aspirations of radicals and democrats. In 1830 republican students and workers, in an episode made memorable by Victor Hugo's *Les Misérables*, took to the streets and reconstructed their revolutionary barricades. The insurrection was crushed effectively but with much bloodshed.

Faced with growing discontent and challenges to rule by property owners, the July Monarchy, despite its liberal foundations, grew more repressive. The turning point occurred in 1835, in the aftermath of a failed attempt to assassinate Louis Philippe. Fearing a widespread conspiracy, the government passed the September Laws, which restricted radical political organizations and censored the press. Ever mindful of the precedents of 1789 and 1830, the radicals looked to revolution as the means out of this political impasse. There would be two more failed attempts at revolution led by Louis Napoléon between 1835 and 1844, then a severe depression in 1845–1847. Bad harvests and high food prices intensified discontent in rural and urban areas. Finally, in 1848, revolution went from radical fantasy to political possibility.

England: Protest and Reaction, 1815–1821

After ending the war with France in 1815, England experienced a lengthy depression until 1821. During these years of intense social conflict, two new classes, a middle class and a working class, came into being. Economic hardship provoked protests, and government repression in turn confirmed the need for reform. Pressure for parliamentary reform had been gaining strength since the 1760s. Population growth and industrial development exacerbated the problem of representation. The rural south was over-represented, whereas the industrial areas of the Midlands and the North were under-represented. Some of the new industrial cities had no members in parliament and, given the local peculiarities of the franchise, many middle-class residents as well as members of the working class were without the vote.

In 1811–1812, an extensive campaign of machine wrecking occurred in the knitting-frame areas of the Midlands and in textile areas in the English North. The machine wreckers claimed to be followers of General Ned Lud, a mythical folk hero and redresser of the wrongs of the poor, fashioned after Robin Hood. The Luddites (the term is still used to describe those who resist technological innovations) attempted to protect jobs and wages being undercut by the new machinery. Claiming to be enforcing existing laws, they justified a campaign of threats and violence against the persons, property, and machines of the owners of the new industries. An anonymous worker wrote of his desperate situation:

> I have five children and a wife. The children all under eight years of age, I get 9d (nine pence) clear (per week) ... I work sixteen hours a day to get that ... It will take 2d (two pence) per week coals, 1d (one penny) per week candles. My family live on potatoes chiefly and we have one pint of milk per day.

WEB CONNECTION

www.mcgrawhill.ca/links/legacy

Go to the site above to find out more about the Luddites.

Following the suppression of the Luddites, widespread political disruptions recommenced during the depression of 1815–1818. These protests took on a new threatening character. Large numbers of people — 20 000 to 50 000 or more — followed a parade of bands and banners to assemble in open spaces near large urban centres and hear speeches by popular orators. On August 16, 1819, sixty thousand gathered at St. Peter's Field, near Manchester, to hear Orator Hunt, when members of a local mounted militia charged into the crowd, killing 11 and wounding over 400. In mockery of Wellington's victory at Waterloo, the radicals named this episode the Peterloo Massacre. It became a symbol of the government's tyranny over popular rights.

The Reform of British Parliament: 1830–1832

In 1830 the accession of a new king, William IV, necessitated an election. In the rural south, riots had aroused fears of an agrarian insurrection, and in July, news arrived that a revolution in Paris had toppled Charles X. Hopeful that the time was ripe, middle-class and working-class reformers revived their campaign for parliamentary reform. Among the parliamentarians, the aristocratic Whigs (later, Liberals), who had been out of office for 40 years, also saw a need for reform.

The reform bill introduced by Lord John Russell tried to bring some order to the archaic mix of constituencies and voter qualifications. The bill proposed an extensive redistribution of seats, in which small boroughs with few or no voters, called pocket boroughs and rotten boroughs, would lose their seats to the new industrial cities. The bill also reformed the franchise, making a net worth of £10 per household mandatory for borough constituencies, and making only modest changes to voter eligibility in rural or county seats.

In parliament, the bill took from 1830 to 1832 to be passed. These years were a period of economic downturn, and the combination of social unrest and a political crisis strengthened the possibility of revolution. The redistribution of seats to the new industrial centres had more immediate significance than the attempt to make the franchise fairer. Despite these changes, rural constituencies still predominated, and over two-thirds of Members of Parliament came from landed interests. Nonetheless, industrial areas at least had a voice in parliament, and the number of voters increased 50 percent to 652 000, or 18 percent of the adult male population.

The question of whom the bill enfranchised and the process of its passage had longer-term consequences. Opponents of reform warned that once the old system was altered, there would be no way to halt further reforms. This fear of the thin edge of the wedge, or of modest reform in 1832 opening the way for democracy, proved accurate. Sir Robert Peel (prime minister 1843–45 and 1841–46) warned that, in making the House of Commons more representative, the Reform Act made the monarch and the House of Lords less important and provided no principled reason for stopping further extension of the vote until Britain was made an "unmitigated democracy." This process was not completed until the twentieth century: All working-class men and women over the age of 30 got the vote in 1918; women over the age of 21 got the vote in 1928, finally achieving equal voting rights (middle-class men had got the vote in 1832).

DEVELOPMENTS IN POLITICAL THOUGHT

The Origins of Socialism

Liberalism, democracy, and socialism were part of the legacy of the French Revolution and its rallying cry for liberty, equality, and fraternity. During the French Revolution, some asked whether universal suffrage was sufficient to give real meaning to these ideals. In this view, the emancipation of all members of society required much more than new constitutions, laws, and ballots. In the first half of the nineteenth century, the growth in population, the impact of industrial change, and the evidence of a growing disparity and conflict between the rich and the poor confirmed the belief of radical thinkers that, beyond democracy, a genuine liberation required a new kind of society.

Role of Key Individuals: Three Utopian Socialists

Count Henri de Saint-Simon

Count Henri de Saint-Simon (1760–1825) was a French aristocrat and an eccentric visionary. He doubted whether changes in constitutions, even the extension of the vote, would make much difference in the material and spiritual well-being of the entire population. Saint-Simon had a keen interest in scientific discoveries and was confident that technological innovations would bring about greater material abundance. The difficulty was to find a way in which wealth would not be possessed by the few but would serve the needs of everyone. He defined this goal according to the principle, "From each according to his ability, to each according to his work." Saint-Simon's contribution lay in the realization that political liberation was incomplete without

social change, and in his vision that technological innovation and social planning would make life more equitable and fulfilling.

Robert Owen

In England, Robert Owen (1771–1858) shared Saint-Simon's optimism about the social potential of industrial technology, but his direct experience as a cotton manufacturer made him extremely pessimistic about the consequences of unrestrained industrial capitalism. He thought that the emphasis of industrial entrepreneurs on individualism and competition, including the effort to maximize profit by demanding optimum productivity for the lowest possible wage, was harmful to the individual and destructive of the fabric of society. He feared the degradation of working people and the rise of sharp class antagonisms, which could result in destructive class warfare. Owen believed in gradual reform, the power of education, and union and model communities.

Pierre-Joseph Proudhon

By the 1830s, socialist ideas began to influence the political demands of radical democrats who hoped to win the vote and then bring about socialist reforms. Pierre-Joseph Proudhon (1809–1865), an influential French radical, addressed the question of the source of violence and repression in society. Contrary to the common view, he claimed that the responsibility for violence and crime lay not with individuals but with governments. The state, through its laws and police force, compelled humans to live in an unnatural condition of inequality and oppression, and the grossest inequality of all was in the ownership of property. His famous pamphlet of 1840 asked the question *What is Property?*, and he answered "All property is theft." A popular revolutionary insurrection, in his mind, should do away with private property and create conditions of social equality. Having removed the source of oppression and violence, the state itself was no longer needed. Unlike most other radical thinkers of his age, Proudhon deeply distrusted the state, and his view of the repressive character of government made him one of the founders of anarchism.

Karl Marx and Friedrich Engels

Anticipating that the deepening economic depression of 1845–1847 would build to a political confrontation, the Communist League, a small society of exiled German radicals, commissioned one of its members to write a pamphlet advising German workers on how to respond to the impending crisis. By February 1848, in just six weeks, Karl Marx (1818–1883), with assistance from Engels, produced *The Communist Manifesto*, one of the most influential pamphlets in modern history. The word "communist" in the title was chosen deliberately to set it apart from other socialist tracts. Those "utopian socialist" works were largely the product of middle-class intellectuals who criticized the capitalist system of private ownership. Communism advocated common ownership of the means of production, but it embraced the power of the new working class and preached that neither reason nor votes but only revolution would bring about the new socialist order.

Lessons of History

If the existing social and political order was oppressive, how did a new liberating social order come into being? Marx believed that the answer to this difficult question lay in history — but the answer was not superficial or simple. *The Communist Manifesto* begins with the famous sentence, "The history of all hitherto existing societies is the history of class struggles." Looking to the French Revolution of 1789, Marx argued that the old order of aristocratic feudalism had reached a point of revolutionary crisis and had been overthrown by the new capitalist order of the bourgeoisie. This new order, most advanced by the Industrial Revolution in England, operated by a competitive spirit in which the rich got richer and the poor got poorer. Furthermore, wealth accumulated in fewer and fewer hands, and producers, growing in number and poverty, were reduced to living solely by selling their labour. The labour of these wage-earning proletarians was actually the source of wealth of the bourgeoisie (factory owners, bankers, and merchants), so the bourgeoisie, he concluded, made its profits by the theft of other people's labour.

Marx applied the concept of the dialectic — a process of change whereby opposing forces of thesis and antithesis come into conflict and are resolved in truth, or synthesis; this was drawn from the philosophy of Friedrich Hegel (1770–1831). Marx claimed that each stage of history gave rise to antagonistic forces that were the source of its destruction. Just as the feudalism of the aristocracy (thesis) gave rise to its antithesis in the capitalism of the bourgeoisie, he predicted that the opposing forces of capitalism (bourgeoisie vs. proletariat), he predicted, would in turn result in the communism of the proletariat (synthesis). These historical contradictions were a product of profound changes working over time, and in the struggle between classes they reached a climax in revolution. Marx called revolutions the "locomotives of history," the great engines that drove the historical process forward.

The first part of *The Communist Manifesto* set out Marx's scheme of history with its emphasis on class struggle and the inevitable outbreak of revolution. Marx claimed that his theory, called dialectic materialism, unlike that of earlier socialists, was not utopian or idealistic but scientific, because it rested on the laws of historical change. In this view, one did not have a choice about political strategy, because revolution was inevitable. The only choice was how one could advance the course of the revolution.

The Communist Manifesto

The Communist Manifesto, published in February 1848, was written by Karl Marx (1818–1883) and Friedrich Engels (1820–1895). Only 23 pages in its first printing, the document is one of the most influential pamphlets in modern history.

Marx and Engels wrote *The Communist Manifesto* for a meeting of the Communist League in 1847. This was a period of severe economic depression and widespread unemployment in Europe, and the Communist League, a small society of exiled German radicals, commissioned one of its members, Karl Marx, to write a pamphlet advising German workers how to respond to the crisis. The manifesto was also intended to serve as a statement of the League's collective principles. Writing quickly to meet the League's deadline, Marx and Engels produced *The Communist Manifesto* within six weeks.

The Manifesto of the Communist Party is a powerful statement of principles based upon an analysis of historical change. The first part of the document offers the authors' analysis of history, with an emphasis on class struggle between the proletariat (workers) and the bourgeoisie, who control the means of production. This struggle, according to Marx and Engels, inevitably leads to revolution. The two men theorized that the proletariat will develop consciousness, overthrow the bourgeoisie, and establish a new, eventually classless society. The second part of *The Communist Manifesto* sets out the program of German communists.

Political philosopher Karl Marx wrote *The Communist Manifesto* in England, where he lived in poverty with his family.

In the years following its publication, *The Communist Manifesto* had a profound intellectual influence on every field, from humanities to social sciences to the natural sciences. In the political sphere, The Manifesto set in motion a movement that radically changed the world. Its fundamental ideas inspired the communist political system, which at its height ruled nearly half the world's population and defined the ideological conflict of the second half of the twentieth century.

The Communist Manifesto

The history of all hitherto existing society is the history of class struggles.

Freeman and slave, patrician and plebeian, lord and serf, guild-master and journeyman, in a word, oppressor and oppressed, stood in constant opposition to one another, carried on an uninterrupted, now hidden, now open fight, a fight that each time ended, either in a revolutionary reconstitution of society at large, or in the common ruin of the contending classes.

In the earlier epochs of history, we find almost everywhere a complicated arrangement of society into various orders, a manifold gradation of social rank. In ancient Rome we have patricians, knights, plebeians, slaves; in the Middle Ages, feudal lords, vassals, guild-masters, journeymen, apprentices, serfs; in almost all of these classes, again, subordinate gradations.

The modern bourgeois society that has sprouted from the ruins of feudal society has not done away with class antagonisms. It has but established new classes, new conditions of oppression, new forms of struggle in place of the old ones.

Hitherto, every form of society has been based, as we have already seen, on the antagonism of oppressing and oppressed classes. But in order to oppress a class, certain conditions must be assured to it under which it can, at least, continue its slavish existence. The serf, in the period of serfdom, raised himself to membership in the commune, just as the petty bourgeois, under the yoke of the feudal absolutism, managed to develop into a bourgeois. The modern labourer, on the contrary, instead of rising with the process of industry, sinks deeper and deeper below the conditions of existence of his own class. He becomes a pauper, and pauperism develops more rapidly than population and wealth. And here it becomes evident that the bourgeoisie is unfit any longer to be the ruling class in society, and to impose its conditions of existence upon society as an overriding law. It is unfit to rule because it is incompetent to assure an existence to its slave within his slavery, because it cannot help letting him sink into such a state, that it has to feed him, instead of being fed by him. Society can no longer live under this bourgeoisie, in other words, its existence is no longer compatible with society.

The essential conditions for the existence and for the sway of the bourgeois class is the formation and augmentation of capital; the condition for capital is wage labour. Wage labour rests exclusively on competition between the labourers. The advance of industry, whose involuntary promoter is the bourgeoisie, replaces the isolation of the labourers, due to competition, by the revolutionary combination, due to association. The development of Modern Industry, therefore, cuts from under its feet the very foundation on which the bourgeoisie produces and appropriates products. What the bourgeoisie therefore produces, above all, are its own grave-diggers. Its fall and the victory of the proletariat are equally inevitable.[2]

---

1. Describe the fears of the English working class in the form of a list of grievances that would address their fundamental concerns.

2. Prepare a role-play that presents the hopes and fears of these sectors of English society in the mid-nineteenth century: aristocrats, middle-class industrialists, urban factory workers, and farm labourers.

3. List the sectors of North American society today.

Review, Reflect, Respond

1. How did the Industrial Revolution change peoples' expectations of the government? Consider the working class, the middle/merchant class, and the aristocracy.

2. How did the Congress of Vienna help prepare the way for both liberalism and nationalism?

3. Which Utopian Socialist philosophy most appeals to you? Explain why.

1848: THE YEAR OF REVOLUTIONS IN EUROPE

In light of his historical understanding, Marx offered advice about the particular circumstances of 1848. The second part of his manifesto set out the program of the German communists. Part of the platform restated well-established radical proposals that went back to the time of the French Revolution: the unification of Germany, universal suffrage, and a progressive tax against the wealthy. Newer socialist objectives included state ownership of banks, mines and railroads, and a more original proposal involved the creation of large-scale, scientific, collectivized agriculture. *The Communist Manifesto* concluded with his advice to radicals and workers: "Workers of the world, unite."

In 1848, Marx had an opportunity to observe several revolutions first-hand. To a certain degree, this year of revolutions confirmed Marx's analysis. Clearly, revolutionary outbreaks were possible, and even common. It was equally evident that historical conditions did not yet exist for the success of a workers' revolution, and, in Central Europe, even bourgeois revolutions achieved temporary but not lasting victories.

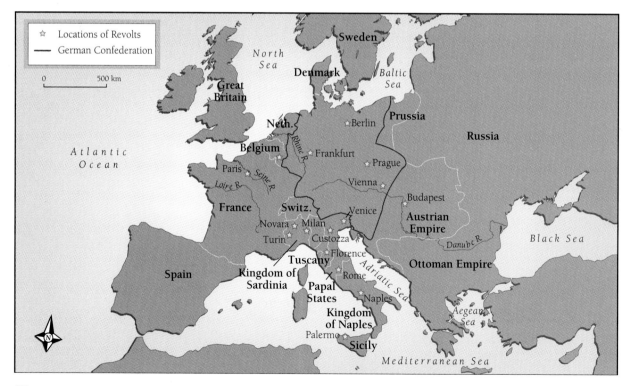

■ **FIGURE 7.2 Revolutions in Nineteenth-Century Europe**
Observe where no revolts of significance took place. Consider why that was so.

Revolution brought down the July Monarchy in Paris in February 1848. In the next few months, an epidemic of revolutions spread from one European capital to another, and, like an epidemic, the revolutions were short-lived. Paris led the way, once again. In June the revolutionaries remounted the barricades but this time met defeat at the hands of a reconstituted government and its armed forces. During the following year, monarchs and generals restored authority and order throughout Europe.

Economic Crisis

The revolutionary outbreaks occurred in response to a serious economic crisis. Over the longer term, a growing population had put pressure on the food supply, and this resulted in a decline in living standards. In the short term, poor harvests and the potato blight in 1845–1847 created a sudden increase in the price of food. In some rural areas of Germany, Central Europe and Italy, peasants struggled to avoid starvation. The year 1846 was also the beginning of the great famine in Ireland that killed thousands as a result of the failed potato crop. At the same time, a financial crisis disrupted commerce and industry and created widespread unemployment among both handicraft and industrial workers in the cities. In France, over a million people were unemployed. The economic distress spilled out into the streets, as people joined in protests seeking a political remedy for their plight.

Revolutionary Spring: February 1848

Liberal and nationalist demands for a new constitutional order, combined with popular discontent in the countryside and in the cities, created the revolutionary crisis of 1848. The first place revolution broke out was in Palermo, Sicily, where there was an uprising against rule from Naples. Then with riots and barricades in the streets of Paris, and a National Guard unwilling and unable to re-impose order, Louis Philippe abdicated on February 24. During the first six months of 1848, similar revolutionary outbreaks occurred in Vienna, Budapest, Berlin, Piedmont, Prague, and various Italian cities.

COUNTEROFFENSIVE: JUNE 1848

France

Following the February Revolution of 1848, a second republic was proclaimed in France. Its provisional government, dominated by moderate republicans and liberal reformers, reluctantly bowed to the popular demand for universal suffrage but resisted the inclusion of radical social and economic reforms. Louis Blanc, one of the two representatives of the Paris working class, managed to gain support for a form of national workshops, a relief program of public works for the unemployed. The April elections confirmed the moderate direction of the Republic, as the radicals elected only about 100 delegates out of a total of 800 members of the Constituent Assembly. In the countryside, small landholders, fearful for their property, grew ever more suspicious of the Parisian radicals.

By June, 120 000 workers, many committed to radical reform, had enrolled in the national workshops. With the support of rural France and middle-class property owners, the government decided to dissolve the workshops. The working class took to the barricades once more, and, between June 22 and 26, a bloody class war was fought on the streets of Paris. During these terrible "June Days," the government and the army prevailed, and over 10 000 people were killed or injured. This bloodshed had a lasting effect on class relations and class politics in the second half of the nineteenth century. In the presidential elections of December 1848, a familiar name returned to French politics — Louis Napoléon Bonaparte, Emperor Napoléon's nephew, won a decisive victory.

The Austrian Empire

In the Austrian Empire, aristocratic officials and military leaders felt more confident when their ineffectual emperor abdicated in favour of Franz Joseph, his 18-year-old nephew. There had been one gain from the reforms of March: The peasantry had been freed of serfdom, with its forced labour and feudal dues. Having achieved their principal objective, the rural population became passive observers of the struggles in the cities.

In battles with civilians on city streets, the military were limited both by the reluctance of the soldiers to engage in this dangerous combat against fellow subjects and by an unwillingness to use artillery (because of its power to destroy not only lives but property). With new determination, on June 17, the Austrian commanders used their cannon to bombard Prague and crushed the revolt of Czech students and radicals. By the end of July, the Austrian forces had a similar success against liberals and nationalists in northern Italy. In October, the army, at a cost of 4 000 lives, reclaimed Vienna from the control of radicals and students.

Italian republican radicals under Giuseppe Mazzini (1805–1872) held out until July 1849, when the French army intervened and restored Pope Pius IX. Hungarian nationalists, having established their own state and army, were the last to fall. The Austrian forces received support from rival ethnic minorities such as the Romanians and Croats, but it took 130 000 Russian troops to bring an end to Hungarian independence in the summer of 1849.

While it may be argued that that the revolutions of 1848 made no lasting historical impression, after the spring of 1848, modern states would never again be so fragile in the face of popular insurrection. The days of absolutism were numbered. Serfdom had been abolished in the Austrian Empire. Monarchs with absolutist pretensions survived in Prussia, Austria and Russia, but having faced revolution, these states had redefined the basis of their authority.

France, the mother of revolution and modern political ideologies, gave birth to the first modern

Giuseppe Mazzini (1805–1872)

politician, Louis Napoléon Bonaparte, who became president by promising a democratic electorate that he would restore order in society and government. The peasantry and the middle class responded to his appeal, and he continued to cultivate their backing as emperor. A democratic electorate transformed the foundation for political legitimacy and proved the secret to stability in modern states.

NINETEENTH-CENTURY WESTERN ART

Through the study of history, we have learned that a large variety of ideologies and beliefs grew out of the challenge of industrial progress. Liberalism, radicalism and socialism, to name a few, were matched by an equal number of "isms" in the world of the arts. Romanticism, realism, naturalism, and expressionism were all offspring of the restless, questioning intellectual climate that pervaded European society in the nineteenth century. Artists abandoned tradition and convention and, perhaps overwhelmed by the number of ideologies confronting them, looked to their personal visions of life and art to find answers.

When romanticism is used in an artistic context, the words freedom, emotion, nature and individual come to mind. The romantic movement, characterized by a highly imaginative and emotional treatment of life, began in the late eighteenth century and continued until the mid-nineteenth century. The early nineteenth century was a time when the romantic aesthetic held sway: Artists explored the subconscious of society through their art.

The eighteenth century is sometimes called the Age of Reason. In a reaction to the rational, symmetrical and formalized classical world, many artists of the late eighteenth and early nineteenth centuries chose to free themselves from the confines and restrictions of the academic world. An artistic revolution would match the political and social revolutions that ended the eighteenth century. Four of the most famous artists of this time were Ingres, Géricault, and Delacroix from France and Goya from Spain. Each painter provides a different perspective on the political and social climate of the time, and each reveals his own inner vision.

Jean-Auguste Ingres

Jean-Auguste Ingres (1780–1867) was heavily influenced by classicism and is close to David in style and technique. He became leader of the academic painters, who disapproved of the art of Delacroix and Géricault, who were painting in a freer, more romantic style. Ingres, for our purposes, is important because of his portraits of the influential people of his time. His portrait of Napoléon as emperor is an interesting counterpart to David's portrait of Napoléon as conqueror. Both artists capture Napoléon's view of himself at different times in his life. David portrays the romantic, heroic aspects of the young Napoléon which captured Beethoven's imagination. Ingres portrays Napoléon the emperor as rigid, self-satisfied, and perhaps even contemptuous of the spirit of the romantics.

This painting by Ingres is titled simply *Odalisque* (1814). An *odalisque* was a woman in a harem. These women were among Ingres's favourite subjects. The artist has exaggerated the length of this woman's spine to get the desired pose.

This large painting (2.67m x 3.45m) by Goya, of the infamous execution of Spanish rebels by French soldiers on the third of May, 1808, was commissioned by the later, liberal Spanish government to commemorate this atrocity of the Napleonic Wars.

Perhaps Ingres's most famous and beloved works are his Odalisques. These nudes are painted in a style recalling the Renaissance, particularly Raphael; however, the subjects, women of a harem, reflect the romantic penchant for the exotic, even erotic elements of romantic thought. The painting, in one sense, may be appreciated almost as a piece of sculpture, yet the elongated body is far from realistic. Although the art of Ingres provokes an immediate intellectual reaction, a closer look takes one into a purely romantic world.

Francisco de Goya

The artistic vision of the Spanish painter Francisco de Goya (1746–1828) is the antithesis of Ingres's ideal classical world. Where Ingres flirted with romanticism,

Goya lived it. Goya is so original that he really belongs to no particular school or style of painting. He was truly a romantic hero in his defiance of the strong authoritarian regime that ruled Spain at that time. It is surprising then, that he spent several years as court painter to the Spanish King Charles IV.

Most importantly, Goya was witness to the brutality of Napoleonic occupation in his country. His series of engravings, *The Disasters of War*, is a collection of prints that depict the horror and cruelty inflicted upon Spain by Napoléon. Goya's most powerful indictment is his painting *The Third of May, 1808*, which depicts a firing squad executing a group of Spanish citizens in retaliation for a shooting incident.

Goya has dramatically reduced the space between the firing squad and its victims, emphasizing the contrast

The Raft of the Medusa is an enormous painting (4.88m x 7.16m) in which Géricault took great risks by using unusual perspective and stark realism in his depiction of this horrifying event that caused a scandal in France.

between the faceless, dehumanized soldiers and the group of townspeople anticipating death. Central to the painting is the man in the white shirt, who flings his arms open in a gesture of defiance and despair. Goya's *The Third of May, 1808* has become an icon of the horror and brutality of war. Goya's dark vision rejected the eighteenth-century view of humanity as reasoned and the nineteenth-century view of humanity as naturally good.

Théodore Géricault

Another painter who was fascinated by the darkness of the human spirit and death was Théodore Géricault (1791–1824), however, where Goya deliberately distorted his human forms, Géricault painted them in the classical style. He depicted the events of his time on huge epic canvases. Whereas Goya the Spaniard vilified Napoléon, Géricault glorified him. He celebrated war as a glorious experience. Géricault's works are powerful and appealed to people because they were an escape from reality, though they depicted real events.

The Raft of the Medusa is Géricault's most famous and most challenging work. The event portrayed was a shocking revelation, the scandalous and horrific details of which were reported in the contemporary press.

The crew of a slave ship, which was foundering in heavy seas, built a raft on which to tow excess human cargo and thus lighten the ship's load. The crew cut the ropes holding the raft and the slaves were left to drift and die. But, there were survivors of the ordeal who lived to tell their horrifying tale, which included cannibalism. Géricault decided to record the event as graphically as possible. He actually had the original carpenter reconstruct the raft. He spent time in morgues drawing dead bodies and severed limbs. The result is a work of epic proportions. His dying slaves are sculptural, in the neoclassical manner of David. They are not shown as the dying men, maddened with thirst and hunger, that they really were.

Eugène Delacroix

Eugène Delacroix (1798–1863) admired the work of Géricault, but he is generally considered to have moved beyond him in his vision of human nature, death, and suffering. He too depicted epic scenes of human suffering, whether real, imagined or inspired by literature; however, his work is infused with his personal belief that the savage, instinctive, and primitive aspects of humanity are what ally us to nature. Delacroix's paintings are dynamic and full of movement. For him, the story was secondary to the emotional intensity of a moment. Like so many of the romantics, he wanted to shock and thrill his viewers in order to capture their imaginations and inspire passion and fear.

Two of Delacroix's great narrative works, one that inspires and one that shocks, are *Liberty Leading the People (see chapter opener)* and *The Death of*

The Death of Sardanapalus (1828) by Delacroix was meant to shock and thrill viewers with its graphic display of barbarism. At 3.06m by 4.8m the impact might have been overwhelming.

Sardanapalus. Liberty is an allegorical figure commemorating the Parisian revolution of 1830.

The picture tells a story, although it records no actual incident. Liberty is symbolized by a partially clad woman reminiscent of the Venus de Milo. She is holding the flag of the revolution and is surrounded by the different types of people who become revolutionaries — a young street boy, a rich dandy, a poor old man. There are echoes of Géricault's *Raft of the Medusa* here as Liberty moves through the dead and dying. The composition is also familiar: Liberty's strong arm, which bears the flag, is reminiscent of the gesticulating arm of the dying sailor on the raft. Both figures are strong symbols of hope in the face of impending death. Delacroix's picture reveals the political atmosphere of the early nineteenth century as one of tension and revolt in all aspects of society.

These two paintings represent the two sides of Delacroix's vision of human nature: On one hand, he immortalizes human bravery in the midst of suffering; on the other, he offers a similar, if not more realistic, view of the human capacity for cruelty.

English Romantic Painting

There is an enormous difference between English and French romantic painting: English romantic painting is much more akin to the works of the German romantic painters like Kaspar David Friedrich (1774–1840). Where the French depicted emotion and action through narrative paintings, English and German painters conveyed their feelings through natural landscapes. This is, of course, allied to the powerful romantic movement in literature — specifically the nature poetry of Wordsworth and Coleridge. The two great English landscape painters for us to consider are John Constable and Joseph Turner.

John Constable

John Constable's (1776–1837) painting may be aligned with the poetry of William Wordsworth: He, too, expresses his deep love of nature through his art.

Constable's landscape paintings show romantic views of the English countryside, often bathed in a golden light, as in this painting of Salisbury Cathedral, dated 1823. What makes this a romantic painting?

Constable was searching for the truth of nature by recording every detail he observed, yet he was not trying to express a completely realistic vision. His approach was at once scientific and poetic. He wanted to record the moods and shifts of the natural processes around him. For example, he painted hundreds of cloud studies to record the movement of mist and atmosphere across the sky. Constable's most famous painting is *The Hay-Wain*.

This deceptively simple work records the passage of a hay cart across a stream. The deceptively simple subject of the painting allows the observer to move through the landscape — foreground to mid-ground and into the distant sky. Constable's paintings are comfortable in their beauty; they are approachable and accessible to the average viewer.

Joseph Turner

Joseph Mallord Turner (1775–1851), on the other hand, was not interested in providing comfort or ease for his audience. In fact, an audience did not interest him at all. Turner was a renegade, a rebel. His personal

Joseph Turner was particularly fond of painting ships at sea, with the play of light and colour on the water. In this painting, called *The Fighting Téméraire* (1838), we see a nineteenth-century English sailing vessel along side a steam-powered ship, the old technology and the new.

Tchaikovsky's *1812 Overture*

Pyotr Ilyich Tchaikovsky (1840–1893) had not started out to be a musician and was tormented by great doubts about his abilities. He often considered quitting composing altogether. But, 1877 marked a dramatic turning point in his life, both for the good and bad.

Tchaikovsky married his 28-year-old former student to quiet the rumours of his homosexuality. He also began a strange relationship with the wealthy widow Nadezhda von Meck, who promised to support him financially for the rest of his life on the condition that they never meet. They did meet once, quite by accident and literally turned and hurried away from each other. Tchaikovsky's marriage proved catastrophic. Within months of the marriage, Tchaikovsky went into a deep depression and attempted suicide. He then left his wife to live on his own. It was von Meck's letters to him that pulled Tchaikovsky out of his depression and back to composing.

Nikolay Rubinstein, a friend of Tchaikovsky, had been given responsibility for planning a grand event, an All-Russia Exhibition of Arts and Crafts. He wanted Tchaikovsky to compose a great work to celebrate the event. Tchaikovsky was not interested. Rubinstein then added a great sum of money to his request, and Tchaikovsky immediately accepted. He was, after all, a freelance musician.

Tchaikovsky (1840–1893)

The commission changed purpose and was now to mark not only the 1882 Moscow Exhibition, but also the consecration of the Cathedral of Christ the Saviour, which was rebuilt to give thanks for the Russian victory in the war against Napoléon. The cathedral was later destroyed during the Russian revolution in 1917.

In its premiere on August 20, 1882, the overture was an immediate success. It became enormously popular and was played not only throughout Russia, but all over the world. In part, its success and popularity stemmed from the fact that its score called for a real cannon to be fired, church bells to be rung, and many cymbals to crash loudly and often. In his own words, Tchaikovsky found it "very loud and noisy."

Russian music under the czars had not made a great impression on the outside world, but by the time Tchaikovsky died, his work had put his country on the world's musical map, not the least because of the great success and popularity of the *1812 Overture*.

The music incorporates the old Russian hymn *God, Preserve Thy People* and the French national anthem, *La Marseillaise*. The work also uses the czarist Russian national anthem, *God Save the Czar*. Interestingly enough, neither of these anthems were actually in use in their respective countries at the time of the famous Battle of Borodino, the historic event that the *1812 Overture* musically celebrates.

---

1. In one or two paragraphs, describe the Battle of Borodino, the historic event that Tchaikovsky commemorated in his overture.

2. Why do you think Tchaikovsky put a passage from *La Marseillaise* in his *1812 Overture*?

vision of nature, specifically the seas and skies with which he surrounded himself, is somewhat akin to that of Delacroix. Turner too was fascinated by the powerful, often destructive forces of nature; however, he had a passion for the science of light and colour, and he performed endless experiments trying to achieve exact renditions of light in his paintings. Turner also took a rather pessimistic view of the fate of humanity. All these facets of Turner's aesthetic and personality made him one of the most powerful painters in the history of English art.

Like many of the romantics, Turner began painting in the classical tradition; but, his fascination with light and colour caused him to move away from tradition into a world of his own peculiar creation. He saw colour as a way to convey deep emotion: His canvases boil with deep reds and oranges to convey war and destruction. Others are filled with dark, sombre shadows of black, purple, and blue to convey sadness and death. The *Fighting Téméraire* is a narrative painting, in which he exploits his colour symbolism to its fullest.

The red-and-orange sunset spanning the sky behind the old vessel symbolizes its days as a warship. The gorgeous blue-black hollow beneath it symbolizes its death and the death of the old world of sailing vessels in the face of the new steam technology of the industrial age. Later painters, most notably the Impressionists, were indebted to Turner for the breakthrough he made in the use of colour and light and for his technique. He underwent such hardship in order to pursue his goals, that we may be justified in calling Turner himself a romantic hero.

Music in the Nineteenth Century

As in art and literature in the nineteenth century, music became part of the culture of all Europeans. Music by nature appeals first to the emotions of the listener. The romantic age, with its focus on the emotions of the individual, was the perfect time for musicians to break free of restrictions and explore their personal artistic visions. Advances in technology, the

A scene of a nineteenth-century *salon* concert, called *Hush! The Concert*. French artist James Tissot takes us inside a fashionable nineteenth-century home, where elegantly-dressed people enjoyed musical as well as literary and intellectual entertainment.

economic shift from aristocracy to middle class, and the philosophy of the age inspired many musicians to enormous achievements.

The Industrial Revolution had a strong influence on the development of music. New technologies produced better and less-expensive instruments. For example, the improvements made to wind instruments allowed horns to play melodies. The creation of the tuba and the saxophone enriched the sound of an orchestra. The piano was improved to give a deeper, more ringing tone; a different type of piano concerto could be developed.

Larger orchestras allowed for a far greater variety of musical compositions. They also had an influence on the type of sound produced. In the eighteenth century, the composer's range had been limited to soft or loud. With the addition of so many instruments to the orchestra, the composer could play with the mood of the audience through contrasts in tempo, harmony, and volume. Orchestras became a new art form. As artists used colour and contrasts in light and dark to portray moods, so did composers. A new vocabulary of musical dynamics developed to convey these emotions.

With the new emphasis on the middle class and the expansion of education came the creation of music schools. Musicians began to receive better training. The composers of the nineteenth century now had excellent performers at their disposal. Their music began to be performed in public concert halls rather than churches, and orchestras grew in size and number, as did audiences. The new freedom to play with form and content was due also to the fact that nineteenth-century musicians no longer had to work for an aristocratic patron. They were now supported by the middle class; their appeal, therefore, was to a far greater audience. Solo performers became stars and were welcomed into fashionable society, but were no longer the glorified servants of the rich.

Musicians soon became educators and founded conservatories in the mid-nineteenth century. Felix Mendelssohn founded the great Conservatory of Music at Leipzig, where Johann Sebastian Bach spent so many years. Franz Liszt, considered the greatest pianist of the age, influenced countless musicians by teaching them his brilliant technique. Richard Wagner opened his own theatrical school, in which he taught his revolutionary kind of opera, called "musical drama." Through printed musical scores and music journals, people could enjoy music in their own homes.

As the opportunities for musical education increased, so did the number of women performers. Many women became accomplished pianists, as society found it socially acceptable for women to play the piano to entertain guests. Women also found musical careers in the opera as singers, although they were not known as composers. Clara Wiek-Schumann (1815–1896), the wife of German composer Robert Schumann (1810–1856), was a renowned pianist and composer in her own right.

In the spirit of the new age of nationalism, musicians incorporated folklore and national idioms into their work. And, because music is so easily able to cross ethnic and cultural boundaries, people were able to enjoy the rhythms and flavours of all areas of Europe. Hungarian, Polish, Bohemian, and Russian folk music was incorporated into music that was heard everywhere. Musicians often went outside their own national identity. Northern musicians were fascinated by the folk music of Spain and Italy, whereas Russian composers looked to Asia as inspiration for their work.

This was the beginning of the huge influence Asian and Oriental music was to have on the composers of the early twentieth century.

LITERATURE OF THE NINETEENTH CENTURY
The Romantic Age

The Romantic movement in literature had its roots in eighteenth-century France and Germany. The writings of the French philosophers Rousseau and Voltaire inspired not only the intellectuals who engineered the French Revolution but also the poets and philosophers of the British Isles. It is interesting that a small group of men and women could put in motion such an enormous change in the thinking and feeling of an entire continent and thus start a literary movement that still influences European and English literature.

It is difficult to characterize the literature of the early nineteenth century because the poets and writers whose work is described as romantic strove to be unique in their art. Nevertheless, think about the words that have been used to describe romanticism: emotion, revolution, freedom, nature, the common person. These concepts are present in much of the literature of the early nineteenth century.

Romantic writers sought to convey intense emotional experience through their works. This intense experience was usually a result of some communication or connection with the natural world. Nature, in the eighteenth century, was subordinate to a greater belief in reason, but nature is not reasonable; it is highly volatile, moody, irrational, even cruel and often dangerous. This is what delighted the romantics about the natural world. Like intense feelings, nature was tempestuous and appealed to the senses, not the intellect.

France and Germany had their own romantic movements. The founder of the French movement was François-René de Chateaubriand, who rejected eighteenth-century society and morality. In his poetry, he explored the worlds of the mysterious and the irrational. He was very much like Byron: restless, moody and despairing of life. Later French romantics included Victor Hugo, author of *Les Misérables*, Honoré de Balzac, author of countless novels that decried the hypocrisy of post-revolutionary Paris, and Alexandre Dumas, author of *The Three Musketeers and The Count of Monte Cristo*.

The romantic movement in Germany was not limited to one circle of writers but extended to different circles in different cities. Most German and French writers recognized the influence of Wolfgang von Goethe, the eighteenth-century philosopher and writer, as the impetus for the romantic movement on the Continent. Goethe's attitude toward nature and freedom prefigured the romantic movement everywhere.

It was the British romantics who had the greatest impact on the literature of the nineteenth century. English romantic poets lived in remoter parts of the British Isles, deploring the cities, which they felt had been ruined by the Industrial Revolution. They also deplored the state of civilization. They rejoiced in Rousseau's idea of the "noble savage." They felt that to know oneself truly, one must move away from the distractions of the city and discover inner truth by seeking out beautiful, natural landscapes. Nature was now an inspiration rather than a nuisance, and this attitude to nature is still an influence on our thinking today.

The major historical impetus for the romantic revolution in literature and the arts was, of course, the French Revolution. Romantic poets, many of whom were actually involved in the revolutionary movement, celebrated the French people's struggle against the aristocracy. They also championed the individual, who they felt had been lost in the vast industrial and social changes that had so affected Britain. Thus, their literature glorified the poor, working-class people who laboured around them. Fifty years before, the great poetic works and writings had dealt solely with the aristocracy; only novels had considered common people as worthy of mention. Now the poorest labourer became the subject of long dissertations on the plight of the everyday person.

William Blake

William Blake (1757–1827), perhaps the most mystical of the early romantic poets, expressed his extraordinary vision in esoteric lyrics whose subject matter ranged from child slavery in the mills of industrial Britain, to the power of nature. Blake's powerful and unusual poetry and painting were completely different from the works of his contemporaries. He was a true revolutionary and could perhaps be seen as the transition-maker from the Age of Reason to the age of romanticism.

William Wordsworth

In any discussion of the Romantic movement in English literature, two names in particular will almost always be mentioned: William Wordsworth (1770–1850) and

God Creating the Universe (Ancient of Days) (1794) by William Blake. Blake's unique style and vision are seen here, in the frontispiece to his book *Europe: A Prophecy*.

Samuel Taylor Coleridge. Their anthology, *Lyrical Ballads*, published in 1798, is considered the definitive collection of romantic poetry.

Wordsworth had also felt the appeal of the revolutionary spirit that pervaded the Continent prior to 1789. He was in France during the early years of the revolution. During the Terror, the situation became too dangerous for him to stay, so he returned to England where, living with his beloved sister Dorothy, he started to write the poetry he is so famous for today. It was during this time that Wordsworth met Samuel Taylor Coleridge. In the preface to their anthology is a treatise on the nature of poetry, which they felt should express "the spontaneous overflow of powerful feelings" and "emotion recollected in tranquility." Yet, each poet had a different vision of the natural world and his place in it.

Wordsworth saw nature as a moral guide. He was a religious man, who hoped to come to a sense of God through emotional communion with nature. He believed that it is through an intense experience with nature that we recapture the innocence — for Wordsworth, the godliness — of our early childhood. His *Ode. Intimations of Immortality* exemplifies this philosophy, which pervades all his works and is often echoed in the works of other poets of his century:

> Hence, in a season of calm weather,
> Though inland far we be,
> Our souls have sight of that immortal sea
> Which brought us hither,
> Can in a moment travel thither,
> And see the children sport upon the shore,
> And hear the mighty waters rolling evermore.
> Though nothing can bring back the hour
> Of splendour in the grass, of glory in the flower;
> We will grieve not, rather find
> Strength in what remains behind ...
> In the faith that looks through death,
> In years that bring the philosophic mind.[3]

Ode. Intimations of Immortality, sts. 9-10 (1807)

As a youth, Wordsworth enjoyed a powerful emotional connection with nature; however, he found that these moments of rapture seemed to lessen in intensity as he grew older. He became frustrated and unhappy until he suddenly rediscovered his youthful passions through experiences such as those he describes in the poetry quoted above.

Samuel Taylor Coleridge

Samuel Coleridge (1772–1834), on the other hand, viewed nature as an inspiration to look deeper into one's self, not in a religious sense, as did Wordsworth, but in a psychological sense. His works are concerned with the metaphysical, supernatural realm, which one reaches through a connection with the physical, natural realm. Coleridge is best known for his lengthy poem *The Rime of the Ancient Mariner*. Below is a small passage describing the mariner's haunted ship and his dying shipmates.

> Water, water everywhere,
> And all the boards did shrink;
> Water, water everywhere,
> Nor any drop to drink.
> The very deep did rot: O Christ!
> That ever this should be!
> Yes, slimy things did crawl with legs
> Upon the slimy sea [4]

The Rime of the Ancient Mariner, pt. 2 (1798)

This long narrative poem is written in the style of a medieval ballad. The mariner may be seen as a modern Ulysses in a quest for his spiritual identity and his connection to the universe. The ship's voyage takes the mariner and his crew around the tip of South America. As they sail near the South Pole, they are followed by an albatross, which becomes a mascot of good luck for the sailors as they struggle with the ice and snow. One day, for no apparent reason, the mariner shoots the albatross with his crossbow. As the ship becomes trapped in the ice, the sailors curse him and hang the dead bird around his neck as penance. The ship, however, sails free of the ice and the superstitious sailors cheer the mariner. But, the ship then quickly moves into the doldrums (where there are no winds) and all the sailors, except the mariner, die of thirst. He is in a

A romantic painting of a romantic poet's funeral - *The Burning of Shelley* (1899). In this painting by Louis Fournser we see the poet Byron standing by as Shelley is consumed in a funeral pyre. Byron himself would have a romantic death, while working for the cause of Greek independence.

living hell, overcome with guilt for his stupid, senseless act. One night, perhaps in a delirium of thirst, the mariner watches the beautiful water snakes swimming by the side of the boat and unconsciously blesses them. The albatross suddenly falls from his neck. The crew return as ghosts and steer the ship to safety. When the mariner reaches his home port, he must tell and retell his tale of the follies of human nature to warn others.

The *Rime of the Ancient Mariner* poses the existential questions: Why are we here? What is our function in the universe? Why do we commit unspeakable acts? How do we pay for these acts? These same questions are explored again and again in the late-nineteenth and early-twentieth-century literature of Joseph Conrad and Jean-Paul Sartre, and the philosophies of Friedrich Nietzsche.

Wordsworth and Coleridge led the way for the next generation of romantic poets, such as Byron,

Shelley, and Keats. These later poets actually lived the romantic adventure, and all three met untimely deaths. Their work shares many of the same general characteristics of early-nineteenth-century verse, yet each poet was an individual in theme and style.

Lord Byron

George Gordon, Lord Byron (1788–1824), is known more for his romantic lifestyle and adventures than his poetry. He took it upon himself to live out the role of a romantic hero. He was notorious for his many love affairs and scandals with members of the aristocracy. Like Géricault, he too courted death and eventually died in his thirties while on a military campaign in Greece to help free the Greeks from the Ottoman Turks.

Byron's poetry belongs more to the eighteenth century than to the nineteenth. His greatest work, *Don Juan*, is a satire on his modern world, written in an epic style. His love poems are similar to the works of the seventeenth-century lyrics of chivalry. Byron's work is important for his exploration of the satanic hero, Don Juan, who is perhaps an extension of his own persona as rebel prince.

Percy Bysshe Shelley

Another romantic rebel was Percy Bysshe Shelley (1792–1822). He was the son of a wealthy man, yet he was determined to dedicate his life to correcting the evils of social injustice and tyranny everywhere. Due to his unorthodox activities at Oxford University and subsequent expulsion, he was vilified by London society as an atheist and revolutionary. He had also left his young wife and two children and formed a relationship with the 17-year-old Mary Godwin, daughter of a political activist. When his wife killed herself out of grief, and Shelley lost custody of his two children, he and Mary married and moved to Italy.

Shelley's life on the Continent was marred by constant struggles with money and the death of his two children. Mary, as a result, went into deep depression. But, it was under these harsh circumstances that he wrote his most interesting poetry. In poems such as *The Cloud,* Shelley developed a new three-line verse form to emulate the movement of clouds. His well-known poem, *Prometheus Unbound,* is a symbolic drama that explores the nature of evil within mankind and celebrates the rebel hero who defied the gods. Shelley felt that the control of evil is the moral responsibility of humanity, and, until that control is established, people will be unable to realize fully their creative potential.

John Keats

Of all the romantics, John Keats (1795–1821) was a true hero in the romantic sense. He was not of aristocratic origin, nor a scholar at one of the large universities; he gave up his career in medicine to become a poet. Unfortunately, Keats only lived to age 26, but even in this short lifetime, his poetic achievement was enormous. Poems such as *The Eve of St. Agnes* and *La Belle*

The Brontë Sisters, Emily, Charlotte, and Anne painted by their brother Bramwell. Do you think the passion in their novels was reflected in their lives?

Dame Sans Merci show a romantic interest in medieval legend. His odes *To Autumn* and *To a Nightingale* are insightful explorations into nature and our existence within it. Although Keats's poetry appeals to all the senses and gives a full appreciation of the poetic experience, there is a sense of power or control over language, felt through the shear craftmanship of his poetry. Sonnets such as *When I have Fears* immerse the reader into a sensuous dream world of love and regret.

Often Keats's poetry is simply the exploration of a beautiful object — a work of art or a piece of nature. Keats is able to lose himself, and the reader, in contemplation of beauty; however, something that leads to exquisite pleasure may also lead to exquisite pain. Like Watteau, Keats was conscious of his approaching death from tuberculosis. Every work that deals with the transitory nature of beauty and happiness is tinged with sadness. For him, both love and death offered escape from the cruel reality of his desperate situation.

The Brontë Sisters

Some of the richest works of art in the early nineteenth century are novels and plays. Anne, a poet and novelist, was less renowned than her two sisters. Sisters Emily (1818–1848) and Charlotte Brontë (1816–1855) gave us the novels *Wuthering Heights* and *Jane Eyre*, respectively, and became two of the best-known writers of the time. *Jane Eyre* depicts controlled passion in its first-person narrator. In contrast, *Wuthering Heights* depicts passions out of control. With its complex narrative frame, the tale of lovers Cathy and Heathcliff has become a literary classic.

Review, Reflect, Respond

1. How successful were the revolutionaries of 1848 in achieving their objectives and bringing about change in Europe?

2. Do you prefer the neoclassical art of the eighteenth century or the romantic art of the late eighteenth and early nineteenth century? Give examples to illustrate your preference.

3. Explain what the term "romanticism" means as it applies to art, music, and literature.

Reflections

The nineteenth century was a time of profound change in the realms of politics, daily life, economics, art, music, and literature. After 1848, the states most successful at unifying territory and consolidating authority — Germany and Italy — shook off the remnants of absolutism and redefined the basis of the state's authority by joining elitist rule with electoral approval by a democratic majority. Regimes such as the Austrian and Russian ones, which clung to absolutism and failed to incorporate a means to win legitimacy from a popular electorate, suffered the consequences: Eventually, the Austrian Empire would be dismembered and czarist Russia would face revolution.

The losers of 1848 would appear to be the real revolutionaries: the socialist radicals and the working class. Yet, 1848 confirmed their belief that universal suffrage by itself would not achieve liberation from social and economic oppression. The experience of 1848 also destroyed the romantic myth that popular insurrection invariably captures the imagination of the people and leads to the overthrow of governments. The people were divided by social class, and, by and large, the middle-class rural landholders and even the poor had a stake in stability rather than change. After 1850, the growth of industry would extend some of its benefits to workers as well as owners, and improvements in living standards dampened political volatility. If the politics of mass democracy made revolution more difficult, it also allowed for the possibility of reform. Contrary to the theory of Marx and Engels, the most advanced industrial society, Great Britain, proved the most impervious to revolution, whereas the least developed, Russia, proved the most vulnerable.

Chapter Review

Chapter Summary

In this chapter, you have seen:

- that 25 years of war and revolution motivated the leaders of Europe to seek peace and co-operation in the nineteenth century
- how and why an understanding of cause-and-effect relationships is an essential tool for understanding the developments during the Industrial Revolution
- the impact of modern Western thought on economic, social, and political developments in the West during the first half of the nineteenth century
- how family structures changed as a result of the Industrial Revolution

People, Places, and Events (Knowledge and Understanding)

1. Understanding the history of the early nineteenth century requires a knowledge of the following concepts and people and their significance in the reshaping of European culture and society. Select and explain at least two from each column.

Concepts	Events	People
dual revolution	First Industrial Revolution	Adam Smith
moral economy	Saint Monday	Friedrich Engels
Multiplier Effect	New Poor Law	John Stuart Mill
cash nexus	Factory Act of 1833	Thomas Malthus
liberalism	July Monarchy	Jeremy Bentham
communism		Luddites
Romanticism		Karl Marx

2. The Industrial Revolution radically altered many facets of life in Europe. Using a mind map, capture all of the ways you can think of that the Industrial Revolution had an impact on European society. Then, using the ideas and information from your mind map, copy and complete the following chart in your notes:

The Impact of the Industrial Revolution on European Society

Political Impact	Social Impact	Economic Impact	Cultural Impact

Doing History: Thinking About the Past (Thinking/Inquiry)

3. In *The Communist Manifesto*, Karl Marx outlined a view of history that suggested that European society had progressed to the point where a revolution that would bring about a classless society was imminent. He wrote:

The history of all hitherto existing societies is the history of class struggles ... Our epoch, the epoch of the bourgeoisie, possesses, however, this distinctive feature: It has simplified class antagonisms. Society as a whole is more and more splitting up into two great hostile camps, into two great classes directly facing each other: bourgeoisie and proletariat.

To what degree does this quote and your knowledge of *The Communist Manifesto* support the idea that it was a product of its age? Or is it an insightful and prophetic work identifying the course of history on a grand scale? Prepare a three-to-five paragraph response.

4. There is no question that the long-term consequences of the Industrial Revolution were to increase the overall standard of living for the vast majority of Europeans. What remains a much more contentious issue is whether the short-term impact of the Industrial Revolution benefited the working class. Based on the evidence, write a short (two pages) essay that addresses this question (a) from the perspective of an industrialist owner and (b) from the perspective of a factory worker or rural labourer.

Applying Your Learning (Application)

5. Eugene Delacroix's *Liberty Leading the People*, seen at the beginning of this chapter (page 242), is one of the best-known paintings of the Romantic movement. Take a look at the painting and then respond to the following questions: How does this painting make you feel? How do you think it was meant to make nineteenth-century audiences feel?
Now, take a closer look at the painting and answer the following questions:

   a)   Was Delacroix a supporter or opponent of the revolution of 1830? Explain your answer.

   b)   Who was his intended audience?

   c)   What was the purpose of this painting?

   d)   How successful do you believe Delacroix was at achieving his goal?

6. The early nineteenth century was an era of rich philosophical thought, as people attempted to understand society and humanity in the midst of unprecedented change. Select any one of the philosophers discussed in this chapter, and, after doing some research, prepare a list of five questions you would ask in an interview. For each question, provide a probable answer based on the research you have done.

Communicating Your Learning (Communication)

7. Using visuals (pictures, symbols, icons) and key words or phrases, illustrate the multiplier effect. Show the relationship between technological innovations and change in society. Be sure to draw on the art included in this chapter for ideas.

8. Write a feature article for the *London Times* newspaper in the 1830s, reporting on working conditions in English factories. Your article of 500 to 750 words must accurately capture working conditions in a manner that would grab and hold the attention of the literate public. Be sure to base your newspaper report on historical evidence and write in journalistic style.

C H A P T E R   8

Nations in Upheaval: Europe 1850–1914

CHAPTER EXPECTATIONS

By the end of this chapter, you will be able to:

- describe the development of modern urbanization

- assess the influence of key individuals and groups that helped shape Western attitudes

- describe a variety of forces that helped to bring about changes in modern Western artistic expression

- demonstrate an understanding of the rise of the modern nation-state in the West and, subsequently, in the rest of the world

"L'Action Feministe" Women in France overturned ballot boxes in protest against elections in which they did not have the vote.

Much of the foundation of our current political, social, and intellectual reality was laid in the second half of the nineteenth century. The preceding period was an age of revolution in Europe, when idealism drove social and political thinkers to imagine and try to implement profound change. From 1850 to 1900, however, the shape of society was influenced less by idealists and revolutionaries, than by seasoned politicians at the national level and political activists in the realm of women's rights and organized labour.

As in all historical periods, certain philosophical concepts fuelled the forces of change. Nationalism fuelled political change at the national level, as countries sought to consolidate and solidify their power. Socialism was the driving force behind changes in society, as labour groups and women's rights activists fought their battles for equality and better treatment under the law. Realism informed the major artistic movements of Europe, as poets and painters aimed to reveal society as it was, not as it should be.

During this period, a number of political leaders throughout Europe attempted to increase and solidify their power by uniting smaller territories into larger nation-states. This ultimately led to the unification of Italy and Germany. Louis Napoléon Bonaparte in France sought to strengthen the authority of the state by seeking popular support for his policies and leadership. Italian nationalists fought to unite numerous disparate states through both popular insurrection and diplomatic negotiations. The framework for what is now modern-day Germany was drawn primarily by one man, Count Otto von Bismarck, who became the driving force in uniting various German states with the military strength of Prussia.

KEY CONCEPTS AND EVENTS

imperialism

Crimean War

Franco-Prussian War

Paris Commune

Third Republic

Dreyfus Affair

second industrial r
   evolution

realism

Women's Social and
   Political Union (WSPU)

KEY PEOPLE

Louis Napoléon Bonaparte

Count Otto von Bismarck

Giuseppe Garibaldi

Czar Alexander II

Benjamin Disraeli

Emmeline Pankhurst

Josephine Butler

Vladimir Ilich Ulyanov
   (Lenin)

Charles Darwin

Marie Curie

Albert Einstein

Friedrich Nietzsche

Wit and Wisdom

The palace is not safe
if the cottage is not
happy.
   **Benjamin Disraeli, Lord
   Beaconsfield (1804–1881)**

TIME LINE: NATIONS IN UPHEAVAL

Louis Napoléon Bonaparte establishes Second Empire in France	1852	
	1854–1856	Crimean War
Charles Darwin: *The Origin of Species by Means of Natural Selection*	1859	
	1863	Edouard Manet: *Le Déjeuner sur L'herbe*
Austro-Prussian War and the Peace of Prague	1866	
	1867	Karl Marx: *Das Kapital*, vol. 1
John Stuart Mill: *The Subjection of Women*	1869	
	1870	Franco-Prussian War; Napoleon III defeated; the fall of the Second Empire
Unification of Italy	1871	
	1878	Congress of Berlin
Claude Monet moves to Giverny	1883	
	1886	Friedrich Nietzsche: *Beyond Good and Evil*
The Dreyfus Affair	1894–1906	
	1897	Auguste Rodin: *Balzac*
Sigmund Freud: *The Interpretation of Dreams*	1899	
	1902	V. I. Lenin: *What is to be Done?*
Marie Sklodowska Curie, Pierre Curie, and Henri Becquerel receive Nobel prize for work on radioactivity	1903	
	1904	Max Weber: *The Protestant Ethic and the Spirit of Capitalism*; Giacomo Puccini, *Madama Butterfly*
Revolution in Russia; Albert Einstein: theory of relativity	1905	

Not to scale.

THE RISE OF THE NATION-STATE

The philosophical concept behind the forces of change during this period was nationalism; however, nationalism, or pride in and focus on the strength of the nation-state, generally did not originate among the people of these nations. Rather, it was ignited and fuelled by individual political leaders driven to consolidate power.

By 1871 this process of consolidation and unification had created modern Germany and modern Italy, significantly altering the balance of power in Europe. Although general European war did not break out until 1914, there was by no means a state of peace up to that time. Where the power of a state had once been gauged by the size of its territory, population and military capacity, after 1871 the size and international scope of its economy became increasingly important.

Thus, the struggle between states for land and wealth occurred primarily outside Europe, in manifestations of imperialism — the process of expanding a nation's territory through the acquisition of colonies and dependencies.

In addition to fuelling the expansion of Europe, nationalism was also a powerful tool used to mobilize the populations of these nations in support of governments and their policies. Since the age of revolutions, most governments accepted the importance of recognizing the sovereignty of the people, if only superficially at times. The ideology of nationalism linked the individual's identity with the state, connecting his or her sense of pride, prestige, and power with the internal and external strength of the nation.

The power of nationalist ideology rested on new historical conditions, a new form of economy and an increasingly urban society, all of which emerged in the

■ **FIGURE 8.1 Political Boundaries in Europe 1871**
Only one country shown on this map, Switzerland, lacks access to the sea. Think about why having access to the sea would be important to a country.

second half of the nineteenth century. Deep and sincere national sentiment was also a factor, but, as history suggests, the success of a nation did not depend upon national sentiment. Rather, political leaders had to be able to harness the power of the people's pride in the state in pursuit of national objectives.

FRANCE: THE ROLE OF KEY INDIVIDUALS

Louis Napoléon Bonaparte

France was one of the only nations in Europe that was no longer a monarchy. It was a republic, a state in which supreme power is held by the people or its elected representatives and not by a monarch. During the second half of the nineteenth century, France was perched precariously on the fence separating democracy and autocracy. It found itself ruled by an autocrat who successfully appealed to the population's sense of nationalism to garner public support for his policies. The nephew of Napoléon Bonaparte (1808–1873), Louis Napoléon Bonaparte showed that popularity depends on success. He ruled as president (1848–1852) and then emperor (as Napoléon III, 1852–1870) of France during years of prosperity, in which Paris was restored as the diplomatic and cultural capital of Europe. But, it would all end in disaster. Prussia's overwhelming victory over France in 1870 brought Napoléon III and his Second Empire to a humiliating end, and would ultimately mark the ascendancy of modern Germany as the dominant power in Central Europe.

Louis Napoléon Bonaparte's election as president of the Second Republic in December of 1848 unexpectedly elevated him from political obscurity. Following the terrible bloodshed of the June Days of the same year, the French electorate was still split between monarchists and republicans. To the monarchists, the name Napoléon offered order in place of republican anarchy; to the republicans, it offered republican virtue in place of aristocratic corruption.

Together, they voted for Louis Napoléon, giving him a lead of almost four million votes over his nearest rival.

For Louis Napoléon, the constitution of the Second Republic had one serious limitation: the president's term was limited to four years, without the possibility of re-election. Ironically, Louis and his supporters attempted to alter this situation by appealing to the people. The National Assembly, dominated by a monarchist majority who were in favour of rule by a kind of emperor, created the possibility of a presidential appeal directly to the people. Still fearful of popular radicalism in Paris, the Assembly censored the press and revised the franchise (the right to vote) by reintroducing a property qualification and arrested leading radical deputies. In a campaign of public speeches, Louis Napoléon linked the memory of his uncle to the principle of popular sovereignty and to his own leadership. In October of 1849, he announced: "The name of Napoléon is in itself a whole program. It means order, authority, religion, popular welfare at home, national dignity abroad."

In an attempt to solidify his power beyond that of a mere president, on December 1–2, 1851, the army occupied Paris and the police arrested 78 National Assembly deputies. Parisians awoke to the news that the president had dissolved the National Assembly and restored universal male suffrage. Although Louis Napoléon and his advisers had wanted a peaceful *coup d'état*, the army killed 200 rioters on December 4, while suppressing a left-wing uprising in Paris.

In engineering this *coup*, Louis Napoléon declared himself emperor and claimed, ironically, to be restoring democratic rights. In fulfilment of this claim, he introduced a new form of election by direct vote, the plebiscite. On two occasions, in December 1851 and December 1852, the French electorate supported Emperor Louis Napoléon and the Second Empire in a plebiscite. This seeming contradiction appeared to be a result of the fact that under Napoléon III's Second Empire, the French populace seemed content with the symbols rather than the substance of democracy. The economy was prosperous, as the boom in railroad construction had a multiplier effect that stimulated

French industries and generated employment. Napoléon III had sound advisers, knowledgeable about the functioning of the economy and interested — partly due to Saint-Simon's influence — in government assistance and planning. Legislative reform facilitated the development of joint-stock and limited-liability companies. The Second Empire created *Crédit Mobilier*, an investment trust in which citizens deposited savings, which in turn financed industrial development. All these signs of prosperity seemed to keep the population satisfied and the desire for true democracy at bay.

The most visible sign of planning during the Second Empire was the transformation of Paris. Starting in 1853, Baron Georges Haussmann, prefect of the Seine region, directed the work of redesigning the centre of Paris by removing crowded tenements and widening narrow streets into broad boulevards. Paris would become one of the splendours not only of Europe but of the world.

Prosperity maintained political peace for a few years. By 1860, financial scandals, dissent over foreign policy, and discontent with a censored press reawakened political criticism. Napoléon III responded with a series of liberalizing reforms that relaxed controls on the press, allowed freer debates in the legislative assembly, made ministers more responsible to elected representatives, reduced the influence of the church on education, made schools more accessible to females, and legalized trade unions and the right to strike. These reforms came into place gradually between 1860 and 1869 and, even though they provoked criticism, Napoléon III remained popular. A plebiscite in 1870 revealed that 7.3 million approved of the emperor's policies and 1.5 million dissented.

Conflict and War

Napoléon III aspired to emulate his uncle in restoring French prestige in Europe. In 1854 he challenged Russia's claim that it was the protector of all Christians in the Ottoman Empire. The ensuing Crimean War of 1854–1856 was actually fought to resist Russian expansion beyond the Black Sea and into the Balkans and eastern Mediterranean. None of the major armies (French, British, or Russian) distinguished itself in battle. Despite incompetent generals, more soldiers died from disease than from gunfire. The horrific conditions were brought to light by the English nursing pioneer Florence Nightingale and by reports from the battlefront from a new breed of journalist, the war correspondent. Politically, the Russians were the great losers in the war, and this time Napoléon III was the victor. The Peace Congress held in Paris in 1856 accepted the Russian concessions and restored Paris as the diplomatic centre of Europe.

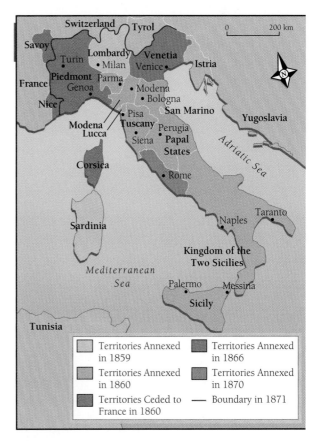

■ FIGURE 8.2 **Italy United**
Examine this map of what was to become Italy. What autonomous regions disappeared in the unification of the Italian states?

ITALY: THE ROLE OF KEY INDIVIDUALS

The struggle for the unification of Italy (1848–1871) involved both an idealistic nationalism seeking liberation through popular insurrection, and an exercise in *realpolitik* — politics based on realities and material needs rather than ideals and morals. Although Italian unification would not have been possible without the idealism of the nationalists and the realism of the politicians, these two factors often acted in conflict rather than in harmony.

The making of an Italian nationality was not a natural or inevitable product of geography or history, but the result of the struggle of Italian nationalists who sought to create a new nation. Unification had to overcome the opposition of Austria and the papacy, as well as the entrenched interests of political leaders attached to the existing fragmented structure of small states.

The *Risorgimento*, or movement for Italian unification, had originated before the French occupation of northern Italy by the revolutionary and Napoleonic armies. After 1815 small groups of intellectuals, students and radicals organized secret societies, the *Carbonari*, and planned insurrectionary outbreaks against Austrian rule in the north, against administrative corruption in the papal states, and against the restored Bourbon monarchy in Naples. In 1820–1821, and again in 1831, such uprisings proved to be isolated and largely futile attacks on entrenched authorities.

Giuseppe Mazzini and Giuseppe Garibaldi

Out of the failed uprisings of 1831, Giuseppe Mazzini (1805–1872), who had himself been arrested as a conspirator, founded the Young Italy society in Marseilles, France. Born in Genoa and the son of a doctor, Mazzini came to personify a romantic revolutionary nationalism not just for Italians, but for all Europeans. Through Young Italy, he publicized the goals of Italian nationalism, which aimed to bring together the principles of nationalism and liberalism. Mazzini's new Italy would

Mazzini and Garibaldi: Founders of Modern Italy. Speculate on the fate of the Italian peninsula had it not been unified.

be both a democracy and a republic; he aimed to achieve that goal through popular insurrection.

In quick succession, members of Young Italy joined popular insurrections in the principal cities, including Palermo, Naples, Rome, Turin, Milan, and Venice. An uprising in Rome established Mazzini as president of a radical, democratic republic. Since Rome was also the seat of the Vatican and the papacy, its status was not just an Italian, but an international, question. In a combined action to restore the Pope to Rome, 30 000 troops from Naples, Austria, and France intervened against the Republic. The defence of the city was led by Giuseppe Garibaldi (1807–1882), a romantic revolutionary and leading nineteenth-century exponent of guerrilla war by irregular forces. Garibaldi led his 10 000 irregulars, known as Red Shirts, in a heroic defence of the Roman Republic, but eventually they were forced to abandon the city and flee to the hills. Shortly thereafter, the last holdout of the 1848 revolutions, the Republic of Venice, surrendered to the Austrians in August of 1849.

www.mcgrawhill.ca/links/legacy

Go to the site above to find out more about Giuseppe Garibaldi and the Red Shirts.

The defeat of the Roman and Venetian republics also defeated Mazzini's vision of the *Risorgimento*. The task of unification needed a more centralized direction and a more expert use of political power. This task was taken up by Count Camillo Cavour (1810–1861), a moderate liberal aristocrat from Piedmont. As prime minister of Piedmont in 1852, Cavour showed that he was not an idealist, but a realist in politics. He secured his political support through astute, even fraudulent, electoral management, and in his foreign policy he used diplomatic cunning and threats of war to pursue his objectives. Cavour realized that he needed the assistance of powers outside Italy. He joined forces with France against Russia in the Crimean War, and later joined Prussia against Austria (both good examples of *realpolitik*). As a result of his diplomatic manoeuvres, Cavour managed to have the Italian question discussed at the Paris Peace Congress in 1856 and, by 1860, to bring about the unification of northern Italy, except for Venice.

The initiative then passed from Cavour to Garibaldi. His Red Shirts had been involved in the campaign in Lombardy, and rather than disband his private army, the guerrilla leader took 1 000 soldiers (called *i mille*) south to Sicily. There, his Red Shirts and peasant brigands defeated the army of the Bourbon king, Francis II. The guerrilla army then invaded the mainland and quickly captured Naples.

Garibaldi's success in the south presented a problem to Cavour's unified northern Italy. The conquering forces of radical republicanism and popular insurrection in the south gave every indication of continuing their northward march. Cavour dispatched the Sardinian army through the papal states, and met Garibaldi south of Rome. Garibaldi, who was more of a soldier than a politician, agreed to the union of north and south on Cavour's terms. In March 1861, the new Kingdom of Italy came into being with Victor Emmanuel II as its constitutional monarch. An assembly was elected on a limited property franchise, with its capital at Turin in Piedmont. Cavour died only 11 weeks after the creation of his Kingdom of Italy.

As it stood in 1861, Italy was still incomplete. Venice remained in Austrian hands, and Pope Pius IX still held the remaining papal states and the city of Rome. Once again, diplomacy and war completed the task of unification. In 1866 Italy supported Prussia in its short, victorious war against Austria, and received Venice as its reward. In 1870 Napoléon III, facing war with Prussia, pulled French soldiers out of Rome. Italian troops occupied the city, the Pope retreated to the Vatican, and Rome became capital of a fully united Italy in 1871. Just as in France, idealistic nationalist sentiment in Italy had been astutely managed by realistic politicians to advance the cause of the greater nation-state.

MODERN GERMANY: THE ROLE OF KEY INDIVIDUALS

Out of the experience of the occupation of German lands by Napoléon, and from the romantic movement's interest in folk traditions and history, there emerged a common culture and tradition of German-speaking peoples. But, the unification of Germany, even more clearly than that of Italy, came not from a popular nationalist movement, but from an exercise in *realpolitik*.

From 1815 to 1848, liberal nationalists dreamed of the creation of a unified Germany under a liberal constitution. There were, however, significant political obstacles to the realization of this vision. The German confederation of 1815 brought together 39 states, including the larger and more powerful Prussia and Austria. The purpose of this confederation was not to unite German states, but to preserve the existing political structure of small states ruled by absolutist princes.

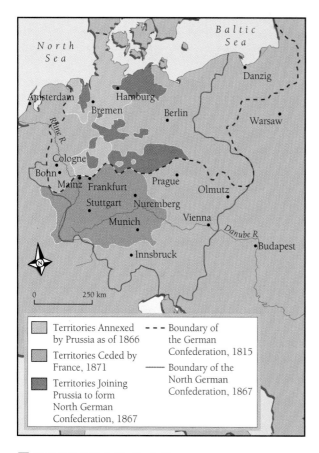

■ FIGURE 8.3 A United Germany
Consider the changing face of Germany as shown on this map. Do you think the changes foretold future problems?

Prussia and Austria were potential leaders of the confederation, and the lesser states were divided in their loyalty to the two rival powers. Social and economic development had begun to break down some of these divisions. In 1834 the *Zollverein*, or customs union, brought the northern German states, including Prussia but excluding Austria, into closer economic association. The extension of railroads and urbanization in the 1840s and 1850s also weakened the parochialism and isolated nature of the regions, and fostered a sense that economic growth and the exercise of diplomatic influence required a larger, more unified nation-state.

The liberal nationalists had an opportunity to give substance to their dream in 1848, but, like their contemporaries in Italy, their efforts ended in failure at this time. As they met in the Frankfurt Assembly, they could not agree on the definition of the new German state. The "Greater Germans," who favoured the inclusion of Austria, were drawn largely from southern Catholic regions. The "Lesser Germans," who favoured the exclusion of Austria and looked to Prussian leadership, were drawn largely from northern Protestant areas. The failure of the Frankfurt Assembly and the reassertion of royal autocracy in Berlin and Vienna in 1848–1849 brought an end to the fusion of liberalism and nationalism in German unification.

Count Otto von Bismarck

Otto von Bismarck (1815–1898), a conservative aristocrat and ardent supporter of the Prussian monarchy against the liberal nationalists of 1848, was the unexpected agent of German unification. A man of exceptional physical strength and vitality, who as a student and as an adult had a well-deserved reputation for his consumption of food and drink, Bismarck was equally known for his astute intellect. Although his memoirs suggest that he followed long-range plans, his real skill was in adroitly adapting to situations in pursuit of the objective of enhancing the power of his beloved Prussia. His flexibility in action also gave him a reputation of paying only lip-service to long-term commitments, and for cunning — even deceit — in his pursuit of immediate goals. Bismarck's contempt for liberalism and his belief in the central role of power in politics and diplomacy were encapsulated in his famous speech to the finance committee of the Prussian diet on September 29, 1862:

> Germany is not looking at Prussia's liberalism but at her power ... Prussia must preserve her power for the favourable moment, which has already several times passed. Prussia's frontiers are not suited to a healthy national life. The great questions of our times will not be decided by speeches and majority decisions — that was the mistake of 1848–1849 — but by blood and iron.

Conflict and German Unification

In 1864 Denmark resurrected its claim to Schleswig and Holstein, two neighbouring principalities with German-speaking populations. Infuriated by this claim, German nationalists called for action. Bismarck took the initiative by arranging for joint Austrian and Prussian military intervention. The short war demonstrated the superiority of the Prussian army (with armaments manufactured by Krupp) over Denmark, but the victors could not agree over the future of the two conquered principalities.

In an endeavour to appeal to German public opinion on this question, Bismarck took the unexpected step of proposing a reorganization of the German confederation, including the creation of a national assembly elected by universal male suffrage. He knew that this proposal, in apparent contradiction to his own well-established conservative principles, would be rejected out of hand in Austria. Liberal opinion was still distrustful of Bismarck and Prussian militarism, but this initiative now raised the possibility that this long-debated and much-needed reform had a better friend in Berlin than in Vienna.

In the Austrian capital, Emperor Franz Joseph and his ministers thought that war was an inevitable consequence of Bismarck's proposal and they, along with informed opinion in general, thought that Austria would win any military contest. The Prussian generals, under the leadership of Helmuth von Moltke, deployed new industrial technology to achieve victory, and pointed the way to modern warfare. Prussian soldiers had the advantage of a new needle gun or breech-loading rifle. The troops were amassed in greater numbers with greater speed by the use of the railroad, and the speed of communications was greatly enhanced by the electric telegraph. Buoyed by their success, the Prussian generals were set to march on Vienna; Bismarck, mindful of future political objectives, negotiated a lenient peace. Within just seven weeks, from June to August 1866, the Austro-Prussian War was over. It was Prussia that defeated Austria in the field and Bismarck reformed the German confederation.

The Peace of Prague of 1866 brought an end to the tussle between Austria and Prussia within the German confederation. The ramifications were far-reaching. First, in keeping with the Italian involvement in the war, Venice was ceded to the kingdom of Italy.

Second, a newly constituted North German confederation excluded Austria and included an enlarged Prussia, which annexed formerly independent states by adding some 3 300 square kilometres and 4.5 million in population. The new association incorporated two-thirds of the former confederation, except for the southern German states. Prussia was the most powerful player in the new confederation, with King Wilhelm I of Prussia heading the government, which had an assembly elected by universal male suffrage. Bismarck was confident that rural voters would elect conservative landholders and not middle-class liberals. Military and foreign affairs were under the direction of the ministers of the confederation, appointed by the king, and also under Prussian control.

Third, the four South German states, Bavaria, Württemburg, Baden and Hesse-Darmstadt, which had remained outside the North German confederation, signed a military alliance with Prussia. With Austria out of the picture, they also had no other option than to develop closer economic and political relations with the Prussian-dominated North German confederation. Bismarck kept a watchful eye on France, realizing that Paris deeply distrusted the new Germany, and would try to exploit the remaining divisions among the German states. When in May 1870, Napoléon III had a resounding victory in a plebiscite, Bismarck, perceiving danger in inactivity, prepared for confrontation with France.

THE FRANCO-PRUSSIAN WAR (1870–1871)

The Franco-Prussian War originated in a diplomatic dispute over the succession to the Spanish throne. The war's origins were petty, but its consequences were profound. In 1868 a revolution in Spain had resulted in the abdication of Queen Isabella II, and Madrid offered the Spanish crown to Prince Leopold of the Hohenzollern house, a distant relative of Wilhelm I of Prussia. The

The French caption reads: *"Here is Bismarck, still with his big broom, who scolds and picks up all of the recalcitrant (stubborn) Germans. Let's go! Go or die! Faster than that! Or the French will eat your sauerkraut!"*

possibility of an ally in Spain had great appeal to Bismarck but it terrified the French, who feared the prospect of a Spanish-Prussian alliance and a two-front war. Newspapers in France and Germany, encouraged by political leaders such as Bismarck, inflamed public opinion by warning that the issue at stake was nothing less than national dignity and prestige.

Meeting with King Wilhelm I in Ems, Germany, the French ambassador succeeded in getting a withdrawal of the Hohenzollern candidate but, in addition, he demanded a commitment that the proposal would not be revived. The king refused this second demand and telegraphed the results of the meeting to Bismarck. Upon receipt of the telegram, Bismarck shortened the text, making the king's refusal seem far more brusque, and released the Ems dispatch to the press. The press

release inflamed French opinion and, on the call to defend the nation's honour, Napoléon III declared war against Prussia on July 19, 1870.

Using the modern methods that had proven so successful against Austria, including the rapid movement of 500 000 troops to the front by railroad, the Prussians achieved a stunning victory in the Franco-Prussian War. The capture of Napoléon III and 100 000 French soldiers at Sedan in September 1870 led to the collapse of the Second Empire. The war continued for another four months. Paris lay under siege, and the population had to resort to eating their pets, even rats, to avoid starvation. The Treaty of Frankfurt, May 1871, imposed harsh terms: The provinces of Alsace and Lorraine were ceded to Germany; France had to pay five billion francs and endure German occupation for the three years it would take to complete the payment. To add insult to injury, it was in the Hall of Mirrors in Versailles, formerly the seat of Louis XIV, the Sun King and the glory of France, that King William I was proclaimed German Emperor over a unified nation.

The Austrian Empire: An Anomaly in Europe

In contrast to the consolidation of the new nations of Italy and Germany, the great autocratic Austrian Empire was weakened rather than strengthened by the forces of nationalism. In the aftermath of the revolutions of 1848–1849, the Hapsburg monarchy appeared victorious over the forces of nationalism and liberalism. In an age of nationalism, however, the Austrian Empire was increasingly becoming an anachronism. It was a dynastic state, not a nation-state. Its territories and peoples were thrown together as part of the hereditary lands of the Hapsburg dynasty. According to Franz Joseph, the young king who gave new resolve to the forces of reaction in 1848 and who would survive as king until his death in 1916, the purpose of Hapsburg rule was to preserve that territorial inheritance and, if possible, to extend its boundaries. For this task, the monarchy had the support of the landed aristocracy, the Catholic Church, and an extensive bureaucracy and army largely under the direction of German-speaking officials.

For the national minorities, Hapsburg rule, in spite of its oppressive qualities, was at least a known quantity. National separation, even if an attainable political objective, presented the prospect of replacing Hapsburg control with the external influence of either the Hohenzollerns from Bismarck's new German Empire, or the Romanovs from czarist Russia. Neither was desirable.

This balance of competing nationalistic and dynastic interests became even more complex with the decline of the Ottoman Empire in the Balkans. There, Slavic nationalism created new possibilities for Russian influence. In Vienna, Francis Joseph and his advisers wanted to fend off Russian intrigue and at the same time exploit the weakness of the Ottoman Turks. This explosive mix of nationalist ambition and great-power rivalry made the Austro-Hungarian Empire and the Balkans what Bismarck called "the powder keg," which would ignite a much larger conflict in 1914.

CZARIST RUSSIA: REFORM AND REPRESSION

Russia, the other great autocratic monarchy, was caught between the desire to preserve a conservative aristocratic order and the need for economic and industrial reform. Russia's defeat in the Crimean War, 1854–1856, demonstrated the need for industrialization of the economy and modernization of the army. Under Alexander II (1855–1881), a cautious but moderate reformer who ruled between 1855 and 1881, the difficult task of reform began.

The most significant change was the emancipation of 22.5 million serfs in 1861. This reform had to satisfy the Russian gentry, however, who feared the loss of their income from land, their control over the peasantry, and their legal privileges. Therefore, the peasantry paid the price of reform: While legally free and in possession of limited plots of land, the peasants had to pay an indemnity to the state for their emancipation.

The gentry and the reformers had feared that emancipation would create a landless and rootless — and potentially dangerous — rural population. Consequently, traditional peasant communes continued to control land usage and restrict the movement of peasants away from communal villages. Thus, the peasantry was still trapped in a poverty made worse by an increase in population. The Russian export of grain grew rapidly with the extension of the railroads, but, at the same time, grain prices fell sharply. Peasants found themselves having to produce more grain for less income, while having to feed larger families and work under a system of land use that discouraged innovation. Under these conditions, the additional hardship of a bad harvest readily transformed discontent into violent protest.

Another wave of discontent was brewing in the urban areas of Russia. With the encouragement of the government, the first wave of industrialization occurred in the 1860s. Railroad construction and associated industrial development led to the growth of cities and to the creation of a new working class. Like the first generation of industrial workers elsewhere, these wage earners experienced exploitative conditions, with low pay and no protection by state legislation. Some working-class leaders began to look favourably on Marx's analysis of industrial capitalism and to a revolutionary solution to their oppression.

Czar Alexander II, his bureaucracy, and the aristocracy had only cautiously introduced reform. When faced with criticism and discontent, and in reaction to a nationalist uprising in 1863 in Poland (which was partly under Russian domination), the czar reverted to a policy of repression. These repressive policies caused the seeds of discontent to grow further among different members of the population.

The small but nonetheless growing ranks of the intelligentsia remained troubled by the backward conditions of their homeland. The populists looked to the peasantry as a source of popular insurrection rehabilitating Russian traditions rather than simply imitating Western practices. Others were attracted to the ideas of the anarchists, and still others saw no hope for change except by violence.

In 1881 a terrorist's bomb succeeded in assassinating Alexander II. Contrary to the assassin's expectations, the death of the czar did not provoke a general uprising, but rather introduced a new and prolonged period of repression under the new czar, Alexander III (?–1917). After 1881 Russia seemed to move in a direction contrary to trends in Western Europe. In Russia, the forces of autocracy grew in strength; in Western Europe, the period after 1870 marked the advent of the new politics of democracy.

Review, Reflect, Respond

1. (a) What is the difference between a nation and a state?

   (b) Based on the examples provided, and the context in which the term "nation-state" is used, write a clear definition of the term.

2. Can the term "nation state" be applied to Canada? Why or why not?

3. How did the situations in Russia and Austria in the late nineteenth century differ from those in most other Western European countries?

DEVELOPMENTS IN POLITICAL THOUGHT: THE ADVENT OF DEMOCRACY

In addition to nationalism, another force was shaping the political landscape of Europe. Democratic principles were being adopted to varying degrees in different nations, bringing them closer to the nations we know today. Between 1850 and 1914, most countries implemented a broad franchise, if not universal male suffrage. In 1871 both the new German Empire and the new Third Republic in France had elections based on "democratic" suffrage of adult male citizens. In Great Britain, after 1867, urban male householders could vote in parliamentary elections. By 1914 even autocratic Russia and Austria had introduced universal male suffrage.

Between 1815 and 1848, the prospect of a mass electorate had terrified conservatives and liberals, yet when democratic politics arrived, the disaster that had been predicted did not occur. In fact, conservative politicians Otto von Bismarck in Germany and Benjamin Disraeli (1804–1881) in Great Britain even granted the vote to the working class. When the widened electorate went to the polls, the winners were conventional politicians drawn largely from the landholders or upper middle class, who espoused conservative to moderate liberal beliefs. The most potent expression of popular feeling was not for radical reform, but for militant nationalism.

France: The Third Republic

Democracy in France faced a number of challenges in the second half of the nineteenth century. These challenges included antagonism between Paris and the provinces, state repression of protesters, monarchists attempting to reinstate an authoritarian government, and anti-Semitism.

In a trend that continues in most countries to this day, the urban centre of Paris found itself at odds politically with the peripheral areas of France. After the collapse of Napoléon III's Second Empire, the new government of the Third Republic was elected on the basis of universal male suffrage. Paris, whose population had been under siege for four months, once again found itself out of step with the provinces. The nationwide elections returned a monarchist majority in the Assembly, which was prepared to accept the German terms of peace; however, to the people of Paris who were opposed to the terms, the politicians were traitors. To make matters worse, the government approved the landlords' claim for back rent accrued during the siege of the city.

The discontent felt by Parisians led to protest and violent repression, further challenging the precarious hold democracy had on the nation. The people of Paris took to the streets to oppose the newly elected government. In 1871 they created the Paris Commune under the leadership of radical democrats, with the backing of the socialists. After six weeks, the army of the Third Republic suppressed the insurrection with unprecedented savagery. In its final days, the Commune killed about 100 hostages, including the Archbishop of Paris. Estimates vary, but from 20 000 to 25 000 Communards were executed as political prisoners in the week following the end of the street fighting, and many of those fatalities came as summary executions without benefit of trial. The experience of the Commune decimated the French left for more than a decade, and it embittered and weakened the radical cause throughout Europe. The Commune became a symbol of Parisian and republican valour, and its memory persisted in the mutual fears and hatreds of the respectable bourgeoisie and the radical working class.

The monarchist majority of the first government of the Third Republic hoped to establish order by restoring the monarchy, but it overlooked the political lesson of the Second Empire. Napoléon III had shown that universal suffrage and authoritarian government were quite compatible, as long as the economy was prosperous and the populace, through the symbols of democracy, was made to feel part of national life. Here, the monarchists were an absolute failure. They had trouble finding a potential king, and the Bourbon candidate was unwilling to accept the tricolour, the national flag and symbol of the Republic of France.

The monarchists on the right wing of the political spectrum had never been comfortable with a republican constitution and made several attempts at reform. In 1879 General Patrice MacMahon (1808–1893), president and formerly marshal of France, failed in his attempt to protect the royalist cause by dismissing the government and influencing the election. A second *coup* from the right also failed in 1889, when General Georges Boulanger (1837–1891) plotted without success to restore a Bonapartist empire. The right wing attracted royalists and Bonapartists — defenders of the Catholic Church against republican secularism — as well as supporters of the army, including nationalists seeking revenge against Germany for the humiliation of 1871. These groups all associated republicanism with national weakness and dishonour. They looked for a scapegoat to blame for the alleged weaknesses of the Republic, and found one in the Jews, whom they blamed for the shortcomings of the nation.

The Dreyfus Affair

Virulent anti-Semitism was yet another challenge to the strength of the Republic and the democratic principles it theoretically espoused. Anti-Semitism reached explosive proportions in 1898–1899 and divided French society during the Dreyfus affair, which lasted from 1894–1906.

In 1894 Captain Alfred Dreyfus (1859–1935), a Jewish officer on the French General Staff, was court-martialed for allegedly passing secrets to Germany. The espionage continued after Dreyfus's imprisonment, and charges were then laid against another member of the General Staff. In court proceedings, army officers attempted a cover-up, even forging evidence against Dreyfus. When these matters came to light, French society was polarized into two hostile camps. On the one side, the patriots of the right defended the charges against Dreyfus; on the other side, the defenders of the Republic exonerated Dreyfus and charged that the conduct of the General Staff had brought dishonour to France. Eventually, Dreyfus was acquitted and re-admitted to the army, but the case had radically polarized French society, and left long-lasting scars.

Socialists of the French left, decimated by the suppression of the Paris Commune in 1871, only began to revive in the 1880s. The socialists were the heirs of the revolutionary tradition and, with memories of the Commune, were reluctant to collaborate with the bourgeois politicians of the Republic. Nonetheless, with the Republic in danger from the right, with Boulanger's failed plot in 1889, and more particularly with the Dreyfus Affair in the 1890s, the socialists came to support Republican institutions.

Ultimately, the minority on the right, still entrenched in the powerful enclaves of landholders, the army, and the church, failed to dismantle the Republic. The strength of the Republic lay in its electoral support among the urban middle class and among the small landowners, independent businessmen, and shopkeepers of provincial France. This mix of political ideology and electoral support created the broad consensus that emerged in support of the Republic.

BISMARCK'S GERMANY 1871–1890

The constitution of the German Empire of 1871 provided a symbolic, rather than substantive, measure of democracy. The democratic element, the parliament or *Reichstag*, was elected by universal male suffrage, but had very limited powers. It could not initiate legislation, but it could obstruct its passage. On financial matters, the *Reichstag* had the power to approve budgets, but it mysteriously failed to do so. Ministers were not responsible to the elected representatives but were appointed and dismissed by the kaiser, who by hereditary succession was the king of Prussia.

In the German constitutional structure, the potential existed for resentment against Prussian dominance, and to avoid this potential for fragmentation, Bismarck worked to secure support for his policies. During the 1870s, his main source of opposition lay in the Catholic or Centre Party, strongest in the Rhineland and the South German states. To counter its influence, Bismarck adopted a national secular policy of *Kulturkampf*, an anticlerical policy limiting the rights of the Catholic Church in Germany. He attempted to restrict church influence on education and on matters such as marriage and divorce. He appealed to the secular views of the National Liberals, who had supported him in the policy of unification in the 1860s. The policy of *Kulturkampf* proved unsuccessful; the Catholic, or Centre Party, continued to grow stronger, and Prussian conservatives, including Lutheran pastors, feared the reduced influence of all churches on the state.

In 1878 Bismarck shifted course by abandoning the policy of *Kulturkampf* and turned his attention to his new enemies, the socialists. In 1875 the Social Democratic Party (SPD) was formed out of a union of Marxists and followers of the German economist Ferdinand Lassalle (1825–1864), who in the 1860s had argued for political action to secure political and social reforms. The SPD quickly built support in urban working-class constituencies. Bismarck, who once called the socialists and their working-class supporters "the menacing band of robbers with whom we share our largest towns," decided to nip the movement in its youth. In 1878 he passed an anti-socialist law that declared socialism to be an enemy of the state; it also restricted newspapers, meetings, and other activities of the social democrats and their allies, the trade unionists. Bismarck recognized that, in dealing with the SPD, a policy of suppression would be insufficient, so, between 1881 and 1888, in an attempt to undermine their influence and transfer public support to himself, he passed the most advanced social legislation in Europe. The legislation introduced universal sickness and accident insurance, and old-age pensions.

Despite Bismarck's strategies to suppress the socialists with rapid industrialization and urbanization in the late nineteenth century, the appeal of the SPD grew until it became the most popular political party in the Empire. Aware of this danger, Bismarck contemplated introducing restrictions on the franchise. The young kaiser Wilhelm II (1859–1941), wanting to be popular and anxious to be free of Bismarck's domineering influence in foreign affairs, dismissed his aged chancellor in 1890. With SPD strength growing, the weakness of the *Reichstag* in relation to the kaiser's ministers was exposed. The German state, its kaiser and his ministers needed a source of popular appeal beyond the domestic politics of social reform. In a climate of intensified international rivalry from 1890 onward, militant nationalism provided the means to unite the German people without meaningful democratic reform.

BRITAIN 1867–1894: DISRAELI AND GLADSTONE

Democracy in Great Britain was not new. Britain had had a long history of peaceful government, comprised of both king and parliament. The tradition of parliamentary rule had shown its capacity for reform. By the mid-1860s, the issue of the vote had been resurrected and the question was not so much whether the vote would be extended, but when, by whom, and to whom. The extension of the vote proceeded in measured stages. In 1867 prime minister Benjamin Disraeli (1804–1881) and the Conservatives passed a Second Reform Act, which granted the vote to male urban working-class householders, thereby adding one million voters to the list. In 1884 prime minister William Gladstone (1809–1898) and the Liberals extended the vote on the same terms to male householders in rural constituencies, thereby adding another two million voters to the list. Throughout the second half of the nineteenth century, however, Britain witnessed a struggle between the forces of change — as social reform — and the forces of continuity, in support for the monarchy and other conservative traditions.

Unlike many in his party, Benjamin Disraeli was an optimist and knew how to seize opportunity. His optimism rested on his belief that a natural alliance existed between a paternalistic landed interest and a deferential working class; whereas a natural animosity existed between workers and the middle-class manufacturers who supported Gladstone's Liberals. In a famous speech at the Crystal Palace in 1872, Disraeli redefined the appeal of conservatism across class lines by calling on tradition, patriotism, and paternalism, embodied in three key terms: monarchy, empire, and social reform.

When Disraeli became prime minister in 1874, he based his policies on these three principles. First, he persuaded Queen Victoria to come out of her reclusive widowhood after the death of her husband Prince Albert in 1861. Through Disraeli's influence, the modern monarchy and the modern royal family became symbols of tradition closely attached to the values of the Conservative Party.

Disraeli also appealed to pride in empire. He made Queen Victoria the empress of India and purchased shares in the Suez Canal. He pursued an aggressive colonial policy, engaging in wars in Afghanistan and southern Africa. His ministry also passed the most innovative social reforms of the second half of the nineteenth century, improving the legal status of trade unions and introducing legislation on consumer protection, industrial safety, and public housing. On this basis, Disraeli helped build the modern Conservative Party by identifying it with traditional institutions such as the monarchy, by making it the party of imperialism, and by linking it to a program of social reform.

Under the leadership of William Gladstone, the Liberals' rallying cry was "Peace, Retrenchment, and Reform." By "peace" they meant free trade and opposition to costly foreign and colonial adventures. By "retrenchment" the Liberals meant a *laissez faire* policy in which the role of government was strictly limited, and costs and taxes were reduced as far as possible. By "reform" they had in mind doing away with outmoded laws that benefited the privileged. Accordingly, the Liberals reformed the army and the civil service to eliminate patronage, enabled students who were not Anglicans to graduate from Oxford and Cambridge Universities, and, in 1870, introduced national primary education.

Ultimately, it was their own slogan of peace that proved to be the Liberals' undoing. When more than 12 000 Bulgarian Christians were killed by Turkish forces in 1876, Disraeli, for strategic reasons, backed the Ottoman Empire in its war with Russia (1877–1878). The enormous public interest in these moral and strategic questions was given a renewed charge by William Gladstone in 1879–1880. For the first time in British and European history, a politician embarked on a modern political campaign. In his Scottish campaign of 1879, Gladstone travelled by train from Liverpool to Edinburgh, stopping at towns on the way, and delivering speeches that condemned the immorality and costs of Disraeli's imperial policy. After a second Scottish campaign in 1880, the electorate tossed out the Conservatives, and gave Gladstone and his Liberals a majority.

Gladstone, who had supported the cause of national liberation in Europe, wrestled with Britain's imperial conflicts in Africa against the Boers, and nationalism in Ireland. When he introduced his Irish Home Rule bill in 1886, he split the Liberal Party. As a result, the Conservatives — the party of patriotism and empire — and their leader Lord Salisbury, became the dominant party in British politics for the next two decades.

The Road to War: 1900–1914

With the spread of industrialization and the mounting economic competition between European states, national rivalry and imperial ambition led to an arms race and the formation of diplomatic alliances in anticipation of war. Nationalism aroused not only loyalty toward an individual's own state and people, but also antagonism toward states and peoples perceived to be threats. John A. Hobson, a liberal British economist and critic of imperialism, observed the jingoistic response of the British populace during the Boer War in South Africa (1899–1902). In *The Psychology of Jingoism* (1901), Hobson commented that aggressive nationalism became "an inverted patriotism whereby the love of one's own nation is transformed into the hatred of another nation and fierce craving to destroy the individual members of that other nation."

National and imperial rivalry put new pressures on domestic politics within states. The Prussian aristocracy, which dominated the offices of state and the army, identified its own power with the pre-eminence of the German nation. With the backing of industrialists anxious to profit from the arms race, politicians and generals wrestled with the problem of Germany's encirclement within Central Europe. They began to see the inevitability of a great war as the way for Germany to assume its rightful and dominant place on the Continent. Consequently, during critical weeks of crisis diplomacy in July 1914, there was a willingness to believe that the time had come for a lasting peace through a victorious war.

In Britain, rivalry with Germany, especially in the naval arms race, fostered a constitutional crisis. The Liberal government needed to finance both warships and new social measures, such as old-age pensions. The People's Budget of 1909, proposed by Chancellor of the Exchequer David Lloyd George (1863–1945), introduced taxes on inherited wealth. In response, the landed aristocracy in the House of Lords defeated the budget and brought down the government. This constitutional crisis, whereby a hereditary peerage brought down a popularly elected government, reflected a new willingness of conservative, traditional interests to challenge the authority of the state.

Nationalism and the Origins of World War I

Aggressive nationalism and the polarization of domestic politics in part explain why European nations were ready to go to war in August of 1914. The popular appeal of aggressive nationalism at least explains why domestic political considerations did not prevent politicians and generals from going to war. It also explains why, when war was declared, recruits readily signed up to fight and die for their country.

Nationalism also accounts for the more immediate cause of the war in a more specific way. Aggressive nationalism presented the gravest threat in the Balkans, where a complex mixture of cultural and linguistic groups and two archaic empires — the Ottoman Empire and the Austro-Hungarian monarchy — had failed to resolve competing claims of various nationalities. These nationalities — Romanians, Bulgarians, Serbs, Bosnians, Croats, and others — were residents of not only the Austro-Hungarian Empire, but also its Ottoman neighbour. After two local Balkan Wars in 1912–1913, the rival ambitions of the nationalists and of great powers such as Austria-Hungary and Russia remained unresolved. The Balkan Wars hardened the resolve of rival nationalists to such an extent that no one was ready to make any concessions or compromises.

In this climate, an isolated spark could and did set off an engulfing inferno: A Serbian nationalist (named

Gavrilo Princip) assassinated the Austrian archduke Francis Ferdinand, heir to the Austrian throne, and his wife at Sarajevo on June 28, 1914. Within six weeks, the incident escalated from a Serbian-Austrian confrontation to a full-blown European and world war. In the new twentieth century, the engine of historical change would not be liberation through revolution, but destruction through total war.

SOCIETY IN MODERN EUROPE

The Rise of a Dominant Middle Class

The political transformations examined so far — the consolidation of nation-states, the appeal of nationalism, and the advent of democracy — occurred within a novel social and cultural context. While many of the features of this new urban and industrial society originated in the period prior to 1850, the process of industrialization was greatly accelerated in the second half of the nineteenth century.

Not only was there remarkable growth in the European population (from 266 million to 401 million from 1850 to 1900), but the economy, whether measured by volume of trade or by value of industrial output, grew at an accelerated rate. Consequently, the standard of living of the majority of people in Western Europe, including landowning peasants and industrial wage earners, improved in the period from 1850 to 1914. The most dramatic increase in living standards occurred between 1873 and 1896, the so-called Great Depression years. In this period, prices fell, partly due to transportation improvements and increased production. As the cost of goods declined, persons with a steady income experienced a remarkable improvement in living standards. Regularly employed, skilled wage-earners in Britain saw their real income increase by 70–100 percent. From the mid-1890s to 1914, however, the trend was reversed: Rising prices and business profits increased and middle-class investors benefited,

whereas working-class consumers faced higher prices and greater employment insecurity.

A distinctive feature of nineteenth-century society was the dominant role that the middle class came to play. As a result of the Industrial Revolution, Europeans experienced a shift from an elitist society (in which the aristocracy dominated) to a mass culture (in which the middle class defined morality, customs, fashions, and trends). Middle-class men and women were not transformed into model citizens, but they did exert considerable influence on the working class. The increase in economic power was accompanied by an increase in political power, enabling merchants, industrialists, bankers and other professionals to play a larger role in defining the society in which they lived. In this way, the rise of the middle class led to profound changes in many aspects of society.

As the size and influence of the middle class grew in the nineteenth century, so too did its sense of self-importance. Members of the middle class became increasingly critical of certain aspects of aristocratic society. Their sense of moral responsibility led to more concern for the poor and a strong emphasis on the middle-class values of sobriety, thrift, hard work, piety, and respectability as a means of providing guidance to the lower classes. Although there were minor variations in what was considered respectable, there were universally condemned behaviours, such as wild drunkenness, godlessness, homosexuality, self-indulgence, flamboyant dress and overt expressions of sexuality, or promiscuity. From a very early age, middle-class children were thus instructed in the behaviour and appearance of the idealized, perfect lady or gentleman.

With the rapid decline in the importance of titles and land, a vacuum was created within the morals and values of European society. The emerging middle class was able to make sense of this new world and base its values on the capacity to live a Christian life without the formal and hereditary trappings of the nobility. A true Christian, it was felt, had to live a spiritual life every minute of every day. Many among the middle class believed society was rotten to the core and blamed this decay on religious emptiness. The aristocracy came under harsh criticism for its acceptance of male infidelity and for politically arranged marriages that belittled the care and companionship that the middle class considered an essential part of the marriage sacrament. This strict sense of morally acceptable and respectable behaviour was the hallmark of the Victorian Age (1837–1901).

SOCIAL ORGANIZATION IN THE NINETEENTH CENTURY

Popular Culture

During the latter half of the nineteenth century, the diversification and enrichment of cultural and leisure pursuits affected the lives and values of the affluent middle class and the lower-middle and working classes. Differences in disposable income and in taste produced two cultures. One appealed to the affluent elite, or what the English called the "classes," and the other served what some derisively called the "masses." By the end of the century, in sports and entertainment, the clear lines that divided the classes were beginning to blur.

The popular institutions associated with nineteenth-century cities — art galleries, museums, libraries, theatres, opera houses, concert halls, and symphony orchestras — reflected a middle-class quest for cultural enrichment (to become more like the upper class). Technical innovations in printing and publishing also made books much cheaper and created a modern reading public anxious for the latest works of well-known authors of the time. In addition to these cultural pursuits, the middle class developed new ways to spend its increased leisure time. The railroad allowed short excursions to picturesque countryside and seaside resorts. Pioneering English travel agent and missionary Thomas Cook (1808–1892) arranged more elaborate holidays to the Mediterranean Riviera, the Alps, or, for the more adventurous, to Palestine and Egypt.

New forms of popular entertainment, combined with the growth of mass-circulation tabloid newspapers and cheap sensational pulp fiction, led moralists to

Pleasures AND PASTIMES

There was a significant push during the nineteenth century to "elevate" the working classes and try to blur the lines that separated them from the upper classes. Sports and other leisure activities were routinely scrutinized in the press to see whether they served to achieve this goal. Cricket — still a staple of the British leisure diet — emerged during the nineteenth century as a popular sport and was deemed worthy of praise for its ability to bring the upper and lower classes together. In 1869 the local press reported that "... cricket recognizes no distinctions of class; that it is, and ever has been, one of the principal agents in bringing the different grades of society into contact, and showing that God's mental and moral as well as His natural gifts, are bestowed alike upon the peasant and the peer." In some parts of England, it was reported that cricketers' belts bore the motto: "The Prince and peasant by cricket are united."

bemoan the degeneration of taste in this new age of democracy and popular culture. To these pessimistic social commentators, the centres of this degeneration were the large cities where all spectators were now equal and traditional values enshrined in religion and custom no longer prevailed.

Technology and Society: The Second Industrial Revolution

Like the first, the so-called "second" Industrial Revolution (1880–1939) was characterized by a number of significant technological breakthroughs and new principles in the organization of production and labour. Some developments that we associate with the early twentieth century actually originated before 1900. It is easy to focus on the new telephone, electric lights, phonograph, motion pictures, and automobile, but we should not forget the less striking but equally significant developments of the late nineteenth century. Inventors were still finding new uses for steam power, and railroad construction proceeded at a faster pace than in the 1840s and 1850s. Between 1850 and 1870, world steam power increased 4.5 times and the length of railway track by eight times.

Although the development of the internal-combustion engine and the automobile can be traced back to the nineteenth century, initially, the motor car was only a luxury replacement for the horse and carriage used by the very rich. The most significant innovations in personal transport in the 1880s and 1890s were the humble but pervasive bicycle, and the electric streetcar. Electric streetcars, including subway systems in London and Paris, transported millions of riders daily by the beginning of the twentieth century.

The second Industrial Revolution involved the use of new sources of energy comparable to steam in the first Industrial Revolution. This time, scientific research played a more significant role. New discoveries in physics and chemistry led to multiple applications of electricity. The development of the internal-combustion engine was dependent on a new fuel: refined petroleum. Germany and the United States took the lead in the new science-based technologies of chemical and electrical engineering. With larger domestic markets, Germany (with a population of 68 million) and the United States (92 million) surpassed Great Britain (45 million) in industrial productivity and technological innovation. London remained the world's financial centre and Britain the dominant player in global shipping, commerce, and investment. Japan also experienced its industrial revolution in this period and became the first non-European state to join the industrial nations.

The new technologies required larger amounts of capital than the pioneering family enterprises of the first Industrial Revolution. Though the small firms employing fewer than 50 people still were more common, the new industrial enterprises, most evident in Germany and the United States, were larger. Krupp, the German steel, engineering and munitions giant of the Ruhr Valley, employed only 72 people in 1848, but

12 000 in 1873. Larger establishments, financed and owned as joint-stock enterprises, began to grasp control of various stages of production in what was termed "vertical integration." Large corporations were now involved in all aspects of production: extracting and processing raw materials, manufacturing the finished goods, and transporting and retailing products. Such concentration of ownership was an increasing trend. In the United States and Germany, the steel, chemical, electrical and petroleum industries were run by large corporations, cartels (monopolies), and trusts. These corporations not only dominated whole sectors of the economy and were interrelated with financial institutions, but their chief executives also had close links with political leaders.

History BYTES

In addition to the great technological innovations of the Industrial Revolution, the nineteenth century also saw many important inventions that do not routinely receive the attention showered on the steam engine and the cotton gin. One of these was the forerunner to the modern-day sewage system. Until the nineteenth century, human excrement was collected in buckets and removed by "night soil men," only to be sold later as fertilizer or collected in a cesspit, which would be emptied once a year into a local river, from which many drew their drinking water. As cities grew increasingly congested, the health implications of these practices — including outbreaks of cholera and typhoid fever — necessitated the development of a city drainage system that would filter and chemically treat human waste and then carry it out to be dumped into the sea.

New machines also facilitated the ongoing transition from craft production to factory manufacture. In the 1870s, American-designed machines replaced hand-made shoes and boots with factory-made products. Cobblers who had practised an ancient and prestigious craft, were reduced to repairing machine-made shoes. Similarly, another American invention, the Singer sewing machine, allowed factories and small work-shops, usually employing women at piecework rates, to replace tailors and seamstresses. The mass production of machine-made clothing went hand in hand with a revolution in retailing. Until the 1870s, clothes were made-to-measure, and poorer people purchased second-hand clothing. Now, new department stores and retail chain stores sold ready-to-wear garments produced by sewing-machine operators.

THE EVOLVING WORLD OF WOMEN

The lower status of women had significant repercussions in the public sphere (politics and employment) as well as the private sphere (marriage and the family). The emergence of feminist movements in the second half of the nineteenth century was a result of dissatisfaction with the subordinate status of women, which was rooted in tradition and enforced by law. This dissatisfaction grew more acute as adult men gained the right to vote and equality before the law. Inequality on the basis of gender was an obvious contradiction of newly established egalitarian principles.

Steps toward the emancipation of women were taken thanks to both the efforts of feminists to change the law, and significant innovations that came with economic and social change. The expansion of the middle classes, the spread of state education, the increase in leisure time and, especially, new forms of employment for women, eased some of the restrictions on the lives of women both in and outside the home. This informal emancipation also brought women face-to-face with the inequality of their legal and political status.

Feminist Movements across Europe

The rallying cry of the suffragists, "votes for women," had both political and psychological significance. The vote offered female electors the opportunity to select politicians who would be more responsive to women's issues. Denying women the vote was the most obvious symbol of women's inequality.

Feminist movements in different countries confronted different obstacles. In Germany, feminists faced the combined obstacles of a conservative, middle-class culture, in which the subordination of women was sanctioned by both Protestant and Catholic churches, and a political structure that made legislative reform extremely difficult. Consequently, the German feminist movement was small and moderate in its goals until the beginning of the twentieth century. Then a radical group of feminists emerged demanding legal equality and the vote, access to birth control, the right to abortion, equal pay for equal work, and state provision of day-care.

In France, the polarized politics of the Third Republic placed the feminists, whose ideology of emancipation had roots in the Revolution, on the left, among the defenders of republicanism. The feminist opposition on the right came mainly from the Catholic Church, which defended the subordinate status of women within the traditional family. Although their anticlericalism may have separated feminists from many French women, the late achievement of reforms in France reflected the immense resistance faced by reformers. French feminists began calling for a reform of marriage law in the 1880s, but married women only became legal persons able to possess property in 1938. Women in France did not get the vote until 1945.

In Britain, the feminist movement originated earlier in the nineteenth century and, by the beginning of the twentieth century, suffrage societies were able to conduct a more sustained political campaign than their sisters on the Continent. In 1857 divorce courts were created; by 1882 married women secured the same rights as single women to own property.

Measures for female voting had been introduced in the British parliament at regular intervals for 30 years beginning in 1867, but were never passed. The frustration of those expectations fuelled a vigorous campaign involving new tactics of both civil disobedience and violence.

In 1903 Emmeline Pankhurst (1858–1928) and her daughter Christabel launched a new suffrage society in Britain, the Women's Social and Political Union (WSPU), dedicated to winning the franchise for women on the

Puck magazine in England carried this anti-suffragette poster calling the women "Jekyll and Hyde militants." It shows suffragettes as having two sides: one ladylike and one like a torch-carrying witch. How has the feminist movement countered these stereotypes?

on hunger strikes in prison and refusing to pay taxes. These measures escalated to violence against property: windows were smashed, male symbols such as golf greens were destroyed, public buildings were set fire to, paintings in art galleries were slashed. Most disturbing was the suicide of Emily Davison, who threw herself in front of the king's horse at the Epson Derby horserace in 1913 as a political protest. But, despite the extent of the feminist campaign and its militancy, the Liberal government remained unmoved.

Review, Reflect, Respond

1. Compare and contrast the styles and policies of British prime ministers William Gladstone and Benjamin Disraeli. Which politician would you have supported? Explain your choice.

2. Explain why many believe the seeds of World War I were planted in the late nineteenth century by listing, in order of importance, four important causes of the war.

3. How are the inequities faced by women today different from those that women experienced in the late nineteenth and early twentieth century?

same limited terms as then existed for men. The members of the WSPU, who became known as "suffragettes," differed from other feminists not so much in their aims as in their methods. The Pankhursts decided on a campaign of vigorous direct action. The campaign began with the questioning of politicians on public occasions, and continued with disruptions of political meetings and mass rallies before parliament. These demonstrations led to confrontations with the police, arrests, and further demonstrations. The suffragettes began to engage in passive resistance, chaining themselves to lampposts, going

Urban Communities and Trade Unionism

Throughout Europe, the law and its administration were biased on the basis of not only gender, but also on social class. Working people had two options for attempting to redress the hardship and inequity of their economic and legal position. They could take direct action to improve wages and working conditions at their place of employment, or they could become active politically to try to change the law.

With further industrialization, working people attempted to make improvements by creating trade unions. Early unions had historical links with

The Fourth Estate: Sarah Josepha Hale

Sarah Josepha Hale (1788–1879) was an American author and editor. Her literary works include *Northwood: A Tale of New England*, which was the first novel to be published by an American woman. She also published several volumes of poetry, one of which includes the classic children's song *Mary Had a Little Lamb* (1830).

Sarah Josepha Hale, publisher and political activitist

But it was as a magazine editor that Hale made her greatest impact. After her lawyer husband died at an early age, she was left with five young children to support. Partially on the strength of her novel's quality, she was offered the editorship of *Ladies' Magazine* — advertised as "the first magazine edited by a woman for women." Hale was editor of the periodical from 1827 to 1836. For 40 years after this she served as editor of *Godey's Lady's Book*, through which she wielded considerable influence over the reading, learning, and political consciousness of American women. *Godey's Lady's Book* was the most popular women's magazine of the era, at its height reaching a circulation of about 150 000.

While the magazine contained fashion plates, sentimental songs, recipes and household hints, it also published serious literary works. It showcased the writing of respected male American authors, such as Edgar Allan Poe, Henry Wadsworth Longfellow, Ralph Waldo Emerson and Nathaniel Hawthorne, and promoted the work of many American women writers.

Hale's editorials exerted considerable influence over her large readership. She used the magazine as a platform to support better education for women. But, Hale's editorial policy was decidedly conservative. She espoused education for women to make them better wives and mothers. In her early editorials, she promoted the idea that women were overseers of the spiritual and domestic realm. She opposed the women's rights movement as an attempt to take women away from their domain — the home, in Hale's eyes.

Later, though, Hale supported the idea of careers for women, when industrialization made employing them necessary. Eventually, she actively promoted the concept of women doctors doing missionary work in Africa.

An excerpt from an 1855 Editorial by Sarah Josepha Hale follows:

What is Needed in America

Thanks to the spirit of Christian freedom, women in our land are favoured above the sex in any other nation. The absurd and degrading customs or usages of the common law, and the partial and, therefore, unjust statutes of kings, brought by our forefathers from England, are fast passing away, or being rendered nugatory by new enactments, more in accordance with reason and righteousness. The Homestead laws, and the security given that the property of a married woman shall remain in her own possession, are great safeguards of domestic comfort. The efforts made to open new channels of industry and profitable professions for those women who have to support themselves are deserving of much praise; but one great act of public justice yet remains undone. Government, national or State, has never yet provided suitably for the education of women. Girls, as well as boys, have the advantages of the free school system; but no public provision has been made, no college or university endowed where young women may have similar advantages of instruction now open to young men in every State of the Union. True, there are very many private institutions devoted to female education; but these are defective for the want of a higher model than private enterprise has yet given. Of course, the better woman is educated the higher she will be estimated, and the more careful will legislators be to frame laws just and equitable which are to guard her happiness and protect her rights; men will thus improve their own *hearts* and elevate their views. The standard of woman is the moral thermometer of the nation.

Holding these sentiments, our "Book" has never swerved from its straightforward course of aiding women to improve themselves, while it has aimed to arouse public sentiment to help onward this improvement. For this, we give patterns and directions for feminine employment, we show the benefits of female education, and for this we have *twice* brought before congress our petition for aid; and now we come a *third* time, intending to persevere till some noble champion arises to advocate the cause and win the victory ...[1]

---

1. Using points raised in this passage, write a one-page response to Hale's argument that "The standard of woman is the moral thermometer of the nation."

2. Which of Hale's suggestions actually came to pass? Why?

HANT TAILORS

UNION

THE ROAD TO SHEFFIELD.

Punch A L. "NOW, THEN, STOP THAT, I SAY! WE'LL HAVE NO INTIMIDATION HERE."

In this political cartoon, a policeman is warning a trade unionist not to intimidate men during riots that were going on in Sheffield, England in 1867. What did the Unionist want?

pre-industrial crafts and guilds. Highly skilled trades attempted to protect their craft and their wages from the competition of new industrial processes. As more people were hired by industry, especially at larger firms employing more people doing similar work, trade unionism spread among the semiskilled. In place of the older craft unions organized by each separate trade, industrial unionism, from the 1880s onward, united all workers employed in a particular industry, such as coal mining or the railways.

The extent of unionization varied according to the level of industrialization. By the early twentieth century, over two million workers were organized in Great Britain, over three million in Germany, and over one million in France. The new industrial unions were very militant. The trade unionists' capacity to organize and put pressure on employers

through strikes and picketing depended upon the law, which in most countries still restricted the actions of trade unions. Consequently, labour organizations had to press for political change, especially where the law was punitive and where qualifications for the franchise still excluded many working people.

DEVELOPMENTS IN POLITICAL THOUGHT: SOCIALISM

Socialism directly addressed the political needs of trade unionists and working people. Apart from the British labour movement, European labour advocates and socialists were strongly influenced by Karl Marx's analysis of industrial capitalism. Marx accurately predicted that industrial capitalism would continue to expand and draw increasing numbers of people to a system of wage labour. Furthermore, his description of the conflict between employers and employees — more generally, between the bourgeoisie and the working class — conformed to the daily experience of many late-nineteenth-century industrial wage earners.

Aside from interpreting capitalism and advocating a proletarian revolution, Marx worked as a political organizer helping to create the First International Workingmen's Association in 1864. This first attempt to build an international socialist political organization was one of the many failures of the Paris Commune in 1871. With its defeat and the collapse of the French left, the First International disbanded in 1876.

The idea of an international organization of socialists was revived with the foundation of the Second International in 1889. By this time, industrialization had expanded in Germany, France, and elsewhere on the Continent; working people were now more widely organized in trade unions and in their own national political parties. This situation offered the possibility that the workers might gain at the ballot box what Marx had said could only be achieved by revolution.

In 1899 German socialist theorist Eduard Bernstein (1850–1932) proposed that socialism could be won gradually by elected governments implementing socialist measures over time. The debate over Bernstein's so-called revisionist strategy deeply divided the Second International as well as various national movements, including the social democrats in Germany and the socialists in Russia. Those still committed to Marx's ideas argued that a socialist restructuring of the economy and society could only be achieved by revolution.

WEB CONNECTION

www. mcgrawhill.ca/links/legacy

Go to the site above to find out more about suffragettes and the early women's movement.

Bernstein and his revisionists lost the debate within the Second International, but the political conditions within which socialist parties functioned meant that they were often revolutionary in ideology but revisionist in practice. The Social Democratic Party in Germany, the most successful socialist party in Europe (4.5 million votes), which became the largest party in the *Reichstag* (German parliament) in 1912, remained committed to revolution in theory, but focussed their energies on conventional electioneering.

The French left remained divided between those nominally committed to revolution but ready to enter electoral politics, and those who looked to direct action in the revolutionary tradition. Radical trade unionists and syndicalists favoured the politics of direct action through strikes and industrial sabotage rather than electioneering. Moderates favoured the open and humanistic socialism of Jean Jaurès (1859–1914), a middle-class philosopher and journalist who became the leading French socialist and orator of the late nineteenth and early twentieth centuries. He built a popular working-class following, but refused to join coalitions with non-socialist parties. In 1914 he campaigned against the dangers of militant nationalism, only to be assassinated by a fanatic nationalist that same year.

The British labour movement, the least influenced by Marx and his revolutionary doctrine, was the most

revisionist in its political strategy. Out of the growth of the trade-union movement, the Independent Labour Party, and other working-class and socialist groups, the Labour Party was created in 1900; it fought the 1906 election as a lobby attempting to secure changes in labour law and social reform. There were also middle-class groups, such as the Fabian Society, whose members engaged in research and made proposals for social legislation. They believed in gradual reforms and sought to permeate the established Conservative and Liberal parties. The leading Fabians, Sidney and Beatrice Webb and George Bernard Shaw, for example, were skeptical about an independent working-class party, and before 1918 had only a limited influence on the Labour Party.

In several European states on the eve of World War I, the revolutionary rhetoric of the socialists and the militancy of the trade unions created a sense that both the economy and the state were potential hostages to direct action by an organized working class. In Western Europe, this perception of an industrial and political crisis was more apparent than real. In Eastern Europe, under more repressive political regimes and less advanced economies, this sense of crisis, even of revolution, had more serious foundations.

The Revolution in Russia, 1905

The socialist debate between revolution and revisionism came to a head in Russia in 1905. In the early 1890s, under Czar Alexander III and from 1894 until 1917 under Czar Nicholas II (the last czar), the contradictory policies of rapid industrial development and continued political repression created the potential for a revolutionary explosion. Under the guidance of the first constitutional prime minister of czarist Russia, Sergey Witte (1849–1915), Russia experienced a second wave of rapid industrial development by relying on financing by foreign capital. With industrialization, the working class grew in size and engaged in clandestine revolutionary activity under the scrutiny of the czar's secret police.

The leading Marxist party, the Russian Social Democratic Party, was in exile in Switzerland. Along with other socialist parties, it engaged in the debate on revisionism, and in 1902, one of its leading militants, Vladimir Ilich Ulyanov, known as Lenin (1870–1924), published an influential pamphlet under the title *What is to be Done?* In defending the necessity of revolution, Lenin argued that it was not sufficient to wait for a spontaneous insurrection of the masses. He advanced the idea that a dedicated core of professional revolutionaries, the vanguard of the party, could use a political crisis to lead the working class into full-scale revolution. In subsequent debates, Lenin and his more militant faction won a small majority and became known as the Bolsheviks; his more moderate social democratic or revisionist opponents constituted a minority that became known as the Mensheviks.

For the Russian socialists, these debates had more than theoretical significance. In 1905 they found themselves in a real revolution. Added to an economic slump that had created extensive hardship among the peasantry and industrial workers, the defeat of Russian naval and military forces by Japan in 1904–1905 created a political crisis. This crisis escalated into revolution when, on Bloody Sunday (January 22, 1905), troops killed several hundred peaceful and unarmed demonstrators who sought to petition the czar at the Winter Palace to grant political reforms and economic relief. A prolonged constitutional crisis, coupled with extensive rural unrest, recurrent general strikes (e.g., 100 000 factory workers struck in St. Petersburg), a mutiny in the navy and incidents of political violence, finally forced Nicholas II to create a *Duma*, or parliament.

Even though the new *Duma*, like the German *Reichstag*, had limited powers, the reform was sufficient to split the forces pressing for change. The social revolutionaries attempted to continue their campaign of strikes, but were crushed by the army at the end of 1905. A regressive reform of the electoral law weighted the *Duma* even more favourably toward conservative property owners. Nicholas II, never fully reconciled to even this moderate degree of constitutional rule, governed in an increasingly autocratic manner. Eventually, a much more severe crisis brought on by the stresses of war launched a full-scale revolution in 1917.

Developments in Religious Thought

The new urban environment was secular, and the churches were losing the battle for the souls of the masses. In England, a religious census in 1851 shocked contemporaries when it revealed that only 50 percent of the population attended church, and in some working-class areas, fewer than 10 percent. In Catholic countries, the church, led by the Pope, pronounced itself the determined opponent of the forces of secularism and modernization. In the *Syllabus of Errors* in 1864, Pope Pius IX rejected any idea that "the Roman Pontiff can, and ought to, reconcile himself and come to terms with progress, liberalism, and modern civilization." The identification of the church with conservatism made anticlericalism in countries such as France and Italy a powerful part of the creed of reason and progress among liberal reformers and working-class radicals.

In the 1880s and 1890s, advocates of social Catholicism in France and Germany criticized the impact of industrial capitalism, and developed programs of social reform addressing the needs of the working class. Similarly, in Protestant countries, churches began to see the need to address questions of social reform. This social gospel, strongest in Britain among Baptists, Methodists, some elements within the Church of England and new religious organizations such as the Salvation Army, created a climate more accepting of social legislation and even of democratic socialism. Nonetheless, these agencies of various churches largely failed to halt the growing indifference toward religion among working- and middle-class city dwellers.

DEVELOPMENTS IN SCIENTIFIC THOUGHT

The New Physics

The most revolutionary challenge to the certainties of science came from scientists themselves. In physics, for example, Isaac Newton's synthesis of the laws of motion in the late seventeenth century had provided a vision of an ordered universe and a model of scientific truth resting on the precision of mathematics. This Newtonian universe now came under scrutiny, as scientists explored those features of the structure of matter and the dimensions of space for which existing explanations were inadequate.

From the work of Marie Curie (1867–1934) on radium and radioactivity, and from other scientists' work on the atom, the old view of matter as being solid was challenged. The subatomic world did not behave like a mini-universe as Newton believed. The mysterious properties of atomic particles could only be explained by the new theory of quantum physics formulated by German physicist Max Planck (1858–1947). Probabilities rather than fixed laws provided a better explanation for the behaviour of matter and energy than did Newton's laws.

The new work at the subatomic level also had implications for the grander dimension of the cosmos. For Albert Einstein (1879–1955), a German mathematician and physicist, the assumption that matter and energy, or time and space, were fixed absolutes failed to explain natural phenomena in relation to the speed of light. In his theory of relativity (1905), Einstein put forward the revolutionary hypothesis that time and space were dependent on the frame of reference of the observer. In his famous equation, $E=mc^2$, he demonstrated the equivalence of matter and energy.

The new quantum physics and the theory of relativity required a grasp of advanced mathematics, which widened the gap between the understanding of scientists and the common-sense understanding of the educated public. The new physics also challenged the idea of an objective, value-free science independent of the observer. In both scientific and humanistic studies, in the study of natural phenomena and human thought, the observer now had a greater role in making these subjects intelligible.

PHILOSOPHY AND SOCIETY

While confidence in reason, science, and progress continued as a commonplace assumption until World War I, a significant minority of creative artists, scientists, and intellectuals of the age began to question this certainty. This pre-1914 generation established the intellectual and cultural framework for the more troubled, skeptical, and disordered world of the twentieth century.

Friedrich Nietzsche

Among those who challenged the belief in progress and human reason, Friedrich Nietzsche (1844–1900), a German philosopher, exerted an unsettling influence on his contemporaries. Even a century later, he continues to cast a critical light on the shallow presumptions of our culture. Nietzsche questioned the emphasis on reason in Western civilization and asserted that creativity rested upon the human will. In his famous phrase, "God is dead," he not only challenged the received wisdom of Christianity, but also argued that the individual could only find meaning and purpose through exertion of the human spirit. He saw that the prevailing trends of the age, the rise of mass culture, the emergence of democratic politics, and the reforming energy of socialism, were all sources of delusion and weakness. He was equally critical of the egalitarian pretences of bourgeois culture, and thought that only exceptional individuals could fulfil their creative potential through superior force of character.

Nietzsche's reputation has been adversely affected by his personal association with composer Richard Wagner (1813–1883), who dedicated his art to German nationalism, and by the subsequent use of

Charles Darwin

The evolutionary theories of English naturalist Charles Darwin had a profound impact on the scientific and religious thought of his day — and Darwin's ideas continue to influence thinking today.

Although Darwin's name is closely associated with evolution, he was not the first to propose the evolution hypothesis. In France, Jean-Baptiste de Lamarck had pioneered the idea of animal evolution early in the nineteenth century. And Darwin was influenced by two English theorists: Thomas Malthus, who raised important questions about population increase and natural control; and Sir Charles Lyell, a geologist, who from his studies of rock strata challenged the biblical notion of earth's relatively recent creation.

The major question puzzling those who supported evolution was: How did it occur? Darwin's great legacy was in proposing the mechanism for evolution — natural selection. His thinking

Charles Darwin changed the way we think of our place in the natural world.

provided sufficient cause, which raised scientific ideas about evolution from hypothesis to a verifiable theory. And in his writing, Darwin provided exhaustive biological evidence, presenting it in a careful, coherent, and persuasive manner that eventually succeeded in convincing almost all biologists of its truth.

Many of Darwin's key ideas about natural selection came from his observation of nature. And a great deal of this scientific observation was done in his capacity as a naturalist on the surveying expedition of the HMS *Beagle*. The ship arrived at the Galapagos Islands, off the coast of Ecuador, in 1835, and Darwin spent about a year studying and recording extensive notes on the varied island species.

Darwin wondered why species living in an area were so closely related to those that were extinct; and why species living in slightly different environments have slightly different characteristics from one another.

Upon returning to England in 1836, Darwin began the painstaking work of cataloguing his specimens and writing short papers on his emerging ideas. By about 1844, he had outlined the principles of his position on natural selection. During the next decade, Darwin condensed and shaped his vast body of notes into the landmark work *The Origin of Species by Means of Natural Selection* (1859).

Very simply put, Darwin's basic theory proposed that life on earth is the result of millions of years of adaptations to changing environments. The ability to adapt distinguishes "successful" species from "unsuccessful" ones. Darwin called this process "natural selection."

In Darwin's second pivotal work *The Descent of Man* (1871), he stated that humans, like every other organism on earth, were the result of evolution:

> We must, however, acknowledge, as it seems to me, that man with all his noble qualities ...
> still bears in his bodily frame the indelible stamp of his lowly origins.

Darwin's ideas were highly subversive: They undermined the biblical view of creation and the centrality of human's position within the universe. Religious individuals and groups vehemently attacked *The Origin of Species*, because it did not agree with the account of creation offered in the Book of Genesis.

Darwin's ideas caused immediate controversy when they were first published and eventually changed the dialogue we use to think about human nature, nature itself, biological processes, and even social relations to this day. One of the liveliest debates took place in Tennessee, where in 1925 teacher John T. Scopes was prosecuted for teaching Darwin's theory of evolution in the classroom. This well-known trial, fought out by renowned lawyer Clarence Darrow and conservative statesman William Jennings Bryan, was widely covered in the press and was even the subject of a famous play called *Inherit the Wind*.

In the latter part of the nineteenth century, some thinkers applied Darwin's ideas to society, politics, and economics. Foremost among them was English philosopher Herbert Spencer, who coined the phrase "survival of the fittest" and developed a school of thought called social Darwinism. In its more extreme form, social Darwinism held that businesses should be allowed to fail, people should be left to starve, and disease and death should be free to weed out the unfit. Spencer's ideas gained popularity during the late nineteenth century in free enterprise and highly individualistic societies such as the United States.

Darwin's theory of evolution was applied by various thinkers and writers to support views about human society. Often these views, referred to as "social Darwinism," were at odds with Darwin's theory, but they reflected the strong influence of the concept of evolution by natural selection. Herbert Spencer advanced the case that individualism and the competitive nature of capitalism were simply the expression of natural laws. In contrast, some followers of Marx, for example Friedrich Engels, claimed that Marx had reached an understanding of the laws of historical development, just as Darwin had perceived the laws governing biological development. Both theories, although they aimed to achieve opposite goals, emphasized the process of progressive change, and both stressed that such changes were a product of conflict and were determined by forces beyond human control.

Late-nineteenth-century commentators applied Darwin's ideas to conflicts between nations and between human groups identified as races. These theorists, including the British statesman and entrepreneur Cecil Rhodes, stressed that struggle was an inherent part of the human condition, and that success went inevitably to the most powerful. Social Darwinism was most influential in two countries: Germany, a new country concerned with its national stature and with the ethnic minorities of Central Europe, and the United States, which was warring with Native Americans, inventing new ways to segregate African Americans after emancipation, and seeking to justify a subordinate status for new immigrants.

In Britain, Victorian society portrayed itself as the pinnacle of human achievement and other peoples were classified as unprogressive barbarians, or as childlike primitives of the human family. These ideas were usefully applied during the new age of imperialism, when European colonial powers were intervening in Asia, Africa, and the Pacific, and reducing once autonomous cultures and peoples to a subordinate status.

1. Do you see evidence of "social Darwinism" in today's society? Where and in what forms?

2. Recreate the setting and a scene from the play *Inherit the Wind* by J. Lawrence and R. E. Lee which is based on the Scopes trial of 1925.

some of Nietzche's ideas to justify atrocities committed by Hitler and the Third Reich. Nietzsche was critical of the militarism, nationalism, and anti-Semitism of his own time. His insight into the limitations of human reason, his perception that science was more a human creation than an objective description of nature, and his effort to come to terms with the sources of human creativity struck a responsive chord in the thinking of other philosophers, artists, and scientists of the time.

Some contemporary thinkers began to explore non-rational sources of human conduct. Emile Durkheim (1858–1917), a French social scientist and one of the founders of the new discipline of sociology, explored the sources of collective consciousness. His interest grew out of studies of individual loneliness and alienation, most dramatically revealed in incidents of suicide. Contrary to conventional liberal assumptions, Durkheim concluded that modern urban, industrial society threatened to create an excessive individualism dangerous to mental health and social well-being. Max Weber (1864–1920), a German liberal economist whose thought had a profound influence on the social sciences in the twentieth century, shared with Durkheim the concern for the individual within an impersonal and secular environment. In his influential work *The Protestant Ethic and the Spirit of Capitalism* (1904–1905), Weber challenged the economic ideas of Marx and argued that religious beliefs and values shape economic organization and behaviour.

Weber was particularly concerned with the basis of political and social action in modern capitalist societies organized on a rational and secular basis. The price of this new, more rational order was the disillusionment of the individual and the growth of bureaucracy. To overcome the rules and regulations of these entrenched bureaucratic structures, Weber looked to the possibility of a dynamic or charismatic leader. He did not predict or advocate the rise of totalitarian dictators, but, in looking for some scope for individual action within impersonal social institutions, Weber thought that such leadership offered the individual a greater purposefulness in modern secular society.

FAMILY LIFE IN THE NINETEENTH CENTURY

During the nineteenth century, women continued to find themselves restricted and exploited in a paternalistic, male-dominated society. During the first half of the century, bourgeois women were commonly involved in the family business by taking on such tasks as keeping the books. By the 1850s and 1860s, business had grown and the bourgeoisie had ceased to live near the family business, choosing the expensive new neighbourhoods instead. Women, consequently, retreated into the home, where they raised the children and tended to household duties such as supervising servants and hosting charitable events and social teas.

Women of the urban working class were also homemakers, which is not to suggest they had nearly the leisure time their middle-class counterparts enjoyed. The list of responsibilities attached to a homemaker of the nineteenth century is staggering. Firstly, she was responsible for the care and supervision of the children. Everywhere a woman went, she took her children with her. Her second function was to care for the family by performing countless household chores. These included: shopping for the lowest-priced food, often bartering and gathering what free items she could find in the city; preparing meals; gathering fuel; fetching water; and washing, tailoring, mending, and patching the family's clothes.

Beyond carrying out household chores, working-class women were often counted on to earn a supplementary income for the family by cleaning the houses of others (no vacuum cleaners yet), taking in laundry (an all-day, back-breaking job), making deliveries (on foot), or selling items at the street corner. During the last 30 years of the nineteenth century, the garment industry began to exploit this pool of labour by having women sew garments in their homes for piecework wages. In time, factory work won out over the unsupervised sweatshops where lower-class women worked.

Childhood

By the end of the nineteenth century, a new science of child-rearing had emerged. During the nineteenth century, children became the centre of the European family; greater interest was placed on child-rearing practices and on how best to educate children. Consequently, among the middle class, breast-feeding by the mother — rather than by a wet nurse (another lactating woman) — became much more common and the practice of swaddling (tightly wrapping infants in blankets to restrict movement) came to an end. By the mid-nineteenth century, the first pieces of social legislation aimed at the welfare of children were being passed. In France, a law was passed in 1841 limiting the hours of factory work for children. Despite its relative ineffectiveness as legislation, it was a symbolic move toward recognizing the need to protect children.

Birth remained a home event during the nineteenth century, although increasingly the well-to-do were employing the help of a male doctor for the delivery, rather than the traditional midwife. Giving birth in a hospital was still considered a sign of poverty or of illegitimacy. The hospital was where unwed country girls went to give birth before abandoning their babies. Following the birth of a baby, the father announced the arrival of the child at the town hall, thus welcoming the child to the family as well as the community.

Prior to the 1800s, childhood was seen as a long stretch of ill-defined time that differed little for boys or girls. By the nineteenth century, childhood was divided into three distinct phases: early childhood (up to age eight), childhood proper, and adolescence. In the child's early years, the task of raising and nurturing was left solely to the mother, since in early childhood all infants were treated as female. Children of both sexes under the age of four wore dresses and long hair and played with dolls that tended to be androgynous. The early education of children was left to the mother.

By the time children reached the age of eight, they were believed to have reached the age of reason. At this point in their lives, young middle-class boys could expect their fathers to begin playing a more active role, sometimes acting as tutors. Middle-class daughters could seldom expect their fathers to play a significant role in their education. By the age of 15, most middle-class daughters were sent away to boarding schools to complete their moral education and prepare them for social life. Boys were often sent to boarding schools at an even earlier age. There they endured barracks-like conditions as they prepared to pass the *baccalaureate*, the distinguishing mark of the bourgeoisie.

WESTERN ART OF THE NINETEENTH CENTURY

Realism

In striking contrast to the romantic qualities of art during the first half of the nineteenth century, the art of the second half of the nineteenth century attempted to portray life more realistically. Interest in science and technology overcame interest in spirituality. Art now searched for truth through the recording of factual rather than personal experience.

Like other artists of his day, Jean-François Millet often painted rural and working class people. This picture, called *Angelus* (1857) shows a poor farm family praying. What impression of the people do you get?

Daumier frequently pictured the working class. How do you think he felt about the people in this painting, called *The Third Class Carriage* (1862).

Jean-François Millet

Jean-François Millet (1814–1875) is known for his depiction of working people, especially peasants. Just as English romantic poet William Wordsworth focussed on the working class in poems such as *The Solitary Reaper* or *The Leech Gatherer*, so Millet conveys a sense of admiration for his subjects through his sculpture-like figures. His work also reflects the socialist ideas associated with the political climate of the time.

Honoré Daumier

Concern with the social problems of the time is also reflected in the work of Honoré Daumier (1808–1879) who, like William Hogarth in the preceding century, used satire to point out social ills. Daumier made no attempt to glorify the lower classes; rather, he depicted them as he saw them: victims of an industrialized society that was slowly dehumanizing the masses. Daumier was also a skilled draughtsman and caricaturist, whose subjects included many of the leading politicians, lawyers, and doctors of the day.

Gustave Courbet

Art had become more concerned with concrete problems than abstract ideas. Two of the great realists who tackled some of these social and aesthetic problems were Gustave Courbet (1819–1877) and Edouard Manet. Courbet represented French society as he saw it. His dark, sombre canvases make no attempt to beautify the French landscape or the French people. He was vilified by both the public and the critics, who felt his work was too ordinary, too crude in subject matter and technique. The lower and middle classes were becoming a political factor and there were those who felt that artists such as Courbet were promoting the working-class cause. His work seems to parallel some of the realist novels of the day, by Balzac, Zola and Dickens.

Courbet's monumental *Burial at Ornans* best exemplifies his vigorous style. He does not seek to astonish or entertain; he makes no concession to the viewer. Courbet simply depicts a small-town funeral in its simplicity of forms and content.

Edouard Manet

Courbet's defiance of popular tastes led the way for the art movement known as Impressionism. Edouard Manet (1832–1883) was one of the founders of this movement. Manet's art also shocked and disturbed the public. He achieved a new perspective on life: Through the use of bright, heavy planes of light, he was able to achieve a detached, distanced view of humanity and nature. His realism is also related to photography: Manet makes no conscious concessions to beauty, yet his works are striking for their unusual composition and subject matter.

Manet sometimes borrowed subjects from other schools of painting. He took a Renaissance work, *Fête Champêtre*, by the Venetian painter Giorgione, and depicted the same figures, not in a pastoral setting, but in a Parisian park. When some viewers considered this work pornographic, Manet would refer them to its predecessor in the Louvre. Manet's bold experimentation with subject and form, and his movement away from the traditional toward the abstract, laid the foundation for what we call modern art. He helped smooth the way for the Impressionists, the next movement identified in Western art of the late nineteenth century.

The Impressionists

The Impressionists were artists who tried to depict contemporary life through artistic impressions that reflected an interest in science and the study of light. Like the romantic poets, Impressionists saw themselves as innovators. Indeed, each Impressionist painter is unique in style, yet has important qualities in common with other Impressionists. Some of the great artists of this school included Auguste Renoir, Edgar Degas, Camille Pissarro, Mary Cassatt, and Claude Monet. Here we focus on the work of Claude Monet.

The Burial at Ornans (1849-50) by Courbet measures 3.14m x 6.63 m. Why might the artist have chosen to paint this seemingly mundane scene on such a large scale?

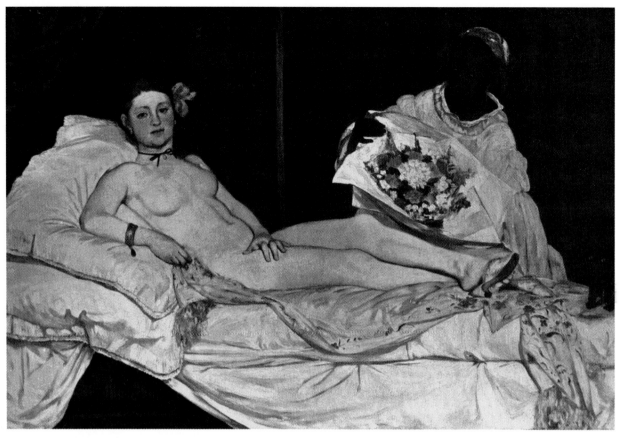

Edouard Manet's *Olympia* (1865) treats an old subject in a new way. Many found this painting offensive because of its overtly sexual connotations. What does this reaction tell you about late nineteenth-century morality?

Claude Monet

Claude Monet's (1840–1926) work combines an obsessive intellectual interest in the properties of light with an emotional interest in the sensations created by those properties. Thus, even his most scientific observations of the qualities and passage of light are infused with deep feeling. In an attempt to record an accurate perception of light, Monet painted some of his subjects, such as the Rouen Cathedral or haystacks in a field, over and over again (up to 40 times). Each time, Monet painted from the same point of view, but under the changing conditions of light and atmosphere in each instant. Monet also experimented with colour by placing complementary colours together using thick, textured brush strokes to create the effect of shadows.

Monet spent the last years of his life painting hundreds of pictures of the garden at his house in Giverny. The huge canvases of his water lily garden are records of pure sensation, the culmination and refinement of Monet's aesthetic vision. He lovingly recorded the colour, light, and texture of the lake in his garden and the trees, plants, and skies reflected there. These works share the essential character of Impressionism but, like the art of other Impressionists, Monet's work is completely his own.

It was this painting by Monet, called *Impression Sunrise* (1873), that gave the Impressionists their name. What makes this painting impressionistic?

Post-Impressionists

Georges Seurat

The Impressionist movement in its pure form was short-lived; however, many artists responded to Impressionist art and broke new ground. Georges Seurat (1859–1891) took a strictly intellectual approach to painting. He practised pointillism, a highly disciplined technique in which the artist uses small dots of colour to create larger forms. This technique was based in Seurat's scientific studies of light and colour, as many artists at this time made use of new ideas about the psychological and scientific aspects of colour.

Sunday Afternoon on the Island of La Grande Jatte (1844-46, 2 m x 3 m) by Georges Seurat. Seurat studied scientific theories of optics and colour. This scene of fashionable people out for a stroll is made up entirely of tiny dots of colour. What types of people are shown?

During the 1880s, Cezanne painted many scenes of the countryside of southern France. He would paint the same landscape several times, exploring shapes, light, colours, and perspective.

Paul Cezanne

Paul Cézanne (1839–1906) was also concerned with conveying the underlying order of nature through his art. His was a classical approach, as he used geometrical forms to create solid, monumental forms. His favourite subject for his experiments with colour and light was the still-life genre, where colour does not move and shift. Cézanne painted in solid colours to enhance the solidity of his shapes. He, like Monet, painted scenes familiar to him such as Mt. Ste.-Victoire, a mountain near his home. Cézanne began painting in a realistic manner, eventually removing all incidental detail in order to reveal the elemental shape and mass of the scene before him.

This painting is called *"Stary Night Over the Rhone"* (1888), by Vincent Van Gogh. How does it make you feel?

Vincent van Gogh

In contrast to Cézanne's intellectual approach is the art of Vincent van Gogh (1853–1890). A popular mythology has grown up around this artist, most of it debatable, if not completely untrue. Do van Gogh's paintings reveal a tormented artist? There can be little doubt of this, given van Gogh's documented history of mental illness and his suicide at the young age of 37. Van Gogh's brushwork, in particular, shows a restless, almost frenzied spirit, but it is the artist's colours that attract people the most. Every generation since the artist's death has been captivated by works such as *Starry Night*, the many paintings of sunflowers and irises, and portraits of the artist himself and his friends. In van Gogh's highly expressive colour and textured brushwork, we experience the personal vision of a complex, intelligent, but tortured human being.

Review, Reflect, Respond

1. How did the second Industrial Revolution contribute to socialist responses in countries such as Germany, France, and Britain?

2. How did V. I. Lenin adapt Marxist theory to make it more practical in the Russian situation?

3. How did the ideas of Nietzche and Darwin challenge the foundations of Western art and society?

LITERATURE IN THE NINETEENTH CENTURY

As England grew prosperous through the mid-nineteenth century, idealism changed to practicality. Just as we saw a shift in the painting of the late nineteenth century from romanticism to realism, we now see a similar shift in the literature of the same period. The literature of the nineteenth century reflects a deep desire to solve the serious problems facing the new, prosperous industrial age.

The literature also explored the conflict associated with religion, science, and the negative effects of prosperity and territorial expansion (i.e., imperialism). Essayists such as Thomas Carlyle (1795–1881), Thomas Macaulay (1800–1859), John Henry Newman (1801–1890), and Thomas Huxley (1825–1895) examined history, science, and education in their works. Theirs were not romantic, ideal explorations of the philosophy of these disciplines; they tackled concrete, practical problems.

Victorian poetry was also concerned with artistically exploring difficult social and moral realities. Victorian poetic structures often reflected the structures of arguments or discussions, yet these poets could also magically transport the reader to other worlds to explore again the age-old problems of love.

Alfred Lord Tennyson

The poet whose work perhaps most exemplifies the Victorian era is Alfred Lord Tennyson (1809–1892). He is best known for his long poem *In Memoriam*, which encapsulates, in form and content, the general tenor of Victorian literature. The work is an extended elegy that records his reaction to the death of his close friend Arthur Hallam.

Tennyson was also interested in myth: *The Lady of Shalott* tells one of the Arthurian legends from a psychological perspective. *Ulysses*, a dramatic monologue, looks to Greek mythology for its inspiration. The narrator is the old Ulysses, who mourns the loss of his past, adventurous life and wants to go out again and risk all he has to undertake new adventures. These lines from the poem are like a credo of the Victorian age:

> One equal temper of heroic hearts,
> Made weak by time and fate, but strong in will
> To strive, to seek to find, and not to yield.[2]

Robert Browning and Elizabeth Barrett Browning

Tennyson's contemporaries were the Brownings: Elizabeth (1806–1881) and Robert (1812–1889). Elizabeth is best known for her *Sonnets from the Portuguese*, a collection of 44 sonnets written to Robert during their courtship. Robert Browning's poetry reflects typical Victorian concerns, but he is perhaps the livelier of the two poets. He perfected a style of poem known as "dramatic monologue." *My Last Duchess* and *The Bishop Orders His Tomb* are among the most celebrated of this genre. These monologues are far more than clever poetic speeches. They are character revelations of the self-conscious narrator, who uses the monologue to tell his own story.

WEB CONNECTION

www.mcgrawhill.ca/links/legacy

Go to the site above to find out more about nineteenth-century English literature.

Charles Dickens

The novels of Charles Dickens (1812–1870) provide us with a series of revealing social commentaries. Dickens, through his complex plots and vivid characterizations, criticized the social injustices to which the poor and working classes were subjected in industrial England. His novels take place in his own time, primarily in urban settings such as the city of London. Some of the best known of Dickens's novels include: *Oliver Twist*, *David Copperfield*, *Great Expectations*, *The Pickwick Papers*, and *A Christmas Carol*.

Thomas Hardy

The novels of Thomas Hardy (1840–1928) focussed on life in rural England, usually Dorset County in the south. Hardy explored humanity's passions and problems, often through the idea of a hero or heroine struggling helplessly against the hand of fate. Hardy was also one of the first novelists to explore human sexuality, specifically female sexuality, as a theme in novels such as *Tess of the D'Ubervilles*, *Far from the Madding Crowd*, and *The Mayor of Casterbridge*.

Émile Zola and Honoré de Balzac

The great French novelists were also exploring similar issues in their works. Émile Zola (1840–1902) and Honoré de Balzac (1799–1850) deplored the hypocrisy and degeneracy of the upper middle class and aristocracy of the nineteenth century. Their works are condemnations of the abuse of wealth and power at the expense of the common people. Like the painters Courbet and Manet, they sought to express truth through realism. They not only portrayed social evils, but also presented deep psychological insights into the human condition. Zola's works include *Germinal* and *Nana*. Among his more than 40 novels are *La comédie humaine* and *Le père Goriot*.

The sculptor Auguste Rodin worked on many different versions of this and other portrayals of the prodigious French writer Honoré de Balzac from 1892 to 1897. The bronze sculpture stands nearly 3m high.

George Bernard Shaw and Henrik Ibsen

Drama also became a venue for social commentary. Two prolific and powerful playwrights were George Bernard Shaw (1856–1950) of Ireland and Henrik Ibsen (1828–1906) of Norway. Shaw satirized society through his comedies, many of which were full of black humour. Among Shaw's plays are *Major Barbara*, *Pygmalion*, and *Caesar and Cleopatra*. Ibsen was a serious counterpart to Shaw. Like Balzac's novels, Ibsen's plays, such as *An Enemy of the People*, *Hedda Gabler* and *The Master Builder*, explored the darker aspects of human nature.

When the nineteenth century came to a close, there was a period of stagnation in literature. Perhaps this was due to the effect of the political problems facing Europe. Perhaps the Victorian writers dominated the literary scene too powerfully to allow any new creative ideas to emerge until the likes of T. S. Eliot and Virginia Woolf emerged in the early twentieth century. Nevertheless, the nineteenth century produced some of the great works of the English language, many still studied and loved, and still an inspiration for writers today.

George Bernard Shaw (1856–1950), was a playwright and social critic.

Reflections

The effects of industrialization and urbanization transformed the workplace and the home during the nineteenth century. Change was far less rapid and revolutionary in rural areas, where the often forgotten peasantry witnessed slow change and little improvement in their standard of living. While political theorists such as Karl Marx and scientists such as Charles Darwin were reshaping the political and intellectual landscape of Europe, a more subtle yet equally profound change was occurring in the home. Family relationships were being redefined, the approach to child-rearing was changing, and a new morality was reshaping values and mores: The middle class established a clear predominance in European culture. Women were beginning to press their demand for equal participation in society. Europe was also on the verge of seeing an end to the perpetual poverty that had afflicted the vast majority of the population in previous centuries. Soon, most homes would be properly heated and ventilated, and an increased awareness of the importance of good hygiene would help to reduce the threat of disease. The nineteenth century had brought European society into a modern industrial age. The century that followed would witness change at an even more rapid pace, bringing with it its own unique problems and rewards.

Chapter Review

Chapter Summary

In this chapter, you have seen:

- how and why an understanding of cause-and-effect relationships is such an essential tool for historical analysis
- the impact of modern Western thought on economic, social, and political developments in the West
- how family structures changed during the nineteenth century
- that social organization and social relationships were altered by the advent of industrialization and urbanization in Europe

Reviewing the Significance of Key People, Concepts, and Events (Knowledge and Understanding)

1. Understanding the history of the late nineteenth century in Europe requires a knowledge of the following concepts, events, and people and an understanding of their significance in the shaping of the history of the world in the later half of the twentieth century. Select and explain two from each column.

Concepts	Events	People
nationalism	Crimean War	Madame Curie
Socialism	Dreyfus Affair	Otto von Bismarck
realism	Paris Commune	Giuseppe Garibaldi
imperialism	second industrial revolution	Giuseppe Mazzini
Kulturkampf		Emmeline Pankhurst
feminism		Friedrich Nietzsche
conservatism		Claude Monet

2. The impact of the Industrial Revolution extended well beyond the factories. In a chart or Venn diagram, explain the impact of the Industrial Revolution on the rise of white-collar work, shopping habits and the retail industry, and changes to daily life.

Doing History: Thinking About the Past (Thinking/Inquiry)

3. The nineteenth century has been called an age of transition for European society — a transition which paved the way from aristocracies to democracies, from elite culture to mass culture, and from cottage industries to industrial factories. Defend or refute the view of the nineteenth century as an age of transition using examples from this chapter.

4. In 1851 the editor of *The Economist*, James Wilson, reflected upon the progress made by England during the first half of the nineteenth century. He concluded his article "The First Half of the Nineteenth Century: Progress of the Nation and the Race" with the following proclamation:

> On no account has this country greater ground for self-congratulation than on the vast improvement which is observable in the CHARACTER and tone of feeling among PUBLIC MEN ... Statesmen have now learned to feel not merely that they are playing a noble game ... but that they are called upon to guide a glorious vessel through fluctuating shoals, and sunken rocks, and storms of terrific violence.

Choose a nineteenth-century politician mentioned in this chapter. Does this person fit Wilson's assessment of the nineteenth-century politician? Defend your answer.

Applying Your Learning (Application)

5. In his book *Darwin, Marx, Wagner: Critique of a Heritage*, Jacques Barzun explains: "To name Darwin, Marx, and Wagner as the three great prophets of our destinies is but to recognize a state of fact." Barzun claims that "should you open any book dealing with the problems of our time, "you will find Darwin and Marx repeatedly coupled as the great pair whose conceptions revolutionized the modern world." Do you agree with the importance Barzun attaches to the ideas of Karl Marx and Charles Darwin, not only to their age but also to ours? Support your answer with historical evidence.

6. Compare Georges Seurat's *La Grande Jatte* (page 323) with Vincent van Gogh's *The Potato Eaters*, which shows a rural family eating potatoes. After examining each painting, bring the scenes to life with a dialogue between characters in the paintings. Use evidence presented in this chapter as the basis of your dialogues. The dialogues should show how daily life differed for the wealthy and the working classes.

The Potato Eaters (1885)

Communicating Your Learning (Communication)

7. Select a CD in your collection and redraw the cover in the style of either Impressionism or post-Impressionism. Once you have completed the image, write a one paragraph explanation of why you believe this style of art does or does not suit the CD cover. Be sure to include in your paragraph response a clear understanding of the reasons artists of the late nineteenth century chose to work in these styles.

8. Imagine you have been commissioned by the WSPU TO WRITE *The Women's Manifesto*. Your task is to capture clearly, succinctly and with passion the goals and demands of the women's movement in the nineteenth century. The manifesto should outline women's grievances as the foundation for both the movement and the manifesto.

Imperialism, Colonialism, and Resistance in the Nineteenth Century

CHAPTER EXPECTATIONS

By the end of this chapter, you will be able to:

- *demonstrate an understanding of the concepts and processes associated with imperialism and of its role in shaping present world relations*

- *explain how and why an understanding of cause-and-effect relationships is an essential tool for historical analysis*

- *describe key conflicts and controversies that arose as a result of resistance to the assertive spread of modern Western ideas*

- *demonstrate an understanding of key forms and styles of artistic expression throughout the world in the nineteenth century*

The image of a non-Western woman, a Tahitian from the South Pacific, as pictured by nineteenth-century French artist Paul Gauguin. *Woman with A Mango* (1897). Do you think the artist was trying for visual accuracy?

The relationship of Western Europe to the rest of the world in the nineteenth century was paradoxical. Within Europe, the enlightenment ideal of democracy and equality continued to spread, while in the colonies abroad, rigid hierarchical power structures prevailed. In the legislatures of the European capitals, the slave trade had been abolished, but slavery continued to flourish in the colonies. The first half of the century saw the retreat of most European powers — with the exception of Great Britain — from imperialist expansion, yet in the final decades, imperialism was revived with more vigour than ever before. What were the forces that fuelled these changes in the nineteenth century, and what factors maintained the continuity of centuries-old modes of thinking and action? What was the legacy of imperialism — economically, politically, and culturally? How does history record the attitudes of Europeans and those of its "conquered peoples" during this time? What role did people living in the colonies play in achieving their independence? These and other questions will be addressed throughout this chapter.

Imperialism is a belief in the desirability of acquiring colonies and dependencies, or extending a country's influence through trade, diplomacy and other means. Although traditionally historians have tackled the subject of imperialism in the nineteenth century as a unique phenomenon with its own reasons for existence, the idea of colonial conquest was certainly not new. Those with greater power have, throughout history, sought to conquer and dominate both weaker neighbours and entire nations oceans away. In this century, however, imperialism took on a new flavour, as it encompassed more territory than it ever had before and spanned almost the entire globe.

KEY CONCEPTS AND EVENTS

East India Company
Opium Wars
Berlin Conference (1884)
Indian Mutiny of 1857
racism
Boer War
Fugitive Slave Act
Emancipation Proclamation
caudillos
Indian National Congress
Pan-African Conference
Russo-Japanese War

KEY PEOPLE

J. A. Hobson
King Leopold II
Toussaint L'Ouverture
Sam Sharpe
Simón Bolívar
Sun Yat-sen

Wit and Wisdom

Revolt is the only way out of the colonial situation, and the colonized realizes it sooner or later... For the colonial condition cannot be adjusted to; like an iron collar it can only be broken.[1]

Albert Memmi, *The Colonizer and the Colonized* (1965)

TIME LINE: IMPERIALISM, COLONIALISM, AND RESISTANCE

Haitian Revolution	1792	
	1810	Argentina and Paraguay gain independence
Venezuela gains independence	1811	
	1818–1825	Northern and western South America liberated by Simón Bolívar
Mexico gains independence	1821	
	1822	Brazil gains independence
Jamaican Slave Revolt	1831	
	1834	Slavery abolished in the British Empire
Opium Wars in China; Treaty of Nanking	1839–1842	
	1857	Indian Mutiny
American Civil War	1861–1865	
	1882	British occupation of Egypt
Berlin Conference organizes imperialism in Africa	1884	
	1896	Battle of Adowa (Ethiopia)
Spanish-American War	1898	
	1899–1902	Boer War
Boxer Rebellion	1900	
	1904–1905	Russo-Japanese War

Not to scale.

IMPERIALISM IN THE NINETEENTH CENTURY

European colonization did not occur at an even pace throughout the century. From the American Revolution in 1776, until 1870, informed political opinion expressed opposition to formal acquisition of colonies, preferring informal trade relationships instead. In 1800, Europe and its overseas possessions constituted 55 percent of the world land mass, and, by 1878, that proportion had risen to 67 percent. European colonization intensified very markedly in the last two decades of the nineteenth century, so that, by 1914, Europe and its possessions accounted for 84 percent of the world's land mass.

Within the evolving, Western-dominated world system, a significant shift occurred in the second half of the nineteenth century. After 1870, and even more dramatically after 1885, there was a remarkable increase in the European acquisition of colonial territories in the South Pacific, Asia, and Africa. In 1870 about 10 percent of Africa had been colonized, whereas by 1895, approximately 90 percent had come under European colonial control. Earlier in the nineteenth century, imperial powers had preferred the techniques of informal empire, in which commercial and political relations were established with the indigenous elite, and formal military conquest and colonization were thought unnecessary. After 1870 European powers began to rely more on colonization or formal empire, than on informal economic ties. This has been dubbed the period of "new imperialism."

Prior to 1815, there were no comparable examples of conquered territories in Asia or Africa. In these continents, Europeans had established commercial relations, usually through strategic coastal enclaves, where indigenous merchants traded local products for European goods. Formal political conquest of territories and populations was limited. In Asia, exceptions were

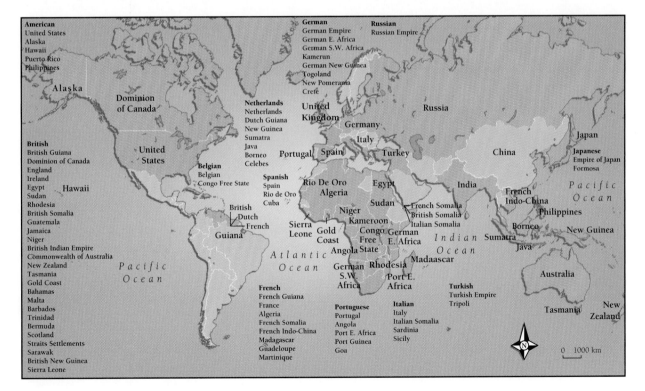

■ FIGURE 9.1 Colonial Empires
Colonialism in the past as shown on this map was highly visible. What types of colonialism, though less visible, are taking place today?

the Dutch-held East Indies, coveted for their spices and other tropical crops, and British-held India, where the East India Company engaged in trade, administered the law, and collected taxes in conquered provinces. Africa's interior was still an undiscovered mystery to Europeans, who had only established slave-trading posts in West Africa and a small settlement at the Cape of Good Hope. In the South Pacific, although trading links existed, British settlement began in Australia only in 1788, with the establishment of penal colonies. Until 1870 Britain had remained the dominant imperialist power. Although it lost significant territory when the United States gained independence in 1776, Britain retained control — formal or informal — in British North America (Canada), Latin America, Australia and New Zealand, the Indian subcontinent, and various parts of Africa. It is literally true that at this time, "the sun never set on the British Empire."

New Imperialism in Asia and the Indies

As the nineteenth century advanced, European nations began to rely less on informal empire and more on formal political control of their colonies. In Asia the British extended their possessions from India into neighbouring Burma (now Myanmar), the Malay Peninsula, and Singapore. Similarly, the Dutch enlarged their formal political jurisdiction in the East Indies, and the French colonized Indochina from the 1850s to the 1880s.

From 1870 to 1914, the other major European powers joined the race to acquire colonies and exert their influence over indigenous peoples. They accomplished this at a remarkable rate, annexing 240 000 square miles per year. In Asia, the British established formal control in India and annexed Burma; the

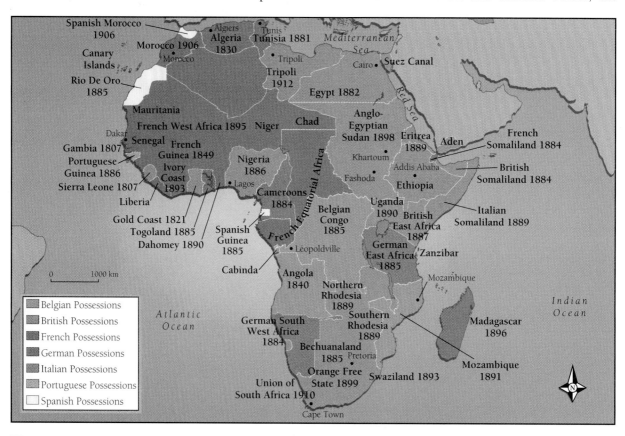

■ **FIGURE 9.2** Africa: Colonial Possessions
The legend on this map speaks to the "possessions" of various nations. How else might this legend be worded?

French took Cochin China (now Vietnam) and Laos; and the Dutch consolidated their power in what is now Indonesia. The Pacific Islands were also divided up among the great powers. The United States, having driven the Spanish out in 1898, exerted greater control in the Americas, annexing Puerto Rico, Hawaii and half of Mexico; it also annexed the Philippines.

China was not formally occupied by a European power but essentially lost control of trade within its own borders as a result of the Opium Wars. The British, French, Germans, Russians and Americans, by and large, controlled trade in China. The Manchu dynasty was pressured by rival European and American interests, and internally by warring factions, until it fell in the revolution of 1911. Japan was the great exception in Asia. It was militarily vulnerable to Western naval superiority, and the arrival of the Americans in 1853 exposed the weakness of the shogunate. Following the Meiji Restoration in 1868, Japan initiated its own program of industrial development and political reform. In this way, Japan not only managed to preserve its autonomy but also, by the 1890s, had become an imperial power in its own right.

The Boers, descendents of Dutch settlers in South Africa, fiercely defended their land during the Boer War (1899-1902). Do you think the partition of Africa was fair?

New Imperialism in Africa

The greatest scramble for control occurred in Africa, which had, until the 1870s, remained largely unconquered — and undiscovered — by Europeans. Beyond the trading outposts and forts established on the west coast, the two principal areas of European settlement in Africa were the Dutch colony at the southern Cape of Good Hope, and French settlement in Algeria, which had begun in the 1830s. During the Napoleonic Wars, the British took the Cape from the Dutch and, until the 1880s, fought a series of local wars to establish a secure frontier against the independent Dutch settlers (the Boers) pushing north in their "Great Trek," and the southward-moving Bantu-speaking Africans, led by the formidable military force of the Zulus. During the 40 years preceding World War I, however, the African subcontinent was almost entirely parcelled out among European nations, with little regard for natural boundaries of geography,

tribes or lineages. From the 1880s onward, the European powers engaged in a frantic competition for colonies in Africa.

The key political event in the race for colonization in Africa was the Berlin Conference of 1884–1885. Bismarck called together representatives of 15 nations to deal with rival colonial claims in Africa, especially with the creation of the Congo Free State by King Leopold II of Belgium. Ignoring the rights of existing African kingdoms and peoples altogether, European powers claimed the right to acquire inland territories by expansion from existing coastal possessions. To avoid dominance by a single state or war between rival colonial powers, the Conference agreed that possession involved more than a "paper partition" based on claims made over a map; they agreed that possession should involve effective occupation of the land and control over the people. After 1885 Africa was swiftly partitioned among the rival European powers.

British soldiers serving in South Africa in 1900. A reconnaissance balloon flies overhead, watching for oncoming Boers. Why were the British fighting the Boers?

The colonizing powers moved outward from their established centres in West and South Africa and from the strategically sensitive area of the eastern Mediterranean, in Suez, Egypt and the Sudan. Once the European powers had established their military and political presence, white traders and settlers followed in the late nineteenth and early twentieth centuries in East and Central Africa, principally Kenya, the Rhodesias (North now Zimbabwe and South now Zambia), and Mozambique, and in the west and south in the Congo, Angola and South African colonies. The discovery of diamond and gold deposits in South Africa made that region important strategically and economically, and the ongoing conflict between the British and the Boers (the descendants of the Dutch settlers in South Africa) led to the Boer War, 1899–1902.

By the end of this period, the British were in both West Africa (Gold Coast and Nigeria) and East Africa (Kenya and Uganda). They also occupied Egypt, the Sudan and Somalia. The French maintained control over a large territory from North to Central Africa. The Portuguese controlled Angola and Mozambique. The Germans, the Italians, and King Leopold II of Belgium also seized control of colonies on the continent.

The Partition of Africa

The partition of Africa is a textbook case of late-nineteenth-century imperialism. The events that brought political and economic imperatives into action occurred not in Europe but in Africa itself. From a British perspective, Africa represented a strategic rather than an economic interest, in that the continent's shoreline was part of the route to India. There were areas of vital concern along this important trade route: the Suez Canal, Egypt, the Red Sea, the Horn of Africa and the Cape of Good Hope, which was a naval and fuelling station.

Britain had the largest established empire and dominated the route to India by defending strategic outposts. This aroused rivalry with other European powers such as France, which had its own interests in Suez, Egypt, North Africa and West Africa. The Germans also sought to establish colonies in southern and East Africa, and King Leopold II of Belgium sought recognition for his Congo Free State. In addition, colonial interests and settlers, including private companies with private armies in West Africa, French colonists in Algeria, and British and Boer settlers in southern Africa, encroached upon African and Arab territory, sparking wars of resistance. These competing interests put strategically sensitive areas of Africa in turmoil. Trying to contend with this unrest, the colonial powers were drawn deeper and deeper into Africa, partitioning the continent at first, and later formally making colonies out of areas of influence.

The turmoil in the periphery was itself a product of the informal influence of the Western economic presence, and the political and economic needs of the colonial powers drew them further into these conflicts. In the frantic rush to obtain colonies in the last two decades of the nineteenth century, European powers intervened in Africa, Asia and the Pacific, not so much in quest of immediate gain as out of fear that a rival power might gain future strategic or economic benefit. Having acquired the colonies on the premise of the prospect of gain, the colonial powers, once they had secured effective occupation, made every effort to make the colony pay back. At this point in the process, the lives of the peoples of Australasia, Asia, Africa and the Americas began to be transformed in new and more substantial ways, and often by force.

CHANGE AND CONTINUITY: CAUSES OF IMPERIALISM

Unequal Power Relations

Traditionally, historians have sought to explain the "new imperialism" of the late nineteenth century as if it had been a unique phenomenon requiring special explanation — especially since it seemed that the great powers were suspending active acquisition of colonies during the first three quarters of the century. Some scholars, however, believe that imperialism is the natural tendency of strong political powers. History is full of examples of peoples — the Greeks, Romans, Mongols, the Ming dynasty, the Ottoman Turks, the Aztecs and the Incas, to name but a few — who tried and succeeded in dominating their weaker neighbours.

The level of success of a dominant power has largely been attributed to its level of technological advancement. Those with more advanced military technology and methods of production have tended to dominate. This is no different from the pattern seen in the nineteenth century. Britain dominated the world of empire building for the first three quarters of the century, while it remained ahead of the other European powers in reaping the rewards of the Industrial Revolution. Its manufacturing and military technologies were far more advanced than those of its neighbours. But, by the end of the century, the countries of the rest of Europe had begun to catch up, and they too joined the race to acquire colonies and build their empires. According to this argument, the "new imperialism" of

the late nineteenth century was simply yet another example of the consequences of unequal power.

Nationalism and Geopolitics

It is useful to understand other causes of imperialism that are generally cited to explain the events of the nineteenth century. This will help build a clearer picture of the world prior to World War I. The explanation for this "new imperialism" has generated much historical literature, partly because the topic remains central to the relationship of the wealthier Western industrial world to the poorer, non-Western, non-industrial world. At the centre of this political debate is the question of whether the new imperialism is a political phenomenon involving the extension of the power of Western nation-states, or an economic phenomenon creating new forms of dependency and exploitation in developing nations.

According to this Eurocentric view, the primary motive for colonization was political. Governments, encouraged by the emerging sense of nationalism and the chauvinism of a mass electorate, enhanced their power and prestige by possessing colonies. Colonies also provided them with a "bargaining chip" at the tables of international conferences. Colonies often also carried with them geopolitical significance. They were important because of their place on the map. For example, the British established control in Egypt in order to pre-serve control of the Suez Canal, which was vital to maintaining a quick trade route to India.

The actual defence of colonial acquisitions was rarely a matter of politics alone. Proponents of empire claimed that the superiority of industrial civilization gave Europeans the right to take over territories. In *The Control of the Tropics* (1898), Benjamin Kidd, a British popular writer on imperialism, stressed that Europe was under an obligation to develop the tropics as "a trust for civilization." He claimed that: "If our civilization has any right there at all, it is because it represents higher ideals of humanity, a higher type of social order." Kidd and other advocates of empire assumed that Western industrial civilization was superior, and that a kind of trusteeship existed in which colonies should be developed for the benefit of the colonizing power and for the subordinate colonized peoples.

The rival Eurocentric view of the new imperialism, the theory of economic imperialism, challenged the claims of Kidd and other advocates of empire. This theory, proposed by liberal English economist J. A. Hobson in 1902, and later used by the Russian statesman Lenin, argued that the primary motive for empire was economic. The main benefactors of imperialism were not the colonized peoples or the White populations of Europe or North America. According to Hobson and Lenin, colonies were acquired as fields for investment, at the urging of capitalists with surplus wealth. These investors, some of whom owned popular newspapers and had an influence on politicians, promoted imperialism to get the state to acquire territories and protect their overseas investments. Lenin identified this form of imperialism with an advanced or monopoly stage of capitalism and predicted that competition for colonies would eventually lead to war and revolution. Like the political explanation of imperialism, which stresses the role of European diplomacy, this economic theory of imperialism is also Eurocentric, in that it focusses on the economies of advanced industrial nations and pays little attention to the economies in the non-Western world.

UNCO-OPERATIVE COLONIES

China

Contemporary explanations of imperialism have again shifted the focus away from metropolitan centres in Europe and North America to events in the periphery: in Australasia, Asia, and Africa. According to this view, the informal free-trade imperialism of the early nineteenth century relied on relationships with collaborators drawn from merchant and political elites within the indigenous populations. As these economic relationships developed, Western influences became stronger; movements to

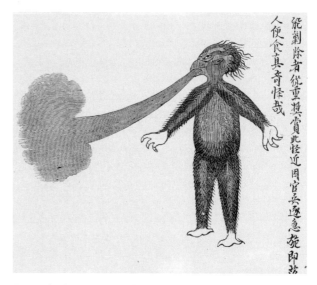

During the Opium Wars, a Chinese artist, perhaps under the influence of the drug, saw a Western soldier as a hairy, fire-breathing creature. Is there another explanation for this depiction?

resist this influence began to develop and networks of collaboration broke down. In order to restore the now necessary economic and political relationships, Western colonial powers resorted to force and imposed formal colonial rule by military conquest.

Many people today assume that free trade is within the natural order, and that economic interests are best served without government regulation. Yet, free trade was a form of commercial relationship created, sometimes by force, by the European powers, chiefly Great Britain. For example, although Western countries wanted access to the enormous market of China, the Chinese were relatively self-sufficient, and the Manchu dynasty discouraged Western trade. To remedy this situation, the British created a demand in China for opium, a drug traded by the British from India and Southeast Asia. When the Chinese government sought to control this trade, the British intervened militarily to defend it as free trade.

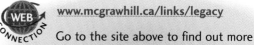

www.mcgrawhill.ca/links/legacy

Go to the site above to find out more about the Opium Wars.

Through the Opium Wars, from 1839 to 1842, the British succeeded in securing their demands for trade and took control of the important trading centre of Hong Kong in the treaty of Nanking of 1842. In response to increased Western influence and trade — and to the internal anarchy of Chinese politics — the anti-monarchist Taiping rebellion erupted from 1850 to 1864. European military forces intervened in support of the Manchu dynasty and helped crush the rebellion, thus winning further privileges for Western traders. In this way, the policy of free trade imposed by Western military force brought China within the informal imperialism of Western power and provoked Chinese resistance to the alien influences on their society.

India: A Case Study

In other instances, the breakdown of collaborative relationships led to the imposition of formal imperial authority. In India the British had been slowly increasing their influence and control since the early 1600s, when they established their first trading post. The function of a British firm called the East India Company was initially only trade, but gradually, over the course of some 200 years, the Company forged alliances with local rulers who were involved in political disputes and wars of succession. The British established a number of puppet governments by militarily and financially supporting a local contender for power, who would then rule according to their wishes and directly appoint British people to various positions of power. The British East India Company had secured an effective, if informal, economic control of the Indian subcontinent by the 1780s.

By means of their overwhelming influence, the British were changing the face of India in a number of ways. The agrarian structure was completely reformed; railways were introduced and transformed the movement of people and goods; the first telegraph lines were laid; and a national postal system was developed, creating new and far more efficient methods of communication.

Along with these progressive reforms, however, British influence also intruded upon many areas of Indian life that were resistant to change. The missionaries, preachers, and lay reformers who had followed the merchants into India succeeded in their attempt to introduce English-language education and, as a result, opened the doors to Western culture and Western ideas about religion and politics. The advent of English education sparked an ongoing internal debate between those who believed that it would pose a threat to the preservation of indigenous culture and those who supported the idea. Indian supporters of English education eventually were able to use their knowledge of English and Western philosophy to deal with the British on their own terms during later movements toward Indian independence.

Pleasures
AND PASTIMES

The Victorian era was notorious for the constraints placed on the pastimes of women. Young ladies who dared to participate in male sports such as target shooting or hunting were considered "fast" — exhibiting improper and unacceptable behaviour for a Victorian lady. Once British women moved with their husbands to the colonies, however, these constraints loosened, and they achieved a certain degree of freedom from the whispers of upper-class society that seemed to judge their every move. British women who accompanied their husbands to India, for example, wrote about roving about on horses in "gypsy fashion," of hunting and even of shooting tigers for sport. In Australia it was the lively (and bloody) kangaroo hunt that drew the attention of thrill-seeking women adventurers.

Concern that the British were slowly making inroads into the local culture and threatening the survival of age-old traditions and social systems escalated as the British implemented new social laws and introduced changes to the army. They had formally abolished the

Hindu practice of *sati*, whereby a widow chose or was required by her family and community to take her own life by throwing herself on the funeral pyre (cremation fire) of her husband. In 1856 the British passed a law that allowed Hindu widows to remarry — an unheard-of practice up to that time.

With respect to the army, the General Service Enlistment Act forced Indian soldiers (called *sepoys*) to accept service anywhere within the vast British Empire. This threatened to cause chaos within Indian society, since social behaviour among Hindus was, and to a lesser degree still is, governed by a rigid social system of castes. The caste system is a complex hereditary system of social hierarchy, which dictates everything from a person's marital prospects to occupation and eating habits. It establishes one's status in society — a status forfeited by those who deviate from accepted behaviour. One of these deviations was the act of "crossing the black waters," or leaving the Indian sub-continent to travel abroad. Thus, when the British required soldiers to accept service anywhere within the empire, they were undermining a basic element of Indian social structure.

The cumulative impact of Westernizing reforms in the economy, in administration, in the law, in education and in religion made Indians fearful of the loss of their rich, varied, and ancient traditions and values. The last straw was the introduction into the army of the new Enfield rifle. Soldiers had to bite the tip off the cartridges used in the rifles when loading and unloading. A rumour spread that the cartridges were smeared with animal fat, and so, if a *sepoy* forbidden by his religion to eat specific types of meat were to put the cartridges into his mouth, he would be violating one of the most sacred customs.

What historians would call the Mutiny of 1857 began when members of an army brigade refused to load their rifles. The British had the defiant soldiers imprisoned. The next day, three regiments rose in revolt while British officers were in church. They freed the prisoners, killed several officers, and marched on the capital, Delhi. In Delhi, the *sepoys* opened the gates for the mutineers and allowed them to bring in and restore to the throne a displaced Mogul ruler. News of the revolt spread and triggered revolts across the country. There was little organization and no common thrust to the rebellions, since they consisted of armies in revolt, peasants resentful for losing their land during agrarian reform, and others protesting excessive taxation. There was no real leadership, no unity, and no real effort made to drive the British out of India.

The British retaliated and the mutineers were put to death. Delhi was recaptured by British and Sikh troops, and battles continued in northern and central India until late 1858. The most important result of the mutiny was the Government of India Act passed by the British Parliament in 1858, which transferred all rights of the East India Company directly to the crown. The

THE CLEMENCY OF CANNING.

Governor-General. "WELL, THEN, THEY SHAN'T BLOW HIM FROM NASTY GUNS; BUT HE MUST PROMISE TO BE A GOOD LITTLE SEPOY."

A political cartoon satirizing British Prime Minister George Canning's attitude of clemency toward Indians who had been involved in the Mutiny of 1857. What is the point of satire?

British government formalized the control it had first exerted through a trading company. All decisions regarding the fate of the Indian people would now be made by the British parliament, in the name of Queen Victoria, the "Empress of India." In this way, a breakdown of existing forms of collaboration and the outbreak of resistance in the form of mutiny led the British to impose formal imperial control.

Jamaica

Developments in Jamaica showed a similar process at work. In 1865 conflict between Black peasants and White landowners over vacant land led to a riot in Morant Bay, where 18 people died. In response, Governor Edward John Eyre imposed martial law for six weeks, during which time 439 people were killed or executed, another 650 were flogged, and over 1 000 peasants' homes were burned. The brutality of the repression raised a public outcry in Britain, but the political repercussions of the rebellion were longer-lasting. In order to preserve Britain's imperial control and to defend the privileged status of White planters against the rising demands of the non-white middle class and peasantry, the elected legislative assembly was disbanded, and Jamaica returned to crown colony status. It would be ruled from London until 1884.

The preceding examples illustrate the theory that the cause of the new imperialism in the latter half of the nineteenth century was the breakdown in collaborative relationships in the colonies, leading European powers to impose imperial control in order to serve their economic interests.

THE LEGACY OF IMPERIALISM

In 1815 there was a striking contrast between the European world and the conquered lands of the Americas and dependent lands of Asia and Africa. In the Americas, conquest and disease had decimated the Amerindian population. The demographic structure was altered by voluntary migration of European settlers and by forced migration of African slaves. By 1815 the trend was clear. Growth in European settlement and capitalist forms of production pushed Native Americans, such as the Cheyenne and Arapahoe peoples, farther into the hinterland (eventually to reserves). Conflicts over land led to bloody wars, and Natives were forced into a dependent economic and political status. In Asia and Africa, imperial control also led to profound changes in the economic, political, social, and cultural lives of indigenous peoples.

The Economic Legacy

In Chapter Six, we began to explore the hypothesis that the foundation of poverty in developing nations today lies in the relationship of dependency and underdevelopment that developed over several centuries. The imperialism of the nineteenth century only furthered this dependent relationship by incorporating the colonies into the capitalist system, undermining indigenous agriculture and production and forcing local peoples into a cash economy.

The Industrial Revolution brought about a transformation in productive capacity and the distribution of wealth. Colonies had formerly served simply as sources of commodities, such as furs, fish, sugar, tobacco, coffee, spices, tea and precious metals. Now they began to represent potential markets for manufactured goods. This shift from commercial capitalism to industrial capitalism created greater differences in wealth, and it transformed relations between the colonizers and the colonized.

Under industrial capitalism and its doctrine of *laissez faire* (no government interference), the restraints of the colonial empires came under attack, and the new idea of free trade became the orthodox economic doctrine. During the globalization phase of the world economy, the policy of free trade took time to be introduced; not surprisingly, its main champion was Great Britain, the leading industrial power, possessing the largest empire.

In the eighteenth century, Britain imported cotton cloth produced by handloom weavers in India. When the cotton textile industry was established in new factories in England, the trade was reversed. In the early nineteenth century, under imposed conditions of free trade, Indian handloom weavers could not compete in price with British manufacturers of cotton cloth, so India became an importer of cotton textiles and an exporter of raw cotton. Under free trade, a form of informal imperialism, industrial societies became economically predominant and colonies in Asia, Africa, and the Americas became dependent sources of raw materials as well as markets for the manufactured goods of the metropolis.

Prior to the development of the dependent relationship of imperialism, most of the people in the non-Western world were involved in subsistence agriculture — farming primarily for themselves. Any surplus produced was generally handed over to whoever formed the ruling group within the local social structure. Imperialist powers succeeded in forcing Native peoples to change to producing agriculture for export. Europe had developed a taste for the foods discovered in the non-Western world, including sugar, cacao, wheat, meat, tea, coffee, coconuts, palm oil, rice, bananas and ground nuts. There was also a voracious appetite for other products such as tobacco, cotton, jute, rubber, wool, tin, gold, silver, bauxite and copper. The imperialist powers needed their colonies to supply raw materials to support the growth of industry in European cities.

This transformation of local production from a subsistence economy to an export economy had various effects. First, as more and more land was used to grow cash crops for export, these territories would become increasingly dependent on imports of both food and manufactured goods. This benefited the colonial powers by providing a large market for their products but had the adverse effect of creating dependency in the colony. In the middle of the eighteenth century, the level of industrialization of countries such as Great Britain, France, and Germany had been pretty much on par with that of China and India. But, over the next 150 years, not only did the industrialization of the European powers "take off," but, more tellingly, the industrial levels of the non-Western world fell dramatically, sometimes to one-quarter of what they had been before being drawn into the modern world system. Mass-produced goods from Europe were far cheaper and often of a better quality than locally produced goods. The indigenous manufacturing sector was thus undermined by the "imperialism of free trade," as there was little incentive for local entrepreneurs to develop the local craft sectors into a thriving industry.

Central to making the colonies profitable for the imperialist powers was the necessity of converting the local people into wage labourers and forcing them into a cash economy. Between 1890 and 1914, colonial developers, such as Cecil Rhodes, faced the problem of changing African populations from traditional pastoral and agrarian economies to wage labour geared for agricultural export, in industrial enterprises such as mines and in large infrastructure projects such as the building of railways. For the colonial government or investor, the task was to bring the resources of the colony — land, natural resources, and labour — into production to gain a profit. Indigenous African societies had their own systems of production and trade that were relatively self-sufficient, and thus they did not necessarily respond to opportunities for trading with European entrepreneurs or for working as wage earners for colonial employers. Colonial developers, therefore, made extensive use of migrant labour and used a variety of strategies to compel Africans into a cash, wage-labour economy. Even though such imposed change was often defended as bringing the benefits of civilization or modernization to "backward" peoples and cultures, the supposed benefits were not readily apparent to those peoples directly affected. In some instances, Africans not only found their lives changed against their will but also came to endure working and living conditions inferior to those they experienced prior to Western intervention.

The process of converting Africans into labourers in a cash economy exhibited its most brutal features in the Congo Free State (today Republic of Congo) between 1885 and 1908. King Leopold II of Belgium

Images of a tea factory in Ceylon (now Sri Lanka) are highlighted on this advertisement for Lipton Tea from 1866. Tea remains a major export for Sri Lanka, where it is grown in the inland hills. Would this advertisement be considered suitable today?

took about half the land into his private ownership or gave it to companies granted concessions in return for railroad development. The Congolese now had more restricted use of land for their own agriculture, while Leopold and the concessionaires compelled the local population to harvest natural rubber.

To satisfy the demand of the industrial world for rubber for pneumatic tires on bicycles and automobiles, Congolese workers had to find and tap the rubber trees in the tropical rain forest. They often had to work far from their home villages, and brutal punishment was inflicted upon them for failure to meet the required quotas. Adolescent boys were punished by mutilation, including the cutting off of ears or hands. Failure of particular villagers to meet quotas resulted in raids on their home villages, where women were raped, children and the elderly beaten and houses destroyed. In 1908 an international crusade of humanitarian agencies

finally pressured Leopold II to turn his private domain in the Congo over to the Belgian government. By that time, the production of rubber on plantations in Malaya had replaced the harvest of "red rubber" (referring to the blood of Africans) in the Congo.

Other methods were used by the European powers to force people into wage labour. For example, they would impose a head tax or hut tax that had to be paid by the local people to the rulers, but it would have to be paid in European currency. The only way for them to acquire European currency was to work for the European colonial rulers in the mines or on the plantations.

In the view of the European powers, colonies were not to be a drain on the treasury of the metropolitan state, but rather the cost of maintaining economic dominance over the colony was to be borne by the colony itself. The costs of colonial administration and military presence were obtained through local taxes.

King Leopold II of Belgium in 1880: International pressure helped put an end to "red rubber", and the cruel exploitation of Congolese workers in Leopold's rubber plantations.

The conversion of peoples into wage labourers and consumers had to overcome a number of substantial obstacles. In some cases, there were not enough suitable labourers. In Queensland, Australia, for example, the local aboriginal population and the White settlers could not meet the needs of the sugar planters. Labour contractors recruited — or captured — over sixty-two thousand "blackbirds," or South Sea Islanders, and brought them to work on the Queensland plantations. Beyond the question of labour supply, self-sufficient peasant cultivators did not respond immediately to the lure of a wage income and a market economy stressing production for export. Labour on plantations or in mines involved more arduous work for longer hours at a lower living standard than could be achieved in a traditional farming or hunting economy.

Facing these obstacles to the supply of labour, colonial developers often resorted to various forms of compulsory labour. The moral prestige of the anti-slavery movement meant that slavery, the traditional form of coerced labour, could not be reinstituted. Furthermore, in the metropolitan industrial world, the principle of free labour and democratic political rights, such as the vote, had been established by the late nineteenth century. The colonial world moved in the opposite direction. Colonial development relied on new forms of compulsory labour, and, apart from White settler communities, the "Natives," or "coloured races," to use the language of colonialism, were subject to discriminatory laws and denied the rights of citizens. These blatant contradictions between Western principle and practice were reconciled by the pervasive racist ideology of the time: Racism gave freedom as a right to the Whites but denied it to non-Whites.

The economic impact of imperialism has had far-reaching consequences. The global economic relations established during this period have shaped the modern world system and, some would argue, are the foundation of poverty in developing nations in the twenty-first century.

For example, the Indian Army, paid for by taxes imposed on the people of India, served the British Empire not only in India but also in Southeast Asia, Hong Kong, Persia, Egypt, and East Africa. Taxes usually involved payment in cash, thus serving the additional purpose of forcing non-Western populations into a cash economy

Review, Reflect, Respond

1. What were the advantages for the European powers in the so-called "scramble for Africa?" Were these primarily economic rather than cultural or political advantages? Explain.

2. What does the Berlin Conference of 1884–1885 tell you about European views and attitudes towards Africa and African peoples in the nineteenth century?

3. Were there any benefits of formal imperialism for colonized peoples? Explain with both African and Asian examples.

The Cultural Legacy of Imperialism

Not only did economic relations and systems change as a result of imperialism, so did the fundamental cultures of peoples subjected to European rule. One of the most important vehicles of culture is language, and, in most former colonies, language has undergone sweeping transformations. As a general rule, the indigenous language of the colony was relegated to second-class status, in favour of the language of the European power that ruled the colony. Thus, the common language today in Central and South America is Spanish or Portuguese, in North Africa is French, in India is English, and so on. Of course, local languages have not been completely abandoned, but they are generally not the languages used in the spheres of politics, economics, or administration.

The Europeans also exported their religion — Christianity — to the colonies, most often with a sense of mission. It altered the lives of the peoples who adopted it, as the local religions tended to be very organic, woven into and growing out of the daily lives and experiences of the people. More importantly, perhaps, is that Christianity was often used as a justification for massacres, racial discrimination, cruelty, and regressive social policies.

Imperialism and Non-Western Art

Indigenous arts felt the impact of imperialism in a number of ways. Art was now produced for export to European nations and, therefore, often needed to reflect European tastes and preferences. Changes in values and the influence of Christianity also had an impact on various art forms. In parts of Africa, for example, where Christianity dates back almost to the time of Christ, Christian missionaries often mistakenly assumed that African sculpture represented idolatry and thus attempted to undermine this art form. On the part of Africans who accepted Christianity, expressions in art changed to include this new belief system. Statues of saints in the European tradition were carved from wood, and angels became subjects of sculpture, albeit with a distinctly African flavour.

In India one of the ways the colonialists had a lasting impact was through the construction of immense buildings steeped in the tradition of Victorian architecture. Throughout India, but particularly in the urban centres, the British built testaments to their glorious empire. Since one of their most lasting innovations in

Built in 1915, the Victoria Railway Terminus in Bombay displays a mixture of Indian and British architectural elements.

India was the introduction of an extensive railway system, it seemed only fitting that this style of architecture would be seen most prominently in the massive railway station in Mumbai (formerly Bombay).

The nineteenth century also saw the continuing fascination with chinoiserie — Chinese art and decoration — in Britain especially. Grand homes were decorated with Chinese objects of art and incorporated elements of Chinese architecture. China had originally mass-produced items for export, such as porcelain and silk, but with the development of industrialization in Europe, the West could now produce many imitation items to satisfy growing consumer demand at home.

The Social Legacy of Imperialism

Finally, the social structure of societies changed drastically as a result of imperialism. Both White and non-White migration changed the ethnic composition of societies. Effective occupation of colonial territories depended upon a European military and administrative presence and transformation of land and population by White immigrants. From 1871 to 1914, Europe's population grew by about 200 million and an additional 30 million migrated overseas. The United States attracted about two-thirds of these immigrants, just under two million came to Canada, and the rest settled in Australia, New Zealand, South America (principally Argentina and Brazil), Algeria and South Africa. There was also an extensive migration of European Russians to Asiatic Russia.

European imperialism and the migration of White populations are usually linked, but the colonial empires were also great agents for forced and voluntary migration of non-European peoples. Although Britain and the United States ceased to trade in African slaves in the first decade of the nineteenth century, the transatlantic slave trade continued, chiefly to Brazil and Cuba. From 1811 until the virtual end of the slave trade by 1870, almost two million Africans were brought to the Americas as slaves. The mid-century gold rushes in California, Australia, and British Columbia attracted voluntary immigrants not only from Europe, but also from China. The demand for labour in mining, railway construction, and agriculture prompted various schemes of voluntary and indentured labour.

The workers who migrated voluntarily were mainly Chinese and South Asians from the Indian subcontinent. This migration was global. Indian immigrants went to Fiji and Queensland, to Southeast Asia, to Mauritius and the Seychelles in the Indian Ocean, to East and South Africa, to the Caribbean (principally Trinidad and Guyana), and to British Columbia. Chinese immigrants went to similar destinations, including Australia, Southeast Asia, South Africa, the Caribbean and, on the west coast of the Americas, to British Columbia, California, Peru and Chile. There were also more localized migrations of South Sea Islanders to work plantations in Queensland, of African West Indians within the Caribbean and Central America, and within Africa an extensive trade in slaves destined for America and the Middle East. Later in the century, African migrant labourers worked on plantations, on railway construction, and in mines in West, Central, and South Africa.

Plantations had been most fully developed in the slave societies of the New World, but in the course of the nineteenth century, colonists adopted the use of gang labour for the production of crops to be exported to Asia, the Pacific, and Africa. These labourers produced tea in Ceylon (present-day Sri Lanka), rubber in Malaya, sugar in Queensland (Australia) and Fiji Islands, sugar in Natal (South Africa), cloves in Zanzibar, cocoa in the Congo and Angola, rubber in the Congo, and palm oil in West Africa. Like the plantations, the mining industry and large construction projects, such as railroads, also used gang labour. By the end of the nineteenth century, there was extensive internal migration in Africa, especially to the gold mines in South Africa and to the copper belt in the Congo and Rhodesia.

Indentured Labour

The most extensively organized system of migrant labour was the trade in indentured labourers from

India and China. The indenture was a contract to work for a specified period of time, usually five years. The contract provided for transportation to the colony, lodging, and wages. The aim of indentured labourers, mostly men, was to work to send money back to their families in India or China. Although technically a voluntary contract labour system, the indenture system was considered by many to be a new system of slavery. Contractors in India and China recruited the labourers from the most impoverished classes. When offered the inducement of a small advance, many recruits, already facing punishment for debt, were entrapped into contracts they did not understand. At the end of their lengthy sea voyage, the labourers faced demanding physical work, lived in crowded barracks, received inadequate food and no health care, and had no normal family life. When they had a conflict with their employers, they faced a legal system and a police force ready to enforce their employers' conditions. Indentured labourers often had to earn money to buy their return passage. In the West Indies, the return could cost an additional five years of labour. Consequently, indenture, though intended to be temporary, often became a permanent migration to a new home.

Between 1830 and 1870, at least one million — and possibly as many as two million — indentured labourers were sent from India to various British colonies. This trade continued into the 1920s, with most immigrants going to Ceylon, Burma, and Malaya (present-day Malaysia), but significant numbers worked on plantations in Fiji, Mauritius and Natal. The longest and most hazardous journey was to the British West Indies. Between 1838 and 1900, two-hundred thousand Indian labourers were settled in British Guyana; another 150 000 were taken to Trinidad. The indenture schemes assumed that the cost of the journey would be borne by the employer, but in the British West Indies, it was paid by the colonial governments out of taxes on consumer goods. Thus, through the taxes they were forced to pay, Black consumers paid for the indentured labourers who competed with them for employment on the plantations.

Chinese migrants more commonly worked in mining and construction than on plantations. In the mid-nineteenth century, there were forty-two thousand Chinese miners in the Australian gold fields, and a total of two hundred thousand Chinese went to California to work in the gold mines and railroad construction and in the growing and processing of fruit. After disease and exhaustion decimated Hawaiian migrants employed in the extraction of nitrate from guano beds (of bird excrement) in Peru, ninety thousand Chinese indentured labourers were recruited for this dangerous work (workers experienced lung damage from toxic fine particles). In Peru, Canada and the United States, Chinese labourers also worked on railroad construction: fifteen thousand were recruited from Hong Kong alone to complete the Canadian Pacific Railway. Chinese labourers were most extensively recruited to work in Southeast Asia, where they would work in the tin mines and on spice plantations in

History
BYTES

Although not a direct cause of imperialism, the European imposition of formal colonial rule was made possible by advances in Western technology. In earlier times, tropical regions had presented a powerful natural barrier to White settlement: disease. With advances in medicine, especially with the use of the antimalarial drug quinine, White soldiers, administrators, traders, and missionaries could now live in regions once considered inhospitable to Europeans. These agents of White empire were also equipped with a new technological capacity — the breech-loading rifle and the machine gun — enabling them to control territories and peoples in a fashion that was not possible even in the first half of the nineteenth century. These technological innovations gave even small brigades of European soldiers a decided advantage over much larger armies of natives equipped only with spears and muskets, as was the case in confrontations such as the British-Zulu War of 1879.

Malaya and Singapore. For a brief period in the aftermath of the Boer War, gold mining companies in the Transvaal recruited over fifty thousand indentured Chinese miners as an alternative to African miners, who were in short supply, demanded higher wages and posed a political threat.

Immigration and the White Dominions

At the same time as the system of compulsory migrant labour existed, voluntary migration of non-Whites to the so-called "White" dominions of the British Crown and the United States was closed off by exclusionary immigration policies. After an initial period of Chinese, South Asian and other non-White immigration, these self-governing colonies — Australia, New Zealand, South Africa, and Canada — instituted "Whites only" immigration policies. These discriminatory restrictions were an embarrassment to the British government, as they contradicted the imperial claim that all persons, regardless of skin colour, were equal subjects of the Queen.

Faced with the protests of the governments of India, China and Japan, the dominions found non-racial ways to exclude non-White immigrants. Australia, New Zealand, and South Africa imposed a literacy test in a European language and allowed wide discretion on the part of immigration officers. For example, when a South Asian or Chinese immigrant with literacy in English applied, Australian officials demanded literacy in another European language. Canada adopted a similar strategy by insisting that immigrants travel directly from their home port to a port of entry into Canada. Since most ships from India and China went via Hawaii, immigrants could not readily pass this entry requirement.

When taken together, exclusionary immigration policies and compulsory migrant labour constitute one of the clearest signs of the Eurocentric racism that characterized the age of imperialism. Racism also constituted one of the most painful and enduring legacies of colonialism. In areas of European settlement, it created the myth that in the past and in the future, these lands were by right "a White man's country." In areas of forced mass migration like Fiji, Malaya, South Africa and Guyana, colonialism left a legacy of communities divided by race and ethnicity.

Global migration created new multiracial and multiethnic societies. Besides throwing peoples of diverse origins and cultures together, imperialism constructed societies in which peoples were unequal in wealth and power, and it fostered racial and ethnic divisions to maintain European authority. Probably the most enduring and destructive legacy of nineteenth-century imperialism is the ideology of racial superiority, known as racism, and the establishment of multiracial societies based on racial inequality.

The rise of industrial economies increased the contrast in wealth between the metropolitan centres and the periphery. The partial implementation of new principles of individual liberty and representative government also increased the contrast between free citizens and mere subjects. In some cases, the law threatened rather than protected liberty and specifically denied particular groups, such as Black slaves and other non-Whites, equality of status and the right to due process. The contrast between the metropolitan areas of North America and Western Europe and the colonized periphery created a world more starkly divided by race.

The economic and political inequalities in the world fostered the illusion that the modern, civilized order belonged to Whites and the servile, colonized order belonged to non-Whites. To defend this illusionary racial order and its denial of the universality of human rights proclaimed by the American and French revolutions, scientific racism (and ideas such as social Darwinism) preached that the privileged status of White males, particularly the middle class, was reflective of a natural rather than a human order. Racist scientists attempted to demonstrate that the inequalities within particular societies were reflective of the differing biological inheritance of human groups. Their science was constructed on false premises, since the evident inequalities in wealth, political power and status between peoples were not products of biology but of history: Global inequalities were the result of past human actions. Racial inequalities in the Americas were the result of the military conquest and enslavement of Amerindians and Africans, and the political power of White elites who constructed a social and legal order that perpetuated their privileged status.

Apartheid: Legacy of Imperialism

In 1867 rich diamond deposits were discovered at Kimberley, South Africa. Mine owners recruited migrant African labour to work the deposits on short-term contracts. In order to prevent the theft of diamonds, they placed labourers in compounds, separating men from their families. This compound system was later adapted in Witwatersrand in the Transvaal, where extensive gold ores were discovered in 1886. Miners from Europe would handle the technology for working underground, and African labourers moved the ore to the surface. In order to recruit workers, poll taxes were levied on Africans to create a need for cash income. Men migrated to the mines, while their families remained in homelands engaged in traditional pastoral and agricultural activities. This system enabled employers to pay Africans less than an economic wage, since, unlike European workers, the Africans did not have to provide for wives and families.

These economic and social changes revived the long-standing conflict between the descendants of the Dutch settlers, the Boers, and the British. The gold mines were financed and administered by British companies and attracted British settlers, but the gold fields were located in the three republics created by the Boers (Natal, Transvaal, and the Orange Free State). Conflicts over control of the gold fields and treatment of British settlers led to the Boer War, from 1899–1902, which ended with the surrender of the Boers.

In the negotiations for the Union of South Africa (1910), the rights and interests of Africans were largely ignored, despite British claims to the contrary. With the exception of the "Cape coloured," who already had the vote, the constitution of the new Union of South

In Johannesburg during the Apartheid years in South Africa, signs like this were common. Photographed in 1956, this sign says "Caution Beware of Natives." How do you think signs like this made "natives" feel?

Africa denied Africans all political rights, including the vote. The new Union also passed laws to institutionalize the practice of a segregated, migrant African labour force. Although Africans constituted about 80 percent of the population, the 1913 Lands Act allocated only 13 percent of the land for African homelands. Africans were also restricted in their freedom to settle in the cities, and laws required them to carry passes for travel and residence outside of designated areas. From these beginnings, the system of apartheid made racial segregation the overriding reality of South African society.

In examining various forms of migratory and compulsory labour, we have focussed on those peoples most dramatically affected by late-nineteenth-century colonialism. Even in 1900, many hunter-and-gatherer and agriculturalist societies in developing nations had only begun to feel the impact of a global market economy. Nonetheless, by 1900 the directions of change were clear. The transition to modern capitalist forms of production often required force; consequently, this modernizing process produced instability and conflict. Colonialism fundamentally altered economic and political relationships as well as the whole fabric of the social and cultural life of communities. Colonized peoples developed their own strategies of resistance in response to Western intervention.

AGENTS OF HUMAN RIGHTS ADVANCEMENT

Resistance to Imperialism

The extraordinary expansion of European empires in the course of the nineteenth century, especially from 1870 onward, did far more than alter the political map of the world. Imperialism involved a social and economic as well as a political transformation. This intrusion of the Western powers into the non-Western world imposed change on formerly autonomous peoples and cultures. At first, the peoples affected tried to restore their traditional ways, but as the transformation to a modern world system took hold, colonized peoples began to develop their own forms of nationalism as they sought new ways to assert their freedom. By 1914 it was already evident that the nineteenth-century age of empire was entering a new phase of crisis and conflict.

The colonized peoples were not simply passive victims, but engaged in a variety of forms of resistance to foreign European intervention and control. This history of resistance laid the foundations for colonial nationalist movements in Asia and Africa. The history of colonization in the nineteenth century encompasses the ways in which the imperialism of European states and the resistance of colonized peoples transformed the modern world system.

The Age of Revolutions in Europe, 1789–1848, had a corresponding revolutionary impact on Europe's relationship with the wider world. In this broader global perspective, some have labelled this the Age of Democratic Revolutions. The first wave of decolonization and emancipation grew out of the new political principles proclaimed by the American and French revolutions and with the new forms of economic and social organization that began with the first Industrial Revolution in Britain, 1780–1850. This birth of the modern world from the dual revolution in politics and industrialization transformed the relationship between imperialist powers and their colonies and dependencies.

The first movement for colonial independence began with the revolution that made the United States independent from Britain. The American Revolution inspired the movement for the liberation of Mexico and the South American republics from Spain (1808–1825). In British North America, this decolonization occurred at a later date and in a peaceful way. The evolution of principles of representative and responsible government within British colonies eventually led to the establishment of the Dominion of Canada in 1867.

The Abolition of Slavery

Great Britain and the United States ended their involvement in the slave trade (1807–1808), and slavery itself was abolished in the British Empire in 1834. The new Latin American republics, in keeping with their liberal founding principles, abolished slavery. France ended slavery in its empire with the Second Republic, founded by the revolution of 1848. Thereafter, the principal slave powers were Cuba, which remained a Spanish colony, Brazil, under the Portuguese Empire, and the United States, ironically the world's foremost liberal democracy.

A closer look at the first wave of emancipation reveals a pattern: In North America, where European settlers were predominant within a capitalist economic order, the United States and Canada became part of the industrialized and metropolitan sector of the modern world. Haiti and the Latin American republics were liberated from colonialism, yet remained part of the economically dependent developing nations. The colonies of the British and French empires in the Caribbean, where slavery had been abolished, remained under the control of London and Paris as part of their dependent, colonized periphery. Similarly, imperial possessions in mainland Asia, the Dutch East Indies, and British India were not part of this first wave of emancipation and, like the former slave colonies in the West Indies, did not achieve independence until after 1945.

The new industrial order stressed both the individualism of the entrepreneur and the value of labour in a modern economy. These values were in direct conflict with the dependence of the older colonialism on the coerced labour of African slaves. During the Age of Democratic Revolutions, the practice of chattel slavery, in which human beings were regarded as merchandise and forced to labour for their owner's benefit, came under attack. In one of the most significant advances for human freedom, slavery, an institution as old as recorded history, came to an end under the combined assault of changing economic circumstances, the rise of an international antislavery movement, and the slaves' resistance to their oppression.

These three factors first became evident in the Caribbean Islands, where the institution of slavery was the most vulnerable to attack: The prime crop of the West Indian plantations was cane sugar, which made extreme demands on the soil and on slave labour (for harvesting and refining cane into sugar). Some historians have argued that both the slave trade and West Indian slavery were already in economic decline by the beginning of the nineteenth century, but recent historians stress the economic viability of both the trade and the system. Consequently, more emphasis has been placed on the political dynamics of emancipation.

Politically, the West Indian colonies were particularly vulnerable. Unlike the United States with its institution of slavery, the West Indies were not politically independent, but were colonies subject to political decisions in London and to events in revolutionary Paris. In those capitals, the antislavery movement pressed first for the abolition of the slave trade and then for the end of slavery itself. The abolitionists, whose campaign began

in the 1770s and continued as a vigorous movement for almost a century, declared slavery to be a violation of human rights as defined by the Enlightenment and as put into constitutional form by the American and French revolutions. British and American abolitionists, such as the Society for the Abolition of the Slave Trade (1787), organized the largest and most effective movements, combining an appeal to human rights and to evangelical Christianity, which declared slavery to be both immoral and unchristian.

The Slave Revolution in Haiti 1791

The balance between the vested colonial interests defending slavery and the humanitarianism of the abolitionists was tilted by the actions of the slaves. The slave revolution in Haiti sent shock waves through the plantation communities throughout the West Indies, South America, and the southern United States. In Haiti a tiny minority of French planters ruled 800 000 slaves, many of whom were newly arrived from Africa. Aware of their African families and communities, these slaves were especially hostile to the oppression of New World slavery and struggled to retain their language, religion, and culture.

The slaves' opportunity came with the French Revolution. Under the leadership of François Dominique Toussaint L'Ouverture, a slave about the age of 50 who was literate and had served as an estate manager, the Haitians defeated French, British, and Spanish attempts to suppress their revolution. Toussaint L'Ouverture helped the French abolish slavery in 1794, and he was made a general. But Napoléon, in response to pressure from the sugar planters, had him imprisoned in France when he declared Haiti a Black republic. Toussaint died in prison in 1803.

Slavery in the British West Indies

In the British West Indies, similar situations existed, as tiny White planter elites faced the potential of a mass insurrection of their slaves. The example of Haiti, and the demand for ships and seamen during the Napoleonic

Wars, gave the abolitionists new practical as well as moral arguments, which led Britain to abolish the slave trade in 1807. Ending the importation of African slaves did not decrease the number of slave insurrections. In the British West Indies, slave uprisings occurred in Barbados in 1816, in Demerara (Guyana) in 1823, and in Jamaica in 1831–1832.

The uprising in Jamaica was decisive for the abolition of slavery in the entire British Empire. The conditions of slavery in Jamaica were similar to those in many other countries: A white minority ruled over a slave population nearly 10 times as large. The exclusion of slaves as witnesses in court was indicative of the assumption that they were creatures of inferior intelligence. Family life was discouraged in order to demonstrate the intrinsically animal nature of the African slave, and the whip as an instrument of punishment struck the terror needed to maintain slavery.

In 1831 word reached the slaves in Jamaica that the British government had passed legislation to end slavery. This rumour was spread by Sam Sharpe, a domestic slave who worked in Montego Bay. Sharpe was intelligent, literate, and ambitious. Although he was himself aware that no such legislation had been passed, he used the rumour to fuel a slave rebellion. Beginning in August 1831, Sharpe and his associates started to organize for a Christmas rebellion. By December 1831, the agitation for revolt was reaching a peak. On December 27, 1831, missionary minister William Knibb tried to warn the African slaves: "I learn that some wicked persons have persuaded you that the King has made you free. Hear me, I love your souls — I would not tell you a lie for the world. What you have been told is false — false as Hell can make it. I entreat you not to believe it, but to go to your work as usual."

Knibb's warning served only to disappoint and anger the slaves, who felt missionaries were concerned with law and order but not with their freedom. On the day of Knibb's warning, a fire on the Kensington estate in St. James, one of the most important sugar-growing parishes, marked the beginning of a slave rebellion that would engulf the western part of the island of Jamaica. The rebellion would last a few weeks but ultimately proved unsuccessful. Lack of unity among various groups, a shortage of weapons, and poor military training all contributed to the ultimate defeat of the rebel slaves.

Despite the failure of the revolt, its significance should not be underestimated. The rebellion contributed indirectly to the abolition of slavery. Following the rebellion, White slave owners blamed missionaries for the rebellion and, in retaliation, destroyed the chapels. This led the missionaries to conclude that the only way they could carry on their work was if slavery was abolished. They therefore sent delegates to England, where they became invaluable propagandists in the fight to end slavery. Slavery was completely abolished in the British Empire on January 1, 1835.

Slavery in the United States

In the United States, the contradictions between slavery and the founding principles of a democratic republic eventually provoked the American Civil War (1861–1865).

Though often seen as a conflict within White America between a pro-slave South and a free North, African-Americans, both slave and free, helped generate the crisis that led to the civil war and then exploited the circumstances of the war to turn the crisis into a struggle for emancipation. Even in the pro-slave South, African-Americans were generally a minority and faced much larger White populations than did the revolutionaries in Haiti or Jamaica. Slave revolts were therefore less frequent in the United States, though some, such as Nat Turner's uprising in Virginia in 1831, were inspired by the example of Toussaint L'Ouverture. Turner's rebellion and others' were repressed, as southern authorities organized a legal reign of terror to deter any sign of slave resistance. Consequently, American slaves sought liberation through escape rather than rebellion. The brave and the lucky escaped north to freedom and to the refuge of free Blacks and abolitionist sympathizers. Some fled the country altogether. The secret flight to the northern United States and Canada, set up by abolitionist sympathizers, was called the Underground Railroad.

To put a stop to the escape of fugitive slaves, southern politicians had Congress pass the Fugitive

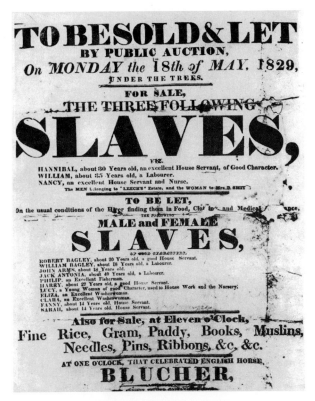

TO BE SOLD & LET
BY PUBLIC AUCTION,
On MONDAY the 18th of MAY, 1829,
UNDER THE TREES.
FOR SALE,
THE THREE FOLLOWING
SLAVES,
VIZ.
HANNIBAL, about 30 Years old, an excellent House Servant, of Good Character.
WILLIAM, about 35 Years old, a Labourer.
NANCY, an excellent House Servant and Nurse.
The MEN belonging to "LEECH'S" Estate, and the WOMAN to Mrs. D. SMIT.

TO BE LET,
On the usual conditions of the Hirer finding them in Food, Clothes and Medical assistance,
THE FOLLOWING
MALE and FEMALE
SLAVES,
ROBERT BAGLEY, about 20 Years old, a good House Servant.
WILLIAM BAGLEY, about 18 Years old, a Labourer.
JOHN ARMS, about 18 Years old.
JACK ANTONIA, about 40 Years old, a Labourer.
PHILIP, an Excellent Fisherman.
HARRY, about 27 Years old, a good House Servant.
LUCY, a Young Woman of good Character, used to House Work and the Nursery.
ELIZA, an Excellent Washerwoman.
CLARA, an Excellent Washerwoman.
FANNY, about 14 Years old, House Servant.
SARAH, about 14 Years old, House Servant.

Also for Sale, at Eleven o'Clock,
Fine Rice, Gram, Paddy, Books, Muslins,
Needles, Pins, Ribbons, &c. &c.
AT ONE O'CLOCK, THAT CELEBRATED ENGLISH HORSE,
BLUCHER,

This 1829 poster advertising a slave auction lists the names of the people being sold, their ages and the type of work they can do. Most are simply named Clara, Hannibal, Philip, Nancy, and so on, with no family names. Rice, muslin (fabric), needles and pins were also being sold, along with a "celebrated English horse." What does this say about the attitudes toward slaves?

Slave Act (1851), which made it illegal to protect fugitive slaves anywhere in the United States and in effect extended the authority of the slave states into the free states of the North. This intervention, however, began to threaten not only the life and liberty of Blacks but also the rights of Whites. Consequently, the institution of slavery was seen to be corrupting the whole country. When it became clear that the country could not be half-slave and half-free, a southern secessionist movement (to withdraw from the Union) formed and the civil war erupted.

At the beginning of the Civil War in 1861, President Abraham Lincoln and the northern forces claimed to be fighting to restore the Union and not to end slavery. In the first two years, the war went badly for the North, and the flight of slaves into areas under Union control made it difficult to re-impose slavery on fugitives. Furthermore, Black regiments had joined the Union army, and there was no doubt that they were fighting for emancipation. African-Americans, abolitionists, and many recruits in the army redefined the struggle as a war against slavery. In January 1863, Lincoln issued his Emancipation Proclamation, which freed the slaves, authorized the creation of Black military units, and changed the war into a struggle against slavery.

Slaves in Cuba and Brazil had a similar role in their own emancipation. The struggle to end race slavery took more than a century, and although often overlooked by White historians, the resistance of the slaves themselves was essential to their liberation. Out of this history of resistance, as we shall see, Black people of the African diaspora to the New World founded a tradition that would both challenge new forms of racist oppression and build an alliance with their African brothers and sisters to mount a nationalist movement against colonialism.

Review, Reflect, Respond

1. Briefly describe the social and cultural legacy of imperialism in Africa, Asia, and India.

2. How did the economic and social impact of imperialism contribute to increasing conflict in the nineteenth century? Refer to Haiti and Jamaica in your response.

3. List and explain the two factors you believe were the most significant in bringing an end to slavery.

THE LEGACY OF EMANCIPATION

The British West Indies

New forms of compulsory labour developed out of the legacy of race slavery. In the British West Indies, former slaves worked as wage labourers on plantations or as small independent cultivators on their own tracts of land. From the 1830s onward, the West Indian sugar industry was in decline due to competition from European sugar beets and Cuban sugar. Still attached to their slave-owning past, the planters held the former slaves responsible for the economic decline. Claiming that the native Blacks were unproductive, costly labourers, estate owners sought alternative cheap labour by importing indentured workers from India. The former defenders of the Black population, the abolitionists, believed that once slavery had ended and individual freedom existed under the law, progress and prosperity would follow. Even though the abolitionists denounced race prejudice, their assault on slavery did not lead to a movement against racism. With the decline in the West Indian sugar economy, many abolitionists began to view emancipation as a failure and became tolerant toward the planters' demands for cheap migrant labour.

Segregation and the American South

British and American observers applied the lessons of the apparent failure of emancipation in the West Indies to policies in the southern United States after the civil war and to British policies in Africa. From 1865 to 1876, the policy of reconstruction was imposed on the South by the victorious North. It included some land redistribution to former slaves and the extension of political and civil rights to African-Americans. As northern reform energy weakened, White southerners reasserted their political power and dismantled the reforms of reconstruction. White control of land perpetuated the former slaves' dependency. The system of sharecropping met the former slaves' desire to be independent cultivators but kept them in chronic debt to White landowners. The southern elite, backed by poor Whites seeking privileges from their racial status, also reasserted their political predominance and excluded Blacks from the political process. Under the Jim Crow legislation of the 1890s, the practice of racial segregation was incorporated into law and enforced within communities by vigilante attacks on Blacks, including widespread lynchings by the Ku Klux Klan and other White racist gangs. The experience of the American

At this Ku Klux Klan meeting in 1925 a man is being sworn into the organization. Members of this and other White racist groups were particularly worried about miscegenation - the mixing of the White race with other races through intermarriage. Are these attitudes still present today?

South influenced developments elsewhere. South Africa and other colonial societies saw that the American South and its policy of segregation provided a model for their own racist, multiracial societies.

Decolonization in Latin America

The Age of Democratic Revolutions gave rise to not only the first wave of emancipation, but also the first movement for colonial independence. The new liberal principles of individual liberty and representative government, and the new economic doctrines of *laissez faire* and free trade challenged the established practices of colonial rule. The old colonialism of conquest was best exemplified by Spain's empire in Latin America. Between 1808 and 1825, political upheaval and armed struggle liberated most of Spain's American colonies.

In the Spanish Empire in the eighteenth century, society was divided into various classes. At the top there were

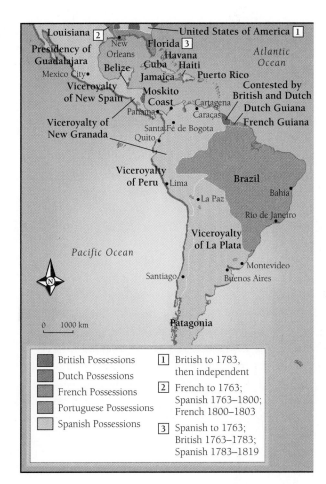

Map labels:
Louisiana [2]
United States of America [1]
Presidency of Guadalajara
New Orleans
Florida [3]
Havana
Atlantic Ocean
Mexico City
Belize
Cuba
Haiti
Jamaica
Puerto Rico
Viceroyalty of New Spain
Moskito Coast
Panama
Cartagena
Contested by British and Dutch
Dutch Guiana
French Guiana
Viceroyalty of New Granada
Santa Fé de Bogota
Caracas
Quito
Viceroyalty of Peru
Lima
Brazil
Bahia
La Paz
Rio de Janeiro
Pacific Ocean
Viceroyalty of La Plata
Montevideo
Santiago
Buenos Aires
Patagonia
0   1000 km

British Possessions
Dutch Possessions
French Possessions
Portuguese Possessions
Spanish Possessions

[1] British to 1783, then independent
[2] French to 1763; Spanish 1763–1800; French 1800–1803
[3] Spanish to 1763; British 1763–1783; Spanish 1783–1819

FIGURE 9.3 Latin America Before Independence
Many of the country names on this map have disappeared and others appeared in their place. Which changes stand out for you?

three sources of authority — the administrative bureaucracy of the Spanish monarchy, the Catholic Church, and the White Creole (born in America of Spanish descent) elite, a landed aristocracy descended from the conquistadors. Together, these authorities ruled over an impoverished Amerindian and *Mestizo* (offspring of White males and Amerindian women) majority. Thus, under a variety of forms of coerced labour, the impoverished majority paid rent and services to the Creole landowners and the Church, and tribute or taxes to the royal officials. In return, the peasantry preserved a measure of cultural autonomy and a protected legal status under the supervision of the Spanish Crown and the

Church. In areas where plantation agriculture existed, African slaves endured a similar oppressed and subordinate condition. Finally, in an ambiguous intermediate status, there existed a *Mestizo* and *mulatto* (offspring of White European and Black African).

The Creole elite living in Latin American colonies wanted greater autonomy from the Spanish Crown as well as greater access to the expanding trade of the Western hemisphere, chiefly with the newly founded United States and with Great Britain. Political reforms granting more autonomy and freedom to the Creoles carried the risk of liberating the subordinate majority of Amerindian peasants and African slaves. The danger of an insurrection from below was made evident by a peasant movement in 1780, led by the Inca Tupac Amaru to restore the ancient rule of the native Incas in Peru, and by the slaves' revolution in Haiti in 1791. Caught between a desire for reform and the need to preserve their authority, the Creoles were split. The majority still supported the Spanish monarchy and the Church, while a minority sought reform in light of Enlightenment ideas and the liberating example of the American Revolution.

Colonization and the Napoleonic Wars

This situation was unexpectedly changed by the French Revolution and the Napoleonic Wars. Previously, the British defeat of the Spanish Armada (1588) and blockade of transatlantic trade had caused a break in commercial relations between Spain and its huge American empire. Then, in 1808, Napoléon invaded Spain and put his brother, Joseph Bonaparte, on the Spanish throne. These events created a crisis of legitimacy within the Creole elite, who were divided between those still loyal to Spain and those seeking independence under a liberal constitution. The resultant civil wars (1808–1820) proved inconclusive until both the royalists and the liberals recognized that the Spanish government was unwilling to extend greater autonomy to its colonies and that appealing to the Crown as a source of political legitimacy was no longer a viable option. The only course was independence, the terms of which would be decided by further armed struggle.

THE STRUGGLE FOR AN INDEPENDENT LATIN AMERICA

In Mexico, the elite chose independence for conservative reasons. They feared reforms from a liberal republican government in Spain and opted for independence in order to preserve the existing social hierarchy. Faced with protracted civil strife that began with an uprising of peasants and slaves in 1810, the Mexican landholders, led by Catholic priest Miguel Hidalgo, declared themselves independent from Spain in 1821.

In South America, the forces of liberalism were at the vanguard of the movement for independence. In the Andes Mountains, José de San Martín (1788–1850) led the armed struggle for the liberation of what is now Argentina, Chile, and Peru. Inspired by the American and French revolutions, San Martín, an Argentine son

This painting of Miguel Hidalgo, hero of Mexican independence, is by the renowned twentieth-century Mexican artist Diego Rivera (1886-1957).

of a Spanish army officer, hoped to establish independent constitutional monarchies in South America, but he failed to do so.

Simón Bolívar: The Great Liberator

Born in 1783 in Venezuela to an elite family, Simón was orphaned at only nine years of age. As a teenager, he was sent to Spain to further his education and polish his social graces. Following the tragic death of his wife, Bolívar returned to Europe in 1803 to complete a grand tour that took him to Paris, Geneva, and Rome. His tour happened to coincide with the period when Napoléon Bonaparte and the armies of France were rearranging Europe into a "continental system."

Bolívar's tour through Europe did much to shape his political ideas and to strengthen his resolve to lead the people of Latin America to freedom. While in Europe, Bolívar was introduced to the ideas of Voltaire and Rousseau, and met with Jeremy Bentham, from whom he seems to have taken a utilitarian philosophy of life. The driving force behind Bolívar's politics was that he never saw freedom as an end in itself; rather, he believed that government existed to maximize human happiness, and that its function was to make policy as well as satisfy interests.

In describing the Spanish-American Revolution, Bolívar said:

> A republican government, that is what Venezuela had, has, and should have. Its principles should be the sovereignty of the people, division of powers, civil liberty, prohibition of slavery, and the abolition of monarchy and privileges. We need equality to recast, so to speak, into a single whole, the classes of men, political opinions, and public custom.

When Bolívar returned from Europe in 1807, he joined a secret organization committed to winning independence from Spain. Bolívar's dream was to unite the Spanish colonial empire, which stretched from California to the southern tip of South America, in an alliance of free and independent states. In 1819, after

Latin revolutionary, Simón Bolívar, ca. 1820: Who might the artist have been thinking of when he or she painted this portrait?

After Independence: Rule by the Caudillos

The newly founded republics developed liberal constitutions but failed to develop political cultures that could sustain that liberalism. Furthermore, civilian governments were subject to interventions by the army and to periods of authoritarian military rule. The wars of independence were really civil wars within the Creole elite. Beyond the quest for autonomy from Spanish authority, the Creoles wanted to avoid any political participation of the *Mestizo* majority. There was no real middle class or working class to sustain pressure for reform based on liberal individualism or egalitarian democracy. In the republics, founded by the liberating armies led by Catholic priest José María Morelos in Mexico and by Bolívar and others in South America, military leaders were drawn from the landed elite. These military men championed the interests of rural society over the cities and headed their own private armies. Appealing to the historical precedents of founding liberators such as Hidalgo, Bolívar and San Martin, they also claimed to be saviours of the nation in crisis. After 1825, military leaders called *caudillos* took over and made dictatorship a part of the political tradition of Latin America.

Latin America and Informal Empire

In the confused aftermath of their foundation, the new republics would have been vulnerable to a restoration of Spanish colonialism, had it not been for the protection of Great Britain and the United States. The British controlled the sea routes between Europe and South America and worked in diplomatic councils to resist any threatened restoration of colonial rule. In 1823 James Monroe, the president of the United States, declared the Western hemisphere a sphere of influence belonging to his government. Known as the Monroe Doctrine, this decree committed Washington to resisting any European intervention.

British and American protection of the new republics preserved their political independence but

years of frustration, defeats and exile, Bolívar addressed a revolutionary council in the Venezuelan town of Angostura (Ciudad Bolívar). Here he outlined his proposal for a nation that would unite what we know today as Venezuela, Colombia, Ecuador, and Panama into a single independent state. This new state would be the cornerstone of the alliance of Latin American states of which Bolívar had dreamed. Over the next six years, Simón spearheaded a revolution that led to the liberation of Venezuela, Colombia, Ecuador, Peru, and Bolivia. Simón Bolívar died in Colombia in 1830, his body destroyed by tuberculosis, his spirit destroyed by bitterness.

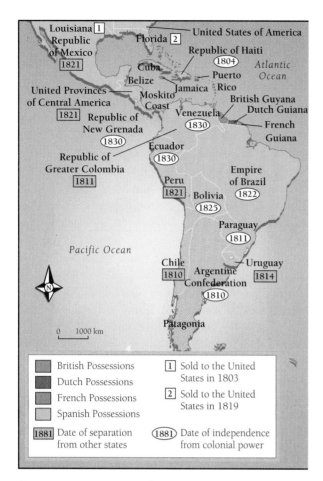

Louisiana 1
Republic of Mexico
1821
Florida 2
United States of America
Republic of Haiti
1804
Atlantic Ocean
Cuba
Belize
Jamaica
Puerto Rico
United Provinces of Central America
1821
Moskito Coast
British Guyana
Dutch Guiana
French Guiana
Republic of New Grenada
1830
Venezuela
1830
Ecuador
1830
Republic of Greater Colombia
1811
Peru
1821
Bolivia
1825
Empire of Brazil
1822
Paraguay
1811
Pacific Ocean
Chile
1810
Argentine Confederation
1810
Uruguay
1814
Patagonia
0   1000 km

British Possessions
Dutch Possessions
French Possessions
Spanish Possessions
1881 Date of separation from other states
1 Sold to the United States in 1803
2 Sold to the United States in 1819
1881 Date of independence from colonial power

■ **FIGURE 9.4** Latin America: After Independence
Areas of North America were sold to the US by the colonizing power. Do you think those sales were legal? Moral?

encouraged new dependent economic relationships. Free from colonial connections with Spain, Latin American republics forged new trade and investment links with the world's predominant maritime and industrial powers. Britain obtained raw materials and agricultural produce largely from Argentina, Chile, Peru and Brazil, the largest South American republics. In return, these republics imported British manufactured goods, and from the 1850s, British firms and technology were used to build railroads and other engineering projects. The British negotiated trade agreements on the basis of free trade, which had the effect of opening Latin American markets to British manufacturers. But, this also slowed Latin American industrial development because British industries could produce goods more cheaply. In contrast, the United States was using protective tariffs to allow its own industries to become established.

In the second half of the nineteenth century, the expansion of the American economy led the United States to overtake Britain as the leading foreign economic interest in Latin America. Under the imperialism of free trade, the South American republics, having established their political autonomy, forged new forms of economic dependency. Eventually, this dependency created U.S. interest in the domestic politics of South America. From the 1890s, especially in the Caribbean and Central America, the United States displayed an increased willingness to intervene both politically and militarily to preserve their own economic interests in Latin America.

WAR AND RESISTANCE TO COLONIZATION

Resistance to colonialism among the peoples of Asia and Africa was contemporaneous with the new imperialism of the nineteenth century. Out of this long struggle emerged the idea that all colonized peoples shared elements of history and identity in common. Consequently, unlike the nation-state nationalism of Europe, colonial nationalist movements developed a sense of belonging to a larger international movement of colonized peoples seeking liberation from colonialism and racial oppression. Anti-Western protests, sometimes called primary resistance movements, organized to expel foreigners and restore the culture to its original state.

The resistance of peoples under threat of colonization accounted for the frequent colonial wars during the age of imperialism. In resisting the encroachment of White settlers, aboriginal peoples engaged in a series of unsuccessful wars in the American West. Similarly, in the 1840s and again in the 1860s, the Maoris of New Zealand fought to preserve their land and culture. The next generation of

Under their leaders Shaka and Cetawayo, Zulu warriors such as these fought off both British and Boer armies during the nineteenth century.

Indian nationalists looked back to the Mutiny of 1857 as the origin of their movement for independence from British rule. In China, the Taiping Rebellion of the 1850s and 1860s was also a reform movement inspired by religious and political ideals in opposition to Western influence.

In the partition of Africa, the contending forces of indigenous resistance and Western encroachment were also at work. In what today is South Africa, Bantu-speaking peoples, most notably the Zulus, were organized by their leader Shaka (1787–1828) into a military caste and conducted a long struggle against both Boer settlers and British authorities from the 1830s to the end of the nineteenth century. Later, under the leadership of Cetewayo (ca 1836–1884), the Zulus defeated the British army at Islandhlwana in 1879, but the British army quickly received a supply of reinforcements and defeated the Zulus a year later. Cetewayo was given back some of his kingdom in 1883 and ruled until his death in 1884.

In West Africa, where trading relationships between local coastal states and Europeans had existed for 400 years, British and French intrusions in search of gold, palm oil, and other tropical products brought those powers into conflict with large and powerful African states. After a series of wars beginning in the 1870s and ending at the beginning of the twentieth century, Britain and France established the colonies of West Africa.

The French advance from Senegal into the interior also brought them into conflict with Islamic states, and in the Sudan, the British confronted Islamic forces attempting to preserve their autonomy from Western influences. In 1885 the Islamic leader, or *Mahdi*, and his followers succeeded in capturing Khartoum and killing its British commander, General Gordon. They controlled the area for more than a decade. In 1898, at Omdurman, a British force equipped with machine guns killed 11 000 Sudanese, lost 28 British soldiers, and put an end to this Islamic revolt. British success antagonized the French, and the two countries came close to war in a confrontation at Fashoda (today Kodok, in the Sudan) in 1898.

COLONIAL NATIONALIST MOVEMENTS

In various parts of the world, the leaders of nationalist movements in the colonies tended to be from the Western-educated elite. In India and Africa, for example, local people were employed in many jobs that required a knowledge of English and some familiarity with Western legal, administrative, and business practices in the army, government, and private businesses. At considerable expense, families had their sons educated at colleges at home or, when possible, in Britain, to make them qualified for employment in these professions. An example was Mohandas Gandhi (1869–1948), the future leader of the Indian nationalist movement, who went to London to train as a barrister. In West Africa, a similar class of Western-educated Africans received their training at mission schools and colleges and, in some cases, went on to study law or medicine at British and European universities.

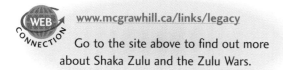

www.mcgrawhill.ca/links/legacy

Go to the site above to find out more about Shaka Zulu and the Zulu Wars.

These Western-educated, highly qualified professionals became disenchanted with European rule and founded nationalist political parties seeking first reform and eventually independence. In the late nineteenth century, European racism intensified and colonial administrators became more authoritarian. They had little tolerance for democracy within Europe — let alone within colonial empires. Consequently, White officials restricted African and Asian professionals to subordinate positions and maintained that equality before the law and the right to political representation were unsuitable for colonial societies or non-European peoples. As victims of the racism practiced by foreign intruders, the Western-educated elite in the colonies developed a legitimate grievance and a desire to be masters in their own lands.

The Indian National Congress

Founded in 1885, the Indian National Congress (INC) was one of the earliest colonial nationalist political parties and one of the most influential examples followed by other nationalist movements. When the INC originated, the Congress was moderate in its proposals for reform, seeking a larger role for Indians within the councils and administrative structure of the British *Raj* (dominion) but not seeking full political independence. From the outset, though, leaders of the Congress questioned the direction of economic developments in India. The modernization of agriculture and the extension of railroads had changed patterns of landholding and had converted some areas to the production of export crops. These reforms had also increased the peasants' indebtedness and their vulnerability to famines that struck in the 1870s and 1880s. Some Indian nationalists charged that the British connection acted as an economic drain on the resources of India. Even

though the leaders of the Congress were moderate and constitutional in their demands, British officials viewed them as unrepresentative troublemakers until more radical voices and popular protests began to change the face of Indian nationalism.

The supporters of the Congress were largely high-caste Hindus with a Western education and representative of urban interests. Their foremost spokesperson was G. K. Gokhale (1866–1915), a constitutional moderate who challenged the conduct of the British administration. A rival and more militant nationalism, associated with the revival of the Hindu religion and with support from rural communities, developed under the leadership of B. G. Tilak (1856–1920). At the cost of his own imprisonment, Tilak championed the freedom of the press and demanded independence from British rule. Popular violence and protests, some involving conflicts between Hindus and Moslems, led the British to propose a partition of the province of Bengal in 1905. This provoked widespread rioting and a boycott of British goods and British institutions. The British proposal to partition Bengal, combined with militant Indian nationalism and the potential for an independent mass movement, radicalized the Indian Congress, and, in 1905, the party committed itself to the goal of Indian self-government.

The Pan-African Movement

The Indian National Congress became a model for other colonial nationalist parties in its creation of a broad-based coalition with the common goal of independence. In July 1900, a group of men and women from Africa or of African descent held the first Pan-African (all African) Conference in London, the capital of the world's largest empire. The Conference was organized by Henry Sylvester Williams, a Trinidadian schoolteacher who had studied law at Dalhousie University in Halifax and King's College in London. Williams brought together representatives from the independent Black states of Abyssinia, Liberia and Haiti, as well as lawyers, clergymen, and journalists from South and West Africa. About 50 people attended the conference, and those from the Americas outnumbered those from Africa. The Rev. Henry B. Brown, an African-Canadian clergyman from Ontario, served as vice-president. The President of the Conference and leading speaker was Bishop Alexander Walters of the African Methodist Episcopal Zion Church of New York, and chairman of the Afro-American National Council. From the United States, young W. E. B. DuBois, who would have a long and distinguished career as a scholar, civil rights activist, and champion of Pan-Africanism, assisted with the preparation of the Conference's "Address to the Nations of the World."

W. E. B. Dubois, chief proponent of the Pan-Africanism Movement. What does Pan-Africanism mean?

This gathering of intellectuals, lawyers, clergymen, journalists, and students gave early expression to the solidarity of African peoples. The participants understood that in the struggle against colonialism and racism, the peoples of Africa and the descendants of slaves transported to the Americas were joined in a common battle. Their liberation could only come with the liberation from racial oppression of all peoples. Although the address itself tried to appeal to liberal and humanitarian opinion in Britain and elsewhere in the Western world, it forthrightly set out the demands of African peoples and of colonized peoples in Asia and elsewhere, for equal and universal rights as human beings and democratic citizens. In a phrase later made famous by W. E. B. DuBois,

The problem of the twentieth century is the problem of the colour line, the question as to how far differences of race — which show themselves chiefly in the colour of the skin and texture of the hair — will hereafter be made the basis of denying to over half the world the right of sharing to their utmost ability the opportunities and privileges of modern civilization.

A small group of Black activists meeting in London in 1900 had little immediate impact, but within the course of six or seven decades, through struggle and many setbacks, the visionary idealists of 1900 helped transform the world.

Colonial Resistance at the Turn of the Century

The Pan-African Conference was unusual in its global vision of how racism and colonialism affected peoples of African descent in particular and colonized peoples in general. Prior to 1914, the more usual pattern had been the outbreak of localized and apparently unrelated uprisings, wars, and revolutions. The causes of these outbreaks might well have been local but knowledge of these conflicts became widespread. The revolution in communications not only enabled the colonial powers to impose their authority more effectively but also enabled colonized peoples to understand the global dimensions of colonial conflict and racial oppression. In Japan, China, India, the Middle East, South and West Africa, the West Indies and in the African-American community in the United States, daily newspapers reported these events from a non-Western perspective. From this point of view, and that of some

Western observers, these localized outbreaks fit into a larger pattern that showed that the face of imperialism and global power would be altered fundamentally in the coming twentieth century:

A quick survey of some of these conflicts in the two decades prior to 1914 provides a picture of this emerging sense of a global crisis.

- In 1898 Spain faced nationalist uprisings in the last strongholds of its empire. Cuban and Filipino nationalists challenged the authority of Spain, only to be faced with the intervention of a former colony that had itself become an imperialist power: the United States. In both instances, the United States intervened, ostensibly to protect American lives and property, and ended Spanish colonial rule in its last two colonies. Filipino and Cuban nationalists now found themselves living in client (dependent) states of the new American power.

- In China in 1899, a secret martial-arts society, known as the Society of Harmonious Fists, or Boxers, conducted a campaign of murder and assault against Westerners in China. Intervention by the Western powers only intensified anti-foreign feelings and weakened support for the Manchu dynasty.

- From 1906 to 1910, Japan, the new Asian imperial power, faced protests and riots from Koreans resisting Japanese rule.

- In India, especially in the province of Bengal, the British faced hostile demonstrations and boycotts.

- In Egypt in 1906, *fellaheen* (peasants, in Arabic) attacked a British hunting party and in retaliation, an innocent Egyptian was beaten to death and another four were executed. This event profoundly alienated nationalist opinion, and in order to control dissent, the British imposed press censorship and detention without trial.

- In 1896, Emperor Menilek of Ethiopia and his army of one hundred thousand soldiers defeated Italian forces at Adowa (Adwa) and preserved the kingdom's ancient autonomy. Ethiopia had a special significance in African culture: It had links with the civilization of ancient Egypt. In the Bible,

Ethiopia was synonymous with all of Africa; and it was also the home of Coptic Christianity. As a reflection of this importance, and in part under the influence of African-American missionaries, South African Christians founded the Ethiopian movement. The founding of an autonomous church independent of European missionaries corrupted by imperialism appealed to African converts throughout the continent.

- The people of the Union of South Africa were innovative in developing strategies to resist oppression. In the aftermath of the Boer War, there were protests against the importation of fifty thousand indentured Chinese labourers to work in the gold mines.

- In Natal, in 1906, Zulus rose in insurrection against efforts to compel them into wage-labour mining.

- The Indian community of Natal and the Transvaal faced racial discrimination in being denied the vote, in restrictions on their businesses, in the obligation to carry identity passes, and in the government's refusal to recognize the legality of both Hindu and Muslim marriages. Mohandas Gandhi, a barrister who went to South Africa to be an advocate for the Indian community, having exhausted conventional legal avenues, launched a campaign on a new set of principles: passive resistance and civil disobedience. When he returned to India, he was already a well-known champion of Indian rights — the Indian press had followed his career — and had protested against the mistreatment of South Asians in South Africa, British Columbia, and elsewhere in the British Empire.

- In 1912, Africans frustrated by the denial of their rights in the constitution of the Union of South Africa, formed the South African Natives National Congress, the forerunner of the African National Congress (ANC).

- In Latin America, the forces of nationalist and popular protest had to contend with the authority of the *caudillos* and the landed elite. They also had to deal with American economic and political influence, which had become more visible with the readiness of Washington to intervene in the domestic politics of the Caribbean and Central America. In addition to American intervention in Cuba and Puerto Rico in the Spanish-American War (1898), U.S. President Theodore Roosevelt (1858–1919) promoted a secessionist movement in Colombia, and intervened in 1903 to establish the client state of Panama to secure lands for the future Panama Canal. American troops also occupied Nicaragua in 1912 to support the United Fruit Company, and invaded the Dominican Republic in 1914, and Haiti in 1915.

- The most significant upheaval occurred in Mexico, where Washington also tried to influence events, but where a revolutionary crisis in 1910–1920 created a social upheaval too large for the simple machinations of an external power. In the North, under the leadership of Pancho Villa, and in the South, under the leadership of Emiliano Zapata, the peasantry struggled to reclaim control of the land. In the course of this revolutionary war, over one million peasants died. In the South, where there was a large Amerindian population, the Zapatistas fought for land and for the preservation of Amerindian culture. The Zapatista movement inspired a new nationalism among Amerindian communities elsewhere in Latin America.

Review, Reflect, Respond

1. Describe the legacy of emancipation in two areas of the world.

2. How did the intellectual movements in Europe during the eighteenth century and early nineteenth century contribute to the goals and ideas expressed by Simón Bolívar. Why did his hopes for a united Latin America fail?

3. What did the Indian National Congress and the Pan-African Movement have in common? Refer to factors such as leadership, goals, political platform, grievances, and the nature of success or failure of each movement.

The Russo-Japanese War 1904–1905

The victory of Japan over Russia in the Russo-Japanese War of 1904–1905 was remarkable in two ways. Firstly, not only had a non-Western power defeated a major European power in war, but the conflict had been fought using the full arsenal of modern military technology. Three hundred thousand troops were engaged on either side, and Japan defeated the modern Russian navy. Here was proof that a non-European power could claim equal standing with a large and powerful nation.

Dr. Sun Yat-sen, first president of the republic of China after the Revolution of 1911. There is a statue of Dr. Sun Yat-sen in Riverdale Park, Toronto.

Leopold von Ranke on Objective History

Von Ranke was a leading German historian of the nineteenth century. He had a formative influence on Western historiography and coined the phrase *wie es eigentlich gewesen* ("show it how it really was"), which became the basis of nineteenth-century attempts to produce objective history. Ranke wanted to understand the actions of God in history but did not believe this could be achieved by using a moralistic approach to history. In his preface to the first edition of the *Histories of the Latin and Germanic Nations from 1494–1514*, von Ranke wrote:

> To history has been assigned the office of judging the past, of instructing the present for the benefit of future ages. To such high offices this work does not aspire: It wants only to show what actually happened.
>
> But whence the sources for such a new investigation? The basis of the present work, the sources of its material, are memoirs, diaries, letters, diplomatic reports, and original narratives of eyewitnesses; other writings were used only if they were immediately derived from the above mentioned or seemed to equal them because of some original information. These sources are identified on every page; a second volume, to be published concurrently, will present the research methods and the critical conclusions. Aim and material mold the form of a book. The writing of history cannot be expected to possess the same free development of its subject which, in theory at least, is expected in a poetical work; I am not sure it was correct to ascribe this quality to the works of the great Greek and Roman masters. The strict presentation of the facts, contingent and unattractive though they may be, is undoubtedly the supreme law. After that, it seems to me, comes the exposition of the unity and progress of events. Therefore, instead of starting as might have been expected with a general description of the political institutions of Europe — this would certainly have distracted, if not disrupted, our attention — I have preferred to discuss in detail each nation, each power, and each individual only when they assumed a pre-eminently active or dominant role. I have not been troubled by the fact that here and there they had to be mentioned beforehand, when their existence could not be ignored. In this way, we are able at least to grasp the general line of their development, the direction they took, and the ideas by which they were motivated.
>
> Finally, what will be said of my treatment of particulars, which is such an essential part of the writing of history? Will it not often seem harsh, disconnected, colorless, and tiring? There are, of course, noble models both ancient and — be it remembered — modern; I have not dared to emulate them: theirs was a different world. A sublime ideal does exist: the event in its human intelligibility, its unity, and its diversity; this should be within one's reach. I know to what extent I have fallen short of my aim. One tries, one strives, but in the [end] one does not attain one's end. Let none be disheartened by this! The most important thing is always what we deal with, as Jakobi says, humanity as it is, explicable or inexplicable: the life of the individual, of generations, and of nations, and at times the hand of God above them.[2]

1. Do you agree with von Ranke's methods when he states: "I have preferred to discuss in detail each nation, each power, and each individual only when they assumed a pre-eminently active or dominant role."? Explain your opinion using examples.

The Russo-Japanese War had important consequences for the direction of world history. Russian interests were deflected from Asia to Europe and added to the buildup of diplomatic tensions that led to the Russian Revolution in 1905, an inspiration for revolutions elsewhere, and to World War I in 1914. The news of the Japanese victory was widely celebrated in the nationalist press of China, India, the Middle East, and Africa. In the European press, journalists worried about the blow inflicted upon the perceived imperial majesty of all Europeans; fanatical racists feared a new Yellow, Brown, and Black Peril sweeping the globe.

A number of events followed close on the heels of the Russo-Japanese War. In Persia (modern Iran), an insurrection in 1905 led to a constitutional revolution that created an elected assembly under the Shah. In 1908 a *coup* by young army officers, the Young Turks, introduced modernizing reforms to the Ottoman Empire. Popular disorder and mounting nationalist pressure led the Dutch to create a People's Council with Indonesian representatives for the East Indies. In India, liberal reforms placed Indian representatives on the Viceroy's Council.

The most stunning change occurred in China: The Revolution of 1911 brought down the Manchu dynasty and proclaimed a new republic based on the principles of nationalism, socialism, and democracy. The first president of the Republic was Dr. Sun Yat-sen (1866–1925), the son of a peasant family who converted to Christianity as a teenager.

Sun Yat-sen had spent many years abroad, living for a time in Vancouver, and received support from expatriate Chinese communities around the world. As recently as 1907, Vancouver's Asian community was the target of a White racist riot.

Reflections

It is important to recognize the global dimension of revolutionary conflicts engendered by Western imperialism and to appreciate the deep historical roots of movements seeking liberation from colonial and racial oppression. It is equally important not to underestimate the power of the colonial empires. On the eve of World War I, these were at the zenith of their power. The transformation of the modern world system in the course of the nineteenth century involved an enormous expansion of the colonial empires and an equally unprecedented increase in their military might and economic power. In the twentieth century, it would take two world wars to shake the foundations of the world's imperialist powers. The colonized peoples played an important role in their liberation from colonial domination and racism. We need to remember the experience of people like Toussaint L'Ouverture, Simón Bolívar, Sun Yat-sen, and Gandhi. People with intelligence, courage and determination — even from obscure backgrounds without access to the power of the state — have risen in times of crisis and conflict to advance the common cause of liberation.

Chapter Review

Chapter Summary

In this chapter, you have seen:

- the impact of Western colonization on both the colonizer and the colonized
- that understanding the importance of chronology is an important tool in analysing historical events
- the key characteristics of and significant ideas emerging from various cultures around the world during the nineteenth century
- that selected non-Western ideas and cultures influenced developments in indigenous societies

Reviewing the Significance of Key People, Concepts, and Events (Knowledge and Understanding)

1. Understanding world history during the nineteenth century requires a knowledge of the following concepts, events and people and an understanding of their significance in the shaping of the history over the past two centuries. Select and explain two from each column.

Concepts	Events	People
Imperialism	Berlin Conference (1884)	J. A. Hobson
East India Company	Indian Mutiny of 1857	King Leopold II
laissez faire	Opium Wars	Toussaint L'Ouverture
racism	Fugitive SlaveAct	Sam Sharpe
Caudillos	Emancipation Proclamation	Simón Bolívar
Indian National Congress	Boer War	Sun Yat-sen
Pan-African Conference	Russo-Japanese War	

2. Throughout the nineteenth century, European imperial powers faced resistance from virtually every corner of the earth. Each time a colonial power encountered resistance, it prompted a reaction. Re-create and complete the following chart in your notes.

Nature of Resistance	Imperial Power	Response of Imperial Power
South America		
Caribbean		
China		
India		

Doing History: Thinking About the Past (Thinking/Inquiry)

3. The struggle for political and economic independence continues in many parts of the world today. The foundations for these movements, however, were laid down in the nineteenth century. How did colonial resistance at the turn of the twentieth century help shape the world today?

4. In an essay entitled "The Development of Underdevelopment," André Gunder Frank suggests that many third-world countries have been intentionally underdeveloped to serve the capitalist needs of the developed world. He argues that Europeans seldom set out to explore the world without the desire to exploit it. To what degree does the history of imperialism and colonialism support Gunder Frank's view?

Applying Your Learning (Application)

5. In February of 1899, English writer Rudyard Kipling's poem "The White Man's Burden" appeared in *McClure's Magazine*. The poem provided defenders of imperialism with the defence of their policies rooted in the noble cause of civilizing the world. Within a few weeks, a response in the form of a poem titled "The Brown Man's Burden" surfaced in magazines such as *Truth*. Consider what these two poems tell us about the attitudes of the colonized and the colonizers in 1899. Did either of the passages surprise you? Explain why or why not.

The White Man's Burden

Take up the White Man's burden —
Send forth the best ye breed —
Go, bind your sons to exile
To serve your captives' need;
To wait, in heavy harness,
On fluttered folk and wild —
Your new-caught sullen peoples,
Half devil and half child.
Take up the White Man's burden —
In patience to abide,
To veil the threat of terror
And check the show of pride;
By open speech and simple,
An hundred times made plain,
To seek another's profit
And work another's gain.
Take up the White Man's burden —[3]

The Brown Man's Burden

Pile on the brown man's burden
To gratify your greed;
Go, clear away the "niggers"
Who progress would impede;
Be very stern, for truly
'Tis useless to be mild
With new-caught, sullen peoples,
Half devil and half child...
Pile on the brown man's burden,
compel him to be free;
Let all your manifestoes
Reek with philanthropy.
And if with heathen folly
He dares your will dispute,
Then, in the name of freedom,
Don't hesitate to shoot.[4]

By Henry Labouchère
Truth (London); reprinted in Literary Digest 18
(Feb. 25, 1899).

6. Considering the two poems cited above and what you have learned from this chapter, prepare two editorials for late-nineteenth-century magazines or newspapers. One of the editorials should be from the perspective of the colonizers, defending imperialism, while the other is to be from the viewpoint of the colonized, showing how colonization has affected their society.

Communicating Your Learning (Communication)

7. Create a concept map beginning with imperialism and its repercussions as the central concept.

8. Select one event you have learned about in this chapter and retell the event in the form of a television news report. You may need to do a little additional research. Remember who your audience is. Your story should not be more than 400 words and should include suggested camera shots for the report.

Unit Review

Reflecting on What You Have Learned (Knowledge and Understanding)

1. The nineteenth century introduced a multitude of new ideas or "isms" to the West, many of which would come to have global implications. For each of the "isms" listed below, provide some background (when developed, by whom, key ideas) and provide a brief comment on the impact of the "ism" on society.

"ism"	"ism" defined	Impact of the "ism" on Society
Communism		
Conservatism		
Darwinism		
Romanticism		

2. Summarize the various consequences of imperialism for Europe and the world in a concept map.

Practising Historical Interpretation (Thinking/Inquiry)

3. It has been suggested that power lay at the root of change in the nineteenth century. Not political or economic power, but the harnessing of steam power and later the internal combustion engine. This meant that for the first time in history, human beings were not limited to human power or work animals. Do you agree that power lay at the root of most of the significant changes in the nineteenth century? Support your answer with historical evidence.

4. By the late nineteenth century industrialization and imperialism had radically altered the relationships between various parts of the world. Explain how and why the world became divided along racial lines. How was science used to support the political ends of the late nineteenth century?

Applying Your Historical Understanding (Application)

5. Read again the definition of genius given in the Unit One Review. Select one of the historical figures from the list below and explain why you believe he or she should be remembered as a genius. If you believe they merit the title of genius, be sure to show clearly how their work had a lasting effect on a particular domain.

Karl Marx	Simón Bolívar	Charles Darwin
John Stuart Mill	Sun Yat-sen	Marie Curie
Thomas Malthus	Emmeline Pankhurst	Albert Einstein
Eugene Delacroix	Josephine Butler	Sigmund Freud
Toussaint L'Ouverture	Vladimir Ilich Ulyanov (Lenin)	Vincent van Gogh

6. When the nineteenth century began, Europe was largely governed by monarchies, industrialization had not spread far beyond England, and the study of science was seen as a way to know God. Considering political, economic, and social developments both within Europe and around the world, can it be argued that the nineteenth century was a transitional age? Defend your answer with historical evidence.

Communicating Your Learning (Communication)

7. Write an "I am ..." poem based on one of the following groups or concepts. For an example of an "I am ..." poem, go to the *Legacy* web site at www.mcgrawhill.ca/links/legacy.
   proletariat
   bourgeoisie
   communist
   suffragist
   Luddite
   impressionist
   imperialist
   colonial

8. Create a set of maps that depict the spread of imperialism between 1815 and 1914. Make effective use of visuals, symbols, and icons as well as clear labels to indicate countries, empires, the exchange of goods between the imperial powers and colonies, and instances of resistance among the colonies.

> * *Now complete Skills Focus Four:*
> **Formulating a Thesis.** *(p. 596)*

The World at War 1914–1945

Chapter Ten
**The War to End War
World War I 1914–1919**

Chapter Eleven
An Anxious Generation

Chapter Twelve
World War II, 1939–1945

Unique Forms of Continuity in Space (1913, bronze, 1.1m high) by Umberto Boccioni. The artist was a member of a group known as the Futurists. In their Manifesto, these artists proclaimed a new artistic language that worshipped speed, technology and war, and scorned women.

The period between the end of the Napoleonic era and the beginning of World War I was relatively peaceful in Europe. Although there were significant wars in the Crimea and the United States, Europe remained largely unscathed. While the nineteenth century was a period of peace and stability, it could also be described as the calm before the storm. A century of industrial growth and innovation, expanding empires and growing nationalism, planted the seeds of destruction that would plague the Western world twice in less than half a century.

Between the two world wars, much of the world experienced an economic boom and bust. The radical swings in the economies of North America and Europe led many to question unbridled capitalism. The suffering experienced by many families during the Great Depression convinced many governments to play a more active role in the social welfare of their citizens.

UNIT EXPECTATIONS

In this unit, you will:

- O evaluate key factors that led to conflict and war or to co-operation and peace

- O demonstrate an understanding of how the historical concept of continuity is used to analyse developments in the West and throughout the world during the first half of the twentieth century

- O demonstrate an understanding of the key Western beliefs, philosophies, and ideologies that have shaped the West and the rest of the world during the twentieth century

- O analyse significant economic developments in the West and the rest of the world during the first half of the twentieth century

- O demonstrate an ability to think creatively, manage time efficiently, and work effectively in independent and collaborative study

This Russian political cartoon shows Kaiser Wilhelm, the German Emperor, on a battlefield with cannons and airplanes, killing Russians. The caption is "merry-go-round of Wilhelm". What was the " merry-go-round"?

The War to End War World War I 1914-1919

CHAPTER EXPECTATIONS

By the end of this chapter, you will be able to:

- *demonstrate an understanding of the key factors that have led to conflict and war*

- *demonstrate an understanding of the consequences of war*

- *assess the extent to which art reinforces and/or challenges prevailing social and political values*

- *describe a variety of forces that helped to bring about changes in modern Western artistic expression*

- *analyse various efforts to create international governmental and judicial structures*

One of many posters urging people to buy government bonds to help raise money for the war effort.

The period of industrial and scientific progress from 1815–1914 ended in a war made more terrible by industry and science. People of the time called World War I the Great War, as it was indeed greater in death and destruction than any war known to that time; however, this "war to end war" would be followed by revolutionary wars and another, even greater world war. Some historians describe a continuum of violence in modern history, running from the mass slaughter of soldiers in World War I to the genocides of World War II. This chapter traces the causes, events, and results of this destruction. It describes the most violent half-century in European history. The changes brought about by the turmoil included the overthrow of monarchies and governments, the decimation of both the ruling classes and the peasantry of some nations, and massive social changes in the lives of European families. A materialistic, confident, and optimistic European era was about to come to a dramatic end. Decades of competition for limited resources, rampant nationalism, and historical antagonisms propelled Europe into an arms race and hostile alliances. The assassination of the heir to the Austrian throne was the fateful spark that ignited the other more complex causes of the war. The harsh reality of modern warfare was an ordeal from which Europe never fully recovered. The story begins when Europe is at the peak of its power.

The causes of the European catastrophe of 1914 must be studied within a historical framework, going back to the German victory in the Franco-Prussian War of 1870–1871. Bismarck had built the new German Empire and he would spend his last years in politics trying to preserve it. France, bitter in defeat and bent on revenge, was looking for allies against Germany. With diplomatic genius, Bismarck kept the French alone and isolated by tying the major powers into alliances with Germany. He brought his country together with Austria (1879) and Italy (1882) to form the Triple Alliance. Finally, in 1887, he joined with Russia in the Reinsurance Treaty. Bismarck, who made his way into history by winning wars, ended by building an alliance system for peace. Ironically, this binding together of powerful nations by permanent military commitments started Europe on the road to war in 1914.

KEY CONCEPTS AND EVENTS

Dreadnought

Schlieffen Plan

Hague Peace Conference

Battle of the Marne

Russian Revolution

The Lusitania

Bloody Sunday

Marxism and Leninism

Treaty of Versailles

League of Nations

KEY PEOPLE

Kaiser Wilhelm II

Archduke Franz Ferdinand

Douglas Haig

Marshal Philippe Pétain

David Lloyd George

Georges Clemenceau

Czar Nicholas II

Rasputin

Leon Trotsky

Woodrow Wilson

Erich Maria Remarque

Wit and Wisdom

War makes rattling good history; but peace is poor reading.
Thomas Hardy, *The Dynasts* (1904)

TIME LINE: THE WAR TO END WAR

Creation of German Empire under Kaiser Willhelm I and Otto von Bismarck	1871	
	1882	Triple Alliance: Germany, Austria-Hungary, and Italy
Lenin, *What Is to Be Done?*	1902	
	1904	Russo-Japanese War
"Bloody Sunday" uprising in Russia	1905	
	1905	*Duma* (Russian parliament) dissolved
Triple Entente: Great Britain, France, and Russia	1905	
	1912–1913	The Balkan Wars
World War I begins	1914	
	1915	Battle of the Somme
United States enters World War I	1917	
	1917	March Revolution in Russia
End of World War I	1918	
	1919	Treaty of Versailles
Civil war and war communism in Russia	1918–1921	
	1924	Lenin dies

Not to scale.

WORLD WAR I
Causes of the War

An event in 1890 changed the game of great-power relations: Bismarck was dismissed from office. The young and ambitious Kaiser Wilhelm II forced the ageing chancellor into retirement and put himself at the centre of German affairs. Advisers convinced him that Bismarck's alliance system was too complicated, and that Austria and Russia had too many quarrels between them to be common allies with Germany. As a result, Berlin stayed with its Germanic partner, Austria, in the older Triple Alliance and let the Reinsurance Treaty with Russia expire. Russia and France, two societies so different from each other, now had something in common. Both were without strong allies. What followed was a revolution in European affairs. In 1894 France and Russia signed a mutual-defence pact. Soon after, Britain began having second thoughts about being isolated from her European neighbours. In need of better relations, the British joined with France (1904) and Russia (1907) in a loose agreement described as an *entente cordiale*. This Triple Entente was a "friendly understanding," a vow of closer association. Now it was Germany's turn to feel surrounded by adversaries.

In the face-off between the Triple Alliance and the Triple Entente, Germany had the weaker allies. Austria-Hungary, under Emperor Franz Joseph I, was a power already in decline due to internal political and economic conflicts. Italy was poised to join the other side at the first chance. Germany, however, made up the difference, since it was the powerhouse of the Continent, the new superpower that challenged the European order. Leading everyone in industry and output, Germany had the best technology, scientists, and universities in the world. Its army was one of the finest. Its population, 65 million in 1914, was the largest in Europe outside Russia. Its steel production was greater than that of Britain, France, and Russia put together. Germany was a new nation, a latecomer, but already its strength was out of proportion to the other powers. Germany was perceived as a nation too big and too powerful for any other nation to face alone.

Under Wilhelm II, German power was enhanced by a driven and blustering ruler. In love with dashing uniforms and dramatic poses, the kaiser brought to foreign relations a bullying style that fostered aggressive German nationalism. At times he wanted to make peace; at times he threatened to make war; at times he wanted to make peace by threatening to make war. To him, the twentieth century was to be "Germany's century." Where Bismarck saw Germany as a contented nation, at peace with its place in the world, Wilhelm saw a nation still rising to greatness. Where Bismarck believed that Germany's greatness was in its army, Wilhelm wanted to make it a sea power that would rival Britain's fleet. Where Bismarck wanted to keep out of competition with France and England for colonies around the world, Wilhelm wanted Germany to have them. The result in Europe was an armed peace, and one war scare after another.

www.mcgrawhill.ca/links/legacy

Go to the site above to find out more about the Schlieffen Plan.

Germany and France appeared on the brink of war in 1905, and again in 1911, when the kaiser threatened to resist French designs on Morocco. His bullying, however, always made things worse. This time he annoyed the British, and brought them closer to the side of France. At this point, German-British relations were already tense over Wilhelm's dream of sea power. German naval planners had convinced the kaiser that sea power was essential to great-nation status, and that battleships were a necessity for power at sea. While Germany built battleships, Britain's plan was to match them two to one. In 1905, the British began work on the dreadnought, the first of a new class of battleship

— larger, faster, deadlier, and far more expensive than anything afloat — that would make all other battleships obsolete. Both nations went back to the starting line and the naval race between Britain and Germany began all over again. Larger ships and larger armies were driving military spending, and military spending was straining national nerves and budgets.

The more governments faced the threat of war, the more they placed their hopes on the military. Military people, in turn, placed their hopes on war plans for victory. The German plan in 1905 was the work of army chief General Alfred von Schlieffen (1833–1913) who designed it to overcome the danger that Germans feared the most — a two-front war against Russia and France. His plan was to beat them one at a time. Schlieffen thought that Russia, could only move slowly and so could be held off for a time by Austria-Hungary.

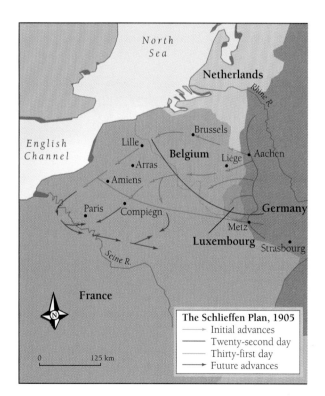

■ FIGURE 10.1 The Schlieffen Plan

Compare the Schlieffen Plan to Hitler's war plans. Where are they similar and where do they differ?

A German attack on France was to be first, fast and fatal, and to be wound up in six weeks. German armies, bursting through Belgium (which was neutral), were to roll past Paris in a vast, wheeled movement, driving the French armies to defeat against the Alps. The Schlieffen Plan was war by timetable. "Do not build forts," said Schlieffen, "build railroads." Trains would speed the mass invasion of France. After victory, trains would then speed the mass transfer of troops to Russia. The Schlieffen Plan, like the war plans of other powers, inspired hope and courted disaster. It was geared to quick success based on the dangerous idea that victory goes to the one who attacks first.

Europe was on high alert. The powers were ready for war — but not for the kind of war that was coming. Europe was ready for another nineteenth-century war, one like the Crimean War, which lasted only a few years (1853–1856), with victory or defeat stemming from a few decisive battles. Wars were a custom of the system of nation-states on the Continent. They were a way for countries to defend their honour and interests after diplomacy had failed.

The nature of war was changing for the worse. The 600 000 dead in the American Civil War (1861–1865) should have been a warning that modern weapons could turn war into mass slaughter. Unfortunately, this overseas warning was too distant to be heard. The alliance system, created by Bismarck to keep the peace and maintain the balance of power, had instead set the stage for great-power warfare on a continental scale. There were dreadnought navies and million-man armies; there was an arms race, naval race, and war plans. There were the high emotions that went with international crises, emotions rising and falling with every war scare. And there was "jingoism," the rowdy, flag-waving patriotism that took its name from a popular British song called *By Jingo!*:

> We don't want to fight
> But by jingo if we do
> We've got the ships
> We've got the men
> We've got the money too

Peace and Co-operation

Movements for peace and disarmament were as much a part of the history of this period as preparations for war. From them came peace ideas of all kinds, ideas for world law, a league of nations, arbitration of international disputes, education for peace, and arms control.

As governments increased military spending, some people of wealth spent their own fortunes on projects for peace. When he died in 1896, Swedish industrialist and inventor of dynamite, Alfred Nobel, for example, bequeathed large sums in the form of yearly peace prizes to support outstanding contributors to world order. In 1910 American steel millionaire Andrew Carnegie established the Carnegie Endowment for International Peace to promote better understanding between nations. The strength of "peace" came from the bottom of the social pyramid as well. Millions of working-class members of Europe's socialist movements identified the cause of socialism with the cause of peace. To them, militarism stirred hatred, turned nation against nation, and defeated the common purpose of working people everywhere to create a better life together. In parliaments, the socialist parties (such as the German Social Democratic Party), following this anti-war line of the Second International Workingmen's Association, voted year after year against conscription and military budgets.

As Europe moved toward war, it was full of illusions about the power of peace. In 1900 a great international exhibit in Paris (held to celebrate the high civilization of the West at the beginning of the new century) drew over 50 million visitors to a vast display of scientific and industrial inventions. Such wonders, and a generation of peace since 1871, encouraged some Europeans to believe that they had advanced too far to return to war again. The structure of peace was too strong. Commerce connected nation to nation. In most capitals, government was still in the hands of aristocrats, people of culture and conservatism with a common interest in the international order. Ruling families shared blood ties. The crowned heads of England, Russia, and Germany were cousins, related through Queen Victoria of England, whose many descendants connected the grand families of the Continent. The strength of peace, some Europeans believed, was that too many had too much to lose in a war.

In 1898 Czar Nicholas II, unable to keep pace in military spending with the Western powers, called for an international conference to limit armaments. The results were the Hague Peace Conferences of 1899 and 1907, the first meetings nations had ever had on the issue of arms control. Delegates debated the same hard questions that such meetings have debated ever since: Do fewer weapons keep the peace or does peace come through strength? Do weapons cause or deter war? Ultimately, the conference left everything important about weapons to national governments to decide on their own. The ideal of international co-operation for arms control was no match for the reality of nations bent on defending themselves.

In the end, the peace movements were overwhelmed by the outburst of popular enthusiasm that greeted the coming of war in 1914. In every capital, as governments read out declarations of war, crowds cheered and sang patriotic songs; socialists embraced

Swedish industrialist Alfred Nobel invented dynamite and instituted the Nobel Peace Prize. Who was the Canadian awarded this prize in the twentieth century?

their nation's cause; labour unions promised to end strikes. World War I began as a people's war and, at the start, Europeans of all classes were in it together. Everyone thought the war would be over by Christmas (1914).

The Outbreak of War

Early in the century, great-power rivalries in Europe were centred in two areas. One was in the West, where France and England confronted Germany. The other was in the Balkans, where three empires, Russia, Austria-Hungary and Ottoman Turkey, struggled for supremacy. Long before 1914, observers had described the Balkans as the real trouble spot, the place where a catastrophe was waiting to happen. When Austria-Hungary appealed to its German ally and France sided with Russia, the two conflict areas — the Balkans and the West — merged into one, and what was to happen in Sarajevo became a major crisis involving all of Europe.

Historically speaking, the trouble in the Balkans began when the Ottoman Empire, after centuries of control over the region, began to weaken. In decline, the Turks were making concessions during the struggle of Balkan peoples for national liberation. The Serbs, a southern Slavic people, broke free of the Ottomans and received recognition from the European powers as an independent nation in 1878. Serbs dreamt of a "Greater Serbia," with borders expanded to the western Balkans to include all the South Slavs. In the fulfilment of this dream, Serbia crossed paths with Austria-Hungary, moving into the area to take the place of the Ottoman Empire in resisting the liberation of the South Slavs.

The Austro-Hungarian Hapsburgs, struggling against the odds to preserve a multinational empire in an age of nationalism, lived in fear of national movements and came to fear expansionist Serbia. Austrian officials saw Serb efforts to arouse the nationalism of South Slavs as a menace that could spread to other peoples under their control. Each nation saw potential danger: Serbia believed that Austria threatened the dream of Greater Serbia; Austria believed that Serbia threatened the future of the Empire. Thus, the mighty Hapsburgs, rulers of over 50 million people, became the enemy of little Serbia, with a population of about three million.

The real danger came when Serbia turned for help to another mighty empire – Russia. The Russians had their own dream about the Balkans, and longed to possess strategic Constantinople (today Istanbul) and the Dardanelle Straits connecting the Black Sea to the Mediterranean. In coming to protect Serbia against Austria, however, Slavic Russia was responding as well to pan-Slavism, the idea of a brotherhood of all Slavic peoples, and to its historic role in protecting them against foreign oppressors.

In 1908 the Russian and Austro-Hungarian Empires came to the brink of war after Austria annexed Bosnia and Herzegovina. These provinces were the home of South Slavs, peoples that Serbia longed to include in the Greater Serbia of the future. After months of crisis, Russia, lacking the support of France and Britain and weak after defeat in the Russo-Japanese War of 1904–1905, decided not to fight. Instead, it issued a warning: next time, there would be war. "Next time" came on June 28, 1914, when Franz Ferdinand and his wife were murdered by a Bosnian revolutionary during a parade at Sarajevo. Within weeks, Europe was spiralling into war and, on August 4, Germany invaded Belgium and World War I had begun.

The July Crisis

Few periods in history have been more closely studied than these last days of peace. Much of the later debate among historians on the war-guilt controversy (over who was responsible for the war) dwelt on the words and deeds of political leaders during this so-called July Crisis. Austrian leaders were certain — but had no proof — that Serbia was behind the assassination of Austria's archduke in Sarajevo. Their intent was to punish Serbia in a brief and overpowering war, and get out before Russia had time to come to its rescue. As insurance against misfortune, Austrian foreign minister Leopold von Berchtold obtained from his German ally on July 6 a promise of full support in dealing with

Serbia. This was the famous "blank cheque," the binding commitment from Germany to back Austria in the case of a Balkans showdown. So armed, on July 23 Berchtold sent Serbia an ultimatum: a list of 10 demands so harsh that rejection was seen as inevitable. Serbia accepted all but two of the demands, those that challenged its sovereignty. Great Britain proposed an international conference on the matter and, just when it appeared that the crisis had passed, Austria declared war against Serbia on July 28 and began bombing its capital, Belgrade, the next day.

Called to the defence of Serbia, Russia now set the stage for disaster. Despite last-minute telegrams from Kaiser Wilhelm pleading with him to negotiate with Austria, on July 30 Czar Nicholas ordered his army to mobilize for war. The czar's advisers had convinced him that Russia had to keep its word to protect Serbia. With this, the clock started running against Germany because the Schlieffen Plan timetable had an essential condition: Germany had to strike first, driving into France while Russia was still going through the motions of preparing for war. The situation was clear: Germany either had to stop Russian mobilization or start the war itself. In an ultimatum on July 31, Germany ordered Russia to halt mobilization within 12 hours. Receiving no reply, Germany declared war against Russia on August 1, and against France two days later. The next day, August 4, German troops were advancing through Belgium.

Next came the turn of the most uncertain player of all: Britain. Other nations were bound to their partners by written treaties, although secret clauses in the agreements kept enemies in the dark about important commitments. Britain, already preoccupied with the Irish Home Rule issue, had only a "friendly understanding" with France and Russia, nothing written and nothing signed. As a result, Germany reasoned that the British, having no stake in the war, would remain neutral. But, Britain declared war on Germany condemning the German invasion of Belgium as the violation of a treaty signed back in 1839 that pledged to respect the neutrality of the Belgian nation. Astonished, German officials denounced this decision to go to war over "a scrap of paper" from the previous century. Had London first warned Berlin of its intention to fight for Belgium, they asserted, there would have been no German attack and no war. Thus, as battle started, all nations had the idea that they were being forced to fight, that their cause was just, and that the other side was to blame.

The Beginning of the War

"The lamps are going out all over Europe," said British foreign secretary Sir Edward Grey on the eve of the war, "and we shall not see them lit again in our lifetime." The event that truly turned out the lights was the Battle of the Marne on September 6–9, 1914, when the German assault on France was stopped in its tracks, within 35 miles of Paris. After marching through Belgium and sending the French reeling in retreat, Germany had over a million soldiers advancing across northern France, when one of its armies attempted a manoeuvre that caused it to veer away from the line of attack. The result was the "Marne gap," an opening in the German lines at the Marne River northeast of Paris. In a savage counterattack, French commander-in-chief Marshall Joseph Joffre (1852–1931) threw into the opening all the reserves at hand, halting the German assault and ending the German illusion of a lightning victory.

Germany now realized that it had to fight a two-front war. When the battle began in the West, the feared Russian army, the largest but worst equipped of the great powers, struck from the East, driving a small German force back into Germany. There, however, at Tannenberg, the Russians fell into a trap. In the first great victory of the war, the Germans destroyed the advancing army with a crushing blow. In the fall and into the winter, the two sides battled back and forth across Russian land, until a loose line of defence came to form the Eastern front. Here, movement and manoeuvring remained possible for most of the war. In the West, on the other hand, the front was solid for the first months.

After the "miracle of the Marne," the two sides were lined up at close range along a front stretching

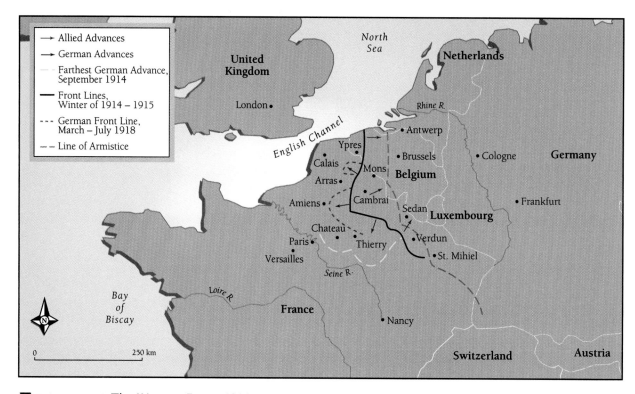

FIGURE 10.2 The Western Front, 1914
Looking at this map, you can see place names that have become memorials to bloody battles. What places witnessed Canadian heroism?

over 725 kilometres from the sea in Belgium to the Alps at the Swiss frontier. It was a front without flanks, gaps, or room to move. Shut in, the soldiers dug trenches and strung barbed wire. There they stayed, separated from the enemy by a "no-man's-land." These trench lines of 1914 moved little in either direction until the last year of the war (1918). Instead of *Blitzkrieg*, or lightning war (as in WWII), fighting in the West was a *Sitzkrieg*, a sitting war or stalemate in the trenches.

In past wars, the charge of soldiers on horseback would break through the enemy line and roll up the flank. War was the art of movement, with all the advantage on the side of the offence. As a result, most of the military held the opinion that the best way to make war was to attack. In the first battles of 1914, however, the cavalry rode into the muzzle of machine guns and rapid-fire artillery; soldiers and horses were

slaughtered immediately. Developments in firepower had taken the "lightning" out of war and shifted the advantage to the defence. Early on, however, the generals held to the old idea of "offence to the limit," using infantry attacks where the cavalry charge had failed. The infantry paid the price in blood.

In 1915 Britain tried to get around this slaughter in France by landing an invasion force on the Gallipoli peninsula in the Turkish Dardanelles. The plan was to open a front in the Balkans against Ottoman Turkey, which had joined forces with the so-called Central Powers, Germany and Austria-Hungary, in 1914. The failure of this operation, however, made it plain that there was no easy way out. The war would be decided by a fight to the finish on the Western front, in which the chances of success depended on bringing more force to bear against the enemy: more soldiers, more material, more allies, more science, more propaganda.

World War I rapidly became a war in the trenches as infantry came up against machine guns, not horses. War in the trenches would prove to be slow, filthy and deadly for millions of soldiers.

In a word, to make total war. By way of definition, total war can be described as a war in which the total resources of society are committed to the fighting effort. Conditions for a war of this nature probably were long present in Europe, but total war first "happened" at this point in World War I because of the determination of both sides to break the stalemate. The effect was to change the war from a fight between European alliances into a world-scale war.

As many as six million soldiers went to war in 1914, and the number increased to over 65 million before the fighting ended in 1918. To keep the soldiers coming, Germany drafted all able males from ages 16 to 50. France made soldiers out of the people in its African and Asian colonies. England called in the Empire, bringing troops from Canada, Australia, New Zealand, India and South Africa. In fact, only industrialized nations could keep up with the demands of the war for supplies and munitions. Nonetheless, both sides worked to win over nations and peoples of every description. Bribes and promises became the stuff of wartime diplomacy.

Italy, having deserted the Triple Alliance in 1914, joined the Triple Entente (called the Allies) after receiving promises in the secret Treaty of London in 1915 of territory to be taken from Austria-Hungary after the war. Germany used the same ploy to bring Bulgaria to the Central Powers. Britain coaxed Arab leaders into rebellion by promising to liberate their lands from the Ottomans. Then London made a bid for Jewish opinion by promising "a national home for the Jewish people" in Palestine (The Balfour Declaration, 1917). Before the war was over, 38 nations, some as far away as Japan and Brazil, were involved in a war caused by the death of an archduke in a corner of the Balkans.

When the Canadian officer John McCrae (1872–1918) wrote his poem *In Flanders Fields* in 1915, the idealism of duty and sacrifice was still strong. Over time, however, the daily slaughter took its toll on the fighting soldiers. Worst were the days of the big offensives, always beginning and ending in the same way: first massive artillery fire to "soften up" the enemy (such was the roar of weapons that on a still day the sound could be heard in London and Paris); then came the massacre, the mad rush of soldiers going "over the top" and into the machine guns and barbed wire. What was left of the romance of war vanished after 1916, when the idea of "offence to the limit" was finally was buried under dead bodies.

That year started with the German assault on Verdun. The fortress of Verdun was a symbol of French military glory, and the German commander believed that the proud French would defend it to the last man. There, he said, he could "bleed them white." In reality, the two sides bled each other. For four months, German metal fell on Verdun like snow: over a million shells, the greatest bombardment in the history of warfare, blasting to pieces fortress, earth, and already-dead bodies. The Germans suffered 280 000 casualties, the French 315 000. The Germans gained seven kilometres.

Notes of a War Correspondent

The following excerpts are from articles by a war correspondent named Will Irwin. He was reporting from France on events during the second Battle of Ypres, in the aftermath of German army attacks that had included the dispersal of chlorine gas on French and Canadian troops.

New York Tribune, April 27, 1915

THE USE OF POISON GAS

North of France, April 24. There is no doubt that the action which has been proceeding about Ypres for a week, and which will probably be known in history as the second battle of Ypres, is the hardest and hottest which has yet developed on the extreme Western front. Indeed, no battle of the war has developed so much action on so concentrated a front. It is the third desperate attempt of the Germans since this war began to break through the combined British and Belgian lines and take the all-important City of Calais ... The nearest British support was a part of the Canadian contingent. Fighting with desperate bravery, the Canadians succeeded in recovering part of the lost ground. They are still at it today. On a favourable wind the sound of cannonading can be heard as far away as the coast towns.

The nature of the gases carried by the German asphyxiating shells remain a mystery. Whatever gas it is, it spreads rapidly and remains close to the ground. It is believed not to be specially deadly — one that rather overpowers its victims and puts them hors de combat without killing many ... That such devices might be used in war has been known for a long time, but the positive prohibitions of the Hague Conference have prevented the more civilized nations of Europe from going far with experiments in this line.

Boulogne, April 25. The gaseous vapour which the Germans used against the French divisions

This soldier is being choked by gas. Do you think gas warfare should be considered a war crime?

near Ypres last Thursday, contrary to the rules of the Hague Convention, introduces a new element into warfare. The attack of last Thursday evening was preceded by the rising of a cloud of vapour, greenish gray and iridescent. That vapour settled to the ground like a swamp mist and drifted toward the French trenches on a brisk wind. Its effect on the French was a violent nausea and faintness, followed by an utter collapse. It is believed that the Germans, who charged in behind the vapour, met no resistance at all, the French at their front being virtually paralysed.

Everything indicates long and thorough preparation for this attack. The work of sending out the vapour was done from the advanced German trenches. Men garbed in a dress resembling the harness of a diver and armed with retorts or generators about three feet high and connected with ordinary hose pipe turned the vapour loose towards the French lines. Some witnesses maintain that the Germans sprayed the earth before the trenches with a fluid which, being ignited, sent up the fumes. The German troops, who followed up this advantage with a direct attack, held inspirators in their mouths, thus preventing them from being overcome by the fumes.

In addition to this, the Germans appear to have fired ordinary explosive shells loaded with some chemical which had a paralysing effect on all the men in the region of the explosion. Some chemical in the composition of those shells produced violent watering of the eyes, so that the men overcome by them were practically blinded for some hours.

The effect of the noxious trench gas seems to be slow in wearing away. The men come out of their nausea in a state of utter collapse. Some of the rescued have already died from the after-effects. How many of the men left unconscious in the trenches when the French broke died from the fumes it is impossible to say, since those trenches were at once occupied by the Germans.

This new form of attack needs for success a favourable wind. Twice in the day that followed the Germans tried trench vapour on the Canadians, who made on the right of the French position a stand which will probably be remembered as one of the heroic episodes of this war. In both cases the wind was not favourable, and the Canadians managed to stick through it. The noxious, explosive bombs were, however, used continually against the Canadian forces and caused some losses.

---

1. The United States did not enter World War I until 1917. The story above was written by an American for an American newspaper. Comment on the reporter's objectivity regarding the events he described.

2. Compose a letter to the editor in response to your reading of this report.

In July came the British offensive at the Somme River, an all-out attack on the Germans, who were entrenched on high ground. There were 60 000 British casualties on the first day. For this, British general Douglas Haig (1861–1928) would be remembered as the leader of the "meat-grinder war." When the fighting ended in November, the Germans counted 450 000 casualties, Britain 420 000, and France 200 000. All told, a million soldiers were dead or wounded. The British gained 10 kilometres. In the trenches, the soldiers sang a song: "If you want to find the old battalion, I know where they are. They're hanging on the old barbed wire." From these disasters came the vision of World War I as a scene of utter destruction, with blasted landscapes, blundering generals and senseless death.

German wartime leaders Paul von Hindenburg and Erich Ludendorff. How did their idea of war compare to the reality?

Review, Reflect, Respond

1. Explain how Germany's Kaiser Wilhelm II contributed to the collapse of peace and the eventual outbreak of war in 1914.

2. Create a time line to illustrate the course of events from an assassination in the remote Balkan city of Sarajevo to a world war engulfing all of Europe's major powers.

3. Explain why Germany expected Britain to stay out of the war and why Britain eventually joined in. Comment on the significance of the British entry into the war.

[WARTIME LEADERSHIP

The butchery of 1916 indicated that the military deadlock was total. It also revealed that the fighting spirit of the soldiers was being worn down. After other bungled attacks early in 1917, mutinies spread in the French trenches. This was not a rebellion, but an outcry by foot soldiers asking their leaders to make war in a different way. In response came a new commander and a different strategy. Marshal Philippe Pétain (1856–1951) was a champion of defensive warfare, "lavish with steel and stingy with men," a soldier's general who promised to end suicidal attacks. Pétain was the first of the new leaders who believed that the way to victory was not mass offensive but firm endurance. The winning side would be the one to hold out the longest. The greater reserves of soldiers and supplies of the Allies, soon to be joined by those of the United States, would mean victory in the end.

In Britain, the idea of making war "to the bitter end" found its leader in David Lloyd George (1863–1945), who became prime minister in 1916. In France, it was Georges Clemenceau (1841–1929), "the tiger," a fiercely patriotic man who was appointed premier the following year. When the war broke out in 1914, most people said that "the boys will be home by Christmas." By 1917, with no end in sight, some were calling for protests and peace talks. The role of Lloyd

George and Clemenceau was to fight against every sign of defeatism in the population. When a high public figure, who had been premier of France, appealed for a compromise peace with Germany to save what was left of Western civilization, Clemenceau had him arrested for treason. "You ask me for my policy," said Clemenceau, "it is to make war. Home policy? I make war. Foreign policy? I make war. Always, everywhere, I make war."

From 1914, war strategists in Berlin were aware that the greater resources of their enemies would endanger Germany in a war that went on "to the bitter end." For victory, Germany needed a breakthrough, a wonder weapon, a gamble that would pay off in quick results. In 1915 Germany was the first to use poison gas in hopes of a dramatic advance in Flanders. But, this new and horrific weapon failed, so Germany looked to another device — the submarine.

Throughout the war, the German high-seas fleet was kept safe in harbour, away from the superior might of the Royal British Navy. Only once, in 1916, did the two fleets meet head on, in the Battle of Jutland in the North Sea. After this encounter, a draw at best, Germany decided not to engage in a second round. Britain then used its sea power to blockade German ports, choking off military and civilian supplies alike. As a result, hunger took hold in the country in the "turnip winter" of 1916, when root vegetables became the main diet of the population. To turn the tables, Germany threw its own "hunger blockade" around Britain with unrestricted submarine warfare, a shocking new strategy. On February 1, 1917, Berlin declared British waters a war zone and threatened to torpedo on sight any ship in the area, enemy or neutral. This provoked the United States, which had been making good profits from sailing supply ships into British ports.

Though neutral, Americans protested the German violation of "the freedom of the seas" from the start. Their indignation increased with the sinking of the British passenger liner *Lusitania* in 1915, which caused the death of some one thousand passengers, including more than one hundred Americans, mostly women and children. Germany decided for a time to call off attacks on neutral vessels. In 1917, desperate to break the stalemate on land, German general Erich Ludendorff (1856–1937) decided to roll the dice in the sea war. Naval officers convinced him that six more months of unlimited submarine warfare would cause the British to starve and that the war would be over before America could arm. "I give Your Majesty my word as an officer," the navy chief told a nervous kaiser, "that not one American will land on the Continent."

The United States declared war on Germany on April 6, 1917. According to President Woodrow Wilson (1856–1924), it did so "to make the world safe for democracy." Now, ammunition from the "arsenal of democracy" began landing in Europe by the boatload. Meanwhile, the Allied invention of the convoy system, merchant vessels sailing in tight formation with warship escorts, soon reduced the threat of German submarines. When American troops finally began landing in France in 1918 at a rate of 300 000 per month, the strength of the Allies broadly surpassed the resources of the Central Powers.

Pleasures
AND PASTIMES

Postcards were an immensely popular form of communication. The only forms of mass communication at this time were newspapers, books, posters, and the mail. Thousands of postcards with a war theme were produced during World War 1. Their main purpose was to demonstrate the patriotism of those who bought and sent them. Both children and adults became collectors. Some cards were humorous depictions of the enemy as misbehaving children, drunkards, or animals (e.g., Britain as a bulldog, France as a rooster, Russia as a bear, Serbia as a pig, Japan as a monkey). Stereotypical and often racist caricatures were used. Still others promoted hatred of the enemy by portraying executions, atrocities, and murderous ambitions. Regardless of the style, all these postcards revealed the feelings and attitudes of people in war-torn nations.

German efforts turned out better on the Eastern front. The Russian Revolution of 1917 overturned the czar and raised hopes in Berlin for victory and an end to the two-front war. The Russians, however, wanted to continue fighting. In response, Germany decided to make use of a Russian revolutionary who talked of leading a more radical upheaval, one that would take Russia out of the war once and for all. Vladimir Ilich Ulyanov, a Marxist intellectual known by his underground name, Lenin (1870–1924), was living in exile in Switzerland when the Germans arranged to transport him by train into the midst of the revolutionary events in Russia. In Lenin, the Germans had discovered an intellectual weapon. Without knowing it, they were setting loose one of the most powerful revolutionaries of modern history.

■ FIGURE 10.3 World War I, the Eastern Front
Compare this map to a map showing the region's topography. Do the battle sites appear to be related to the nature of the terrain?

WAR AND REVOLUTION IN RUSSIAN

The Russian Revolution of 1917 was one of the pivotal events of modern history. For some it was a socialist's dream, for others a legacy of brutal dictatorship. To all, it demonstrated a radically new model of the relationship between state and society.

The nature of communist rule in Russia was shaped by a long revolutionary struggle against the old czarist regime. The Russian empire in the nineteenth century was big and sprawling, with a vast mix of peoples, languages, cultures and religions. To keep order in such diversity, the czars believed that all authority had to come from above. As a result, Russian revolutionaries faced a large and stubborn enemy. The revolution at first had been a story of failure, of small numbers of radicals fighting against overwhelming odds. The state was too strong to overturn, the population too traditional to change, and the weight of the past too heavy for czar and people alike. These conditions left the revolutionaries with a central question: What is to be done? How is revolution to come to Russia?

Some radicals said that the way was to "go to the people," to change their way of thinking and bring them to revolt. The result was the Populist Movement of the 1870s, when thousands of Russian youths went to live and work with peasants to educate them for revolution. The peasants scorned them and reported them to the police. This failure of youthful idealism caused other revolutionaries to back away from the idea of turning the peasants and the people away from their ignorant and backward ways. The revolution would have to be made by the revolutionaries themselves.

The ideal revolutionary was fully committed, devoid of softness, ready to kill for the cause, and ready to die for it. One of these was Alexander Ilich Ulyanov, eldest brother of Lenin, hanged in 1887 for plotting to assassinate the czar. Lenin himself decided to make revolution in a different way. He started by embracing Marxism, a set of ideas that was just beginning to circulate in Russia.

As a Western philosophy based on the idea that communism would come first in the most advanced capitalist nations, Marxism would seem to have had little appeal for Russian intellectuals. Their country was still a peasant land, with a small capitalist class and only the beginnings of industrial development. Marx had said, however, that capitalist development was a way out of backwardness and toward communism. Thus, when George Plekhanov (1857–1918), the father of Russian Marxism, founded what was to become the Russian Social Democratic Party in 1883, this was the idea at the core of the movement. The rise and fall of capitalism was the route by which backward Russia could move toward communism. The destiny of Russia depended on it becoming a modern state.

The same idea was driving the czarist government — but for very different reasons. After defeat in the Crimean War against France and England in 1856, the czars recognized that backwardness was putting their nation at risk. To continue as a great power, Russia had to catch up with the industrialized countries in the West. Thereafter, the czars rushed toward modern development at one moment and backed away from it at the next. Count Sergei Witte, minister of finance from 1892 to 1903, borrowed heavily from abroad to finance a program of industrial growth; however, when protests and strikes occurred, Czar Nicholas II dismissed Witte and called for more time. Two years later, in the Russo-Japanese War, Russia was defeated by an Asian nation.

Czar Nicholas II (1868–1917) was a weak personality trying to rule with a strong hand. He never really recovered from defeat in the Russo-Japanese War (1905), or from the revolution at home that followed it. In panic, he granted his subjects a constitution and the right to elect a parliament, called the Duma. But thereafter, he tried year after year to undo his own reforms. In this he was encouraged by his German-born wife, Alexandra, and the strange, religious man Rasputin (1872–1916) who was her favourite in the royal court. This character, accused of every sexual vice, was despised by court and country alike. The czar and empress adored him, mostly for his mystical power to stop the internal bleeding of their hemophiliac son, the Czarevitch Alexis. This ruling family was one of the most unpopular in Europe.

www.mcgrawhill.ca/links/legacy

Go to the site above to find out more about the role of the United States in World War I.

Even in Russia, however, public discontent was overcome by the patriotic emotions of 1914, when that nation entered the World War I. But, when discontent returned upon news of Russian defeats, Nicholas II took personal command of his armies. At court, loyal supporters hoping to rid the czar of a pernicious influence, eventually murdered the sinister Rasputin. This did not, however, save Nicholas from war. An Allied summer offensive against Austria-Hungary in 1916 began with smashing success and ended in disaster and a million casualties on both sides. Austria, near exhaustion, asked for German support to stay on its feet. The Russian collapse came in the following spring, beginning in the cities at the rearguard.

Russian cities in 1917 were places with bread lines, labour strikes, and peace demonstrations. Large numbers of factory women were working long shifts in war industries in place of soldiers. There were army deserters by the thousands as well — soldiers in uniform living outside the law and on the run from authorities. On March 8, 1917, women in Petrograd marched in an International Women's Day demonstration for "Peace and Bread." The march turned into a riot, the riot into a revolt. Military units, ordered to put down the crowds, lost control, and some soldiers took the side of the revolt. Without the power to restore order, Nicholas abdicated on March 15. This was the March Revolution of 1917, a political surprise, swift and unplanned, when the Romanov dynasty, after ruling Russia for three centuries, was brought down in one week.

Power now passed to two very different organizations. One was the provisional government, a group of mostly middle-class politicians from the last *Duma* who wanted to introduce liberal reforms. The

The Romanovs, family of the Czar. Assassinated and placed in an umarked grave in 1918, members of the Russian Imperial family were officially buried in St. Petersburg in 1999. Do you think killing the Czar was inevitable?

other was the Soviets (councils), large assemblies of delegates elected by workers, peasants and soldiers, and inspired by socialist ideas. Despite their differences, both organizations wanted to continue the war. To lose it now, most believed, was to lose everything won in the March Revolution. The new leaders wanted to fight; but the soldiers had had enough. Were it not for the soldiers' thirst for peace, Lenin might have passed unnoticed in history.

Lenin the Revolutionary

Born in 1870 into the family of a minor civil servant in rural Simbirsk on the Volga River, Lenin trained for the law before devoting his life to revolutionary politics. After this activity landed him in a Siberian prison colony between 1895 and 1900, he fled to exile in Western Europe. There he lived the life of that subclass of intellectuals and professional people that

Russians call the intelligentsia. His formative years were spent in debates with other Marxists before World War I, and he was already 47 at the time of Red October in 1917. His whole life had been a preparation for that moment. "There is not another man who for 24 hours of the day is taken up with the revolution," a companion wrote of Lenin in exile, "who has no thoughts but thoughts of revolution, and who even in his sleep, dreams of nothing but revolution."

What made this "compulsive revolutionary" different from most other Russian Marxists was his idea that the revolution would be led not by the working class but by Marxist intellectuals. In a famous tract in 1902 called *What is to be Done?* Lenin said that the workers, left to themselves, could think only of better pay and small improvements in the conditions of labour under capitalism. It was the intellectuals, he claimed, who could see beyond the capitalist system and lead the workers to overthrow it. At issue was a struggle for the soul of Russian Marxism. Plekhanov had created the movement to advance the democratic development of the labouring people of the nation. Lenin said simply that democratic methods would not work in the Russian police state. Against czarism, success could

come only from an organization of the best revolutionaries, a party of a single truth, small, secret, directed from above and closed to opposition groups within. "Give us an organization of revolutionaries," he wrote "and we will turn Russia upside down."

Meeting in exile in 1903, the Russian Social Democrats split over the issue of party organization. Lenin came away with a majority in one of the votes and took the name Bolsheviki (majority) for his followers. Lenin's ideas were made for the needs of revolution in Russia. There, public affection for the czar was destroyed on Bloody Sunday in 1905, when troops slaughtered an unarmed, peaceful crowd of 200 carrying a petition to the imperial palace. The 1905 Revolution, crushed by loyal regiments, revealed the weakness of the Russian government, behind its police and prisons; but, it revealed as well the weakness of the forces that had attempted to overthrow it. Lenin now decided that the Bolsheviks would have to do the work themselves.

When he arrived in Petrograd in April 1917, his political party had little more than 20 000 members, the Bolsheviks. This small band of intellectuals liked to think of itself as "the vanguard of the proletariat." In reality, it was the minority wing of the small party of Russian Marxism, the Social Democrats. Known for their dogmatism and ironclad organization, the Bolsheviks had appeared out of date in the previous period of democratic socialism in Europe. Now, in the crisis conditions of the war, Lenin's methods turned out to be an advantage. The provisional government wanted to concentrate on fighting the Germans and to put off the hard questions facing the nation until the election of a constituent assembly to be held in the coming months. Lenin, however, had immediate answers. His slogan was "Land, peace, bread": immediate distribution of land to the peasants, immediate peace with the Germans, immediate Marxist revolution in Russia, and "All power to the Soviets."

The Bolsheviks, now 200 000 in number and growing, took control of the Soviets in the fall of 1917. On November 7, in a swift coup organized by Lenin's brilliant lieutenant Leon Trotsky, the Bolsheviks seized

Lenin shown addressing a crowd of revolutionaries in a 1917 propaganda image. What type of image is Lenin given?

power from the provisional government. Its last leader, Alexander Kerensky, the final hope of the democratic ideals of the March Revolution, escaped into exile. The March Revolution against the czar had been the spontaneous uprising of a suffering people. In contrast, this November Revolution — called "Red October" in accord with the old Julian calendar then in use — was a planned operation. A revolutionary minority grabbed power from a more democratic government that had lost the support of a people weary of war. This was the "Red Miracle" of 1917, the birth of communism in one of the most unlikely nations, according to the predictions of Marx — Russia was, after all, an agrarian, not an industrialized country.

The Bolshevik victory in 1917 was a result of World War I. Lenin ordered an assault upon a government that had lost the support of an army and a people exhausted by war. The significance of this event was not long in coming. The previous government had simply put off the great questions of the day. The leaders of the March Revolution wanted these questions answered by a future constituent assembly. This was to be Russia's first experiment in democracy, a body chosen in a free election by a free people. In fact, the election took place on November 25, 1917, three weeks after the Bolshevik coup. The vote confirmed that Lenin's party, with 25 percent of the ballots, remained a minority in the country. Sixty percent went to a combination of other socialist parties. Lenin insisted, however, that Bolshevik rule, called "the rule of the working class," was "a higher form of democracy" than that of an elected majority. No sooner had the constituent assembly met on January 18, 1918, than he ordered armed guards to close its doors for good. This assembly, elected to begin a Russian democratic republic, sat for only one day.

Lenin knew that the task of holding power would be enormous. Bolshevism would need the advantages of unlimited force, terror, and dictatorship. To support this, he made use of an idea found in Marx's writing called the "dictatorship of the proletariat." This involved was the concept of a temporary dictatorship coming after the revolution, when the communists would use the power of the state to crush any remaining opposition. Writing

American propaganda focussed on liberty and preparedness. What do you think about linking the Boy Scouts to war?

in 1917, Lenin made the mission of this dictatorship vast and enduring. Now he gave his party the role of "leading the whole people to socialism, of directing and organizing the new system, of being the teacher, the guide, the leader of all the working and exploited people in organizing their social life ..." The party leads, the people follow. In building the Bolshevik party, Lenin had created a power machine greater than anything in the hands of the czars. In the idea of its leading role in society, he gave the party the myth that was to support its long rule over the nation. After this, Lenin's ideas could no longer be described by the term Marxist alone. They were different enough to need a new name of their own: Marxist-Leninist.

What Lenin had invented was the kind of leader-centred, mission-driven, vanguard party characteristic of many one-party dictatorships in the twentieth century. According to Lenin, this type of organization was needed in the beginning to make revolution in Russia in the first place. Later it was needed to lead the people to socialism. The historic mission of the party had become, in part, the same task that czarist reformers had set for themselves in the past — the economic development of the country.

Significantly, this new regime was born fighting. Its enemies immediately fell upon it from all sides, beginning the Russian civil war that would last four years (1918–1921). The war with Germany, however, was over and done with. On March 15, 1918, Lenin signed the Treaty of Brest-Litovsk, taking Russia out of the war in defeat and humiliation. Finland, Poland, Ukraine, and the Baltic provinces were stripped away from the old Romanov Empire. At last, one of Germany's gambles seemed to have paid off.

Lenin wanted the new communist state to be a turning point in history. To that end, the Bolsheviks changed its name from Russia to the Union of Soviet Socialist Republics (1922). They wanted their U.S.S.R. to be a new star in the East, a sign for exhausted peoples in the West to rise up against the war. The day after coming to power, Lenin issued his Decree on Peace, calling for immediate peace without victory or defeat for either side. To stir anger, he published documents found in czarist files, revealing the secret treaties between the Allies to divide the spoils of war. In effect, communist peace propaganda was the first Soviet challenge to the Western world.

World War I: *The Last Days*

The propaganda war between the Allies and Central Powers had been fought as hard as the war at the front. The difference was that governments aimed most propaganda not at the enemy, but at their own people. Citizens wanted to know what they were fighting for, what this war over the death of Franz Ferdinand was all about. British soldiers sang a song to explain why they were in the trenches: "We're here because we're here, because we're here, because we're here ..." Hard pressed to answer, their government said the reason was German war crimes and atrocities.

On January 8, 1918, President Woodrow Wilson of the United States announced the famous "Fourteen Points," or conditions for peace on America's terms. In part, this was a reply to the challenge of Lenin's propaganda. Where Lenin denounced the war as a struggle between capitalist powers for markets and profits, Wilson defended it as "a war to make the world safe for democracy." Both demanded an end to secret treaties made by aristocrats behind closed doors. Both called for more open and democratic world diplomacy,

How does the image in this Soviet propaganda poster differ from the American example?

for government under the eyes of the citizens. The debate between Lenin and Wilson on communism and freedom was the first battle of modern propaganda war between the Soviet Union and the United States, one which was to continue through most of the century.

Review, Reflect, Respond

1. Compare the attitudes of the public in Britain, France, and Germany toward going to war in 1914?

2. Explain why the sinking of the *Lusitania* is considered a turning point in World War I.

3. List in order of significance five factors you believe contributed to the success of the Russian Revolution. For each, provide a reason for your choice and ranking.

THE SOCIAL IMPACT OF THE WAR

The social impact of war changed attitudes toward leaders and governments, and beliefs in human dignity and progress. The destructive potential of technology was also clearly demonstrated during the war. English writer Thomas Hardy summarized new attitudes toward civilization and technological progress in his poem *Christmas: 1924.*

> "Peace upon earth!" was said. We sing it,
> And pay a million priests to bring it
> After two thousand years of mass
> We've got as far as poison gas.

Many soldiers recalled not hating the enemy but hating the new kind of war. Bravery counted little; what counted were industry, technology, and steel. The result was horrible to see and hear. Soldiers described a "symphony of hell," the sound and fury of modern weapons: machine guns, powerful explosives, heavy artillery, and — loudest of all — the 20-tonne German cannons called "Big Bertha," which fired shells weighing over a tonne. French war writer Henri Barbusse wrote that even the dead could not sleep. He remembered watching enemy fire rip and tear at already-dead bodies. Under this storm of metal, dead soldiers stirred as if coming back to life.

Terrible weapons caused terrible losses. More than 10 million lives were lost. Observers said that Europe was destroying its youth, whose talents would have enriched the life and culture of the Continent. Soldiers who survived described the misery, mud, rats, and lice of the trenches. As doctors, nurses, ambulance drivers and volunteers at the front, women also encountered the horrors of battle. Through all this, however, most armies fought well and followed orders. Most were loyal to their country and leaders. In some cases, Italian and Russian troops mutinied and many French troops refused to fight under certain generals unless guaranteed that there would be no more large offensives. Austrian and German troops also became increasingly desperate for an end to the fighting.

The war experience influenced men and women in different ways. To some, it was civilization gone mad; to others, it was men at their most manly. German-born American novelist Erich Maria Remarque, who was wounded several times, said that the war was the ruin of his life. Future German Nazi dictator Adolf Hitler (1889–1945), though wounded and gassed several times, said it was "the greatest and most unforgettable time of my earthly experience." British nurse Edith Cavell, who had harboured Allied soldiers behind German lines in Belgium, proclaimed before her execution by a German firing squad: "I know now that patriotism is not enough, I must have no hatred and no bitterness towards anyone." Some feared that the individual's sense of identity and worth would be crushed under the sheer weight of mass armies and mass death. Others recognized that the fighting created proud new identities.

Canadian soldiers entered the war as part of the British army and distinguished themselves fighting for King and Empire. In April 1917, in a striking victory at Vimy in northwestern France, Canadians swept the enemy from Vimy Ridge, a stronghold on high ground where German defenders had held off every other attacking force for two years. Wrote one historian, "Canadians then and later knew that they had done a great thing and that on such deeds nations are built." The victory at Vimy Ridge is considered a crucial, formative event in the development of Canada's nationhood.

As leaders realized that the conflict would be long and hard, they recognized that war production at home was as important as sending soldiers to the trenches. This was a war of industrial peoples. The least advanced — Austria-Hungary, Russia, and Italy — were the first to show the strain. No nation, however, could continue "business as usual." People, resources, and production all had to be organized, managed and driven as never before. The result was an increase in government controls of society, wages, prices, profits, opinions, and news. Governments had to partner with labour unions and private businesses to mobilize the workforce.

As the war became total, so did the power of the state. Germany, landlocked by the British naval blockade, became a fortress under siege. The home front was mobilized like the war front, with the economy under military command and all males between ages 16 and 60 bound by the Support Services Law to accept work in war industries. But, if Germany came closest to the later, totalitarian vision of the state-as-war-machine, its enemies were showing some of the same signs. Britain, Australia and Canada chose to treat those who were not citizens, such as Germans and Ukrainians, as enemy aliens and restricted their civil rights. In the most extreme cases, German and Ukrainian nationals were interned in government-operated labour camps in remote parts of Canada such as Banff, Alberta.

In many nations, the war helped to make life at home more egalitarian. Because of the dramatic increase in the demand for labour at home, many working-class people attained a higher level of income than ever before. Each family, whether aristocratic or working-class, faced the rations and hardships of war equally — this "equality of sacrifice" included the

death of loved ones. While profiteering did occur, most people were equally affected by the war.

By 1917 groups of civilians in every home-front nation, suffering from war weariness and frequent hunger, took to the streets to engage in strikes and protests. Despite absolute censorship by the state, there was no longer denial of the negative effects of the war. People who had nationalistic dreams also saw the war as an opportunity to advocate separation. In 1916 a week-long, bloody uprising by Irish nationalists was crushed by British forces. Czech and Yugoslav leaders strongly voiced their desire for independence.

Women had special importance in this total war. In Britain, in the period before the 1916 conscription law, the government looked to women to persuade men to get into uniform. Patriotic organizations told women to keep their distance from men in civilian clothes, and to disgrace them on the street by giving them a white feather, a symbol of cowardice and dishonour. Government and industry also needed women to replace men in many lines of work.

Italian women assembling bombs as part of the war effort. The war changed the lives of many women, but most returned to their pre-war status after the armistice. How do you think that made the women feel?

During the war, women took on jobs usually done by men: ambulance driving, factory work, construction, and banking. Nevertheless, in many European countries, women did not get the right to vote until after World War II. When did Canadian women get the vote?

History
BYTES

Often forgotten among the casualties of total war are the tens of thousands of animals that were pressed into work alongside soldiers at the front. Trained homing pigeons were used to carry messages to and from the front lines. In 1915 the Canadian units alone used 100 pigeons per day. Some pigeons were actually cited for military honours. Dogs were also used to carry communications on battlefields. Bloodhounds hunted for wounded soldiers and those that lay buried in the mud. In Belgium, dogs pulled machine-gun carts. The Red Cross used dogs to aid soldiers and medical staff. Horses continued to play an important role in warfare, although cavalry, once considered the elite of any army, were now hopelessly vulnerable against the new machines of war. Aside from their uses in communication and transportation, animals were companions for the soldiers. War memorials in many nations recognize the contribution of animals in war.

The war economy opened up opportunities to women as never before. In Britain, about 1.5 million new female workers entered the labour force. In 1917 over 43 percent of the labour force in Russia were women. Many found jobs in war industries and the number of female workers increased in every sector of the economy. Women replaced men as plumbers, mail carriers, bank tellers, labourers, truck drivers, factory workers, and police officers. Over 100 000 British women joined the military units established for women by the armed services. Often, changes in women's lifestyles and dress resulted from their new roles and independence. Many wore pants, shorter skirts, and cosmetics; some took to drinking, smoking, and experiencing "night life." The war allowed women to enter areas of work and leisure that they had once been kept out of by men.

Female workers, however, were still treated unequally. Women's wages were lower than those of the men who had been doing the same work. When women demanded equal pay for equal work, men argued that this would keep them from returning, after the war was over to their roles as mothers and wives. Men also worried that cheaper female labour would threaten their own pay scale. In any case, when peace came in 1918, governments, employers and labour unions banded together to return men to work and women to the home. The workingwomen of World War I had been treated as substitutes for workingmen. When the fighting stopped, both returned to traditional roles.

All sides in the war wanted to reward women for doing their patriotic duty. Before 1914 the suffragette struggle for the right to vote had met hard resistance. Beginning in Russia in 1917, the great powers, with the exception of France, extended the franchise to women. All told, the war was a force for change in women's history, but it was proof of the strength of gender discrimination as well. In the voting booth, women became citizens. In the world of work, they remained disadvantaged.

| WARTIME ARTISTS

When novelist Erich Maria Remarque (1898–1970) published *All Quiet on the Western Front* in 1929, it became an immediate bestseller with sales of 3.5 million in one month. Remarque was 18 years old when he went to fight, and his book caused immediate debate. Was it an honest version of the horrors of war, or was it a consciously anti-war novel that shamed veterans? In this passage, Remarque's wounded main character describes his arrival in a field hospital:

Day after day goes by with pain and fear, groans and death-gurgles ...

On the next floor below are the abdominal and spine cases, head wounds and double amputations. On the right side of the wing are the jaw wounds, gas cases, nose, ear, and the neck wounds. On the left the blind and the lung wounds, pelvis wounds, wounds in the joints, wounds in the testicles, wounds in the intestines. Here a man realizes for the first time in how many

places a man can get hit ... A man cannot realize that above such shattered bodies there are still human faces in which life goes its daily round. And this is only one hospital, one single station; there are hundreds of thousands in Germany, hundreds of thousands in France, hundreds of thousands in Russia. How senseless is everything that can ever be written, done, or thought, when such things are possible. It must all be lies and of no account when the culture of a thousand years could not prevent this stream of blood being poured out, these torture chambers in their hundreds of thousands. A hospital alone shows what war is.[1]

All Quiet On The Western Front by Erich Maria Remarque. "Im Westen Nichts Neues," copyright 1928 by Ullstein A.G.

Poetry at the beginning of the war was patriotic. John McCrae's famous poem *In Flanders Fields* typifies this style: "Take up our quarrel with the foe: To you from failing hands we throw the torch; be yours to hold it high." British poet Rupert Brooke's (1887–1915) nationalistic poem *The Soldier* was read on Easter Sunday, 1915, from St Paul's Cathedral in London as national preparation for war: "If I should die, think only this of me: / That there's some corner of a foreign field / That is forever England.[2]"

As the war continued, poets such as Wilfred Owen (1893–1918) and Siegfried Sassoon (1886–1967) used stark realism in their poetry to describe the horrors that the common soldier faced. These poems were radically different from the Victorian and Edwardian poetry, in both theme and style. Here is an excerpt from *Dulce et Decorum Est*, by Wilfred Owen:

If you could hear, at every jolt, the blood
Come gargling from the froth corrupted lungs
Bitter as the cud
of vile, incurable sores on innocent tongues,
My friend, you would not tell with such
high zest
To children ardent for some desperate glory,
the old lie: *Dulce et decorum est*
Pro patria mori [3]

Canadian War Artists

Women Making Shells by H. Mabel May. What impression do you get of the women seen in this picture?

For What? by Frederick H. Varley ca. 1918. What was the artist referring to?

Similar to the changing themes found in wartime poetry, music at the beginning of the war was blatantly patriotic and attempted to rouse enthusiasm for the cause, it became increasingly critical as the war dragged on. The titles of the songs at the start of the war reveal their tone and intent: *It's a Long Way to Tipperary*, *Alexander's Ragtime Band*, *Keep the Home Fires Burning*, and *Pack up Your Troubles*.

Most war songs were not composed by professional musicians, but created by soldiers. These songs, in contrast to the nationalistic ones, were marked with bitterness and irreverence. Often the satirical verses were sung to the melodies of well-known hymns and earlier patriotic songs. The words often changed over time and were unique to each unit's fighting experiences. Some of the allied troops' favourites included *Oh It's A Lovely War!*, *When this Lousy War is Over*, *Hush, Here Comes a Whizzbang*, and *Hanging on the Old Barbed Wire*.

Canadian visual artists and Group of Seven members A. Y. Jackson (1882–1974) and Frederick H. Varley (1881–1969) evocatively captured scenes of war using a variety of techniques such as impressionism

and realism. Varley was an official "artist overseas" during the war, painting battlefields and cemeteries. Jackson echoed the concern of many visual artists when attempting to reconstruct scenes of devastation: "What to paint was a problem for the war artist ... The old heroics, the death and glory stuff, were gone forever; the impressionist technique I had adopted in painting was now ineffective, for visual impressions were not enough." Hundreds of European artists worked on or near the front lines, others depicted scenes of the home front such as Canadian H. Mabel May in her impressionistic work *Women Making Shells*.

[THE END OF THE WAR

In April 1917 the Americans declared war on Germany. In December of the same year, they declared war on Austria-Hungary. This turned the course of the war in favour of the Allies because the Americans brought fresh troops and resources into the equation with the Supreme War Council of the Allies in December 1917. The German spring offensive in the West in 1918 heightened war activity. Strengthened by

Igor Stravinsky's *The Rite of Spring*

The first performance of *The Rite of Spring* (*Le sacre du printemps*) by Igor Stravinsky (1882–1971) nearly caused a riot. This infamous performance on May 29, 1913, was actually a collaboration of Stravinsky the composer, Serge Diaghilev, producer of the Ballets Russes, and Vaclav Nijinsky, his renowned young Russian dancing star. The audience was shocked not only by the dissonant, unpredictable and loud music, but also by the ballet's choreography, which was seen as lewd and unnatural for the human body. Yet, this was not the first joint effort by these innovative and sometimes flamboyant artists. Diaghilev, Stravinsky, and Nijinsky had earlier produced two critically and publicly successful ballets, *The Firebird* and *Petrouchka*.

The first thing about *The Rite of Spring* the audience might have been wary of was the sheer size of the orchestra. The composition requires an enormous number of instruments with extra violins and timpani (large kettledrums). Some instruments, such as the bassoon, make sounds almost unrecognizable to the ear. The musical language involves many layers of sound and rhythm, and challenges the listener whether it is played with the ballet, or without, as a purely orchestral work.

The ballet celebrates the coming of spring in pagan rituals involving worshipping the Earth and the sacrifice of a woman at the climax of the performance. The choreography is difficult and demanding, as dancers must do unusual steps and tableaux. At first the dancers move slowly and rhythmically, with movements sometimes suggesting sexual union between worshippers. The first part ends fast and furiously as the young pagans dance with primitive abandon. Then, in the second part, the sacrificial victim dances herself to death and is carried high in the air by the young male dancers.

While audiences today do not react with the same hissing and shouting that occurred at the original performance, *The Rite of Spring* is so powerful and evocative that audiences even today are amazed and sometimes shocked by its powerful effects.

1. If you were designing costumes for a performance of *The Rite of Spring*, what type or style of costume would you choose? Try doing a few sketches of your ideas.

2. Find a biography of any one of the three artistic personalities mentioned above and do a one-page summary of his life and achievements.

Dancers in an early performance of *Rite of Spring*. How do you think audiences would react today?

troops returning from victory in Russia, Ludendorff's "all-or-nothing" assault brought his armies close to Paris. They suffered heavy casualties for every mile of the advance. This time, there were no replacements. After four years of effort, the German superpower was out of soldiers and low on endurance. The Allies struck back in July, beginning a grinding offensive that continued to the last day of the war. By this time, the generals had new ideas and new weapons for offensive warfare. The British had high hopes for the tank, and even though some German soldiers were reported to have surrendered at the sight of them, these iron "motor-monsters" were too slow and trouble-prone to make much difference in this war. The difference now was that the Allies had more of everything and their enemies had less. The Germans did not crack, they simply fell back. When the fighting ended, the exhausted troops were still on French soil, while their own country had remained largely untouched by the war.

Ludendorff, his nerve broken, told Kaiser Wilhelm II on September 29, 1918, that the war was lost. The general advised the Kaiser to seek an armistice and appoint a new government of democratic leaders to open negotiations for peace on the terms of President Wilson's Fourteen Points. Later, critics would say that Ludendorff had wanted to shift responsibility for defeat from the military leaders to the democratic politicians. The most important of these politicians were moderate socialists of the Social Democratic Party, who had at first supported the war in 1914. Later, they turned away, and warned that the nation's leaders would be made to account for the suffering of the people. "Now," said Ludendorff, "they will eat the soup that they cooked for us."

The new leaders were handed a nation on the edge of revolt and ruin. Sailors had mutinied; revolutionaries were fighting in the streets. The Social Democrats managed to pick up the pieces — and make enemies on

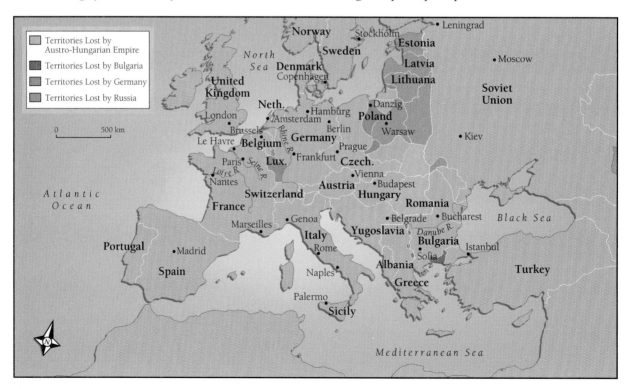

■ FIGURE 10.4 Political Boundaries in Europe, 1919
Consider which countries on this map are land-locked, that is, have no access to the sea. Do you think that is important?

every side. On November 9, 1918, they proclaimed their nation a republic, ending the German Empire and the Hohenzollern dynasty. Bitterly, Wilhelm II abdicated and left the country his ancestors had created in the previous century. He would die in exile in Holland. On November 11, 1918, representatives of the new German republic met Allied officers in France and, in a railway car, signed the armistice that ended World War I. Angry voices on the right blamed the socialists and the Jews for Germany's defeat and accused the politicians of a crime against the nation for surrendering a German army that was still fighting on foreign soil.

Soon enough, the new republic had enemies on the left as well. These were radical Social Democrats who had rebelled against the "treason" of the party's decision in 1914 to support the war. Some, inspired by the Bolshevik revolution in Russia, now became the first members of the new Communist Party of Germany, called the Spartacists. In Berlin, this party was led by two militants who soon became cult figures in the history of modern communism: Rosa Luxemburg and Karl Liebknecht. In January 1919 these radicals attempted to take power. Against this revolution from the left, the new government turned for support to army leaders and the volunteer bands of armed veterans known as the Free Corps. These tough street fighters crushed the uprising, murdered Luxemburg and Liebknecht, and moved quickly to restore order throughout Germany. The German communists would remember this as more treason by the Social Democrats against the working class. Thus, even as it was being born, the new Germany republic created enemies on the left and the right who would hound its political life to the end.

When Germany signed the armistice, the defeat of the Central Powers was complete. Bulgaria and Turkey had given up the fight. The Austro-Hungarian Empire, or what was left of it, signed an armistice on November 4, 1918. Already the Czechs, Poles, and South Slavs were creating their own nations in the old Hapsburg lands. Even before the peacemakers met at Paris in January 1919 to redraw the map of Europe, the people were remaking the Continent themselves.

THE TREATY OF VERSAILLES, 1919

Twenty-seven Allied nations participated in the drawing up of the Treaty of Versailles, so named after the magnificent palace outside Paris where the final document was signed on June 28, 1919. In reality, most decisions at the Paris Peace Conference were made by the so-called Big Four: Britain, France, the United States, and Italy. But, Italian premier Vittorio Orlando (1860–1952) soon complained of being slighted by his powerful partners. As a result, Italy came away disappointed and carried its resentment about the Paris peace agreement into the postwar period. The achievement of the conference was to bring together different views, from the hard-line demands by Clemenceau to dismember Germany, to the more moderate aim of Lloyd George to keep Germany and France in balance. Added to this was the idealistic plan of Woodrow Wilson to contain Germany by bringing it into a new world order of democratic, independent nations. Observers called the result a compromise peace. The compromise, however, was only between the victors. The defeated nations were given no place and no voice at the peace table. To Germany, the treaty was a Diktat, a peace dictated by the Allies. Germany itself, of course, had dictated a much harder peace to the Bolsheviks at Brest-Litovsk in 1918.

Critics said that the Versailles settlement, in contrast, was both hard and soft at the same time. The reason was that Europe itself was of two minds. Many people were moved by Wilson's ideal of a just peace but they were also out to punish Germany. The Allies were going to "squeeze Germany like a lemon," said one British leader, "and keep squeezing until you can hear the pips squeak." The Versailles Treaty reflected both the toughness and the moderation of these public moods.

Whom to Blame?

After their victory, the winners said it was the losers, who were to blame and tried to make the point stick by writing the responsibility of Germany and its allies into the Versailles Treaty itself (article 231): "The Allied and Associated Governments affirm that Germany accepts the responsibility of Germany and its allies for causing all the loss and damage to which the Allied and Associated Governments and their nationals have been subjected as a consequence of the war imposed upon them by the aggression of Germany and its allies." This so-called "guilt clause" did not end disagreement over the causes of the war; instead, it started a quarrel between nations and historians that continued for most of the century. As emotions cooled, the early verdict against Germany gave way in Western countries to a more balanced judgment. Most historians eventually agreed that every power had some responsibility for the catastrophe of 1914. Nations miscalculated their enemies; failed to restrain their allies; became captive to rigid war plans. Recent scholarship supports the old argument that Germany was most at fault. Few, however, want to oversimplify the question of guilt. There was little innocence and enough guilt to go around in 1914.

The victors slashed Germany's military strength to ribbons, reducing its army to 100 000 troops. Germany lost Alsace and Lorraine to France. It lost eastern territory to the revived state of Poland, which was also granted a land corridor to the Baltic Sea. This corridor separated East Prussia from the rest of Germany. Germany lost its colonies around the world but the country itself was not dismembered. The German population of 60 million remained larger than any of its neighbours; its factories and mines — some temporarily under French control — remained capable of returning the nation to the status of an industrial power. The German giant had been defeated but it was still a giant.

Austria paid a higher price in the Treaty of Saint-Germain. (Separate treaties were signed with each of the defeated powers.) Western liberals had viewed Austria-Hungary as a land of repressed minorities, peoples longing for nationhood. In Woodrow Wilson's mind, this repressed nationalism had been the cause of the Sarajevo assassination, of the war, and of European discontent. The way to peace, he believed, was to complete the revolution of nationalism in Europe and give the right of self-determination to all peoples. The result was the dismemberment of the old Hapsburg Empire and the emergence of the new nations of Hungary, Czechoslovakia, Poland, and Yugoslavia. When the Big Four were finished, the empire of Austria-Hungary had disappeared from the map. What remained was Austria itself, now a little republic of less than seven million, forbidden to ever unite with Germany again.

Time was up for the Ottoman Empire as well. Despite Allied promises to recognize the independence of Arab lands after the war, most lands were taken over by Britain and France as mandates of the new League of Nations. The mandate system, designed to do away with old-style imperialism, included a provision for the great powers to govern particular regions during a period of development. Britain, given a mandate over Palestine, kept its wartime promise to provide for a Jewish national home in the Holy Land. The Balfour Declaration of 1917 laid the foundation for the future state of Israel. Arab peoples, for their part, saw little difference between old-style imperialism and new-style mandates. To them, the right of self-determination appeared to be only for Europeans.

The peacemakers were more interested in an old empire closer to home, wherein communism had replaced czarism in the largest country on Earth. In 1917 Allied troops had already been sent to Murmansk, Archangel, and Vladivostok to prevent supplies being sent to Russia from falling into German hands and to keep Russia in the war against Germany. Afterward, with fears rising that communism could spread to the West, troops stayed on through most of the Russian civil war. These troops from Britain, Canada, France, the United States and Japan — about 100 000 in all — were warriors in the dark, since half were involved in supporting the czarist, "White" armies under General Larr Kornilov (1870–1918) in their fight against the communist Red forces, and the other half were trying to stay out of the way.

With the Bolsheviks tied down in a fight for survival, new nations were able to emerge in the old Romanov lands in the West: Finland, Estonia, Latvia,

Lithuania, and Poland. As the old empires broke into pieces, the result was the most enormous shuffling of borders in the history of the Continent.

THE CONSEQUENCES OF THE WAR

The Europe of kings and emperors gave way to the sovereignty of the people. France and Portugal were the only republics in Europe before the war; after it, there were more republics than monarchies. Many, however, were weak and defenceless, and most had troubles with minorities within their borders. The different peoples of the Continent were too entangled to make it possible for all the different peoples to have their own states. Despite Wilson's ideal of self-determination, large minorities, such as

Germans living in Czechoslovakia, continued to live unhappily outside the country of their choice. With the fall of the old empires, the middle of Europe was thus made up of small inexperienced states with revolutionary Bolshevism on one side and a discontented Germany on the other. Critics of the Versailles Treaty, such as the French marshal Foch (1851–1929) argued that this new Europe was more unstable than the old one. Foch would claim, "This is not a peace treaty, it is an armistice for 20 years." In other words, the settlement of World War I planted the seeds for World War II.

The American president was aware of the problems of the peace. He believed that they could be set right by the League of Nations in the coming years. The League was Wilson's idea — a way to bring international co-operation to a jumbled world. Wilson first included his idea in his Fourteen Points and, in Paris,

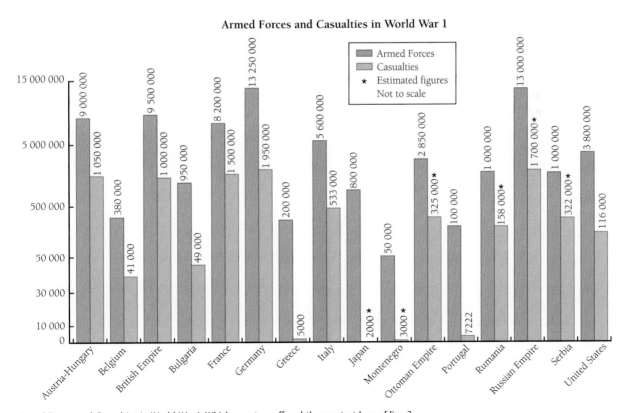

Armed Forces and Casualties in World War I. Which country suffered the greatest loss of lives?

worked successfully to establish the League as part of the Versailles settlement. After a history of American isolation from Europe, Wilson led his country into the affairs of the Continent. Many Americans did not want to stay. When the Republican-led United States senate refused to ratify the peace treaty or let the country join the League, the country returned to its original isolation and left the problems of European security to the Europeans. Britain, in turn, decided to go back to its own isolation and left the problems to France. The real trouble with the Versailles peace, some historians have concluded, was that the peacemakers did not stick around to enforce it.

WEB CONNECTION

www.mcgrawhill.ca/links/legacy

Go to the site above to find out more about the League of Nations.

The result was that the German problem came back to challenge Europe all over again. The "war to make the world safe for democracy" made Germany a difficult place for democrats. Leaders of the new Weimar Republic (named for its beginnings in the city of Weimar) wanted to show the world a Germany of culture and peace. The defeat, however, left behind too much resentment. The Versailles *Diktat* and the guilt clause added more. Allied experts set the cost of reparations at 33 billion dollars. Some economists, even in Allied countries, warned that the sum was too high and ruinous for all concerned. The English economist John Maynard Keynes, in his pamphlet *The Economic Consequences of the Peace*, believed that the enormous reparations would only slow down Europe's economic recovery. In Germany, anger over the reparations was added to the anger of a defeated and humiliated nation. The Weimar Republic was on the verge of self-destruction.

The guilt clause of the Versailles Treaty was not included merely to humiliate Germany but to give a legal basis to Allied claims for reparations. The costs of

the war had been huge. It had been financed on the Allied side by loans, especially from the United States, turning the countries involved into debtor nations. The logic of the guilt clause was plain: Germany was guilty of starting a war of aggression, so Germany was responsible for the damages. Yet 12 years earlier, nations at the Hague Peace Conference had considered war an accepted instrument of state policy.

How and why was this war different? The new level of violence, the horror of gas weapons, the attacks on civilians by submarines and aircraft, all made war on this scale appear to be a threat to civilization itself. A war of this kind could not be accepted as "the continuation of foreign policy by other means." The guilt clause thus represented a different principle for the twentieth century. To wage an aggressive war was now in violation of international law. World War I had changed the way the West viewed war and peace.

Review, Reflect, Respond

1. List and describe three ways in which World War I had a lasting impact on Western societies.

2. How did wartime poetry and music change over the course of the war? What did the changes reflect? Use specific examples of poetry, songs, or other works in your answer.

3. Do you believe that the Allied powers achieved a "just peace" at the end of the war? Explain your answer using specific examples.

The Results of the War

World War I was a great divide in history. It ended a period of relative peace and began a period of total war and totalitarian regimes. The war and revolution of 1914–1918, in turn, unleashed more wars and revolutions that would shape the rest of the century:

- The communist revolution
- The fascist revolution
- A revolution in military technology

It is important to point out that these revolutions all arose from the death and destruction experienced in World War I. The most outstanding characteristic of this war was death on a previously unheard of scale. In all, some 10 million were killed, including roughly two million Russians, two million Germans, 1.5 million French, and nearly a million British. Perhaps 30 million were wounded, though the number is uncertain. From all this destruction came forces and feelings that no peace settlement could overcome. Although the war appeared to be a victory for democracy, it gave rise to two radical movements that would carry state power over the individual to new limits. Both communism and fascism had their origins in the previous century, but the war gave them new form and passion. After the Allied victory of 1918, the real challenge for democracy was still to come.

Some historians use the term "the second Thirty Years' War" to refer to this period, and "the German problem" that challenged Western democracy between 1914 and 1945. They mean that only a brief peace separated World War I (1914–1918) from World War II (1939–1945). The enemies were the same; what changed was the scale of devastation. From 1914 onward, a momentum toward greater and greater destruction became obvious as military leaders, with the Western front in deadlock, extended the war into the civilian population by using submarines and aircraft. To military strategists, new weapons and easier targets appeared to be the way out of the stalemate.

The result was a revolution in military technology, brought about in particular by the development of air power. The first flight had come only 11 years before 1914 — in 1903, thanks to the Wright brothers in the United States. Not surprisingly, airplane design and technology advanced rapidly during the war. From simple reconnaissance work, pilots moved on to strafing (shooting at people on the ground) and bombing behind the lines. Total war blurred the distinction between military and civilian targets. If total war meant war in which the total resources of a nation were engaged, then all these resources — military and civilian — had now become targets as well.

Reflections

In the wake of World War I, an epidemic of influenza, the worst on record, circled the Earth in 1918–1919. The toll was 20 million dead, twice as many as those killed in the war. Yet the influence of this much greater human loss simply could not match the influence of the Great War on history. It was said that the most important casualty of the war had been the Western mind. Wounded was the pride and confidence of Europeans in themselves and their values. Now Western thought was overtaken by pessimism, by concern with violence and the irrational in human behaviour. As Europe appeared to lose mastery, the other peoples of the globe began to stir, making ready for the revolt against Western control over their lives. In the results of the war were the conditions, which, over time, would bring the end of the European Age in world history.

Chapter Review

Chapter Summary

In this chapter, you have seen:

- that in an age of conflict and war, key factors motivated some to seek peace and co-operation with others
- the impact of elements and characteristics of historical change, particularly regarding changes brought about by the Russian Revolution
- the consequences of war for human life and property, power structures and regimes, social structure, and gender relations and expectations
- how important modern philosophies, such as Marxism and Leninism, have shaped Western thought
- that art and literature in various forms reinforced prevailing social and political values during the period of World War I

Reviewing the Significance of Key People, Concepts, and Events (Knowledge and Understanding)

1. Understanding the history of World War I, its underlying causes, course of events and consequences, requires a knowledge of the following concepts and people, and an understanding of their significance. Briefly explain three items from each column.

Concepts/Events	People
Dreadnought	Alfred Nobel
Schlieffen Plan	Douglas Haig
Hague Peace Conference	Kaiser Wilhelm II
Battle of the Marne	Archduke Franz Ferdinand
Marxism and Leninism	Georges Clemenceau
League of Nations	Rasputin
Russian Revolution	Leon Trotsky
Bloody Sunday	Woodrow Wilson
Treaty of Versailles	Erich Maria Remarque
Lusitania	

2. The late nineteenth century was an era of technological innovation. Much of this technology was devoted to increasing the destructive power of war machines. Create a concept web that shows at least four technological developments and how each altered the nature of warfare. Prepare a two-paragraph response to the question: How did technological developments make World War I the first modern war?

Doing History: Thinking About the Past (Thinking/Inquiry)

3. What do you believe should be the primary objective of a peace treaty? Do you think the Treaty of Versailles was a fair and effective treaty? If it was not, how should the Allies have treated the defeated nations? Respond to these questions in a short essay of 500 to 700 words. Be sure your essay has a clear thesis and supporting arguments.

4. At the time of World War I, Bertrand Russell (1872–1970) was one of Britain's leading philosophers and its most famous pacifist. Russell wrote the following passage shortly after the end of the war. Write a response Russell's ideas:

   > In times of excitement, simple views find a hearing more readily than those that are sufficiently complex to have a chance of being true. Nine people out of 10 in England during the war never got beyond the view that the Germans were wicked and the Allies were virtuous (crude moral categories, such as "virtuous" and "wicked," revived in people who, at most times, have been ashamed to think in such terms) ...
   >
   > To stand out against a war, when it comes, a man must have within himself some passion so strong and so indestructible that mass hysteria cannot touch it.

Applying Your Learning (Application)

5. Write two arguments. one for and one against the following statement:

   At the root of all the death, destruction, and madness of World War I was the ideology of capitalism. In light of the mayhem resulting from capitalism's destructive forces, communism appeared to be a sane and rational alternative.

6. What elements in western society today are similar to or different from those in pre-war western society?

Communicating Your Learning (Communication)

7. As the lead writer for a new television series called "Confronting the Past," you are to prepare an interview with one of the people listed below. This entails writing eight to 10 interesting and engaging questions that the host will ask the historical guest. Write a response you think your guest might make to each question. This will involve the use of historical fact and speculation, plus some additional research. Possible guests: Kaiser Wilhelm II, Georges Clemenceau, Edith Cavell, Czar Nicholas II, Lenin, Douglas Haig, Rasputin, Rosa Luxemburg.

8. Review the description of World War I propaganda postcards (Pleasures and Pastimes, page 389) given in this chapter. Create two of your own postcards, one that is patriotic and one that portrays the enemy in a negative way. Avoid racially demeaning stereotypes.

CHAPTER ELEVEN

Between the Wars:
An Anxious Generation

CHAPTER EXPECTATIONS

By the end of this chapter, you will be able to:

- *assess the reasons for the failure or success of various approaches to maintaining international order*

- *evaluate key elements and characteristics of the process of historical change*

- *describe the main tenets of key modern beliefs and philosophies and explain how they have shaped Western thought*

- *compare the various political opinions that are understood to constitute the "political spectrum," taking into account the ideological positions and political methods associated with them*

Many believed that the Munich Agreement of 1937 had halted the march toward war. Adolf Hitler did not. Why not?

Democracy in Europe was the legacy of World War I. In the years after the war, all the Western powers had liberal constitutions and free markets. A revolt against this democratic order, however, was not long in coming. It came most clearly in 1922 with the rise of fascism in Italy. Italy's leader Benito Mussolini used the word "totalitarian" to describe a form of state power in stark contrast to liberal and democratic ideals. Gone was the difference between public and private life. "For the fascist," said Mussolini, "the state is all-embracing; outside it no human or spiritual values exist."

After the Great Depression of the 1930s, the real challenge to democratic beliefs came from totalitarian regimes in the Soviet Union and Germany. In these countries, the side-by-side evolution of the dictatorships of Joseph Stalin and Adolf Hitler was one of the most important historical phenomena of the twentieth century. Both these regimes carried out some of the worst crimes against humanity in their own and other countries. The regimes of Stalin and Hitler resembled the nightmare world of George Orwell's novel *1984* and the possibilities of total control of society. Against these two leaders in the 1930s, democratic peoples were forced onto the defensive and feared for the survival of free institutions. "Do you want to know what the future looks like?" asked a character in *1984*: "Imagine a boot being ground in your face, forever." After two decades of devastation, the boots of fascism were destroyed during a second bloody world war.

It is sometimes said that Western democracies won the war and lost the peace. The defeat of Germany in 1918 was not final and the apparent victory of democracy was not apparent for long. In 1919 France in particular was filled with illusions of victory. With Germany beaten and disarmed, France appeared once again to be the greatest power in Europe. In reality, the nation was weaker than before. With the lowest birth rate of the great powers, France was seriously affected by the human losses of the war. Once a creditor nation, it was left with a war debt of over seven billion dollars. Its currency, one of the most solid in Europe before 1914, was losing value year after year. Also, Germany and Britain were virtually untouched by the destruction, whereas France had been a battlefield. Now, after the Versailles Treaty, this great but wounded nation was left alone by its allies to enforce the peace with Germany.

KEY CONCEPTS AND EVENTS

Dawes Plan

fascism

Mein Kampf

Locarno Pact

New Economic Policy (NEP)

Five-Year Plan

terror famine

Great Purge

Stalinism

Rapallo Agreement

National Socialism
    (Nazism)

Dachau

Nuremberg Racial Laws

Kristallnacht

cubism

KEY PEOPLE

Benito Mussolini

Joseph Stalin

Adolf Hitler

John Maynard Keynes

Franklin Delano Roosevelt

Leon Trotsky

Pablo Picasso

Gustav Mahler

T. S. Eliot

Virginia Woolf

Wit and Wisdom

We are living in a demented world. And we know it.

Johan Muizinga, *In the Shadow of Tomorrow*, 1936

TIME LINE: AN ANXIOUS GENERATION

John Maynard Keynes, *The Economic Consequences of the Peace*	1919	
	1920	Germany given a bill of 33 billion dollars for war reparations
Benito Mussolini comes to power in Italy; Germany proposes a moratorium on reparations payments	1921	
	1922	Locarno Pact signed; Mussolini's March to Rome
The Ruhr is occupied by French and Belgian forces	1923	
	1924	Dawes plan accepted: occupation of Ruhr ends and a sliding scale of reparations is granted to Germany; Adolf Hitler, *Mein Kampf*
Locarno Pact signed	1925	
	1927	Joseph Stalin consolidates power in the Soviet Union
Great Depression in Europe and North America; Stalin's first Five-Year Plan begins	1929	
	1932	Nazis become largest party in German parliament
Great Purge begins in Soviet Union; Hitler appointed chancellor of Germany; Nuremburg Laws deprive German Jews of all civil rights; Night of the Long Knives	1934	
	1935	Italy invades Ethiopia; Spanish Civil War begins; Stalin's show trials

Not to scale.

▌A CHALLENGE TO PEACE

Relations between France and Germany were at the centre of European events in the postwar years. The most contentious issue between the two nations was war reparation. France was determined to make Germany pay for the war. Moreover, the French needed to feel secure against a possible revival of German power. For this, they wanted to keep their enemy poor, weak, and disarmed. Georges Clemenceau, premier of France, said, "Peace is the continuation of war by other means." Just as France was determined to enforce the Versailles Treaty to the letter, so Germany was determined to defy it at every opportunity. French fears increased in 1922, when Germany signed the Rapallo Agreement with the Soviet Union. With this accord, the two defeated nations exchanged promises of support. Involved in this new relationship, the French believed, were secret arrangements to permit Germany to conceal weapons and train soldiers behind the scenes in Soviet territory.

A showdown between France and Germany occurred the following year. After Germany failed to deliver shipments of coal as part of a reparations payment, the new French premier Raymond Poincaré (1860–1934) decided on a tough response: French troops would go into the German mining area in the Ruhr Valley, occupy it, and bring out the coal themselves. On January 11, 1923, French and Belgian troops entered the Ruhr Valley to begin a long and difficult military occupation. In response, German leaders called for passive resistance and a strike by Ruhr workers. Defiantly, they printed piles of paper money to support the resistance and pay the strikers. What followed brought tragedy to both sides.

The cost of the war had already set off galloping inflation in Germany. Rising prices and a bloated currency were bringing misery to families living on savings, pensions, and fixed incomes. The massive release of new money into the economy brought on a ruinous inflationary spiral. The Great Inflation of 1923 left a scar on the mind of the nation. In November of that year, the German mark, falling in value to four trillion to the American dollar, became virtually worthless. Radical movements were rising left and right. In the Ruhr, French troops faced riots, sabotage, and a failed mission.

Massive inflation in Germany in the early 1920s made it more economical to decorate with money than to buy wallpaper.

The Search for Peaceful Co-existence

The experience of the Ruhr occupation was the turning point in relations between France and Germany. The French had second thoughts about using strong-arm methods to force reparations out of Germany. These methods had already brought criticism from the United States and Britain. As wartime emotions cooled in these countries, more citizens were having doubts about the Versailles settlement. They criticized the idea of blaming Germany for the war and charging it for all the damages. They criticized France for keeping Germany out of the League of Nations and for using the League to enforce strict obedience to the Versailles Treaty. After a "war to end war," they condemned

France as well for disarming Germany without disarming itself. France had said that it would disarm when Germany backed down and paid up. The trouble in the Ruhr, however, brought home a hard lesson: Germany would not pay at the point of a gun — and could not pay so long as it was poor and miserable.

An idea was becoming fixed in Western opinion: reparations had been set too high for Germany to bear. As mentioned previously, important to this was the influence of the British economist John Maynard Keynes (1883–1946), whose 1920 pamphlet *The Economic Consequences of the Peace* warned that reparations would impoverish Germany and other nations. A prosperous Europe, said Keynes, needed a prosperous Germany.

In 1923 a new leader who recognized the need for Germany to come to terms with the Versailles Treaty appeared in Berlin. Gustav Stresemann (1878–1929), made chancellor in 1923, called for an end to the resistance in the Ruhr and began work to restore order to German life. Under Stresemann, a new "politics of understanding" began between Germany and France. By agreement, a committee of experts in international finance, led by the American banker Charles Dawes, put together a plan to end the Ruhr occupation and restore the German economy. The Dawes Plan, which stretched out reparations payments and arranged foreign loans for the reconstruction of German industry, set the stage for economic recovery. With it, Europe turned from the protest and rage of the postwar years to a period of peace and order.

Democratic Governments

The period of peace and order between 1924 and 1929 was the high point of Western democratic institutions in the years between the two world wars. Underlying it was an economic prosperity that temporarily overcame the bitterness left by the Great War. From near disaster, the German economy took off after the burden of reparations was lightened. In France, inflation was eventually controlled. In England, the final rumble of social unrest came in 1926, when millions of workers tried to shut down the country in a massive general strike. Called to support miners suffering through the decline of the coal industry, the strike instead rallied the public behind the Conservative government, led by Stanley Baldwin (1867–1947). When the strikers gave up, the Labour Party decided against revolutionary protests as a means of promoting change. After years of strikes and struggles, a calm settled over the West.

With peace at home came the opportunity to make peace abroad. The result can be described as the first period of appeasement in the relations of France, Britain, and Germany. In a conciliatory gesture, France and Britain responded to Germany's need to rise from defeat. In turn, Germany responded to the need for guarantees of peace and security in France and Britain. Three men who made "appeasement" a word of honour in foreign relations were involved. One was Gustav Stresemann, who had now moved to the post of foreign minister at Berlin. In Paris, Aristide Briand (1862–1932), foreign minister in a new middle-of-the-road government, convinced French leaders that Germany could not be held down forever as a second-rate power. The way to keep the Germans at peace, he believed, was to make a peace that was worth keeping. In London, British foreign secretary Austen Chamberlain (1863–1937) was working on his own project to reconcile France and Germany. Today, historians believe that the three men had hidden agendas to advance the interests of their own nations.

Delegates to the Locarno conference. What was the Spirit of Locarno?

At the time, however, these were the "good Europeans," the three statesmen honoured in the press for bringing a new era of peace to the Continent.

When the stock market crashed in 1929 people tried to get money any way they could. Could the "Crash of '29" happen again?

Their greatest achievement was the Locarno Pact of 1925. In this non-aggression agreement, Germany promised to accept its new boundaries in the West and to respect the demilitarization of the Rhineland. England, for its part, agreed to act against all violation of these arrangements. The Versailles settlement, it appeared, was secure in the West. Observers noted with unease that Germany made no commitment to accept its eastern borders with Poland and Czechoslovakia. Stresemann promised, however, that any changes would be by peaceful means. Finally, it seemed that Europeans had put World War I behind them. In London, *The Times* reported on the Locarno Pact under a banner headline: "Peace at Last."

Between 1925 and 1929, the three men were part of "the spirit of Locarno." For their work, Chamberlain, Briand and Stresemann received the Nobel Peace Prize, and the spirit of Locarno became the spirit of the time. France withdrew more occupation troops from German soil. In 1926 Germany was admitted to the League of Nations. Two years later, Briand and American Secretary of State Frank B. Kellogg (1856–1937) drafted an international agreement, called the Kellogg-Briand Pact, outlawing wars of aggression. Some 60 nations agreed to its terms. Finally, in 1929, came the Young Plan, a schedule for a softer settlement of the reparations problem. Drawn up by American lawyer Owen D. Young and a panel of experts, the plan tried through "wise business sense" to take the heat out of the reparations debate by reducing the total amount and extending payments far into the future — all the way to 1988. The Great Depression would have to come first.

ECONOMIC RUIN: THE GREAT DEPRESSION

October 29, 1929, was "Black Tuesday," the day the New York stock market crashed and the "roaring twenties" gave way to the "dirty thirties" in the United States (and Canada). It was the beginning of the end for the economic recovery that had sustained peace and optimism. Pessimists had already warned that this recovery was on shaky ground because large amounts of American capital had been invested overseas, chasing high interest rates in Europe. As a result, industry on the continent was being propped up by American money, but the money was going around in a circle. Dollars invested in Germany were used to pay reparations to France and Britain, and these nations, in turn, paid war debts to the United States. Thus, when Americans in the 1929 Wall Street crash withdrew their investments, the circle was broken and European nations started sliding toward bankruptcy.

It started with the collapse of Austria's largest bank in May 1931 and spread outward in a ripple effect across Europe. The impact was uneven. France, with a large sector of small-scale enterprises sheltered behind tariff walls, took longer to get into the Depression and longer to get out of it. The British were harder hit. A worldwide empire of free trade, Britain was driven to raise tariffs on foreign goods and close doors to foreign immigrants. The British pound sterling, the proudest currency in Europe, was taken off the gold standard and reduced in value when the nation was forced to sell off its gold reserves. Worse was the case of Germany, where the Depression went deeper and was more devastating than anywhere else in Europe. But, every country except the Soviet Union showed the same signs of the worst depression on record: falling production, falling prices, falling profits, and falling wages.

The only thing that went up was unemployment. The number of jobless hit a peak at the same time as the Depression hit bottom in 1932. In Britain, some regions suffered as much as 35 percent unemployment; up to 32 percent in Germany; and, in the United States, at times as much as one third of the total labour force was unemployed. With this came the misery of homelessness, bread lines, soup kitchens, and millions of destitute people.

What went wrong? Most Western leaders thought that the downturn was part of the normal boom-and-bust cycle of a *laissez faire* economy. This time, however, the old remedies of tariffs and spending cuts did not work. To ease the debt burden on Europe, American president Herbert Hoover (1874–1964) in 1931 called for a temporary moratorium on reparations payments and war debts. What was "temporary" became permanent. When Germany stopped paying reparations to the other powers, they, in turn, stopped paying war debts to the United States. In sum, the result of the moratorium was a massive default on reparations and war debts alike — leaving the Americans holding the bill. So ended the tug-of-war over the financial settlement of the Versailles peace — with resentment all around.

In the United States, the new president, Franklin Delano Roosevelt (1862–1945), elected in 1932, decided to set the country on a course of reform. He called this the "New Deal." The idea was to get citizens working and buying again. Roosevelt plunged into deficit spending, pouring dollars into public works, government loans, farm subsidies, and a system of welfare payments for the aged, disabled, and unemployed. The result was economic recovery, along with bigger

People called him "FDR." US President Roosevelt gave Americans a New Deal that would get them working and spending again. What was the result of the New Deal?

government, regulation, debt, and taxes. Some Americans never forgave Roosevelt for these radical changes and the way his government intervened in the free-market economy. Nevertheless, he was re-elected president three times. He died during World War II, near the start of his fourth term in office.

In Europe, neither France nor Britain would go as far as Roosevelt. The new Popular Front government in Paris, a coalition of centre and left-wing parties elected in 1936 to resist fascism, passed laws to improve labour conditions and control the banking industry. In Britain, parliament mostly fought the Depression in the old-fashioned way, through less spending and more tariffs. The rise of the Labour Party, however, which had passed the Liberals in 1922 to become the official opposition, indicated that many British were also looking to government to take a larger role in social welfare. In general, the effect of the Great Depression was to bring back to government some of the control over the economy that it held during World War I.

In the making was the modern welfare state. In 1936 John Maynard Keynes was the spokesperson for "the new economics," the ideas for public management of a private-enterprise economy. In his prescription, government bureaucrats took the place of the "free forces" of the marketplace. The way out of the Depression, Keynes argued in his book *The General Theory of Employment, Interest and Money*, was for government to put money into the economy to drive up spending and demand. More demand would bring more supply; more supply would mean more production, investment, and employment. In the new economics, the role of the state, said Keynes, was to keep a steady course between inflation and depression, to take money out of the economy when the economy heated up, and to put money in when it cooled down. Some economists said Keynes saved capitalism from death and disgrace in the Depression. He had explained how to make private enterprise work again. His theory would end the boom-and-bust cycle of capitalism, a system predisposed to roaring out of control, piling up private wealth and spreading public misery. In contrast, some thought his theory was the road to ruin. Keynes's ideas would increase the size, cost and power of government, and replace the good old values of saving and thrift with an easygoing philosophy of tax-and-spend.

As a result of the Depression, governments had caught on to the new economics before Keynes wrote about it. His ideas came mainly to provide the supporting theory for the rising welfare state. The increase in state spending that was to bring the West out of the Depression went to supporting an armaments industry to fight off a new danger: the rising dictatorships.

WEB CONNECTION

www.mcgrawhill.ca/links/legacy

Go to the site above to find out more about fascism.

Depression and Dictatorships

One by one, the nations of Eastern Europe, beset by weak economies, minority problems and border disputes, turned from democracy to dictatorship. Most dictatorships were right-wing; the military took power while claiming to save the nation from communism and enemies within. The first dictator appeared in Hungary, where the navy leader Admiral Miklós Horthy (1868–1957), an anti-Semite and anti-communist, took charge of the country as early as 1920. Next, after Benito Mussolini (1883–1945) ended democracy in Italy, came Marshal Joseph Pilsudski (1867–1935) in Poland in 1926, the royal dictator King Alexander in Yugoslavia in 1928, and King Carol in Romania in 1930. Others appeared in Bulgaria, Greece, and eventually in the three Baltic states, Estonia, Latvia and Lithuania. The result was a clean sweep for dictatorship in Eastern Europe, with strongmen ruling the whole area from the Baltic Sea to the Mediterranean.

Depression also brought dictatorship to Central Europe. Only Czechoslovakia, under its liberal leaders Thomas Masaryk (1850–1937) and Edvard Benes (1884–1938), stood against the tide. In Germany, Adolf Hitler (1889–1945) ended Weimar democracy in 1933. Austria fell to its own fascist leader, Engelbert Dollfuss (assassinated in 1934), the following year. Democracy, once in style across the Continent, had been pushed back into the West. There, weak and divided, it was in for the fight of its life.

[THE RISE OF FASCISM

It is difficult to come up with a satisfying political definition of fascism. The word fascism goes back to an ancient Roman symbol of authority — the *fasces* — a bundle of sticks bound around an axe, and carried in the presence of a magistrate. The symbol is meant to evoke the idea of strength through togetherness. As Europeans became increasingly disgruntled with their new postwar liberal governments, many chose fascism (as opposed to communism) as an answer to economic, political and social problems. A rejection of

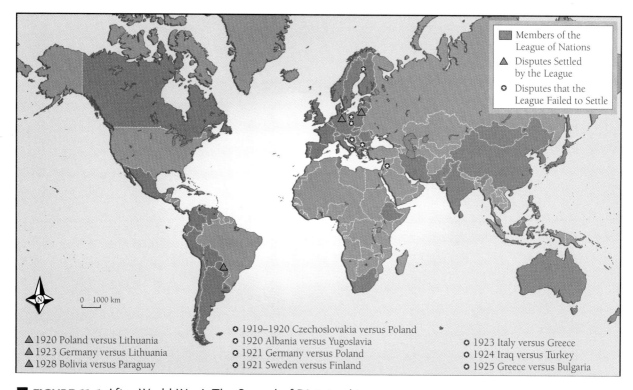

■ Members of the League of Nations	
▲ Disputes Settled by the League	
✪ Disputes that the League Failed to Settle	

0 1000 km

▲ 1920 Poland versus Lithuania
▲ 1923 Germany versus Lithuania
▲ 1928 Bolivia versus Paraguay

✪ 1919–1920 Czechoslovakia versus Poland
✪ 1920 Albania versus Yugoslavia
✪ 1921 Germany versus Poland
✪ 1921 Sweden versus Finland

✪ 1923 Italy versus Greece
✪ 1924 Iraq versus Turkey
✪ 1925 Greece versus Bulgaria

■ **FIGURE 11.1** After World War I: The Spread of Dictatorships
Many argue that the League of Nations was doomed from its inception. Why do you think many people believed this?

liberalism, of the ideas of the Enlightenment and the French Revolution, was at the root of fascist beliefs. Fascists saw democracy as a greedy, individualistic system that sacrificed national interests for class and party concerns. Democracy, to the fascist, breeds alienation and loss of community — fascism inspires citizens to acts of loyalty, honour, and heroism for the state. As nationalist movements, fascist parties everywhere identified themselves with the histories, traditions, and symbols of their own people.

At the same time, all forms of fascism shared some common characteristics: hypernationalism, anti-Marxism, anti-liberalism, anti-conservatism (though some had working relationships with the conservative elite), a *Führer* (leader) concept, a cult of youth and male dominance, a paramilitary group, and a fixation for flag rituals, Roman salutes and coloured shirts. Fascists glorified violence and action. Indoctrination, propaganda, and terror were

means to ensure that people were supportive of the state. From Britain to Romania, each country had its own version of fascism. In general though, European fascism was a tale of two cities: Rome and Berlin, Mussolini, and Hitler.

Hitler and Mussolini were two dictators, different men from different movements. Mussolini's fascism was full of swagger and fanfare; Hitler's had a dark and menacing quality that stirred terror in his enemies. Mussolini wanted colonies in Africa and more power in the Mediterranean. What Hitler wanted was limitless. In his book, *Mein Kampf* (My Struggle) he wrote about Germany's need for *Lebensraum* (living space) in the East. As a German of Austrian birth, he cherished the Pan-German dream of bringing all Germans "home to the *Reich*," of annexing Austria and "liberating" German minorities in border areas. As well, he wanted to settle the score with France for his nation's defeat in World War I. He wanted to tear up the

Versailles Treaty and change the boundary lines in Europe; and he wanted to do something about the Jews. The era of fascism became the story of Germany's revival, rearmament, and return to the struggle for mastery on the Continent.

In communism and fascism, the Continent had two anti-democratic forces rising at opposite extremes. Outwardly, the communists claimed to be struggling for the "real democracy" that would come with human equality in a communist future. In contrast, the first fascists presented themselves as enemies of democracy, equality, and the tradition from which they came. In this period of new "isms," fascism was the one that broke most radically with the nineteenth-century legacy of liberty because it had no ideology; it simply wanted to take power. Fascism, said Mussolini, was not about thinking; it was about acting.

Benito Mussolini was born in 1883, the son of a village blacksmith. He left a failing career as a schoolteacher to start a promising career in the Italian

The fascism of Benito Mussolini, shown here leading his black-shirted troops, was full of flag-waving, goose-stepping show. What kind of government did he run?

Socialist Party. The war turned his life around. Between 1914 and 1919, Mussolini changed from a socialist against the war to a nationalist in support of it; and from wounded soldier to angry war veteran. After the fighting, the country was full of discharged soldiers. Some on the left wanted to bring Bolshevism to Italy. Some on the right wanted to take revenge against the Versailles Treaty for cheating Italians out of their victory in the war.

From his beginnings on the radical left, Mussolini now joined veterans on the radical right. Together, they combined socialist jargon and nationalist passions into a hot mix of war cries that passed for the ideology of a new movement: fascism. Some in the ranks wore the black uniforms of the *Arditi*, the Italian elite shock troops of World War I, and soon the black shirt became the symbolic dress of the Italian Fascist Party. During the "red years" of 1919–1920 (years of strikes and left-wing protests), the Black Shirts organized themselves in fighting squads to take on the socialists and labour unions. Region by region, they beat down the "Reds" with fists, clubs, knives, and revolvers. Fascism thus came into existence in the curious guise of a radical movement in defence of law and order.

Fascists received support from those who lived in fear of revolution in Italy. Money came from business and landholding interests; political protection came from important military and government figures. The left said that the fascists were doing the dirty work of capitalism. The fascists, supported by some in the Catholic Church, said that they were saving Italy from communism — and had earned the right to power as a result. By 1922 certain leaders in government were ready to agree. When Mussolini ordered his followers, about 200 000, to begin "the march on Rome," the country's political elite simply stepped aside. King Victor Emmanuel III (1900–1946) made this fascist "revolution" legal by appointing Mussolini as the new prime minister. Without resistance, the Black Shirts paraded in triumph upon the capital city.

After three years in power, Mussolini closed down what was left of democracy in Italy. In 1924 the fascists — a small minority when they took power in

Time Magazine

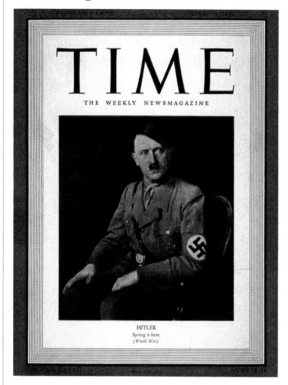

TIME

THE WEEKLY NEWSMAGAZINE

HITLER
Spring is here.
(*World War*)

Over the years, *Time* magazine has been one of the most influential news magazines in both its style and content. The first issue of the weekly appeared in March 1923 and the American publication quickly achieved popularity, reaching a circulation of 175 000 by 1927. *Time* was founded by two young, Yale-educated journalists, Henry R. Luce (1898–1967) and Briton Hadden (d. 1929). Initially, Hadden was the magazine's editor and Luce served as its business manager, but when Hadden died in 1929, Luce assumed the role of editor-in-chief until 1964.

Henry Luce created the periodical as a means of educating what he considered a poorly informed American public, especially in international affairs. Luce wanted to produce a magazine that would inform busy readers about current events in the United States and the rest of the world in a systematic, concise, and well-organized style.

From the magazine's inception, the contents of *Time* consisted of many short articles, summarizing information on subjects of importance and general interest. These articles were organized into departments covering national and international affairs, business, education, science, medicine, law, religion, sports, books, and the arts. Part of the magazine's broad appeal came from Hadden's formative editorial direction, which offered a lively layout and focussed on personalities.

After Luce took over the editorship and exerted his considerable influence, *Time* increasingly reflected his moderately conservative political viewpoint, which included support for the Republican Party, anti-communism and internationalism. Luce was considered the most influential magazine publisher in the United States. In articles during the Luce era, *Time* often suggested what readers should think about the subjects covered. Luce believed that objective reporting was impossible, and he encouraged editors to express his views, which appeared unsigned in the magazine. By the 1970s, however, the magazine assumed a much more neutral tone.

Time magazine's highly successful and profitable format has spawned many imitators, including *Newsweek*, founded in 1933 by Thomas J. C. Martyn, a former foreign-news editor for *Time*. In Canada during the 1960s, *MacLean's* magazine patterned itself after *Time* and created Canada's first news magazine. The first Canadian edition of *Time* appeared in 1943, and in 1961 the first edition of *Time* Canada was published in Canada. Eventually, the practice of publishing *Time* in Canada raised a controversy over "split-run" magazines — Canadian editions of foreign magazines. Many Canadian magazine publishers strongly feel that these split-runs threaten the financial well-being of Canadian magazines.

Person of the Year

For over 70 years, a highly popular feature of *Time* has been the issue entitled "Man of the Year" (as of 1999, "Person of the Year"). The figure who graces this issue's cover is *Time's* idea of the single person — man, woman, child, or even idea — who for better or worse has most influenced events in the preceding year.

In 1927 Charles Lindbergh was the first Man of the Year. Other notable figures to appear include Mohandas Ghandi (1930), Franklin Roosevelt (1932, 1934, 1941), Adolf Hitler (1938), Joseph Stalin (1939, 1942), Winston Churchill (1949), Charles de Gaulle (1958), and Martin Luther King (1963). Wallis Warfield Simpson, the woman for whom King Edward VII abdicated the British throne (1936), and Queen Elizabeth II (1952) are among the famous and influential women who have qualified as Man of the Year! Some ideas represented on the "Man of the Year" cover are Hungarian Freedom Fighters (1956), the generation of people 25 and under (1966), American Women (1975), the Computer (1983), and Endangered Earth (1988).

To mark the end of the twentieth century, *Time* selected a "Person of the Century," who "for better or worse personified our times and will be recorded by history as having the most lasting significance." *Time* editors chose Nobel-Prize winner Albert Einstein. Einstein's scientific genius, said the managing editor, "touched the most important fields of technology: nuclear weapons, television, space travel, lasers, and semiconductors."

1. Think about which person you would nominate as "Person of the Century." Do you agree with *Time's* choice of Einstein? Why? Why not?

2. Do you think magazines like *Time* give an objective view of the news stories they cover? Is there such a thing as "objective" news? Discuss this question as a class.

3. Criminals and terrorists also shape the world. Should they be "Persons of the Year" too?

1922 — won an impressive election victory (65 percent of the vote). This election, full of Black Shirt brutality and fraud, demonstrated nonetheless that Mussolini was swinging the country to his side. Suddenly, in 1924, opinion turned on the fascists after the murder of Giacomo Matteotti, a popular socialist who was murdered after speaking out against Mussolini. Defiantly, Mussolini now declared himself dictator and, with state power in hand, began to build his version of the fascist state.

The Fascist Party was merged with the Italian state. Police powers were increased across the board. Public propaganda made a cult of Mussolini as *Il Duce*, the leader of the Italian people. On the street, uniforms, parades and the raised-arm salute infused pageantry into everyday life. In public schools, indoctrination was aimed at developing "the new fascist man" of the future, and the young were organized into movements to carry fascism to the next generation.

Italian fascists had a simple saying: "Mussolini is always right." Mussolini actually ruled by consent. His government rested on the support of the traditional institutions and elite of the country. In this connection, his most popular move was to sign the Lateran Accords with the Catholic Church in 1929, bringing fascism to terms with the papacy and the religion of the Italian people. Mussolini now recognized the independence of Vatican City; Pope Pius XI, in turn, called on the Italian people to support fascist rule. The effect was to end a quarrel that had divided church and state in Italy since 1870.

[THE RISE OF STALIN

In Russia, war, civil war, revolution and famine resulted in the deaths of some 15 million people between 1914 and 1921. At the same time, the fall of the Romanov dynasty after three centuries of rule raised hope in the Russian people for freedom and representative government. In these circumstances, resistance to the rising communist dictatorship ran wide and deep in the nation. In 1918, for example, an assassination attempt against Lenin himself left the communist leader

severely wounded. In the end, the Bolsheviks overwhelmed the opposition (the "White" armies) by greater violence and terror. The result, however, was a separation between the state and the people that remained a lasting feature of Soviet history.

Czarist Russia, the most conservative state in Europe, became Bolshevik Russia, the first Marxist state. It began in the civil war between 1918 and 1921, when one army of Russians lined up against another, Reds against "Whites." In the conflict, the communists found themselves fighting alone against all their enemies together, from old czarists to left-wing radicals. Foreign troops from France, Britain, the United States, Canada, Poland, Czechoslovakia and Japan entered the country in 1918 in an attempt to bring Russia back into the war against Germany, and keep arms stockpiles out of the hands of the communists. The Bolsheviks believed, though, that troops had been sent to kill communism in its cradle. The effect of this Allied intervention in the civil war was to raise a wall between communism and the West, setting them apart in suspicion and distrust for most of the twentieth century.

Joseph Stalin, the "man of steel" would cultivate a fatherly image and so was sometimes called "Papa Stalin." He tried often to be photographed with Lenin. Why?

Led skilfully by Leon Trotsky, Commissar of War, the Red Army fought its enemies. Numbering as many as five million in 1920, the Red Army conquered piece by piece most of the country that the Bolsheviks were eventually to govern. Their victory meant defeat for the Ukrainians, Georgians, and other non-Russian peoples who had once had hopes for homelands of their own. Behind the lines, the *Cheka*, the new Bolshevik political police, spread the Red Terror, shooting opponents and suspects in droves. Included were the whole family and household staff of the fallen czar Nicholas II, on July 17, 1918. *Cheka* gunmen said that they had shot the "class enemies" of the revolution.

As the communists tightened their hold on power, the reality of one-party rule became clear to those who had fought to free the country of the czar. Revolutionaries who struggled beside Lenin in 1917 now struggled against him. Men and women once locked up in czarist jails were now locked up in communist jails. As these jails filled, prisoners were transported to forced labour camps in remote areas. In effect, this was the beginning of what writer Aleksandr Solzhenitsyn called the "Gulag Archipelago," the chain of concentration camps for political dissidents that soon spread across the country.

The ruin caused by the civil war came on top of the ruin caused by the Bolshevik economic plan known as "war communism." In this headlong leap into communism, the party in 1918 had taken command of the whole economy. The result was a catastrophe of falling production and human suffering. Armed squads of communists from the cities seized "surplus" crops from starving peasants. Between 1920 and 1922, a famine in the countryside took at least five million lives. Resistance was everywhere, and in 1920 alone, nearly half of the Red Army was needed to hold down peasant protest in the villages.

In 1921 Lenin announced the New Economic Policy, a return to more free-market methods. The government kept control of large industry, banking and foreign trade, but other activity was opened to private buying and selling, a concession to peasants who had opposed the requisitioning of crops. The result was an economic recovery at a time when the party needed it most. Within seven years, production was returning to pre-1914 levels. More importantly, the peasants were at peace with the regime. In their hands at last was the soil of Russia. This truce however, would not last for long. Many party members were not at peace with the NEP, since true communism had not been achieved.

First they needed a new leader. From the moment that Lenin suffered a paralytic stroke in 1922, a fight for leadership began among the top personalities in the party. Everyone looked to the intellectuals, men like Lenin himself, educated, skilled in Marxist theory and familiar with European culture. The best and brightest was Leon Trotsky, brilliant in revolution, victorious in command of the Red Army and the favourite of left-wing circles in the West. Other Bolshevik leaders, however, remembered him as one who came late to Leninism. Moreover, the arrogance of this clever man set them on edge. Trotsky did not have the patience for bureaucratic battles; this was the strength of his rival, Joseph Djugashwili, known as Stalin (1879–1953), the "man of steel."

Born in Georgia in 1879 to a poor family, Stalin was studying to be a priest before he was expelled from the seminary, probably for misbehaving. He then turned to revolutionary activity. Before 1917, while other Bolshevik personalities lived in exile abroad, he worked in the party underground in Russia, and was arrested seven times as a result. After the revolution, Stalin advanced because of his talent for paperwork and, in 1922, became the general secretary of the party. Stalin's control over the machinery of the party (the *apparat*, or apparatus), especially by appointing friends and allies to key positions, was the secret to his coming success.

What allowed Stalin to rise was the change in the party from a small, radical movement to a large ruling state bureaucracy. The primary need was no longer for revolutionary intellectuals but for day-to-day organizers. At this work, the plain and plodding Stalin showed true genius. Lenin, before his death in 1924, warned that Stalin was taking too much power and that he should be removed from the post of general secretary. But, the other men competing in the leadership race had more fear of each other than of this ordinary man. As they attacked one another, Stalin quietly took the party in hand.

At a time when Mussolini in Italy set the style for fascist dictators, with shiny uniforms, dramatic poses and speeches full of bluster, Stalin gave communist leadership an entirely different image. He was an "office dictator," simple in dress and lifestyle, a ruler poor at public speaking and without charisma. His power was in the *apparatchiki*, the people of the apparatus, the full-time bureaucrats who did the everyday work of the party, who knew the organization inside out, and who made it run. For this work, Stalin chose personalities like himself, individuals without formal learning, without experience in the world outside Russia and without interest in anything beyond politics. The party's grassroots organizations, called "cells," were located in every institution and area of life, in all the neighbourhoods, villages, factories, military units, police detachments and youth groups. The dictator sat in the Kremlin, the centre of government in the communist capital of Moscow, but his eyes and ears were everywhere.

Essential to Stalin's success in the leadership struggle was the lesson that Lenin had taught every Bolshevik: the duty of absolute loyalty to the party. Now, in a way, the party had become Stalin. To lay claim to the Bolshevik legacy, he made a cult (religion) of the dead Lenin. The body of the first Bolshevik leader was embalmed and displayed like a sacred relic in a tomb in Kremlin Square. Party propagandists made clear the connection between the old leader and the new. "Stalin is the Lenin of today," they said.

Between 1924 and 1928, the struggle for leadership in the party was hidden behind a debate on the New Economic Policy. Trotsky pressed the hard Marxist line that communism could not be made from scratch in a peasant society. What was needed, he insisted, was industry at home and revolution abroad, an immediate crash program to industrialize the Soviet

Leon Trotsky—why didn't the party choose him as their new leader?

Union, and an immediate push in the Comintern to carry revolution to the capitalist countries in the West. Arguing against this was Nikolay Bukharin, the champion of the NEP. Peace with the peasants, he said, was the safest way to advance the country. Trying to start revolutions abroad — certain to bring retaliation from the great powers — was the sure way to ruin it.

Stalin's first Five-Year Plan of 1928–1932 was the true dividing line between the old Russia and the new. After defeating his rivals and ending the NEP, Stalin put at risk all that he had gained by plunging into a vast economic transformation of Russian society. He forced the country through an agricultural, industrial, and social revolution all in one. By concentrating on building "socialism in one country," Stalin at the same time brought into Soviet communism a spirit of nationalism that changed the nature of the movement. In a speech to party members in 1931, he described how throughout Russian history, backwardness had brought military defeat, and how, without success in the Five-Year Plan, their new "socialist fatherland" would be defeated again. "We are 50 or 100 years behind the advanced countries," he said. "We must make good this lag in 10 years. Either we accomplish this or we will be crushed."

The First Five-Year Plan, 1929–1932

With the start of the Five-Year Plan on December 27, 1929, a sweeping process of collectivization brought all industry, commerce, and agriculture under state control. The result was a command economy in which production was regulated by a central plan and the labour force driven by production quotas. These quotas, set high and beyond the capacity of most workers and managers, started the economy racing at breakneck speed. Electrical power plants, for example, were ordered to increase output by 400 percent, heavy industry by 300 percent, and agriculture by 200 percent. Consumer goods had low priority, and the goods themselves were often shoddy and unfinished. Resources were directed instead to megaprojects: hydro-electric plants, tractor factories, and new industrial cities built up out of the wilderness.

Party leaders later criticized the first Five-Year Plan for having too many boundless goals and massive projects. As it turned out, the goals could not be met. Yet, at a time when capitalism in the West was paralysed by the Great Depression and millions of workers were idle, communism in the Soviet Union made remarkable advances in industry — and there was no unemployment.

Stalin mobilized his people for industrialization in the way a nation mobilizes for war. State propaganda urged men and women to work hard and sacrifice to the "production front." In factories, medals were given to "the heroes of Soviet labour," women and men who exceeded their production quotas. Those who were late,

lazy, or absent met with punishments and police measures. Long hours, low wages, poor housing — this was the lot of Soviet labour during the Five-Year Plan. Since no Western bank would make loans to a communist government, especially one that had refused to repay the czar's state debts to foreign creditors, to get money for industry, Stalin had to brutalize his own people.

In particular, Stalin fell upon those in the countryside, where close to 80 percent of the population lived and worked the land. Here, the state took everything: land, livestock, and farm equipment. According to plan, the nation's 25 million peasant farms were collectivized into large common farms where the peasants worked as field hands under a party manager. Their task was to meet production quotas dictated from above. At harvest, the state carried off the quota, sold it at steep prices in the cities, or exported it for hard currency and poured the money into more industrial growth. Those on the collective farms lived or died on what was left in the fields.

Against this, the peasants reacted with fury; they burned crops and slaughtered their own livestock. Between 1929 and 1932, the Soviet Union lost 50 percent of its horses and cattle and 60 percent of its sheep and goats. The party responded with still greater fury, as the Five-Year Plan in the countryside was declared a form of class war against the *kulaks*. The *kulaks* generally were described as rich capitalist peasants, a class living off the rural poor and profiteering on the harvest. The word *kulak* actually had a loose meaning, and came to be used by the communists to describe any peasant who opposed them. Stalin ordered the liquidation of the *kulaks* as a class. Army and police units raided villages, forced peasants off their lands, and shot them in droves. In the process, some two million to three million people were packed off to forced labour in the gulags of Siberia.

Famine was an even greater killer. Left without food when the party confiscated entire harvests, an estimated 3.5 million to 7.5 million rural people starved to death between 1931 and 1933. The death toll was especially high in Ukraine, where Stalin wanted to crush peasant resistance and Ukrainian nationalism at the same time. Some called this "the terror famine." Stalin's policy against peasant opposition was simply to starve people to death or exile them to Siberia. The result, in any case, was one of the largest mass deaths in modern history.

Review, Reflect, Respond

1. Why was post–World War I Europe susceptible to radical political movements? Were these movements inevitable? Explain.

2. Create a three-column chart that lists the causes of the Great Depression. Describe the effect of each cause, and explain the various remedies.

3. Briefly describe how Stalin won power in the Soviet Union. Was he the best person for the job? Explain.

Life Under Stalin

Life in the Soviet Union prior to World War II was difficult, as people experienced a decline in their standard of living from the previous decade. There was a constant shortage of food. A shortage of housing meant there were, on average, four people per room in every urban dwelling by 1940, up from 2.7 in 1926. Those who were not fortunate enough to find an apartment, built themselves scrap-lumber shacks or dug underground shelters in the shantytowns around the cities. There were some incentives for workers under Stalinism: Unemployment was virtually unheard of and important social benefits such as health care, education and day care, as well as old-age pensions, were freely available to all Soviet citizens.

There were important gains for women under the communist regime but they did not last. Immediately following the revolution, equal rights for women were proclaimed. During the 1920s, divorce and abortions became easy to obtain and women were encouraged to work outside the home. Implicit in the new-found freedom for women was an increase in sexual freedom. Women also found numerous career and educational

opportunities open to them as they began to attend university and acquire jobs in fields that had been restricted to men. By 1950, for example, 75 percent of doctors in the Soviet Union were women. Millions of women began factory work and heavy construction, building roads, mills and dams.

These new gains for women had their disadvantages. In many cases, women did not have a choice about whether to work or stay at home. Wages were so low that a family required two incomes to survive. After toiling at their jobs all day, women still carried the heavy burden of maintaining the home and caring for the children. Finally, in 1929 the *Zhenotdel*, the organization that led the campaign for women's emancipation was abolished. It was declared that the liberation of women had been achieved. The socialization of child care and housework, once central issues to many Marxists, were forgotten. Stalin now wanted to boost the birth rate, so divorce became less accessible and abortions became illegal. The family became the fundamental institution of the Soviet State.

THE GREAT PURGE, 1935–1938

The first Five-Year Plan was celebrated as a success when Stalin called an early end to it in 1932. In fact, the Kremlin was left with production problems in agriculture that would last as long as the Soviet Union itself. In industry, however, the changes brought by the modernization drive shifted great-power relationships in Europe. The Soviet Union had entered the industrial age and by 1939 had surpassed England in overall production. But, the years of crisis had put the Soviet system under severe strain.

Reports of suffering in the countryside had apparently brought tension into Stalin's own household, even causing his second wife to commit suicide in 1932. As opposition and discontent threatened to spread disorder, Stalin took measures to put Soviet society under tighter control. His method was to bring the state into more and more areas of public and private life.

The Five-Year Plan had transformed the Soviet Union into a totalitarian society. The state now controlled virtually all aspects of life in the U.S.S.R..

The process of repression was soon carried into the party itself. A key event was the assassination in Leningrad of Sergei Kirov, a rising star in the communist leadership, on December 1, 1934. Caught red-handed, the assassin confessed on the spot to acting for opposition elements in the party. The following year, the secret police, now called the NKVD (the name of the secret police often changed; the organization was permanent), reported the discovery of a "terrorist centre" in the party, bent on murdering Soviet leaders and destroying the new Five-Year Plan.

What followed was a wave of arrests, murders, and executions that swept over party members and the Soviet elite. These purges served to remove upper- and middle-level officials in government, the military and cultural positions. Stalin replaced these people with younger, loyal followers who would obey his demands. New laws ordered the death penalty for citizens who failed to inform on others. Children over 12 who failed to report the crimes of their parents were punished. Before this Great Purge of 1935–1938 was over, an estimated one million victims were dead and another four million to six million were put in forced-labour camps.

The most sensational drama of the Great Purge were the show trials of party leaders. Most of the leaders were tough old Bolsheviks who had lived for the revolution and once stood at Lenin's side. Now they confessed in open courtrooms to the blackest crimes against the Soviet Union: terrorism, sabotage, and spying for capitalist countries. Worse, they confessed links to the "traitor" Trotsky. This once great revolutionary — now in exile — had become the target of Stalin's paranoia. In the show trials, horror stories on the evils of Trotskyism made up the most bizarre part of courtroom testimony. Western writers wondered why innocent men and women confessed to such vile crimes. Much later, after Stalin's death in 1953, one of his successors gave an explanation from the inside. Soviet leader Nikita Khrushchev

(1894–1971) told party members in 1956 that Stalin had a simple method to get confessions out of his enemies: "beat, beat, and once again beat" and that the accused were "no longer able to bear such barbaric tortures."

From Khrushchev came details on the path of destruction throughout party ranks. He reported that out of the nearly 2 000 members who attended the XVIIth Party Congress in 1934, 1 108 ended up in the hands of the secret police. Out of the 139 individuals elected at that time to sit on the Central Committee of the party, 98 were arrested and shot. Behind it all, Khrushchev claimed, was the personality of one man.

Western observers concluded, however, that such massive terror could not be caused by one personality alone. Stalin needed the secret police, the party organization, the powers concentrated in the Kremlin, and the support of an ideology that appeared to justify the use of such extreme force. The cause of the Great Terror, they believed, was not the dictator alone, but a broader system of power and ideas. They called it totalitarianism. By 1938, in any case, fear, conformity and silence had become a way of life in the Soviet Union. In the gulags, there were as many as eight million prisoners, many from influential elements of the population. The regime, for example, had turned on its own military leaders, arresting or killing about half of its high officer corps, including 90 percent of its generals (some 30 000 officers in total). Then with the rise of fascism in Europe, the Soviet Union had to bring an end to the terror and waste of its own people.

Already the Nazi rise to power in Germany in 1933 had spread panic among communist leaders. Communism had met a force more radical than itself. As fascist movements were growing in Western countries as well, communist parties in democracies were suddenly on the defensive. Now communist parties everywhere called on all democratic parties to join them in a Popular Front against fascism. None of this, however, turned back the march of fascism. More and more, the march of fascism came to mean the march of Hitler and National Socialism in Germany.

HITLER AND THE RISE OF NATIONAL SOCIALISM

Adolf Hitler was born on April 20, 1889, in an Austrian village near the German border. He was the son of a minor Austrian customs official, a man of peasant stock who had made his way into the lower middle class. Later, there would be rumours of a Jewish grandfather in Hitler's family tree, but no hard evidence was ever found. Dreaming of becoming an artist, Hitler was crushed by his failure to gain admission to the Imperial Academy of Fine Arts in Vienna in 1907. An angry youth, he stayed on in Vienna and became steeped in the national hatreds that divided the peoples of the Hapsburg Empire.

Hitler's ideas were a jumble of old Central European hatreds: hatred of Marxists, Slavs, and Jews. Other nineteenth-century thinkers had already dressed these hatreds in the language of Darwinism and the "science" of race. They had described history as a "struggle for existence," pitting race against race, blond Aryans against dark Semites, and the German master race against "subhuman" Slavs, Jewish "parasites" and faceless socialist hordes. Hitler brought to these ideas a deeper hatred and a way with words that somehow released the same hatreds in his listeners.

In 1913 Hitler left Vienna for the German city of Munich. The next year, as a common soldier in the German army, Hitler proved his courage on the Western front, where he was one of the few enlisted men to be awarded the Iron Cross, first class, for bravery under fire. He would describe his ordeal in World War I as the supreme experience of his life. Word of the German defeat came as he was being treated for temporary blindness as the result of an Allied gas attack. Full of anger, he set himself upon a path of revenge against those politicians at home whom he believed had betrayed the German army. To him, this "stab in the back" was the work of the same enemies of his people he had discovered in Vienna: the Marxists and Jews, but especially the Jews. To fight them, he said, had become a sacred duty. "By defending myself against the Jew," he wrote in *Mein Kampf*, "I am fighting for the work of the Lord."

In 1919, in a Munich beer hall, Hitler attended a meeting of the German Workers' Party, a small group — scarcely 50 people — who talked of combining nationalism and socialism into a movement to defend the German workingman against Jews, Marxists, and foreigners. Within a year, Hitler made the organization his own. He changed its name to the National Socialist German Workers' Party (in German, NSDAP) and developed it into a leader-centred movement with himself as its *Führer* (leader). From him came Nazism's black symbols and menacing features. He introduced the wearing of uniforms, the swastika emblem, the *Sieg Heil* salute, and the display of flags, standards and marching men. In 1921 he added a paramilitary squad, the *Sturmabteilung* (SA), or storm troopers, also known as Brown Shirts. These tough veterans in brown shirts and jackboots stood guard at party meetings and engaged in brawls with Hitler's enemies.

At this early stage, however, the Nazis were not much different from the many other small right-wing parties of postwar radicalism. A change came after what was called the Beer Hall *Putsch* (revolt) in 1923. In a show of force, Hitler had led about 2 000 followers on a protest march through the streets of Munich. When police fired upon the march, the Nazis broke and ran. With this failure, Hitler gave up on thoughts of seizing power by revolutionary means. At his trial for treason after the *Putsch*, he turned failure into success. His defiant speeches in the courtroom made front-page news and gained him national attention for the first time. Now, he decided that the road to Nazi dictatorship led through Weimar democracy.

New supporters came to Nazism in part because of the electioneering genius of Joseph Goebbels (1897–1945). Named by Hitler in 1929 to be the new Nazi propaganda chief, Goebbels took over just in time to exploit the resentments caused by the Depression. Far from the Nazi ideal of the tall, blond, Nordic man, Goebbels was small, dark and wiry, with a clubfoot. He had a talent for exciting

Adolf Hitler and Joseph Goebbels, Nazi propaganda chief. When does information become propaganda?

human emotions, and believed, as did Hitler, that the role of propaganda was not to stimulate thought but to stop it. Goebbels had a trick for making Nazi ideas sound nationalistic, socialistic, capitalistic, or anti-Semitic, according to crowd demand.

Scholars once concluded that Nazi votes came mostly from the lower middle class, but further research has revealed that the party appealed to all levels of the population. By the end of 1932, however, Goebbels's propaganda had reached its limits. The Nazis then had 450 000 party members and 400 000 SA Brown Shirts, a paramilitary force four times the size of the German army. In the November election of that year, the Nazis received 12 million votes. This,

however, was almost two million less than they had received four months earlier. The movement had peaked. The plan to win power by winning elections had fallen short. The Nazis never received more than 37 percent of the German vote. Now, however, with his party losing momentum, Hitler got the break of his life: he was handed power in a political deal.

Conservative politicians around Reich president Paul von Hindenburg (1897–1934) had tried for some time to convince this grand old World War I general to come to terms with the idea of a Hitler government. One of them in particular, the Prussian aristocrat Franz von Papen (1879–1969), argued that Hitler could be "used." The Nazis had the support of the masses. Thus, only a deal with Hitler, Papen concluded, could bring this mass support to the side of the conservative forces in the country. Hindenburg, however, wanted no part of the vulgar Hitler. Only when the Nazis started to decline at the polls — and Hitler became easier to handle — did Papen wear down the resistance of the old soldier-president. Papen promised Hindenburg — now nearly senile at age 84 — that a Hitler government would be surrounded and controlled by conservative politicians. Under the agreement, Hitler promised to appoint a majority of conservative ministers to his cabinet (of 12) — and only three Nazis. In return, President Hindenburg appointed the Nazi leader Chancellor of Germany on January 30, 1933. Said von Papen, "Within two months, we will have pushed Hitler so far into a corner that he will squeak."

Hitler called his victory "the triumph of the will," the victory of a party of iron determination over a weak opposition. He went on to build his party into a propaganda machine. Historians have agreed that Hitler's most clever ideas, and the most interesting pages of *Mein Kampf*, are on the art of mass propaganda. These pages reveal his contempt for the intelligence of the common people, and his view that the best propaganda is that directed at the least intelligent among them. The message, he said, must be simple, emotional and totally one-sided; most of all, it must be repeated, again and again and again. Hitler believed, above all, in the power of the spoken word.

Fascism in Power: The Third Reich

The compromise with the conservatives that brought Hitler to power was important to the shaping of the Third Reich, the name given to Nazi rule in Germany from 1933 to 1945. Like the fascists in Italy, the Nazis had to live with their conservative allies. Therefore, as Hitler's followers moved into position as a new political class in Germany, the old elite held their place in society. Over time, state regulation increased, police powers grew, the opposition was beaten into submission, and the conservative elite came one by one to its knees before Hitler. By 1938 Germany had become "the Hitler state," a form of dictatorship far more totalitarian than the fascist regime in Italy.

The push toward total power began in the first months of Nazi rule. When fire gutted the *Reichstag* building in Berlin on February 27, 1933, and a communist youth was arrested on the spot, Goebbels screamed about communist plots. Many suspect it was the Nazis who started the fire (though it proved to be the actions of a single, deranged person). In the uproar, Hindenburg gave Hitler emergency powers to suspend civil liberties and maintain order in the country. The SA then began arresting communists and socialists. With a new Germany in the making, an election on March 5 — which Hitler made sure would be the last — again left the Nazis short of a majority at 44 percent. But, the support of Hitler's conservative allies gave the government a majority in the *Reichstag*. Hitler pushed through the Enabling Act, the legislation which, in giving him power to rule without parliament, completed the "legal revolution" that brought dictatorship out of a democratic system.

With power in hand, the Nazis began the process of bringing the organized life of the country under political rule. Institutions, labour unions, professional societies, women's movements, along with sports, youth and volunteer groups of all kinds now became National Socialist organizations, or were closed down as private bodies existing apart from the state. Hitler's purpose was not only to spread Nazi control but also to carry the ideas of his movement into the group life of the nation. One result was the dramatic night ceremony called "The Burning of the Books." On May 10, 1933, youths of the new student organization threw into huge bonfires the great books of Western culture, including the works of Jewish writers.

From the start, Hitler's conservative allies called on him to restore order in the nation. Hitler responded by naming his second-in-command, Hermann Göring, to the police post of Minister of the Interior for Prussia. Göring lost no time in making the secret state police, known as the *Gestapo*, the most feared organization in Europe. Much of the disorder in the country, however, came from the Brown Shirts. Their leader, Ernst Röhm, in particular, was a bully who always urged Hitler to take more radical action. But, Hitler now needed a professional army more than Röhm's street fighters. Early on June 30, 1934, in a bloody purge known as "The Night of the Long Knives," Nazi detachments fell upon the SA leaders, murdered Röhm and his lieutenants, and ended the power of the Brown Shirts.

Those who did the dirty work of purging the SA were the *Schutzstaffel* (SS), or security section, an elite branch of the SA distinguished by their black uniforms and iron discipline. In contrast to the emotionalism and random violence of the SA, the SS was taught to be passionless, hard, and obedient. After 1934, as the SA was withdrawn from the streets, the SS took over the work of political police. As the role of the SS increased, the power of its leader, Heinrich Himmler (1900–1945), increased along with it. Himmler was both a racist and a supreme organizer. Named by Hitler as Reich Leader of the SS and Chief of German Police, he came to control the entire police apparatus of party and state alike. Included was control over a concentration camp system that eventually became a Nazi version of the Gulag Archipelago.

The first concentration camp was opened at Dachau, near Munich, in March 1933, and it became a model for the many camps to follow. As many as 6 000 prisoners went through these camps in the early years. Most were political opponents of Nazism, largely communists, socialists and intellectuals. By 1935 Himmler's SS had broken any remaining organized resistance to Hitler's destruction of Weimar democracy, and the number of arrests actually declined.

While the true measure of public consent to Nazism is uncertain, it appears that the regime enjoyed wide popularity during these early years. A 1934 state plebiscite (opinion poll) showed that 85 percent of the population approved of Hitler as *Führer* of the nation after Hindenberg's death. The popularity of Nazism was based on more than police and parades. There were also jobs, profits, and prosperity. Hitler's programs for rearmament and public works, including the construction of superhighways (*Autobahnen*), brought the country out of the Depression and into a period of economic recovery and high employment.

While many under Nazi rule feared the *Gestapo*, did not want to go to war, and despised Nazi party bosses, they were grateful for the economic recovery and the resurgence of German power that accompanied the rise of Adolf Hitler.

Hitler's War Against the Jews

Just as Hitler had used the German constitution to give himself ultimate power, he also used legal means to destroy the lives of Jews. The Nazis wanted to isolate Jews from mainstream society. Beginning in April 1933, shops and businesses owned by Jews were boycotted. A legal definition of who was a Jew was established in the same year (a legal Jew had at least one grandparent who was Jewish). Restrictions were placed on the number of Jews admitted to public education. On September 15, 1935, Hitler passed the Nuremberg Laws on Citizenship and Race. These laws stated that in order to be a citizen of the German Reich, you had to be "of German or kindred blood" and your behaviour had to demonstrate that you were "both desirous and personally fit to serve loyally the German people and the Reich." Only those granted citizenship would enjoy full political rights. Jews were denied their citizenship — they could not vote, hold public office, or be protected by other laws. Jews could easily be identified by the yellow Star of David they were forced to wear on their clothes. Left defenceless

before any violent or discriminatory action that the Nazis might use against them, many Jews left the country.

Still hesitant to leave behind their homes or extended family, and unwilling to believe that the racism would continue, other Jews quietly resisted the persecution. By January 1937, Jews had been banned from most professions (teaching, dentistry, accounting). As it happened, the assassination of a German diplomat by a Jewish student living in Paris set off a wave of mass violence against the Jewish community. On the night of November 9, 1938, gangs looted and burned hundreds of synagogues, and smashed windows of Jewish shops during what became known as *Kristallnacht*, or "the night of broken glass." Jews were fined one billion *Reichmarks* to pay for the damage and 30 000 Jewish males were rounded up and sent to concentration camps. Soon it became extremely difficult for Jews to leave Germany.

Historians debate whether totalitarian states derive their strength from terror or popular acquiescence, or both. Were average German citizens afraid to help their neighbours, the Jews? Or did they agree with the persecution, either by ignoring the actions of Nazis or by complying with them? One historian, Saul Friedlander, argues that some people felt sympathy towards the Jews, but the majority were not sympathetic because this would have meant they distrusted the "rightness of

The aftermath of *Kristallnacht*, "the night of the broken glass," when synagogues and shops owned by Jews were vandalized.

Hitler's ways," of which they approved. He also points to the failure of German religious, artistic and intellectual figures to provide moral, religious or humane leadership or guidance during the persecutions.

More Victims of the Third Reich

Although racism and annihilation were the least publicized aspects of Nazism, they formed the core of Third Reich politics. Those who failed to live up to the competitive criteria of National Socialism became the first targets of the Nazi regime. These people can be broken into three main groups:

- ideological enemies such as communists
- those who did not follow traditional social norms, such as homosexuals and Roma people (gypsies)
- biological outsiders who were considered a threat to the continuation of the German race.

The third category included two main groups: those who were non-Aryan and therefore considered undesirable, and those who carried hereditary defects. Of the persecution of the Jews, Roma (gypsies), and other peoples, much is known. Less has been written about those who were exterminated by the Nazis because of their "bad genes."

The theory of eugenics, which promotes the strengthening of a race through selective breeding, had become popular in many European countries during the 1920s and 1930s. In the 1920s, some German doctors encouraged "negative selection" (as opposed to the Darwinian idea of natural selection) as a means to improve or protect the gene pool. By sterilizing those with hereditary defects, they believed they could eventually weed out defective genes among the Germans. The Nazis put this suggestion into practice within six months of their coming to power in 1933. From 1934 to 1945, nearly 350 000 men and women were legally sterilized.

The Nazis carried their program of negative selection further by exterminating thousands of people who were considered unfit. Between 1939 and 1945, approximately 5 000 children were murdered, either by lethal injection or by malnutrition, because they suffered from severe handicaps. At least 50 000 people were murdered on the grounds of mental illness. The first gas chambers, later used to exterminate the Jews, were actually developed in six mental hospitals to handle the large number of mental patients to be killed.

WEB CONNECTION

www.mcgrawhill.ca/links/legacy

Go to the site above to find out more about eugenics.

Family Life under Nazism

The tumultuous years of the Weimar Republic, 1918–1933, had changed the life of the traditional German village. Most homes, while remaining part of the traditional village economy, required a second income, often earned by one member of the family employed in an office or factory. Despite the obvious move towards an industrial economy, village life and status within the village continued to be centred around land ownership.

One of the most profound changes to village life brought about by the Nazi regime was that the political power structure within the village began to lose its paternalistic, land-based nature. Young people could no longer see a relevant connection in their lives to inheriting land (nor the wealth and power that accompanied land ownership) and instead became attracted to Nazism. Some among the older generation remained skeptical of the Nazis, and this led to conflict within households. These divisions within the home and village deepened as the Third Reich increasingly insisted on loyalty to the party and state above all else. Excitement, rapid change, as well as the opportunity for personal advancement appealed to young Germans.

The Nazi state also came to replace the role of the nuclear family in the rearing and training of children.

Schools became the ideal institution to promote racial propaganda and to train young minds to be receptive to the militarism of the Third Reich. Over time, children became involved in paramilitary exercises and practised survival techniques instead of working on the land. There was little open hostility to the increasing role of the state in the lives of children and in village life. Most people had been indoctrinated with the notion that "everyone's welfare was at stake," and that to show concern for individual needs was to be socially

irresponsible. Hitler was also clear in his beliefs about women in Nazi society. First, he believed that women needed physical training in order to become good mothers. He encouraged people to have large families and supplied better health care to facilitate a higher birth rate. Abortions were outlawed, except for non-Aryan women and those with physical or mental "defects." Women were encouraged to be leaders within the party only at the beginning of the regime. Once in power, the party gave women limited political roles; they were expected to be the moral backbone of the regime, while men were the all-powerful warriors.

A poster for the Nazi Youth movement. Two-thirds of Nazi party members were under 40 years of age. The Nazi elite was largely composed of young, not highly educated, lower–middle class people, like Hitler. Why do you think that was so?

Review, Reflect, Respond

1. Describe three important events that contributed to the rapid rise of the Nazi Party.

2. From what you know about Adolf Hitler, do you think he was an original thinker or simply a skilled orator who borrowed and adapted the ideas of others? Explain your answer.

3. How were the totalitarian regimes of Hitler and Stalin alike, and/or different? Provide specific examples in your answer.

POSTWAR NORTH AMERICA, 1920–1939

The Roaring Twenties

While much of Europe attempted to rebuild after the devastation of the Great War, North Americans enjoyed the fruits of an economic boom during a period often referred to as the "Roaring Twenties." Many industries in Canada and the United States benefited from Europe's rebuilding process by supplying construction materials and expertise. Although prosperity returned after the war, the innocence and optimism that had characterized the turn of the century became a casualty of war, like the thousands of young soldiers who had died in it. The result was a decade of rampant materialism during which new fads, new fashions and new trends in music suggested a carefree attitude, as many North Americans tried to forget the horrors of war and live life with reckless abandon.

Consumerism

The late nineteenth and early twentieth centuries had witnessed the rapid development of technological innovations. Thomas Edison had invented the light bulb, the phonograph, and other devices; Guglielmo Marconi had sent the first radio message from Signal Hill in Newfoundland; Alexander Graham Bell had developed the telephone; and Canada's Reginald Fessenden had developed sonar. In the years between 1790 and 1860, the United States Patent Office issued 36 000 patents. By comparison, in the 40 years from

What are the values being reflected here?

1860 to 1900, there were 676 000 patents granted. By the 1920s, hydro-electric power had reached most areas of Canada and the United States, revolutionizing factories and providing homes with the electricity needed to power the multitude of gadgets and labour-saving devices being churned out by North American industries. Refrigeration allowed North Americans to eat fresh fruits and vegetables year-round. Improvements in packaging gave rise to a wider variety of packaged foods including the revolutionary new sliced bread. Consumers all over North America were purchasing electric irons, vacuum cleaners, washing machines, toasters, and refrigerators. Even leisure time was being radically changed by the widespread purchase of radios and phonographs and the building of movie theatres.

The consumer revolution that occurred in the 1920s was not merely the result of a rapid increase in the number of products available; it was also the result of a sudden growth in advertising. For the first time, advertising was actually creating consumer demand, rather than simply informing the public about products, services and prices. Middle-class consumers, especially women, were being inundated with messages about products to improve their appearance. They were also being told how they could become more efficient as wives, mothers and homemakers, by using new products and time-saving appliances. This revolution in advertising was aided by the emerging mass media: newspapers, radio stations, billboards, and national magazines.

Another radical change that helped drive the consumer revolution was the practice of buying on credit. For the first time, consumers were able to put down a deposit and pay the balance in instalments. The opportunity to buy a new phonograph for "$5 down and $5 dollars a month" was irresistible to many North Americans. In 1928, records show that 85 percent of furniture, 80 percent of phonographs, 75 percent of washing machines and radios, and 70 percent of refrigerators were bought on credit. Buying on credit also brought automobile ownership within reach for many ordinary North Americans. The earliest automobiles had been expensive luxury items restricted to the rich. This changed with the introduction of assembly-line manufacturing by Henry Ford in 1908. By the 1920s, a Ford Model T could be purchased for $300, well within the budget of the average family.

The car changed North American culture in many ways: dating habits of young people, family vacations, Sunday outings, and even where people lived. North Americans could now visit far-off places or go on day trips on weekends. Their increased mobility allowed people to move away from the industrialized centres of cities to houses in the quieter suburbs. The affluence of the 1920s and the opportunity to buy on credit helped bring on North America's love affair with the automobile.

A Revolution in Leisure

The 1920s also saw a revolution in how North Americans spent their leisure time. Movie theatres were a place to escape the real world, radios kept North Americans in touch with major events, spectator sports provided much-sought-after heroes, and blues and jazz music caught the ear of the rebellious youth.

Movies became a national pastime that attracted people from all backgrounds and ages. An ad in the *Saturday Evening Post* urged Americans to "Go to a movie ... and let yourself go!" Movie stars became idols for North Americans in the 1920s. When the silver screen's leading heartthrob, Rudolph Valentino, died suddenly at the age of 31, nearly thirty thousand tearful fans attended his funeral. Movies came to be so much a part of North American culture that the Hollywood stars became the major trendsetters, transforming tastes and behaviours. A new hairstyle worn by Gloria Swanson, or a new dress style worn by Mary Pickford, would become the rage, and thousands of women would want the same look.

Spectator sports also experienced tremendous growth during the 1920s. Baseball, football, boxing, and hockey all produced heroes, such as Red Grange and Babe Ruth. Now, women actively participated in the sports craze by joining women's leagues in

Canadian actor Mary Pickford became known as "America's Sweetheart."

baseball, hockey and track. North Americans were able to follow the triumphs and defeats of their heroes by attending sporting events, listening to radios, or reading newspaper and magazine articles.

Changes in the Family

Families in North America moved from the cities into suburbs, where they experienced emerging new attitudes about traditional gender roles and expectations. Already in the nineteenth century, suburbs were beginning to emerge around several Canadian and American cities, as new methods of transportation allowed people to live farther away from their place of work. By the early twentieth century, suburbs had become more than just a place to live; they had become a new way of life. Accessible to white-collar workers of the middle class, such as bank clerks and businesspeople and more affluent, skilled members of the working class,

History

Clarence Birdseye, an American naturalist with an interest in biology and business, was the inventor of the "Multiplate Quick Freeze Machine" (1925), the machine that created the frozen-food industry. Birdseye, while working in Labrador as a naturalist for the U.S. Geographic Service in 1912, noticed that fish caught by Inuit people would freeze and then be consumed days later with no noticeable change in taste or texture. Birdseye figured out how food could be rapidly frozen at extremely low temperatures without destroying its cellular structure. After years of experimenting, Birdseye's Freeze Machine successfully packaged prepared foods such as peas, spinach, cherries, as well as meat and fish, into waxed cardboard cartons which were flash-frozen under high pressure. Consumers were skeptical at first, but sales grew steadily through the 1930s and 1940s to become the enormous industry frozen food is today. The advent of frozen foods saved people time and energy and improved the health of consumers, since valuable nutrients were preserved in the freezing process.

suburbs became a symbol of the ideal life for the modern family. In 1903 *Cosmopolitan* magazine described the suburbs as a "compromise for those who temper an inherent or cultivated taste for green fields ... with an unwillingness to entirely forgo the delights of urban gaiety." Women, especially, felt less isolated in their new suburban homes, because they now had the use of the automobile, radio and telephone.

The roles of men and women within the family were changing by small degrees. A man was still considered the breadwinner and authority figure in the home. A woman was expected to offer nurturing support. But, more middle-income women now held jobs outside the home. These jobs tended to be in domestic service, factories, and as clerks in offices and stores. The majority of women working outside the home were single (marriage usually meant the end of a woman's career) and young, between the ages of 20 to 24. Ethnic and non-White women faced employment discrimination and often found work only in their own communities. Lower-income, poorly educated women continued to work for extremely low wages while still maintaining a home, often without electricity and running water. Women's wages were 54–60 percent of the earnings of men.

Changes in the lifestyles of young people came with the new affluence of this period. Single women with disposable incomes often became "flappers" — bobbing (cutting short) their hair, wearing short skirts, bangles and beaded necklaces, applying make-up, smoking, drinking and dancing at bars. Young men were similarly lured into fashion trends (greased hair, pencil-thin mustaches, flashy suits) and lifestyles that included entertainment in nightclubs, speakeasies (illegal drinking places), and sporting events. Views toward sexuality were changing and use of chaperones and arranged marriages declined sharply.

Popular women's magazines, such as *Women's Weekly* and *Cosmopolitan*, which outlined new "scientific" methods of child care, influenced the raising of children. Women were expected to follow new formulas for child rearing and ignore traditional advice from previous generations. Young girls and boys went to the same schools to learn reading, writing and mathematics but girls were enrolled in domestic-science classes, while boys took classes in manual training. The new morality and limited economic opportunities aside, a woman's life continued to be defined by her traditional role as wife and mother, and a man's by his role as husband, provider and privileged citizen.

Family Life in the Great Depression

There were many social consequences of the Great Depression. Entire families packed up their belongings and endlessly moved around in search of employment. Young people in search of work stowed away on trains

WASH AWAY FAT
AND YEARS OF AGE
With La-Mar
Reducing Soap

The new discovery. Results quick and amazing—nothing internal to take. Reduce any part of body desired without affecting other parts. No dieting or exercising. Be as slim as you wish. Acts like magic in reducing double chin, abdomen, ungainly ankles, unbecoming wrists, arms and shoulders, large busts, or any superfluous fat on body. Sold direct to you by mail, post paid, on a money-back guarantee. Price 2/- a cake or three cakes for 4/-; one to three cakes usually accomplish the purpose. Send postal or money order to-day. Surprising results. LA-MAR LABORATORIES, Ltd., 48, Rupert Street (110L), London. W.1.

REDUCE!

Popular women's magazines began to feature beauty products and cosmetics. Do you suppose "Reducing Soap" really worked?

from coast to coast in Canada and the United States. "Hobo jungles" sprung up along riverbanks and rail lines. Hungry, unemployed people formed long lines in hopes of getting a bowl of soup and a warm place to sleep. How did these lean years affect the family?

Like the economic systems of the Western world, families would survive the Depression years by changing and adapting. One result of the crisis was a new type of family, one supported by two wage earners. Prior to the Depression, the family unit of the early twentieth century was one in which the father was the breadwinner, while the mother was a homemaker and full-time mother. Economic realities forced men to accept the idea of women contributing to the family income, and encouraged women to find jobs or pursue careers. As a result, more women began to move outside the home, although they seldom found their workload at home significantly reduced.

The Great Depression also had an impact on marriage and divorce rates. During the 1930s, the marriage rate in the United States plummeted, as many young men chose to remain single, fearing they would not be able to support a family. The sharp decline in marriages became a grave concern for many educators and church officials who feared delayed marriages would lead to more liberal sexual behaviour outside of marriage. To prevent young people from becoming sexually active prior to marriage, governments were encouraged to provide subsidies to young couples wanting to marry. The decline in the marriage rate was accompanied by a decline in the birth rate, and a further increase in the rate of divorce. Many marriages collapsed under the strain of the economic depression.

DAILY LIFE IN EUROPE 1900–1939

Life Among the Working Class

The stock market crash and the Great Depression also affected families in Europe. Throughout the first half of the twentieth century, the basic design of the homes of the middle and upper classes was markedly different from those of the working class or rural people. In general, overcrowding was the norm in most areas of Europe prior to 1950. According to a 1906 census, 26 percent of those living in cities larger than 5 000 people lived more than two to a room, while a further 36 percent lived more than one to a room. Between 1900 and 1950, there were few improvements in home comfort and conveniences in European homes, other than the introduction of electricity.

With overcrowding such as this, individuals enjoyed little privacy within the home. Members of a family had to dress in front of family, bathe in a wooden tub in the common room, and no one had the luxury of sleeping alone. In many homes there would be only one bed shared by as many as five people. Living conditions made it difficult to keep many private belongings or have private conversations. Sexual

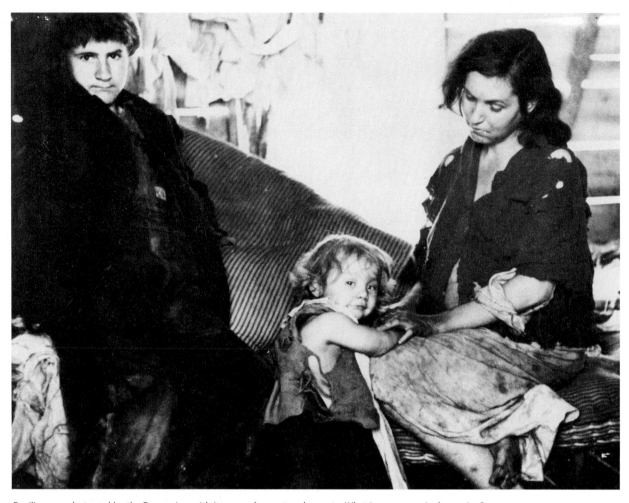

Families were destroyed by the Depression, with its unemployment and poverty. What is an economic depression?

intimacy took place either in secluded public spaces or discreetly in the home, despite the presence of family. Thus, during the first half of the twentieth century, the private lives of the European peasantry and working class was indistinguishable from family life.

Children

Among all classes in Europe during the first half of the twentieth century, children had no right to a private life. All aspects of children's lives were closely monitored and controlled by their parents. Spare time after school was most often taken up by the chores parents gave their children. When they did find leisure time to spend with friends, families could be very selective about which children would make suitable playmates. Making new friends in public places, something very common among young children today, was not allowed.

Parents also took it upon themselves to plan their children's futures by selecting which university they would attend or in which trade they would apprentice. Among the middle and upper classes, where considerable wealth was at stake, marriage was also a family concern in which parents exercised considerable influence. When planning a marriage, protecting the family fortune and status carried more weight than the emotional bond between the prospective bride and groom.

Marriage and Divorce

The changes in attitudes toward marriage and divorce during the twentieth century reveal a great deal about the evolution of the family in Europe. During the first half of the century, the purpose of marriage was still to establish a household and have children in order to carry on the family name and inheritance. Therefore, when selecting a marriage partner, professional prospects, wealth and morality were seen as more important than appearance or love. In fact, many couples considered a successful marriage one in which a man and woman were able to understand, appreciate, and respect each other. While love was not considered a prerequisite for marriage, many entered into a union hoping that, over time, they would grow to love their spouse.

Given this attitude toward marriage, divorce was quite rare in Europe. Marriage was considered a permanent contract that could only be broken in very severe cases where the husband or wife was seen as guilty of grave misconduct. At the turn of the century, there were fewer than fifteen thousand divorces in France; in 1940 there were still fewer than thirty thousand. When granted, divorces usually involved an abusive, alcoholic husband who had not only been unfaithful to his wife but also had become a financial burden to the family. Incompatibility was simply not sufficient grounds for divorce. Mental or physical cruelty, or adultery, was often not sufficient grounds for the termination of a marriage either.

By the 1930s and 1940s, attitudes toward both marriage and divorce in Europe were beginning to change and become more liberal. More rapid change, however, had already begun in North America. By the turn of the century, Americans were also witnessing a rapid rise in the divorce rate. In the years between 1867 and 1929, the population of the United States increased 300 percent, the number of marriages increased by 400 percent, and the number of divorces skyrocketed (an increase of 2 000 percent). By 1929 in the United States one in six marriages was ending in divorce, the world's highest divorce rate.

VISUAL ART OF THE EARLY TWENTIETH CENTURY

Symbolism

In every Western country at this time, there was an outpouring of artistic expressions in every form and medium. Symbolist art was a carry-over from the romantic period and used themes related to dreams and emotional experience. The symbolists also often looked to the arts of other cultures or other times, such as Asia, the South Pacific, the Middle East, the medieval and the Byzantine eras. In symbolist paintings, objects decorate a flat surface, often without perspective. While the figures may be realistic, instead of reality they seem to exist in a world of dreams. Some symbolists were influenced by the psychological theories of Sigmund Freud (1856–1939), and especially his book *The Interpretation of Dreams*.

The Dream, a symbolist work by artist Henri Rousseau (1844–1910). How is this painting dreamlike?

Fauvism and Expressionism

The first real art movement that wholly belonged to the early twentieth century involved a group of artists who called themselves *Les Fauves* (wild beasts, in French). They considered themselves wild and rebellious, defying the traditions and aesthetics of the previous century. Fauvism signalled a definite change from the predominant styles of late-nineteenth-century romantic art. The Fauves overtook the Impressionists and post-Impressionists, with their technique and bold use of colour.

German expressionist artist Käthe Kollwitz is known especially for her paintings of the tragedies and pain of war and poverty.

Henri Matisse, master of *Les Fauves*, had a long, and distinguished career working in many art forms: painting, ceramics, stained glass, sculpture, and fabric design. This is a painting of Madame Matisse.

Colour actually became the subject of Fauvism because it expressed and was meant to evoke deep emotion. The Fauves wanted to convey deep feeling through bright colour and strong imagery. On its own, Fauvism did not last long (1900–1910). But, its main proponent, Henri Matisse (1869–1954), was faithful to its aesthetic much longer. His art expressed a continuation of the basic Fauvist principles of colour and form.

At this time, an important German artistic style called expressionism emerged. Its paintings, characterized by dark colours and violent imagery, are in the tradition of German styles as far back as the medieval and Renaissance periods. The works of Käthe Kollwitz (1867–1945) show us the darker side of human emotions and the pain and struggle of war, poverty, and the working class.

German and Austrian painters explored the disasters, distress and suffering of people through bizarre, chaotic paintings that reflected the political and social chaos brought on by the war and the rise of Nazism. These paintings were considered "degenerate" by Hitler and many expressionist artists would have to flee Germany.

Russian painting, too, was affected by the new expressionist movement. The work of Russian painter Wassily Kandinsky (1866–1944), for example, completely abandons recognizable subject matter. Kandinsky saw the use of colour and abstract forms as a way to express ideas and feelings beyond physical reality, into the unconscious mind. According to the nineteenth-century philosopher Nietzsche, civilization is simply a lie, used to cover up the reality of our primitive, irrational human nature. In creating or expressing the irrational through colour on the canvas, the artist expresses the truest reality of himself or herself, and thus human nature in general.

The twentieth-century art movement that really left behind the artistic conventions that began in the Renaissance was cubism. Cubism took its inspiration from the work of Paul Cézanne in the late nineteenth century. Cézanne intellectualized nature into geometrical forms to fit them onto a two-dimensional canvas. This aesthetic philosophy was promoted by two

The Blue Rider (1911) by Kandinsky. Eventually this Russian artist's work become totally abstract, with no recognizable objects.

extremely influential and important painters: Spanish painter Pablo Picasso (1881–1973) and French painter Georges Braque (1881–1963).

Guernica is a mural-sized painting (3.4m x 7.7m) by Picasso. Does the cubist style effectively convey the subject and emotion behind this work?

To get a sense of the major trends in modern art, one needs only look at the career of Pablo Picasso. He experimented constantly and changed styles many times, matching the philosophies and the historical "isms" of late-nineteenth- and twentieth-century Europe — a world in upheaval and transition. Picasso began painting in a realistic mode but his work gradually became more and more abstract. In the early l900s, he was influenced by the art of Africa and Oceania, as were other artists and musicians. This influence allowed him to break away from the Western academic tradition. Like Cézanne, he began to reduce what he saw to abstract planes.

One of Picasso's most passionate works is the mural entitled *Guernica*. The painting is an indictment of the 1937 bombing of the small Basque town of Guernica during the Spanish Civil War. Hitler's *Luftwaffe* practised bombing techniques on the population; this large painting, done in somber black and white, depicts the resulting carnage.

The devastation of war affected many artists. The senselessness of war led some artists to create what has been called an anti-art movement known as Dadaism. The Dada artistic and literary movement began in Switzerland during World War I. Hans Arp, one of the early Dadaists explained the movement as follows:

> Revolted by the butchery of the 1914 World War, we in Zurich devoted ourselves to the arts. While the guns rumbled in the distance, we sang, painted, made collages and wrote poems with all our might. We were seeking art based on fundamentals, to cure the madness of the age, and a new order of things that would restore the balance between heaven and hell.

Dadaist artist Marcel Duchamp created what he called "Ready-mades" works of art made from everyday objects, to which Duchamp adds titles or other commentary. Despite their seeming absurdity, some of Duchamp's works are based on historic art. This work is called *Bicycle Wheel* (1963).

The emergence of psychology as a new science was a powerful influence on all aspects of the arts. Under this influence came another important art movement in the early twentieth century — surrealism. The discovery of new realities by scientific research was parallelled by the discovery of the inner realities of the human psyche, especially through the studies of Sigmund Freud. A whole new plane of existence — altered states of consciousness — became subject matter in all The arts. Indeed, art became an effective method for self-discovery and revelation. Surrealism, then, was a movement designed to explore altered states of consciousness, and the unconscious mind, through many artistic forms.

The painter most people associate with surrealism and Freud's concept of the unconscious mind is Spanish artist Salvador Dalí (1904–1989), whose work tries to redefine our sense of beauty. His paintings, in one sense, are lyrical, colourful and romantic, but the realistic objects are placed together in bizarre relationships. Like a dream, they exist in and of themselves in a strange landscape. .

There was also a huge outpouring in the art of sculpture. Auguste Rodin (1840–1919), for example,

Salvador Dali called this painting *Autumnal Cannibalism* (1936). What do you see?

LE PENSEVR

The Thinker in bronze and executed in 1880, is Rodin's most recognized work. How is this sculpture unrealistic?

had an enormous influence on modern sculptors. His rebellion against the classical world, and the expressionistic character of his works, attracted young sculptors who wanted to break new ground. Many painters tried sculpture as well. Impressionists Degas, Renoir, and the more modern Matisse, Joan Miró (1918–1959) and Picasso, all produced interesting sculptural representations of the imagery found in their paintings. All of these artists, through their sculpture, presented abstractions in a three-dimensional, concrete form. Although concrete in shape and texture, these works are able to express timeless and universal abstract ideas.

Early Twentieth-Century Music

Just before the onset of World War I, there was a reaction against romanticism in music. This desire for change affected all the arts. Painters presented new planes of existence; writers presented new points of view. In music, the traditional major-minor scales began to be considered obsolete. Among other things, Impressionist composers and musicians looked to the construction of religious music, of the Middle Ages for inspiration. Non-Western music was also a strong influence in music as it was in painting. Japanese and Chinese instruments were incorporated into Western works. Dissonance, or non-harmonic music, and new sounds and tones became acceptable. Composers put together unusual combinations of sounds, just as Monet created unusual combinations of colours to express his vision.

Impressionist composers allowed themes and melodies to flow into each other subtly. Unlike Romantic concertos and symphonies, which are full of climaxes and mood changes, Impressionist works use short lyric forms such as preludes, nocturnes, and arabesques — titles often used for paintings as well. And, as in painting, Impressionist music had Romantic qualities and an emphasis on mood and atmosphere.

Just as French painters dominated the art scene, so French (rather than Austrian or German) composers dominated the music scene. Claude Debussy

Sigmund Freud Frees the Unconscious

Austrian scientist Sigmund Freud (1856–1939) revolutionized our understanding of the human personality through a system of treatment he founded called psychoanalysis.

I received the profoundest impression of the possibility that there could be powerful mental processes which nevertheless remained hidden from the consciousness of man.

Sigmund Freud, 1889

Early in his career, Freud worked with French neurologist Jean Charcot (1825–1893), who used hypnosis to treat various abnormal mental conditions. Freud experimented with hypnosis, but found that its beneficial effects did not last. He then became interested in the ideas of Josef Breuer, who had discovered that when he allowed hysterical patients to talk freely about the earliest occurrences of their symptoms, the symptoms sometimes disappeared. From this insight, Freud developed the idea that many neuroses had their origins in deeply traumatic, childhood experiences that were now hidden from consciousness.

Look into the depth of your own soul and learn first to know yourself, then you will understand why this illness was bound to come upon you and perhaps you will thenceforth avoid falling ill.

Sigmund Freud, One of the Difficulties of Psychoanalysis

Psychoanalysis

In 1896 Freud coined the term psychoanalysis to describe the "talking cure" he had developed. Very simply, according to psychoanalytic theory, there are three important parts to the personality. The "id" is the largest and most important part of the unconscious, containing the drives for pleasure and aggression. The "ego" is the self we think we are; and the "superego" is the moral sense of a personality.

Acting on the assumption that repressed conflicts are buried in the deepest recesses of the unconscious mind, Freud had his patients relax, and then encouraged them to speak freely, in the belief that he could thereby discern the unconscious forces lying behind what the patient said. This method is called free association. Through free association, and by analysing dreams, Freud proposed that the screening mechanism of the superego is moderated, and material that would otherwise be completely repressed is allowed to filter through to the conscious ego. Once inner conflicts become conscious, the patient can be treated effectively.

Critical Reaction

Freud's ideas were controversial in his time and have continued to be the subject of intense debate. There are disturbing implications to psychoanalytic theory. For example, according to such a theory, humans are not just physical beings, but complex psychological entities controlled by powerful urges from within, which are largely unconscious.

Several medical colleagues had difficulty with Freud's theoretical emphasis on sexuality, particularly the idea of sexuality in childhood. It was not until 1908, with the first International Psychoanalytical Congress, that Freud's importance became recognized. His reputation was greatly enhanced in 1909, when he was invited to give a course of lectures in the United States.

From 1910 on, Freud's reputation grew enormously, and he continued to write prolifically until his death, producing more than 20 volumes of theoretical works and clinical studies. Part of the reason Freud commanded such widespread attention was that he was a graceful speaker who skilfully presented his arguments.

Still, some medical practitioners doubted Freud's seriousness as a therapist because his name was still associated with the then disreputable subject of hypnotism. And, other contemporaries rejected his ideas because they could not be tested by traditional scientific methods.

There were problems with Freud's psychoanalytic theory as well. For instance, it relied on male sexuality as the norm of development. Many women found such assumptions shocking for an analyst who treated many women patients.

The great question ... which I have not been able to answer, despite my thirty years of research in the feminine soul, is, What does a woman want?

Sigmund Freud

Still others objected to Freud's ideas because of their own blind prejudice. When the Nazis took over Germany, for example, Freud's books were among the first to be banned as the fruits of "Jewish science." When Hitler invaded Austria, Freud was forced to flee to England, where he died of cancer in 1939.

What progress we are making. In the Middle Ages they would have burned me. Now they are content with burning my books.

Sigmund Freud, Letter (1933)

Freud's Legacy

The impact of Freud's work went beyond medicine and psychotherapy. It also profoundly influenced literature, art, religion, anthropology, and education. Great film directors such as Federico Fellini and Ingmar Bergman have used dream sequences in their work, with many allusions to the Freudian concept of dreams in both their content and structure.

After Freud's death, numerous Freudian schools of thought emerged to develop psychoanalysis in different directions. But, despite ongoing and sometimes compelling challenges, Freud has remained one of the most significant thinkers in the intellectual landscape of the twentieth century.

1. Do some research to find out the meaning of the expression "Freudian slip."

2. Do you think dreams reveal what goes on in the unconscious mind? Try to analyse or explain one of your own, or a friend's dream.

Pleasures
AND PASTIMES

In the 1920s, Berlin rivalled Paris as the artistic and cultural centre of the Western world. To some, however, Berlin was the "Babylon of the world" — a city of four million, racked with unemployment, crime, prostitution, drugs, riots, strikes and political unrest. In the midst of all this turmoil, three dozen theatres thrived. One form of musical theatre, the cabaret, was a reflection of the bitter, ironic irreverence of the times. Sex, politics, and religion were all fair game for sharp-tongued singers and actors who donned flamboyant costumes and wore theatrical make-up. Talented American Jazz artists such as Duke Ellington toured the cabarets in the 1920s. Each cabaret was known for its particular specialty. The Apollo, for example, had nude dancers of both sexes and the services of prostitutes upon demand. The Eldorado was well known for its transvestite actors. The Resi and Femina installed telephones at all tables so patrons could call each other. The cabaret prided itself in breaking all traditional morals and social conventions. When Hitler took power in 1933, the cabaret was one of the first victims of National Socialism. Producers and performers (many were Jewish) either fled the country, were arrested and sent to concentration camps, or committed suicide.

(1862–1918) wrote music that was shockingly contrary to the strict academic rules of the French Conservatory of Music. Debussy was also influenced by the French symbolist poets. Their literary movement tried to present poetic images similar to the art of the symbolist painters. They, too, wanted to move language away from its intellectual use — conveying a meaning — to its symbolic use — presenting an idea. Their free-verse forms were echoed in Debussy's musical language. His best-known orchestral works are *Afternoon of a Faun*, *La Mer*, and *Nocturnes*. Debussy also experimented with the solo piano and tried to capture a moment in time through his abstract pieces. His most famous piano work is

probably *Clair de Lune*, which tries to capture the beauty and evanescent quality of moonlight.

Perhaps the most important of the French post-Impressionist composers was Maurice Ravel (1875–1937). Like Debussy, Ravel was attracted by the art of the Impressionists. He was also influenced by Spanish music and the music of the nineteenth-century Romantics. He was deeply affected by World War I; although over 40 years old, Ravel served as a driver in the army but had to be discharged due to ill health. One of his most famous works is *Concerto for the Left Hand*, written for a concert pianist who had lost his right hand in the war.

EARLY TWENTIETH-CENTURY LITERATURE

In the world of literature, artists no longer wanted to associate themselves with Victorian conventions and respectability, or with bourgeois materialism. They wanted to isolate themselves from middle-class values. One method was to live as a "bohemian" in physical isolation, as artists who deliberately chose to live in poor areas and in poor housing did. Writers did not want to think of themselves as catering to the crass tastes of the middle class, so another tactic was to provoke outrage.

Other features of early-twentieth-century art and literature were pessimism and stoicism. The fatalistic novels of Thomas Hardy (1840–1928), such as *Tess of the d'Urbervilles*, portray characters who see themselves as pawns in a huge chess game, perpetual victims of fate. As the Victorian age drew to a close, there was an even stronger reaction against its restrictions and conservatism. People were in the mood for a freer society. The political situation in England added fuel to this fire, as people protested the Boer War and imperialism in general. Writers too became involved in these issues. For example, Irish playwright George Bernard Shaw (1856–1950) championed women's rights. The Irish struggle for independence was supported in the works of James Joyce (1882–1941) and

William Butler Yeats (1865–1939). These writers worked hard to keep Irish culture alive by encouraging a renaissance in Irish literature.

Poetry

During the early years of the twentieth century, imagist poetry (based on clear imagery) arose in reaction to the emotional qualities of Romantic poetry. As a literary movement, it coincided with similar movements in the visual and performing arts. Just as Debussy and Picasso were influenced by Oriental rhythms and African motifs, imagist poets used Oriental modes such as the *haiku* to express their complex visions in deceptively simple forms.

Consider the following imagist poem by the American poet Ezra Pound (1885–1972). The poem was inspired by a scene he experienced in a Paris subway station. It is called *In the Station of the Métro*. Note the simplicity of this poem in its hard, clear, and precise images.

> The apparition of these faces in the crowd;
> Petals on a wet, black bough.

Poets began to experiment with language, juxtaposing poetic language with the language of everyday conversation, including slang. The result was a highly intellectualized attempt at creating poetry that reflected emotional qualities of real life. The poet T. S. Eliot (1888–1965) spearheaded this movement, which revolutionized the way artists wrote and people thought about poetry for the rest of the century.

WEB CONNECTION

www.mcgrawhill.ca/links/legacy

Go to the site above to find out more about early-twentieth-century literature and poetry.

Eliot is considered the foremost English-speaking poet of the twentieth century. Like Ezra Pound, he was an American, but lived and worked in England. Eliot started with the intellectual, imagist approach but took it many steps further. His poetry is compelling in its ability to stir both the emotions and intellect of his readers. He experimented with poetic forms, language and the structure of poetry, even exploring how a poem actually appeared on the page.

One of Eliot's most celebrated works, *The Love Song of J. Alfred Prufrock*, is actually a journey or odyssey of a man who feels isolated and alienated in a society for which he feels no affinity but longs to join it. The poem's structure meanders over the page, just as its narrator wanders in search of love or at least companionship. The poem combines rich language and imagery with bizarre scenes or fragments of conversation. The poem forces the reader to think, while being conscious of and sympathetic to the painful self-consciousness of the narrator, Prufrock. His demeanour is that of a man in a middle-age crisis.

> Let us go then you and I
> While the evening is set against the sky
> Like a patient etherized upon a table;
> Let us go, through certain half-deserted streets,
> The muttering retreats of restless nights in one-night cheap hotels
> And sawdust restaurants with oyster shells:
> Streets that follow like a tedious argument
> Of insidious intent
> To lead you to the overwhelming question ...
> Oh do not ask, 'What is it?'
> Let us go and make our visit.
> In the room the women come and go
> Talking of Michelangelo.[1]

Another extremely influential and important poet of the twentieth century was W. B. Yeats, who also was Irish. He began his career in the 1890s, at a time when the "art for art's sake" aesthetic dominated the literary scene. Yeats soon developed his own particular aesthetic and style of poetry. Like the eighteenth-century poet and forerunner of romanticism William Blake, he developed his own mythology and symbolism based on Byzantine and Celtic imagery. His interest in Irish mythology led him to become a champion of the Irish independence movement. His poem *Easter 1916* commemorates the attempted Irish nationalist revolt against the British government in 1916. The poem ends with references to the men involved in the uprising, some of whom were known to Yeats:

> MacDonagh and MacBride
> And Connolly and Pearse
> Now and in time to be,
> Wherever green is worn,
> Are changed, changed utterly:
> A terrible beauty is born.[2]

Review, Reflect, Respond

1. Describe four ways in which the technology that developed in the late nineteenth and early twentieth century changed daily life for the average North American.

2. Describe three major changes in the family structure or the daily routines of family members that occurred in the first half of the twentieth century.

3. In your opinion, did art, music, and literature reflect or shape values and attitudes in the inter-war years? Respond with supporting examples.

The Novel

Just as artists reacted to the war with art movements such as Dadaism and expressionism, many writers, disillusioned and horrified by the loss of so much life, looked to the political left for some sort of justification of existence. Many intellectuals from all over Europe and North America joined the Republican army in the Spanish Civil War (1936–1939) but soon realized their resistance was futile against the ultra-right.

The novel underwent a transformation in the early twentieth century. Four of the most important English novelists of this time were Joseph Conrad (1857–1924), James Joyce (1882–1941), D. H. Lawrence (1885–1930), and Virginia Woolf (1882–1941). In keeping with the new psychological theories of Freud and Jung, and with the changes in poetry, these novelists sought to develop a technique that allowed them to capture a sense of the human condition. One way was to present a narrative or situation in layers, using multiple points of view. This allowed the novelist to present a total experience.

Virginia Woolf used multiple points of view to express a total reality in her novel *The Waves*. The novel tells the story of six children who move from childhood to adulthood. Each character presents his or her perception of certain situations. The reader puts these situations together to obtain a complete picture of the life surrounding the characters and a realistic picture of the characters themselves. Other works by Woolf include *Orlando*, *To the Lighthouse*, and *A Room of One's Own*.

Virginia Woolf, an influential novelist of the early twentieth century.

James Joyce's novel *Ulysses*, based on Homer's classical epic *The Odyssey*, details an extraordinary day in the life of an ordinary man as he journeys through Dublin having various adventures. The whole novel is one experiment after another with technique. In one chapter, for example, Joyce bases his narrative on the musical score of a Bach fugue. A *leitmotif* (recurring theme) is expressed through the repetition of words and rhythms throughout the novel. The last 70-odd pages of the novel are pure stream-of-consciousness technique. Joyce eliminates all punctuation in an attempt to record the actual thought patterns of the character Molly Bloom, the wife of the hapless hero.

D. H. Lawrence was more concerned with exploring human relationships than technical experimentation. He was interested in all combinations of relationships: mother and son, lover and lover, friend and friend. Lawrence adopted a Freudian approach to human sexuality. In the novels *Lady Chatterley's Lover*, *The Rainbow*, and *Women in Love*, he attempts to relate the physical as well as emotional experiences of women in sexual relationships. These novelists laid the foundation for modern writing; however, they are only three of many whose works from this time became building blocks for future generations of writers.

Reflections

The years between 1918 and 1939 were trying and anxious times economically, socially, politically, and culturally. Artists responded with dramatic new forms of expression in an attempt to comment on the new realities. The economic roller coaster that took people from the boom of the 1920s to the Great Depression first created a demand for consumer goods and then forced people to search for drastic solutions to survive. In Europe, the totalitarian regimes in Italy, Germany, and the Soviet Union attempted to crush all opposition in a desire for a new relationship between citizen and state. Depression, warfare, and totalitarianism all posed a great threat to democratic citizenship — a threat that was turned into a battle with the coming of the next world war.

Chapter Review

Chapter Summary

In this chapter, you have seen:

- how key factors such as demographic pressures, racial issues, and clashing ideologies have led to conflict and war
- the importance of chronology as a tool in analysing the history of events in the West in the early twentieth century
- that several key factors such as racial bias and authoritarian governments have slowed or blocked the advancement of human rights
- that key social developments have occurred as a result of Western technological innovations

Reviewing the Significance of Key People, Concepts, and Events (Knowledge and Understanding)

1. Understanding the history of World War I, its underlying causes, events and consequences, requires a knowledge of the following concepts and people, and an understanding of their significance. Select and briefly explain three from each column.

Concepts and Events	People
Mein Kampf	Benito Mussolini
Lateran Accords	Joseph Stalin
Locarno Pact	Adolf Hitler
New Economic Policy (NEP)	John Maynard Keynes
Five-Year Plan	Leon Trotsky
Great Purge	Pablo Picasso
National Socialism (Nazism)	T. S. Eliot
Nuremberg Racial Laws	Virginia Woolf
cubism	

2. How should history judge the regimes of Mussolini, Hitler, and Stalin?

   Construct a matrix to help you analyse these regimes. Your matrix should include: Economic Prosperity, Technological Advances, Human Rights and Freedoms, Strength and Stability of the State, and Standard of Living. Once your matrix is complete, write a one-paragraph summary of your overall conclusions.

Doing History: Thinking About the Past (Thinking/Inquiry)

3. How did the ideologies of fascism and communism respond to the pessimism and disenchantment many felt towards democratic-capitalist systems? Why, in your opinion, did both systems ultimately fail despite making considerable material progress? Respond in two to three paragraphs supported with evidence.

4. On the twenty-fifth anniversary of King George V's reign in England, British historian Sir Ernest Barker offered this reflection on the changes sweeping Western society:

> A gust of mechanical changes has produced a revolution in our material way of life ... The pace of life has been quickened by the motor-car, the aeroplane, the telephone, the wireless [radio] ... Perhaps some of the social and political movements of our time on the continent of Europe are connected with the physical revolution through which we are going. They tend towards idolization of the group — the race, the nation, the class. They use the new physical means of mass propaganda ... to produce the temper and feeling of the group.

Explain why you agree or disagree with Barker's assessment of the impact of physical change on European society and politics.

Applying Your Learning (Application)

5. Pablo Picasso's *Guernica*, shown in this chapter (page 441), is an example of art as political message. Picasso loaned the work to New York's Museum of Modern Art with the proviso that it remain there until democratic government was restored to Spain. *Guernica* was returned to Madrid in 1981.

Imagine you are viewing this huge painting. Describe what you think your initial reactions would be and then answer the following questions:

(a) Why do you think Picasso chose to create this work in shades of grey, black and white?

(b) The painting includes images of hope as well as despair. What do the various figures represent? Describe three figures and what you think they mean.

6. Imagine that you are poor, unemployed and living in London, England, in the early 1930s. You have been approached by different groups promoting the advantages of communism and fascism. Prepare four questions you would ask each group to help you decide whether you have any interest in joining their political movement.

Communicating Your Learning (Communication)

7. Prepare a map of Europe using colours and symbols to indicate the type of government and leader in the following countries in 1935: England, France, Germany, the Soviet Union, and Italy. This map should capture the division in Europe between democracies and totalitarian regimes. Try to make effective use of images, relevant colours, and symbols.

8. Select a significant event or accomplishment that occurred in the 1920s or 1930s in one of the countries listed below, and write two newspaper stories about them. Write the first article from the perspective of an British or Canadian reporter. Write the second article from the perspective of the "official" press in Germany, Russia, or Italy.

CHAPTER TWELVE

World War II 1939–1945

CHAPTER EXPECTATIONS

By the end of this chapter, you will be able to:

- *demonstrate an understanding of the consequences of war*

- *demonstrate an understanding of the key factors that have led to conflict and war*

- *describe the main tenets of fascism and Nazism*

- *demonstrate an understanding of how the policies and actions of Nazi Germany blocked the advancement of human rights*

The mushroom cloud from the explosion of the second atomic bomb dropped on Japan in August, 1945, at Nagasaki.

Twenty years after World War I ended, Europe plunged back into war with battle lines drawn in similar patterns. Once again, Germany, Italy and the Austro-Hungarian Empire were allied against Britain and France. It appeared that four years and several million lives lost had done little to resolve the issues that divided Europe. Europe in 1939, however, was profoundly different from what it had been a quarter-century earlier. When war erupted in 1914, Europe had still been governed predominantly by monarchies. By 1939 most of the monarchies of Europe had fallen. In some cases, they were replaced by democracies, but in others, dictators such as Hitler and Stalin had come to power. Amidst the apparent continuity in Europe a dramatic ideological shift was taking place. World War I had pitted European countries with essentially similar ideological perspectives against each other. World War II would bring distinctly different ideologies into conflict. At the outset of the war, while democratic states were allied against the fascist forces of Europe, the communist Soviet Union negotiated a deal with Nazi Germany that effectively kept it out of the war. By the end of 1941, Japan would enter the war allied with the fascists, while the Soviet Union would be drawn into the war as an ally of the Western democracies.

While countries re-aligned much as they had during the first war, World War II would be a dramatically different confrontation. In addition to the usual horrors of war, the Nazis would carry out genocide on a scale never seen before. During the course of the war, the Nazis would undertake the systematic extermination of European Jews, along with Roma (gypsies), communists, homosexuals and liberal intellectuals. Never before had so many innocent people been victims of organized hatred and racism; and never before had so many civilians died at the hands of ideological fanatics.

KEY CONCEPTS AND EVENTS

Dieppe

Blitzkrieg

Spanish Civil War

Munich Agreement

Dunkirk

Battle of Britain

Operation Barbarossa

Pearl Harbor

Operation Overlord

Yalta Conference

Hiroshima

Holocaust

Potsdam Conference

KEY PEOPLE

Neville Chamberlain

Adolf Hitler

Joseph Stalin

Winston Churchill

General Dwight Eisenhower

Emperor Hirohito

Harry Truman

Wit and Wisdom

The murderers are loose! They search the world

All through the night, oh God, all through the night.[1]
Murder by Gertrud Kolmar, a Jewish writer who perished in Auschwitz

TIME LINE: WORLD WAR II

Adolf Hitler establishes alliances with Italy and Japan	**1935**	
	1936–1939	Spanish Civil War
Munich Agreement; Germany annexes the Sudetenland (Czechoslovakia)	**September 29, 1938**	
	November 9, 1938	*Kristallnacht.* Nazi gangs shatter Jewish store windows and burn synagogues
Germany invades Poland	**September 1, 1939**	
	September 3, 1939	Britain declares war on Germany; Canada declares war one week later
Germany quickly achieves victory in France	**May 1940**	
	July 10, 1940	Battle of Britain begins
Operation Barbarossa; Germany invades the Soviet Union	**June 22, 1941**	
	December 7, 1941	Japanese attack the United States fleet at Pearl Harbor, Hawaii
Operation Overlord, the invasion of Normandy	**June 6, 1944**	
	April 30, 1945	Adolf Hitler and his mistress, Eva Braun, commit suicide
VE Day; Germany surrenders unconditionally	**May 7, 1945**	
	August 6, 1945	United States drops first atomic bomb on Hiroshima, Japan; three days later a second is dropped on Nagasaki
VJ Day; Japan surrenders, World War II ends	**August 14, 1945**	

Not to scale.

CONFLICT AND WAR: EUROPE, 1939

When war returned to Europe in 1939, a mere two decades had passed since the "war to end war" had concluded. The peace established in 1919 by the Treaty of Versailles did little to restore prosperity and stability to Europe. So little had been accomplished by four years of war and the ensuing peace, that historians increasingly viewed World War II not as a second world war, but as the continuation of a European civil war with global consequences. Yet, despite the severe restrictions imposed by the Treaty of Versailles, Hitler managed to rejuvenate the German economy by initiating a public works program and building up the military strength of the Third Reich.

The Politics of Appeasement

Students studying the history of World War II often ask why Hitler was allowed to rearm, in obvious violation of the Treaty of Versailles. In hindsight it is easy to be critical of the leaders of France and Britain for their failure to enforce the treaty early in the rule of Adolf Hitler. Appeasement is the term used to describe the type of diplomacy used in the 1930s by the Western powers of Europe (those who signed the Treaty of Versailles) on the Third Reich. Simply put, appeasement was an attempt to avoid conflict through compromise. By allowing some violations of the Treaty of Versailles, Britain and France hoped that Germany would be calmed and conflict could be avoided. There was also a general feeling that the terms of the Treaty had been too harsh. It was through diplomacy that Hitler was able to re-introduce conscription in 1935, while at the same time rapidly rearming Germany.

In 1935 Hitler and Mussolini established their alliance of fascist states known as the Rome-Berlin Axis, and signed a similar pact known as the Anti-Comintern Pact (anti-Soviet) with expansionist Japan. In 1936 Hitler re-occupied the Rhineland (an area bordering France) — demilitarized under the Treaty of Versailles — with no reaction from either Britain or

France. By early 1938, he had concluded that his opposition at that time was neither united nor prepared to stand up to an aggressive Germany.

Women in Britain protesting war with Germany. How does this demonstration compare to those of today?

At a meeting of top military officials in November 1937, Hitler made it clear that he believed the increase in food production necessary to support the growing German population could not be achieved on the available arable land. Hitler concluded that " ... the only remedy, and one which might appear to us visionary, lay in the acquisition of greater living space ... " To acquire greater living space, known in German as *Lebensraum*, Hitler pointed out that "Germany's problem could only be solved by means of force and this was never without attendant risk." Throughout this meeting, Hitler stressed the need to seize land aggressively, and to do so no later than 1945.

Correctly sensing that he would face little opposition, Hitler planned for the annexation of Austria and Czechoslovakia. In February 1938, Hitler met with Kurt von Schuschnigg (1897–1977), Chancellor of Austria, at his private retreat in the Bavarian Alps. At this meeting Hitler demanded that Austrian Nazis be provided better treatment, and coerced von Schuschnigg into taking Arthur Seyss-Inquart, an Austrian Nazi, into his cabinet. Shortly after their meeting, Austrian Nazis began to make demands for union with Germany, prompting von Schuschnigg to call a national plebiscite. The people of Austria said no to union. As a show of force and intimidation, Hitler delivered an ultimatum and amassed troops along the Austrian border. This action became known as the *Anschluss*, the "Annexation."

On March 11, 1938, von Schuschnigg resigned and was replaced as chancellor by Seyss-Inquart, who promptly declared union with Germany. On March 14, with the union complete, Hitler rode triumphantly through the streets of Vienna. During the month that followed, violence was unleashed against Jews and all those who opposed the Nazis. When a plebiscite was held again a short time later, 99.7 percent of Austrians gave their approval to union with Germany. Britain and France, while lodging ineffective formal protests with the League of Nations, took no real actions against the now openly aggressive Germany.

Maintaining International Order

Why did the Western powers remain virtually silent while Hitler rearmed and openly prepared for war? Public opinion had much to do with the decisions made by the United States, Britain, and France. Immediately following the end of World War I, the United States had reverted to its isolationist policies of the prewar years. Events in Europe, it was argued, were of no concern to Americans. Leaders in Britain and France also sensed there was little support among the public for a war against Germany.

Public opinion is usually a complex mixture of ideas springing from a wide variety of experiences and prejudices. To some degree, support for the policy of appeasement in the 1930s was built on ignorance. The limited information provided to the public about the injustices being committed in Germany was reported with indifference by newspapers such as *The Times* of London. As a result of such reporting, many people were led to believe that the Nazis wanted only to regain self-respect for Germany and redress grievances

over the Treaty of Versailles. Even Canada's prime minister, William Lyon Mackenzie King (1874–1950), following a meeting with Hitler on June 29, 1937, recorded in his diary, the following sentiments:

> I spoke then of what I had seen of the constructive work of his regime, and said that I hoped that work might continue. That nothing would be permitted to destroy that work. That it was bound to be followed in other countries to the great advantage of mankind.

Obviously there was limited support for any actions that might lead to bloody conflict with Germany. Instead, public opinion, while divided, seemed to favour appeasement.

Even in France, where hostility toward Germany was much higher, there was a reluctance to take actions that would prompt war. Instead, France adopted a

Fellow fascists Adolf Hitler and General Francisco Franco. How did Western nations respond to Franco's *coup*?

defensive mentality in the 1930s, hoping to avert any future war on French soil. During the 1930s, France committed virtually all its defence budget to the building of the Maginot Line. The Maginot Line, which spanned the length of the French-German border, consisted of hundreds of concrete structures designed to withstand bombardment, and heavily armed to defend against German attack. While the Maginot Line would have been effective against advancing troops in 1918, it would prove useless against the type of warfare that Hitler would unleash on France. Thus, Britain, France and the United States were unwilling to stand against the boundaries of German lands as long as the injustices being committed were against only German citizens. For this same reason, the Western powers also stayed away from the situation in Spain, where sides representing fascism and democracy were fighting a civil war.

The Spanish Civil War: 1936–1939

By 1936 the young Spanish Republic, a coalition of republicans and moderate socialists, was in jeopardy. The democratically elected Popular Front government had failed to live up to its promises and many people in Spain, especially in the countryside, were growing restless. In 1936 General Francisco Franco (1892–1975) led a fascist *coup d'état*. Rather than quickly toppling the government, the fascist forces under Franco initially met stiff resistance from the republican government. The result was a three-year civil war in Spain. Spain was actually a microcosm of Europe in the 1930s and the Spanish Civil War might have alerted the Western world of the impending crisis. Instead, the Western powers chose to remain on the sidelines, despite the support Franco received from Hitler and Mussolini. Only the Soviet Union sent aid to the Popular Front to assist in its struggle against fascism.

Many British, Canadian, American, and even anti-Nazi Germans fought against Franco as volunteers. Without the support of their governments, these soldiers fought out of idealism. This was the famous International Brigade against fascism. To many, the Spanish Civil War was the "Last Great Cause." Nevertheless, the governments of the countries that would face the fascists on the battlefields of Europe only a few years later, had little interest in the struggle for democracy in Spain.

WEB CONNECTION
www.mcgrawhill.ca/links/legacy
Go to the site above to find out more about the Spanish Civil War and the International Brigade.

A Spanish Republican propaganda poster. What symbols and images have been used? Are they effective?

EL FRENTE POPULAR DE
MADRID
AL FRENTE POPULAR DE
EUROPA

The significance of the Spanish Civil War goes beyond a clash of ideologies. Spain would become the testing ground for Nazi weaponry and tactics that would later be used with tremendous success against other European nations. For example, on April 26, 1937, the small city of Guernica, near Bilbao, became the target of the first strategic bombing raid by the *Luftwaffe* (the German air force). The world was shocked by this attack, not only because of the carnage, but also because Guernica was an undefended civilian city with no strategic importance. Despite atrocities such as Guernica, and the support the fascists received from Germany and Italy, both Britain and France avoided being drawn into the conflict, still convinced that the policy of appeasement could prevent war.

Peaceful Co-existence? The Munich Agreement

The policy of appeasement pursued by Britain reached its climax with the signing of the Munich Agreement on September 29, 1938. In the days that immediately followed, British prime minister Neville Chamberlain (1869–1940), who was a strong supporter of appeasement and an architect of the Munich Agreement, was widely applauded as a man of fortitude and diplomatic skill for his dedication to securing peace. This gratitude and praise was short-lived. In less than a year after Munich, Europe was once again at war. Chamberlain's negotiations with Adolf Hitler now appeared naive and short-sighted.

Hitler and the Sudetenland

Czechoslovakia, under its leader Edvard BenesWhen Hitler met with Chamberlain on September 15, 1938, he made it clear that he was prepared to risk war over the issue of the Sudeten Germans, but that this would be the "last major problem to be solved." Convinced that an agreement on the Sudetenland was the only way to ensure peace, Chamberlain, with the support of the French prime minister Eduoard Daladier, managed

Neville Chamberlain proclaims peace with the Munich Agreement. Why did it fail?

to persuade the Czech prime minister to hand over the territory in return for some compensation and an international guarantee of Czechoslovakia's defence.

When Hitler increased his demands a week later, insisting that Czechoslovakia sign over the territory by October 10 and agree to Polish and Hungarian demands on Czech territory, Chamberlain was shocked. These new demands amounted to the dismantling of Czechoslovakia. Rather than attempt to extract further concessions from the Czechs, Chamberlain and Daladier decided to leave Benes out of any further negotiations arising from Hitler's new demands. In an attempt to resolve the crisis without conflict, Chamberlain and Daladier, with the support of United States president Franklin Roosevelt, asked that Hitler attend a final conference.

At the resulting Munich Conference on September 29, 1938, Chamberlain, Daladier, Mussolini and Hitler formally agreed to transfer the Sudetenland to Germany by October 10 and to deal with Polish and Hungarian claims at a later date. Czechoslovakian prime minister Benes was left with the option of accepting the agreement or fighting Germany alone. He chose to sign the agreement and shortly thereafter resigned. Chamberlain, believing that the Munich Conference had indeed succeeded in swaying Hitler, issued a joint declaration with him guaranteeing that Britain and Germany would never "go to war with one another again." This declaration allowed Chamberlain to return home jubilant, declaring, "I believe it is peace in our time."

Any relief felt as a result of the Munich Conference was short-lived. Less than a month later, following the assassination of a Nazi diplomat in Paris, Hitler unleashed the reign of terror against German Jews called *Kristallnacht* or "the night of broken glass." Synagogues were burned and thousands of Jewish people were brutally beaten, shot, or dragged off to concentration camps. A few months later, on March 16, 1939, the Third Reich claimed what was left of Czechoslovakia by announcing the German protectorate of Bohemia and Moravia. There was no longer any doubt in Britain and France that war with Germany was imminent.

Signs of things to come: Jewish property and synagogues vandalized during *Kristallnacht*. Why didn't more Jews flee Germany?

Nazi-Soviet Non-Aggression Pact

At the end of World War I, the old Hapsburg Empire had been dismembered and several new nations created: Yugoslavia, Latvia, and Poland. Poland's rebirth as a nation came at the expense of both Russian and German territory and, in 1939, Poland found itself caught between two disgruntled nations. Shortly after taking Czechoslovakia, Hitler turned his attention to Poland to right a wrong that he believed had been committed against Germany in the Treaty of Versailles. During the spring of 1939, Hitler brought much pressure to bear on the Polish government, demanding territorial concessions that the Poles repeatedly rejected. Having been stung by Hitler's lack of integrity, both Britain and France had by now abandoned appeasement and were guaranteeing Polish borders.

By the summer of 1939, it appeared the outbreak of war was only a matter of time. Poland's poorly equipped army of about one million soldiers would be no match for the efficient and modern German army. This left any hope of resistance dependent on help from Britain and France. In a bid to avoid a two-front war (facing pressure in the West from Britain and France and from the Soviet Union in the East), Germany stunned the Western world by signing a non-aggression pact with its enemy, the Soviet Union. On August 23, 1939, the Nazi-Soviet Non-Aggression Pact laid the basis for a division of Poland that would follow a joint Nazi-Soviet invasion. It also gave the Soviet Union a free hand in Finland, Estonia, Latvia and Lithuania, in return for Stalin's assurance he would not oppose Germany's aggression in Western Europe.

WEB CONNECTION

www.mcgrawhill.ca/links/legacy

Go to the site above to find out more about Canada's participation in World War II.

Why would these enemies agree to help each other? Did this agreement spell the end of ideological war? Were fascists and communists now working together? An argument can be made that the Nazi-Soviet Pact, although Machiavellian in nature, was consistent with ideologies on the right and the left. Hitler's ultimate goal was to conquer Europe. Fighting a two-front war would lessen his chance of success. By negotiating a pact with Stalin, whose previous attempts to negotiate with Britain and France had been rebuffed, Hitler could first turn his attention to Western

Europe. He would then be able to turn around and throw the might of the German army, combined with the resources of the conquered nations, against the Soviet Union. Stalin, meanwhile, may have seen the pact as an opportunity to prepare for communism's ultimate spread worldwide. By avoiding conflict with Germany, Stalin not only bought more time to build up the Soviet Union's military strength, but also pitted the Nazis against the capitalist West. After years of war, the West would be exhausted and the way would be clear for the spread of communism throughout Western Europe.

Regardless of the rationales of Stalin and Hitler, the pact left Western Europe stunned. Appeasement was no longer an option, so Britain and France had no choice but to support Poland against Nazi aggression. When the German army rolled across the Polish border in the early hours of September 1, 1939, Chamberlain briefly wavered in his support for the Poles. Facing near-rebellion in the House of Commons, the British government sent Germany an ultimatum: agree to withdraw from Poland by 9:00 a.m. on September 3 or face the consequences. Receiving no reply, Britain declared war on Germany the same day. Britain was joined by France, Australia, New Zealand, and, on September 6, South Africa. Canada would declare war seven days later, after a brief debate in the House of Commons and a nearly unanimous vote. One member who voted against Canada's declaration of war was J.S. Woodsworth (1874–1942), the pacifist leader of the CCF (Co-operative Commonwealth Federation). His opposition to the war would cost him the leadership of his party. Despite this declared support, Poland quickly fell and was carved up by the Soviets and the Nazis. It would be another six months before war would reach Western Europe.

WAR AGAIN

Total War Through Technology

Although World War II followed closely on the heels of World War I and pitted essentially the same enemies against each other, developments in technology ensured that this war would be no mere repetition of its predecessor. While World War I had introduced tanks and aircraft to warfare, it was World War II that witnessed the horrific potential of these and other weapons of mass destruction.

Aircraft were first used in World War I for reconnaissance. By the end of the war, guns synchronized with the propellers had been mounted on the airplanes and pilots could drop small bombs from the sky. During the inter-war period, the British were the first to develop the idea of "terror bombing." Although it was the British who first discussed the idea of terror bombing, it would be the Germans who made the first, and most effective, use of this weapon. Key to the effectiveness of terror bombing was the development of long-range bombers that allowed pilots to fly well behind enemy lines and target cities that previously had been safe from enemy fire. Developed alongside long-range bombers were incendiary bombs that ignited firestorms. The temperature at the centre of these infernos could reach as high as 4000° Celsius.

The targeting of civilians would become one of the most disturbing features of World War II. No longer was warfare about pitting army against army. Now, every citizen, no matter how young or old, was a target. By the end of the war, both sides had engaged in extensive terror bombing of civilian targets. London and Coventry in England, Dresden and Hamburg in Germany, Osaka and Tokyo in Japan, are just a few of the cities that suffered extensive damage from long-range bombers. While the dropping of atomic bombs on Hiroshima and Nagasaki in August 1945 introduced a new and more powerful weapon of mass destruction, the targeting of civilians was not a new tactic. Total war, a war in which countries marshal all of their resources to defeat the enemy and make everyone and everything a target, would be a permanent legacy of World War II.

The Invasion of Poland

The world was stunned by the Nazi invasion of Poland, not so much for its aggressiveness as for the

Members of the Polish cavalry in training, 1938. This old-style army would come up against Hitler's mechanized war machine.

speed with which Hitler's armies were able to secure victory. Trench warfare in World War I had resulted in agonizingly slow movements of troops; while few believed Poland could win a war against Germany, no one anticipated that the invasion would take less than four weeks. Utilizing a new kind of mechanized warfare called *Blitzkrieg* (lightning war), the German military quickly destroyed Poland's small and largely obsolete air force, and rolled over the ill-equipped Polish army. *Blitzkrieg* was a coordinated attack strategy using *Panzer* (armoured tank) divisions supported by ground troops and an umbrella of air support. By using fighter-bombers such as *Stukas* and *Heinkel* airplanes instead of long-range artillery, as used in WWI, the German *Luftwaffe* was able to create chaos on the ground. By targeting civilians, terror bombing used psychological effects to implant defeatism into the minds of the general population, and to ensure disarray among the opposing armies. The key to the success of the *Blitzkrieg* was that the attack was lightning-swift and could exploit the enemy's weak points. Surrender had to come early or the advantage gained by catching the enemy off guard would be lost. The early success of the *Blitzkrieg* was due in part to the lack of preparedness of its targets. It would take nearly three years for the Allied forces (Britain, France, the U.S., Canada, etc.) to come to grips with this new type of warfare and to prepare effective tactics against it.

On September 25, the Soviets and Nazis signed an agreement that divided the spoils of war by dismantling the Polish state. The city of Warsaw would fall on September 27. Hitler immediately began eliminating Polish intellectuals and any others who might oppose Nazi control. He then started the process of turning Poland into a worker state devoted to supplying the needs of the Third Reich.

The Phony War

Despite declaring war in September 1939, neither the British nor the French would be actively involved in the war until the spring of 1940. They immediately began their preparations for war, including rationing supplies and moving children to the countryside to be safe from possible aerial raids. Since no one was actually fighting, this activity during the fall of 1939 and the spring of 1940 earned the name the "phony war."

The term "phony war" is somewhat misleading, as it applies only to Western Europe. Throughout the winter of 1939–1940, both Germany and the Soviet Union aggressively continued to seize more territory. After a failed attempt at bullying Finland into allowing naval bases there, and surrendering a strip of land along the Finnish-Soviet border near Leningrad, Stalin concocted a border incident that gave him the justification for ordering an invasion in November 1939. Despite committing a million troops to the invasion of Finland, the Soviet army faced stiff resistance and numerous setbacks at the hands of the 175 000 skilled and determined Finnish soldiers. By the spring of 1940, Finland could no longer hold out and on March 12 agreed to a peace treaty, accepting Stalin's earlier demands. In the

History
BYTES

To people today, the swastika is a symbol inextricably linked with the Nazis and associated with hatred, anti-Semitism, and violence. Yet, the swastika is an ancient symbol going back as far as the Indus Valley civilization in the second millennium BCE. The swastika has been found in the art and decorating objects of many Eastern cultures, including India, China and Japan. The word for the symbol comes from the ancient Sanskrit language and usually meant things like "good luck" and "strength." Various groups in Germany in the nineteenth century used the swastika as an insignia (we would say a logo), but Hitler adopted the symbol for his movement in 1920. The difference between the way the ancient swastika was usually shown and how the Nazis used it is the orientation of the cross. The ancient symbol was usually shown as a cross with its arms bent 90 degrees while the Nazi version usually turned that cross on its end.

fall of 1940, the Baltic states of Estonia, Latvia and Lithuania would also be absorbed by the Soviet Union.

During the winter of 1939–1940, Germany also prepared to make further invasions. Coincidently, on April 9, 1940, the day Germany planned its full-scale invasion of Denmark and Norway, the British and French were preparing to tighten a blockade around Germany by seizing the Norwegian port of Narvik and laying mines in the Norwegian channels that separated the offshore islands from the mainland. Denmark fell in one day, and Norway, despite a determined effort from its army, was defeated by early May, though not before members of the government and the royal family had escaped to Britain. Hitler established a puppet government headed by the Norwegian Nazi leader Vidkun Quisling, whose name has become synonymous with treason and treachery. The victory over Norway was not without its costs to Germany. The loss of a heavy cruiser, two light cruisers, and ten destroyers shifted the naval balance in favour of the Allies.

The defeat of Norway would also have political consequences, prompting the resignation of British prime minister Neville Chamberlain. Seen by the public and his own Conservative Party as indecisive, Chamberlain handed over the reigns of power to Winston Churchill (1874–1965) on May 10, 1940. Churchill had long been an ardent opponent of the policy of appeasement. He would now emerge as one of the most important wartime leaders in British history and one of the dominant figures of the twentieth century. While Churchill was forming a new national government comprised of members of the Conservative, Liberal and Labour parties, Hitler had turned his armies to the Netherlands. By May 15, the German *Blitzkrieg* had smashed the Netherlands and Belgium, and was poised to invade France. Western Europe was facing its darkest hour.

THE FALL OF FRANCE

The collapse of the French army came with surprising speed. By June 1940, France had fallen to the Nazis and the Allied armies had been pushed to the English

A British anti-Nazi cartoon. What do you think the "when" referred to?

Channel. Few people expected the Germans to win so quickly. In the aftermath of the war, many historians have tried to determine the reasons behind the stunning Nazi victory over the apparently ill-prepared Allied forces.

The long hard winter of 1939–1940 and the drawn-out phony war, during which soldiers had waited in anticipation, likely created boredom among the French troops, resulting in low morale. Evidence was seen in the failure of soldiers to salute officers, soldiers abandoning their posts, widespread pillaging of evacuated areas, abuse of alcohol, and a general lack of discipline. Indeed, this malaise seems to have permeated French society. Many French citizens believed it was their government's duty to avoid war. French communists also played a role in denying the

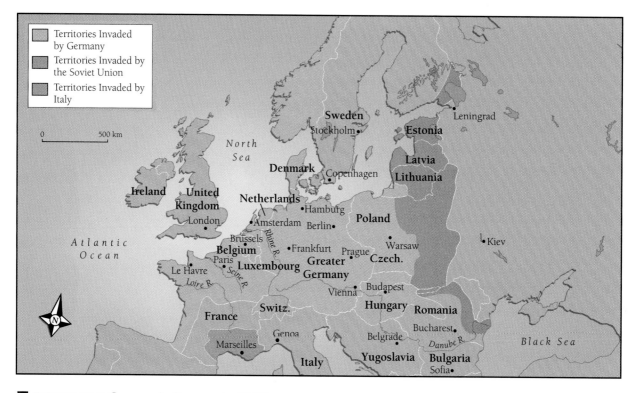

■ FIGURE 12.1 Germany's Conquests, 1939

Switzerland was not invaded by Germany. It was both neutral and a major world banking centre. How could a neutral Swiss government help the German war effort?

French government the full support of the people. By opposing the war on the grounds that it was an imperialist war, serving only the needs of the bourgeoisie, the communists were able to undercut government efforts to arouse support for the war. The lack of conviction extended even to the leaders of the French nation, resulting in confusion. It appears that many French leaders wanted to pick up where France had left off in 1918, to rely heavily on the Maginot Line, rather than adapt to the new realities of war.

In the end, it would appear that several factors contributed to Germany's stunning victory over France. The effectiveness of the German attack, the greater familiarity of the Germans with the new style of warfare, and the lack of committed Allied support all seem to have contributed to the decline in French morale and the defeat of France. Poor leadership by both the French government and the French generals,

as well as inadequate preparation, further contributed to the lack of resolve displayed by French soldiers. Other factors, such as effective German propaganda and a defensive mentality created by the Maginot Line, also contributed to the collapse of the French army in the face of the German attack.

The French were forced to sign the terms of the surrender on June 22, in the same railway coach where the German delegates signed the armistice in 1918. France was humiliated. The Germans occupied all of northern France, while a small part of the south was left in the hands of World War I hero Marshal Pétain. This area came to be known as Vichy France, after the small spa town that became its capital. Pétain would blame the collapse of France, in part, on the moral decay brought about by democracy.

By June 1940, Hitler and his fascist allies controlled all of Western Europe, while the Soviet Union dominated the East. Until the entry of the United States into the war in December 1941, Britain and the Commonwealth countries stood alone in the West, valiantly trying to stem the Nazi tide.

The Miracle of Dunkirk

Sensing the inevitability of defeat in France, the British government began planning the evacuation of the British Expeditionary Force (BEF). Admiral Bertram Ramsey and his chief of staff, Captain Day, would be responsible for the evacuation of the BEF and Operation Dynamo, the code name given to the plan. The most optimistic estimates suggested that no more than 45 000 troops could be rescued from the French coast. By the end of May 1940, rescued troops numbered 338 226. The soldiers were plucked from the beaches of Dunkirk by an array of boats ranging from destroyers to sightseeing boats, fishing vessels, and pleasure craft. The outstanding success of the evacuation earned Operation Dynamo the more familiar nickname of the Miracle of Dunkirk.

There are at least three explanations for this surprising turn of events. The *Luftwaffe*, which was to have prevented any evacuation from Dunkirk, seems to have been hampered by heavy fog and by the efforts of Britain's Royal Air Force (RAF). At the same time, the often rough English Channel was relatively calm, thus allowing a wide variety of boats to cross. Finally, a surprise "stop order" given to the *Panzers* on May 23 by the German commander, and supported by Hitler, gave the British the opportunity to reach safety behind the Canal Line. Although Hitler's fear that the *Panzers* would get bogged down in the canals and rivers around Dunkirk was justified, the result of his stop order (revoked two days later) was to allow the part of the British army that Germany needed to destroy, to escape to safety. This decision would return to haunt Hitler and the German army later in the war. The extraordinary military evacuation gave the Allied forces a boost in morale following a disastrous campaign.

Winston Churchill seized on the success of Operation Dynamo to provide inspiration and incentive to the remaining Allied forces. As Operation Dynamo drew to a close, Churchill declared to the House of Commons: "We shall go on to the end. We shall fight in France, we shall fight in the seas and oceans, we shall fight with growing confidence and growing strength in the air; we shall defend our Island whatever the cost may be."

> ## Review, Reflect, Respond
>
> 1. Explain why some, especially Neville Chamberlain, believed appeasement was the best route to take in dealing with Germany in the 1930s.
>
> 2. List and briefly explain what you believe were the three most important factors leading to the early and stunning success of the Nazi army in Poland and France.
>
> 3. Was peace between Britain and Germany possible in June 1940? Explain your answer.

THE BATTLE OF BRITAIN

Hitler's last remaining enemy in the West was the island of Great Britain. It would appear that Hitler had hoped to work co-operatively with the British rather than humiliate them as he had the French. Following the Dunkirk evacuation, Germany waited nearly a month for the British to seek peace. Until May 1940, Hitler had never even contemplated an invasion of Britain, and when he did, it was with some misgivings. When the order to plan for an invasion of Britain was issued on July 2 and the preliminary directive was signed on July 16, Hitler still held out hope that an air assault, backed by the threat of a full-scale invasion, might be enough to prompt the overthrow of the Churchill government by a party in favour of peace. A month after the Battle of Britain had begun, Hitler continued to cling to the illusion that the Third Reich could co-exist and co-operate with the British Empire. Confiding in Vidkun Quisling (1887–1945), leader of the Nazi Party in Norway, Hitler mused, "After making one proposal after another to the British on the reorganization of Europe, I now find myself forced against my will to fight this war against Britain."

The key to success for Operation Sea Lion (the code name for the German invasion of Britain) was command of the skies. Without the *Luftwaffe* in control, Germany could not launch an invasion of Britain with any hopes of success. Thus, the Battle of Britain would mark a turning point in the history of warfare. Unlike the Battle of France, which was essentially a conventional military ground operation (despite the *Blitzkrieg*), the Battle of Britain marked the first time aircraft would be used as the primary instrument to destroy the enemy's will and capacity to resist. When Hitler issued the *Führer* Directive (No. 16) on "Preparations for a landing operation against England," officials within the *Luftwaffe* were alarmed at the scope of the task set before them. The *Luftwaffe* was to establish the preconditions for victory before the army or navy were ever involved. By early August, German naval authorities were claiming that Göring, commander of the *Luftwaffe*, was not directing air attacks with the aim of facilitating an invasion; he was fighting a total war in the air.

Britain's success against Operation Sea Lion was largely a result of the resilience of the British people

A Messerschmitt 109, Germany's weapon in the Battle of Britain. What airplanes did Britain use?

and the heroic defence provided by the Royal Air Force (RAF). In the final days of the Battle of France, Churchill had wanted to send six squadrons to France. The commander-in-chief of Fighter Command for the RAF, Sir Hugh Dowding (1882–1970), had opposed him. Dowding had correctly guessed that the RAF would be essential to Britain's defence, and argued that committing the six squadrons to France would be a vain attempt to help an ally. Eventually, the British cabinet agreed with Dowding, and some have described this as one of the best strategic decisions in history.

When the Battle of Britain began on July 10, 1940, Britain held a few important advantages. Whereas the German *Luftwaffe* used airfields they had recently captured and quickly adapted for their own use, the British squadrons were operating from home bases they had occupied for some time. Furthermore, being on the defensive, any British pilot who was forced to crash-land or bail out of a damaged aircraft did so over friendly soil, while German pilots were either taken prisoner or drowned in the English Channel.

The first phase of the Battle of Britain, which began July 10, was known as *Kanalkampf* (Channel Battle). This phase focussed on the English towns of Plymouth, Weymouth, Falmouth, Portsmouth, and Dover. Hitler became impatient with the aerial stalemate that developed and ordered a change in strategy. Based on the assumption that the British were already defeated but refused to admit it, Hitler issued Führer Directive No. 17, which ordered the Luftwaffe to "overpower the English air force with all the forces at its command in the shortest possible time." This phase of the battle, known as Operation Eagle, began on August 13, 1940, and focussed on the airfields of Britain in an effort to knock out the raf. Any success of the Luftwaffe came at a high price, but, by early September, the Luftwaffe had begun to take the upper hand. The victory was too slow in coming for both Hitler and the commander of the German Luftwaffe, Hermann Göring.

Although the German planes outnumbered British planes 930 to 650 when the battle began, the British overcame this disadvantage under the leadership of

Hermann Göring (right), head of the German air force, the *Luftwaffe*.

Canadian-born Lord Beaverbrook (1879–1964). By July 1940, Beaverbrook, the minister in charge of aircraft production, had geared up factories to produce 500 Spitfire and Hurricane aircraft a month. At the same time, German factories could turn out only 140 Messerschmitt 109 and 90 Messerschmitt 110 aircraft per month. The British had also developed radar (radio detecting and ranging), a system that enabled pilots to detect the distance and speed of aircraft in their area. This was particularly important because it allowed British pilots to evade German aircraft and defend themselves during nighttime bombing raids. Radar was crucial not only to the defence of Britain, but also to the final outcome of the war.

The bombing of London was calculated to break the will of the British people. Out of fear that the opportunity for a land invasion could be lost due to autumn winds, the focus of the *Luftwaffe*'s efforts shifted from the airfields of Britain to the city of London on September 7, 1940. An order dated August 24, 1940, stated: "Attacks against the London area and terror attacks are reserved for the *Führer*'s decision." Hitler delayed giving this order, still hoping to get Churchill to the negotiating table to avert retaliation on German cities. Finally, in early September, Hitler could wait no longer. The order was given to bomb London, and the Battle of Britain entered a new phase.

Hitler's decision to shift the *Luftwaffe* to the densely populated area in and around London took the pressure off the British airfields. Although over 30 000 Londoners would die during the blitz, the British people remained steadfast and courageous. During the heavy air raids, Londoners turned "lights out" in their homes and took shelter in the underground tube stations (what Londoners call their subway). Rather than breaking the will of the people, Hitler's attack on London strengthened their resolve and allowed the RAF to rebuild. Furthermore, in retaliation Churchill ordered the bombing of Berlin, leading to the first civilian deaths in Germany as a result of enemy bombing.

On September 17, 1940, Hitler announced the postponement of Operation Sea Lion until further notice. Assuming Britain was already defeated, Hitler turned his interests eastward. This did not mean the end of bombing raids in Britain; Hitler wanted to keep the pressure on Churchill. Nighttime raids became the norm by October.

[WIDENING AGGRESSION
The Tripartite Pact

With Western Europe defeated, and believing that Britain was all but finished, Hitler realized that only the United States, should they choose to enter the war, could offer serious opposition to his aggression. Meanwhile, Japan was continuing its aggression in China and the Pacific, and shared a similar concern about American opposition. In an effort to guard against any future challenges, the fascist states of Germany and Italy, along with Japan, signed the Tripartite Pact in September 1940, guaranteeing mutual support in the event of an attack from any new enemy. To the small countries of Eastern Europe, Soviet aggression posed a greater threat than the expansion of the German empire. Consequently, Romania, Hungary and Slovakia all sought and were granted admission to the Tripartite Pact by November 1940.

The first concrete action of the Tripartite Pact came in October 1940, when Mussolini's forces invaded Greece. Unlike Hitler's peaceful takeover of the rest of

Eastern Europe, the Italian campaign was a disaster, requiring help from Germany to subdue the defiant Greek forces. When Britain sent ground troops and aircraft to help the Greeks, Hitler feared that crucial oil production in Romania could be cut off by Allied support in the Balkans. To ensure the Third Reich was not denied the critical flow of oil, Hitler ordered the invasion of Yugoslavia while the army was en route to support the Italians in the Greek campaign. Although the Germans were ultimately successful at driving out the British and occupying both Greece and Yugoslavia, Hitler's armies were never able to put down resistance in the Balkans. For the duration of the war, the Balkans witnessed a bitter guerrilla war, which tied down 500 000 of Germany's best soldiers, committing Hitler to a Mediterranean theatre of war he had not anticipated.

Operation Barbarossa

Regardless of the Nazi-Soviet Pact signed in 1939, Hitler's grand design had always included the conquest of the Soviet Union. Discussions in *Mein Kampf* regarding Lebensraum (living space) clearly indicate Hitler's belief that the Third Reich would eventually control large tracts of land in Eastern Europe as far as the Ural Mountains, which were rich in natural resources. With the fall of France, Hitler believed the war in the West was over. Assuming Britain always preferred to have others fight for them, he could not understand why the British continued to fight after the defeat of France. Hitler rationalized Britain's resolve to continue fighting by believing the British still expected support to come from elsewhere, most likely the United States or the Soviet Union. Consequently, Operation Barbarossa, the

■ **FIGURE 12.2** German Conquests to 1942
Some countries were occupied by Germany while others were allied to the Reich. Explain the difference.

code name given to the Nazi invasion of the Soviet Union, was a strategic move designed to fulfil Hitler's vision of *Lebensraum*, strike a blow at his most hated rivals, the communists, and deny the British support from the Soviets. He expected this to convince Britain to follow the lead of France and agree to peace terms with Germany. Furthermore, if Germany launched a massive invasion of the Soviet Union, Stalin would have to deploy his military strength in Europe, thus giving Japan a freer hand to expand in the Pacific. Japanese aggression in the Pacific would ensure the United States were preoccupied, and therefore less likely to become involved in a European war.

The German attack on the Soviet Union was also prompted by racist fervour, which would make Operation Barbarossa like no other military action in modern history. Barbarossa, from the outset, was to be total war with the aim of exterminating "undesirables" such as communists, Jews, and people with Asiatic features. Hitler's intent was not merely to defeat the Soviet state, but to annihilate large portions of the Soviet population. Hitler planned to ignore accepted conventions of war, and in the process change the nature, purpose and outcome of wars between states. The Soviets would follow the Nazi lead in that they imitated their cruelty. Partisans (resistance forces) also came to play a prominent role in the outcome of this war. For the first time since the Treaty of Westphalia in 1648, war involved interest groups fighting for themselves rather than leaving the fighting to the state. Operation Barbarossa would mark the high point, and the beginning of the end for interest warfare. It would also mark the beginning of warfare that involved governments, armies, and partisan organizations seizing the state's exclusive right to wage war or use violence to achieve its objectives.

Planning for the invasion of Russia had been under way as early as 1934, when Germany began photographing the Soviet Union. By 1940 the *Luftwaffe* was gathering photographs two or three times a day. These photos provided the Germans with vital information for the target-bombing of factories and defensive works. Despite relatively widespread intelligence-gathering, racist preconceptions prevented the Nazis from asking the key question: Can we win a war against the Soviet Union?

The scale of Operation Barbarossa was enormous. On June 22, 1941, armies of three million troops on either side, with air and naval support, spanned the length of the German-Russian border, covering half of Europe. Hitler had expected the Russian campaign to last no longer than six weeks and had not considered the consequences should the first strike fail to defeat the Red Army and topple the Soviet government of Joseph Stalin. Given the success of the German army in rolling over Western Europe, and the initial success in Eastern Europe, these expectations were not unreasonable. Several of Hitler's top advisers urged a continued focus on England, fearing an attack on the Soviet Union at this point would involve Germany in a two-front war.

Initially, the success enjoyed by the German army in Western Europe seemed about to be duplicated in the East. During the summer and fall campaigns, Germany opened gaping holes in the Soviet defences, capturing Minsk, Smolensk and Kiev, and sending the apparently ill-prepared Red Army reeling backward. The critical first-strike success of a *Blitzkrieg* failed, however, as the Soviet army was able to retreat over the vast expanse of Russia. As it retreated, the Red Army followed a strategy that had been used in Russia for centuries — the "scorched earth" policy. This practice of destroying everything of any value while pulling back would prove particularly effective against the German *Blitzkrieg*. The success of *Blitzkrieg* relied on the immediate collapse of the enemy, making victory less likely as time dragged on. The *Blitzkrieg*, so well suited to the more compact Western Europe, was plagued with difficulties in the vast expanse of the Soviet Union. The farther the German army pursued the retreating Red Army, the more difficult it became to supply the army and service the Panzer divisions.

In late August of 1941, Hitler made what many historians agree was a critical mistake. The drive toward Moscow was to be halted while the German army headed south. Hitler explained his decision to his commanders by emphasizing the economic aspects of war and the need to capture the Soviet Union's crucial economic zone, from Kiev to Kharkov. The Germans would be highly successful in their drive south, destroying five Soviet armies and 50 divisions; but, the attack on Moscow now faced a critical delay.

Despite the difficulties faced by the German army, by December 1941 they had made considerable progress. They had advanced beyond the Sea of Azov in the south, surrounded the city of Leningrad in the north, and reached the western suburbs of Moscow. As well, nearly three million Soviet soldiers had been captured, of which half a million would die from lack of food or shelter in the first three months of winter. Victory still seemed possible, but it would not be the easy campaign Hitler had imagined. Arrogance had led the Germans to make no preparations for a winter campaign. Delayed by the diversion south, the German army that reached the suburbs of Moscow by early December was greeted by the icy grip of an early winter. Without proper clothing and no cold-weather grease for the Panzers (tanks), the German army ground to a halt. Emerging from the Kremlin after a month in seclusion, Stalin ordered the transfer of six Siberian divisions from Asia to head a massive counterattack. Led by General Georgy Zhukov (1896–1974), the Soviets were able to stop the Nazi advance, winning a great psychological victory and handing Germany their first major setback of the war.

WAR IN THE PACIFIC

The Sino-Japanese War

Although allied with both Italy and Germany, neither Emperor Hirohito nor the minister of War, General Hideki Tojo, was fascist or pro-Nazi. The Japanese, while strongly anti-communist, were also strongly anti-Western and determined to defeat the Western nations and establish a Japanese sphere of influence in the Pacific. This would then allow Japanese access to vital natural resources such as oil, rubber, and mineral ores. Japan's decision to join the Tripartite Pact was for purely practical reasons: An alliance worked to Japan's

advantage, since the dominant Western powers in the Pacific were the French, the British, and the Americans.

Throughout the 1930s, Japan had increased its presence in Asia, beginning with the invasion of Manchuria, China, in 1931. In the years that followed, Japan expanded and consolidated its hold over large sections of China. In 1937 a skirmish between Chinese forces and the Japanese army escalated into a full-scale war. Initially, the war swayed back and forth, but ultimately the Japanese broke through the Chinese defence and quickly captured the capital city of Nanking. Over the next four months, a brutal and bloody massacre took place.

The Rape of Nanking

When the Japanese forces entered the city of Nanking, they embarked on a campaign of rape, murder, and looting. Between December 1937 and March 1938, some 250 000 to 300 000 people were killed, many of them women and children. Estimates of the number of Chinese women raped by Japanese soldiers range from 20 000 to 80 000. Thousands more women were forced to serve as "comfort women" for the Japanese soldiers; some women would be raped several times a day. Journalist Tillman Durdin of the *New York Times* reported on the early stages of the massacre. He wrote:

> I was 29 and it was my first big story for the *New York Times*. So I drove down to the waterfront in my car. And to get to the gate I had to just climb over masses of bodies accumulated there. The car just had to drive over these dead bodies. And the scene on the riverfront, as I waited for the launch ... was of a group of smoking chattering Japanese officers overseeing the massacring of a battalion of Chinese captured troops. They were marching about in groups of about 15, machine-gunning them.[2]

After World War II, Azuma Shiro, a Japanese soldier who took part in this "rape of Nanking," confessed his part in the massacre. Describing one episode, Shiro recalled:

> There were about 37 old men, old women and children. We captured them and gathered them in a square. There was a woman holding a child on her right arm ... and another one on her left. We stabbed and killed them, all three — like potatoes in [sic] a skewer. I thought then, it's been only one month since I left home ... and 30 days later I was killing people without remorse.[3]

Despite such confessions and other eyewitness accounts such as Durdin's, the Japanese government has never issued an apology or offered compensation to those who suffered the soldiers' actions.

The Attack on Pearl Harbor

The defeat of France in 1940, coupled with British war-cabinet reports passed along by the Germans, indicated that the British could neither oppose the Japanese in Indo-China nor send a fleet to the Far East. This gave Japan the opportunity to secure southeast Asia and, with it, the resources necessary to maintain itself as a great power. By 1941, however, Japan's occupation of Indo-China had prompted the United States to impose a trade ban between the two nations. Furthermore, the Two Ocean Naval Expansion Act, passed by the United States Congress in July 1940, served notice to the world that the Americans intended to build a fleet that would rival any of the world's naval powers. By 1944, the United States navy

The Japanese bombing raid on Pearl Harbor. Did the Japanese provoke a war they knew they could not win?

would outnumber the Japanese navy by a ratio of 10:3. According to Japanese calculations, a minimum ratio of 10:5 was necessary for them to fight a successful defensive campaign in the western Pacific. Tojo, as minister of war, harboured no illusions that the Japanese could defeat the United States in a full-scale war, but if war with the United States was inevitable for Japan to achieve its national objectives, it would have to happen soon.

The Japanese realized that their best hope for success was to conquer southeast Asia quickly and thereafter establish a defensive perimeter around their gains, where they would fight the Americans to a standstill. By striking at the United States naval base in Pearl Harbor, Hawaii, it was hoped enough damage could be inflicted on the Americans to discourage them from continuing a costly war.

Japan's surprise attack on Pearl Harbor came early Sunday morning, December 7, 1941. It lasted only a little more than two hours but inflicted heavy losses on the American navy. Of the eight battleships in the harbour, four were sunk and four severely damaged. Ten other warships were sunk or destroyed; 188 planes were destroyed and a further 159 damaged; 2 403 Americans were killed and 1 178 wounded. To the disappointment of the Japanese, none of the American aircraft carriers had been at Pearl Harbor. This prompted the architect of the surprise attack, Japanese commander Admiral Isoroku Yamamoto to remark: "We have succeeded only in awakening a sleeping bear." The war, which had begun as a European conflict, now took on global proportions. Britain, in support of the United States, declared war on Japan, while Italy and Germany, honouring the Tripartite Pact, declared war on the United States.

Following the attack on Pearl Harbor, the Japanese moved quickly to conquer almost all of the western Pacific and southeast Asia, including the Philippines, Hong Kong and Singapore, in the first six months of 1942. Using its navy to both spearhead the attack and transport the army, Japan was able to establish a vast Pacific empire it referred to as the Greater Asia Co-Prosperity Sphere. The stage was now set for a long and bitter war in the Pacific.

DIPLOMACY AND COALITION WARFARE

The United States Enters the War

Germany's invasion of the Soviet Union and Japan's surprise attack on Pearl Harbor had brought much needed aid to the British. A short time later the three Allied powers, Britain, the Soviet Union and the United States, would refer to themselves as the United Nations. Given the economic resources and military strength of the United States, the tide had certainly shifted in favour of the Allied forces. The great challenge that lay ahead was for the Allied powers to make diplomacy work.

By 1941 Britain was economically exhausted and would rely on support from Canada and the United States to survive the rest of the war. It was therefore in the interests of Canada and the United States that the war be as short as possible. The United States, meanwhile, hoped for a postwar world in which it would have access to world markets and that would be comprised of fellow bourgeois democracies. Consequently, the primary American aim was to ensure not only the defeat of Nazi Germany, but also the survival and spread of democracy in the postwar world. It was well understood by the American military that any aid given the Soviet Union was for purposes of defeating Germany, not for helping the communists. The beleaguered Soviet Union also placed its own survival at the forefront. Only after the German army was being driven from their land did the Soviets begin to plan for the postwar period. These conflicting objectives would present Roosevelt, Churchill, and Stalin with diplomatic hurdles to overcome if their alliance against fascist aggression was to be successful.

Although it was the Japanese attack on Pearl Harbor that brought the United States into the war, Roosevelt believed the defeat of Nazi Germany was America's most pressing task. Although he faced opposition in Congress, Roosevelt seemed to realize that Japan posed no immediate threat either to the United States or Western democracy. He therefore committed the United States to what became known as the Europe First Policy. Roosevelt's decision not only helped to assure the survival of Britain, but also helped seal the fate of the Third Reich. Roosevelt, Churchill, and Stalin would meet several times over the next few years as they plotted to defeat Hitler and planned the postwar world. Coalition warfare would require a good deal of compromise and a careful balancing act as each leader attempted to pursue political and ideological goals without losing sight of the primary objective, the defeat of Nazi Germany.

Strategic Disputes

Despite their close military co-operation from 1941–1944, a major strategic dispute dominated the relationship between the Americans and the British. Whereas the British favoured an indirect or peripheral approach to victory in Europe, the Americans favoured a direct approach through a massive invasion of north-western France. Although several American strategists agreed with Stalin that a large-scale invasion in the West was the best strategy to defeat Germany, the earliest the United States could launch such an attack was the spring of 1943. Needing to solidify his support at home for the Europe First Policy, Roosevelt decided a show of force somewhere in Europe would be necessary in 1942. The details of a combined British-American counteroffensive in the Mediterranean for 1942 were worked out in Washington at a meeting known as the Arcadia Conference. This meeting between Churchill, Roosevelt, and their respective war planners would be the first of several.

The Critical Juncture

Stalin realized that 1942 would be a critical year for the Soviet Union. Following the spring thaw, the Russian winter could no longer be counted on to impede the progress of the German army. In meetings with Churchill and Roosevelt, Stalin demanded a second front be opened in Western Europe to help draw pressure off his besieged nation. This request would not be met for over two years. Meanwhile, in May 1942 Hitler made a surprise change in direction. Rather than attempt to finish the drive to Moscow, he suddenly diverted the German army south to the Crimea and the oil fields. Hitler's rationale was that by

Hitler's generals were not prepared for winter at the Russian front. Can you think of another army that was defeated by a Russian winter?

seizing control of the critical oil reserves, the Soviet Union's lifeline would be severed, forcing it to surrender.

Despite the heavy losses inflicted by the German army on the Soviet Union, the *Blitzkrieg* failed to provide the quick victory essential to the long-term success of Hitler's master plan. By the spring of 1942, the Soviet Union had managed to regroup, bolster its troops and artillery, and launch a defence with a ferocity not seen in the previous fall campaign. There are several reasons given for this renewed vigour. During the winter of 1941–1942, Stalin began to appeal to Russian nationalism by urging a fight for the motherland rather than an ideological war. As part of this appeal to the Russian people, and to assure his new allies in the West, even churches that had been closed since the revolution were reopened. Another possibility is that suspected victims of purges in the 1930s had not in fact been killed, but rather imprisoned in remote gulags. By releasing these highly trained soldiers, and appealing to their Russian nationalism, Stalin may have given the country the boost it needed.

By October 1942, the German advances had been halted. The Soviet Union had withstood devastating attacks on major cities such as Stalingrad and Leningrad and were now beginning to hand Hitler his first setbacks of the war. When the winter of 1943 began, the German army was cut off from all supplies. This time they would not survive the winter. By the end of January 1943, the German Sixth Army, which had laid siege to Stalingrad, was forced to surrender. An army of 650 000 was reduced to 90 000, of which only 5 000 would ever return to Germany. The German army, which only two years earlier had seemed invincible, was dealt a crippling blow.

The Raid at Dieppe

One of the most controversial military decisions of World War II was the ill-fated raid on the small French town of Dieppe, on the northwest coast of France. After weeks of delay, the assault was finally launched in the early morning of August 19, 1942. After nine hours of fierce fighting, the Battle of Dieppe ended in disaster. It was to be the bloodiest nine hours in Canadian military history. Of the 6 086 troops sent to Dieppe, nearly 5 000 were Canadian. Of these, over 900 were killed, 500 were wounded, and 1 874 taken prisoner. The Allies also lost 106 aircraft and 81 pilots, of which 13 planes and 10 pilots were Canadian. German losses were light by comparison. Why had things gone so terribly wrong?

Dieppe was a strongly fortified defensive town held by the Germans. Aside from the high cliffs overlooking the beaches, it was protected by concrete pillboxes, artillery positions and barbed wire. In addition, the Germans had nearly 50 field and coastal guns and Howitzers (small artillery to fire shells), three anti-aircraft guns, and a few anti-tank guns. Against this strong position, the Allies sent troops with no battle experience, supported by only eight destroyers, but no battleships and no heavy aerial bombardment. When the attack began, the German defence forces fired down on the landing craft from the high cliffs above the beaches. Many of the soldiers were killed before they even made it to the beaches, while scores of others died as they raced for cover. The soldiers who did manage to get ashore faced overwhelming odds against the well-fortified German troops.

Why was an assault against such odds launched? Why were untried Canadian troops given such a difficult assignment? These and several others questions continue to be debated. One reason for the Dieppe raid was to appease Stalin's demand for a second front. By carrying out the attack on Dieppe, the Soviet Union, at that point in a desperate struggle against the Nazis, would get some relief as German troops would be drawn from the Russian front to defend positions in the West. The Dieppe raid was also to act as a trial run for the full-scale invasion that was to occur later. Finally, the decision to use untried Canadian troops seems to have been made for two reasons. First, the Canadian troops were among the best-trained troops in the world, despite their lack of battlefield experience. Second, the Canadians, who had been training in England for nearly two and a half years were eager to see active duty. In the end, we are left with several unanswered questions. Could any degree of success be expected with untried troops against a strongly fortified Dieppe? Were the Canadian troops sacrificed to appease Stalin? Was Dieppe a necessary disaster for the later D-Day assault to be successful? Did any experience gained contribute to success in 1944?

1942: A Turning Point

By the fall of 1942, the Allies had reached a turning point in their war against Germany by successfully counterattacking on three fronts: Egypt, North Africa, and Russia. On October 23, the British launched a successful offensive in Egypt against the overextended *Afrika Korps*. Two weeks later, a combined British and American attack in North Africa soon closed in on General Erwin Rommel's armies. While these victories signalled a positive shift in the war, they also presented the Allies with a problem. Soviet victories and assurances to Stalin that a second front in the West would be opened put pressure on Britain and the United States to launch an assault in northern France. But, the success in the Mediterranean prompted Roosevelt and Churchill to consider further Mediterranean offensives, rather than the opening of a second front in Europe.

The Casablanca Conference

Early in 1943, Churchill and Roosevelt met in Casablanca (Stalin was not invited), recently liberated by American troops under General Eisenhower. During the Casablanca Conference, the two leaders mapped out the future direction of their combined war efforts. Despite mounting pressure from Stalin to open a second front in Europe, Churchill continued to press for an indirect strategy designed to weaken the German army to the point where a cross-Channel invasion of France would be a guaranteed success with minimal losses. The British delegation at Casablanca demonstrated more experience than their American counterparts and dominated the planning sessions. In the end, the only concession the Americans were able to achieve

was a joint declaration that stated that the Western Allies would accept only an unconditional surrender from the Axis powers. This declaration was intended to appease Stalin by offering some reassurance that the West would not sign a separate peace pact with Germany and leave the Soviet Union on its own.

Other than the joint declaration, Churchill was successful at achieving his demands for continued peripheral warfare. Arguing that the Germans were still not driven out of North Africa, and that time and shipping constraints made an attempted cross-Channel invasion unlikely in 1943, the British suggested the Allied forces continue to fight the Germans in North Africa, Sicily, and possibly the Italian mainland. If successful, they would be able to gain control of vital shipping lanes between Europe and the Middle East, while at the same time tying down a large portion of the German army.

When the threat of an Italian invasion of Egypt arose in June 1940, it prompted a clash between the British and Italian forces in North Africa. Italian defeats in both Africa and the Balkans brought Germany into the Mediterranean theatre of war, drawing troops away from Europe and lending some credibility to Churchill's peripheral warfare strategy. But, the Allies would find that fighting fascism in the Mediterranean was no easy task.

Operation Husky: The Invasion of Sicily

By May 1943, the Germans and Italians had been driven out of Tunisia, their last hold on North Africa. Within a few months, a combined force of American, British and Canadian troops had launched Operation Husky, the invasion of Sicily. The invasion caught Hitler somewhat off guard, in part due to a brilliant plan of deception. A corpse carrying fabricated top-secret papers was planted for the Nazis to find. These papers convinced Hitler that any Allied invasion fleet seen in the Mediterranean would be heading for Greece. After six weeks of fighting, the island of Sicily fell and the Allied forces began their preparations for the invasion of mainland Italy.

The successful Allied invasion of Sicily left Italy in turmoil. Italians who had followed Mussolini into war had never expected it would be fought on their own soil. This turn of events led the Fascist Grand Council to withdraw its support of Mussolini. On July 25, he was asked to resign as prime minister. After being summoned to the royal palace by the king, Mussolini was imprisoned and King Victor Emmanuel III assumed direct command of the armed forces and Marshal Pietro Badoglio took over as prime minister. Immediately, the new government began secret negotiations with the Allies for surrender, despite publicly announcing continued support for Hitler. When Badoglio realized the Allies were demanding an unconditional surrender, he stumbled in his negotiations. Meanwhile, the Germans sent additional troops to the south of Italy to intercept the Allied forces that had begun crossing the Straits of Messina on September 3. The Germans arrived in Italy prepared to fight a defensive war, while the Allied forces committed minimal troops and resources — they were now planning for the cross-Channel invasion, code-named Operation Overlord. As a result, the Italian campaign became a long, indecisive, and costly affair that would not end until the collapse of the German army 18 months later. The campaign would cost 250 000 lives.

Canada's Role in Italy

Canadians played a crucial role in the hard-fought struggle for Italy. After their first experience in Sicily, Canada's First Division became the spearhead of the Allied drive toward Rome. The Canadians encountered German resistance unlike anything they had seen before. The fierce fighting around the small Adriatic town of Ortona was described by one soldier this way: "Amid the olive groves and vineyards, every farmhouse became a bastion. Every yard of ground was ravaged by shellfire. The rain pelted down. Mines were everywhere." CBC war correspondent Mathew Halton's report of the fighting around Ortona read:

Soaking wet, in a morass of mud, against an enemy fighting harder than he's fought before, the Canadians attack, attack, and attack. The enemy is now fighting like the devil to hold us. He brings in more and more guns, more and more troops. The hillsides and farmlands and orchards are a ghastly brew of fire.

The persistence of the Allies, especially the Canadian troops, eventually paid off. The road to Rome was eventually opened and, after ten months of fighting, victory was at hand on June 5, 1944, one day before the massive D-Day landing at Normandy. Unfortunately, neither the capture of Rome nor the successful D-Day invasion would bring an end to the fighting in Italy. The stubborn German army would fight on until the spring of 1945. By the end of the war, the Italian campaign had claimed the lives of more than 5 000 Canadians and left more than 25 000 wounded.

Canadian troops in Italy—what was their role?

Total War and Strategic Bombing

What had begun in Guernica as a heartless atrocity had become the norm by 1943. Total war, in which civilians became legitimate targets, was a strategy employed by both sides. Beginning in 1942, the Allies put a great deal of faith and money into a strategic bombing offensive. Strategic bombing involved nightly raids by the RAF intended to destroy German factories, thereby destroying the productive capacity of the Third Reich. German cities also became targets of these nightly raids, as the Allies attempted to break the spirit of the German people. In many ways, the nightly terror of strategic bombing provided the second front Stalin had wanted. Operating out of Britain, the RAF, later supported by the American Flying Fortress B-29 bombers, dropped 48 000 tonnes of bombs on Germany in 1942 and 207 000 tonnes in 1943.

The chief proponent of the strategic bombing offensive was British air marshal Arthur (Bomber) Harris. He believed that by maintaining nightly terror bombings of German cities, the Allies could bomb Germany out of the war, either by knocking out their industrial capacity or by forcing German civilians to demand that their government surrender. Bombing raids that included incendiary bombs virtually obliterated several German cities such as Cologne, Dresden and Hamburg, and killed hundreds of thousands of civilians.

During the war, few questioned the morality and effectiveness of strategic bombing. Questions do remain, however. Could the money spent on bombing have been better spent on tanks to support ground troops, which, in the end, defeated the German military? Was total war and the use of terror bombing to achieve the Allied victory morally defensible?

The Teheran Conference

The first meeting of all three leaders of the major Allied nations, Stalin, Roosevelt and Churchill, took place during November 1943 in Teheran, Persia (now Iran). By this point in the war, events had turned decidedly in favour of the Allies, and the leaders of the "Big Three" nations were able to plan the final defeat of Nazi Germany. Churchill pressed for continued support for his Mediterranean strategy, arguing that fighting Germany from the south through Italy and the Austrian Alps would ensure the greatest success. Stalin had grown tired of the delays in the opening of a second front in the West to relieve pressure in the Soviet Union, and now he had support from

Roosevelt. Through negotiation, a reluctant Churchill was convinced to agree to an invasion from the West. The cross-Channel assault would take place in the late spring or early summer of 1944. Despite Churchill's agreement to take part in Operation Overlord, he did not abandon his Mediterranean policy and Allied soldiers would continue to fight in this theatre of war.

The Big Three leaders agreed that when the war was over, the Soviets would be allowed to move their borders west at the expense of Poland. Poland, meanwhile, would be given a part of eastern Germany as compensation. Although no details were worked out at Teheran, it was apparent that a defeated Germany would be severely punished by the Allied powers. In return, Stalin assured Roosevelt that once Germany had surrendered, the Soviet Union would enter the war in the Pacific to bring about a rapid defeat of Japan.

Review, Reflect, Respond

1. Explain and rank in order of importance the three key factors you think changed the direction of the war, and led to the defeat of Nazi Germany.

2. How did the entry of the United States affect the outcome of the war?

3. Can the indiscriminate damage done by strategic bombing be morally justified? Defend your answer.

OPERATION OVERLORD: THE NORMANDY INVASION

Immediately following the Teheran Conference, the British, Americans and Canadians began planning for the cross-Channel invasion. Churchill and Roosevelt had appointed American general Dwight D. Eisenhower (1890–1969) supreme Allied commander at a conference held at Québec earlier in 1943. In preparation for the launching of the second front, Eisenhower directed British field marshal Bernard Montgomery (1887–1976) to prepare detailed invasion plans and act as commander of the invasion ground forces. The invasion of

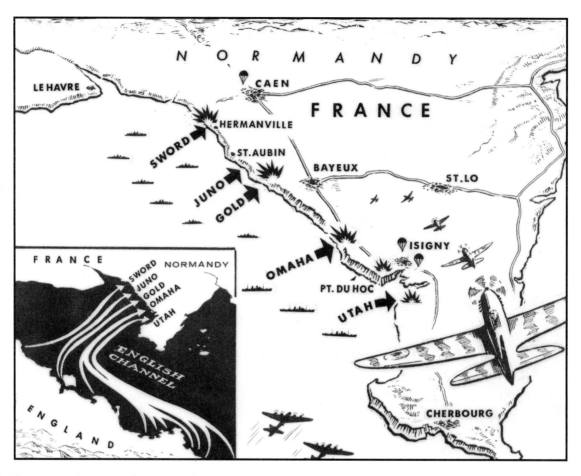

The Allies Forces in the Invasion of Normandy. Where did Canadian troops come ashore?

France across the English Channel would be supported by a naval bombardment and air support from American and British aircraft. The crossing would not be easy. The English Channel can be a difficult body of water to cross at the best of times, and the Germans had constructed a formidable series of defences along the northwestern coast of France. The Allied invasion was also supported by Allied successes at disguising their intentions. The most logical place for an invasion to land would be at Calais, France where the Straits of Dover are the narrowest and the beaches are flat. Nevertheless, it was decided that the invasion would take place on the beaches of the Normandy coast.

By the time the landing on the beaches of Normandy came in the early morning of June 6, 1944, the Allies had amassed one of the largest invasion forces in history. The 156 000 British, American, and Canadian troops were transported to beaches called Sword, Juno, Gold, Omaha, and Utah, under cover of heavy air bombardment. The convoy transporting the troops and armoured vehicles comprised 6 500 naval and transport craft, divided into 75 convoys, while the air support was made up of 12 000 aircraft. The German military, caught off guard, could muster only 425 fighters, and by nightfall the Allies had secured all beachheads and defeated an attempted German counterattack. By June 10, the separate beachheads had been consolidated, giving the Allies a solid base from which to begin pushing back the German army.

Throughout July, Germany would mount a determined resistance, especially by the Twelfth SS Hitler *Jugend* (Hitler Youth), fanatics who would neither take prisoners nor surrender. Hitler refused to allow his armies to retreat and launched several desperate counterattacks in an attempt to stem the tide of Allied forces. During the Allied drive into France, the German military unleashed a new weapon, the first guided missiles (V1 and V2 rockets). These bombs proved inaccurate and were thus of little consequence. Meanwhile, Allied strategic bombing during the summer of 1944 had begun to have an impact, as the productive capacity of Germany began to weaken. German scientists scrambled to develop a superweapon to save the Third Reich from imminent collapse. No such weapon would be developed in time to save Hitler's crumbling empire.

By the end of July 1944, the Allied forces had secured the area around Caen and were able to begin their drive toward Paris. The landing at Normandy would spell the beginning of the end for Nazi Germany, but the cost was high. Of the 1.3 million Allied troops who had landed, there were 120 000 casualties. During the same time, there were 500 000 German casualties.

Hitler's Last Stand

Hitler's armies were now being squeezed both from the East, where the Soviet Red Army had pushed the Germans back to the Polish frontier, and by the Allied armies driving hard from the West since the Normandy invasion. Many of his top military com-

Members of this group of Canadian soldiers landed carrying bicycles that would allow them to move quickly through the French countryside after the Normandy invasion.

Allied soldiers search German soldiers who have surrendered. Many German prisoners of war would be shipped to England after the invasion. How old do you think this soldier is?

manders knew defeat was inevitable, but Hitler, with the support of the state police (the *Gestapo*) and the SS, continued to control military and political decision-making. Hoping to negotiate peace before Germany was crushed, a group of army officers attempted to assassinate Hitler. On July 20, 1944, Colonel Claus von Stauffenberg placed a briefcase containing a bomb beside Hitler prior to a meeting in the map room of his East Prussian headquarters. Just before the bomb detonated, Hitler moved the briefcase to the other side of the table leg. Although injured, Hitler miraculously survived the blast. The repercussions of this failed attempt were immediate and severe. At least 5 000 officers and suspected conspirators were executed, among them were Field Marshal von Kluge (1882–1944), the Normandy commander-in-chief. Field Marshal Erwin Rommel (1891–1944), who had earned the nickname "Desert Fox" for his campaign in North Africa, was allowed to commit suicide. Despite the dramatic turn of events against the Third Reich and the rapidly declining morale among German troops, Hitler refused to admit defeat.

To complement Operation Overlord, the Allies had also launched an invasion of southern France on August 15 and began driving northward. By late fall, Paris had been liberated as had Belgium and the Netherlands. Yet, Hitler stubbornly refused to accept defeat and the Allies would consider nothing less than an unconditional surrender. Although defeat was certain, Hitler would launch one final counteroffensive and drag the war on a further six months, while bringing about the total destruction of Germany and the loss of millions of more lives.

Gathering what strength the German army had left in the West, Hitler launched an attack on the Ardennes region, along the German-Belgium border on December 16, 1944. Although the counteroffensive met with some initial success, the strength of the Allies soon overwhelmed what remained of the German army. In January 1945, German defences collapsed, as 180 Russian divisions crossed the Vistula River into Germany. In the West, the Allies crossed the Rhine by March. From this point onward, there would be no pause in the Allied offensives in the East and West until Germany surrendered.

The Big Three at Yalta. Would all of them survive the war?

REORGANIZING EUROPE

The Yalta Conference

With victory all but certain, Churchill, Roosevelt and Stalin met once more, at Yalta in the Crimean Peninsula, from February 4 to 11, 1945. This would be the last meeting of the three leaders, since Roosevelt, who suffered from polio, was gravely ill. Unlike their previous meeting, during which they mapped out a strategy to bring about the defeat of Germany, the focus at Yalta was to decide the fate of a defeated Nazi Germany. Roosevelt had declared earlier that "the German people as a whole must have it driven home to them that the whole nation has been engaged in a lawless conspiracy against the decencies of modern civilization." Stalin certainly agreed with Roosevelt's sentiments, insisting that Germany pay 20 billion dollars in compensation for the destruction it had brought to Europe, and that half of this be given to the Soviet Union for the carnage the Nazis had caused in Russia. Stalin also reminded Churchill and Roosevelt of the Teheran agreement to partition Poland and compensate it with part of eastern Germany. Churchill, suspicious of the Soviet leader, balked at this demand. Although Roosevelt was more accepting of Stalin's request, the three decided to put off any final decision until the war ended. The major agreement to come out of Yalta was that a defeated Germany would be demilitarized and the Nazis routed. Furthermore, Germany was to be divided into four zones of occupation, a zone for each of the Big Three powers and a zone for France. Berlin would be similarly occupied.

The United Nations is Born

The other major development to come out of the Yalta Conference was the foundation for a new organization to replace the failed League of Nations. The countries allied against the Axis powers were to be invited to a meeting in San Francisco in April 1945. Wanting to be part of the emerging new world order, several other countries joined in the war against Germany for the last few months. The new organization, known as the United Nations, would replace the League of Nations and its mandate. It would comprise a General Assembly, in which all member countries would have equal voting rights, and a Security Council of five permanent members: Britain, the United States, China, the Soviet Union, and France. The Security Council would be given the power to decide if the United Nations should intervene in disputes that threatened international peace and security. Each member of the Security Council had a veto, or the right to overturn a decision.

Two other organizations would also play a crucial role in the rebuilding of Europe and the bringing about of stability and order in the postwar world. Following a meeting at Bretton Woods in the United States in 1944, the Americans and British set up the World Bank and the International Monetary Fund. The function of the International Monetary Fund was to lend money to countries whose economies were in trouble, in order to prevent the wild fluctuations in world currencies that had played such havoc with world economies in the 1930s. The World Bank would lend money to war-torn Europe to assist in the rebuilding, and to poor countries for economic development. It was hoped that these two organizations would help to ensure stability and prosperity in the postwar era and avoid the chaos and destruction that had plagued the first half of the twentieth century.

Hitler is Destroyed

The Third Reich, which Hitler had boasted would last 1 000 years, had completely crumbled by the spring of 1945. During the final days, Hitler wavered between plans to continue resistance or withdraw his remaining troops to the Alpine areas of southern Germany and Russia. In the end, he decided to remain in Berlin, where he attempted to implement scorched-earth orders and contemplated the use of new and deadly gases and the massacre of all prisoners. Finally, on April 22, Hitler seemed to realize his defeat and, in a fit of temper, abandoned all his powers, only to resume

Adolf Hitler and his companion Eva Braun, shortly before they committed suicide in May of 1945.

them the next day. On April 25, Soviet and American troops met at Torgau on the river Elbe in central Germany. By this time the Italian front had also collapsed, leaving only a few blocks of Berlin as the remnants of the former Nazi empire.

On April 30, Hitler and his mistress, Eva Braun, withdrew into the air-raid shelter of the Reich Chancellory in Berlin. With the sounds of the Soviet Red Army advancing in the background, Hitler nominated Admiral Karl Dönitz as his successor and then the *Führer* and Braun committed suicide. Their bodies were never recovered from the bombed shelter. On May 8, 1945, called VE Day, the German forces surrendered unconditionally. Germany was left without a government, its cities and factories lay in ruins, its transportation system was destroyed, and its fate was in the hands of the victorious Allies.

THE HOLOCAUST: A WAR WITHIN THE WAR

World War II was not just a war of territorial conquest or an ideological clash; it was a war of racism, hatred, and genocide. The people who would suffer the most during the 12 years of Nazi rule were the European Jews. When the war began, Europe was home to approximately 12 million Jews. By the end of the war, the Nazis had exterminated half of this Jewish population. Millions more were homeless and had spent several years in deplorable conditions in concentration camps where the Third Reich had used them as slave labour. Only 10 percent of the Jewish children living in occupied Europe survived the Holocaust (from the Greek for "whole burning"), the name now given to this genocide of Jewish people.

The Holocaust is generally seen to have gone through three phases: deportation, "ghettoization," and extermination. The first phase, deportation, occurred prior to the outbreak of war, as the German government attempted to drive Jews out of Germany.

The entrance to Terezin concentration camp in Czechoslovakia. As at other concentration camps, the entrance gate reads "Work Makes Freedom."

Once the war broke out and Germany began to roll over much of Europe, millions more came under the heel of the Third Reich. Initially, Hitler's reaction was to concentrate Jews in huge ghettos, tightly regulated and guarded by soldiers. In one such ghetto, in Warsaw, Poland, the Jews, starving and exhausted, organized themselves and rose up against their Nazi captors. The story of this heroic uprising is dramatically told in the novel *Mila 18* by Leon Uris. It all ended in September 1943, when the fighters in the Warsaw ghetto were finally defeated, worn down by Nazi troops and Polish police.

The Final Solution

The Final Solution refers to the Nazi's plan to exterminate all European Jews. At a meeting in January 1942, in the Berlin suburb of Wansee, top SS officials gathered to work out the details of the *Endlösung*, or "final solution" of the Jewish problem. What was the most efficient way to kill large numbers of people? What could be done with the bodies? Who is a Jew? Did someone with one Jewish parent or grandparent qualify as a Jew?

While there is a general agreement among historians as to the horrors perpetrated on the European Jews by the Nazi regime, a wide range of opinion exists over when and why the extermination of Jews took place. Historian Lucy Dawidowicz has argued that the Holocaust was a part of Hitler's grand design as early as 1919. Certainly *Mein Kampf,* which Hitler published in 1925, contains numerous examples of anti-Semitism, and Jewish Germans faced persecution under the Third Reich. There is no doubt that the ideology of the Nazis was based in anti-Semitism, but the question remains, at what point did the extermination of Jews become a planned, systematic operation?

WEB CONNECTION
www.mcgrawhill.ca/links/legacy
Go to the site above to find out more about the Holocaust.

Christopher Browning, author of several books on the Final Solution, accepts that anti-Semitism played a role in the eventual attempt at genocide, but rejects Dawidowicz's view that the Final Solution was already a fixed goal before the war began. Instead, Browning argues that the Final Solution was a product of a series of events over a number of months, with the period between the fall of 1941 and the spring of 1942 bringing as the critical transition to genocide. Browning writes:

> The intention of systematically murdering the European Jews was not fixed in Hitler's mind before the war, but crystallized in 1941 after previous solutions proved unworkable and the imminent attack upon Russia raised the prospect of yet another vast increase in the number of Jews within the growing empire.[4]

Concentration camp prisoners are freed by Allied troops. Many of the prisoners still alive at the time of liberation were so sick or starving that they were beyond help and died a short time later.

Historian Arno Mayer has suggested that the Final Solution came about even later. He contends that the Final Solution was a result of the failure of Operation Barbarossa. With Nazi Germany stretching its resources to the limit, it could no longer afford to guard and feed Jews in concentration camps and ghettos.

Once the decision was made to carry out the extermination of European Jewry, the Nazis wasted little time in putting their plans into operation. Scores of specialized death camps, such as Auschwitz, Dachau and Treblinka, were set up to handle the mass murder. The first Jews to be selected for the gas chambers were those who were too young or frail to work. Others were used as slave labour, given little to eat, and when

A mass grave at the Nordhausen concentration camp in Germany. Prisoners at this camp did not die in gas chambers; they starved to death.

their strength was gone, sent to the gas chamber, hundreds at a time. Many were used as human guinea pigs in unethical medical experiments.

The decision to use gas chambers as the means of mass execution came about because of psychological problems that had arisen among the middle-aged family men — Nazi soldiers — who were expected to shoot women and children. The use of the gas chamber was considered a more humane method of killing. Killing by means of gas was first conceived of in September 1939, to carry out the Nazi policy of euthanasia for "unworthy life," that is, those in mental hospitals. After the killing, bodies were burned in large ovens or thrown into mass graves.

Adolf Hitler is the single-most obvious explanation for the Holocaust. Too often the blame for the atrocities is placed on him and to a lesser extent on his top officials, such as Himmler and Göring. While the Nazi leadership might have decided on the physical extermination of the Jews, it was the willing collaboration of many individuals that allowed the plan to be put into effect. Throughout Eastern Europe, the Nazis were able to exploit centuries-old anti-Semitism, and in countries such as Lithuania, people from all levels of society collaborated with the Nazis to rid the nation of the "Jewish vermin." The Final Solution was the product of anti-Semitism in its ultimate form — genocide. Hitler may have given the orders for the extermination of Jews, but many others must also be held accountable.

There were others who suffered in the concentration camps and were murdered by the Nazis. Just as Jews wore the yellow Star of David, other types of prisoners could be identified by their badges, creating a sort of hierarchy within the camps. Political prisoners wore a red triangle; homosexuals wore a pink triangle; Jehovah's Witnesses, imprisoned for refusing to serve in the army, wore a purple triangle; common criminals wore a green triangle, and there were several other categories of people persecuted and exterminated by the Nazis. All these types were considered degenerate or undesirable in German and European society.

Historiography: *Inside the Third Reich*, by Albert Speer

> In writing this book my intention has been not only to describe the past, but to issue warnings for the future.
>
> **Albert Speer, Inside the Third Reich**

The original title of this book, first written in German in 1969, was *Erinnerungen*, or simply, *Memoirs*. What are memoirs? In this case, they are the written remembrances, or memories of the admittedly ambitious young man who was Adolph Hitler's architect, the designer and builder of monumental structures that would express and serve the *Fuhrer's* vision of a new Germany. Speer eventually became Hitler's Minister of Armaments and War Production and knowingly used slave labour and concentration camp prisoners in the factories that built Hitler's war machine. All this, Speer described and took responsibility for (unlike others accused) during the Nuremburg Trials, in which he was a defendant. Speer was convicted of war crimes, and crimes against humanity, and served every day of his 20-year sentence in Spandau Prison in Germany.

Like all memoirs, Speer's book is a type of personal history, of which he is both subject and historian. His story is biographical and historical, and as an active participant in many of the events and processes described in his memoirs, he has a unique perspective. Unlike most writers of memoirs, Speer had to write his in secret, using only his memory, but with the knowledge that there were documents that would prove the truth of much of his account. Much of this documentation was eventually used by Speer in writing his book when he was released from prison.

Albert Speer was not the only person to write memoirs about the events of World War II. Among others, Prime Minister Winston Churchill wrote his memoirs, as did General (later President) Dwight D. Eisenhower, General George S. Patton, and Major General Bernard Law Montgomery, all important men on the side of the Allies. Speer's memoirs are one of the extremely rare first-hand accounts of the events of WW II from the perspective of someone inside the Third Reich; he was there, making history, however infamous, alongside Hitler and others on his elite staff — Himmler, Göring, Rommel, Hess, Goebbels — none of whom survived the war or its immediate aftermath.

Imagine then what immensely helpful primary sources memoirs can be to the work of the historian. Memoirs have been written by all kinds of people, and not just famous or historic personalities. For virtually every period in history and from many walks of life, there are memoirs, first-hand accounts based on memories of people who made history.

Hitler and his personal architect, Albert Speer looking over blueprints.

---

1. At the library, or on the Internet, find the memoirs of a famous person and write a one-page summary, including how they might be of use to a historian.

2. If you were going to write your own memoirs, how might you begin? Do a concept map to organize your thoughts.

The Death Toll

At the end of the war, the death toll was staggering. Aside from the six million Jews who died at the hands of the Nazis, nearly 14 million Russians, six million Poles, and 1.7 million Yugoslavians died as a result of the war. In addition, 600 000 French, 357 000 British, 405 000 Americans, and 109 000 soldiers from British Commonwealth nations lost their lives. When these numbers are added to the loss of life in Axis countries, the death toll for World War II approaches 40 million people.

PLANNING THE POSTWAR ERA

The Potsdam Conference

As the defeat of Nazi Germany approached, postwar realities began to become clear. The Soviet Union would emerge as a great power. Furthermore, its critical role in the defeat of Germany, and its desire to ensure postwar security would lead to aggressive Soviet demands at the diplomatic table. This forced the Western Allies to once again revise their view of the Soviet Union. In a few short years, Western perceptions of the Soviet Union and Joseph Stalin had changed radically: from an evil, repressive regime, to a heroic ally, and then a suspicious ally. By 1944 the Western Allies, aware of the crucial role the Soviet Union had played in the defeat of the Third Reich, were now seeing the potentially dominant force the Soviet Union could become in the postwar world. This would lead both Britain and the United States to view the Soviets with caution and mark the beginning of the Cold War rhetoric that would dominate postwar diplomacy and international politics for many years.

When the three Allied leaders, Stalin, Churchill and Harry S. Truman (1884–1972), Roosevelt's replacement, met at Potsdam near Berlin on July 17, 1945, major changes were in the wind. As a result of the Manhattan Project, the Americans had just tested the world's first nuclear weapon in a remote part of New Mexico, and Winston Churchill had been defeated in a general election. The newly elected British leader, Clement Attlee (1883–1967), would join Churchill at the Potsdam Conference. As the sole member of the original Big Three powers left at the diplomatic table, Stalin would attempt to use the sudden changes to his advantage. He had already established a puppet government in Poland and ruthlessly dealt with any opposition there. The Soviet Union clearly would act to consolidate gains in Eastern Europe regardless of any opposition from the West.

An Iron Curtain Descends

Little was actually accomplished at the Potsdam Conference. The administration of Germany was given to a Control Council made up of the four military commanders in the occupied zones. In addition, the decision was made to arrest former members of the SS and wartime leaders of the Nazi Party. They would be tried before a special tribunal set up at Nuremberg, Germany. Many would be charged with "crimes against humanity" and sentenced to death or imprisonment for life.

Each power was allowed to take what it wanted from its zone of occupation as reparation payment, while the Soviet Union would also be allowed to seize a quarter of the industrial equipment in the British and American zones. For the most part, the Potsdam Conference revealed a disintegrating alliance, not one that promised postwar harmony among the great powers. In fact, there were no discussions of the fate of Eastern Europe or Germany. These issues had been settled by the positions of the Allied armies when Germany surrendered. Europe was now clearly divided between the communist-controlled East and the democracies of the West. Churchill, prior to the Potsdam Conference, lamented the fate of Europe when he wrote to Truman, "I view with profound misgivings ... the descent of an iron curtain between us and everything to the eastward." For the next four decades, this iron curtain would stand between the East and the West. The Cold War era had arrived.

THE IMPACT OF WAR ON SOCIETY

Mobilizing a country for war requires its citizens to make considerable material sacrifices. For most Europeans, these sacrifices accompanied living in constant fear of attack, whether from the sky or the ground. Advances in military technology made World War II the first war in which living hundreds of kilometres from the front lines was no guarantee of safety.

For all societies involved in World War II, food rations became a way of life. To feed and equip a large modern army properly, enormous resources had to be devoted to the war effort. Consequently, governments throughout the world imposed rations on their citizens to ensure badly needed supplies would be available for their soldiers. In North America, car production virtually ground to a halt during the war years as car factories were converted to munitions factories producing weapons and machinery. As the war dragged on and more and more of Europe lay devastated or destroyed, food became increasingly scarce and rationing placed tighter restrictions on consumers.

Germany imposed the War Economy Decree on September 4, 1939. This decree closed down all production of consumer goods except for essentials, and imposed rationing on the people. The average citizen was now allowed 250 grams of meat and one egg per week. Most Germans survived on a diet of little more than black bread and potatoes. In the cities, hot water was rationed to a couple of days a week, and families were allowed only a single bar of soap per month. Towards the end of the war, as the bombing of German cities progressed, consumer goods became even more scarce. Despite these severe restrictions there was virtually no starvation among German citizens during the war. Those who attempted to profit from the consumer shortages through the black market were dealt with

harshly, in some cases even executed. Foreign workers and prisoners of war felt the shortage of goods most acutely. Given the limited supply of food, they were at the end of the German food chain and often food destined for them was sold or stolen; many of them would die of starvation.

Changes in the North American Family

North Americans also endured rationing to support the war effort. Despite the restrictions on material goods, the war years led to an interesting phenomenon among North American families. In the years between 1940 and 1943, over one million more families were formed than in normal years. During the war years, the birth rate went up, the marriage age went down, and the number of marriages rose significantly. Several reasons help to explain this rapid growth in the number of families. Financial problems brought about by the Depression were eased by the war, and unemployment was virtually eradicated. Couples facing separation sought to solidify their relationships, and widespread propaganda urged people to support soldiers fighting to protect their families. Emphasis on the importance of the family created a popular culture in which marriage and family were highly valued.

With millions of men enlisted in armies, women had to keep the farms and the factories going. Not surprisingly, public opinion supported women in the workplace during the war. Whereas 82 percent had opposed woman working outside the home the previous decade, opposition to women being employed plummeted to only 13 percent by 1942. Despite this change, the war did not bring about significant, long-lasting change in women's employment. Immediately following the end of the war and the return of the men from overseas, the majority of the women who had joined the workforce during the war returned to their homes, and men resumed their status as the primary breadwinners. Real and lasting change would not come for another quarter of a century.

VICTORY IN THE PACIFIC

Immediately following the Potsdam Conference and the defeat of Germany, the world leaders turned their attention to the Pacific, where the war against Japan dragged on. Since the bombing of Pearl Harbor, the Americans, British, Australians and New Zealanders had waged a relentless and tiring war against the Japanese. Over the course of the war, fierce fighting had spread through the jungles of Burma and Borneo and the numerous islands of the South Pacific, reaching as far as the Aleutian Islands off the coast of Alaska. Concerned that an invasion of Japan could cost a further two million American lives, President Truman called for Japan's surrender on July 26, warning it would face "prompt and utter destruction." In response, Japanese Prime Minister Kantaro Suzuki (1868–1948) said of this demand that his government would "kill it with silence," or *mokusatsu*, in Japanese.

The Nuclear Age Is Born

Truman and his military advisers weighed their options and in the end decided against a mere demonstration of the force of an atom bomb. Instead, they would drop an atomic bomb on a Japanese city. On

Hiroshima after the first atomic bomb explosion. Do you think President Truman did the right thing in ordering the bomb to be used?

August 6, 1945, the city of Hiroshima became the first target of a nuclear attack. At 8:15 a.m., an American B-29 bomber called the *Enola Gay* dropped a 3.2-metre-long bomb that exploded in the air above Hiroshima. Silent lightning was followed by a supersonic shock wave, and then a fireball that was hot enough to melt iron spread over the land. People at the centre of the blast were immediately vaporized, while others suffered agonizing deaths as their clothes ignited and their skin melted from their bodies. By the end of the day, 70 000 people had died, some from radiation burns, others from being buried in the rubble of collapsed buildings. Another 61 000 were injured, many of whom would soon die from their wounds. By the end of the year, the death toll in Hiroshima would reach 140 000, as radiation, burns and infection claimed more lives.

When the Japanese failed to announce an immediate surrender, a second bomb, claiming 40 000 more lives was dropped on the city of Nagasaki. Great controversy still surrounds Truman's decision to drop the second bomb. Many feel the bombing of Nagasaki had little to do with pressuring Japan to surrender and more to do with making a show of force to the Soviet Union to keep the communists in check in the immediate postwar years.

This is the Peace Park in present-day Hiroshima. What does a monument such as this say to people today, now that a number of nations have nuclear weapons capability?

WEB CONNECTION www.mcgrawhill.ca/links/legacy

Go to the site above to find out more about the Manhattan Project and the development of the first atomic bomb.

Following the destruction of Hiroshima and Nagasaki, Japanese Emperor Hirohito (1901–1989) accepted the Allied terms of surrender. On August 14, 1945, the war in the Pacific was over; it was VJ Day. Six years of brutal war had come to an end. The United States, which had won the war in the Pacific, dictated the peace. Japan was to be demilitarized, and democracy put in place under the guidance of a military government headed by General Douglas MacArthur (1880–1964), supreme commander for the Allied Forces.

Reflections

The world in 1945 was quite different from the one that had preceded the war. It was now a world divided between the communist East and the democratic and capitalist West; it was a nuclear world in which future wars could spell the end of civilization as people knew it. Peace had been restored, but it was, once again, a tenuous peace. This time, however, it would last. The world had entered World War II reluctantly, still mournful over the heavy losses of war a generation earlier. By the time peace had returned, the nuclear age had made future world war virtually unthinkable. The development of the nuclear bomb would lead to an uneasy peace in the new era known as the Cold War.

Chapter Review

Chapter Summary

In this chapter, you have seen:

- that efforts to create international governmental and judicial structures were spurred on by the events of World War II
- that some sought peace and co-operation before, during and after the war, with various results
- that efforts to establish international order failed to prevent a second world war, but were renewed following the defeat of fascism
- that war had a dramatic impact on family structures during the war years, but little lasting impact

Reviewing the Significance of Key People, Concepts, and Events (Knowledge and Understanding)

1. Understanding the history of World War II requires a knowledge of the following concepts, events, and people and an understanding of their significance in the shaping of the history of the world in the later half of the twentieth century. Explain two from each column.

Concepts	Events	People
Lebensraum	Munich Agreement	Neville Chamberlain
Blitzkrieg	*Kristallnacht*	Adolf Hitler
total war	Battle of Britain	Joseph Stalin
Holocaust	Operation Barbarossa	Winston Churchill
	Pearl Harbor	General Eisenhower
	Operation Overlord	Emperor Hirohito
	Hiroshima	Harry Truman

2. For each of the planned attacks listed below, identify the date and location, the primary objectives, the outcome, and at least two of the most crucial factors determining the outcome.

Operation	Location and Date	Primary Objectives	Outcome	Factor #1	Factor #2
Operation Sea Lion					
Operation Barbarossa					
Operation Husky					
Operation Overlord					

Doing History: Thinking About the Past (Thinking/Inquiry)

3. In *Origins of the Second World War*, English historian A. J. P. Taylor wrote:

    The First [World] War explains the Second, and in fact, caused it, insofar as one event causes another. The link between the two wars went deeper. Germany fought specifically in the Second War to reverse the verdict of the First and to destroy the settlement that followed.

    Was World War II a historical inevitability, or did Hitler intentionally bring it about? Explain your answer.

4. Carefully review the copy of the Hossbach Memorandum given to you by your teacher. Does this document prove that World War II was premeditated? To respond to this question, select four key statements from the memo that support your viewpoint.

Applying Your Learning (Application)

5. In 1945, during World War II, Randall Jarrell, an American poet, novelist and teacher, served in the Army Air Corps. Read and reflect on his poem below. What do you think Jarrell is comparing to the death of the ball turret gunner? How might you illustrate this poem?

    ### The Death of the Ball Turret Gunner
    From my mother's sleep I fell into the State,
    And I hunched in its belly till my wet fur froze.
    Six miles from earth, loosed from its dream of life,
    I woke to black flak and the nightmare fighters.
    When I died they washed me out of the turret with a hose.[5]

6. Imagine you are a reporter interviewing Churchill, Stalin and Roosevelt 1943. The central question you want them to answer is: "How can the defeat of Germany be brought about quickly and with the smallest loss of life?" Create four more questions related to this issue, and some responses you might get from the three leaders. The answers should be based on historical evidence, but some informed speculation will be necessary.

Communicating Your Learning (Communication)

7. Visually chronicle the events of World War II from September 1, 1939, to August 9, 1945, using symbols, icons, drawings (of your own or copies of others), photos, cartoons, or other artwork. Your chronicle must include two to three key events per year and should be laid out in an original and creative way. You should label and date each event but you are not to include any captions. The visuals must convey the key ideas.

8. Today, groups such as Amnesty International work on behalf of those suffering human rights abuses. Often this involves letter-writing campaigns to influential people. Write a letter to someone of influence about a group whose human rights were being violated in World War II. Your letter should outline the violations and what should be done about them. Groups to consider are: Jews, *Roma* (gypsies), homosexuals, Korean women, Canadians in Japanese prisoner-of-war camps, Japanese-Canadians in internment camps.

Unit Review

Reflecting on What You Have Learned (Knowledge and Understanding)

1. The twentieth century opened on a note of optimism. Rapid developments in technology had had an impact on many aspects of life. Show that technology was an important agent of change during the period 1914–1945 by copying and completing the following chart in your notes.

Era	Technological Development	Impact or Change that Occurred
World War I		
1920s		
1930s		
World War II		

2. Summarize the various consequences of both World War I and World War II for Europe and the world in a concept map. If you are unfamiliar with concept maps ask your teacher to explain them and give you instructions.

Practising Historical Interpretation (Thinking/Inquiry)

3. To what degree do you believe the occurrence of two world wars in the first half of the twentieth century was a result of nineteenth-century forces? Explain your views in a three-to-five paragraph essay.

4. The traditional political spectrum places communism and fascism at opposite ends, left and right. Some see the two ideologies as more similar than different because of the totalitarian nature of the governments both brought about. Argue for or against a political spectrum that places communism and fascism at opposite ends. Be sure to consider the ideological foundations of both "isms," as well as the nature of the government and society each gave rise to in the twentieth century.

Applying Your Historical Understanding (Application)

5. Check the definition of genius given in the first Unit Review. Select one of the historical figures given below and explain why you believe he or she should or should not be remembered as a genius. Be sure to give specific examples to support your view.
T. S. Eliot
Virginia Woolf
Joseph Stalin
Lenin
Winston Churchill
Adolf Hitler

6. Did the "modern age" reach its zenith in the early twentieth century and then implode between 1914 and 1945? To answer this question you will need to review carefully the material in this unit and decide whether or not the beliefs and values of the modern age were destroyed by war, revolution and economic depression. Respond with a clear thesis statement and three-to-five supporting paragraphs.

Communicating Your Learning (Communication)

7. Write three diary entries from the perspective of someone who was a teenager in the mid-1920s. The three entries must address life in the 1920s, 1930s, and 1940s. One entry should reflect the impact of World War I on culture and society. Decide and explain the gender, nationality, ethnicity, and other characteristics of your diarist. Each diary entry should be 250 to 400 words in length. While fictional, each entry must incorporate historical evidence.

8. Along with technological innovations and ideological shifts, the early twentieth century witnessed several new and dramatic styles of art, from cubism to abstract expressionism. Select a case from your CD collection and redraw the cover art in a style popular between 1914 and 1945.

---

* Now complete Skills Focus Five (p. 597):
Organizing Your Essay from Cue Cards to Outline.

The New World Order

Chapter Thirteen
**The Western Experience,
1945 to Today**

Chapter Fourteen
**Challenge and Change
in the Global Village**

The New York skyline as it appeared before September 11, 2001.
The World Trade Center towers stand in the centre.

After a generation of war, much of Europe lay in ruins. The task of rebuilding the devastated cities and countryside would be monumental. The "superpowers" of the past few centuries — Britain, France, and Germany — had lost too much to be able to dominate the postwar world; by 1945, they were eclipsed by the United States and the Soviet Union.

The postwar world was divided along ideological lines: Western capitalism against East European communism. Now, with the advent of atomic weapons, a confrontation between superpowers became a threat to humankind. For the first time, human beings had the ability to annihilate their own species. The decades following 1945 were thus a time of uneasy peace in Europe, a time when the cost of open warfare between the major powers was too high. This did not, however, prevent limited though costly wars between smaller satellite states.

The changes that were reshaping Europe were also having an impact on much of the world. The age of European colonialism had finally come to an end. In the decades following World War II, European empires were dismantled and former colonies achieved independence. The process of decolonization proved volatile, and ethnic rivalries often erupted into civil war. Former empires split into independent states, many of which would join larger trading blocs in order to survive.

Perhaps the least tangible but nonetheless most profound change to occur since 1945 has been in our perception of the world: Our religious and philosophical beliefs, assumptions about family structures, the roles of the sexes, the role of science in society, and the nature of education have all come under scrutiny in the past few decades. Space travel, feminism, existentialism, the global village, and the computer revolution have all contributed to our rethinking of the way the world works and our place in society. While the Renaissance and the scientific revolution laid the foundations for the modern world, the latter half of the twentieth century saw the beginning of the end of the modern age.

UNIT EXPECTATIONS

In this unit, you will:

O evaluate the key factors that have led to conflict and war or to co-operation and peace

O demonstrate an understanding of the importance and use of chronology and cause and effect in historical analyses of developments in the West, and throughout the world, during the second half of the twentieth century

O demonstrate an understanding of ideas and cultures that have influenced the course of history during the second half of the twentieth century

O analyse significant economic developments in the West and the rest of the world since 1945

O critically analyse historical evidence, events, and interpretations

CHAPTER THIRTEEN

The Western Experience, 1945 to Today

CHAPTER EXPECTATIONS

By the end of this chapter, you will be able to:

- *demonstrate an understanding of the development of different types of communities such as environmentalists, feminists, and human rights activists*

- *identify the forces that facilitate change, the influence of key individuals in promoting change, and the characteristics of change*

- *assess key modern beliefs and philosophies and explain how they have shaped Western thought on economic, social, and political developments*

- *describe the efforts of individuals and groups who facilitated the advancement of individual and collective human rights*

- *identify individuals and groups who have worked for the advancement of the status of women*

The Berlin Wall: Why was it built? Why did it fall?

Seven years of world war had utterly devastated the European continent. "What is Europe now?" asked British prime minister Winston Churchill mournfully. "A rubble heap, a charnel house (morgue), a breeding ground of pestilence and hate." By the end of World War II, because of massive air raids during the war, conditions in Europe were far worse than after World War I. Almost every major city in Europe had been devastated. Bridges and railroads in many areas were non-existent, and vast stretches of Central and Eastern Europe resembled a lunar landscape. In addition to the material damage, there had also been an immense human cost. About 40 million Europeans died in World War II, four times the number in the previous war. Six million of the dead were Jewish victims of the Holocaust. A year after hostilities ended, untold millions had to survive on rations that provided little more than a starvation diet. An estimated 40 to 50 million displaced persons had fled or lost their homes.

Europe's status had also been significantly weakened. Decisions regarding its future lay in the hands of two superpowers: the Soviet Union and the United States. The Soviets, with several million soldiers in Eastern Europe, dominated the Continent militarily; the Americans dominated economically. The need to defeat Nazi forces during World War II had made allies of these two disparate nations. Their wartime collaboration had been an uneasy one and once the fighting had stopped, the profound differences between the Americans and the Soviets complicated the process of drawing up a postwar settlement.

Thanks to American aid and to their own strenuous efforts, the nations of Western Europe recovered relatively quickly. Eastern Europe, under Soviet domination, got back on its feet more slowly. In international affairs, however, tensions between the two superpowers created the Cold War, and its "battles" dominated European and world politics for at least a generation. Only after communism collapsed in 1989 did the Cold War come to an end. At that time, many people looked forward to a new era of peace and prosperity, but economic uncertainty and ethnic unrest brought a fresh set of problems for Europe.

KEY CONCEPTS AND EVENTS

Cold War

International Monetary
  Fund (IMF)

Marshall Plan

North Atlantic Treaty
  Organization (NATO)

Warsaw Pact

Cuban Missile Crisis

Strategic Arms Limitation
  Treaty (SALT)

Solidarity

Chernobyl

Organization of Petroleum
  Exporting Countries
  (OPEC)

KEY PEOPLE

Charles de Gaulle

Harry Truman

Fidel Castro

John F. Kennedy

Mikhail Gorbachev

Rachel Carson

Nikita Khrushchev

Martin Luther King, Jr.

Lech Walesa

Boris Yeltsin

Wit and Wisdom

Cold War methods, methods of confrontation suffered a strategic defeat. We have come to this realization. And common people have realized this, perhaps even better ...

Mikhail Gorbachev, Malta Summit, December 1989

TIME LINE: THE WESTERN EXPERIENCE

International Monetary Fund/World Bank is established	1944	
	1945	Yalta Agreement ends World War II in Europe; United Nations is formed
Communists take over Czechoslovakia; civil war in Greece; Palestine is partitioned, creating the state of Israel	1948	
	1949	NATO is established; Simone de Beauvoir publishes *The Second Sex*
North Korea invades South Korea	1950	
	1953	Joseph Stalin dies
Warsaw Pact is signed	1955	
	1956	Suez Crisis
Soviets launch Sputnik satellite	1957	
	1961	Berlin Wall is erected
Cuban Missile Crisis	1962	
	1964	Vietnam War begins
Arab-Israeli Six-Day War	1967	
	1969	American astronauts land on the moon
The Oil/Energy Crisis	1973	
	1974	The Watergate scandal
Helsinki Agreement signed; Vietnam War ends	1975	
	1985	Soviet communism collapses in Poland, Hungary, East Germany, and Czechoslovakia
Reunification of Germany; Boris Yeltsin is first democratically elected Russian president	1985	
	1991	The U.S.S.R. is dismantled
UN conference in Brazil on Environment and Development	1991	
	1999	The Euro introduced as the common European currency
Terrorist attacks on United States lead to a "War on Terrorism" centred in Afghanistan	2001	
	2002	Escalating violence in the Middle East

Not to scale.

EUROPEAN RECOVERY

The Marshall Plan

Planning for the future began in 1944, when representatives from 44 Allied countries met in New Hampshire to discuss financial policy. They set up institutions that still function today. The International Monetary Fund, a kind of international insurance fund, helped stabilize world financial systems, while the World Bank provided low-cost loans for reconstruction. All the countries present at the conference had agreed to contribute funds to start up these two organizations, but since the United States had contributed about one-third of the total, it dominated both bodies. American predominance was evident in that the headquarters for both the IMF and the World Bank were in Washington, D.C., and the American dollar became the currency against which all others were measured.

Another key contribution to European economic recovery was the European Recovery Program, commonly known as the Marshall Plan. Proposed in 1947 and named after George C. Marshall, the American Secretary of State from 1945 to 1947, the plan made over 13 billion U.S. dollars available to rebuild industry with up-to-date technology. Such aid, along with food and raw materials, was crucial in the years immediately following the war. Recovery was slow, and political turmoil in France, Italy, and other Mediterranean countries threatened the stability of a world only recently at peace.

Aid offered under the Marshall Plan was not merely a handout. The Americans insisted that Europeans take responsibility for planning their economic recovery. All European nations were invited to participate. Those participating had to allow the U.S. government to supervise their budgets and agree to purchase American exports. Not unexpectedly, the Soviet Union refused to take part in the Marshall Plan. Soviet leader Joseph Stalin would accept American financial assistance only if it came with no strings attached. Soviet allies in Eastern Europe took their cue from the Soviets and also turned down Marshall Plan assistance. Moscow organized a rival organization, Comecon (1949), which integrated the economies of Soviet bloc countries.

The United States took on the lion's share of responsibility for helping to reconstruct European economies for several reasons. Compassion certainly played a part; but so did economic and political considerations. The war had made the United States the world's richest nation, accounting for 50 percent of the world's gross national product (GNP). American leaders realized that the U.S. could not prosper for long in a ruined world marketplace.

Plowing the soil of Europe the old way and the new way, after the Marshall Plan of 1945-1947. Who benefited most from the Marshall Plan?

The beginning of the Cold War and the prospect of communist dictatorships persuaded American legislators to grant the billions needed to help restore Europe. The Marshall Plan was one of the most successful foreign-aid programs ever undertaken by any country and served as a model for Western European co-operation in other areas.

In 1951, France, West Germany, Belgium, Luxembourg, the Netherlands, and Italy formed an organization to co-ordinate the production of steel and coal in Europe. Seven years later, this body, known as the European Coal and Steel Community (ECSC), expanded into a free-trade region called the European Economic Community (EEC). In this large, tariff-free market, businesses could cut costs, lower the prices of consumer goods, and raise the standard of living. By the late 1960s, Western Europe had become an economic powerhouse. The creation of the EEC was also significant because it showed that European states, most notably the long-time enemies France and West Germany, could put aside national rivalries in the interest of their common welfare.

World Peace and the United Nations

Constructing a stable international order in 1945 was another important issue on the Allied agenda. A number of questions had to be resolved. What could be done to prevent future wars? What should be done about Germany? What kind of border changes should be made in Central Europe? There was strong disagreement on these issues between the Soviet Union on the one hand, and the United States and the United Kingdom on the other. Reaching a consensus would not be easy.

American president Franklin Roosevelt believed that maintaining world peace required an international body that could restrain aggressors effectively. "All nations of the world must be guided in spirit to abandon the use of force," he had declared in 1941. In 1944 Roosevelt outlined his idea for a new international organization, later to be called the United Nations. In some ways, it was similar to the League of Nations created in 1920, in that each member would have a seat in the General Assembly. In addition, there was to be a Security Council of the world's most powerful nations; this body would have the authority to punish aggressors with "immediate bombardment and possible invasion" if necessary.

The nucleus of the UN was the Security Council, in which China, France, Britain, the United States, and the Soviet Union received permanent seats

Membership and Presidency of the Security Council in 2002		
Month	Presidency	Membership Term Ends
January	Mauritius	31 December 2002
February	Mexico	31 December 2003
March	Norway	31 December 2002
April	Russian Federation	Permanent Member
May	Singapore	31 December 2002
June	Syrian Arab Republic	31 December 2003
July	United Kingdom	Permanent Member
August	United States	Permanent Member
September	Bulgaria	31 December 2003
October	Cameroon	31 December 2003
November	China	Permanent Member
December	Colombia	31 December 2002
	Guinea	31 December 2003
	Ireland	31 December 2002
	France	Permanent Member

The structure of the United Nations Security Council. Who are the permanent members today?

(some seats were allotted to smaller powers, which held office for two-year terms). The permanent delegates each had a veto power over Security Council decisions. This arrangement was made to accommodate Stalin, who opposed any scheme that gave smaller powers an opportunity to restrict Soviet freedom of action in international affairs. Since the Americans and the Soviets almost always disagreed, joint action to restrain aggressors proved almost impossible. Too often, the United Nations became an arena for verbal confrontation between the superpowers and their allies.

DEALING WITH A DEFEATED GERMANY

The Occupation

Within Europe itself, the most pressing question was what to do with Germany. Stalin wanted to deindustrialize Germany and return it to a kind of primitive agricultural state. His allies went along with this goal at first, before deciding that a modernized, demilitarized Germany under Allied control would be a better guarantee of peace. In accordance with the 1945 Yalta Agreement, the Allies divided Germany into four zones of occupation (at British insistence, France was allotted a zone too). The former German capital, Berlin, was partitioned in a similar fashion. Once Germany was denazified and a suitable system of government put in place, the occupying forces could withdraw. The whole process, it was hoped, would take no more than four years.

Unfortunately, friction between Allied leaders scuttled those plans. The issue of how much Germany should pay in reparations provoked dissent. A figure of 20 billion dollars was agreed on, half of which would go to the Soviet Union. The Soviets, however, wanted more than money. In defiance of their allies, they began to confiscate German industry and factories. In order to speed up the expropriation process, the Soviets also widened the gauge of German railroads to correspond to Soviet tracks. In the Soviet view, German property was the spoils of war, to which they were entitled as the victor who had lost the most during the war.

Meanwhile, the Western Allies took steps that alarmed the Soviets: They instituted a new currency system in their zones and encouraged German leaders to start drafting a new democratic system of government. After the Berlin blockade of 1948 (in which the Soviet Union blockaded the land routes leading to the Allied sector of Berlin), the Americans, British, and French merged their zones of occupation into one unit, creating the Federal Republic of Germany. The Soviets, in turn, established the communist German Democratic Republic in the area that they controlled. The city of Berlin, which lay inside the communist German Democratic Republic, was also divided, so that East Berlin was communist-controlled while West Berlin was in the hands of the Federal Republic of Germany. This created the awkward situation of a free and democratic West Berlin surrounded by communist-held territory.

The Nuremberg Tribunal

Aside from territorial and monetary concerns, there remained a critical justice issue — what would be done with former Nazis? There had been almost eight million officially registered in the party, from all walks of life. Stalin, who preferred quick solutions, suggested rounding up fifty thousand Nazi leaders and shooting them. After much discussion, the Allies set up a war crimes tribunal in the German city of Nuremberg. They identified three categories of crimes: crimes against peace, crimes against humanity, and war crimes. Of the 24 Nazi leaders tried in Nuremberg in 1945 to 1946, three were acquitted, 12 condemned to death, and the rest sentenced to life imprisonment. Other trials followed. Between 1945 and 1949, over five thousand Nazi leaders were caught and convicted. This prosecution of high-ranking Nazis did facilitate some world co-operation and helped to strengthen the belief that both military leaders and common soldiers should be held accountable to global standards of human rights that are outside the realm of traditional international and domestic law.

When the Cold War began, the West shifted its attention to fighting communism. Much the same happened in East Germany. The Soviets were not inclined to look into peoples' pasts as long as they agreed to co-operate with communist regimes. As a result, many former Nazis quietly resumed their lives and hid the details of their criminal pasts. Dozens of Nazi scientists and espionage experts actually escaped persecution and were knowingly employed by Soviet and American space and intelligence agencies.

THE NEW FACE OF EUROPE

The Union of Soviet Socialist Republics

Stalin's goal to regain the territory that Russia had lost at the end of World War I was another source of friction. The three Baltic republics — Estonia, Lithuania, and Latvia — which had once been part of czarist Russia, were incorporated into the Soviet Union along with a large part of eastern Poland. By way of compensation, Poland received a slice of eastern Germany. The Soviets set up puppet governments under their control in Czechoslovakia, Romania, and Finland. With these changes, the boundaries of the Soviet Union were more or less the same as those of czarist Russia in 1914.

National security was a second Soviet concern. The German invasion in 1941 marked the second time in the twentieth century that Russian soil had felt the tread of German boots. Driving out the invaders cost the lives of some 27 million Soviet soldiers and citizens.

Nazi occupiers had treated the Slavic peoples brutally. They had driven millions of Ukrainian and Russian civilians into slave labour camps, where they manufactured goods for the German war effort. Given the Russian experience with Germany, it is not surprising that Stalin wanted a protective barrier of "friendly" states in Eastern Europe in the event of another invasion. He was successful in attaining this objective, and, by 1949, a buffer zone of six satellite states — East Germany, Poland, Czechoslovakia, Romania, Hungary, and Bulgaria — covered the Western-Soviet border. For a time, it seemed that Yugoslavia would also be part of the Soviet empire in the eastern part of the Continent, but Yugoslav communist leader Josip Broz, known as Tito, successfully challenged Stalin's attempt at domination by asserting Yugoslavia's independence. Finland also managed to retain its independence. The Western Allies did not like

FIGURE 13.1 The Face of Europe Post World War II
Russia feared European invasion. How did the creation of the USSR help remove some of those long-held fears?

the changes that the Soviets had imposed upon Central and Eastern Europe. But short of going to war, there did not seem to be much that they could do. The presence of several million Soviet troops meant that Eastern Europe was part of the Soviet sphere of influence.

Parliamentary Democracy in Europe

Germany

After the war, many nations had to refashion their systems of government along democratic lines. In 1948 the three Western Allies directed German leaders to begin drafting a new system of government. The basic law guaranteed German citizens fundamental rights and provided the framework for a democratic constitution. A federal system of government was put in place with a *Bundestag*, or lower house elected by the people, and an upper house representing the states. One important provision of the law stipulated that a party had to win five percent of the popular vote before its delegates could sit in the *Bundestag*. This law prevented the kind of chaotic situation that had characterized the Weimar Republic, when a large number of small antagonistic splinter parties had destabilized the political process. The courts also now had the power to outlaw extremist parties. It was this situation that had given Hitler his opportunity to gain power. Consequently, both communists and neo-Nazis were prevented from sitting in the *Bundestag*. The parties that dominated West German politics were the Christian Democratic Union and the Social Democratic Party.

For 17 years, from 1946 until his resignation in 1963, Christian Democratic chancellor Konrad Adenauer (1878–1967) dominated West German politics. Adenauer's goal had been to restore respect for Germany by co-operating with the U.S. and with Germany's neighbours, especially France. Under Adenauer's leadership, Germany took some responsibility for the atrocities of the past and offered an apology, along with financial compensation, to Holocaust survivors. West Germany also adopted a generous asylum law allowing refugees from other parts of the world to enter freely, though they were not readily able to gain citizenship.

Italy

Italy, too, underwent a profound change. In 1946, Italian voters decided to abolish the monarchy in favour of a republican form of government. The Italian political scene was characterized by constant changes of government, although the Christian Democratic Party remained dominant.

France

After its liberation from Nazi rule, France adopted a new constitution, known as the Fourth Republic. In contrast to the stable West German situation, the French political scene was volatile: A multitude of parties resulted in a series of short-lived coalition governments, and virtual paralysis of decision-making. In 1958, war in its Algerian colony brought the Fourth Republic to the brink of collapse. The army called on General Charles de Gaulle (1890–1970), who had been the leader of the French resistance to Nazi Germany during the war, to assume the position of president. De Gaulle supervised the preparation of a new constitution, the Fifth Republic, which increased the power of the president, including increasing the term of office to seven years.

Restoring respect for his country was de Gaulle's primary goal, just as it had been for Adenauer in Germany. First, de Gaulle stabilized the French franc, encouraged state-controlled enterprises, and took other measures to strengthen the economy. Under de Gaulle, the French economy achieved one of the highest rates of industrial growth in Europe. But where Adenauer had made Germany into a loyal ally of the U.S., de Gaulle rejected "American hegemony." De Gaulle took France out of NATO (North Atlantic Treaty Organization), developed an independent French nuclear force, and tried to make France into a "third force" in international politics.

European Politics

As far as the political situation in the rest of Western Europe was concerned, in the immediate postwar period there was a move toward the political left. Socialist parties formed governments in Britain, Italy, and the Scandinavian countries. By the 1950s, the mood of the voting public shifted to the right and conservative parties came to power — but they did not dismantle the socialist states and accepted the need for government control of the economy.

During the 1960s, socialist parties once again found themselves in office, but they had to adjust to their new situation. Automated factories had cut down on the number of blue-collar jobs (labourers, people in trades), while the number of white-collar workers (technicians, office workers, clerks, healthcare workers) increased. In effect, a new class structure had emerged. Under these new circumstances, socialist politicians could no longer rely on appeals to class struggle or revolution in order to win votes. They realized that their political platforms had to appeal to a broader range of the electorate.

Until the 1970s, communist parties managed to hang on to some popular support. Communists had been very active in the resistance against the Nazis, and their efforts had earned them a great deal of prestige. Growing tensions between East and West diminished the appeal of communism but did not eliminate it entirely as a political force. This is especially true of France and Italy, but there were significant differences between the two. The French Communist Party followed Moscow; the Italian Communist Party, by contrast, rejected Moscow's domination. The Italians worked hard to come up with practical election platforms that addressed voters' concerns. Though Italian communists were never elected to national office, they regularly won municipal elections.

Whatever the form of government or party in power, the politics of postwar Western Europe had re-affirmed the values of parliamentary democracy. The two notable exceptions were Spain and Portugal, where dictatorships remained in place until the 1970s.

In Spain, Generalissimo Francisco Franco ruled with an iron hand until his death in 1975. Then, under the guidance of newly restored King Juan Carlos, Spain made a peaceful transition to a democratic system of government. In Portugal, a revolution overthrew the dictator Antonio Salazar and opened the way for a democratically elected republican government.

THE COLD WAR

The Iron Curtain

"From Stettin in the Baltic to Trieste in the Adriatic, an iron curtain has descended across the Continent." So declared Winston Churchill in a speech given in Fulton, Missouri in 1946. This famous speech marked the beginning of the Cold War, a period of tension and confrontation between the Soviet Union and the United States, though short of actual war. Allied disagreements at Yalta in February 1945, and at Potsdam, had already foreshadowed the Cold War. Soviet refusal to join the Marshall Plan and disputes over Germany and Eastern Europe made it a reality. Until its end in 1989, the Cold War was the most critical feature of international politics.

American-Soviet Relations

In the prewar years, Americans had been very suspicious of the Soviets and relations between the two nations had not been cordial. The need to defeat Hitler had made them allies and, for a while, goodwill prevailed. American political leaders such as Franklin Roosevelt and Harry Truman convinced themselves that Stalin was essentially a reasonable person. But a Soviet attempt to infiltrate Iran, and then Turkey, at the end of the war, irritated the Americans.

During the war, the Allies had agreed that the people of Eastern Europe would be allowed to establish "democratic institutions of their own choice." When Stalin, in total defiance of this aim, forcibly installed communist governments in one state after another, the

West became alarmed. Press reports from journalists who had spent time in the postwar Soviet Union made it clear to the American public that the Soviet Union was a repressive dictatorship. This was not exactly new information, but the friendly feelings inspired by fighting a common enemy had temporarily made people forget about the darker aspects of Stalin's rule.

The Soviets distrusted most Western allied actions. The delay in starting the second front against Germany during World War II was an especially sore point. The Soviets felt that the Western Allies had not shown sufficient concern for the tremendous human and material losses the Soviet people suffered in pushing back Nazi armies and turning the tide of the war. No bombs had hit American factories; no invading armies had crossed its borders; and American civilian populations had not been targeted. The U.S. had prospered as a consequence of war. In the Soviet view, American prosperity had been gained through Soviet sacrifice. This is why Stalin had denounced the Marshall Plan as an American plot to extend American economic domination over Europe. He also believed that American capitalism was doomed to collapse.

On a more general level, the Cold War was a manifestation of the clash of two rival worldviews. Each superpower felt that it had a special role to play in history. Many Americans felt they had a mission to spread their form of democracy to the rest of the world. As for the Soviet Union, it too had a sense of mission. After 1917, communist leaders envisioned a global proletarian revolution under their leadership. The organization of the Communist Information Bureau (Cominform) in 1947 united all European communist parties under Moscow's dominance and was regarded by the West as confirmation of Soviet worldwide intentions.

Bloc Politics

The Cold War divided the world into two rival blocs, each headed by one of the two superpowers. It was a war punctuated by a series of crises, all of which kept international relations at the boiling point. The year 1948 was particularly critical. Communists took over Czechoslovakia, the one country in Eastern Europe with a democratic tradition. In Greece, an ongoing civil war pitted communist guerrillas (supported by the Soviet Union) against forces loyal to the Greek government. American president Harry Truman regarded communism as "bacteria" that had to be "contained" before the infection spread to the whole world. Truman dispatched a naval squadron to the Mediterranean and began to supply arms to the Greek government. Faced with the prospect of war with the U.S., the Soviets stopped supporting the guerrillas. Truman's policy of containment, as it was named, became the basis for American policy toward the U.S.S.R. in the years that followed. In addition to sending military assistance as they had done for Greece, the Americans made arrangements with other countries, allowing the U.S. to build military bases around the world. From these bases, the U.S. could launch bombers against the Soviet Union. The Soviets regarded containment as a threat to their security.

The Berlin Blockade

The Berlin blockade and the Allied airlift in 1948 was a dangerous crisis. When the Western allies merged their zones into a new country called the Federal Republic of Germany (West Germany), the Soviets responded by closing roads and railways linking West Berlin with West Germany. For almost a year, Allied planes flew in massive amounts of supplies to the besieged population. At one point, cargo planes landed every few minutes in the Templehof airport, 24 hours a day. After 300 days, when they realized that the Allies were not going to back down, the Soviets capitulated. Such confrontations, along with the victory of Mao Zedong in China in 1949 and the North Korean communist invasion of South Korea in 1950, persuaded many people in the West that communism had become a major threat to the free world.

The North Atlantic Treaty Organization

In response to communist actions in 1949, the United States, Great Britain, France, Canada, Portugal, Italy, the Netherlands, Luxembourg, Norway and Iceland formed the North Atlantic Treaty Organization. Greece and Turkey were admitted in 1952, West Germany in 1955, and Spain in 1982. The members of NATO agreed to come to the assistance of any member that was attacked. The decision to allow Germany to join NATO in 1955 prompted the communist countries into a similar alliance of their own, called the Warsaw Pact. Barely 10 years after the end of World War II, Europe was again divided into hostile alliances, just as it had been so many times in the past. Contact between the two blocs dwindled to a minimum; trade dried up; no tourism was allowed. In the Soviet bloc, Western books and newspapers were banned and Western radio programs like the Voice of America and the British Broadcasting Corporation (BBC) jammed.

WEB CONNECTION

www.mcgrawhill.ca/links/legacy

Go to the site above to find out more about Cold War politics and the nuclear arms race.

The Arms Race

A rapidly escalating arms race accompanied this political activity. The Soviets exploded their first atomic bomb in 1949; the Americans countered with a much more powerful hydrogen bomb in 1951; and the Soviets followed with another one a year later. Both superpowers developed sophisticated intercontinental ballistic missile (ICBM) systems. Soon, there was enough firepower to destroy the world several times over.

Governments worldwide promoted civil defence plans by building bomb shelters for government members, encouraging large numbers of people to build their own, creating emergency broadcast systems, and increasing public awareness through television, radio, comic books, and portable exhibits. The peace movement got started when activists cried "ban the bomb" and tried to tell people that all these measures would be useless against the force of a nuclear attack and the radioactive fall-out that would follow. American children of the 1950s became familiar with Bert the Turtle, a cartoon character who demonstrated the "duck and cover" strategy. Children from kindergarten on were made to perform drills in which they would duck under their desks and cover their heads with their arms in preparation for an enemy attack.

A fallout shelter sign. The number of people the shelter will hold is marked. Signs like this appeared on buildings in cities all over the United States in the 1950s.

KOREA AND VIETNAM

The 38th Parallel

During World War II, Korea, which had been annexed by the Japanese, had sided with Japan and the other Axis powers against the Allies. Like Germany, Korea was partitioned into American and Soviet zones, and the dividing line was the 38th parallel. When the superpowers withdrew from Korea, they left behind two heavily armed, mutually hostile governments: a Soviet-supported regime in the North and an American-supported regime in the South. Both claimed the right to govern the entire Korean peninsula.

In 1950 troops from North Korea invaded South Korea and captured its capital, Seoul. The American government saw this action as proof of the Soviet intention to extend its power in the Far East. American president Harry Truman said, "if we aren't tough now, there won't be any next step." Since the Soviet delegate was boycotting the Security Council at the time, the United States succeeded in persuading the UN to send military assistance to help South Korea repel its northern invaders. Led by American general Douglas MacArthur, the UN troops would achieve their goal.

When MacArthur decided to penetrate deep into North Korea and unify the two Koreas, the Chinese became alarmed. In August 1951, 200 000 Chinese

What were readers supposed to think when they saw this front cover of *Picture Post*, about the Korean War?

soldiers crossed the Yalu River separating North Korea from China and reversed the tide of battle. President Truman was unwilling to continue a lengthy war, and so decided to seek a negotiated settlement. The Soviets, who feared that the Korean conflict might escalate into a major war, also gave their support to a cease-fire. In the end, after more than 35 000 Americans, 516 Canadians and more than a million Korean and Chinese soldiers and civilians were dead, the border between the two Koreas remained where it had been, roughly at the 38th parallel. In Europe, the impact of the Korean War was to strengthen the military influence of NATO and accelerate rearmament. In the East, a similar organization, the South East Asia Treaty Organization (SEATO) was formed in 1954.

History BYTES

As the two superpowers threatened the world with nuclear annihilation, the anxiety that people felt was often tempered only by advice on how to protect themselves from the effects of an atomic explosion. The suppliers of bomb shelters could barely keep pace with demand. From the most flimsy plywood construction in a family's suburban backyard, to massive underground steel containers placed metres below ground, bomb shelters became bestsellers in America. Some people became so paranoid that they hid from their neighbours the fact that they were constructing a shelter.

Vietnam

Vietnam proved to be a bloodier battleground than Korea. Initially, it was part of the French colonial empire in Indochina. At the end of World War II, Vietnam was partitioned into a communist-ruled North supported by China, and a non-communist South supported by France. In 1950, at the height of the Korean War, the United States decided to help the French. By the last stages of French occupation, the U.S. was underwriting more than half of French military expenditures in South Vietnam.

When the French withdrew from Southeast Asia in 1957, the United States assumed France's role as supporter of the non-communist South. Even though the South Vietnamese government was corrupt and repressive, the U.S. did not feel it could abandon the South. This was because of a belief in the "domino theory," which held that if one country in Southeast Asia were to fall to communism, neighbouring states would also soon fall. The U.S. dispatched increasing numbers of "military advisers" in order to bolster the South Vietnamese government.

In 1964 North Vietnamese warships fired on American vessels in the Gulf of Tonkin and the nature of American participation changed dramatically. As the action spread into neighbouring Laos and Cambodia, a stronger peace movement developed in the U.S. The Gulf of Tonkin incident persuaded the American Congress to accept President Lyndon Johnson's (who had succeeded the assassinated John F. Kennedy) plan to bomb the North. Two years later, the United States had over half a million soldiers in the region. In the course of hostilities, the U.S. dropped more bombs on Vietnam than the Allies had dropped on Germany and Japan combined during World War II.

In the U.S. and throughout the world, television coverage of the Vietnam war eroded support for American involvement. The anti-war movement in the U.S. gained strength and eventually influenced policy decisions. Corruption in the South Vietnamese government also destroyed the Americans' image. In 1968 the Vietcong communist rebels undertook the Tet Offensive into the South, and although this attack was repelled, the fact that the Vietcong could launch such a massive offensive showed that their strength had not diminished. This was the beginning of the end of the war. In 1972, a generation after the U.S. first became involved in Vietnam, the defeated Americans began peace talks, and in 1973, they pulled out entirely.

[FROM CRISIS TO DÉTENTE

The Berlin Wall and the Cuban Missile Crisis

Another Berlin crisis occurred in 1961. Throughout the previous decade, nearly three million East Germans had fled to the West via Berlin. In order to halt this flow of escapees, the East German authorities built a concrete wall separating the two sectors of Berlin and then constructed barriers all along the border with West Germany. Many would die attempting to scale or circumvent the Wall.

The most critical event of the Cold War occurred a year after the building of the Berlin Wall. The Soviet-supported communist government of Fidel Castro was in power in Cuba, and from photos taken by spy planes, American intelligence learned that the Soviets had constructed missile silos on the island, only 150 km from U.S. territory. After six tense and frightening days, U.S. President John F. Kennedy decided to order a naval blockade of Cuba. In the end, the Soviet leader Nikita Khrushchev capitulated and agreed to remove the offending weapons.

Although people were very frightened and had anticipated the worst, it is only since the release of classified documents in 1998 that historians and the public became fully aware of how close the world came to nuclear war. After the crisis, the United States and the Soviet Union began taking steps to reduce tensions. They set up a hotline between the White House and the Kremlin in order to improve communication between the two governments. By 1963 the United

The United States government faced public opposition to its decision to blockade Cuba in 1962. What is the current state of Cuban—U.S. relations?

States had agreed to sell wheat to the Soviets and other trade agreements would follow. Tourism and cultural exchange between the two countries were encouraged.

Strategic Arms Limitation Treaty

In 1963 Soviet and American leaders (along with those of several other nations) signed a treaty to limit the testing of nuclear weapons in the atmosphere, in outer space, and under water. China joined the nuclear "club" in 1964. Despite the treaty, the Soviets succeeded in achieving nuclear parity with the Americans, largely due to the American preoccupation with Vietnam. In 1972 the two superpowers signed the Strategic Arms Limitation Treaty, under which they agreed to limit the production of defensive missiles. When Soviet leader Leonid Brezhnev visited Washington to sign the treaty, some optimistic observers declared that the Cold War was over and a new era of world peace had dawned.

These hopes proved premature, and the arms race continued under a new guise. The superpowers intensified the firepower of existing weapons and developed new ones, such as the stealth bomber, the low-flying cruise missile, and the neutron bomb (which destroys people, but not property). By 1978 the arms race had reached the MAD (mutually assured destruction) level. This meant that each superpower had the capability to destroy one-quarter of its enemy's population and one-half of its industry.

New sources of disagreement fuelled international tensions. American president Jimmy Carter crusaded for human rights; the Soviets invaded Afghanistan in 1979; the Americans boycotted the Moscow Olympics in 1980; President Ronald Reagan described the Soviet Union as an "evil empire" and pushed for the development of a "Star Wars" defence system (SDI). Yet, despite these and other conflicts, the temperature of international relations did not drop to the frosty depths of the early postwar period. Various factors worked to bring about moderation, and some historians believe that the reality of mad and the destruction it might cause kept the Unites States and the Soviet Union from taking any actions that could have led to war.

During the 1960s and 1970s, trade between the two blocs increased. Nations in the Western bloc began to export technology and extend loans to countries in Eastern Europe. West German chancellor Willy Brandt made attempts at détente (easing of tensions) by reaching out to the East, and in 1972 the two Germanys signed a treaty recognizing each other's borders. In 1975 East and West signed the Helsinki Agreement guaranteeing human rights. Such non-military developments helped build bridges between West and East.

The European Response

For Europeans, the Cuban Missile Crisis underlined the fact that foreign policy was decided in Moscow and Washington. Western Europeans were very much the junior partners in NATO, which was headed by American generals. In his handling of the Cuban crisis, President Kennedy had not consulted with NATO governments, and, although they had supported his position, they were alarmed at the possibility that Europe could become a nuclear battleground. But since European nations were unwilling to build up their armies to counter the Soviet forces massed in Eastern Europe, they tacitly accepted the American nuclear umbrella, even though both Britain and France now had their own nuclear arsenals.

POSTWAR EUROPE 1950-1970

During the first postwar generation, Europe enjoyed a booming economy: All figures measuring economic activity climbed. By 1949 industrial production had regained the levels of 10 years earlier and continued to climb for the next 20 years. Between 1953 and 1964, West Germany led the way with an annual growth rate of six percent. Considering the destruction caused by bombing during the war, this growth rate seemed like an economic miracle. The same trends were seen in Italy, whose economy expanded at a rate of 5.6 percent during this period. France followed with 4.9 percent, and Britain with 2.7 percent.

In human terms, these rates of economic activity meant a shorter workweek, higher wages, and longer paid holidays. Prosperity created demand for all kinds of household appliances, consumer goods, and, above all, automobiles. By 1960 the European auto industry had produced 45 million cars, up from five million in 1940. Owning a car was no longer a privilege enjoyed only by the rich. Not only that, a mass market in cars required roads, and all European nations either expanded existing roads or constructed networks of superhighways. The most famous were the German *Autobahnen*, four-lane highways on which people could drive at speeds of up to 220 km/h.

There was virtually no unemployment in the West during the 1950s and 1960s. The demand for labour was so great that Western Europe became a magnet for people in search of a better life. Italians and Portuguese found work in France and Germany; East and West Indians migrated to Britain; Turks went to Germany as guest workers; Arabs and West Africans migrated to France.

Pleasures
AND PASTIMES

Comic books have been immensely popular since their widespread publication in Europe and North America began in the 1930s. Only in recent years have people analysed mainstream comics for how they reflect and reinforce the beliefs and concerns of society. The Cold War affected comic book genres, and a new breed of superheroes and villains emerged. These figures reflected people's anxieties and fears of a nuclear attack. Now superheroes owed their superhuman powers to radiation accidents. Spiderman had his unique set of powers because he had been bitten by a radioactive spider, and the Incredible Hulk had his "anger management" problems and superhuman strength because he had been exposed to gamma rays.

The Welfare State

As European leaders planned the postwar economic recovery, they were determined to avoid the economic catastrophe that had marked the years after World War I. Governments adjusted tax rates to encourage investment, regulated the money supply, and imposed price and wage controls to control inflation. One of the first steps taken in 1945 by the newly elected British Labour government was to nationalize the Bank of England, the coal and steel industries, public transportation, and public utilities. Britain also took the lead in developing the welfare state. Parliament passed the National Health Act, which provided universal health care, and helped the unemployed, the aged, and other less fortunate citizens. Eventually, subsidized housing, assistance to the handicapped, and improved educational opportunities followed.

The postwar welfare state covered people "from the cradle to the grave" and grew out of a conviction that society as a whole was responsible for the welfare of its members. It was felt that since all citizens had shared in the hardships of wartime, all should share in the benefits of peace. Elsewhere in Europe, governments followed the British example. Old age pensions, healthcare, family allowances, unemployment benefits, state-supported childcare all became commonplace, as did improved access to higher education.

All over Europe, new universities were built and financial support extended to all qualified students. Between 1940 and 1960, student enrolment tripled in Europe, with many of the students now coming from the middle and lower classes. Going to university was no longer a privilege of the rich. These social programs had to be paid for with higher taxes, but they were popular with the electorate in all countries, and no government dared tamper with them.

Social changes thus made European society more egalitarian. Class barriers remained but were less pronounced. The population grew, and society became more urbanized. Automobiles made society more mobile as well, and more people were driving long distances to work. The workplace changed as well: women entered the work force in increasing numbers, particularly in the growing government and social service sectors. While automation lightened the work of many blue-collar workers, in some cases it eliminated jobs. Over time, the number of rural farmers declined, while the number of industrial and service workers increased.

EDUCATION, ALIENATION, AND REVOLT

Existentialism

With the prosperity of the 1950s and 1960s came movements that questioned the status quo, including existentialism, neo-Marxism, the feminist movement, and environmentalism. These philosophies and ideologies challenged prevailing values to an unforeseen degree.

The word "existentialism" comes from the German *Existenzphilosophie*, or the philosophy of existence, which emerged during the 1930s. Its forerunners included nineteenth-century philosophers such as Friedrich Nietzsche (1844–1900) and Søren Kierkegaard (1813–1855). Existentialism was very much a product of the postwar world, and its most important exponents in the years after 1945 were French writers Jean Paul Sartre (1905–1980), Simone de Beauvoir (1908–1986), and Albert Camus (1913–1960).

Existentialism proposes that each of us is alone in a universe that is totally indifferent to our needs and wants. No religion, philosophy, or traditional set of values can provide us with answers to the big questions such as "What is the meaning of life?" Life has no predetermined meaning: it is absurd, senseless. While this can be profoundly depressing, it can also be liberating. "Life begins on the other side of despair," wrote Sartre. We may be alone, but we are also free; free to determine our own destiny; free to choose the kind of

Jean Paul Sartre and Simone de Beauvoir were key figures in the postwar European intellectual community. Are there any philosophers in the news today?

person we want to be. There are limits, but within those limits we can still make choices. To make excuses is to be guilty of what some existentialists called "bad faith." Sartre said at one point, "Make up your own mind; just be sure you are totally sincere and do not live by rules made by others."

There was a great deal of ambiguity in Sartre's advice. It could lead one person to become an aimless drifter, and another to seek a more positive, socially useful life. Sartre, who had fought in the French Resistance against the Nazis, eventually became a communist. His choice was not an unusual one for the time. As has been said, communism enjoyed a great deal of support after World War I. Only when the Soviet Union invaded Hungary during the Hungarian Revolution of 1956 did Sartre abandon the communist cause. Sartre's ideas are expressed in his works such as *Being and Nothingness*, his plays *The Flies* and *No Exit*, and his novels *Nausea* and *Intimacy*.

For Albert Camus, disillusionment with what he called the "concentration camp socialism" found in the Soviet Union came much earlier. Camus affirmed a belief in human dignity in a universe filled with evil. He wrote several novels and essays including *The Plague*, *The Stranger*, *The Myth of Sisyphus*, and *The Rebel: A Study of Man in Revolt*.

Neo-Marxism

Another critique of society, which overlapped to some extent with existentialism, came from a new brand of Marxism, called neo-Marxism, or the New Left. Among the more popular neo-Marxist writers was Herbert Marcuse, an exile from Nazi Germany who found refuge in the United States. Marcuse's immensely popular *One-Dimensional Man* (1964) presented a wide-ranging critique of contemporary capitalism and its "contradictions." According to Marcuse, capitalism, as an economic and technological system, was immensely productive and efficient but ultimately debased human values. Instead of making it possible for people to live rich, multi-faceted spiritual and intellectual lives, capitalism transformed people into willing conformists and docile workers. It bought people off with material goods. Capitalism led people, in Marcuse's words, to "find their soul in their automobile, hi-fi set, split-level home, [and] kitchen equipment." In Marcuse's view, the emphasis on individual values within capitalism brought about a breakdown in the sense of social cohesiveness, and people were alienated from one another.

What thinkers such as Marcuse would have put in the place of capitalism was not entirely clear. Nor did criticism of Western capitalism translate into admiration for Soviet-style communism. Neo-Marxists regarded it as even more repressive and dehumanizing than Western capitalism, and a perversion of genuine Marxism. Their philosophy, with its numerous insights into the depersonalized nature of modern industrialism, was a critique of society rather than a blueprint for change.

The Feminist Movement

Women had been active in the war effort, particularly by doing work usually done by men. Nevertheless, once the fighting was over and the men were home, women re-assumed their traditional roles. Legislation encouraged women to stay home and raise a family; fashion also reinforced traditional femininity in the image of the New Woman — with her tiny waist and full skirt.

When French feminist Simone de Beauvoir published her book *The Second Sex* in 1949, it did not provoke much of a response outside of France; but today it is a classic of feminist thought. Challenging the Freudian premise that "biology is destiny," de Beauvoir wrote in *The Second Sex* that the image and status of women had been institutionalized in society rather than predetermined by gender. As an existentialist, she was concerned with women's destiny as human beings, which she saw as being hindered by the definition of their social roles as wife and mother.

The perception of women's roles would change by the 1960s, as a powerful feminist movement appeared throughout Europe. This movement has been called "second-wave" feminism, the struggle for greater social, economic, and political equality. First-wave feminism had focussed on women gaining the vote and the basic right of citizenship. Second-wave feminist writers and leaders included Betty Friedan (*The Feminine Mystique*, 1963) and Germaine Greer (*The Female Eunuch*, 1970).

To a great extent, Western women's grievances had an economic basis; as they were entering the work force in ever-increasing numbers, only to be concentrated in poorly paid jobs. Fighting for higher wages and access to better-paying jobs was an important goal of the feminist movement. It was, however, only part of the feminist critique of society, as can be seen from the following statement issued by a British Women's Liberation Workshop in 1969:

> We are economically oppressed: in jobs we do full work for half pay; in the home we do unpaid work full time; commercially exploited by advertisements, legally we often have only the status of children. We are brought up to feel inadequate, educated to narrower horizons than men. This is our special oppression as women.

In order to bring about change, women's groups organized and pressured politicians to abolish repressive laws. (For example, in Canada until 1969 it was illegal to disseminate information about birth control.) They opened shelters for abused women and their children. They published newsletters, demanded women's studies courses at colleges and universities, and organized consciousness-raising sessions to promote awareness of injustices.

Feminism also raised the consciousness of society as a whole. Several countries passed legislation granting women pay equity, wider access to birth control, abortions and daycare. Changes in social attitudes made it easier for women to pursue non-traditional careers such as broadcasting, surveying, engineering, and auto mechanics. The invention of the birth control

pill meant more reliable family planning and greater sexual freedom, at least for Western women. As more women worked outside the home, many opted for later marriage and fewer children. In short, the feminist movement helped bring about what is probably the most important social revolution of our time.

American writer Gloria Steinem remains an important voice in the North American feminist community. How would you characterize today's feminism?

In Eastern Europe, change in the status of women took longer than it did in the West. On paper, women had the same rights as men, but the realities of Soviet life, in particular, made it impossible to enjoy such rights fully. Standing in line for food took hours out of a woman's day. While occupations such as practicing medicine and teaching were dominated by women, these women enjoyed little prestige. As in the West, the sphere of politics was still reserved for men in the Eastern bloc, and women still shouldered the double burden of housework and full-time jobs outside the home.

Youth in Revolt

Europe had a lively tradition of student protest dating back to the mid-nineteenth century. But the generation that reached maturity in the 1950s was not inclined to take to the streets or erect barricades. After years of depression and war, the chance to have a job and a settled life was more appealing.

In the 1960s, young people began to criticize the materialism of their parents' generation, many adopting to a great extent the neo-Marxist critique of capitalism. Herbert Marcuse and Jean Paul Sartre became the heroes of the student avant-garde. Students supported, and demonstrated in favour of,

national liberation movements in developing countries. American students protested their country's involvement in the Vietnam War, and this encouraged European students to launch their own protests. Youth groups were also essential advocates for universal human rights.

The most dramatic student protest occurred out in France. In November 1967, students and professors at the newly built university of Nanterre, in the outskirts of Paris, went on strike. Overcrowded classrooms and too few professors made learning difficult, they claimed. In addition, they objected to the theoretical subject matter being taught, which they felt was irrelevant to a modern society.

In the course of their revolt, students gathered support from intellectuals, ordinary citizens, and young workers who had their own grievances against

Workers and youth rioting in Paris in 1968 influenced the government's overhaul of the education system in France. Why did the riots get started?

the system. In the new year, 10 million workers went on strike. Trains did not run, airplanes were grounded, and post offices were shut down. In the *cafés* of Paris, a carnival atmosphere reigned; patrons felt that they were witnessing the first stages of a cultural revolution that would usher in a more democratic world. The collapse of President de Gaulle's government seemed imminent. But when police moved to restore order, the revolt collapsed almost as suddenly as it had begun.

The collapse of the revolt can be attributed to various factors. Vandalism and destruction of property, which were rampant in the poorer sections of Paris, alienated potential supporters. Students started out by asking for specific reforms in university life but proceeded to demand the destruction of the whole capitalist system. This frightened a significant sector of the population, especially since the students had no clear vision of the new social structures that would replace the old. A split occurred between the students, many of whom came from affluent middle-class families, and the young workers who sought job security within the system, not its overthrow.

Even if the 1967–1968 student revolt in Paris did not bring about a cultural revolution, it certainly did cause significant change. The French government introduced long overdue reforms in the education system. The revolt contributed indirectly to the resignation of President de Gaulle, who left office within a year. Shock waves from the revolt reverberated throughout Europe, encouraging similar, though less dramatic events elsewhere. It also accelerated the decline in communist political influence. Party members came from an older generation and did not have much sympathy for the young rebels who, in turn, no longer looked to the political left for leadership or inspiration.

Human Rights Movements

World War II brought universal human rights into the global consciousness. The idea that all human beings should have equal rights and be protected from discrimination in all its forms began to gain support worldwide. The expansion in mass communications made it possible for people around the world to learn about the struggles of others and to support those struggles effectively. Leaders such as American civil rights activist Martin Luther King, Jr. (1929–1968), South African political leader Nelson Mandela, Czech President Vaclev Havel, and Aung San Suu Kyi of Burma (now Myanmar) gained international support (led by Canada) and recognition for their causes through coverage in the mass media, and through the actions of brave and committed supporters within local communities and worldwide. How a government treats its citizens became a new, legitimate matter of international concern and gained momentum from the 1950s onward.

After the *Universal Declaration of Human Rights* was adopted by the United Nations in 1948, its principles became a standard of achievement in human rights for all nations. Over 185 nations have incorporated the *Declaration*'s spirit and principles into their own constitutions. The UN has issued over 20 treaties elaborating on human rights, including the *International Bill of Human Rights*, *the Convention on the Rights of the Child*, and the *Convention on the Elimination of All Forms of Racial Discrimination*.

While world governments often professed adherence to human rights agreements, it took the efforts of individual citizens and groups to guard these rights and expose violations. Non-governmental organizations (NGOs) proliferated in the 1960s. Groups such as Amnesty International, Human Rights Watch, International Working Groups on Indigenous Affairs, and nuclear abolition movements all worked to pressure governments to adhere to specific categories of human rights. A key example of the power of NGOs was revealed in the 1995 UN Conference on Women, held in Beijing. As world leaders discussed women's issues within the confines of the conference, NGO members raised awareness about serious violations of women's human rights in nations that claimed none existed. Worldwide membership in NGOs has been increasing steadily since the 1960s, reflecting the egalitarian belief that all human beings must have the same

The Universal Declaration of Human Rights

On December 10, 1948, the General Assembly of the United Nations adopted and proclaimed the *Universal Declaration of Human Rights*. Portions of the text appear below. Following this historic act, the Assembly called upon all member countries to publicize the text of the *Declaration* and "to cause it to be disseminated, displayed, read and expounded principally in schools and other educational institutions, without distinction based on the political status of countries or territories."

Preamble

Whereas recognition of the inherent dignity and of the equal and inalienable rights of all members of the human family is the foundation of freedom, justice and peace in the world,

Whereas disregard and contempt for human rights have resulted in barbarous acts which have outraged the conscience of mankind, and the advent of a world in which human beings shall enjoy freedom of speech and belief and freedom from fear and want has been proclaimed as the highest aspiration of the common people,

Whereas it is essential, if man is not to be compelled to have recourse, as a last resort, to rebellion against tyranny and oppression, that human rights should be protected by the rule of law,

Whereas it is essential to promote the development of friendly relations between nations,

Whereas the peoples of the United Nations have in the Charter re-affirmed their faith in fundamental human rights, in the dignity and worth of the human person and in the equal rights of men and women and have determined to promote social progress and better standards of life in larger freedom,

Whereas Member States have pledged themselves to achieve, in co-operation with the United Nations, the promotion of universal respect for and observance of human rights and fundamental freedoms,

Whereas a common understanding of these rights and freedoms is of the greatest importance for the full realization of this pledge,

Now, Therefore, The General Assembly *proclaims*
THIS UNIVERSAL DECLARATION OF HUMAN RIGHTS as a common standard of achievement for all peoples and all nations, to the end that every individual and every organ of society, keeping this *Declaration* constantly in mind, shall strive by teaching and education to promote respect for these rights and freedoms and by progressive measures, national and international, to secure their universal and effective recognition and observance, both among the peoples of Member States themselves and among the peoples of territories under their jurisdiction.

Article 1.

All human beings are born free and equal in dignity and rights. They are endowed with reason and conscience and should act towards one another in a spirit of brotherhood.

Article 2.

Everyone is entitled to all the rights and freedoms set forth in this *Declaration*, without distinction of any kind, such as race, colour, sex, language, religion, political or other opinion, national or social origin, property, birth or other status. Furthermore, no distinction shall be made on the basis of the political, jurisdictional or international status of the country or territory to which a person belongs, whether it be independent, trust, non-self-governing or under any other limitation of sovereignty.

Article 3.

Everyone has the right to life, liberty and security of person.

Article 4.

No one shall be held in slavery or servitude; slavery and the slave trade shall be prohibited in all their forms.

Article 5.

No one shall be subjected to torture or to cruel, inhuman or degrading treatment or punishment.

Article 6.

Everyone has the right to recognition everywhere as a person before the law.

Article 7.

All are equal before the law and are entitled without any discrimination to equal protection of the law. All are entitled to equal protection against any discrimination in violation of this *Declaration* and against any incitement to such discrimination.

Article 8.

Everyone has the right to an effective remedy by the competent national tribunals for acts violating the fundamental rights granted him by the constitution or by law.

Article 9.

No one shall be subjected to arbitrary arrest, detention or exile.

Article 10.

Everyone is entitled in full equality to a fair and public hearing by an independent and impartial tribunal, in the determination of his rights and obligations and of any criminal charge against him.[1]

---

1. How might the *Declaration* be useful to someone studying the legal, moral, and human rights situation in a given country or state?

2. Given that the *Declaration* was composed in 1948, do you feel it still adequately deals with all possible human rights violations? In your opinion, is anything missing?

human rights. Governments are now faced with considerable opposition from their citizens over trade, military, and cultural dealings with governments with questionable human rights records.

THE AMERICANIZATION OF CULTURE

Let the Good Times Roll

In the West, a shorter workweek and longer holidays allowed more time for leisure activities. One of the most popular was going to see the latest Hollywood movies. The "American way of life" portrayed in movies had an appeal that went beyond entertainment. America was perceived as a free society where every person had a chance to succeed, a society very different from that of class-conscious Europe. America stood for democracy, which was what the Allies had fought to keep.

American society was prosperous and looked to the future. The casual approach to life taken in the United States seemed so much more attractive than the stiffness and formality still prevalent in much of European society. American music — jazz, rock, and pop music — was also popular with Europeans. Though not all Europeans appreciated what they called the "Americanization" of European culture, the presence of American troops in Europe and American Armed Forces Radio made it difficult to avoid American influences.

Rock-and-roll is a good example of the American-European cultural exchange. In the late 1950s, the music of Elvis Presley, Little Richard, and Chuck Berry swept through Europe. The British group the Beatles reinterpreted the rock idiom, creating a musical explosion that reverberated throughout the world. The Beatles' 1967 album *Sergeant Pepper's Lonely Hearts Club Band* was, according to one critic, "the greatest force for bringing European civilization together since the Congress of Vienna." Other British rock bands soon followed, including The Who, The Rolling Stones, and The Animals. Their music reflected the more permissive, sexually liberated society that was emerging.

Three American popular music giants: Little Richard, Elvis Presley and Aretha Franklin. These performers gained world wide fame in the 1950s and 60s and remain influential in popular music today. Who are the pop music giants of tomorrow?

Television and the Cold War

By the 1970s, an increasingly large number of people were spending their leisure hours in front of the television. American exports, such as the prime-time soap opera *Dallas*, drew enormous audiences. The British Broadcasting Corporation found that imports cost one-tenth the price of producing home-grown programs. To counterbalance the American cultural invasion, government-regulated networks in European countries began offering a variety of domestic programs. Some of these, such as *Monty Python's Flying Circus*, were also well received by viewers in North America. And everywhere, sports telecasts, especially soccer, attracted ever-expanding audiences. As one historian put it: "The age of television turned the game into great theatre and the soccer players into superheroes. The teams had their own battle colours, legends, superstitions, groupies, and sacred victories."

The subtitle of the anti-war satire *Dr. Strangelove* is How I Learned to Stop Worrying and Love the Bomb. What does the subtitle say about the mood of the times?

The Beatles led what became known as the "British Invasion" of rock groups in the early 1960s. Forty years later, the two surviving band members, Paul McCartney and Ringo Starr were still part of the popular music scene around the world.

Both older and newer cultural media reflected the anxieties and opposing ideologies of the Cold War. The U.S.S.R. and the U.S. portrayed each other as aggressive and evil. All forms of culture, from live theatre to comic book heroes became outlets for this propaganda. Arthur Miller's *Death of a Salesman* (1949) became a hit in live theatre in Moscow in the 1960s, along with Soviet plays promoting the socialist agenda. Soviet leaders felt that Miller's classic play displayed the true, darker character of capitalist society.

The Soviet government, in turn, promoted classical Russian texts that glorified the history of the nation. The works of Maxim Gorky (1868–1936) and Nobel laureate Mikhail Sholokhov (1905–1984) were printed in the millions. Novels that were considered too "pessimistic" such as those written by Fodor Dostoyevsky (1821–1881) and Alexander Solzhenitsyn were kept from the public. One notable exception was Solzhenitsyn's *One Day in the Life of Ivan Denisovich*, a story about forced labour camps under Stalin, which was authorized by Premier Khrushchev in his own fight against Stalin's political legacy. Not until Mikhail Gorbachev came to power in 1985 were restrictions on what Soviet citizens could read gradually lifted.

Cold War fiction of the West written by British authors Ian Fleming, John LeCarré, and Frederick Forsyth was immensely popular, selling in the millions. Another bestselling Cold War tale was Nevil Shute's *On the Beach* (1957), the story of how radioactive fall-out destroyed life in the northern hemisphere after a nuclear attack. Many of these novels would become popular films such as *The Spy Who Came in from the Cold* and *From Russia with Love*, a James Bond movie with several Soviet villains.

In Hollywood, the Cold War was reflected in blatantly nationalistic films such as *Big Jim McLain* (1952), starring John Wayne hunting for "commies" in Hawaii, and *I Married a Communist* (1950), which warned against the threat of communist sympathizers in local communities. The tone changed in the 1960s, when political satire became fashionable. Examples of this are *Dr. Strangelove* (1963), the final scene of which shows a crazed American pilot riding like a cowboy on a nuclear bomb headed for the U.S.S.R., and *The Manchurian Candidate* (1962), about a decorated veteran of the Korean War who is programmed or "brainwashed" by the enemy to assassinate politicians.

America was not without its own period of censorship and political persecution in the name of national security. In the early 1950s, the House Un-American Activities Committee, guided by Senator Joe McCarthy, descended on Hollywood and Capitol Hill looking for suspected "commies" and "reds" (it was illegal to be a member of a communist party in the U.S. at that time). The lives and careers of numerous "blacklisted" Hollywood writers and actors were ruined during this campaign, considered one of the darkest periods in the history of the United States.

Popular television shows of the 1950s such as *Leave it to Beaver* and *Father Knows Best* were pure escapism and promotion for traditional family values. Cold War themes were later woven more explicitly into the story lines of shows of the 1960s and 1970s, such as *All in the Family*, M*A*S*H, and *Star Trek*.

Popular Soviet music was expected to centre on the superiority and beauty of life under socialism. In the Soviet Union, protest songs had to be sung in private. In North America, protest songs could go to the top of the pop charts. Barry McGuire's 1965 hit *Eve of Destruction* was a number-one hit in the folk-rock category. Among Bob Dylan's many songs of rebellion and protest, *A Hard Rain's A-Gonna Fall* (1963) was inspired by the Cuban Missile Crisis. Anti-war songs, inspired

by the Vietnam War, were a nearly inseparable part of youth culture of the 1960s. A resurgence of Cold War–type songs occurred in the 1980s with bands such as Britain's The Clash with *London Calling* and Germany's Nena with its international hit *99 Luftballons* — a protest song about children accidentally triggering a nuclear holocaust with their toy balloons.

Review, Reflect, Respond

1. Explain why the Cuban Missile Crisis was a turning point for East-West relations.

2. In what ways did the arts, and pop culture in particular, reflect the anxiety generated by the Cold War?

3. If you were a teenager in the 1950s or 1960s, which movement(s) might you have found the most appealing — existentialism, the women's movement, or the human rights movement? Explain your answer.

BIG SCIENCE

Space

The years after 1945 were years of complex and expensive scientific and technological innovation, hence the term "big science." Science was viewed as a tool to make life better and safer for consumers and citizens. The space programs of both the United States and the U.S.S.R. were based on great advances in pure science, applied technologies, and enormous government funding. Governments in Europe also invested large sums in research and development programs. The number of scientists grew tremendously in the postwar years, and increased specialization led to the development of co-operative and competitive scientific communities and bureaucracies. In the late 1950s, the Soviets launched the Sputnik satellites into orbit around the Earth. This would lead U.S. President John

F. Kennedy to proclaim in 1961 that the United States would put a man on the moon and return him safely to Earth by the end if the decade.

Computers

One major technological development was the computer. During World War II, for instance, British mathematician Alan Turing helped design a computer that the Allies used to decode German intelligence messages. The first computer as we think of them was nicknamed "Colossus" because it was huge, noisy, and slow. Rapid advances in computer technology soon made Colossus look like an antique. Digital electronic circuits embedded on tiny microchips replaced the radio tubes used in earlier generations of computers. The microchip shrank computers from the size of a gymnasium in the 1940s, to the size of a small desk in the 1970s, and the size of a briefcase by the 1980s. Not only were computers getting smaller, they also became faster, more powerful, and inexpensive enough for ordinary consumers to buy. The effects computers have and will have on our society are only beginning to be understood. Computers have revolutionized nearly every aspect of life on (and sometimes off) our planet.

Biotechnology

Dramatic developments in biology also took place after World War II. Beginning in 1951, and based on the work of British biophysicist Rosalind Franklin,

This computer from 1955 took up an entire room but was less powerful than a desk top computer today. What invention allowed computers to get smaller, faster, and cheaper?

scientists Francis Crick and James Watson uncovered the molecular structure of DNA (deoxyribonucleic acid), the chemical that makes up the genetic structure of all living things. This discovery made the identification and manipulation of genes possible, and has led to a multitude of applications in agriculture and medicine, and a new field called biotechnology. The Human Genome Project, ongoing since 1990, now has a map of all human genes. This project, initiated by departments in the U.S. government can only lead to further exploration and understanding of the nature of human life. Along with these developments, the field of bioethics must try to keep up with and keep open the moral and ethical questions that arise as a result.

Lasers moved out of the realm of science fiction into daily life; an especially important application developed was the use of lasers in micro-surgery. New materials, such as plastics and optical fibre, appeared on the market for numerous purposes, from communications to toys. Chemical fertilizers increased agricultural yields dramatically. Antibiotics were mass-produced and many infectious diseases became curable. The contraceptive pill gave women greater control over their fertility. Sixteenth-century thinkers had dreamed that science would one day allow people to control nature and improve human life. At no time did this dream seem closer to reality than in the first generation after World War II.

www.mcgrawhill.ca/links/legacy

Go to the site above to find out more about DNA and biotechnology.

Environmentalism

Cold War scientific research was overwhelmingly geared to military purposes, and according to one estimate, one-quarter of all scientists in the United States and the U.S.S.R. were conducting military research. The weaponry of the Cold War cost the U.S. and the U.S.S.R.

trillions of dollars. But the downside of technological progress soon became clear. The run-off from farms using chemical fertilizers damaged streams and polluted drinking water. Genetic engineering facilitated the development of biological weapons.

It became increasingly obvious that unbridled technological progress could be dangerous to our health. The millions of cars on European roads gave their drivers mobility but also contributed to traffic congestion and air pollution. Nitrous oxide emissions and factory gases fell as acid rain that "killed" lakes, rivers, and forests. In response to decreasing world air quality and after deadly smog outbreaks in London, New York and Los Angeles, the First International Air Pollution Conference was held in 1955.

The 1960s and 1970s saw increased awareness of the need for environmental management and protection. The "oil crisis" of the 1970s, when the price of oil skyrocketed and fuel was in short supply, forced many people to conserve energy out of economic necessity. Greenpeace and other NGOs received a great deal of attention with their dramatic tactics for protecting whales. The U.S. Environmental Protection Agency was born, as natural habitats, food, and water supplies became affected by toxic chemicals.

By the late 1970s, a variety of groups began to raise their voices in protest against environmental degradation. Not all environmental groups had the same goals: some were nature conservationists; more radical groups wanted a return to a simpler way of life, going "back to the land"; still others felt that it was possible to balance economic growth with a concern for the environment. Environmentalists became a major political force.

The 1980s produced a number of large-scale environmental catastrophes. In 1984 a lethal chemical leak in Bhopal, India, claimed eight thousand lives initially, and eventually affected over five hundred thousand people. The Chernobyl disaster (1986) caused radioactive material to contaminate Belarus in the Ukraine for 10 days. Some six hundred thousand people were involved in the clean-up and many died or developed various radiation-related illnesses. According to CNN sources, the Ukrainian government now says that hundreds of thousands of people today still suffer Chernobyl-related illnesses. A decade later, many babies born to inhabitants in the Chernobyl area were being born deformed as a result of radiation. In 1989 the *Exxon Valdez* oil tanker leaked 11 million gallons of crude oil onto Alaskan shores, severely damaging the ecosystem for years to come.

Many thoughtful people began to question the values of industrial society and the damage to the environment it was causing. "The modern industrial system," wrote British economist E. F. Schumacher (1911–1977) in his popular book *Small is Beautiful* (1973), "consumes the very basis on which it has been erected." This happens through wasteful use of fossil fuels and other natural resources. What was needed was a new lifestyle, one that relied on "small-scale ... relatively non-violent technology." Schumacher described this as "technology with a human face." His new philosophy of life led many people to change their lifestyles to varying degrees, from abandoning city life to live in the country, to buying only "organically grown" vegetables from the supermarket.

Rachel Carson, a biologist and writer, is said by many to have launched the environmental movement with the publication of her ground-breaking book *Silent Spring* (1962). In her book, Carson challenged the common belief that science was always a force for good, and called for a change in the way the public, scientists, and governments viewed the natural world. Technological developments that caused the destruction of nature could no longer be called progress.

Many environmentalists point to the first photographs of the Earth, taken during space flights in the 1960s, as another impetus for a pivotal change in public attitudes. Never before had people seen their little blue planet in all its beauty and fragility. The traditional Western view of the Earth as an inexhaustible resource exclusively at the disposal of human need was increasingly unacceptable. In the 1990s, environmental issues received more attention than ever before. In June 1992, the UN Conference on Environment and Development, later named the "Earth Summit," was held. Over 178 nations met to discuss sustainable development. This gathering represented the first attempt at global environmental co-operation.

THE POST-STALIN SOVIET UNION

Party Politics

On paper, the Soviet Union appeared to have one of the most democratic constitutions in the world. In reality, the Communist Party dominated the political system. It was a very select group comprising about 10 percent of the population. Within the party, the post of general secretary was the most important. From 1922 until the time of his death from a heart attack in 1953, Joseph Stalin held this post. Stalin rewarded very generously the members of the party whose loyalty was unquestioned. They enjoyed many privileges: jobs, good apartments, country homes, travel privileges, better education for their children, and access to shops selling Western goods. But privileged positions depended on Stalin's whim. A secret police force reporting directly to Stalin kept tabs on potential dissidents. A misstep of some kind, a remark made to the wrong person, could result in instant dismissal, trial, a sentence to work in a labour camp, or even death.

Soviet citizens had little freedom of movement. Peasants could not leave their farms because they lacked the necessary papers giving them permission to move, and workers had to carry their job record with them at all times. Many Soviet soldiers came home from German prisoner-of-war camps only to find themselves shipped off to labour camps. This was because, in Stalin's view, soldiers who surrendered — even if they had no choice but to do so — were traitors whose exposure to Western ways undermined their loyalty to the Soviet system.

After the Iron Curtain descended, contact with non-communist countries was severely restricted. No dissent of any kind was tolerated. Children were encouraged to inform on their parents; neighbours on one another. And yet, when Stalin died, thousands of people filled the streets of Moscow to mourn him, and

Rachel Carson

> The more clearly we can focus our attention on the wonders and realities of the universe about us, the less taste we shall have for destruction.[2]
>
> *Rachel Carson*

In 1992 a panel of distinguished Americans declared Rachel Carson's *Silent Spring* the most influential book of the past 50 years. Published in 1962, this landmark work is credited with launching the modern environmental movement.

Biologist, writer, and ecologist Rachel Carson (1907–1964) earned a bachelor's degree in biology and a master's degree in zoology from Johns Hopkins University. She then began a 15-year career in the United States federal service as a scientist and editor, and rose to the position of Editor-in-Chief of all publications for the United States Fish and Wildlife Service.

In her private time, Carson wrote many successful and critically acclaimed books that combined her knowledge of science with her highly poetic writing style. Among these were *Under the Sea Wind* (1941) and *The Sea Around Us* (1951). In 1952 she retired to write full-time and produced *The Edge of the Sea* in 1955. But Carson's most controversial and thought-provoking work was *Silent Spring*.

Rachel Carson told the world about the dangers of pesticides.

Immediately after World War II, the pesticide DDT had been hailed as a "saviour of mankind" for its success in controlling disease-carrying mosquitoes. A friend of Carson's, Olga Owens Huckins, who had established a bird sanctuary in Massachusetts, noticed that after government airplanes sprayed DDT over salt marshes to kill mosquitoes, the winds carried the spray over the surrounding area, killing grasshoppers, bees, and birds. Huckins asked Carson to petition federal authorities to investigate the widespread use of pesticides like DDT.

Carson thought the most effective tactic would be to write a magazine article, and this eventually grew into her book *Silent Spring*. She drew on her contacts in the scientific community, consulting biologists, chemists, entomologists and pathologists, and spent four years meticulously gathering and analysing data.

Silent Spring appeared in the *New Yorker* magazine in a three-part condensed version beginning June 16, 1962. The entire book was published in September, and in it Carson identified the damaging, long-term effects on the environment of pesticides such as DDT.

When portions of *Silent Spring* first appeared in the *New Yorker*, they drew an aggressive response from the chemical industry. Carson's opponents questioned her data, her interpretation of the data, her scientific credentials, and then dismissed her as a food-faddist, bird watcher, and "nature nut." They ignored her university degree and experience as a Fish and Wildlife Service biologist, and a *Time* magazine review described Carson's argument as "unfair, one-sided, and hysterically over-emphatic."

> *Silent Spring* caused more uproar ... than any book by a woman author since *Uncle Tom's Cabin* started a great war.[3]
>
> *Reporter Adela Rogers St. Johns*

Rachel Carson, the mother of environmentalism

The powerful pesticide industry grossly distorted Carson's work. It claimed that if her demand to ban all pesticides — a demand Carson never actually made — were followed, America would plunge into a new Dark Age. Insect pests would devour the U.S. food supply and insect carriers, such as mosquitoes, would spread disease everywhere. One chemical corporation even sent a letter to Carson's publisher recommending that the company abandon its plan to publish *Silent Spring*, implying that the work was part of a communist conspiracy.

One obvious way to try to weaken a cause is to discredit the person who champions it. Anyone who really read the book knows that I criticize the modern chemical method not because it controls harmful insects but because it controls them badly and inefficiently and creates many dangerous side effects in doing so.

Rachel Carson, 1962 Speech to Women's National Press Club

Unbiased commentators and reviewers, however, applauded Carson's courage for writing a book on such a difficult and controversial subject.

Despite her battle with breast cancer, Carson participated in a promotional book tour for *Silent Spring* and made public appearances to defend her views. A special CBS television broadcast, "The Silent Spring of Rachel Carson," which aired on April 3, 1963, pitted Carson against a chemical company spokesman. Carson's cool-headed and well-reasoned approach won her many fans and brought national attention to the problem of pesticide use.

Largely as a result of the public outcry generated by Carson's book, President John F. Kennedy appointed a special panel of his Science Advisory Committee to study the issue. The panel's 1963 report supported most of Carson's conclusions, and in 1969 the United States government took steps to ban the use of DDT. In addition, many laws were passed regulating the use of other chemicals that could harm human beings and the environment. In 1970, largely due to Carson's influence, the United States Environmental Protection Agency (EPA) was formed.

Perhaps Carson's most important legacy lies in her reshaping of the way the American public views nature and the environment. Before Carson's *Silent Spring*, for many Americans, the notion of spending time and effort to keep the atmosphere and water supply clean was almost incomprehensible.

Conservation is a cause that has no end. There is no point at which we will say "our work is finished."

Rachel Carson, on receiving an Audubon Medal

1. Why did the chemical companies react so aggressively to Carson's book?

2. Investigate an NGO involved in protecting the environment in some way and write a one-page summary of its activities. Possible organizations include: The World Wildlife Fund, The Sierra Club, Greenpeace, Pollution Probe, or other similar groups.

hundreds were trampled to death in the rush. Even prisoners in camps wept. Stalin had dominated Soviet society and government for so long that people could not imagine life without his leadership.

Nikita Khrushchev took the post of secretary of the Communist Party in 1954. Born to a peasant family, he had risen through the ranks to the post of party secretary in Ukraine. In style, Khrushchev was different from Stalin: He mingled with people on the street, laughed, joked, and argued with them; he was more of a Western-style politician.

The differences between Khrushchev and Stalin went beyond political style. This became clear when Khrushchev delivered his 1956 "secret speech" to the 20th Party Congress. To a largely incredulous audience, Khrushchev denounced the cult of personality fostered by Stalin. He described in gruesome detail the cruel repression, the mass arrests and deportations, and the executions without trial that had decimated party ranks during the 1930s. Khrushchev exposed Stalin's refusal to believe the intelligence reports warning of a German invasion in 1941. He accused Stalin of perverting the Leninist heritage. Though Khrushchev made no mention of the millions of ordinary people who had died in the camps, news of his secret speech leaked out and shook Soviet society. A policy of de-Stalinization had begun.

Khrushchev ended Stalin's politics of terror. He dealt with two of his rivals by making one ambassador to Outer Mongolia, and the other a manager of a hydro-electric station; Stalin would have had both of them shot. Stalin's portraits and statues disappeared from public places; history books were rewritten; people were released from labour camps and their reputations rehabilitated. More freedom of thought was permitted. "Readers should be allowed to make their own judgments," declared Khrushchev. Some authors had their works published for the first time. Alexander Solzhenitsyn's novel *One Day in the Life of Ivan Denisovich* overwhelmed readers with its description of life in a labour camp. Poet Yevgeny Yevtushenko published *Babi Yar*, a poem describing the slaughter of Jews by Nazis during the war, and their burial in a mass grave near Kiev. Indirectly, it suggested that anti-Semitism was still alive in the U.S.S.R., since the grave near Kiev was being used as a garbage dump.

Such changes marked an easing of repression, not the creation of an open society. Dissidents criticizing the system were still persecuted. Some were confined to psychiatric hospitals for re-education, while others were ridiculed by the press or, as in the case of the physicist Andrei Sakharov, exiled to a remote town.

Khrushchev's de-Stalinization program contributed to his own downfall by threatening the privileges and positions of high party officials, many of whom had gone along with Stalin's use of terror. Moreover, Khrushchev's rather crude political style was not always in good taste. When he pounded his shoe on his desk to make a point during a speech to the UN General Assembly in 1960, his colleagues cringed with embarrassment. The details of his secret speech leaked out, encouraging rebellion. Strikes and demonstrations broke out in Poland, and when Hungary rose up in revolt in 1956, Soviet troops invaded to restore order. Khrushchev also failed to prevent a rupture with China in 1961. The confrontation over Cuba in 1962 ended in a humiliating retreat for the Soviet Union. And his attempts at economic reform did not live up to expectations. For all these reasons, Khrushchev's colleagues in the Communist Party ousted him in 1964. The official party newspaper denounced Khrushchev's "harebrained schemes."

Change and Continuity: Brezhnev Takes Control

One of those who had conspired against Khrushchev was his successor, Leonid Brezhnev. Brezhnev's tenure as general secretary of the Communist Party and premier of the Soviet Union (1964–1982) marked a trend toward a more collective style of leadership. The good-natured Brezhnev collected luxury cars and believed in "live and let live." What this meant in practice was that Communist Party members enjoyed more privileges. He did not continue Khrushchev's de-Stalinization

U.S. President Jimmy Carter and Soviet Premier Leonid Brezhnev. Brezhnev ordered the invasion of Afghanistan in 1979. What was the result?

policy but he did not fill the labour camps again. Brezhnev's most notable failure was the invasion of Afghanistan in 1979, a war that for the Soviets, was in many ways comparable to the American intervention in Vietnam. After the attack on the World Trade Centre in New York City on September 11, 2001, war in Afghanistan resumed, this time with the United States and its allies east and west fighting what was called the "War on Terrorism."

In the mid-1970s, public confidence in the communist system plummeted. The Soviet Union was unwilling or unable to suppress dissent by force. Developing nations also lost faith in the communist system. Overly centralized economies had not proven successful at improving standards of living. Defectors to the West, among them Alexander Solzhenitsyn, all had their own stories of persecution to tell. *Samizdat* (secret publications), books, articles, and newspapers linked dissenters in an underground network of opposition. Many Soviet citizens became increasingly disturbed by the growing corruption in the Party and

very cynical about the values of communism. The momentum for change was building.

The Soviet Bloc

All Soviet satellites had a common postwar experience. At first, Soviet troops were welcomed as liberators from Nazi brutality, but liberation soon turned into occupation and the imposition of a communist government. This process also went through three stages: first, communists co-operated with other parties to form a "popular front," then coalition governments were formed in which communists held key posts. Finally, a communist-dominated government led by a "little Stalin," a puppet approved by Moscow, was permanently installed.

What made the process of imposing communist governments easier was the lack of democratic traditions in Eastern Europe. Nevertheless, it was not possible to repress all opposition. Strikes and demonstrations did break out from time to time and were put down by force if necessary. In Poland, the Catholic Church served as a focus for opposition. In all countries, an underground literary network similar to that in the Soviet Union began to grow in importance, and on occasion, Soviet-bloc countries introduced policies that ran counter to Moscow's initiatives. For example, in 1956 Khrushchev's secret speech on de-Stalinization prompted Hungarian leaders, led by Imre Nagy to de-collectivize agriculture, leave the Warsaw Pact, and declare Hungary a neutral state in October 1956. The Soviet response was an invasion and a return to the old system.

Another example was Czechoslovakia in 1968. Alexander Dubcek, the Czech leader, decided to introduce what he called "socialism with a human face." The purpose was not to eliminate the communist system but to liberalize it, and with the Hungarian experience in mind, Dubcek declared that Czechoslovakia would remain within the Warsaw Pact. Even so, Moscow became alarmed. The period of reform, the so-called "Prague Spring" ended abruptly when Soviet tanks rolled into Czechoslovakia. The Soviets justified their intervention with the Brezhnev doctrine: "Every communist party was responsible not only to its own people but to those of other socialist countries." In other words, the Soviet Union had the right to intervene to bring any disobedient satellite back into line.

The Two Communist Societies

By the 1970s, a clear division between those who enjoyed the good life and those who continued to eke out a difficult existence had developed in the Soviet Union. This division was based on position in, and loyalty to, the Communist Party. The average Soviet citizen lived in a congested apartment and had to stand in long lines to get limited quantities of substandard food. Having lived through harder times in childhood, many were content to simply have food, a roof over

their heads, and work — regardless of what went on politically. Give us the material minimum. We won't ask for more." Few Soviet citizens complained openly of their situation. Many were content with a system that provided low-cost housing, free medical care, education, and a guaranteed job.

There was no shortage of material goods for the elite members of the Communist Party. Stores, open only to a select few, were shelved with luxury foods and items imported from the West, such as Belgian chocolate, French wine, Scotch whisky, American cigarettes, Italian ties, and Japanese stereos — all at cut-rate prices. Party leaders lived in large, often hidden, mansions provided free by the state. Some even had private beaches.

By the 1970s, rumblings of discontent were heard among the youth of the Soviet Union. Not having experienced the hardships of earlier generations, young people of the 1970s and 1980s were less willing

■ FIGURE 13.2 Europe in the Year 2000
Some people contend that the major wars of the twenty-first century will be economic ones. Is there current evidence that this is true?

to accept the long lines and lack of material goods, and unwilling to ignore the obvious discrepancies between the Communist Party elite and the majority of Soviet citizens. Although the authoritarian nature of the regime allowed little room for protest, the seedbed for change had been planted.

Life Behind the Iron Curtain

After World War II, the Soviet people were told that restoring the economy required sacrifices equal to those of war. As a result, the standard of living was barely better than it had been early in the century. Because so many men had died in the war, much of the burden fell on Soviet women, who performed up to 40 percent of heavy labour. Producing for export left little to invest in consumer goods or home construction. Urban workers lived in one-room apartments with a communal kitchen and bathroom. Those were the lucky ones, as many workers had to make do with shacks built of earth, cardboard planks, or anything else they could find. During the war, agriculture had been privatized to some degree, and peasants hoped that this trend would continue. Stalin, however, insisted on reinstating the collective farm system, with its low prices and quotas for the state. No exceptions were allowed under any circumstances. In 1946 drought gain hit Ukraine, the main grain-producing area of the Soviet Union. After giving their allotments to the state, millions were left to starve.

Even without natural disasters, under Stalin, agricultural productivity never did rise significantly. At the time of his death in 1953, grain production had dropped to 1913 levels, and there were fewer head of cattle than in 1916. The only sectors that showed improvement were heavy industries: iron, steel, and weapons.

Realizing the gravity of the situation, Nikita Khrushchev undertook an energetic program of economic reform. Khrushchev decentralized the economy and put more emphasis on the manufacture of consumer goods. He raised the prices paid to peasants and gave them more independence in managing the collective farms. During his visit to the United States,

Khrushchev was impressed by the vast fields of corn in the American Midwest. He encouraged Soviet farmers to plant corn to be used as cattle feed, but because the Soviet climate is colder than in the American Midwest, most of the corn froze. The Soviet Union found itself in the embarrassing position of having to import grain from its capitalist rivals the United States and Canada. Nevertheless, Khrushchev's reforms did bring improvements in the Soviet standard of living. The number of housing units doubled, and more consumer goods did become available.

Leonid Brezhnev did not do much more for the daily life of a Soviet citizen. The command economy with its five-year plans designed in Moscow was too rigid and could not be fixed by piecemeal reforms. Soviet citizens devised their own ways of coping and a flourishing underground economy developed. Private plots, which made up two to five percent of the agricultural land, produced 25 percent of the Soviet Union's food supply. Life was better in Eastern Europe, but not by much.

Communist leaders tried to persuade the people that socialism was a more just way of life and that capitalism was too materialistic. Because no contacts with the West were allowed, many Soviet citizens were persuaded that theirs was a superior system. By the 1970s, however, as channels of communication with the West opened and as the Cold War thawed, such propaganda became less and less convincing.

EUROPE: 1970s TO 1990s
The Oil Crisis

The Middle Eastern oil crisis of 1973 marked a turning point. Egypt and Syria attacked Israel, hoping to regain lost territory. Their offensive failed but the oil-producing countries of the Middle East, members of OPEC (Organization of Petroleum Exporting Countries), put an embargo on crude-oil shipments to Europe to show their dissatisfaction with the support that Western nations were showing Israel. OPEC eventually lifted the embargo but raised oil prices considerably. The price of oil went from US$2 a barrel to US$30 within a few years. The higher price for oil soon translated into higher prices for consumer goods and greater wage demands.

In addition to the oil price hike, other factors contributed to an ongoing recession. The demand for consumer goods, which had fuelled the European economy in the postwar period, slowed down. European manufacturers found themselves competing against more aggressive manufacturers in Southeast Asia and Japan. Factories shut down and people lost jobs, and unemployed workers cannot afford consumer goods. The end result was called "stagflation": a stagnant economy with rising prices.

Europe in the 1980s

Some measure of prosperity returned in the 1980s but not to all sectors of European society. High unemployment, averaging 11 percent, persisted. "Deindustrialization" began to transform the European workplace. New computer-assisted technologies needed fewer workers, and these workers needed different skills. European nations turned increasingly to international trade agreements to stabilize and stimulate their economies. The European Union was formed in 1993 by 12 European nations. The aim of the union was to create a Europe without borders, with a common currency, financial and immigration policies, and a military force. The currency, called the "Euro," was introduced in January 1999 to 11 EU members and replaced national currencies in 2002. The United Kingdom was among the nations that chose not to introduce the new currency at that time.

The World Trade Organization (WTO) and the Group of 20 (G20) are two other major economic organizations. The purpose of the WTO and Group of 20 is to develop a stable and predictable global economy. Vocal critics claim that these organizations represent only the interests of Western developed nations, that they are anti-democratic in their structure and policies and that they are a threat to national sovereignty and represent a potentially cruel and extreme form of free enterprise that will harm millions

Conservative Prime Minister Margaret Thatcher of Britain meeting here with Mikhail Gorbachev, Communist Party Secretary of the Soviet Union.

of people worldwide. Supporters say they have a positive mandate in promoting fair trade, arms control, anti-terrorism, and greater economic growth for all nations. These differing world visions (globalization versus "anti-globalization") are the main source of conflict in international disputes. An alliance of all G20 nations and others to fight terrorism after the attacks on New York in September 2001 demonstrates a new collective will to eradicate threats to democratic governments and global economic stability.

Political Action

By the end of the 1970s, a growing number of people, especially the unemployed, felt alienated from a society that had no place for them. Respect for traditional institutions declined. In one country after another, people felt a growing sense of frustration with political systems that did not seem to offer voters much choice. Over the years, both socialists and conservatives had moved their platforms toward the middle of the political spectrum: Conservatives could support the welfare state while socialists could accept some forms of capitalism.

Frustration found various outlets. In Italy, the so-called "hot autumn" of 1969 brought with it a wave of strikes and demonstrations. Terrorism became more common during the 1970s, especially by the Baader-Meinhof Group in Germany, which attacked American army bases and assassinated industrialists, judges, and political leaders. Computerized tracking of suspects eventually brought an end to this movement.

In Italy, a similar situation arose with the terrorist Red Brigades. Like the German terrorists, Brigade members came from affluent middle-class families and believed that, without revolutionary terrorism, capitalism would never change. The climax of their terrorist campaign came in 1978, when they kidnapped and killed former Italian prime minister Aldo Moro. This act of terror turned public opinion against the activists. Organizations such as the Irish Republican Army (IRA) and various other terrorist groups with Middle Eastern connections carried out acts of violence designed to draw attention to their demands.

The appearance of various environment-oriented parties throughout Europe signalled yet another trend. The Green Party, an environmental group in Germany, was first elected to the *Bundestag* in 1983. The Greens' unconventional dress (jeans) symbolized their determination not to act like a regular political party. But unlike the student radicals of the 1960s, the Greens rejected confrontational tactics.

German government reports on the environment had shown that an alarming number of trees were sick or dying; much of the famous Black Forest in southern Germany was damaged. Initially, the Greens attracted support from the German public, but they failed to maintain it. Divisions between those who wanted fundamental change and those who were prepared to work within the system persisted in the movement. By the 1990s, the Greens and their allies were still a part

of the German political scene, but their concerns did not dominate to the extent they had in the 1980s.

Yet another significant political trend was a re-evaluation of the welfare state. A depressed economy and an aging population made it more expensive to maintain, while a declining birth rate lowered the tax base. Governments faced a dilemma: either cut back on the benefits provided by the state or raise taxes.

Just as Britain had led the postwar introduction of the welfare state, so it led in its partial dismantling. In 1979 the Conservative government of Margaret Thatcher trimmed health and unemployment benefits and cut back on university funding. Prime Minister Thatcher also abandoned interventionist economic policies. She sold off municipal housing to working-class people and privatized industries. She went on to defeat the coal miners' union in the course of a long and bitter strike. At first, the British economy, aided by the North Sea oil fields, responded to the hard medicine of the "Iron Lady" and productivity soared. By the 1990s, however, Britain was once again in a recession. Thatcher's failed attempt to introduce an extremely unpopular poll tax forced her to resign. Nevertheless, her neo-conservative approach found followers even in socialist circles. Governments in other parts of Europe began to adopt similar policies. In France, the socialist government of François Mitterrand began its 14-year term of office in 1981 with a socially progressive political program but was forced to make modifications. In Sweden, where the welfare state had been most highly developed, cutbacks were also imposed.

Regardless of the political turmoil that Europe experienced during the 1970s and 1980s, the commitment to democracy in Europe remained firm. Social and economic problems did not lead to dictatorships. In France, Georges Pompidou succeeded de Gaulle after the 1968 student revolt, but the Fifth Republic did not fall. Despite the rise of neo-Nazi groups, Germany remained committed to democratic values and integration with Europe. Italy was plagued by corruption and constant changes of government, but no Mussolini stood in the wings waiting to exploit the situation. This is in marked contrast to the events of the

1930s, when some European nations chose authoritarian solutions to their political and economic problems.

Review, Reflect, Respond

1. What are some of the potential dangers that can arise when advances in technology are not accompanied by changes in government policies?

2. How did communist countries try to convince their citizens of the superiority of the communist system? Did they succeed?

3. Do the events of the 1970s and 1980s suggest that the welfare state is unsustainable? Explain the ideological shift that brought the welfare state under attack.

THE COLLAPSE OF COMMUNISM AND THE END OF THE COLD WAR

The U.S.S.R. in Decline

In Eastern Europe and the Soviet Union, fragmentation rather than unity characterized the political scene in the 1980s. The collapse of the communist system in the U.S.S.R. and the Soviet-dominated Eastern bloc was one of the most dramatic and unexpected political processes of the twentieth century.

By the time of Leonid Brezhnev's death in 1982, conditions in the Soviet Union had deteriorated dangerously. Despite attempts at reform, the country remained economically backward compared with Western Europe. The problems within Soviet society seemed endless and insurmountable: too much spending diverted to military purposes, the failure of collectivized agriculture, inefficient central planning, rampant industrial pollution, and widespread alcoholism. It was against this backdrop that Mikhail Gorbachev arrived on the scene. No one would have guessed that the likable party man Gorbachev was a revolutionary in the making. He believed in the superiority of communism but, at the same time, he was ready to confront his country's problems and was sure that they could be overcome. He had charm and made skilful use of the mass media in trying to get his views across. After his election in 1984 to the post of Communist Party Secretary, Gorbachev began to implement reforms.

Gorbachev's Second Revolution

Gorbachev's "second revolution," as he described it, was based on two principles. One was *glasnost*, or openness. This meant free expression of political opinions, the loosening of centralized Communist Party structures, and more democracy in political life. The second principle was *perestroika*, or rebuilding. It entailed decentralizing the Soviet economy, putting more stress on personal initiative, and curtailing vodka sales. Taken together, the changes proposed by Gorbachev amounted to the most important reform package since the ill-fated attempt by Khrushchev to change Soviet society 20 years earlier.

Unfortunately, what happened was called, by some, "catastroika." Stalin had established a centralized command economy. No one republic was self-sufficient; all had to rely on others for goods and services. For example, all of the Soviet Union's locomotives were assembled in Ukraine but 800 different factories throughout the Soviet Union supplied the parts. The problems involved in transforming this method of manufacturing were tremendous. Gorbachev did propose a 500-day plan in 1990 to privatize 80 percent of the economy, but he encountered a great deal of opposition from party officials opposed to reforms. The transition to privatization risked throwing many out of work. Mismanagement and distribution problems worsened the situation. In some areas, crops rotted in the fields; in others, farmers withheld grain from the market. As a result, the Soviet Union experienced the worst economic conditions since 1945. The visible signs of this deterioration included beggars in the streets, shortages of housing, food, basic commodities, a booming black market, and a decline in the quality of healthcare.

The Chernobyl nuclear disaster in 1986 and the withdrawal of the Soviet army from Afghanistan added to the demoralization in Soviet society. While Gorbachev became a hero to the West, to Soviet citizens he was a failure.

The Rise and Fall of Boris Yeltsin

Before long, Gorbachev lost control of the situation. *Glasnost* led ultimately to a rejection not only of Stalinism but also of Leninism and the communist system. In 1990 Boris Yeltsin, chairman of the Russian parliament, took Russia out of the embattled Soviet Union and resigned from the Communist Party. The following year, he was elected president of the Russian Republic. Disgruntled army officers attempted to reverse the reform process by forcing Gorbachev from office. Yeltsin became the focus of resistance, and the revolt collapsed. The Communist Party was disbanded and Gorbachev, premier of a non-existent Soviet Union and head of an illegal party, was out of a job. Boris Yeltsin sustained several key changes in the new Russia. Freedom of speech and of the press, freedom of political opposition, and the introduction of private property and a market economic were indeed revolutionary changes for the Russian people. By the end of 1991, 13 of the 15 Soviet republics had declared their independence.

The U.S.S.R. had been a multi-ethnic empire consisting of 92 nationalities and 112 languages. The Communist Party in Moscow had repressed religious, ethnic, and national feelings with an iron hand and used propaganda to promote the concept of the Soviet citizen. With *glasnost* and the relaxation of central control, old tensions surfaced. Nationalist movements called for independence. Fourteen former republics obtained independence, including the Baltic areas, Ukraine, Belarus, Georgia, and the Muslim republics in the south. The Soviet Union was dismembered in 1991 and replaced with the Commonwealth of Independent States.

The end of communism brought sighs of relief to many. In their euphoria, however, people failed to realize how hard it would be to transform a command economy into a free-market system. In the meantime, the output of Russian factories fell dramatically after 1990. For many Russians, especially for the poor and elderly, living conditions continued to worsen. Inflation made their savings worthless; crime became a problem. Racism against *Roma* (gypsies) and other ethnic and religious minorities increased. Alcoholism reached critical proportions (two-thirds of Russian men die as a direct result of drunkenness). To complicate matters, Russians had to devise a democratic political system at the same time as they reformed their economy. They had no democratic traditions in their past to guide them. With free elections, all kinds of splinter parties appeared, creating confusion and cynicism among the people. Not surprisingly, for many people a nostalgia for Stalin and the days when the Soviet Union was a feared and respected superpower remained.

Continual political and economic crises, personal health problems and several failed impeachment attempts challenged Yeltsin's leadership. In March 2000, Yeltsin finally resigned and Vladimir Putin was elected president. Putin, a former secret service head, seemed determined to build a stronger central government in Moscow to tackle Russia's complex problems. He wanted to reform ancient tax laws, encourage foreign investment, boost exports, and provide social programs. Conflict with rebels in Chechnya who wanted to secede from the Russian Federation brought Putin popular support at home but international criticism for Russia's excessive use of force against rebels and civilians. Russians wanted peace but at the same time feared that other ethnic areas would demand independence, and create more problems for the new Russian state.

The end of the communist regime and the introduction of democracy and free enterprise has thrust Russians into a world of choices completely new to them. The challenges they face in the coming decades, as they embrace the virtues and vices of free enterprise and individual freedoms, will more profoundly reshape Eastern Europe than any other event in the past five centuries.

SOCIAL CHANGES AT THE TURN OF THE MILLENNIUM

Redefining the Family

Since the 1950s, we have developed a much broader concept of family. By the 1980s, two-parent families would occupy a mere 15 percent of North American households. Almost half of the children born in the 1980s would spend some of their early years in a single-parent environment, and the number of couples choosing to live together rather than marry quadrupled. By 1988 the number of married women working outside the home had risen to 60%. Some moralists see these changes as a loss of universal "family values" and blame the ills of society on changes to the traditional family. Others view these changes as progressive, beneficial, or merely part of a natural evolution of society.

Redefining Feminism

First-wave feminists focussed on achieving political rights. Second-wave feminism focussed on social and economic rights. The focus of third-wave feminists on individualism, sexuality, and power in the 1980s and '90s caused some feminists to feel that the movement was over. Others applauded this broader definition of feminism. It included racial, class, and global issues along with personal interests in culture, beauty, and sexuality.

A sampling of feminist literature in the 1990s reveals the broadening of feminist thought. Naomi Wolf, American author of *The Beauty Myth* (1990), said that women are extremely powerful and must use their power to bring about practical changes. Wolf discusses society's obsession with beauty and sexuality, and the negative impact this can have on even the most independent woman. Camille Paglia, a professor at the University of the Arts in Philadelphia, is a controversial feminist and writer who believes women must claim more personal responsibility for their lives and accept the dominant social position afforded women because of their sexuality. A woman named bell hooks [*sic*] is a professor and writer on gender, race, and mass media who, as a protest against patriarchy, does not capitalize her name. She critiques the idea of a "White Supremacist Capitalist Patriarchy" to stress the interconnectedness of the economic, social, and political issues she examines. The media, hooks asserts, makes feminism a struggle only against men and ignores the crucial factors of class and race. The work of Wolf, Paglia, and hooks demonstrates how women are exploring multiple perspectives on an expanding number of feminist issues.

THE ARTS AT THE TURN OF THE MILLENNIUM

High Art, Popular Art

Since World War II, art has taken many directions. Though artistic movements may often be reactions to previous art, artists remain occupied by all aspects of society — people, politics, religion, beauty, and truth. The viewers of art, listeners of music, and readers of literature have become increasingly viewed as consumers. It is often difficult to distinguish between "high" art and popular art. Artists respond increasingly to consumer demands.

Governments, corporations, and individual patrons remain important sources of funding and support for artists. The debate continues about what constitutes "real" art, music, and literature as opposed to what is commercially popular in a free market. Some would claim that there is no difference, and that those who attempt to distinguish high art from more accessible, popular works are supporting an artificial artistic elite.

Visual Art

Contemporary visual artists are so diverse that it is impossible to discuss all styles, techniques, and movements. Postmodernism is an artistic movement that rejects modernist art and its formal abstraction,

Study after Velasquez's Portrait of Pope Innocent X (1953) by Francis Bacon. As expressionist art, what feeling does this painting convey?

intellectualizing, non-emotional content, and rigid rules. Realism in various styles remains popular in the works of American artists such as Andrew Wyeth and Edward Hopper (1882–1967), and Canadians Alexander Colville, Christopher and Mary Pratt, and wildlife painter Robert Bateman. A return to the landscape genre may mirror the environmental concerns of the West in the past two decades.

Art that expresses strong feeling, called expressionism, was a direction in art that flourished after World War II. Typically, these paintings picture humanity as tormented, fractured and full of suffering. A work by Frances Bacon (1909–1992), *Study after Velasquez's Portrait of Pope Innocent X* (1953), depicts a screaming Pope, seemingly at the moment of his execution in the electric chair. Like Goya in the nineteenth century, Bacon condemns church and state in this work. Bacon's negative, even repulsive vision of

This construction is a white fabric fence that stretches 39 kilometres through two counties in California. In 1995, Christo, the artist, also finished the complete wrapping of the *Reichstag* in Berlin. It took 24 years and over a hundred thousand square metres of polypropylene fabric. What type of art would you call this?

the human condition expresses the effects of two horrific world conflicts on all the arts of Europe.

The second generation of postwar European artists freed itself from the first by establishing a Dada-like movement in art. For the most part, straight pictorial representations were abandoned. Artists made use of objects taken from everyday life, industry, and nature. Performance art had its beginning here with elaborate, theatrical presentations often involving other media. The main art movements during this time were new realism, pop art (popular art), constructive abstraction, op art (optical art), and kinetic art. The new realism involved the use of stark, shocking images often presented as pieces of theatre or sculptures made up of scrap or "junk." Bulgarian artist Christo is an example of a new-realist artist. Pop art, popularized by the works of Andy Warhol (1928–1987), reflected society's obsession with images in advertising and signs. English pop art championed by artists David Hockney and Allen Jones became a significant movement in the 1960s, coinciding with the emergence of the Beatles.

In the face of all these new experimental art forms, a group of artists, the Concrete Abstractionists, continued to express art in rigid, intellectual style involving hard, clean lines.

In a huge array of artistic styles, techniques, ideas, one truth exists — that all art portrays an adventure into or out of the human condition.

Contemporary Music

The music of the second half of the twentieth century can be divided into three types: classical, jazz, and rock. All three types have influenced each other and continue to do so. The new directions in the art world have been roughly parallelled by new directions in classical (some say "serious") music. Contemporary compositions may employ traditional instruments but forge new musical ideas. For example, some composers employ several instruments at once, each playing its own rhythm, which fluctuates at its own pace.

Others try to create a geometric pattern in their scores (the musical notation). Some combine these avant-garde elements with traditional pieces. In the decades after the war, in keeping with the new classicism in abstract painting, a movement developed to give greater structure to sound. The chief inventor of this movement was the German composer Arnold Schönberg (1874–1951). The result is a highly rational form of music based on very strict organization of all aspects of the piece.

In a completely opposite direction, there is the music of American composer John Cage. Just as French visual artist Marcel Duchamp wanted to let his work change or develop by chance, so John Cage's aim is to create music by chance. Cage is best known for his experimental works. For example, he may simply set a radio between stations and allow the resulting static to be his composition. In these types of works, the emphasis is on form. As in many types of contemporary art, content or meaning plays no role at all in the composition. The artist wants to express absolute freedom; the work of art creates its own pattern, its own structure. In contrast to the intellectual and experimental composers, was the composition and performance of the soft music of the new Romanticism. The new Romantic composers want to take music back to its traditional roots and appeal to the emotions again. Some composers of note are Samuel Barber (1910–1981), Ned Rorem, and Thea Musgrave.

Electronic Music

In the years following World War II, there was a technological revolution in the field of music. The first great advance was the use of magnetic tape to record sound, which made the manipulation and recording of sound much easier. Now artists could use not only natural sounds but also artificial sound. This, then, led to the development of instruments and equipment to create these sounds. One of the chief proponents of this experimental technique was Karlheinz Stockhausen in Germany in the early l950s. Production studios sprang up in Europe and the

United States. Composers immediately took advantage of these new opportunities to create new music.

The invention of synthesizers allowed composers to make sound and play with it all in one system, which made it easier to compose music; of course, smaller synthesizers could actually be played on stage. Today, the computer has become an important factor in musical composition of all genres, from classical to rock to jazz. One of the greatest proponents of electronic music was Edgard Varèse (1883–1963). Varèse rejected sounds made by traditional instruments; he wanted to create musical sounds that had never before been heard. He used a great deal of percussion to emulate the sounds of the urban landscape: horns, sirens, industrial tools at work. His music has been compared to abstract painting in its layering of sounds and rhythms.

Blues and Jazz

One of the most important types of contemporary music is jazz. This genre continues to grow in style and technique as it too has been influenced by postwar technology. Understanding the roots of jazz makes it easier to understand. At the beginning of the twentieth century, African-American music began to have a profound influence on the music of Europe and America. One of the first black American composers was Scott Joplin (1868–1917). Joplin made ragtime famous. He even wrote an opera based on ragtime forms. Stravinsky and Debussy were two European composers who were influenced by Joplin's music.

Blues developed from African-American folk music and spirituals. It is a simple, repetitive type of music that comes from the songs that American slaves sang at work. Blues varies in style from region to region in the United States. For example, the blues of the Mississippi Delta, sung by men such as Robert Johnson, has different characteristics from the blues of Chicago.

Jazz was born of a combination of blues, ragtime, and spirituals and is a music based on improvisation. New Orleans was the first great centre of jazz. Some of the most famous and influential musicians to come out of New Orleans were trumpeter Louis Armstrong (1901–1971) and his band, clarinetist Sidney Bechet (1897–1959) and pianist "Jelly Roll" Morton (1890–1941).

The 1920s and '30s came to be known as the big-band era. Big bands involve a much larger number of instruments than ragtime or jazz bands. There is usually a number of saxophones, trumpets, trombones, and lots of percussion. Big-band music is international, but it was the United States that again exerted the greatest influence. Duke Ellington (1899–1974) was a brilliant pianist; he was also a composer and orchestrator because the development of big bands meant that the music had to be written down. Other big bands of note were those of Tommy Dorsey (1905–1956), Woody Herman (1913–1987), and Glenn Miller (1905–1944).

The next important movement in jazz was bebop, which developed in the 1940s in reaction to the music of the big bands. Bebop jazz involved much smaller groups of musicians and much more improvisation. Great bebop musicians were Charlie Parker (1921–1955), Thelonious Monk (1917–1982), and Dizzy Gillespie (1917–1993). Their work is still a major influence in jazz today.

Rock-and-Roll

Like jazz and classical music, rock-and-roll has evolved to include a wide variety of styles, themes, and instrumentation. Rock-and-roll had its roots in American music and became a genre unto itself in the 1950s with artists such as Elvis Presley (1935–1977), Chuck Berry, and Buddy Holly (1936–1959). It appealed, for the most part, to youthful audiences and became, in one sense, a voice for youth. It was, and perhaps still is, a way for youth to express its concerns about life and love.

From the mid-twentieth century onward, every decade seems to have its own great rock movement. The music of the 1950s changed dramatically in the 1960s with the "British invasion" led by the Beatles. In the U.S., the late 1950s and early 1960s saw a revival of folk music. The advent of the hippie movement led

Alanis Morrisette is one of many Canadians to become music stars. Who are some of the others?

to psychedelic music. And, of course, all of these styles interacted with each other. The music of the l970s has been denigrated for its disco movement. In the late 1960s and early 1970s, popular music took a very serious turn when some musicians used it as a vehicle for protest against the war in Vietnam. The impetus for this protest was the huge rock festival in 1969 at Woodstock in New York. For three days, thousands of people gathered to celebrate life and music and give vent to the frustrations that had been voiced by the various protest movements of the 1960s, such as feminism, the struggle for civil rights, and the peace movement.

The 1980s saw a strong movement in popular music known as "new wave," or punk rock, which had its roots in England. Alternative music has come to refer, in a broad sense, to music that is not in the mainstream of popular culture. In the U.S. specifically,

alternative music refers to the "garage bands," such as Pearl Jam. However, there is also a powerful alternative movement in the popular music of Europe. In the mid-1990s, there continued to be a variety of styles, from a revival of regional folk music, to the birth of grunge and the popularity of rap music. Grunge is the name for a musical style. Rap music had its roots in street music in the African-American ghettos. African music, especially that of South Africa, has had a strong influence on all musical styles. Nevertheless, all musicians since the postwar era owe a debt to rhythm and blues, which remains a strong, steady force in music while fads and stars come and go.

One of the more recent phenomena in popular music is fusion. Fusion music is a blend of musical traditions from around the world. The African, Indian, and Cajun are just some of the musical traditions and techniques used. A growing number of classical, jazz, and rock musicians are now experimenting with new combinations of world music styles.

Contemporary Literature

New forms of literature have led to a new way of looking at literature. In the latter half of the twentieth century, literary criticism has become a genre unto itself. The various movements parallel similar movements in the art world. It is useful to discuss these movements, rather than try to discuss actual authors and works for two reasons. First, the literature of the last decades of the twentieth century is difficult to discuss in objective terms because we are still trying to place it in a context relevant to us. Second, many movements under critical discussion are linked to social and political movements and so are relevant to the study of history.

Theories of Literary Criticism

Just as expressionism opposes abstraction in art, subjectivism opposes objectivism in literature. Objectivists want readers to view the text as having its own language or set of signposts, ones we have not encountered before. They think that our approach to literature should be similar to our approach to mathematics. Readers should not project their own experiences onto the literature. The reader must be completely objective while analysing a work of literature; only then can he or she find the truth of a text.

Subjectivists feel that the reader is just as important as the author in the analysis of a literary work. Two major types of subjectivism include psychological criticism and historical criticism. Psychological criticism asserts the importance of the psyche of the author. The psychological theories of Freud and Jung are often applied to the behaviour of the characters in the literary work. Historical criticism looks at literature in a historical context. There are several approaches that involve history and culture:

- Dialoguism, the study of language and its importance to individuals and culture
- Marxist criticism, an analysis of literature in the context of class struggle and as a product of the struggle between classes

- Feminist criticism, the belief that literature reflects society and has an influence on society and all the resulting issues involving women
- New historicism, the belief that all literature is equally important for critical analysis, even those considered part of "popular culture"
- Deconstructionism, a literary theory that maintains that meaning in a text can only be derived from context and the relationship among words
- Postmodernism rejects all-encompassing theories such as modernism and Marxism and embraces diversity and multiple points of view

The many ways of viewing literature reflect social and political movements and issues. Regardless of the type of criticism the reader embraces (if any), the popularity of things such as television, on-line book discussion groups, and community book clubs reflects a renewed interest in fiction and the great impact that literature has on people's lives.

Reflections

In the postwar generations, Europe experienced a bewildering array of changes. Wartime devastation was followed by a spectacular economic recovery, domination by the superpowers, tensions arising from the Cold War and the breakup of the Soviet Union. Increasing globalization will also add to a multitude of challenges to established values and social structures.

Chapter Review

Chapter Summary

In this chapter, you have seen:

- How certain factors led to conflict and war during the Cold War era
- The influence of key individuals in promoting change, and the key elements and characteristics of change
- The extent to which art reinforces and/or challenges prevailing social and political values
- How national and international bodies attempted to recognize and enhance human rights

Reviewing the Significance of Key People, Concepts, and Events (Knowledge and Understanding)

1. Understanding the history of the Western world during the latter half of the twentieth century requires a knowledge of the following concepts, events, and people and an understanding of their significance in the shaping of the history of the contemporary Western world. Select and briefly explain two from each column.

People	Concepts	Events
Harry Truman	Cold War	Cuban Missile Crisis
Senator Joe McCarthy	International Monetary Fund	Chernobyl Disaster
Fidel Castro	Marshall Plan	Earth Summit
John F. Kennedy	North Atlantic Treaty Organization	
Mikhail Gorbachev	SALT	
Simone de Beauvoir	OPEC	
Rachel Carson	EU	

2. In a chart, list five examples of efforts undertaken since the end of World War II to seek and sustain peace. Explain each, and explain the reasons for their success or failure at maintaining international order.

Doing History: Thinking About the Past (Thinking/Inquiry)

3. Throughout this textbook, there has been an emphasis on ideas that have shaped the world. Historian Roland Stromberg wrote: "If the most urgent task confronting us is the organization of our ideas that they may be creatively used, and if these ideas indeed are 'the invisible powers that govern men,' then the systematic study of ideas would seem to be not the least important of the many studies currently pursued." Do you agree with Stromberg's assessment of the importance of the study of ideas? Defend your answer using historical evidence.

4. During the 1970s and 1980s, a debate emerged over whether deterrence (MAD) or disarmament was the best means to ensure peace. Explain which you believe was more important in preventing a major conflict between superpowers: the reality of MAD or efforts such as the SALT talks to limit the production of weapons?

Applying Your Learning (Application)

5. Andy Warhol used universally recognized images to comment on the mass reproduction of cultural icons. Do you think paintings such as *100 Cans* are great art? Explain your response to this painting. What message about society and its values do you find in this painting?

6. Were young people in the 1960s naive idealists? Did they succeed in bringing about significant change? Keeping these questions in mind, prepare 10 questions you might ask someone who was a young adult in the 1960s. Make sure that your questions address several of the important political, social, and economic issues addressed in this chapter.

Communicating Your Learning (Communication)

7. Create a poster that promotes one of the following themes or movements from the 1960s: environmentalism, existentialism, feminism, or the human rights movement.

8. Write a humorous or satirical dialogue between two adults in their fifties (i.e., baby boomers) who are reflecting on their youth. Be sure to address political issues, the environment, women's rights, and human rights issues. Try to include references to film, music, and fashion.

100 Cans (1962) by Andy Warhol (1.82 x 1.32 m)

CHAPTER FOURTEEN

Challenge and Change in the Global Village

CHAPTER EXPECTATIONS

By the end of this chapter, you will be able to:

- *describe factors that have prompted and facilitated increasing interaction between peoples during the latter half of the twentieth century*

- *demonstrate an understanding of key characteristics of and significant ideas emerging from various cultures around the world*

- *demonstrate an understanding of the consequences of global economic interrelationships that developed in the twentieth century*

- *evaluate key elements and characteristics of the process of historical change*

In the 1960s Canadian scholar Marshal McLuhan said "The medium is the message." What does this phrase mean? Does this idea still work today?

Since the end of World War II, the relationship of the West to the rest of the world has in some ways changed substantially, and in others remained the same as for the past 500 years. The forces of change and continuity have worked together to shape the world as we know it today. Change on the political front has been enormous over the past six decades, as entire continents broke ties with imperialist powers to achieve political independence. Although there has not been a global war since World War II, it has certainly not been a time of peace. In the aftermath of colonial independence movements, there have been large-scale conflicts and civil wars in the non-Western world. Nations, large and small, have worked together to create global institutions committed to protecting national security and economic interests of member states. These changes have had a profound impact on the development of relationships between nations.

Although formal imperialism collapsed during the twentieth century, what many have called "economic imperialism" has endured and strengthened the ties that powerful states have with their weaker neighbours. The economic and military alliances forged by the affluent, industrialized nations have most often been about protecting their own interests — sometimes at the expense of developing nations. These alliances have been furthered by the globalization of the market-place, the ownership of the mass media, and the power over world affairs wielded by a few nations.

Throughout this textbook, the term "the West" has usually been used to mean Western Europe. In the twentieth century, however, "the West" has increasingly come to mean the industrialized, affluent nations of the northern hemisphere. Furthermore, since the end of the Cold War, the world has been dominated by a single superpower — the United States of America. Hence, "western" values, ideology and way of life, more often than not, now refers to the American way of life.

KEY CONCEPTS AND EVENTS

Global village

Muslim Brotherhood

satya graha

British Commonwealth of Nations

La francophonie

Suez Crisis

International Law of the Sea Treaty

New world order

Summit of the Americas

KEY PEOPLE

Frantz Fanon

Ho Chi Minh

Marshall Tito

Slobodan Milosevic

Marshall McLuhan

Ken Saro-Wiwa

Naomi Klein

Wit and Wisdom

Workers will have to realize that they are now competing for jobs against people who ride to work every day on bicycles ... and are prepared to live with their families crammed into tiny apartments.

**Robert Brusca,
Chief Economist,
Nikko Securities, 1995**

TIME LINE: CHALLENGE AND CHANGE IN THE GLOBAL VILLAGE

France occupies Saigon, Vietnam	1945	
	1946	The Philippines becomes independent from the United States
India achieves independence from Britain	1947	
	1948	United Nations proclaims *Universal Declaration of Human Rights*; the state of Israel is created
China becomes a communist state under leadership of Mao Zedong	1949	
	1950	Korean War begins; Indonesia gains independence from the Netherlands
Egypt ends its status as a British protectorate	1952	
	1954	French defeated at Dien Bien Phu
Suez Crisis	1956	
	1957	Gold Coast (Ghana) achieves independence from Britain
The Congo achieves independence from Belgium	1960	
	1964	Palestine Liberation Organization (PLO) founded; Marshall McLuhan coins the term "global village"
Civil war in Pakistan ends in creation of Bangladesh	1971	
	1973	Yom Kippur War
Frantz Fanon, *The Wretched of the Earth*	1975	
	1980	Josip Broz (Tito) dies, leading to ongoing crises in Yugoslavia
Collapse of Soviet communism in Poland, Czechoslovakia, Bulgaria, Hungary, Albania, and Romania	1989	
	1991	Iraq invades Kuwait, precipitating the Gulf War
Civil war begins in Rwanda	1993	
	1997	British colony of Hong Kong returned to China
Massive protests rock the World Trade Organization in Seattle, Washington	1999	
	2001	Terrorists attack the World Trade Center in New York City
Elizabeth, the Queen Mother dies at the age of 101	2002	

Not to scale.

FORCES OF CHANGE THE COLLAPSE OF COLONIALISM

Early traces of today's global village appeared in the sixteenth and seventeenth centuries, as Europeans leapfrogged throughout the globe, establishing trading posts and colonies. By the eighteenth century, the Americas, Southern Africa, Australia, and New Zealand were settled by Europeans.

In the nineteenth century, Africa and Southeast Asia were carved up into European colonies and spheres of influence. China, though nominally independent, was forced to make humiliating concessions to European and American powers anxious to penetrate the Chinese market. By the beginning of the twentieth century, Western nations controlled nearly 85 percent of the globe. The race for empire brought into being a network of villages connected by a web of railroad lines, telegraph cables, and steamship routes. European languages, systems of government, social structures, and values dominated, pushed aside, or blended with non-European cultures.

European empires began to crumble after World War I, and the process of decolonization picked up momentum after 1945. By 1975 most former colonies, representing about one-third of the world population, were independent of their European masters. The reasons for such a startling collapse involved two sets of factors: colonial peoples (African, Arab, Asian) organized independence movements, and there were changes in European attitudes toward empire.

Independence Movements

As European nations were extending their power over the globe, non-European powers, such as the Moguls in India, the Ottoman Turks in the Middle East, and the Manchu rulers in China, succumbed to European dominance. Europeans were convinced that their power rested on their racial superiority: Arabs were seen as "devious"; Orientals were labelled "clever, crafty, and cruel"; Indians were derided as "lazy and backward." Blacks ranked the lowest in European estimation.

Civilization was viewed by imperialists as a race up a mountain, and Europeans felt they had already reached the summit. Even though the so-called lesser races had achieved higher than European levels in some aspects of civilization, Europeans felt a moral duty to help their colonies catch up. The British government took over India in 1858 and built railroads, developed industry, and educated Indian students for positions in the Indian civil service. British authorities also put an end to *sati*, the practice of burning a widow on her husband's funeral pyre. They repressed *thagi*, the ritual assassination of travellers by roving bands who sacrificed them to their goddess. The British unified the many small states of the Indian subcontinent by imposing their version of law and order and, most significantly, their language.

Except for the Spanish and the Portuguese (who intermarried with the native populations of their colonies), Europeans set up barriers between themselves and the peoples they ruled. British settlers in India lived in their own separate compounds, excluding even the best-educated or most-refined Indians. The relations between other colonial powers and their subjects were no different. In certain Chinese cities, Europeans inhabited separate quarters and were governed by their right of extraterritoriality, meaning they were not subject to Chinese laws. Independence movements owed much of their original energy to European-educated leaders who were slighted, scorned, and mistreated by Europeans. Memories of such discriminatory attitudes continue to poison European relations with other peoples in countries where the populations did not intermarry.

Economic exploitation intensified the bitterness aroused by racism and insensitivity. Imperial powers extracted the resources of their colonies for their own benefit, leaving the native populations to a life of poverty. Often the growth of a European-dominated world economy forced the integration of non-Europeans into an economic system over which they had no control: The Chinese silk industry produced silk to suit the tastes of the European consumer and the specifications of European textile mills; Kenyan farmers gave up their traditional agriculture in order to produce cash crops such as coffee for an overseas market; in India, cheap cotton manufactured in England flooded the Indian market during the nineteenth century, undermining the Indian textile industry.

Advancing Human Rights in the Colonies

The expulsion of European occupiers became the goal of colonial peoples around the globe during the twentieth century. Violence was common. One particularly bloody example was the 1899–1900 Boxer Uprising in China. Disgusted by the way in which Europeans and Americans had divided China into their own economic spheres of interest, and ashamed of their government's weakness, the Chinese "fists of righteous harmony" (Boxers) rose up against the "foreign devils." Eventually, the Chinese government suppressed the rebellion but only with military help from Europe and the United States.

In some cases, European disdain of non-European culture aroused a reaction in defence of historic ways of life. Indian spiritual leader Mohandas Karamchand Gandhi (1869–1948) urged Indians to reject British culture and return to traditional Indian lifestyles. Gandhi set an example by weaving his own cloth and dressing in traditional native clothing. In contrast to traditionalists such as Gandhi, modernizers such as Gandhi's successor, Jawaharlal Nehru (1889–1964), believed that adapting to the modern world was a more effective way of dealing with European imperialism.

In Turkey, a group calling itself Young Turks sought to build a thoroughly modern, secular Turkish society. Their role model was Japan, whose surge to world power status showed that it was possible to beat the Whites at their own game. After American commodore Matthew Perry blasted his way into Tokyo Bay in 1853, Japan had undertaken a thorough reconstruction of its political, military, and educational systems.

Jawaharlal Nehru believed that modernization was the way India could counter European imperialism. Given current news from India, is Nehru's belief coming true?

Reform began in earnest after 1868, and the period is known as the Meiji Restoration. Borrowing and adapting extensively from the West, Japan transformed itself into a modern industrial nation without abandoning its own religion, traditions, and culture. The takeover of Formosa from China in 1884–1885 propelled Japan into the ranks of the imperial powers. Much to everyone's surprise, the Russo-Japanese War of 1904–1905 ended in a decisive Japanese victory and destroyed the myth that European nations could not be conquered.

In the Middle East, the Muslim Brotherhood won many followers during the 1950s and 1960s. Rejecting the European way of life, the Brotherhood envisioned a just society based on Islamic values as outlined in their sacred book, the Qu'ran. The leaders of the Muslim Brotherhood also came from an educated elite and attracted Arabs who had been shut out of English or French society.

Frantz Fanon, a West Indian psychoanalyst and social philosopher from Martinique, spoke eloquently in the 1960s of the need for a "counterculture" based on ideals radically different from those of European society. The conclusion of his book *The Wretched of the Earth*, published in 1975, reads:

> The European game has finally ended; we must do something different. We today can do everything, so long as we do not imitate Europe, so long as we are not obsessed by the desire to catch up with Europe ... The Third World today faces Europe like a colossal mass whose aim should be to try to resolve the problems to which Europe has not been able to find answers ... If we want humanity to advance a step further, if we want to bring it up to a different level than that which Europe has shown it, then we must invent and we must make discoveries.

Changes in Europe

Colonial peoples' desire for independence accompanied shifts in European attitudes. In the years following World War II, imperialism was no longer as fashionable as it once had been. In Europe during the 1970s, Fanon's message captured the imagination and support of many intellectuals and student protesters. In 1948, fifty countries signed the United Nations *Universal Declaration of Human Rights*, which, among other things, recognized "the equal rights of ... nations large and small." For how much longer could Europeans, who prided themselves on being democratic, and who had just fought a brutal war to defend freedom, justify their claim to rule other peoples?

A second reason for ending imperialism was financial. As discussed earlier, European nations faced the enormous expense of economic reconstruction after 1945. Building the welfare state took priority over maintaining an imperial presence abroad. The economic miracle of Germany and Italy, both countries that no longer had colonial empires, proved that having colonies was not vital to prosperity.

THE PROCESS OF DECOLONIZATION

The examples of decolonization considered below focus on the colonies of two major imperial powers of the twentieth century: Great Britain and France. Sometimes the route to colonial independence was relatively peaceful; on other occasions violent. Much depended on whether a colony had a large European settlement or not. Moreover, the Cold War often complicated the process of decolonization.

India: The Jewel in the Crown

Britain was the greatest imperial power at the beginning of the twentieth century. In one form or another, its empire encompassed territory all over the globe. Canada and Australia were self-governing dominions. Rhodesia enjoyed a limited degree of self-rule. Hong Kong, seized from China during the Opium War of 1841–1842, was a crown colony administered by a British governor, as were West Indian islands. Egypt was a protectorate, in theory an independent state, but in practice subject to British military and financial control. Of all British possessions, however, the Indian subcontinent was the largest — the "jewel" in the British crown. British India consisted of India proper, present-day Pakistan, Myanmar (formerly Burma), and present-day Bangladesh. A British viceroy ruled the subcontinent with the assistance of an Indian civil service.

In the 1880s, a nationalist movement under the leadership of the Congress Party won the backing of many educated Indians. Mohandas Gandhi, an upper-class Indian trained as a lawyer in Britain, became the Congress Party's leader in 1925. He had already earned a reputation as a champion of immigrant Indian labourers when he was living in South Africa. It was in Africa that Gandhi developed his revolutionary vision of peaceful protest and passive resistance as an alternative to violence.

Gandhi realized that the success of the independence movement depended on mass participation. In order to build a broad base of support, he visited towns and villages all over India. He welcomed all castes, women, and Muslims to join the cause of independence. Gandhi's philosophy of life, known as *satya graha* (Hindi for "insistence on truth"), was based on *ahimsa* (the Sanskrit word for non-violence). He called for individual spiritual renewal, and moral awakening, which, in his view, formed the only sound basis for national independence and stability.

Gandhi was not only a philosopher but also a shrewd political leader. He was quick to realize that after World War I the mass media played an increasingly influential role in political affairs, as was seen in Gandhi's highly publicized 1930 protest against the salt tax. Gandhi argued that a tax on such a basic commodity was not only a burden to poor people, but also violated civil rights. To protest the repressive salt tax, Gandhi and a group of followers began a 300 km march to the Indian ocean. Led by Gandhi, they waded into its waters, filled a pitcher, and boiled the water down to extract the salt. This symbolic action was the signal for a nationwide strike and a boycott of British goods. The resulting press coverage generated widespread public support for Indian self-government, while the boycott of British goods threw textile workers in Britain out of work and added British political pressure to the campaign for Indian independence. Gandhi had become a revered holy person, or *mahatma*, to his own people, and an admired hero to many British people, who threw their support behind his cause. The outbreak of World War II, however, delayed Indian independence until 1947.

With India independent, self-rule for other parts of the empire was only a matter of time. Well before the outbreak of World War II, British colonial authorities drew up plans to prepare their colonies for self-rule. They thought that the process might take several decades but the rising tide of post–World War II nationalism and the Cold War forced them to speed up their schedule. The Soviets spread the message that the West was to blame for the misery in which many colonial peoples lived. Fear of communism and the possibility of anti-Western, pro-Soviet uprisings prompted British leaders to grant early independence to several more colonies.

The Gold Coast, renamed Ghana, was the first African colony to break colonial ties with Britain. The year was 1957. Soon others followed. In Egypt, charismatic leader Gamal Abdel Nasser engineered a revolution in 1952 that eventually forced Britain to end its Egyptian protectorate. The major exception was the crown colony of Hong Kong, which, due to a long-term agreement with Britain, was not returned to Chinese sovereignty until 1997. The British Empire, upon which, at one time, the sun never set, was reduced to just a few pushpins on the globe.

The French Experience

Vietnam

After Britain, the second-largest imperial power was France. Most of its possessions were in Africa and Southeast Asia. Long before the Americans became involved in Southeast Asia, Vietnam had been a battleground between a French government intent on keeping its colony and Vietnamese rebels (Vietminh) determined to drive out the French. The French established their empire in Indochina (Southeast Asia) after 1858, but during World War II, Japanese armies overran Indochina. After Japan surrendered, France repossessed Vietnam bit by bit, occupying the city of Saigon in 1945 and Hanoi a year later. At the same time, the French government reached an agreement with Ho Chi Minh (1890–1969), the Vietminh leader, to grant independence to the North. Eventually, it was hoped, the whole Vietnamese peninsula would become united under an independent government. The fact that Ho Chi Minh was a communist did not seem to matter at the time.

Some French leaders objected strongly to this arrangement. The humiliating German occupation of France in 1940 probably contributed to the French determination to hang on to its overseas empire in the postwar period. In defiance of official government policy, the French viceroy in Vietnam allowed local leaders to set up a separate state of South Vietnam. Peace talks broke down and confrontations between the Vietminh and French troops followed. When a French

The mausoleum of Ho Chi Minh, leader of the Vietminh, rebels who fought for and won independence from France for North Vietnam in 1945. Why did France lose control in Vietnam?

In 1954 the French military decided to make a stand at the fortress of Dien Bien Phu, which sat astride the Vietminh supply route to China. An over-confident French commander made mistakes in planning Dien Bien Phu's defences and, after three months of fighting, the French conceded defeat. Out of an occupying force of twenty thousand, only three thousand survived. The whole Dien Bien Phu episode was a political as well as a military catastrophe. France had no choice but to withdraw from Indochina. The 8_year Vietnamese War cost France 8.5 billion dollars and over two hundred thousand casualties. Indochina suffered about forty-three thousand casualties.

Algeria

French society had barely enough time to recover from the Vietnam debacle before the country found itself fighting to keep Algeria. Few French nationals had settled in Vietnam. Algeria, on the other hand, was an overseas department of France that had elected delegates to the National Assembly since 1871. It had close economic and cultural links with France but in truth was controlled by the French minority.

Nationalist groups had begun to agitate against the French presence in Algeria in the last months of World War II. Tens of thousands were killed by the French army. A well-organized and dedicated Muslim-led independence movement, known as the Front de Libération Nationale (FLN), gathered force in the years after the war and began a campaign of violence in 1954, their anger fuelled by French economic exploitation and cultural domination. French settlers, or *colons*, and their descendants formed 10 percent of a population of nine million. Most *colons* were poor but those at the top owned the best land and controlled most of the industry. French was the language of instruction imposed on the Arab majority. The two largest cities, Algiers and Oran, were mainly French in culture, and the mosque in Algiers had been turned into a cathedral.

When the FLN began its terrorism campaign the *colons* retaliated in kind. The colons undertook "rat-hunts" against rebels as reprisals for FLN café bombings

warship fired on the port of Haiphong in November 1946, killing 6 000 people, the communists declared a war of liberation.

Three years later, in 1949, the situation became more serious, as China, under Mao Zedong, became communist and began supporting Vietnamese rebels. A year later, the Korean War broke out. With the Cold War raging in Europe, the U.S. came to the aid of the French in order to counterbalance Chinese forces. The domino theory guided their thinking: If one country succumbed to communism, others would follow. Before long, the United States was financing about 80 percent of the French military budget in the Vietnam. This aid prolonged the war.

Children and their FLN volunteer teacher in an Algerian school in 1962. Without such volunteers, Algerian children would have had no education.

in Algiers. The FLN cut off noses of Muslims suspected of sympathizing with the French. The *colons* threatened to upset any French government inclined to grant concessions to the Muslim rebels. A demoralized French government could not cope with the situation. President de Gaulle, who initially seemed to favour the *colons*, ended the war by negotiating Algerian independence in 1958. In so doing, he had the support of most mainland French who felt that keeping Algeria was not worth the expense. In any case, independence did not dissolve the economic links between Algeria and France.

In contrast to the Algerian blood bath, two French colonies in North Africa, Morocco and Tunisia, as well as French colonies south of the Sahara, became independent through negotiations. The French authorities co-operated with Algerian leaders, who were educated in France, in the transition to self-government.

Other imperial powers retreated from their overseas possessions. The United States withdrew from the Philippines in 1946 and pressured its European allies to grant independence to their colonies. The Netherlands gave up its control of the Dutch East Indies (today Indonesia) in 1950; Belgium left the Congo (today Zaire) in 1960; and Portugal reluctantly withdrew from Angola, Mozambique, and Guinea-Bissau in the mid-1970s. The nineteenth-century network of nations whose "capitals" were in Europe became a relic of the past.

IMPERIALISM AND ITS LEGACY: AFTER INDEPENDENCE

Unfortunately, political independence did not generally result in a better life for the people of these newly independent countries. In too many cases, it brought chaos and fragmentation. Pre-colonial Africa had been a jumble of city-states, small kingdoms, and tribal territories. Europeans, in carving out their empires in Africa, paid no attention to existing arrangements, often including long-time enemies and peoples of different ethnic backgrounds in their new divisions. Ethiopia, for example, encompassed many ethnic groups and languages. The period of colonial rule (by Italy) had been too short to impose any kind of unifying set of traditions.

With the end of imperialism, long-repressed hatreds resurfaced. Angola, a former Portuguese colony, turned into a bloody battleground between rival political groups. In the 1970s, Ugandan dictator Idi Amin expelled Asian Ugandans *en masse*. A bloody civil war broke out in Nigeria, the most populous country in Africa, when the more prosperous and Christian South attempted to secede from the less prosperous and largely Muslim North. The fighting that broke out in 1993 in the Central African country of Rwanda also had origins in inter-tribal rivalry.

Failure to resolve the major Hindu-Muslim conflict forced Britain out of India. The creation of a separate Muslim state of Pakistan, to the east and west of India, brought a temporary peace. In 1948 Gandhi, the Hindu champion of non-violence, was shot by a Hindu fanatic who thought he was too soft on Muslims. After independence, various minority groups agitated for greater autonomy and religious freedom. When Sikhs living in the Punjab failed to obtain greater autonomy, they turned to violence. In 1971 civil war ripped through Pakistan and the eastern portion of the country emerged as the nation of Bangladesh. A dispute over the Kashmir region in the north of India continued and in 2002, threatened to escalate to nuclear warfare.

The American withdrawal from Vietnam did not bring peace to Indochina either, where feuding between competing communist groups meant continued warfare for this troubled region. In Cambodia, radical communist leader Pol Pot and his Khmer Rouge fighters murdered one million people and dispossessed many others. In Ceylon (today Sri Lanka) friction between the Buddhist Sinhalese majority and the Hindu Tamil minority seeking independence sparked a guerrilla war that continues today. This pattern of violence has been endlessly repeated in many former colonial territories with the end of the Cold War. Rapidly growing populations, poverty, economic stagnation, and political corruption have worsened the situation.

A young Cambodian soldier. The Khmer Rouge took one million lives on the "Killing Fields" of Cambodia from 1975-1979. What is the situation in Cambodia today? How can we put an end to recruitment of "child" soldiers?

ARTISTIC MOVEMENTS IN THE NON-WESTERN WORLD

Post-Colonial Literature

Throughout the period of colonization and formal imperialism, the images of non-Western peoples in the minds of Europeans were largely created by European writers. Joseph Conrad's *Heart of Darkness* (1899) created a picture of Africans as an exotic, mysterious, and dangerous race. Daniel Defoe's *Robinson Crusoe* (1719) portrayed the colonizer — represented by Robinson Crusoe — as adventurous, resourceful and humanitarian, and the colonized — represented by Crusoe's Black servant Friday — as willing, subservient, and ignorant. These authors and many others wrote about colonized peoples but did not give them a voice; nor write from their perspective or experience. Post-colonial literature, in general, has worked against this paradigm in an attempt to give a voice to the oppressed. This sometimes has taken a very direct approach as in J. M. Coetzee's novel *Foe* (1986), which tells the Robinson Crusoe story from the perspective of Friday.

www.mcgrawhill.ca/links/legacy

Go to the site above to find out more about Post-colonial literature.

Post-colonial authors explore various themes, which they feel have been undermined as a result of the cultural impact of colonialism. These themes include myth (usually replaced by Christianity), the oral tradition (which tended to be non-linear, collective and holistic), ritual (the basis of values), and language (most often replaced by the language of the colonizer).

Language, particularly, has posed a difficult problem for authors of post-colonial literature. Some have argued that nationalist literature should be written in a local language. This belief is based on the idea that since language is the vehicle for ideology, to write in

English is to accept the worldview of the oppressor. Writers from formerly colonized nations, however, tend to be of the Western-educated elite whose main language is English. They also argue that after hundreds of years of being subjected to English rule, language and society, the original "pure" pre-colonial culture no longer exists. Post-colonial societies have a new hybrid culture that the original indigenous languages do not seem able to express. Furthermore, many post-colonial writers see their writing as a teaching tool that informs and educates the public about the impact and legacy of colonialism. If this is the case, then writing in an indigenous tongue would only serve to limit a writer's audience.

Because of these factors, authors have looked to reject the colonial paradigm through style rather than language — specifically, rejecting realism as a writing style. Realism in literature includes the use of a linear story line, a traditional plot, and simple and easy to understand concepts. It implies a "master narrative" where the author is all-seeing, all-knowing and can "enlighten" the reader about the "truth." Post-colonial authors have identified this notion of truth as the Western worldview and have, therefore, rejected realism as an attempt to reject the Western worldview. This has resulted in novels that tend to be complex in style and structure — often mixing reality with fantasy and using a non-linear story line such as in Nigerian author Ben Okri's *The Famished Road* (1991), where the spirit world intermingles with the corporeal world. The idea behind the rejection of realism as a style is that reality cannot be understood from the simple, linear perspective of a Western colonial power.

In the final analysis, however, it is misleading to use the term "post-colonial literature," since it seems to link very different types of literature from various parts of the globe. It is impossible to simplify the writing and experiences of writers as diverse as Nigerian authors Chinua Achebe and Ben Okri, Indian authors V. S. Naipaul, Anita Desai and Salman Rushdie, and Caribbean authors such as Derek Walcott by painting them all with the same brush; however, one can say that all have been profoundly affected by colonial experiences and used those experiences to produce enduring, award-winning literature.

World Music

The idea of music travelling across cultures and transcending language barriers is certainly not new to the twentieth century. For centuries, different musical styles have emerged as peoples of various cultures migrated and mixed with each other. Flamenco, for example, although thought of as a typically Spanish form of music, actually has its roots in music from Morocco, Egypt, India, Pakistan, and Greece. It is believed to have been brought to Spain in the fifteenth century by Gypsies and has also been influenced by Jewish and Muslim cultures.

Spanish Flamenco dancers and musicians found their inspiration in music of many cultures, some as far away as the Middle East and Pakistan.

World music seems to have emerged in three different ways:

- First, as in the case of Flamenco music, one culture's musical style is influenced by others.
- Second, music indigenous to one culture or region becomes popular and is enjoyed in another part of the world.
- Third, it is a phenomenon largely of the late twentieth century — and particularly since the 1990s — that musicians from different parts of the world, playing very different styles and instruments, come together to collaborate and create a unique sound.

Non-Western music is commonly thought of as having first reached mainstream Western culture in the 1960s. British pop band The Beatles' famous collaboration with Indian classical musician Ravi Shankar created an entire generation suddenly interested in Indian music and philosophy. Young people of the 1960s began travelling to India, seeking out gurus (spiritual teachers), and searching for spiritual awakening.

This was not the first time non-Western music had made a splash in the West. As early as 1916, Hawaiian music was fashionable in the United States. Although Hawaii is now America's 50th state, it was only annexed by the U.S. in 1898. This Polynesian culture's music was originally focussed on vocal music and drumbeats but was influenced by the West in a number of ways. Missionaries from New England brought hymns and vocal harmonies. Cowboys from the American Midwest introduced the guitar, and Portuguese sailors brought over an early relative of the ukulele. As a result, a new Hawaiian music emerged that enjoyed unprecedented success on the mainland. By 1916 more Hawaiian music records were being sold in the U.S. than any other type.

Other non-Western musical styles to be integrated into mainstream Western music include reggae from Jamaica and *bhangra* music from Northern India. Reggae originated in Jamaica as the musical expression of Rastafarians, a religious group constituting less than 15 percent of the population but exerting a disproportionately great influence over the country's musical scene. Although reggae emerged as a new musical style in the 1960s, it soared to the top of Western music charts in 1975 with the release of the album containing *No Woman No Cry* by Bob Marley, Jamaica's most famous rasta musician.

Bhangra is currently enjoying success on dance floors in the West, particularly in Britain, a far cry from its origins in the rural farming communities of Punjab State in northern India. It was originally a form of dance music performed during *bisakh*, the celebration of the end of the harvest. Often the crop being harvested was hemp, or *bhang*, hence the name. *Bhangra* became popular in the towns and cities of Punjab about 200 years ago and in the 1970s entered the British music scene as young British Indians adopted it as the music of their roots.

World music is not simply confined to the popularity of non-Western music in the West; it is a fusion of different cultural musical styles. This has resulted

Pleasures
AND PASTIMES

Although for centuries people have travelled the globe seeking new and exotic experiences, in the year 2001, adventure tourism reached new heights — literally. The second half of the twentieth century saw an increase in the number of tourists willing to pay exorbitant prices in exchange for being guided to remote or exotic locations. Thrill-seekers — often inexperienced — paid tens of thousands of dollars to be guided up Mount Everest or through African safaris or to the most remote corners of the Antarctic. Adventure tourism seemed to reach its height, however, in 2001, when American millionaire Dennis Tito paid millions of dollars to the cash-strapped Russian space program for the opportunity to hitch a ride to the unfinished International Space Station. Amid a great deal of controversy about the appropriateness of this move and potential safety hazards, he became the first space tourist.

Rastafarian musician Bob Marley gave reggae music from Jamaica to North America. Who are the Rastafarians?

in many unique and innovative collaborations. Guitar player Ali Farka Toure of Mali plays with Ry Cooder, an American blues guitar musician. Indian *tabla* (a type of drums) player Zakhir Hussain has collaborated with many different Western musicians, including jazz guitarist John McGlaughlin. Bands such as the Afro-Celt Sound System fuse together such disparate styles as African drum beats with Celtic fiddle. The Toronto Tabla Ensemble is a troupe of *tabla* players whose band also consists of a rock drum set, African drums, the occasional jazz singer or upright bass player — they even play their own version of Beethoven's Ninth Symphony.

The Cinema

Hollywood has long been fascinated by the non-Western world, with its exotic cultures and potential for colourful costume design and lavish sets. Hollywood movies have brought the world to our local big screen, and right into our living rooms, by VCR and DVD.

The Hollywood film industry has also been accused of being exceedingly Eurocentric. Historian J. M. Blaut has said that Eurocentrism presents "the colonizer's model of the world" and this has certainly been true of many movies. Movies have tended to minimize the oppressive practices of the West, effectively sanitizing Western history, while at the same time presenting non-Western cultures in a patronizing, or even demonizing way.

Films made early in the twentieth century often focussed on Native Americans as the archetypal "exotic" culture. The entire genre of film known as "the western" typifies attitudes to peoples of non-European descent, portraying aboriginal peoples as "noble savages" as in *The Last of the Mohicans* (made into a movie four times between 1920 and 1992) or *How the West was Won* (1963).

Another common paradigm is that of the European or American hero travelling to a new land and becoming its saviour in one way or another. It has been pointed out that in *Lawrence of Arabia* (1962) the hero "inspires and leads the passive Arab masses." The more recent Indiana Jones series, *Raiders of the Lost Ark* (1981), *Indiana Jones and the Temple of Doom* (1984), and *Indiana Jones and the Last Crusade* also depicts a Westerner making important discoveries in non-Western lands, and saving those discoveries from destruction for the sake of the locals.

Films dealing with historical events are often criticized for the creative reconstruction of history they often portray. For example, the film *1492: The Conquest of Paradise* (1992) is only one of a number of films about Christopher Columbus that portrays the colonizer as a hero. Historically, Hollywood films have painted a picture of the non-Westerner as passive, underdeveloped and backward, while the Westerner is productive, creative, efficient, and pioneering.

Once considered "art" films for a limited audience, foreign films such as *Crouching Tiger, Hidden Dragon* (2000) are attracting Westerners and turning into box office hits. What do you think the attraction was? Do such films help decrease American cultural dominance?

In more recent decades, films from the non-Western world have been widely praised and accepted. The Academy Awards have even honoured directors of foreign films such as Akira Kurosawa. This renowned Japanese filmmaker has produced a number of films, including *Ran* (1985), and won several Academy Awards. Kurosawa's *Ran* is actually based on the plot-line of Shakespeare's *King Lear*. In India, Satyajit Ray has been an acclaimed director since his debut film, *Pather Panchali* (1955). He was even honoured with a Lifetime Achievement Award by the Academy.

Even more recently, Iranian, Russian, Chinese and Indian films, to name a few, are making their debuts to critical acclaim on Western screens. *Crouching Tiger, Hidden Dragon* (2000), from China, is a good example of a recent foreign "blockbuster" movie. Deepa Mehta, a Canadian filmmaker of East Indian descent, has gained recognition for her films, *Earth* (1996) and *Fire* (1998). Although only a small number of these foreign films ever reach the big screen in North America and are still largely considered to be "art films," many have enjoyed greater success in Europe and are slowly gaining recognition in the West. Witness the burgeoning phenomenon of the Indian film industry, referred to as "Bollywood," in the early twenty-first century. "Film is perhaps the most influential of all art media, and we can expect it gradually to move further away from the "colonizer's model of the world" toward a more accurate portrayal of non-Western cultures.

Review, Reflect, Respond

1. Why did the process of decolonization rapidly accelerate after 1945?

2. Why did political independence in former colonies not immediately lead to a better life for the majority of people in these countries?

3. How does non-Western literature and music reflect the desire of post-colonial artists to reject the cultural impact of colonialism?

INTERNATIONAL EFFORTS FOR PEACEFUL CO-EXISTENCE

Since 1945 the forms of interaction between the West and the rest of the world have changed dramatically in some ways. In others, they remained remarkably the same as for the past 500 years. Interaction between the West and the world in recent decades has taken place largely through formal international institutions (e.g. the United Nations, the Commonwealth, etc.), involvement in domestic conflict and war, trade agreements and economic alliances (NAFTA, APEC, etc.), and the activities of multinational corporations.

The British Commonwealth of Nations

As the European colonial system fell apart, new forms of international organization took its place. One example was the British Commonwealth of Nations, which now consists of 49 independent nations (at one time representing one-quarter of the world's population) and symbolically headed by the British monarch. Most former colonies joined the Commonwealth; the major exception was Burma, today called Myanmar.

The English language is the unifying basis of the Commonwealth. In multilingual India, for example, English remains the official language of law, commerce, government, and education. Cultural and sports events involving all Commonwealth nations, such as the Commonwealth Games, academic scholarships, and conferences on topics of common interest (e.g., agriculture, technology, medicine), create bonds among the widely diverse peoples.

Although meetings between government heads to discuss issues of shared interest are common, peace and harmony have not always prevailed in the Commonwealth. When Commonwealth leaders condemned South Africa's apartheid policy, South Africa angrily left the Commonwealth in 1961. Economic sanctions enforced by the Commonwealth were an important factor in South Africa's decision (under Frederik

W. de Klerk) to dismantle apartheid, and release from jail its most famous opponent, Nelson Mandela. With the democratically elected Mandela as president, South Africa again joined the Commonwealth in 1994.

In post-apartheid South Africa, these Black South Africans patiently wait in line to vote for the first time in their lives, in 1994. How might these people have felt while waiting?

La francophonie

Like Great Britain, France now relates to its former colonies on an equal footing. Unlike Great Britain, France continues to maintain close economic and cultural ties with its former African colonies. The community of French-speaking countries is called *La francophonie* and members include Belgium, Cameroon, Canada, Morocco, Tunisia, Gabon, and Luxembourg. These nations maintain ties and participate in conferences, events and organizations such as the athletic games known as Les Jeux de la Francophonie and a commission dealing with the problem of anti-personnel mines.

The United Nations

The UN is the most prominent organization of the twentieth century. From its initial membership of fifty countries, the UN has grown to over 180 members, many of which were former colonies. Some took new names to symbolize the rejection of an unpleasant past: Zimbabwe was Rhodesia; Sri Lanka was Ceylon; and Myanmar was Burma. In the UN General Assembly, all members, regardless of size, have a vote and a voice. Major decisions are made by the Security Council, but the Assembly, which is a kind of global-village meeting, provides a forum for small countries to express their views.

For the UN, however, acting as a world community is another matter. Restraining aggression was one of the original goals of the UN. The Charter states that, "the Security Council shall determine the existence of any threat to the peace, breach of the peace, or act of aggression, and shall make recommendations, or decide what measures shall be taken in accordance with Articles 41 and 42" (these articles refer to the preference for first using measures that do not involve the use of armed force). But the UN has rarely intervened against aggressors since both the United States and Russia (previously the U.S.S.R.) are permanent members of the Security Council and have vetoed motions on several occasions, especially during the Cold War. In 1950 the UN dispatched an army under American general Douglas MacArthur to help South Korea, which had been invaded by North Korea.

On many occasions, nations have bypassed the United Nations when deciding whether to use armed force in a given situation. The world community considers these nations "rogue states" who act outside of the UN Charter. In its actions in Kuwait, Iraq took the role of a rogue state. Political analysts have pointed out, however, that the United States, too, has acted as a rogue state. During the 1998 Iraq crisis in which Iraq refused to allow United Nations inspectors access to what they suspected were chemical warfare plants, the United States insisted it reserved the right to act unilaterally, without United Nations approval, to use armed force to make Iraq comply. The United States has also vetoed resolutions of the United Nations, such as the Security Council resolution that required all states to observe International Law. This veto followed shortly after a 1986 decision by the World Court condemning the "unlawful use of force" by the United States in Nicaragua. The Court also ruled that the United States should desist and pay reparations to Nicaragua.

Band-Aid Treatments?

Since ancient times, singers, called balladeers or troubadours, were important carriers of information of all kinds: historic accounts of heroes and villains, current events, songs of love, political intrigue, and gossip of course. You could buy a song praising yourself and your accomplishments and have it sung in the market square. Or you could secretly commission a song that exposed the foibles or evildoings of a rival. This was an important function of popular music. Today, popular music has become much more than the information arm of the young — consider the political and social issues that rap and hip hop music communicate. Even so, until fairly recently, pop music remained basically non-political. But that situation changed when one generous and socially conscious musician decided that he could use his talent and fame, and that of his musical friends, to help those in need.

The musician who first took up this form of social activism was George Harrison (1943–2001), the guitarist and composer whom many called "the quiet Beatle." In 1970 Harrison was witness to the vast problem of starvation in the poverty-stricken nation of Bangladesh, formerly known as East Pakistan. Harrison organized a concert of many of the top names in popular music, and the proceeds were then given to help relieve the famine in Bangladesh. Since then, musicians have felt free to organize events or make recordings or

videos to raise money in response to a specific need or to a charitable organization. Musicians now can and do openly identify themselves with a particular cause or charity. There have been aid concerts and videos produced to help American farmers (FarmAid), for AIDS research (e.g. Artists Against AIDS), relief concerts for refugees and displaced children (e.g., Pavarotti and Friends, Live Aid, Band Aid, USA for Africa) and on and on. Most recently, a number of musicians have recorded a version of the classic Marvin Gaye song *What's Goin' On* to raise funds not only for AIDS research (Global AIDS Alliance) but also to help victims of the September 11, 2001, attacks in New York City and Washington. The musical world is directly responding to historical events.

Jennifer Lopez was one of the pop artists to record the *What's Goin' On* video to raise funds for AIDS and victims of September 11 attacks.

1. How will historians look back on this phenomenon and the society that created it?

2. Should pop artists be involved in political or social issues? Explain your answer.

Thousands of Hutu refugees hoping to escape the violence in Rwanda flooded across the border with Tanzania. The UN sponsored the International Tribunal for Rwanda to investigate the genocide and crimes against humanity that occurred in 1994. What more could the international community have done to prevent this situation?

United Nations peacekeeping, rather than action against aggressors, has gained increasing significance since peacekeeping forces were first deployed. Canadian statesman and prime minister Lester B. Pearson was responsible for proposing the first deployment of a UN peacekeeping force during the Suez Crisis in 1956, for which he received the Nobel Peace Prize. Peacekeeping forces consist of troops from many countries sent to separate countries in conflict so they can work out a peaceable solution to their dispute. United Nations troops have intervened in many trouble spots, including the Congo, Rwanda, the Kashmir (on the Pakistan-India border), Cyprus, and Bosnia-Herzegovina. When Yugoslavia disintegrated, UN peacekeepers also intervened to provide humanitarian aid to civilian populations.

Unfortunately, persistent national and ethnic conflict frequently frustrate UN efforts at peacekeeping. Intervention in the Suez Crisis did not bring peace to the Middle East. Thirty years after UN forces entered Cyprus in 1963, they are still policing the so-called Green Line dividing Turkish and Greek sectors. Nevertheless, despite such setbacks, in 1988 UN peacekeepers were awarded the Nobel Peace Prize, an award that recognized the importance of their work. More successful but less spectacular is the UN's role in improving people's lives throughout the world. The World Health Organization (WHO), United Nations Relief and Rehabilitation Agency (UNRRA), United Nations Children's Fund (Unicef), Food and Agriculture Organization (FAO), and World Population Fund are all organizations staffed and supported by member nations. There are of course hundreds of non-governmental organizations (NGOs), such as Greenpeace, the Red Cross/Red Crescent, Amnesty International, and Oxfam, that link peoples from different parts of the world for humanitarian purposes.

The European Union

Ever since the Middle Ages, the vision of a united Europe has stirred the European imagination. Unfortunately, bitter rivalries — economic, religious, and national — have repeatedly frustrated dreams of a united continent. Two immensely destructive world wars, caused in part by national rivalries, began to change people's thinking. Peace could become a reality if Europeans could construct a European federation capable of resolving tensions before they reached a flashpoint. Plus, the superpower confrontation that resulted from the Cold War brought home the uncomfortable truth that Europe was at the mercy of the two great powers (the U.S. and the U.S.S.R.) and their competing interests. Only by building a new Europe could it regain some measure of independence.

As mentioned earlier, a first step was the European Coal and Steel Community, which, by integrating West Germany, France, and other nations economically, diminished the long-standing fear of German dominance. The 1957 Treaty of Rome transformed the ECSC into a wider economic union: the European Economic Community, initially consisting of its founder, France, plus West Germany, Italy, the Netherlands, Belgium, and Luxembourg. Steps toward political unity followed with the creation of a European parliament in 1962. The EEC's economic success was the model for the European Free Trade Area (EFTA), with the so-called "outer six" made up of Britain, Ireland, Denmark, and the Scandinavian countries.

Progress toward European unity hit occasional obstacles. National rivalries did not subside easily. France, under President de Gaulle, twice opposed Britain's entry into the EEC. By 1973, Britain, Ireland, and Denmark had finally joined. During the 1980s, the EEC inched toward a more integrated economic community with uniform product standards and freer circulation of money, goods, and services. In 1992 delegates from 12 European nations met in the Dutch city of Maastricht to hammer out the plan for a closer federation. The treaty increased the powers of the European parliament, introduced the basis for a common currency (the Euro), a common banking system, and a common passport, all of which are functioning today. Delegates also dealt with a broad range of social and cultural issues. They drew up policies protecting workers' rights, regulating television programming, controlling pollution in automobiles, and even standardizing health warnings on cigarette packages. Based on the idea of French political economist Jean Monnet (who was the first president of the ECSC), the European union created by the Treaty of Maastricht was a federal system similar in many respects to the existing Canadian confederation.

On July 1, 1994, the European Union (EU) was proclaimed. This was a major historical event. The EU now rivals North America and Japan in terms of its potential economic clout. It has a large territory with many resources and a highly educated population. It controls one-third of the world's trade and is home to some of the largest banks and insurance companies. Seven of the world's top-ten trading nations are European. European auto, pharmaceutical, and engineering industries are world leaders. The Maastricht Treaty also provides for the inclusion of other nations, extending into the Mediterranean basin and Eastern and Central Europe.

Formulating a common foreign policy for the EU is potentially difficult. The EU put up a united front in protest when Canada apprehended a Spanish trawler fishing inside Canadian waters in 1995. On the other hand, Europeans were not united in their response to the Gulf War and have thus far reached no consensus on how to deal with the problems resulting from the break-up of Yugoslavia.

CONFLICT AND WAR: NEOCOLONIALISM AND REVOLUTION

China

China and Latin America have been areas of turmoil and internal conflict during the latter half of the twentieth century. Although China was never a European colony (it was, however, subject to informal imperialism) and most Latin America countries threw off the bonds of colonialism in the nineteenth century, both underwent revolutionary changes after World War II — largely in response to Western encroachment into their economic and social spheres.

As we saw in previous chapters, the ruling Manchu dynasty fell from power in 1911 and a republic was declared in 1912 with Sun Yat-sen as its first president. Throughout the first half of the twentieth century, power in China alternated between attempts to maintain a republic, the rule of warlords, and rule by the Nationalist Party, culminating in 1949 when Mao Zedong (1893-1976) became the head of a new communist republic. This was by no means a peaceful political development but, rather, the result of years of war. After World War II, China had been left devastated and the United States stepped in to provide more aid for reconstruction to China than it had to any other country. This included 50 000 Marines, and planes and ships to help transport Nationalist forces to regions being evacuated by the Japanese. It also included $1 billion worth of military supplies. The Nationalist forces, however, proved inefficient and incompetent, and support for the Communist Party of China grew among the population. The conflict that followed was one of the largest of the twentieth century and ended in victory for the Communist Party in October 1949.

Although Mao admired Lenin and Stalin, communism in China under Mao was significantly different from Russian communism. "Maoism," as his brand of communism came to be called, focussed on the revolutionary role of peasant farmers rather than the industrial working class. It also emphasized the role of the People's Liberation Army, and, finally, it relied on the elevation of Mao himself to cult-like status.

The first step towards social justice and equality was the Agrarian Reform Law (1950–1956), which redistributed millions of acres — almost half of China's arable land — so that all rural households owned a plot of land. This succeeded in destroying the class of landlords and rich peasants. Ultimately, a system of

Party Chairman Mao Zedong developed his own style of communism. In a series of revolutionary programs, he transformed Chinese society. Describe current Canada—China relations.

rural collectives known as communes was established. This system was one of the cornerstones of the Great Leap Forward (1957–1959), a radical reorganization of village life designed to modernize China and move it closer to true communism. Unfortunately, for various reasons, this was a disaster. Agricultural production fell sharply, which, combined with poor harvests and bad weather, led to massive famine. Though Mao stepped down from power as a result, he stayed on in the powerful position of Party Chairman; soon he would reassert himself in an even bolder undertaking.

During the first 10 years of communist rule, fundamental change occurred in agriculture and cities were reorganized as industry was nationalized. Political reforms sought to eliminate rival ideologies through often violent and brutal measures taken against "counter-revolutionaries." Within the family, major changes were also taking place as the communists focussed on equality of rights for women. Social reforms abolished infant and forced marriages, concubinage, and infanticide. Divorce and abortion became legal. Birth control was promoted to curb rapid population growth, and drug addiction was attacked as a social evil and vastly reduced.

After a brief hiatus, Mao Zedong re-emerged with a new plan for what he saw as the goals of the communist revolution. He felt that many of those in power had become complacent, corrupt and unresponsive to the needs of the people. With this in mind, he launched the Great Proletarian Cultural Revolution (1966–1969). The Cultural Revolution aimed to eliminate the emerging new bourgeoisie and restore the ideals of communism. No aspect of Chinese society remained unaffected as party institutions were destroyed, education was reorganized, and traditional culture was attacked.

The "little red book" called *Quotations from Chairman Mao* was published in many languages as a guide to revolutionary movements. It became a best seller in North America.

Mao had faith in the masses — particularly the peasantry — to mobilize effectively and carry out necessary changes. He also targeted Chinese youth who, in their fervour to root out deviants and detractors, became an aggressive revolutionary force that swept the countryside. High school and university education were paralysed for 10 years as students studied only

Mao's "little red book" — a collection of his beliefs to guide this new movement. The political and social turmoil caused by the Cultural Revolution threw China into a state of chaos from which it would not emerge until Mao's death in 1976. Since that time, China has created greater links with the international community, joined the United Nations, and modernized society based on a more Western model, though retaining its socialist flavour and Communist Party rule.

Latin America

Almost all of Latin America had been independent since 1820. The course taken by Latin American countries in the twentieth century was therefore significantly different from those of Africa and Asia. As Spain and Portugal retreated as colonial powers in the region, first Britain and then the United States asserted their interest in the area. Neither country entered into formal imperial relations with Latin American countries but, rather, developed a relationship that some analysts have called "neocolonialism." Neocolonialism is the tendency of some nations to control and dominate other nations, not through direct rule but by supporting the ruling power economically and militarily. When the dominant nation's interests are threatened, it will often intervene. In this case, the U.S. adopted a neocolonial relationship with Latin America (the Monroe Doctrine, 1823) which included intervention to protect its economic interests in the region. This was similar to the U.S. Cold War policy of fending off and undermining possible communist regimes.

In Latin America, neocolonialism, combined with the characteristics and challenges of domestic South American politics, have led to turbulent and violent times in the latter half of the twentieth century. Latin America has a long history of favouring rule by military leaders or *caudillos* and this trend continued with a proliferation of military dictatorships. These often brutal and violent regimes were perpetuated by the United States, which allied itself with dictators who were friendly to U.S. policy and interests.

U.S. Intervention in Guatemala, Chile, and Nicaragua

The history of Guatemala since 1948 clearly illustrates the policy of U.S. interventionism. In 1948 Guatemalans elected a government formed of a coalition of reform liberals, socialists, and communists. Its leader was Jacobo Arbenz, and its primary objective was social reform, particularly by means of land reform. The idea of redistribution of land to the masses was particularly threatening not only to the Guatemalan elite, but also to the military and the church, both of which opposed radical reform. Strong opposition also came from the American-owned United Fruit Company, which was the principal landowner in Guatemala.

Understanding the powerful forces of opposition and fearing a U.S.-sponsored military *coup*, Arbenz decided to buy arms to protect his country's democratically elected government. Because those arms were bought from communist states, the U.S. claimed he was a Soviet ally and made it a priority to prevent this movement from escaping the U.S. sphere of influence. The CIA trained and equipped members of the Guatemalan elite living in exile to stage a *coup*, and the U.S. ambassador in Guatemala convinced the military not to protect the government when the coup took place. When the exiles invaded in 1954, Arbenz was forced to flee and his government fell. The new government installed was a U.S.-backed military regime, and one of its first acts was to ban the Communist Party and restore land to the United Fruit Company. The term "banana republic" was henceforth used to describe a puppet government put in place by the U.S. to ensure access to indigenous resources such as banana and other fruit crops.

A similar situation occurred in Chile in the 1970s when the democratically elected socialist government led by Salvador Allende was toppled by a military *coup* — again backed by the U.S. The 15 years of military rule that followed led to the implementation of capitalist policies but, unfortunately, did not seem to benefit the country economically. The regime was also notoriously brutal. General Augusto Pinochet led a

Augusto Pinochet was charged with war crimes in Chile. What is his status today?

reign of terror against opposition, and this led to the imprisonment, torture, and murder of political prisoners. In 1988 the country returned to democratic rule as a result of popular pressure, and Pinochet was defeated in 1989. He was arrested while travelling in Britain in 1998 to be tried for crimes against humanity. Pinochet avoided being extradited to Spain for trial in March 2000 and has since returned to Chile where charges against him were pursued.

Nicaragua had also experienced U.S. intervention in domestic politics dating back to 1909. The U.S. Marines actually occupied Nicaragua until 1933 to ensure the stability of a government friendly to U.S. interests. From 1933 to 1976, Nicaragua was ruled by military dictator Anastasio Samoza Garcia and, later, by his two sons. The Samozas were client politicians of the U.S. and ruled to further their personal interests and monetary gain. In 1961 the Sandanistas, a rebel group named after Augusto Cesar Sandino who had organized opposition during the years of U.S. occupation, began an insurgency. Samoza aggressively countered their actions. Finally, in 1978 the murder of newspaper editor Pedro Joachim Chamorro prompted a war of liberation, forcing Samoza out of the country to seek refuge in the U.S. The new president, Daniel Ortega, was soon faced with civil war (1981) against the "Contras," a rebel group that was supported financially and militarily by the United States.

These examples illustrate the willingness of the United States to intervene in Latin American domestic politics when it serves American economic or foreign policy interests. This is not a tendency confined to the countries of Latin America but, rather, a general tendency of the West in its relations with the non-Western world.

THE MIDDLE EAST

Although more than 55 years have passed since the end of World War II, the second half of the twentieth century has not been a time of peace. While Western nations have avoided another world war, conflict is ongoing in the non-Western world. Religious and political interests have clashed repeatedly in the Middle East, the crossroads of East and West. Under tolerant Ottoman rule, Muslim, Christian and Jewish communities had co-existed peacefully. In the nineteenth century, however, an intellectual import from the West — the concept of the nation-state — spread throughout the Middle East. The Young Turks, under the leadership of Kemal Atatürk, thoroughly westernized Turkey beginning in 1909. Nationalism also inspired various Arab groups. Meanwhile, in Europe, the Jewish people, who were still subjected to widespread anti-Semitism, began to dream of a Jewish state where they could live without fear of persecution. For historical reasons, the most logical location for a Jewish homeland was Palestine, which had been under British mandate since 1916.

Dreams of nationhood, whether Turkish, Arab or Jewish, clashed with European imperial plans. As Ottoman Turkish authority weakened in the last decades of the nineteenth century, Britain and France seized the opportunity to extend their influence in the Middle East. They especially wanted to protect access to the Suez Canal, which lay on the route to India and the Far East, and where both countries had imperial possessions. The discovery of oil in the region added another critical factor to the situation.

From 1915 to 1916, the British planted the seeds of the Arab-Israeli conflict that still plagues the Middle East. Secret negotiations between Sheri Hussein (1853–1931), the Arab ruler of Mecca in the Arabian peninsula, and the British High Commissioner led to a

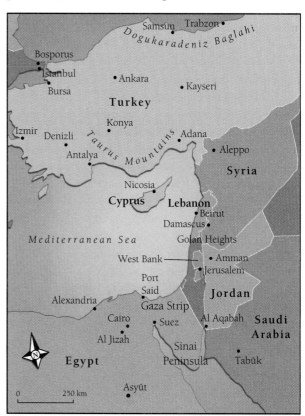

■ FIGURE 14.1 Key Territories in the Middle East
How might you have drawn the borders of a modern Israeli state in order to minimize the potential for conflict?

belief that Arab independence would follow when the fighting in Europe was over. The British fostered anti-Turkish feelings among the Arab countries ruled by the Ottoman Turks because they wanted to bring them into the war against Germany. In the end, the secret Sykes-Picot Agreement divided up the Middle East between Britain and France.

The Balfour Declaration of 1916 announced British support for "a national home for the Jewish people" in Palestine. Though not specified in the Declaration, many people, both Jewish and non-Jewish, assumed that "national home" meant an independent state. The Arab majority of Palestine had not been consulted. A small number of Jewish people had always lived in Palestine, but the Arabs constituted 90 percent of the population, and they too had inhabited the region for many centuries. A wave of Jewish immigration from Europe during the 1920s and 1930s increased the Jewish population considerably. The Arabs regarded Jewish immigrants as Western intruders.

Since Palestine was a British protectorate, the British needed to balance competing Arab and Jewish claims. In 1939, even though Jews were being persecuted by the Nazis, Britain decided to limit the Jewish population in Palestine to one-third of the total and to restrict Jewish land purchases. The Holocaust in Europe changed public opinion in the West in favour of an independent Jewish state in Palestine. In the meantime, Jewish settlers were moving into the area in defiance of British attempts to keep them out. Terrorist attacks made it increasingly difficult for the British to maintain order, and Britain appealed to the United Nations. The UN proposed that Palestine be divided into Arab and Jewish sectors, with the city of Jerusalem, which was sacred to both Jews and Muslims, remaining an international zone. All three areas were to be linked in an economic union.

The Jews reluctantly accepted this proposal, but the Arabs did not because it gave them less land than they already occupied. In frustration, the British simply pulled out in 1948. Immediately after their departure, the Arab residents attacked, and the first Arab-Israeli War broke out. In the midst of hostilities, the Jews announced, on May 14, 1948, the creation of the independent state of Israel, with David Ben-Gurion as its president. When the fighting stopped, the Israelis had expanded their territory by one-third. Thousands of Arab Palestinians fled to the Gaza Strip and the West Bank (of the Jordan River), where they set up huge refugee camps. The Israelis regarded the refugees as potentially disruptive, while the Arabs believed they should be returned to their homelands.

Arab nations refused to recognize the state of Israel and tensions continued. One of the most dangerous episodes in Arab-Israeli relations was the Suez Crisis in 1956. That year, Egyptian president Gamal Abdel Nasser nationalized the Suez Canal. His action infuriated British and French investors who owned shares in the Canal. The Israelis suspected that Egypt was supporting Palestinian guerrillas. A combined Israeli, British, and French force landed in the Canal

Leaders at the Camp David Accord: President Carter mediated as Prime Minister Begin gave back Israeli land and President Sadat recognized the state of Israel. Why is there still no peace in the region?

zone. The rest of the world was shocked at British and French intervention, and in a rare show of agreement, both the U.S. and the U.S.S.R. expressed strong disapproval of the British-French action. Mediation by Canadian External Affairs minister Lester Pearson paved the way for the arrival of a UN peacekeeping force, whose presence allowed British, French, and Israeli troops to withdraw peacefully.

No peace treaty was signed after the Suez Crisis and both sides expected that a war would flare up again. In 1967 Nasser demanded the withdrawal of the UN peacekeepers and called for a joint Arab (Egypt-Jordan-Syria) attack against Israel. The Israelis moved swiftly and decisively to defend themselves against the Arabs before the latter even had a chance to mobilize. In the course of what became known as the Six-Day War, Israel captured the Golan Heights from Syria, the Sinai peninsula and adjoining Gaza Strip from Egypt, and the West Bank of the Jordan River, tripling the size of the Israeli state and increasing the number of Palestinian refugees. It was a humiliating experience for the Arab countries involved. As a result, the Palestinian Liberation Organization, a force founded in 1964 to reclaim the Palestinian homeland from Israel, became more militant. The UN called for the Israelis to withdraw from the occupied territories in return for Arab recognition of Israel's right to exist, but the Arabs refused to recognize Israel and guerrilla fighting continued.

A decade later, in 1973, on the eve of Yom Kippur, a Jewish high holy day, Egypt and Syria attacked Israel and again Israel succeeded in driving them back. In retaliation, the largely Arab Organization of Petroleum Exporting Countries imposed an oil embargo against Europe and the U.S., which had backed Israel financially and militarily. Attempts to find a negotiated settlement went on for several months until Egyptian president Anwar Sadat (1918–1981) took a dramatic and courageous step: He made a personal visit to Jerusalem and addressed the *Knesset* (Israeli parliament). This was the first time an Arab leader had travelled to Israel. His goal was peace. Eventually, thanks to the patient mediation of American president Jimmy Carter, Israel's prime minister Menachem Begin and Sadat met at Camp David in the

U.S. in 1979 and signed a peace treaty. Israel handed the Sinai back to Egypt, and Egypt recognized the existence of the state of Israel. The Camp David Accord did not resolve the Palestinian refugee problem, nor the dispute over who owned the Gaza strip.

Limited as it was, the Camp David Accord angered the Arab world. From the Arab point of view, Egypt had betrayed the Arab cause. President Sadat was assassinated in 1981, but his successor, Hosni Mubarak, continued the policy of peace with Israel. It was not until 1991, after the Gulf War, that Israel and the PLO began to negotiate. By 2002, despite periodic attempts at negotiation, the situation in the Middle East remains unstable. Frequent Arab terrorist bombings in Jerusalem and elsewhere are followed by swift Israeli reprisals. Negotiations between the leader of the Palestinian Authority, Yassar Arafat, and the Israeli prime minister Ariel Sharon are at a bitter standstill.

THE COLLAPSE OF COMMUNISM

In 1989 the Soviet Union collapsed, and the ensuing turmoil reverberated throughout the Soviet bloc. In the case of Poland, where hatred of Soviet domination went back to the early postwar period, the unravelling of communism had begun before Gorbachev came to power. The Catholic Church in Poland, which claimed the allegiance of 25 million people out of a population of 28 million, served as a rallying point for Polish dissent. In 1979 the newly elected pope John Paul II, who was Polish, visited his homeland and gave moral support to a trade-union movement called Solidarity, which had originated in the Gdansk shipyards. Its leader, Lech Walesa, demanded recognition of Solidarity as an independent (non-communist) trade union. As had happened in the past, the government countered with repressive measures and outlawed Solidarity in 1981.

During the 1980s, the Polish government failed to govern effectively and could not crush the Solidarity movement. As a last resort, Polish communist leaders called upon the Soviet Union for help. But unlike previous Soviet leaders, Gorbachev refused to intervene.

■ FIGURE 14.2 1989: Turmoil in Eastern Europe

How do you think the new European economic union might succeed where military alliances have failed to maintain peace and order?

He advised the Polish communist government to solve its own problems, in effect repudiating the Brezhnev Doctrine. There would be no repetition of the invasion of Hungary in 1956 or of Czechoslovakia in 1968. Polish leaders had no choice but to legalize Solidarity and hold free elections. To no one's surprise, Lech Walesa was elected president. His government successfully negotiated a peaceful end to communist rule in June 1989. Such an outcome would have been unthinkable a decade earlier.

Elsewhere in Eastern Europe, a similar pattern was repeated as one communist government after another collapsed. In November 1989, East German authorities dismantled the Berlin Wall, preparing the way for German reunification a year later. In Czechoslovakia, the transition from one-party rule to democracy, under President Vaclav Havel, was so smooth it was called "the Velvet Revolution." Bulgaria, Hungary, and Albania also managed to transfer power from communist to non-communist parties relatively peacefully. The only exception was Romania, where dictator Nicolae Ceausescu's refusal to leave office led to an armed revolt and his (and his wife's) summary execution in 1989.

No one would have predicted that communist systems could have collapsed so suddenly with so little resistance. Europeans were euphoric, for it seemed that an era of peace and reconstruction had finally replaced communism and the last lingering tensions of the Cold War.

Ethnic Tensions

As in the former Soviet Union, the sober reality of rebuilding society replaced some of the optimism created by the fall of communism. One of the most intractable problems was ethnic tension, which caused Czechoslovakia to break up into two independent states, and Romanians to turn against their Hungarian

Breaking down the Berlin Wall in 1989. What impact did the reunification of Germany have in Europe?

minority. Perhaps the most tragic example of the impact of ethnic unrest is in what was formerly known as Yugoslavia.

The independent Kingdom of Yugoslavia came into being in 1921. It fell apart during World War II but emerged again in 1945 as an independent republic. The Yugoslav federation consisted of six republics: Serbia, Croatia, Bosnia, Montenegro, Slovenia, and Macedonia. The people were Slavic (Yugoslav means South Slav) of three religions: Eastern Orthodox, Roman Catholic, and Muslim. Its undisputed leader was a staunch communist named Josip Broz, usually called Tito.

A major problem facing Tito and his country was nationalist tension. Its roots lay deep in history, but most serious was the postwar animosity between Serbs and Croats. During World War II, Croatians and some Muslims had collaborated with the Nazis to exterminate an estimated 1 million Jews and Serbs. In trying to overcome the legacy of bitterness, Tito (a Croat) insisted that Yugoslavs put the past behind them. He preached a message of "brotherhood and unity" and tried to balance the interests of major ethnic groups. He reduced Serbian influence in Belgrade and promoted Serbs to power in Croatia. Tito was a skilled politician and popular because of his wartime leadership of the Partisans, who had resisted the Nazis. He also took Yugoslavia out of the Soviet orbit in 1948, an impressive move that appealed to Yugoslav national pride. He decentralized the economy to an extent unknown in Soviet-bloc satellites and established links with the West.

After Tito's death in 1980, the tensions repressed by his authoritarian regime exploded. Tito's successors lacked his political skill and failed to deal decisively with the country's economic problems. Tito's major failing was probably his unwillingness to transform the nation into a truly democratic society. Communism had served as a repressive glue that held enemies together. In the 1980s, communism lost its appeal, and for want of a unifying ideal, local leaders fell back on strident nationalism, which divided Yugoslavia further. Slovenia declared its autonomy in 1991, followed by Croatia, then Bosnia, reducing Yugoslavia to Serbia, Montenegro, and Macedonia, which constituted 40 percent of its former territory.

Serbian president Slobodan Milosevic aimed to build a greater Serbia on the ruins of Tito's Yugoslavia. He incited the Serb minorities in Croatia and Bosnia to rebel and demand Serbian protection. Initially, most Serbs did not respond to his nationalist propaganda, but an intense media campaign changed their minds. Croatia's Nazi past and murder of thousands of Serbs did not help the cause of reconciliation. The Bosnian declaration of independence prompted Serbian military intervention. Ostensibly, Milosevic acted to protect Bosnian Serbs but a brutal policy of "ethnic cleansing" against Bosnian Muslims accompanied military intervention. What resulted was war and the ruthless destruction of the Bosnian Muslims and their rich heritage. The beautiful and historic Bosnian capital, Sarajevo, was destroyed beyond recognition by Serbian fire.

The public was horrified by the degree of brutality they saw on television and the policy of ethnic cleansing, but no consensus evolved on how to deal with the situation. United Nations peacekeepers tried to set up safe havens; diplomats made one attempt after another to mediate the dispute; the UN distributed humanitarian aid. These efforts all came to nothing. Unlike in the Persian Gulf, military intervention was difficult because of the mountainous terrain. Furthermore, Western nations, as part of NATO, could not agree on how to proceed in the region and sometimes were blinded by their own interests in the conflict.

In 2000 a popular uprising removed Milosevic from power and he was arrested by Yugoslav authorities and charged with corruption, abuse of power, and inciting violence. The UN war crimes tribunal demanded that he be handed over to The Hague to stand trial for war crimes, although the Yugoslav government did not immediately comply. By the end of 2001, Milosevic was in custody and standing trial at the International Court at The Hague for war crimes.

With the end of the Cold War, people had hoped that the world could enter a new era of peace and prosperity. Yet, the situation in Yugoslavia, the continuing tensions in the Middle East and the ethnic and religious rivalries elsewhere remind us that the era of peace has yet to arrive.

Review, Reflect, Respond

1. If someone unfamiliar with the United Nations asked you to explain briefly what it is and what it does, how would you respond?

2. To what degree could one argue that the ongoing conflict in the Middle East is a legacy of imperialism and the difficulties of decolonization?

3. Many people living in the former Yugoslavia feared the Yugoslav federation would not survive the death of Tito. What made Tito the glue that held the federation together?

TERRORISM AND ITS ROOTS

Terrorism is not new, and has been used by many societies throughout history. Terrorism is defined as the use of methods that cause extreme fear in an attempt to govern or coerce governments or communities. Those who use terror often believe that by inflicting suffering and pain on civilians, governments will change their policies or be overthrown. Terrorist groups generally claim to represent some greater political goal. It is important that both elements — targeting civilians and political motivation — be present for an act to be labelled terrorist.

One usually thinks of terrorism as committed by individuals, but as the definition suggests, terrorism can also be carried out by a government seeking to instill fear in its own people or its enemies. For example, in 1972, Palestinian guerillas kidnapped and killed Israeli athletes during the Olympic games, and, in reprisal, the Israeli government bombed Palestinian refugee camps. Since 1945 there have been countless terrorist attacks on citizens. The situation in the Middle East has given rise to scores of suicide bombings, car bombings, and other terrorist acts. Elsewhere in Europe, the Irish Republican Army, whose cause is the unification of Northern Ireland and the Irish Republic, have taken responsibility for innumerable terrorist acts, as have Irish Protestant militia groups and Basque separatists in Spain. In Canada, in October

Prime Minister Chrétien brings the support of Canadians to the site of the 9/11 attacks. How did Canadians help?

1970, the FLQ (Front de libération du Québec) launched a series of terrorist bombings and kidnapped a British trade official named James Cross. The FLQ, during what became known as the October Crisis, also kidnapped and murdered Canadian reporter Pierre Laporte. Etched in recent memory are the September 11, 2001 attacks on buildings in the United States. Hijacked airplanes were deliberately crashed into the World Trade Center in New York and the Pentagon in Washington, DC, killing thousands of civilians, police officers, firefighters and military personnel.

What do these attacks have in common? They are all sudden, horrifying acts of violence with tragic consequences. What causes people to commit such terrible acts? The root cause of terrorism seems to be fanaticism — excessive zeal for an idea or goal. In many cases, fanaticism presents itself as the irrational commitment of an individual to a cause. More recently, however, acts of terrorism have involved the careful co-ordination of larger numbers of people, as was the case in the September 11 attacks in the United States and the bombing of American embassies in Kenya and Tanzania.

The question then becomes: How are a few fanatics able to recruit people to their cause? A particular climate must exist in order for this to happen. Such climates or situations generally include two key elements. The first is despair. People may be easily recruited to commit extreme acts if they feel they are in a situation from which there seems to be no escape — extreme poverty, destitution, or oppression. Secondly, they may have real or perceived grievances against those who are their targets (for example, the imposition of economic sanctions on one country by one or more other countries, or the oppression of one group or people by another). How terrorism is recalled in history, however, can be a relative matter. For example, Nelson Mandela was jailed for what was called terrorism against the apartheid regime of South Africa. Years later, however, he was hailed as a national hero and eventually became president of an apartheid-free South Africa. As historians then, how do we view situations like this, where one group's terrorist is another group's freedom fighter?

Global Economic Relationships

Corporate profit and consumer demand have always fuelled global economic relations, but in the last half of the twentieth century, these forces have developed and changed the way they have an impact on world relations. For centuries, depletion of resources in Europe led to a search for new sources, which in turn led to new trading relationships between Europeans and other peoples. For example, when the Europeans exterminated their own beaver populations, they found an alternative supply in the New World. The resulting fur trade brought together native hunters, European merchants, and consumers into a wide trading network.

In the sixteenth century, Europeans acquired a taste for sugar. To satisfy this demand, sugar plantations spread throughout the Caribbean. At the height of the plantation system, a three-cornered trading pattern linked Europe (source of trade goods) with Africa (source of slaves to work the plantations) and the Americas. By the mid-nineteenth century, Britain could not grow enough grain to feed its population and was obliged to import it from Russia and North America. In the 1960s, the Soviet Union, despite efforts to grow more grain during the Khrushchev years, also had to buy wheat from North America.

The current global economic system is, in some ways, different from that of earlier centuries. First, the whole world is involved in this system. One is hard-pressed to think of a country unaffected by the machinations of global trade. Second, the financial base for the current system draws funds from all major industrial nations and from the oil-producing lands of the Middle East. These funds are then invested where there is cheap labour and/or profitable markets. Third, governments of leading industrial states have tried to coordinate their efforts to ensure the stability of the global economy by creating trade organizations and agreements such as the International Monetary Fund (IMF), the World Bank, the World Trade Organization, the G7 (later G8 with the addition of Russia), the Organization for Economic Cooperation and Development (OECD), the Asia Pacific Economic Co-operation Forum, and so on.

Some of these organizations have been formed, in part, to deal with conflict that arises when nations compete for a share of a dwindling resource. The European appetite for fish and the depletion of herring stocks in the Baltic by the sixteenth century prompted sailors from France, Spain, Portugal, and England to sail for the Grand Banks of Newfoundland, where they found abundant cod. For centuries, there was enough cod for everyone, but by the end of the twentieth century, intensive fishing techniques and a growing world appetite for fish had depleted fish stocks, including the once plentiful cod. Competition for remaining fish stocks off the Grand Banks has led to confrontations between Canada and Spain. Similarly, as coal reserves in Europe dwindled during the post-World War II period, Europeans imported oil from the Middle East to meet their growing needs. In 1973, however, OPEC imposed an oil embargo on exports from the Middle East. The scarcity of oil caused the price to skyrocket from US$2.00 to US$30.00 per barrel, traumatizing the European economy and sending shock waves throughout the world.

The resources of the world's oceans may be worth trillions of dollars. Whom should they benefit? Industrialized nations which have the technology to exploit them? Should industrialized nations share resources with poorer countries? At the Law of the Sea Conference convened in 1974 to discuss ocean resources, the Maltese delegate, Dr. Arvido Pardo, suggested that the ocean beds be declared the "common heritage of humankind" and their riches diverted to a UN agency to help the poorer countries. He was opposed by developed nations determined to defend their national interests. When the International Law of the Sea Treaty came into effect in 1994 after 20 years of negotiations, it gave maritime countries (such as Canada) jurisdiction over the continental shelf along their coastlines. Conflicting interests in resources can divide nations just as needs and wants can bring them together through trade.

The Multinational Corporation: A New Imperialism?

When Europeans disbanded their colonial empires in the postwar period, they retained economic links with the newly independent countries. Trade knits together consumers, producers, suppliers, and governments from different countries into a single economic system. Globalization blurs the question of whether a product is made in one country or another. Consider the case of Chevrolet's Geo Metro. This car was designed in Japan and built in Canada using Canadian- and Japanese-made parts at a Canadian factory managed by Japanese executives. Is the Geo Metro a Canadian or a Japanese car?

This Ford automobile is being assembled in Mexico. Is it a Mexican car?

The vehicle for economic globalization is the large international, or multinational, corporation. McDonald's, with its more than 3 000 franchises throughout the world, is one very well known example, as are Boeing, General Motors, Nissan, Nortel Networks, and others whose names appear in the headlines of the business section of the newspaper. These corporations wield enormous power and are wealthier than some countries. General Motors, for example, has a budget that is bigger than the economies of Saudi Arabia, South Africa, Thailand, and Indonesia combined.

It is important to note that the leading one hundred multinational corporations are all located in the West. Generally, their headquarters and planning, marketing and advertising divisions are in a Western industrialized nation while their manufacturing is based in a developing nation. Nike makes 40 million pairs of shoes per year, none of which are manufactured in the United States, where its offices are based. Why do multinational corporations choose non-Western, developing countries as the bases for their manufacturing? First, they are a source of cheap labour; Nike can pay workers in Indonesia an average of 82 cents per day. Moreover, this factor is not limited to unskilled labourers. A computer programmer in India draws a salary equivalent to only about $10 000 per year, perhaps a tenth of what she or he would earn in the U.S.

In addition to cheap labour, developing nations generally have far fewer environmental and social regulations than Western nations. The exploitation of these regulations (or their lack) by multinational corporations has come under fire, particularly during the 1990s, as working and living conditions in these areas of the world are more exposed in the Western media. Many leading brand-name manufacturers like The Gap and Wal-Mart have been accused of using sweatshops to manufacture their products in "free trade zones" (also known as "export processing zones") in the developing world. These factories generally employ young women at very low wages, make them work long hours, subject them to sexual harassment and respond aggressively, often violently, to attempts by workers to form unions. Since the multinational corporation does not own, but rather contracts the sweatshops, critics charge that this allows corporations to abdicate responsibility for inhumane working conditions.

To operate successfully, multinationals require an open business environment that allows them to choose the locations of their manufacturing and markets. It is no coincidence that the integration of the world economy has marched in step with international accords promoting free trade. The best known is the General Agreement on Tariffs and Trade (GATT), now known as the World Trade Organization (WTO). Its aim is to eliminate tariff barriers and other trade restrictions between member nations. The North American Free Trade Agreement (NAFTA), the European Union, and Asia-Pacific Economic Co-operation are regional agreements to reduce barriers to trade.

Garment workers in Asia. What might be the hopes and expectations of these people?

In developing countries, multinationals and the world economic system are often regarded as a sophisticated form of Western imperialism, or a kind of neo-colonialism. In order to obtain badly needed foreign exchange, developing nations grow crops in demand in the West even if doing so comes at the expense of feeding their own people. In the Philippines, for example, half the bananas, sugar and pineapple are exported, while many Filipino children are malnourished. In Africa, land that could be used to sustain local populations is used instead to produce goods such as tea, coffee, cacao, and palm oil for export.

Developments such as these have often been in response to the requirements of a worldwide financial network. In 1944 the International Monetary Fund and the World Bank were created by the Western powers to monitor the world's currencies and provide loans to developing countries. Although these are not democratic institutions and, therefore, not directly accountable to the citizens of any country, they wield enormous power. During the 1970s, Western banks extended loans to several developing countries that had immense reserves of oil. During the 1980s, the price of petroleum fell. A rise in the prices of manufactured goods and imported food aggravated the situation. Debtor countries could not repay their loans on schedule. They renegotiated loans through the IMF, which demanded that countries restructure their economies in return for such loans. These Structural Adjustment Programmes became the standard protocol for developing countries requiring loans to deal with their balance of payment problems. The Structural Adjustment Programs generally require governments to agree to meet certain conditions in order to receive a loan from the IMF/World Bank. These conditions can include the devaluation of currency, the encouragement of foreign investment, decreased government spending on social services, increased interest rates and taxes, decreased wages, deregulation, and privatization.

Such structural reforms weigh most heavily on the poorer sectors of society. Unicef has noted these effects and reported that in the 1980s, average incomes in Latin America and Africa decreased by 10 to 25 percent. Unicef also found that in the 37 poorest nations, government spending on health decreased 50% and on education 25%. It estimates that 500 000 children die per year due to the measures imposed as a result of debt. Global markets may give the consumer greater choice and cheaper prices, but the benefits of greater choice are available only to a small proportion of the world's population. The gap between rich and poor continues to widen. In 1960 the average annual income in the poorest countries was estimated at one-thirtieth of the income in the wealthiest; by 1990, it had widened to one-sixtieth.

Global Economics and the Environment

Ecological issues are related to the utilization of resources. The list of ecological concerns keeps getting longer. With tourism, germs can hitch a ride to all parts of the globe. Ballast dumped by ocean-going merchant vessels introduces species to territories where they have no natural predators to keep their populations in check. The zebra mussel, which has invaded the Great Lakes from its native Europe, is one example. Disposal of nuclear wastes, oil spills in ocean waters, deforestation, and industrial emissions are other examples of transnational environmental problems caused by human activity.

Global warming is probably the most alarming phenomenon of ecological interdependence. The primary contributor to warming is carbon dioxide (CO_2), followed by methane and chlorofluorocarbons (CFCs). Human activities from all parts of the globe contribute to atmospheric warming. Factory and automobile emissions and burning coal release CO_2 into the atmosphere. Deforestation and overgrazing by animals remove the plant cover that utilizes CO_2.

Reforestation programs, the use of alternative energy sources, energy-efficient technologies, and responsible forms of agriculture could minimize the effects of global warming. Energetic action to stop emissions requires global co-operation, which is politically difficult to accomplish. Citizens of rich countries are reluctant to make lifestyle changes, since very few would readily turn in their cars for ecologically friendly bicycles. Developing countries that want to enjoy a higher standard of living resent being told by wealthier nations that they must adopt costly environmental regulations. The Rio Summit in 1992 made

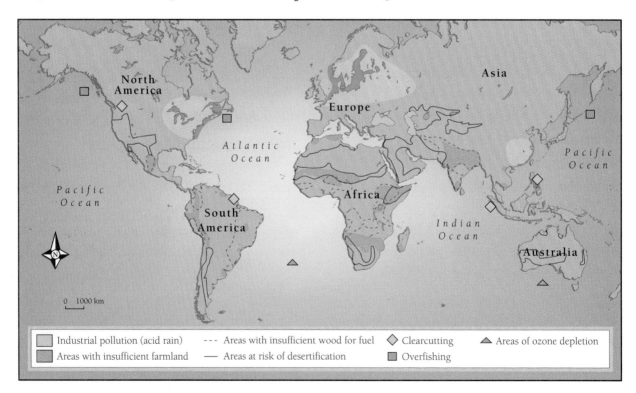

Industrial pollution (acid rain) — - - Areas with insufficient wood for fuel ◇ Clearcutting ▲ Areas of ozone depletion

Areas with insufficient farmland — Areas at risk of desertification ■ Overfishing

■ FIGURE 14.3 Global Environmental Damage

Most industrial nations share the responsibility for this environmental destruction and now want to place world-wide controls on industry. Many emerging nations say these rules unfairly hurt their economies. What do you think should be done?

these differences quite clear. Brazilian delegates insisted that the industrialized world had no right to demand that Brazil stop cutting the Amazonian rain forest, since they were contributing the lion's share of pollutants to the atmosphere with their excessive consumption of energy. Corporations such as pulp and paper companies or oil and gas companies are powerful lobby groups that fight environmental regulations.

Environmental priorities vary widely from one part of the globe to another. For the industrialized world, control of population is a primary concern because of the strain huge numbers of people put on resources. In developing countries, however, large families ensure the survival of the family unit since infant mortality can be higher. While in the developed world, many are worried about global warming and the resulting hole in the ozone layer, for poor peasant families in the developing world, the most pressing environmental problems are getting enough clean water, food, and firewood or other fuel to survive.

History
BYTES

What do corn, cotton, soybean, and canola have in common? They are all genetically engineered crops. Genetically modified (GM) foods have quietly become pervasive on supermarket shelves. In fact, over 60 percent of all processed foods contain one or more of these four crops. The revolutionary technology employed in GM foods takes DNA from one organism and transfers it to another (usually unrelated) organism. The aim of GM foods has been to produce crops resistant to herbicides or viruses, or that are able to produce their own pesticides. Although manufacturers claim that GM foods will have a revolutionary effect on feeding the world's population and even go as far as saying that they can solve the world's hunger problems, skeptics point to the unknown effects of these new food products on the environment and on human health.

IN THE GLOBAL VILLAGE, WHO OWNS THE MASS MEDIA?

During the Cold War, the Iron Curtain separated Eastern Europe from the West. Little news of the outside world reached Soviet bloc citizens and the West knew little about them. It is unlikely that an Iron Curtain could ever come down again because the world has witnessed an explosion in communications technologies: television, tape recorders, videos, fax machines, personal computers, and, of course, the Internet. All of these contribute to a worldwide exchange of information beyond the control of any government.

In 1964 Canadian professor Marshall McLuhan published *Understanding Media*. One phrase from that book became part of everyday language — "global village." McLuhan predicted that as communications systems became more efficient, people would be brought closer together and cultural distinctions would diminish, creating a world community or global village. McLuhan's prediction has become a reality to some extent. Satellite communication enables television networks to deliver instantaneous coverage of world events to millions of TV viewers. Stock exchanges from Tokyo to Vancouver and from New York to London are linked into one global 24-hour financial market. Multinational corporations do business without regard to national boundaries. Environmental problems are also globally shared; witness the fallout from the Chernobyl nuclear catastrophe in Ukraine, which spread 50 tonnes of radioactive waste over northeastern Europe. Fallout in the soil even contaminated food exported from Chernobyl to different countries. We seem to have become a "McWorld tied together by technology, ecology, communications, and commerce," wrote Benjamin Barber in the *Atlantic Monthly* for March 1992.

Television has also been instrumental in creating a snowball effect when it comes to political and social change or revolution. A French satellite photographed

Noam Chomsky

Noam Chomsky and the Media, *Manufacturing Consent*

Do we live in a truly democratic nation? Are freedom of speech and freedom of the press protected so that they remain the safeguards of democracy? Noam Chomsky, a leading intellectual and political analyst in the United States, would answer "no." He focusses his attention primarily on the motives and actions of the United States in determining both its domestic and foreign policies. He argues that the nature of democracy in countries such as the U.S. and Canada is very limited: Our political system and the mass media that supports it are geared towards preserving and enhancing the power of the elite groups in society — not the average person.

On the role of the mass media, Chomsky writes:

Those segments of the media that can reach a substantial audience are major corporations and are closely integrated with even larger conglomerates. Like other businesses, they sell a product to buyers. Their market is advertisers, and the "product" is audiences, with a bias towards more wealthy audiences, which improve advertising rates ... It would hardly come as a surprise if the picture of the world they present were to reflect the perspectives and interests of the sellers, the buyers, and the product ...[1]

Mass Media and Big Business

The influence of advertisers is sometimes far more direct. "Projects unsuitable for corporate sponsorship tend to die on the vine," the *London Economist* observes, noting that stations have learned to be sympathetic to the most delicate sympathies of corporations. The journal cites the case of public TV station WNET, which "lost its corporate underwriting from Gulf+Western as a result of a documentary called *Hunger for Profit*, about multinationals buying up huge tracts of land in the Third World." These actions "had not been those of a friend," Gulf's chief executive wrote to the station, adding that the documentary was "virulently anti-business, if not anti-American." "Most people believe that WNET would not make the same mistake today," *The Economist* concludes. Nor would others ...[2]

Bias in the Media: A Case Study

History doesn't offer true controlled experiments but it often comes pretty close. So one can find atrocities or abuses of one sort that on the one hand are committed by official enemies and on the other hand are committed by friends and allies or by the favoured state itself — by the United States in the U.S. case. And the question is whether the media accept the government framework or whether they use the same agenda, the same set of questions, the same criteria for dealing with the two cases as any honest outside observer would do.[3]

Chomsky argues that the media treat these two types of cases very differently. He offers the examples of atrocities committed by the Khmer Rouge in Cambodia versus the Indonesian invasion of East Timor. Both happened during the same time period and had comparable levels of violence and death, but received very different levels of media coverage.[4]

Early seventies Cambodia (and) Timor are two very closely paired examples. Well the media response was quite dramatic. THE NEW YORK TIMES INDEX 1975–1979: "TIMOR" 70 COLUMN INCHES " CAMBODIA" 1,175 COLUMN INCHES.[5]

A propaganda model provides a ready explanation for this quite typical dichotomous treatment. Atrocities by the Khmer Rouge could be attributed to the Communist enemy and valuable propaganda points could be scored, although nothing useful could be done, or was even proposed, for the Cambodian victims. The image of Communist monsters would also be useful for subsequent U.S. participation in terror and violence, as in its crusades in Central America shortly after ...[6]

Atrocities in East Timor, however, have no such utilitarian function; quite the opposite. These atrocities were carried out by our Indonesian client, so that the United States could readily have acted to reduce or terminate them. But attention to the Indonesian invasion would have embarrassed a loyal ally and quickly disclosed the crucial role of the United States in providing military aid and diplomatic support for aggression and slaughter. Plainly, news about East Timor would not have been useful, and would, in fact, have discomfited important domestic power groups.[7]

By 1978 it [the killing in East Timor] was approaching really genocidal levels. The church and other sources estimated about two hundred thousand people killed. The U.S. backed it all the way. The U.S. provided 90 percent of the arms. Right after the invasion arms shipments were stepped up. When the Indonesians actually began to run out of arms in 1978, the Carter administration moved in and increased arms sales. Other Western countries did the same. Canada, England, Holland, everybody who could make a buck was in there trying to make sure they could kill more Timorese.[8]

It wasn't that nobody had ever heard of East Timor; crucial to remember that there was plenty of coverage in the *New York Times* and elsewhere before the invasion ... After the Indonesians invaded the coverage dropped. There was some, but it was strictly from the point of view of the State Department and Indonesian generals. It was never a Timorese refugee.

As the atrocities reached their maximum peak in 1978 when it really was becoming genocidal, coverage dropped to zero in the United States and Canada, the two countries I've looked at closely. Literally dropped to zero.[9]

1. Who decides what is *news*?

2. If we accept Chomsky's analysis, how might it change the way we use the media as a source of information? How can you be sure you are getting a balanced picture of a news event?

3. Consider an important event that received extensive media coverage, e.g., September 11, the bombing of Afghanistan, the healthcare system in Canada, and so on. Given Chomsky's assertion that the media's purpose is to protect and promote the interests of the government and business elites, how might this have affected the way the event was covered? What questions were not asked? What alternatives were not considered? Whose point of view prevailed?

the 1986 Chernobyl nuclear disaster and broadcast the photos to all parts of the world. Despite their government's attempts to limit access to satellite signals, Soviet citizens improvised ingenious ways to bypass these restrictions, such as fashioning satellite dishes from the seats of children's sleds. Television captured the Tiananmen Square protests in China. The images of demonstrators and tanks were seen all over the world, including China. In Europe, during the Year of Revolution (1989–1990), television coverage of the destruction of the Berlin Wall built up an unstoppable momentum for change.

A striking example of the effect of television on international affairs was the CNN (Cable News Network) coverage of the 1991 Gulf War. "The Gulf War," claims one media expert, "established CNN as an entirely new kind of global information system — an intelligence system that serves not only 70 million households but also world leaders." Knowing that American chiefs of staff watched CNN, Iraqi officials often delayed press conferences until CNN reporters arrived. American officials did much the same.

A world audience from 103 countries watched the Gulf War. As the U.S. bombed military targets near Baghdad, a dazzling show of firepower lit up the Baghdad sky. This was followed by pictures of Scud missiles exploding and computer-generated images of "smart" bombs targeting Iraqi cities. Television images were carefully constructed and, many say, used as propaganda by the U.S. government to drum up support for the war effort without providing much in the way of substantial analysis or dissenting opinions.

Networks increasingly rely on "parachute journalism" (sending a video team to an ongoing-news spot) because it is cheaper than maintaining a foreign news bureau. It also means that reporters no longer need to establish their own local contacts and must rely on official sources for information. None of the CNN reporters covering the Gulf War could speak Arabic or knew much about military affairs. Their ignorance of such matters left them ill-equipped to question the UN and U.S. military, who had learned how to present the

military viewpoint using the latest TV technology in a very sophisticated way.

An important and often overlooked aspect of the mass media is the concentration of ownership of the media in the hands of relatively few large corporations. In North America there are over 1 800 daily newspapers, 11 000 magazines, 11 000 radio stations, 2 000 TV stations and 2 500 book publishers. This totals over 28 000 media entities; but over half of these are owned by only 23 for-profit corporations. Does the concentration of corporate ownership of the media compromise the "truth" that is presented to the public? Noam Chomsky, American political analyst and leading intellectual, writes in his book *Manufacturing Consent* that understanding the motivations and machinations behind media coverage of any story is essential to being a savvy and aware consumer of the media. He points to various filters that work to distort the facts and shape media coverage including the necessity of being attractive to potential advertisers and the tendency to support the political and economic status quo.

[A CORPORATE AGENDA?

Proponents of globalization claim that trade organizations and agreements will ultimately benefit all nations — rich and poor — since they create a level playing field by removing trade barriers and inconsistencies in government policy. They argue that by creating an integrated global economy, the developing world will "catch up" to the nations of the West by adopting similar policies.

WEB CONNECTION

www.mcgrawhill.ca/links/legacy

Go to the site above to find out more about Noam Chomsky and *Manufacturing Consent*.

Opponents of these global trade agreements claim that the economic policies promoted favour large corporations, not citizens. They point to policies that encourage unlimited export of profits, privatization of state assets and social services, a low wage and de-unionized labour force, and unlimited exploitation of natural resources. They maintain that the social impact of such policies includes increased inequality and poverty — particularly for children, women, and indigenous peoples — and decreased affordability and accessability of essential services.

Furthermore, opponents of free trade claim that global trade agreements in their current form pose a serious threat to national sovereignty. For example, the proposed Free Trade Agreement of the Americas, which seeks to bring all the nations of the Western Hemisphere (except Cuba) into NAFTA, includes a section that opponents fear would seriously undermine a government's ability to determine policy for its own country. Paragraph 11 of the proposed agreement would allow corporations to sue governments for implementing domestic policy that compromises their ability to generate profits. Hypothetically, this could mean that a pulp and paper company could sue a government for passing laws to protect rainforest from being clearcut.

One of the most extreme examples of the power of corporations over governments concerns Royal Dutch/Shell in Nigeria. Shell is an oil and gas company that has been drilling for oil in the Niger Delta since the 1950s. Although its presence has been central to the Nigerian economy (80% of the nation's revenues come from oil), it has been disastrous for the Ogoni people who live on the land where the drilling has taken place. The Ogoni's land has been polluted by gas fires, open pipelines, and oil spills. Although the yearly extraction of oil is worth billions of dollars, the Ogoni people still suffer from poverty and lack of services.

To protest Shell's presence and practices, internationally acclaimed author Ken Saro-Wiwa led a protest movement called MOSOP (Movement for the Survival of the Ogoni People). The world was shocked when, in November 1995, Saro-Wiwa and eight other Ogoni leaders who had protested against Shell were executed by the Nigerian government. The military regime headed by General Abacha claimed the execution was the sentence for murder, of which a military tribunal

People protesting the activities of the Shell oil company in Nigeria.

had convicted Saro-Wiwa. Human rights groups around the world, along with the governments of Canada, Australia, Germany, and France had attempted to pressure the Nigerian government to withdraw this sentence. The pressure was based on the revelation that the Nigerian military had been acting on behalf of the corporation in squashing protest. Shell blamed the conflict on ethnic tensions.

These concerns have led to the creation of innumerable citizens' groups that have focussed their energies and resources on altering what they perceive as a corporate agenda. They charge that this corporate agenda is forcing the hands of governments around the world to adopt policies and support practices that are ultimately harmful to citizens.

PROPOSING A CITIZENS' AGENDA

The 1990s has seen what may be the most vigourous protest activity since the 1960s. Protest movements, however, are somewhat different from those in the 1960s. In the past, targets of protest tended to be governments that were using aggression or oppression to achieve their ends. Since then it has become clear that multinational corporations wield more power than some governments, while not being subject to the same democratic controls. Today, multinational corporations are more often the targets for protest movements around the world.

In her book, *No Logo*, Canadian author Naomi Klein pointed to three campaigns in particular that illustrated the potential impact of a citizens' agenda: the campaigns against Nike, McDonald's, and Shell. The opposition to Nike has centred on its use of sweatshop labour in the developing world. McDonald's has long been a target of protesters for various reasons, but came into the limelight especially during a court case that came to be known as "McLibel." McDonald's sued four local activists in London, England, for libel when they were handing out a brochure in front of their fast-food restaurants. Unfortunately for McDonald's, the ensuing court case lasted seven years and became a forum for exploring and exposing a vast number of misdemeanours and questionable practices of the corporation. Although the activists were ultimately ordered to pay damages, they claimed a victory since they were able to open up a multinational company to serious public scrutiny.

Finally, the protest movement against Shell focussed on the right to protest and free speech, which was undermined by the execution of Nigerian Ken Saro-Wiwa and other Ogoni leaders. All these campaigns made extensive use of the Internet to reach thousands of people across the world and co-ordinate efforts on a global scale. The Internet has been called "the most potent weapon in the toolbox of resistance" since it allows citizens groups from different continents to share information instantly and without having to rely on the mass media to cover their side of a story.

These movements are examples of a larger, growing sentiment: many citizens are understanding the impact that multinationals have on our lives and are attempting to wrest power from corporate hands and place it squarely in the hands of the public. Protests have taken the form of worldwide boycotts, political pressure on governments, and exposure of unfair corporate practices in the mainstream media. Schools, universities, and municipal governments are rejecting sponsorship or donations from corporations whom they feel are guilty of social injustice.

Meetings of global trade organizations and alliances such as the G8 and APEC are regularly faced with massive protests. People from all over the world gathered at Seattle, Washington, in 1999 at a meeting of the World Trade Organization and took the world by surprise at the size, organization, and vehemence of their protest. As a countermeasure, governments hosting these meetings are creating larger barriers and using increased security to keep the protesters out. In Quebec City — the site of the Summit of the Americas in 2000 — concrete barriers and barbed wire fences earned the scorn of protesters who dubbed the city "Fortress Quebec." The clashes between security forces and individual protesters are also becoming increasingly violent, a situation protest organizers fear will undermine their actions.

Review, Reflect, Respond

1. Given the roots of terrorism, what do you believe is the most effective action governments can take to eradicate terrorist activity?

2. Terrorism has been described as the weapon of the weak against the strong. Does this justify its use? Explain your answer with historic examples.

3. Explain why multinational corporations often choose to locate manufacturing facilities in the developing world.

The Future of the West?

In 1918 an unknown German high-school teacher, Oswald Spengler, published The Decline of the West. Spengler believed that, like living organisms, civilizations go through a cycle of birth, growth, and decline. He believed that European civilization, which began to take shape in the Middle Ages, had reached the final stage of its development: It lacked vitality and its creativity was gone. Spengler's book became a spectacular bestseller in the 1920s and was translated into many languages. Its gloomy tone coincided with the pessimism that pervaded Europe after the Great War.

Had Spengler lived to see the carnage of World War II, he might have been too appalled to write. The destruction inflicted on the European continent, in both human and material terms, exceeded that of World War I. The emergence of two superpowers, the United States and the Soviet Union, diminished Europe's international influence to a point lower than that of 1918. The process of decolonization further undercut European hegemony. Although European nations recovered some degree of their former power in the post–World War II period, the forces working toward the creation of a global village make impossible the kind of world domination Europe enjoyed at the turn of the century. Other regions (China, Japan, the Americas) have emerged as powerful competitors for global dominance, and the commercial interests and profit motives of multinational corporations transcend national boundaries anyway.

Reflections

Does this mean that European, Western civilization is doomed? And has it been possible, as Frantz Fanon hoped, to take a step beyond Europe? As we struggle to formulate an answer to these questions, we should keep in mind two generalizations: Cultural change is ongoing, and cultures do not evolve in isolation. The Europe of the 1990s is far different from the Europe of 500 years ago, when explorers and adventurers began the process of world conquest and domination. As history marches forward, will multinational corporations continue to gain pre-eminence over democratically elected governments? Is the anti-corporate protest movement the newest form of nationalism? Are we witnessing the emergence of a new form of personal identity — the global citizen?

Chapter Review

Chapter Summary

In this chapter, you have seen:

- how the process of imperialism and decolonization has played a role in shaping present world relations
- the variety, intensity, and breadth of change that has taken place during the past half-century
- that key forms and styles of artistic expression reinforce and/or challenge prevailing social and political values
- a variety of government responses to the social consequences of key economic changes in the West and the rest of the world

Reviewing the Significance of Key People, Concepts, and Events (Knowledge and Understanding)

1. Understanding the emergence of the global village over the past half century requires knowledge of the following concepts, events and people and an understanding of their significance in the shaping of the history of the world in the latter half of the twentieth century. Select and explain two from each column.

Concepts	*Events*	*People*
Global Village	Suez Crisis	Frantz Fanon
Balfour Declaration	The Gulf War	Mohandas Gandhi
satya graha	Summit of the Americas	Ho Chi Minh
British Commonwealth of Nations		Lech Walesa
La francophonie		Naomi Klein
UN Security Council		Ken Saro-Wiwa
OPEC		
WTO		

2. The process of decolonization, although playing out differently in various parts of the world, has not been without its challenges and conflicts. Copy and complete the chart below in your notes. This chart will provide a summary of the process and impact of decolonization in many areas of the world.

Area of the World	Challenges Posed by Decolonization	Nature of Conflicts (if any)	Current Situation
Latin America			
Far East			
Africa			
Middle East			
South Asia			

Doing History: Thinking About the Past (Thinking/Inquiry)

3. Given what you have learned about European imperialism and colonialism from 1500 to the twentieth century, can you think of reasons why philosophies of non-Western peoples are generally not taught in Western schools? Support your answer with historic material.

4. In the prologue to his provocative book, *Millennium: A History of the Last Thousand Years*, Felipe Fernandez-Armesto offered these observations on the study of history:

   > As the end of the millennium draws on, it is already apparent that the preponderance of Atlantic civilization is over and that the initiative has shifted again, this time to some highly "developed," technically proficient communities of the Pacific seaboard ... History is a state of near-equilibrium, punctuated by ... spasmodic change. Most of the long-term trends and long-term causes conventionally identified by historians turn out, on close examination, to be composed of brittle links or strung together by conjecture between gaps ... The experience of changes — bewilderingly fast, barely predicted — in our own time, has helped curtail the hunt for long-term trends...

   Comment on how the study of history might change if we embrace the ideas and assertions of Fernandez-Armesto quoted above.

Applying Your Learning (Application)

5. Often, when nations are in conflict, they try to demonise the other side. This is done through editorials that are very one-sided, political cartoons lampooning the enemy's leaders, news stories that are biased, and TV coverage that emphasises the right of one side versus the wrong on the other. Research your local papers, magazines or TV news coverage about an ongoing conflict. Detail, with evidence, the different ways in which the coverage clearly is supporting one side in the conflict.

6. Imagine you are a mediator between some Western power and or institution (e.g., IMF, World Bank, and so on) and a terrorist organization that uses violence to achieve some political or economic goal. Prepare four questions you would ask each side before beginning the talks. For each of the questions, provide a response you would expect based on what you have learned in this chapter. Finally, write a one-paragraph assessment of the likelihood of success for the mediated talks.

Communicating Your Learning (Communication)

7. Create a two-panel poster that depicts the world at the dawn of the new millennium. On one panel, show the world as it is, and on the other panel, show the world as it could be — free from war, intolerance, poverty. The poster should communicate the two views of the world using symbols, pictures, key words, and appropriate titles and subtitles.

8. Write and design a flyer that promotes the advantages of either the corporate or citizens' agenda. Alternatively, create a flyer advocating a compromise solution that meets the objectives of both agendas. Pay close attention to the purpose and audience for the flyer so it achieves the greatest impact.

Unit Review

Reflecting on What You Have Learned (Knowledge and Understanding)

1. While consumers around the globe eagerly embrace icons of American culture — from Big Macs and Coca-Cola to Hollywood movies — there are those who criticize the Americanization of European culture. Do you think the export of American products poses a real threat to other cultures? Should governments provide funding for "home-grown" entertainment or block the importation of American culture to protect their own?

2. In the decades following World War II, several international organizations were created to provide stability and to help avoid future conflicts. For each one listed below, briefly describe its purpose and assess its success at meeting its goals.

International Organization	Purpose	Assessment
United Nations		
NATO		
International Monetary Fund		
World Bank		
Warsaw Pact		

Practising Historical Interpretation (Thinking/Inquiry)

3. Was the Cold War the product of clashing superpowers intent on empire building, or clashing ideologies that made co-operation virtually impossible? Could a world divided along diametrically opposed political lines have found a way to work harmoniously?

4. "McDonald's in Moscow and Coke in China will do more to create a global culture than military colonization ever could." Explain why you agree or disagree with this statement. Be sure you think about economic, cultural, and political factors.

Applying Your Historical Understanding (Application)

5. Check the definition of genius given in the Unit One Review. Select one of the historical figures from the list below and explain why you believe he or she should be remembered as a genius. You may need to do additional research on some individuals.

   Jean Paul Sartre

   Simone de Beauvoir

   The Beatles

   Margaret Thatcher

   Mohandas Gandhi

   Albert Einstein

   Marshall Tito

6. When historians a century from now reflect on the past few decades of the twentieth century, what will they write about? What are the lasting achievements and developments that will shape the world over the next century? Write a two- or three-paragraph response supported with factual evidence.

Communicating Your Learning (Communication)

7. Write an exchange of letters between two imaginary siblings. Assume one of the siblings lives in either North America or Western Europe and the other sibling lives in Eastern Europe, Asia, Africa, the Middle East, or Latin America. Your letters must clearly establish when the exchange is taking place (between 1950 and 2000) and where the siblings live. Make sure historical events and trends are clearly reflected in the letters. The letters should reflect the political, economic, and cultural situation in the particular area of the world being discussed.

8. Create a political cartoon, 3-D model, or drawing that captures the essence of the global village. Be sure your model, cartoon, or drawing clearly shows the ways in which different parts of the world are interconnected.

---

* Now complete Skills Focus Six (p. 599):

The Final Edit: Revising, Editing and Polishing Your Essay.

The Lessons of History

CHAPTER EXPECTATIONS

By the end of this chapter, you will be able to:

- *critically analyse historical evidence, events, and interpretations*

- *demonstrate an understanding of ideas and cultures that have influenced the course of world history since the sixteenth century*

- *demonstrate an understanding of the importance of cause and effect in historical analyses of developments in the West and throughout the world since the sixteenth century*

- *evaluate the key factors that have led to conflict and war or to co-operation and peace*

Eurodisneyland located in France has not been the success its builders had hoped for. Can you think of why many Europeans might not embrace the Disney enterprise?

LEARNING FROM HISTORY

The lessons of history are of global significance but require individual attention and action to learn. Each of us can reflect on how the events of the past led us to the present and how they might shape our future. Is history made by the actions of individuals, or is humanity swept along by the magnitude of certain events? Does the power of an individual or an event to shape history suggest an ordered unfolding of historical events? Or is history by nature random and chaotic?

When we pause to reflect on the lessons we can learn from a study of the past, what do we find? Does history offer us a moral guide by which to live our lives, or insights into the challenges ahead? Does your familiarity with past individuals and events help you to make sense of a world that can often seem devoid of meaning?

What follows is a guide to the lessons you have learned from this study of history. Consider each section carefully and form your own opinions and beliefs. Then ask yourself: How has history helped me define myself and my place in the world? How has becoming aware of past events, the origins of ideas, customs and rituals helped me to understand my own culture, beliefs, and values? You may find that some of the sections have little relevance to you, and that there are issues and ideas missing from this book. What do you think might have been included?

History can be a powerful tool to guide or misguide people. A little knowledge of the past is a dangerous thing; a good knowledge of history is one of the best safeguards against repeating the mistakes of the past. For example, in 1855 Comte Joseph-Arthur de Gobineau extolled the virtues of the Aryan race when he wrote:

> Everything great, noble, or fruitful in the works of man on this planet, in science, art, and civilization derives from a single starting point ... History shows that all civilization derives from the White race, that none can exist without its help, and that a society is great and brilliant only so far as it preserves the blood of the noble group that created it.

In the latter half of the nineteenth century, many Europeans (and North Americans) embraced these ideas and argued that Europeans (i.e., Whites) were vastly superior to other races. Questionable science and manipulations of history were often used to support blatantly racist theories. None of the writers trumpeting the superiority of the Aryan race bothered to mention that the Aryans appeared on the historical horizon in India about 2500 BCE. They also ignored the debt the West owed to Islam, to the Chinese, the Japanese and other peoples for their many scholars, inventors, and explorers. For generations, history has been used selectively to justify atrocities and to legitimize actions that denied basic human rights to millions of people. A knowledge of history makes us aware of the dangers of charlatans purporting to know the truth, and helps us guard against such abuses.

History and the Dangers of Cupidity

Cupidity means an insatiable desire to acquire possessions and material wealth — greed, in other words. While much can be said of the tremendous scientific and technical advances of the past half millennium, the modern age, by and large has been shaped by the cupidity of European powers. From the voyages of exploration in the fifteenth century, through the partitioning of Africa in the nineteenth century, to the current forces of globalization, greed has been a driving force. Some may argue that the quest to improve the material well-being of human beings has been an impetus for entrepreneurs and innovators whose work has ultimately improved the quality of life for millions of people. But what about those who have suffered because of cupidity? Was cupidity a contributing factor to the slave trade that decimated African societies and denied millions their basic human rights? Was it cupidity that led Belgium's King Leopold to exploit the Belgian Congo and its rubber trade with little regard for the lives of the workers? Could cupidity explain the outbreak of World War I? Have we ignored the lessons of history, or have we learned about the destructive effects of cupidity on the lives of the less fortunate and on the Earth that sustains us?

Folly in the Course of History

When we make a choice based on limited or misleading information, we may be accused of making a poor decision. When we ignore the evidence and take actions contrary to our interests or the interests of others, it may be folly. Folly is a foolish or senseless act or behaviour. In her book *The March of Folly*, American historian Barbara Tuchman suggests that throughout history, decisions contrary to the interests of governments and institutions have been made despite ample warnings of the dire consequences that could follow.

Consider the Renaissance popes, for example. Martin Luther was only one of many calling for reforms and an end to the abuses of the Church. Did the popes respond to these concerns, or did they stubbornly forge ahead, seeking to silence their critics? Was the American Revolution an inevitable consequence of London's refusal to attend to the repeated complaints of the colonists? Was there no warning that Vietnam was an unwinnable war? Why did presidents Kennedy and Johnson spend billions of dollars and sacrifice thousands of lives in a conflict their advisers urged them not to pursue. Were these acts of folly? Did folly contribute to the lack of preparedness on September 11, 2001, when Al Quaeda terrorists attacked the World Trade Center in New York and the Pentagon in Washington?

Before concluding that folly played a significant role in any of these events, we must look at the evidence. As the expression goes: "Hindsight is 20/20." It is easy to look back and suggest what actions should have been taken. It is far more challenging, and worthwhile for us to try to understand the perspective of the people responsible for security at the time. Did they ignore warnings and evidence of an imminent attack? Or were the attacks totally unpredictable? If Tuchman is correct, that many such major events are, to some degree, products of folly,

what can we learn from them to guide us in the future? How will you avoid acts of folly in your own life?

History and Chaos

History is often presented as a neat package, conveniently broken down into periods and studied according to themes. This orderly arrangement helps make the past intelligible and easier for the student of history to follow. It can, however, lead to a belief that history actually unfolds sequentially, as if some guiding hand were leading us through time. Many of us take comfort in knowing that the apparent chaos of our day-to-day lives does make sense in the grand unfolding of historical events. But is this a fallacy and merely some attempt to bring order out of apparent chaos? Perhaps history really is random events, from which little can be predicted. It is only by working in hindsight that we can take disparate events and shape them into a meaningful narrative. If history is in fact more chaotic than we want to believe, what lessons can we draw from the randomness of the past?

Ingenuity and Inhumanity

Over the past 500 years, humanity has conquered many diseases that once ravaged or wiped out whole societies throughout the world. Advances in technology allow us to travel long distances in short periods of time; we can even venture into space. Human ingenuity has led to revolutions in agriculture, medicine, communications, and manufacturing. Yet, over the same span of time, human beings have brought previously unimaginable levels of efficiency and sophistication to the technology of warfare. While advances in medicine have saved lives, advances in military technology have claimed millions. While developments in transportation allowed human beings to step onto the moon, the same technology can launch lethal bombs over thousands of kilometres to precise targets. The work of Charles Darwin helped us unravel the mysteries of life on Earth, yet it has been twisted and manipulated into a justification for genocide. The great human paradox would appear to be that humanity's seemingly unlimited ingenuity and resourcefulness can destroy as many lives as it can save. Could human ingenuity be harnessed solely for the purpose of improving life for everyone? For now, at least, human ingenuity and inhumanity seem destined to travel together through time.

Cultivating a Sense of "Shared Humanity"

Philosophers have used the concept of a "state of nature" to describe human history prior to the development of social organizations. Scientists and philosophers agree that humans are social beings. While Hobbes believed that life in the state of nature was "short, nasty, and brutish," Locke believed it offered humanity limitless freedom. But both agreed that the greatest good would be realized when humanity acted collectively, as a community. It is this shared sense of humanity that allows society to move forward, building upon the advances made by earlier generations.

Such idyllic societies, in which the common good prevails, have been rare in history. Has the capitalist system of the past few centuries always paid heed to morality? Are the forces of globalization considering the human toll as well as the bottom line? Can economic efficiency and human rights co-exist? What has history taught us about the interrelationship between economic systems and safeguarding the rights of the most vulnerable? Does history suggest that the greatest hope for the future lies in the pursuit of individual wealth or in a shared sense of humanity? Can these co-exist?

Humility: History's Most Important Lesson?

Napoleon believed he was unstoppable. The Titanic was believed to be unsinkable. World War I was to be the war that would end war. North Americans believed the 1920s was the first decade of perpetual prosperity. Adolf Hitler proclaimed a Reich that would last a thousand years.

Napoleon was defeated, the *Titanic* sank, wars continue to this day, the economy crashed in 1929, and Hitler's Third Reich lasted barely a decade. What does all this suggest? Perhaps, that humility is the greatest lesson of history? Human arrogance has us led to believe that it is our right to rule over all other creatures. At times, this arrogance has extended to inhumane dominance of fellow human beings. Consequences of such arrogance have included the loss of countless species of plants and animals, and the genocides of entire peoples such as the Arawak of South and Central America and the Beothuk, original inhabitants of Newfoundland. Not to forget the Holocaust, the killing fields of Cambodia, ethnic cleansing in Bosnia-Herzegovina, and massacres in Rwanda, East Timor, and Stalinist Russia.

Modern human beings have inhabited Earth for a mere 35 000 years. Relative to the almost 200 million years the dinosaurs lived, and the five billion years of Earth's history, this is a minuscule amount of time. The belief that we can endlessly harvest Earth to meet our needs, and use and abuse nature as we see fit, reflects a dangerous arrogance that could hasten our own demise. A little humility would remind us that we share this planet with other human beings and all other species of creatures and plants, and that the greatest hope for a prosperous future, indeed any future, lies in co-operation and mutual respect. Think about the past five centuries and ask yourself how events might have unfolded had individuals acted with greater humility and respect for others? Can we learn from past mistakes? Which models from the past should guide our actions in the future?

Using History As Our Guide

It is often said that history repeats itself. This is not true. The study of the past *can* help us better understand the present and prepare for the future. It can never enable us to predict the future. The study of history can help identify certain relationships and trends that may allow us to plan our actions more logically and humanely.

A mural painted by Canadian children for Canada Day.

Yet another fallacy of history is that certain events were inevitable. Nothing is ever inevitable. Certain factors can render an event likely, but to suggest inevitability is to imply the course of history is predetermined. This denies the role of chance and a multitude of other human and non-human interventions — madness, greed, luck, natural disasters. So, a study of history can shed light on how chance and human participation influenced the events that shaped the world we live in today. It may even light the path to the future.

Is History Progressive?

In the introduction to this book, we raised the question of whether or not history unfolds progressively. Conflicting views on this issue were presented. Western logic leads us to believe that history should be progressive, with each generation building on the discoveries of its predecessors. But is this the conclusion you would draw now, after a study of five centuries of history?

Facing the Challenges of Tomorrow

In the post-industrial world we inhabit, where all countries are linked by satellites and international trade agreements, we can no longer ignore events outside of Canada. We live, for better or worse, in a global village where our actions and those of others have implications beyond our borders. Our lives are interrelated. To respond to the challenges that lie before us, we must accept the pluralism of our world and work toward a harmony that embraces religious and cultural differences.

Notes

Prologue: Making History in the West

1. For a translation of Vico see Giambattista Vico, *The New Science of Giambattista Vico*, translated from the 3rd edition (1744) by Thomas Goddard Bergin and Max Harold Fisch. (Ithaca: Cornell University Press, 1948)

Unit One: The World Re-invented 1450-1700

Chapter One: Renaissance and Reformation 1450-1600

1. Thomas V. Cohen and Elizabeth S. Cohen, *Words and Deeds in Renaissance Rome: Trials Before the Papal Magistrates*. (Toronto: University of Toronto Press, 1993), gives a very full discussion of the workings of honour and tells lively tales that exemplify it.

2. E. A. Wrigley, *Population and History*. (New York, 1969) is a very clear introduction to the whole science of historical demography.

3. See Geoffrey Parker, *The Military Revolution, Military Innovation and the Rise of the West, 1500-1800*. (Cambridge: Cambridge University Press, 1988).

4. Elizabeth Eisenstein, *The Printing Revolution in Early Modern Europe*. (Cambridge: Cambridge University Press, 1983) offers an excellent overview and some fine images of Renaissance books and their ornaments.

5. For a complete version of *The 95 Theses see Project Wittenberg* at www.iclnet.org/pub/resources/text/wittenberg/luther/web/ninetyfive.html.

Chapter Two: The Age of Absolutism 1600-1715

1. See *A History of Russia, Fifth Edition*, by Nicholas Riasanovsky. (New York: Oxford University Press, 1993).

2. Quote by Karl van Mander from Laurie Schneider Adams, *Art Across Time*. (New York: McGraw-Hill, 1999) 645.

3. Passage from *Song for St. Cecilia's Day* excerpted from *Eighteenth-Century Literature*, edited by Geoffrey Tillotson et al. (New York: Harcourt Brace Jovanovich, 1969) 167.

Chapter Three: Contact and Conflict 1450-1715

1. See John C. Ricker and John Saywell, *Europe and the Modern World*. (Toronto: Irwin &Co., 1969) 289.

2. See James Michener, *Caribbean*. (New York: Fawcett Crest Books, 1989) 75

3. Excerpted from *The Cambridge History of English and American Literature (1907-21), Volume IV. Prose and Poetry: Sir Thomas North to Michael Drayton*, available at www.bartleby.com/214/0305.html.

4. Anthony Pagden, *The Fall of Natural Man: The American Indian and the Origins of Comparative Ethnology*. (New York: Cambridge University Press, 1982)

5. Quotation by John Lok[sic] from *Hakluyt, Voyages and Discoveries*, edited by Jack Beeching. (Harmondsworth: Penguin Books, 1987) 67.

Unit Two: An Age of Enlightenment and Revolution

Chapter Four: The Enlightenment 1700-1789

1. An English translation of Kant can be found in Immanuel Kant, *Immanuel Kant's Critique of Pure Reason translated by Norman Kemp Smith*. (New York: St. Martin's Press, 1965).

2. See O. Wade, *Studies on Voltaire: with Some Unpublished Papers of Madame du Châtelet*. (Princeton: Princeton University Press, 1947).

3. See "Frederick II, Political Testament," in George Mosse et al, *Europe in Review*. (Chicago: Rand McNally, 1957) 110-112.

4. See *A Source Book for Russian History, Vol. 2*, G. Vernadsky trans. (New Haven: Yale University Press, 1972) 453-454.

Chapter Five: Revolution to Restoration 1789-1815

1. Madame Roland lived in Lyons at the time of the Revolution. She was a vocal and leading defender of the cause of liberty, and was openly critical of the Terror.

2. Jack Zipes trans., *The Complete Tales of the Brothers Grimm*. (New York: Bantam Books, 1987).

3. Mercier describes life in Paris in Louis-Sébastien Mercier, *Panorama of Paris*, Helen Simpson trans. (University Park: University of Pennsylvania Press, 1999).

4. Passages about the Paris *salons* in Bonnie Anderson, *A History of Their Own Vol. I*. (New York: HarperCollins, 1988).

5. John Trusler, *Honours of the Table*, 1788.

6. An English translation of *Emile* found in Jean-Jacques Rousseau, *Emile, or On Education*, Alan Bloom trans. (Basic Books, 1979)

7. *The Memoirs of Madame Roland*, translated and edited by Evelyn Shuckburgh. (London: Barrie & Jenkins, 1989)

8. Charles Maurice de Talleyrand-Perigord (1754-1838). Through skill and cunning, Talleyrand managed to survive the reign of Louis XVI, the Revolution and the Terror, the Directory, the rule of Napoléon, and the reigns of both Louis XVIII and Louis Philippe. He became one of the most important diplomats in Europe during the late eighteenth and early nineteenth centuries. At the Congress of Vienna in 1814, Talleyrand fought to re-establish France as a political power equal to any on the Continent.

Chapter Six: The World in the Eighteenth Century

1. See Stephen Hay ed., *Sources of Indian Tradition, 2nd ed., Vol. 2: Modern India and Pakistan*. (New York: Columbia University Press, 1988) 13-14.

2. Quoted in André Gunder Frank, *ReOrient: Global Economy in the Asian Age*. (Berkeley: University of California Press, 1998) 279.

3. Cited in Garfield Newman and Cynthia Grenier, *Impact: Western Civilization and the Wider World*. (Toronto: McGraw-Hill Ryerson, 1996) 72.

4. Quoted in André Gunder Frank, *ReOrient: Global Economy in the Asian Age*. (Berkeley: University of California Press, 1998) 279.

Unit Three: Modern Europe, 1815-1900

Chapter Seven: The Birth of Modern Industrial Society: Europe 1815-1850

1. Friedrich Engels quote from Mark Kishlansky et al., *Societies and Cultures in World History.* (New York: HarperCollins College Publishers, 1995) 737.

2. The complete text of the Manifesto of the Communist Party can be found at: www.anu.edu.au/polsci/marx/classics/manifesto.html.

3. William Wordsworth, "Ode, Intimations of Immortality from Recollections of Early Childhood" in *The New Oxford Book of English Verse 1250-1950.* (New York: Oxford University Press, 1972) 512.

4. Samuel Taylor Coleridge, "The Rime of the Ancient Mariner Part II," in *The New Oxford Book of English Verse 1250-1950.* (New York: Oxford University Press, 1972) 529.

Chapter Eight: Nations in Upheaval: Europe 1850-1914

1. Information on Sarah Josepha Hale available at www.uvm.edu/~hag/godey/ shtable-1-56.html.

2. See "Ulysses" in *The New Oxford Book of English Verse 1250-1950.* (New York: Oxford University Press, 1972) 646.

Chapter Nine: Imperialism, Colonialism and Resistance

1. Albert Memmi quoted in John Isbister, *Promises Not Kept: The Betrayal of Social Change in the Third World.* (West Hartford CT: Kumarian Press, 1991) 100.

2. Passages by Leopold Von Ranke are from the Preface to the first edition of *Histories of the Latin and Germanic Nations from 1494-1514* (October 1824) found at web site *Europe in the Age of Revolution:* www.ucl.ac.uk/history/course/europe/weeks/ranke.htm.

3. See Rudyard Kipling, "The White Man's Burden." *McClure's Magazine* 12 (Feb. 1899) at: http://www.boondocksnet.com/ai/kipling/kipling.html. In Jim Zwick, ed., *Anti-Imperialism in the United States, 1898-1935.* http://www.boondocksnet.com/ai/ (March 30, 2002).

4. See Henry Labouchère,"The Brown Man's Burden." *Literary Digest* 18 (Feb. 25, 1899). http://www.boondocksnet.com/ai/kipling/labouche.html. In Jim Zwick, ed., *Anti-Imperialism in the United States, 1898-1935.* http://www.boondocksnet.com/ai/ (March 30, 2002).

Unit Four: The World at War 1914-1945

Chapter Ten: The War to End War, World War I 1914-1918

1. Quote from Erich Maria Remarque, *All Quiet on the Western Front.* "Im Westen Nichts Neues," (Ullstein A.G., 1928)

2. Rupert Brooke, "The Soldier" in Rupert Brooke, *1914 and other Poems.* (London: Sidgwick & Jackson, 1915).

3. Wilfred Owen, "Dulce et Decorum Est," in Wilfred Owen, *Poems by Wilfred Owen with an Introduction by Siegfried Sassoon.* (London: Chatto and Windus, 1921) 15.

Chapter Eleven: Between the Wars: An Anxious Generation

1. T. S. Eliot "The Lovesong of J. Alfred Prufrock," in *T. S. Eliot, The Complete Poems and Plays 1909-1950*. (New York: Harcourt, Brace & World, 1971) 3.

2. William Butler Yeats, "Easter 1916," in *The New Oxford Book of English Verse* (New York: Oxford University Press, 1972) 818.

Chapter Twelve: World War II 1939-1945

1. Excerpted from Gertrud Kolmar, *Dark Soliloquy, Selected Poems of Gertrud Kolmar*, trans. Henry A. Smith. (New York, 1975)

2. Tillman Durdins report and information about the massacre at Nanking is available at the BBC News web site: http://news.bbc.co.uk/hi/english/world/newsid_223000/223038.stm.

3. Azuma Shiros account at: http://news.bbc.co.uk/hi/english/world/newsid_223000/223038.stm

4. See Christopher R. Browning, *Fateful Months: Essays on the Emergence of the Final Solution*. (New York: Holmes & Meier, 1985).

5. Poem by Randall Jarrell in Randall Jarrell, *Complete Poems*. (New York: Farrar, Strauss & Giroux [1970])

Unit Five: The New World Order

Chapter Thirteen: The Western Experience 1945 to Today

1. The complete text of the *Universal Declaration of Human Rights* and more information is available at: http://www.un.org/rights/50/decla.htm.

2. Quote by Rachel Carson in Marty Jezer, *Rachel Carson*. (New York: Chelsea House, 1988).

3. Quote by Adela Rogers St. John in Judith Harlan, *Sounding the Alarm, A Biography of Rachel Carson*. (Minneapolis: Dillon Press)

Chapter 14: Challenge and Change in the Global Village

1. Noam Chomsky, *Necessary Illusions: Thought Control in Democratic Societies*. (Montréal: CBC Enterprises, 1989) 8.

2. Edward S. Herman and Noam Chomsky, *Manufacturing Consent: The Political Economy of the Mass Media*. (New York: Pantheon Books, 1988) 298.

3. Ibid, 298.

4. Chomsky, 8.

5. Mark Achbar, ed. *Manufacturing Consent: Noam Chomsky and the Media*. (Montréal: Black Rose Books, 1994) 94

6. Ibid, 107.

7. Herman and Chomsky, 302.

8. Achbar, 102.

9. Achbar, 103.

Skills Focus One

Laying the Foundation: Developing Inquiry Skills

The basis of any good research project, whether a report, essay, or documentary film, is a set of significant inquiry questions that provide a focus for your research. Although this may seem like the easiest step in preparing your research essay, it is probably the most important, and it requires considerable thought.

Select your topic carefully. You will enjoy the task of researching and writing a history essay and will be much more successful if you are working on a topic that is of genuine interest to you. You will find many suggestions as well as several sample inquiry questions in the Prologue and the Epilogue of this textbook. As well, spending a few minutes leafing through the pages of *Legacy: The West and the World* will help you generate many ideas for engaging research topics.

Effective inquiry questions are primarily analytical, not factual. Read the following questions. Based on whether each is mainly analytical (a good inquiry question) or factual (a poor inquiry question), decide which ones would be a good basis for a research paper and which would not.

1. When did the slave trade begin and end, and how many slaves were shipped from Africa during that period?

2. What impact did the slave trade have on African societies and are these effects still being felt today?

3. How did Napoleon manage to gain power, and what did he do with the power once he had it?

4. Did the *Code Napoléon* and the Concordat with the Catholic Church further the ideals of the French Revolution or betray them?

5. How wide is the gap in GDP between wealthy industrial countries and underdeveloped poor nations? What factors contribute to this gap?

6. How have historical forces such as imperialism contributed to the gulf between rich and poor nations? How is the current trend toward globalization increasing or decreasing that gap?

Notice that the odd-numbered statements are essentially factual. To answer these questions would simply require a quick look in a textbook or an encyclopedia. The questions do not require any critical analysis of the research and they would not allow you to develop a good thesis.

The even-numbered questions are more thought provoking and open-ended. They require a careful scrutiny of the evidence. They may also lead to much stronger thesis statements.

Now it is your turn. To get your research focussed and under way, write down your topic. Below it, list five significant inquiry questions. Once you have selected your topic and created your inquiry questions, share them with someone in the class to get feedback. Based on this feedback, revise or replace your topic or inquiry questions, if necessary.

Maintaining a Processfolio

Create a *processfolio* to hold all the steps you will complete on the way to writing your research paper. A *processfolio* is, in essence, a portfolio in which you keep your work in process. A binder set aside specifically for this work will serve as an excellent *processfolio*. Separate each step of the process with a divider, and **be sure you date each piece of work.**

Your work on your topic and your inquiry questions form the first section of your *processfolio*. Label it "Topic." Remember to date all of your work.

Skills Focus Two

Sleuthing Through the Ages: Bibliographies and Notes

Research is the foundation of historical studies. What we know about the past, we know because historians have invested countless hours doing research. As part of your historical studies, you too are expected to delve into historical records. Gathering research material is one of the most important steps in preparing an effective research paper. Insufficient evidence can lead to erroneous assumptions or faulty conclusions. How many sources are needed? Why are some sources more important than others? How can you possibly read so many books? How are some sources different from others? The following guidelines will help you carry out effective historical research.

Keys to Good Research

Variety and depth are the keys to good research. Relying too heavily on only a few sources means you may have a narrow perspective on the issue. This can leave you open to being duped by biased reporting of the evidence. It is best to start with a few general sources such as textbooks and general histories, in order to establish a context for your essay. This context will help you expand your search to other relevant and useful sources. Once you have a good grounding in your topic, you will find the primary documents and more detailed studies easier to understand and digest.

Preparing a Bibliography

Building a strong bibliography is a critical step in preparing to write a research essay. You must examine a variety of sources for your research to be valid. When building your bibliography, try to include both primary and secondary sources. When possible, use all types of sources available: print, video, oral history, and electronic information.

Remember...
1. Never number items in a bibliography.

2. Arrange sources in your bibliography alphabetically by author, or by title if no author is stated.

3. Include the name of the author (last name first), the title, where the source was published, the name of the publisher, and the year of publication.

4. Underline or italicize titles of books and periodicals (magazines, journals, reports).

5. Always follow an accepted format for a bibliography. Ask your teacher which format he or she would like you to use.

Sample bibliographic entries

One author:
Newman, Garfield. *Legacy: The West and the World.* Toronto: McGraw-Hill Ryerson, 2002.

Two authors:
Anderson, B. and Zinsser, J. *A History of their Own: Women in Europe Vol. II.* New York: Harper and Row, 1988.

More than two authors:
Bennett, Paul et al. *Canada: A North American Nation.* Toronto: McGraw-Hill Ryerson, 1995.

Section from a book:
Pierce, Charles Sanders, "The Fixation of Belief" in Donald C. Abel, *Fifty Readings in Philosophy.* New York: McGraw-Hill, 1994.

Periodical article:
Jones, Amanda. "The Retreat from Moscow," *Journal of Napoleonic Studies* 25 (October 1997): 101-126.

Your bibliography is the second section of your *processfolio.* **Label it "Bibliography." Remember to date all your work.**

Notes: Citing Your Sources

Notes are used to indicate sources of facts or quotations and to credit ideas borrowed from other authors. Notes are numbered and placed in the order they appear in your essay. They may be placed at the bottom of the page as footnotes, or at the end of the essay as endnotes. Here are some examples; **note how these citations differ from those in a bibliography:**

For a book:
3. Garfield Newman, *Legacy: The West and the World.* (Toronto: McGraw-Hill Ryerson, 2002) 72.

For a periodical article:
24. Amanda Jones, "The Retreat from Moscow," *Journal of Napoleonic Studies* 25 (October 1997): 101-126.

Your notes form the third section of your *processfolio.* **Label it "Notes." Date all your work.**

Skills Focus Three

Working With Primary Sources

Primary Sources: Primary sources are things recorded at the time of an event. They may include diaries, newspaper articles, government documents, pamphlets, or letters. Primary sources give us a first-hand account of an event or personality. Some provide limited analysis or carry the bias of the person reporting/recording the event.

Secondary Sources: Secondary sources tell us about past events; they are second-hand accounts. This textbook is a secondary source. Other secondary sources include books about an event, person or time period, encyclopedias, documentaries, and CD-ROMs. Secondary sources are interpretations of the past and may carry a bias or relate only selected aspects of the past. They are good sources to begin with, though, and can quickly establish a context for your research.

Form = Purpose + Audience

This simple equation is a useful tool to help you analyse and interpret primary documents. Always remember that the form of the document was determined by its purpose and audience. It should be read and studied with this in mind. For example, consider a diary (form). Its purpose is to record the events in someone's life. The writer was its intended audience. How would considering purpose and audience help in understanding an entry in Napoléon's diary? If we changed its form to an official company or government document, instead of a diary, how would this change in purpose and audience change how you interpret this document?

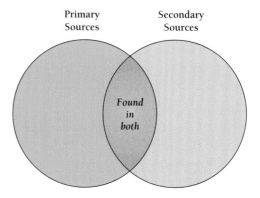

Working with Primary Sources

Primary Sources · Secondary Sources · *Found in both*

Working with Maps

Form = Purpose + Audience

This equation is also a useful tool for extracting information from maps. Maps provide the historian with a great deal of vital information. Just as with written documents, maps can be either primary or secondary. A map prepared during the early sixteenth century by European explorers is a primary source, while maps created for a text such as *Legacy: The West and the World* to illustrate sixteenth-century voyages are secondary sources. Compare the map shown here with the map on page 219. Keep in mind that all elements of a map have relevance and meaning. Never dismiss illustrations or icons as mere filler. They may convey important information.

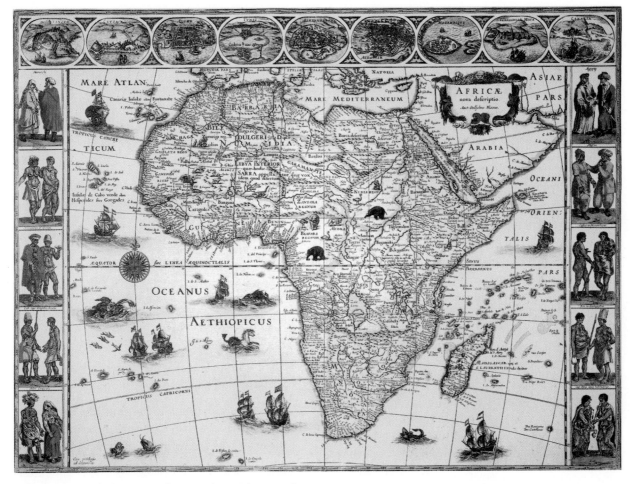

Blaeu's 1630 Map of Africa. How is this so much more than a map?

Review your inquiry questions in light of your analysis. After examining your material, and applying the equation Form = Purpose + Audience, are there any important questions for which you have no information? Do you need to do additional research or take your essay in a slightly different direction from what you previously thought?

Bias

Just as you read in the prologue of this text, with all historical material, both primary and secondary, you must always be on the alert for bias. It is important to remember that every source reflects a bias — the particular perspective, point of view, or experiences of the people involved in the creation of a source. No source can be bias free — not even the essay you are writing.

Skills Focus Four

Formulating a Thesis

A thesis is a statement of intent that clearly defines the central argument you will present in your research paper. A good thesis does not merely identify the central topic but rather sets out a position taken by the writer with respect to that topic, usually in one or two sentences. To be effective, a thesis must be stated clearly in the introduction and all the information and analysis in the essay must clearly connect to it. The sole purpose of any information and analysis a writer presents in a research paper is to support the thesis.

Now that you have completed all of your research, and carefully reflected on the evidence you have gathered, you are ready to formulate a thesis. When writers establish a thesis too early in the process, it can bias their research as they attempt to find the evidence to support the thesis they have created. Simply put, this is bad history-making. In searching for historical truths, the historian must always allow the evidence to speak and shape the thesis, not the other way around.

Below are two lists of thesis statements. Which list contains effective thesis statements? Defend your answer by explaining the strengths of at least two statements and the weaknesses of at least two statements.

List A

1. Despite his failure to establish a republic in Upper Canada, William Lyon Mackenzie was one of the most important Canadian political figures of the nineteenth century.

2. Considering the treaties signed in the eighteenth and nineteenth centuries, the First Nations land claims must be recognized by the government of Canada.

3. Canadian immigration policies at the beginning of the twentieth century were clearly discriminatory and reflected racist attitudes.

4. Louis Riel was a heroic figure who should be celebrated in Canadian history. His hanging was a great injustice.

List B

1. Elizabeth I of England enjoyed one of the longest reigns of all British monarchs.

2. China is a very rich and ancient civilization.

3. The medieval feudal system served a variety of purposes and had both good and bad points.

4. Ancient Egypt sprung to life along the banks of the Nile. Over a span of several thousand years, the Egyptians created buildings and works of art.

The statements under List A are sound thesis statements, as each of them clearly states an argument or point of view that could be supported with evidence. The statements under List B are factual statements that leave little or no room for discussion and do not require supporting evidence to prove them in an argument.

Add two more examples to each list to further illustrate the differences between a sound thesis and a weak thesis.

Your thesis statement is the fourth section of your *processfolio*. Label it "Thesis Statement." Date all work filed in your *processfolio*.

Skills Focus Five

Organizing Your Essay: From Cue Cards to Outline

Now that you have selected a topic, formulated your thesis statement, narrowed your focus through inquiry questions, and prepared a bibliography that includes a variety of sources, you are ready to begin preparing research notes. Perhaps the most effective and efficient way to record your research notes is to enter the information/ideas into a database. If you are unfamiliar with how to use a database for doing research, ask your teacher librarian for assistance.

An alternative, effective, and easy way to organize your research is to use cue cards. By putting main points on cards, you can easily arrange your information in the proper order for your essay. Below is a sample cue card. You will need a number of cue cards to build up your essay. When you are finished, review your inquiry questions to see if you need to add, delete, or revise any of your cue cards.

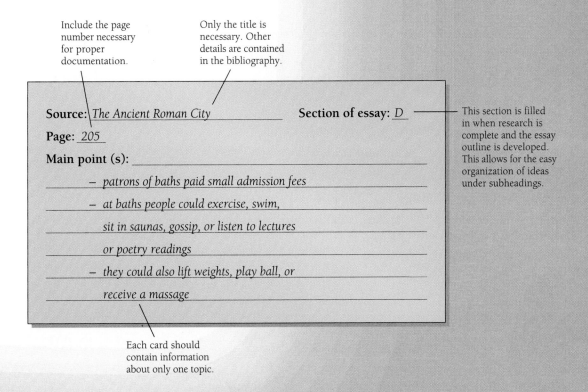

Include the page number necessary for proper documentation.

Only the title is necessary. Other details are contained in the bibliography.

Source: *The Ancient Roman City*   **Section of essay:** _D_

Page: _205_

Main point (s): _____

      — *patrons of baths paid small admission fees*

      — *at baths people could exercise, swim,*

        sit in saunas, gossip, or listen to lectures

        or poetry readings

      — *they could also lift weights, play ball, or*

        receive a massage

This section is filled in when research is complete and the essay outline is developed. This allows for the easy organization of ideas under subheadings.

Each card should contain information about only one topic.

Preparing an Essay Outline

Now that you have your notes in order, you can organize your history essay.

Below is a flow chart to help you get started. Follow these steps from Introduction to Conclusion.

Your essay outline is the fifth section of your *processfolio*. Label it "Essay Outline." Date your work.

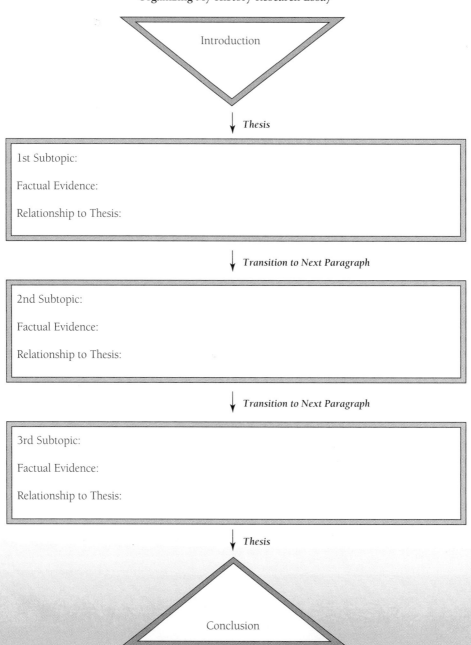

Organizing My History Research Essay

Introduction

↓ *Thesis*

1st Subtopic:

Factual Evidence:

Relationship to Thesis:

↓ *Transition to Next Paragraph*

2nd Subtopic:

Factual Evidence:

Relationship to Thesis:

↓ *Transition to Next Paragraph*

3rd Subtopic:

Factual Evidence:

Relationship to Thesis:

↓ *Thesis*

Conclusion

Skills Focus Six

The Final Edit: Revising, Editing, and Polishing Your Essay

Once you have completed a draft of your essay, you will need to have it reviewed for feedback on how to improve it. Many people can help in this process. Consider asking parents, siblings, and friends to take a look at your essay and provide constructive criticism on how you can improve the quality of your analysis and writing.

Too often the revision process is oversimplified, leading to poor feedback for the writer. If you ask your reviewers to focus on a particular aspect of your essay, you are more likely to receive a useful response. Consider breaking the process into three distinct phases and ask your reviewers to read the essay with a specific focus each time. You might want to try this approach:

The Final Edit Phase One

Revisions: Focus on the big ideas
- Have you maintained a focus on your thesis throughout the essay?

- Have you provided sufficient evidence to support each of your arguments?

- Have you presented your arguments in a logical and coherent manner?

The Final Edit Phase Two

Editing: Focus on paragraph and sentence structure
- Do your paragraphs have clear topic sentences?

- Are there effective transitions from paragraph to paragraph?

- Does each paragraph develop one central idea?

- Are your sentences properly constructed?

- Do your sentences vary in length?

The Final Edit Phase Three

Polishing: Focus on grammar and spelling
- Is your essay free of grammatical errors?

- Is your essay free of spelling errors?

- Have you used language appropriate for your purpose and audience?

- Are your pages and footnotes or endnotes properly numbered?

- Have you created a title page for your essay?

This section of your *processfolio* is labelled "Drafts." Remember to place and date all drafts of your essay, including the final polished version, in this section of your *processfolio*.

Glossary

aesthetic A philosophy of the perception of beauty. The study of the qualities of a work of art that make it beautiful.

annex To add, as an addition or minor part, to existing possessions; particularly used in the context of the government of a country seizing, taking over, invading, and claiming as its own parts or the whole of another country.

Apartheid Racial segregation and discrimination supported by government policy, as against non-whites in the Republic of South Africa.

appeasement The policy of making territorial or other concessions to potential aggressors in order to maintain peace.

arabesque In music, an intricate musical piece using stylized motifs, based on a flowing, ornate, usually floral pattern in painting, as found in Islamic art.

archaic Outdated; no longer in use; belonging to a former period.

archetype The original type or model from which copies are patterned. For example, in Western Christianity, the snake is an archetypal image of evil.

bipolar Having two opposite opinions, points of view, or ideologies.

bourgeoisie Refers to European middle class, used by Marx to refer to the capitalist, manufacturers and bankers who dominated the new industrial age

bureaucracy A system of administration in which government officials employees work collectively

civil war A war between to factions or regions in the same country

collectivization Refers to a system of agriculture in which all land is taken out of private hands and controlled by the state. Agricultural workers work as employees of the state.

conquistador The Spanish conquerors of the Americas in the sixteenth century (from Spanish *conquistadores*).

constitutionalism Refers to a system of government or belief in a system of government based on the principles established in a constitution.

courtiers Attendants at a royal court.

dialectic The art or practice of examining statements logically, as by questions and answers, in order to establish validity.

deist Someone who believes in God based only on reason and not on revelation.

dramatic monologue A first-person poem in which the narrator, in supposed conversation with a silent listener, reveals his or her character to the reader.

elegy A work of literature that may be a memorial to a dead person or simply a sad, contemplative lyric.

emancipation The release/freedom from bondage, oppression, or authority.

eugenics The study of how to improve the human race through selective breeding

evangelical Of or relating to the four Gospels of the New Testament; the doctrine of Protestant churches that salvation is attained chiefly by faith in Christ.

feudalism The social system of western Europe which developed during the 8th and 9th centuries in which vassals were protected by their lords in exchange for service on their land and in war.

franchise The right to vote; suffrage.

fraternal Brotherly. (Note: a fraternal order—a brotherhood of men organized to further their mutual benefit or to attain a common goal.)

guild Association of merchants or craftsmen established in medieval times to provide economic protection for their members and to regulate their practices.

hegemony Domination or leadership, especially the predominant influence of one state over others.

heresy An opinion or doctrine contrary to the official beliefs sanctioned by a church or religious body.

historiography The study of the writing of history. Opposing interpretations and methodology are considered.

Huguenots French Protestants who followed the teachings of John Calvin.

imperialism The policy or practice of extending a states control of other territories.

indigenous Having originated, developed, or been produced in a particular land, region, or environment.

intellectual Those who make public issues a matter of private concern.

intendant Provincial or colonial official of France, Spain or Portugal.

inveterate Firmly established by long continuance; deep-rooted.

KGB The Commission of State Security of the Soviet Union: an agency charged with detecting and countering security threats from abroad.

laissez-faire A belief in unrestricted freedom in commerce including the exchange of goods and the accumulation of wealth.

Meiji Restoration Period in Japanese history beginning in 1867, during which the emperors powers were restored and the dominance of the Shogun declined. Period of rapid reform and an opening up to the outside world.

metropolis The central country, city, region, etc. of an imperialist system which directly or indirectly controls other areas where it may have colonized, established trade, or exploited that areas natural resources.

Moors Muslim from North Africa who are of mixed Arab and Berber descent.

multi-national Corporations whose operations span many countries throughout the world and with little or no allegiance to any particular country.

mysticism A system of contemplative prayer aimed at achieving direct intuitive experience of the divine.

nation A group of people sharing a common language, heritage and customs, i.e. Jewish Nation.

nation-state A geographical area that is usually inhabited by an ethnically homogenous people and that is politically autonomous.

nocturne A short, lyric piano piece of the nineteenth century. It literally means "of the night" in French. There is often a melancholy aspect to nocturnes.

nouveau-riche A person who comes by wealth through commerce rather than title or inheritance. The nouveaux-riches were often resented and spurned by the aristocracy.

oratorio A sacred piece of music, usually narrating (through song) a story from the Bible. A religious opera.

pagan Non-believer, heathen; often said by Christian Europeans of the ancient Greeks and Romans.

papacy The term used for the office of the pope

passive resistance A method of protest against authority that uses no violence. Used successfully by Gandhi in securing independence for India.

paternalist Used to describe a country, community, group of employees, etc. that is cared for or controlled in a manner suggestive of a father looking after his children.

periphery Countries, regions, villages, etc. that are controlled through colonization, exploitation of natural resources, and trade by the metropolis within an imperialist system.

philanthropist One who embodies and demonstrates good will toward humanity by performing charitable or benevolent acts.

plebiscite An expression of the popular will by means of a vote by the whole population.

pluralism The existence in society of groups having distinctive ethnic origins, cultural norms or religious beliefs and practices.

precept A rule prescribing a particular kind of conduct or action; a proverbial standard or guide to morals.

prelude In music, a short introduction to a larger piece; a short lyrical piece.

primogeniture The practice of passing on the family estate and/or title to the first born son.

proletariat Term used to describe the all wage-earners. Used by Marx to describe the industrial workers whose only possession of material value was their labour.

proselytism The making of converts to a religion, sect, or party.

quasi-military mobilization The organization of society in a manner similar to that which may be necessary at the time of war; usually in reference to Russia under Stalin.

reconnaissance in force A military strategy of launching an initial assault primarily for the purpose of gathering information for a future attack upon the same site.

republic A form of government in which the people or their elected representative holds supreme power.

revolution A far-reaching and dramatic change in theory, practice or form of government.

salon A room where an intellectually oriented hostess would entertain selected guests.

schism A division between opposing factions within an organization.

secular Not religious; worldly.

social Darwinism The application of Darwins theory of evolution to human society. Used to justify exploitation or some and the extermination of others.

stalemate A tie or deadlock in a war or competition.

state Refers to a political entity defined by borders and which has its own government and sovereignty.

suffrage The right to vote.

syncopate In music, starting a note on an unaccented beat and continuing on the accented.

tithe A tenth of the yearly agricultural yield; personal income or profits paid as a tax or donation for the support of the church and clergy.

tribute A payment made by a ruler or state to another state or ruler, usually as a sign of submission. Can be in the form of a tax levied by one ruler or state on another.

triptych A set of three panels side by side with pictures or carvings, often an altarpiece.

universal suffrage The condition under which all members of the population have the right to vote.

vernacular The commonly spoken language or dialect of a particular people or place.

world-economy Refers to an economic system based on the exchange of goods and labour from many areas of the world.

List of Maps

Unit One The World Reinvented 1480-1715

Chapter One: Renaissance and Reformation 1450-1600

1.1 Religions in Europe in 1600   59

Chapter Three: Contact and Conflict 1450-1715

3.1 World Wide Exploration in the Fifteenth and Sixteenth Centuries   109

3.2 European Expansion to Seventeen Hundred   122

Unit Two An Age of Enlightenment and Revolution

Chapter Four: The Enlightenment 1700-1789

4.1 Geopolitical Boundaries in Europe, 1715   138

Chapter Five: Revolution to Restoration 1789-1815

5.1 The Crisis in 1793   188

5.2 The Napoleonic Wars 1796-1802   196

5.3 Europe Under Napoléon, 1810   197

Chapter Six: The World in the Eighteenth Century

6.1 European Possessions Overseas, ca. 1713   211

6.2 Geopolitical Boundaries in Europe, 1714   214

6.3 African and Overseas Slave Trade   219

6.4 The Ottoman Empire 1500-1900   224

Unit Three Modern Europe, 1815-1900

Chapter Seven: The Birth of Modern Industrial Society: Europe 1815-1850

7.1 The Industrial Revolution in Europe   245

7.2 Revolutions in Nineteenth-Century Europe   270

Chapter Eight: Nations in Upheaval: Europe 1850-1914

8.1 Political Boundaries in Europe 1871   291

8.2 Italy United   293

8.3 A United Germany   296

Chapter Nine: Imperialism, Colonialism and Resistance

9.1 Colonial Empires   333

9.2 Africa: Colonial Possessions   334

9.3 Latin America Before Independence   355

9.4 Latin America: After Independence   358

Unit Four The World at War 1914-1945

Chapter Ten: The War to End War, World War I 1914-1918

10.1 The Schlieffen Plan   376

10.2 The Western Front, 1914   380

10.3 World War I, The Eastern Front, 1914   386

10.4 Political Boundaries in Europe, 1919   498

Chapter Eleven: Between the Wars: An Anxious Generation

11.1 After World War I: The Spread of Dictatorships   414

Chapter Twelve: World War II 1939-1945

12.1 Germany's Conquests, 1939   460

12.2 German Conquests to 1942   464

Unit Five The New World Order

Chapter Thirteen: The Western Experience 1945 to Today

13.1 The Face of Europe Post World War II   598

13.2 Europe in the Year 2000   524

Chapter Fourteen: Challenge and Change in the Global Village

14.1 Key Territories in the Middle East   560

14.2 1989: Turmoil in Eastern Europe   563

14.3 Global Environmental Damage   570

Index

Abolitionist movement, 222
Aboriginal persons, history, 13–14
Absolutism, 69
  defined, 77
  Eastern Europe, 83–85
  foundations in France, 77–83
  France, 77–83
  Russia, 83–85
  time line, 70
Act in Restraint of Appeals (England), 60, 61
Addison, Joseph, 164
Adenauer, Konrad, 499
Afghanistan, 494
Africa
  art, 223–224, 345
  colonization, 221–222
  communities, 218
  Dutch, 335
  Eighteenth Century, 218–224
  Fifteenth Century, 106
  imperialism, 342–344
  nationalism, 360, 362
  new imperialism, 334–336
  partition of, 336–337
  Sixteenth Century, 116–119
  slavery, 116, 219–220
  social culture, 218–219
  society, 218–219
  trade, 218–219, 233–234
African diaspora, 25, 354
African National Congress, 362
Age of Democratic Revolutions, 350
Age of Enlightenment. See Enlightenment
Age of Reason, 273
  See also Eighteenth Century;
  Enlightenment
Age of Revolutions in Europe, 350
Agrarian Reform Act, 557
Agriculture, 104, 570
  communism, 524–525
  Eighteenth Century, 136, 175–176
  global environment, 570
  Industrial Revolution, 247–248
  New World, 121–122
  Ottoman Empire, 225
  Russia in 18th Century, 152
  trade, 121–122
Alexander I (Russia), 199, 260
Alexander II (Russia), 299, 300
Alexander III (Russia), 300, 313
Algeria, 545–546
Allende, Salvador, 559

Allies, 387, 392
American Civil War, 223, 332, 352–354, 376
American Declaration of Independence, 182
American Revolution, 16, 134, 210, 217, 247
American Revolutionary War, 5, 173, 179
Amin, Idi, 546
Amnesty International, 509, 555
Anabaptist movement, 28
Anabaptists, 54
Anglicanism, 60
Angola, 336, 545–546
Anschluss, 450, 452
Anti-Comintern Pact, 451
Anti-Semitism, 478, 479
  France, 301–302
Anticlericalism, 50
Apartheid, 349–350
APEC, 14, 576
Appeasement, 451, 452, 454
Arab-Israeli Six-Day War, 494
Arafat, Yasser, 562
Arbenz, Jacobo, 559
Arcadia Conference, 469
Archbishop Fenelon, 83
Argentina, 342
  independence, 332
Aristarchus of Samos, 71
Aristotle, 41, 73–74, 123, 124
Arkwright, Richard, 136
Arms control, 377–378
Arms Race, 502
Art
  Africa, 223–224, 345
  China, 230, 346
  Eighteenth Century, 152–156
  expressionism, 436–437
  fauvism, 436–437
  French Revolution, 203–205
  imperialism, 345–346
  impressionists, 321
  India, 226–227, 345
  millenium, 530–532
  Moghul Empire, 227
  Nineteenth Century, 272–278, 319
  post-impressionists, 323
  realism, 320
  Renaissance, 42–45, 152–153
  Seventeenth Century, 90–96
  symbolism, 435
  Twentieth Century, 435–440, 530–532

World War I, 395–398
Asia, new imperialism, 334
Asia-Pacific Economic Cooperation Forum, 567, 569
Asiento, 116, 215
Astrolabe, 108
Ataturk, Kemal, 560
Atawallpa, 104, 114
Attlee, Clement, 482
Augustan Age. See English Restoration
Australia
  beginning of World War I, 381
  imperialism, 344–345
  prelude to World War II, 456
Austria
  beginning of World War I, 381
  Eighteenth Century, 214
  empire, 298–299
  nationalism, 262, 305
  prior to World War I, 375, 379
  Revolution of 1848, 272
  succession, 215
  universal male suffrage, 300
  World War I, 378
Austro-Hungarian Empire, 378
Austro-Prussian War, 290, 297
Aztec, 25, 113–114, 118, 120
  Fifteenth Century, 106

Baader-Meinhof Group, 527
Bach, Johann Sebastian, 156, 280
Bacon, Frances, 531
Bacon, Francis, 73–74
Badoglio, Marshal Pietro, 472
Bailly, Jean Sylvain, 190
Bailly, Sylvain, 180
Baldwin, Stanley, 409
Balfour Declaration, 381, 400, 561
Balkan Wars, 304, 374
Balkans, 378
  prior to World War I, 379
Banana republic, 559
Bank of England, 247
Baptists, 54
Barber, Benjamin, 571
Barber, Samuel, 532
Barbusse, Henri, 392
Barlow, Maude, 15
Baroque art/music/style, 91, 95–96, 152
Barrett Browning, Elizabeth, 325–326
Barzun, Jacques, 77
Bastille, storming of, 181
Bateman, Robert, 531

Battle of Adowa, 332
Battle of Borodino, 278
Battle of Britain, 450, 461–463
Battle of Jutland, 385
Battle of Plassey, 210
Battle of Sekigahara, 116
Battle of the Marne, 379
Battle of the Nations, 199
Battle of the Nile, 198
Battle of the Somme, 374
Battle of Trafalgar, 199, 217
Battle of Waterloo, 170, 187, 200, 260
Beatles, 533, 554
Beaverbrook, Lord, 463
Beccaria, Cesare, 131, 145
Bechet, Sidney, 533
Becquerel, Henri, 290
Beer Hall *putsch*, 424
Begin, Menachem, 562
Belgium
    European Union, 556
    free-trade region, 495
Bell, Alexander Graham, 430
Ben-Gurion, David, 561
Benes, Edvard, 413, 454, 455
Bentham, Jeremy, 145, 257, 258, 354
Bergman, Ingmar, 441
Berlin Blockade, 497, 501
Berlin Conference, 332, 335
Berlin Wall, 494, 504
Bernini, Gianlorenzo, 91–92
Bernstein, Eduard, 313
Berry, Chuck, 533
Bill of Rights (England), 87
Biotechnology, 517–518
Birth rate
    Great Depression, 433
    World War II, 482
Black Death, 28, 37
Black Hole of Calcutta, 226
Black Shirts, 415
Black Tuesday, 411
Blake, William, 281, 443
Blaut, J.M., 550
Bligh, William, 232
Blitzkrieg, 380, 457–459
Bloody Sunday, 314, 374
Blues and jazz, 533
Boer War, 304, 332, 336, 349, 362
Boers, 335, 337
Boleyn, Anne, 28, 58, 60
Bolingbroke, Lord Henry, 143
Bolivar, Simon, 332, 356–358
Bolivia, independence, 357
Bolsheviks, 314, 389
Bonaparte, Louis Napoleon, 271, 290, 291, 293, 295, 297, 298

Bonaparte, Napoleon, 131, 146, 170, 187, 195–199, 244
    exile, 200, 201
Book publishing, 139
Bosnia, 564
Bossuet, Jacques-Benigue, 222
Boucher, Francois, 231
Boulanger, General George, 301
Boxer Rebellion, 241, 332, 362
Brahe, Tycho, 72
Brahms, Johannes, 161
Branch Davidians, 19–20
Brandt, Willy, 505
Braun, Eva, 450, 477
Brazil, independence, 332
Breuer, Josef, 440
Brezhnev, Leonid, 505, 522, 525, 528
Briand, Aristide, 409, 411
Brissot, Jacques Pierre, 187, 223
British Commonwealth of Nations, 552–553
British East India Company, 226, 229
British North America Act, 76, 142
British West Indies
    emancipation, 351–352
    slavery, 349–350
British-Zulu War of 1879, 346
Bronte, Charlotte, 244, 285
Bronte, Emily, 244, 285
Brooke, Rupert, 395
Brown Shirts, 424, 425, 426
Brown, Henry B., 359
Browning, Christopher, 479
Browning, Robert, 323–324
Broz, Josip, 498, 540, 564
Bryan, William Jennings, 317
Bubonic Plague, 28, 29, 37
Bulgaria, 498
Bundestag, 499
Burke, Edmund, 146–148
Byron. See Lord Byron
Byzantine Empire, 104, 112, 225

Cabot, John Sebastian, 111
Cage, John, 532
Calas, Jean, 144
Calvin, Jean, 54
Calvinism, 54
Camp David Accord, 562
Camus, Albert, 507–508
Canada
    abolition of slavery, 351
    beginning of World War I, 381
    constitution, 142
    Great Depression, 416
    invasion of Italy during World War II, 472

NATO, 502
    prelude to World War II, 456
Cape of Good Hope, 111, 221
    slavery, 221–222
Capitalism, 5, 508
    Fifteenth Century, 107–109
Caravaggio, 93-94
Caravels, 108
Cardinal de Richelieu, 58, 70, 77, 78
Carlsbad Decrees, 263
Carlyle, Thomas, 250, 257, 325
Carnegie, Andrew, 377
Caroso, Fabritio, 36
Carr, E.H., 6, 12
Carson, Rachel, 519, 520–521
Carter, Jimmy, 505, 562
Cartier, Jacques, 104, 111, 122
Cartwright, Edmund, 134
Cary, Elizabeth, 96
Casablanca Conference, 471
Castiglione, Baldassare, 28, 46
Castro, Fidel, 504
Catherine II (Russia), 151, 217
Catherine of Aragon, 58, 60
Catherine the Great (Russia), 134, 145, 151
Catullus, 42
Caudillos, 358
Cavell, Edith, 392
Cavendish, Margaret, 96
Ceausescu, Nicolae, 563
Cetewayo, 359
Cezanne, Paul, 324, 437
Chadwick, Edwin, 258
Chamber of Deputies, 263
Chamber of Peers, 263
Chamberlain, Austen, 409–411
Chamberlain, Neville, 450, 454, 458–459
Chamorro, Pedro Joachim, 560
Charcot, Jean, 440
Chardin, Jean-Baptiste-Simeon, 156
Charles I (England), 58, 70, 75, 86
Charles II (England), 58, 70, 86, 157
Charles V (England), 234
Charles V (Germany), 51, 56, 62
Charles V (Spain), 57
Charles X (France), 263, 264
Chechnya, 529
Chernobyl nuclear disaster, 518
Children, 177, 319, 320, 434
    Great Depression, 434
Chile, American intervention, 559–560
China, 332
    art, 230, 346
    colonization, 359
    communism, 545, 557
    communities, 228
    economic system, 229–230

Fifteenth Century, 106
human rights, 542
imperialism, 338
indentured labour, 347
Jesuits, 228
neocolonialism, 556–558
new imperialism, 334
Opium Wars. *See* Opium Wars
revolution of 1911, 364
Seventeenth Century, 231
Sixteenth Century, 115
social system, 228
trade, 229–230, 231
war with Japan, 465
Chomsky, Noam, 572–574
Chopin, Frederic, 244
Church of England, 60, 61
Churchill, Winston, 417, 450, 458–462,
 468, 471–475, 480, 482, 493, 500
Cicero, 3, 42
Cisalpine Republic, 195
Civil Constitution of the Clergy, 184
Civil War in England, 86
Clemenceau, Georges, 384, 399, 409
Clement VII (pope), 46, 60
Code Napoleon, 170, 198, 255
Coetzee, J.M., 547
Colbert, Jean-Baptiste, 80
Cold War, 493, 495, 500, 501
 end of, 528–529
 television and, 514–516
Coleridge, Samuel Taylor, 259, 276,
 282, 283
Collectivization, 421
Colombia, independence, 357
Colonialism, collapse of, 541
Colonization
 Africa, 221–222
 Napoleonic wars, 357
 resistance to, 358–359
Columbus, Christopher, 57, 103–105,
 108, 110–112, 118, 122, 233
Colville, Alexander, 531
Comecon, 495
Cominform, 501
Committee of General Security, 190
Committee of Public Safety, 186, 190
Communism, 267, 415, 419
 agriculture, 524–525
 China, 545, 557
 collapse of, 528–529, 540, 562–565
 decentralization, 525
 Europe, after World War II, 500
 Five-Year Plans, 421–422
 France, after World War II, 500
 Italy, after World War II, 500
 Poland, 562

Russia, 419
 society, 523–524
Communist League, 268–269
Communist Manifesto, 244, 267,
 268–269, 270
Communities
 Africa, 218–219
 China, 228
Compulsory education, 177
Computers, 517
Comte de Mirabeau, 185
Concentration camps, 426
Confucius, 228, 231
Congo Free State, 335, 342
Congress of Berlin, 290
Congress of Vienna, 170, 200, 244, 260, 262
Conrad, Joseph, 282, 444, 547
Constable, John, 276
Constantine XI (Byzantine), 112
Constituent Assembly, 184–185
Constitution, 5, 76, 142
 American, 5, 76, 142
 Canadian, 76, 142
 France, 184–185, 263, 264
 Germany, 302
 political basis for, 74–77
 Spain, 262
 United States, 5, 76, 142
Constitutional monarchy, 70, 85
Constitutionalism, 69
 England, 85–88
Contras, 560
Cook, James, 228, 231
Cook, Thomas, 306
Coolidge, Calvin, 431
Copernicus, Nicolaus, 71
Corday, Charlotte, 204
Cortes, Hernan, 110, 114, 120
Cotton industry, 249
Council of Trent, 55, 56
Counter-Reformation, 55–57
Couperin, Francois, 230
Courbet, Gustave, 320–322
Crick, Francis, 518
Crimean peninsula, 217
Crimean War, 290, 293, 376, 387
Croatia, 564
Cromwell, Oliver, 86
Cromwell, Thomas, 60
Crusades, 105
Cuba, abolition of slavery, 349
Cuban Missile Crisis, 494, 504, 505
Cubism, 438
Cult of the Sun, 121
Culture
 Americanization of, 514–516
 Europe, after World War II, 505–506

imperialism, 345
 India, 340
 Industrial Revolution, 246
 Millenium, 530
 Nineteenth Century, 306–308
 Seventeenth Century England, 88
 Sixteenth Century, 120–122
 United States, 514–516
Curie, Marie Sklodowska, 290, 315
Curie, Pierre, 290
Cuxco, 113
Czechoslovakia, 498, 523, 563
 prelude to World War II, 454–456

d'Alembert, Jean, 140
d'Avity, Pierre, 124
d'Happoncourt, Francoise, 162
D-Day, 473–476
da Gama, Vasco, 104, 110, 230
da Vinci, Leonardo, 28, 43–47
Dadaism, 437
Daladier, Eduaord, 454
Dali, Salvador, 440
Danton, George Jacques, 193
Darwin, Charles, 17, 290, 315–317
Daumier, Honore, 320
David, Jacques-Louis, 133, 170, 203–204
Davison, Emily, 312
Dawes Plan, 409
Dawidowicz, Lucy, 479
de Balboa, Vasco Nunez, 110
de Balzac, Honore, 280, 326
de Beauvoir, Simone, 494, 507–508
de Champlain, Samuel, 122
de Condorcet, Marquis, 131, 148, 184,
 191–193, 223
de Gaulle, General Charles, 417, 499,
 511, 545–546
de Goya, Francisco, 244, 274
de Klerk, Frederik W., 552–553
de Las Casas, Bartolome, 104, 123
de Montcalm, General Louis Joseph,
 216–217, 231
de San Martin, Jose, 357, 358
Debussy, Claude, 439–442
Declaration of Independence, 134, 210
Declaration of the Rights of Man and of
 the Citizen, 182–183, 193, 200
Decolonization, 354–356
 India, 543–544
 process of, 543–546
Deconstructionism, 535
Defoe, Daniel, 162–163, 231, 547
Deforestation, 570
Degas, Edgar, 321, 439
Deindustrialization, 526
Deism, 141

del Monte, Cardinal, 93
Delacroix, Eugène, 244, 276
Democracy, 261–262
    England, 303
    evolution of, 5
    Germany, 302
    post-World War I, 409–410
    Russia, 529
    universal male suffrage, 300
    voting, 300
Demography, 257
    Reformation, 37–38
    Renaissance, 37–38
Dependency theory, 212–213
Desai, Anita, 548
Descartes, Rene, 70, 74
Developing nations, 15, 211
    economic structure, 211–212
Diaghilev, Serge, 397
Dialoguism, 535
Dickens, Charles, 257, 326
Diderot, Denis, 134, 140, 151, 171, 174
Dieppe, 450, 470
Diet of Worms, 51
Directory, 194
Disraeli, Benjamin, 257, 300, 303
Distribution of wealth, 13–14
Divorce
    Great Depression, 433, 435
    Industrial Revolution, 254
    Nineteenth Century, 308
Djugashwili, Joseph. See Stalin, Joseph
Dollfuss, Engelbert, 413
Domino theory, 504
Donitz, Admiral Karl, 478
Donne, John, 96
Dostoyevsky, Fodor, 515
Dowding, Sir Hugh, 462
Dowry, 36
    Renaissance, 35
Dramatic monologue, 325
Dreadnought, 376
Dreyfus Affair, 290, 301
Dryden, John, 96–98
du Chatelet, Marquise, 149–150, 162, 176
du Halde, Jean-Baptiste, 228
Dualism, 41
Dubcek, Alexander, 523
DuBois, W.E.B., 358–360
Duchamp, Marcel, 532
Duke of Marlborough, 154, 214
Duke of Richmond, 158
Duma, 314, 374, 387
Dumas, Alexander, 281
Dunkirk, 450, 461
Dutch East India Company, 137

Dutch United West India Company, 120
Dylan, Bob, 516

Earl of Sandwich, 159
East India Company, 119, 226, 339, 340
Eastern Europe
    absolutism, 83–85
    politics, 64
    Reformation, 64
Ecology, 570
Economic system/structure, 13–14
    American, post-World War I,
    430–431
    China, 228–230
    communism, 524–525
    developing nations, 211–212
    Eighteenth Century, 211–213
    England, 87–88, 303
    Europe, after World War II, 506–507
    France, 293
    global, 567
    Great Depression, 412–413, 433
    history, 6
    imperialism, 341–345
    India, 226
    Industrial Revolution, 245–246
    Nineteenth Century, 306–307
    post-World War I, 409
    Russia, 299
    World War I, 393–394, 402–403
Ecuador, independence, 357
Edict of Nantes, 28, 58, 79
Edison, Thomas, 430
Education
    compulsory, 177
    Eighteenth Century, 177
    France, 197
    French Revolution, 197
Edward VI (England), 58
Edward VII (England), 417
Egypt, 336
    British occupation of, 332
    independence, 544
Einstein, Albert, 290, 315, 417
Eisenhower, Dwight D., 471,
    473–474, 480
Electronic music, 532
Eliot, T.S., 327, 443
Elizabeth I (England), 58, 85, 117, 258
Elizabeth II (England), 417
Emancipation
    British West Indies, 353–354
    United States, 354–355
Emancipation Proclamation, 354
Emerson, Ralph Waldo, 310
Enclosure, 136
Encyclopedia, 140

Engels, Friedrich, 244, 250,
    267–269, 317
England, 87
    abolition of slavery, 350–351
    beginning of World War I, 379–380,
    381
    Civil War, 86
    constitutionalism, 85–88
    democracy, 303
    economic structure/system, 87–88, 303
    economy after World War II, 506–507
    Eighteeenth Century, 246–248
    European Union, 556
    Great Depression, 412
    Industrial Revolution, 245–248
    industrialization, 250
    literature, 48–49
    nationalism, 304
    NATO, 502
    parliamentary reform, 265
    politics, 58–59
    population, 249, 251
    prelude to World War II, 451–456
    prior to World War I, 375, 379
    Reformation, 58–59
    religion, 303
    Romanticism, 276–277
    Seventeenth Century, 85–88
    social conflict, 264
    socialism, 313
    socialism after World War II, 500
    suffrage, 265, 309
    taxation after World War II, 506–507
    textile industry, 248–249
    unionism, 313
    universal male suffrage, 300, 303
    universal suffrage, 308–312
    voting, 265, 303, 308
    welfare state, 527
English Restoration period, 97
Enlightened despotism, 151
Enlightenment, 10–12, 133, 139–140
    religion, 141, 150
Entente cordiale, 375
Environment, 570
Environmental Protection Agency
    (EPA), 521
Environmentalism, 518
Erasmus, Desiderius, 48, 50
Estates General, 170, 179, 180, 184, 185
Estonia, 498
Ethiopia, 546
Ethnic cleansing, 565
Euro (currency), 494, 526, 556
European Coal and Steel Community
    (ECSC), 495, 556

European Economic Community (EEC), 496, 556
  tariffs, 496
European Free Trade Area, 556
European parliament, 556
European Recovery Fund, 495
European Union, 526, 556, 569
  economic system, 556
  trade, 556
Existentialism, 507–508
Export processing zones, 569
Expressionism, 436–437

Factory Act (of 1833/1847), 244, 253, 258
Family
  America, 431–433
  Eighteenth Century, 176–177
  Great Depression, 433
  Millenium, 530
  Renaissance, 35
  Twentieth Century, 529–530
  World War II, 483
Family life
  Nineteenth Century, 319
  Seventeenth Century England, 88–89
Famine, 30
Fanon, Frantz, 540, 543
Far East Company, 120
Fascism, 407
  Italy, 415–418
  nature of, 413–415
  rise of, 413–415
Fauvism, 436–437
February Revolution (1848), 271
Federal Republic of Germany, 497
Feminist criticism, 535
Feminist movements, 508–509
  France, 308
  Nineteenth Century, 308–312
  suffrage, 308–312
  universal suffrage, 308–312
  voting, 308–312
Ferdinand and Isabella (Spain), 28, 57, 122
Ferdinand II (Germany), 63
Ferdinand VII (Spain), 262
Fernandez-Armesto, Felipe, 12, 124
Fessenden, Reginald, 430
Feudalism, 38
  abolition in France, 184
  France, before the Revolution, 173
  lessons of, 267
  Renaissance, 35–36
Fielding, Henry, 165
Fifteenth Century
  Africa, 106
  Aztec, 106

capitalism, 107–109
  China, 106
  Europe, 106–109
  exploration, 107–111
  geography, 106–108
  Inca, 106
  religion, 109
  South America, 106
  technology, 106, 108
Fifth Republic (France), 499, 527
Final Solution, 478–479
Finland, 391, 498
  World War II, 458
First International Workingmen's Association, 313
First Treaty of Paris, 259
FLQ crisis, 16
Flying shuttle, 248
Foch, Field Marshal, 401
Food and Agriculture Organization, 555
Ford, Henry, 431
Forsyth, Frederick, 515
Fourmont, Etienne, 229
Fourth Estate, 572–573
Fourth Republic (France), 499
Fragonard, 133
France
  abolition of feudalism, 184
  abolition of slavery, 210, 223, 349
  absolutism, 77–83
  anti-semitism, 301–302
  art of the Twentieth Century, 437, 438–439
  beginning of World War I, 379–380, 381
  communism after World War II, 500
  constitution, 184–185, 263, 264
  economic reforms, 80
  economic structure, 293
  economy after World War II, 506–507
  education, 197
  Eighteenth Century, 214
  European Union, 556
  fall of, during World War II, 459, 460
  February Revolution (1848), 271
  feminist movements, 308
  Fifth Republic, 499, 527
  Fourth Republic, 499
  free-trade region, 495
  Great Depression, 412
  Industrial Revolution, 246
  industrialization, 249, 250
  literature, 48–49
  monarchy, 292
  multiplier effect, 293
  nationalism, 262
  NATO, 499, 502

parliamentary democracy, 499
  politics, 57–58
  post-World War I, 409
  prelude to World War II, 451–456
  prior to World War I, 375, 379
  Reformation, 57–58
  religion, 185
  Second Republic, 292
  slavery, 170, 210
  socialism, 313
  suffrage, 271
  Third Republic, 300
  unionism, 313
  universal male suffrage, 292, 300
  universal suffrage, 271
  voting, 271, 292
Francis Ferdinand (Austria), 305
Francis II (Austria), 187, 199
Francis II (France), 295
Franco, Generalissimo Francisco, 453, 500
Franco-Prussian War, 290, 297–298, 375
Frank, Andre-Gunder, 213
Franklin, Rosalind, 517
Franz Ferdinand (Austria), 378, 391
Franz Joseph (Austria), 272, 297–299, 375
Frederick II (Prussia), 151, 215
Frederick the Great (Prussia), 134, 144, 145, 151, 215
Frederick William II (Prussia), 177
Free Trade Agreement of the Americas, 575
Free Trade Area of the Americas, 15
Free trade zones, 569
Freemasonry, 140, 161
French East India Company, 120
French Republic, 170
French Revolution, 11, 16, 133, 134, 147, 169, 170, 241
  abolition of monarchy, 187
  art, 203–205
  conscription, 190
  Convention, 187–188
  Directory, 194
  education, 197
  execution of Louis XVI, 189
  measurement of time, 189–190
  metric system, introduction of, 189–190
  music, 203–205
  private life, 201–202
  Prussian invasion, 187
  reign of terror. See Reign of terror
  religion, 202, 203
  September Massacres, 187
  war on Austria, 186–187
  women, 192–193
Freud, Sigmund, 290, 435, 438–441
Friedan, Betty, 509

Friedlander, Saul, 427
Frobisher, Martin, 111
Fronde, 78
Front de liberation du Quebec (FLQ), 566
Fugitive Slave Act (1851), 353
Fugue, 157

G7/G8, 567, 576
Galapagos Islands, 316
Galiano, Dionisio Alcala, 227
Galilei, Galileo, 17, 69, 70, 71, 72
Gallipoli, 381
Gandhi, Mohandas, 359, 362, 543, 544, 546
Garcia, Anastosia Samoza, 559, 560
Garibaldi, Giuseppe, 294–295
Gauguin, Paul, 233
General Agreement on Tariffs and Trade
    (GATT), 569
General Service Enlistment Act, 340
Genetic engineering, 518
Genetically modified foods, 17, 571
Gentileschi, Artemisia, 93–94
George I (England), 158
George II (England), 159
George III (England), 137, 261
George IV (England), 261
George, David Lloyd, 304, 384, 399
George, Dudley, 14
Gericault, Theodore, 275–276
German Democratic Republic, 497
Germany, 497, 556
    Baader-Meinhof Group, 527
    beginning of World War I, 379–380,
    381
    constitution, 302
    defeat in World War II, 473–476
    democracy, 302
    Democratic Republic, 497
    economy after World War II, 506–507
    European Union, 556
    Federal Republic of, 497
    free-trade region, 495
    Great Depression, 412
    Green Party, 527
    Industrial Revolution, 246
    inflation, 409
    Jews, 427–428
    literature, 48–49
    nation-state, 291, 295–296
    nationalism, 262, 302, 304, 375
    NATO, 502
    Nazis, 418, 424–426
    parliamentary democracy, 499
    population, 251
    post-World War II administration,
    481, 497
    prior to World War I, 375, 379

racism, 424–428
Reformation, 62
socialism, 302, 313
taxation after World War II, 506–507
Third Reich, 426–428
unification of, 297
unionism, 313
zone of occupation, 481
Gestapo, 426
Gibbon, Edward, 134, 177, 234
Girondins, 146, 186
Gladstone, William, 303, 304
Glasnost, 528, 529
Global village, 14, 540, 571
Globalization, 526
    corporate agenda, 575–577
    multinational corporations, 568–569
Glorious Revolution, 70, 86, 134
Goebbels, Joseph, 424, 426, 480
Goethe. *See* von Goethe
Gokhale, G.K., 360
Gold Coast, 336
Gorbachev, Mikhail, 515, 528
Göring, Hermann, 426, 462, 463, 480, 481
Gorky, Maxim, 515
Government in the Eighteenth Century,
    137–138
Government of India Act, 340
Goya. *See* de Goya, Francisco
Grand Duke Leopold (Tuscany), 145
Grand Exchange, 233
Grange, Red, 431
Great Britain. See England
Great Depression, 371, 407, 408,
    411–413
    birth rate, 433
    children, 434
    dictators, 413
    divorce, 433, 435
    economic system, 412, 413, 433
    Europe, 433
    family, 433
    marriage, 433, 435
    stock market crash, 433
    unemployment, 412
    women, 433
    working class, 434
Great Leap Forward, 557
Great Proletarian Cultural Revolution, 558
Great Purge, 408
Great Trek, 335
Great War. See World War I
Greater Asia Co-Prosperity Sphere, 468
Greece
    independence, 262–263
    NATO, 502
    Ottoman Empire, 262–263

Green Party, 527
Green Revolution, 17
Greenpeace, 555
Greer, Germaine, 509
Grey, Sir Edward, 379
Grimm, Jacob and Wilhelm, 172
Grimm, Melchior, 229
Group of 20 (G20), 526
Grunge, 534
Guatemala and American intervention,
    559–560
Guilds, 308–312
Gulag Archipelago, 419
Gulf of Tonkin incident, 504
Gulf War, 540, 574
    mass media, 574
Gutenberg, Johann, 28, 43

H'si, Kang, 231
Hadden, Briton, 416–417
Hague Peace Conference (1899/1907),
    377, 403
Haig, Douglas, 384
Haiti
    abolition of slavery, 351
    Slave revolt, 351–352
Haitian Revolution, 332
Hale, Sarah Josepha, 310–311
Hall of Mirrors, 298
Halton, Matthew, 472
Handel, George Frederick, 133, 156–158
Hapsburg-Valois Wars, 57, 62
Hapsburgs, 378
Harald, (England), 5
Hardy, Thomas, 326, 392, 442
Hargreaves, James, 248
Harris, Arthur (Bomber), 473
Harrison, George, 554
Harrison, John, 228
Harvey, William, 70, 73
Haussmann, Baron George, 293
Havel, Vaclav, 511, 563
Hawthorne, Nathaniel, 310
Haydn, Franz Joseph, 157, 160
Hegel, George Wilhelm Friedrich, 7,
    201, 267
Helsinki Agreement, 494, 505
Henri II (France), 57
Henri III (France), 58
Henri IV (France), 58
Henry the Navigator, 109
Henry VIII (England), 28, 48, 58, 60, 85
Heresies, 50
Herman, Edward S., 572–573
Herman, Woody, 533
Hess, 480
Hidalgo, Miguel, 356–358

Hierarchy, 41
Himmler, Heinrich, 426, 480, 481
Hirohito, Emperor, 466, 485
Historians, kinds of, 9
Historiography, 12, 365
Hitler, Adolf, 318, 392, 407, 408, 413,
    415, 417, 424–426, 450–452, 454–457,
    462–463, 474–481
Hobbes, Thomas, 16, 74–76
Hobsbawm, E.J., 243
Hobson, John A., 304, 338
Hockney, David, 532
Hogarth, William, 250, 320
Holly, Buddy, 533
Holocaust, 478, 561
Holy Alliance, 260
Holy Inquisition, 71
Holy Roman Emperor, 62
Hong Kong, 543
Honour Code, 34
Hoover, Herbert, 412
Hourani, Albert, 112
House of Orange, 64
Huckins, Olga Owens, 520
Hudson, Henry, 111, 120
Hugo, Victor, 281
Human Genome Project, 517
Human rights, 15, 222, 505, 543
    advancement of, 350
    China, 542
    colonies, in the, 542
    developing countries, 542
    India, 542
    Japan, 542
    nationalism, 360
    slavery, 222–223
    Turkey, 542
    universal, 511–513
Human Rights Watch, 511
Humanists, 42, 50
Hume, David, 146
Hungary, 498, 523
    nationalism, 305
    prior to World War I, 377
    revolt of 1956, 523
Hussain, Zakhir, 551
Hussein, Sheri, 560
Hutterites, 54
Huxley, Thomas, 325

Ibsen, Henrik, 327
Iceland and NATO, 502
Ieyasu, Tokugawa, 104, 116
Immigration, exclusionary/white-only
    policy, 348
Imperial Guard, 198
Imperialism, 16, 291

Africa, 342–344
Apartheid, 349
art, 345–346
Australia, 344–345
causes of, 337
colonial development, 344–345
culture, 345
economic system, 341–345
India, 339–342
industrialization, 341–345
Jamaica, 341
laissez faire, 341–345
legacy of, 341–352, 546–547
multinational corporations, 568–569
nationalism, 337
Nineteenth Century, 333, 334
resistance to, 350
social legacy, 346–347
wage labourers, 344
Impressionists, 321
Inca, 25, 113, 114, 118
    culture, 120–121
    Fifteenth Century, 106
    Spanish exploration, 114
    tribute system, 121
Indentured labour, 346–347
Index of Prohibited Books, 56
India
    art, 225–227, 345
    beginning of World War I, 381
    British control, 226
    caste system, 340
    colonization, 359
    culture, 340
    decolonization, 543–544
    economic system, 225–226
    Eighteenth Century, 225–227
    human rights, 542
    imperialism, 339–341
    independence, 543–544
    mutiny of 1857, 340
    nationalism, 360, 361
    new imperialism, 334
    religion, 339–341
    social system, 340
    trade, 226
Indian National Congress, 360
Indonesia, 545–546
Indulgences, 51–54
Industrial Revolution, 11, 16, 245,
    250, 281
    agriculture, 247–248
    child labour, 253
    city life, 250–251
    culture, 246
    divorce, 254
    economic system, 245–246

employment, 250
England, 245–248
Europe, growth in 18th Century, 136
family life/violence, 253–255
France/French Revolution, 246
gender roles, 254–255
Germany, 246
government regulation, 257–258
growth of British industrial cities,
    251–252
infant mortality, 253–255
Italy, 247
length of working day, 253
Nineteenth Century, 306–307
role of government, 256–259
rural homes, 252–253
social conflict, 264
social impact, 250
social legislation, 258–259
social system, 245–246
Soviet Union, 421
Spain, 247
standard of living, 250
textile industry, 248–249
transportation, 247
women, 254–255
working conditions, 253
Industrialization, 245, 308–312
    continental Europe, 249–250
    England, 250
    Europe, 246
    France, 249, 250
    Germany, 249
    imperialism, 342–345
    Nineteenth Century, 307–308
    role of government, 256–259
    Russia, 299, 391
    social conflict, 264
    unionism, 308–312
Inflation in Germany, 409
Ingres, Jean-Auguste, 244, 273–274
Intendant, 77, 80
Intercontinental ballistic missiles, 502
International Brigade, 453
International Law of the Sea Treaty, 567
International Monetary Fund, 14, 477,
    494, 495, 567, 569
International Working Group on
    Indigenous Affairs, 511
Ipperwash Tragedy, 14
Ireland and the European Union, 556
Irish Home Rule (Bill), 304, 379
Irish Republican Army (IRA), 527, 566
Iron Curtain, 500
Irwin, Will, 382–383
Isabella II (Spain), 297
Islam, 224–225

Italy, 294
  abolition of monarchy, 499
  beginning of World War I, 381
  communism after World War II, 500
  economy after World War II, 506–507
  European Union, 556
  fascism, 415–418
  free-trade region, 495
  Industrial Revolution, 247
  invasion of, during World War II, 472
  nation-state, 291
  nationalism, 262
  NATO, 502
  parliamentary democracy, 499
  politics, 59–62
  prelude to World War II, 451–456
  Reformation, 59–62
  Renaissance, 46–47
  Revolution of 1848, 272
  unification, 293–294
Ivan IV (Russia), 64
Ivan the Terrible, 64

Jackson, A.Y., 396
Jacobins, 145, 146, 185–187, 192, 195
Jamaica, 341
  imperialism, 341
  slavery, 352
Jamaican Slave Revolt, 332
James I (England), 58, 77, 85, 117
James II (England), 70, 86
Japan
  Eighteenth Century, 232–233
  human rights, 542
  Nineteenth Century, 335
  prior to World War I, 379
  religion, 116
  Seventeenth Century, 232–233
  Sixteenth Century, 116
  World War II, 482–483
Jaures, Jean, 313
Jefferson, Thomas, 134, 210
Jesuits, 56
  China, 228, 229
  Japan, in, 116
Jews, 477, 478
  Germany, 427–428
Joffre, Marshall Joseph, 379
John Paul II (pope), 562
Johnson, Lyndon, 504
Johnson, Robert, 533
Johnson, Samuel, 165
Joint stock companies, 120, 137, 293, 307–308
Jones, Allen, 532
Jonson, Ben, 96
Joplin, Scott, 533

Joseph II (Austria), 151
Joyce, James, 8, 442, 444, 445
Juan Carlos (Spain), 500
Julius II (pope), 46
July crisis, 378
July Monarchy, 264, 270

Kaempfer, Engelbert, 210, 232–233
Kandinsky, Wassily, 438
Kant, Immanuel, 147
Kay, James, 136, 248
Keats, John, 284
Kellogg, Frank B., 411
Kennedy, John F., 504, 505, 516, 521
Kenya, 336
Kepler, Johannes, 72–73
Kerensky, Alexander, 390
Keynes, John Maynard, 402, 408, 409, 413
Khrushchev, Nikita, 423, 504, 520, 524, 525
Kierkegaard, Soren, 507–508
King, Martin Luther, Jr., 417, 511
King, William Lyon Mackenzie, 452
Kirov, Sergei, 423
Klein, Naomi, 576
Kollwitz, Kathe, 436
Korea, conflict/partition of, 503
Korean War, 540
Kornilov, General Larr, 400
Kristallnacht, 427, 450, 455
Kulturkampf, 302
Kurosawa, Akira, 551–555
Kyi, Aung San Suu, 511

L'Ouverture, Toussaint, 223, 351–352
La Francophonie, 553
Laissez faire, 137, 257, 303, 412
  imperialism, 341–345
Laporte, Pierre, 566
Lassalle, Ferdinand, 302
Lateran Accords, 418
Latvia, 498
Lawrence, D.H., 444, 445
Le Tellier, Francois-Michel, 79
League of Nations, 401, 409, 411, 452, 477
LeCarre, John, 515
Leisure
  America, 431
  Nineteenth Century, 306–307
Lenin, V.I., 290, 314, 374, 385, 388–390, 419
Leo X (pope), 46
Leopold II (Austria), 187
Leopold II (Belgium), 335, 342–344
Levi-Strauss, Claude, 6
Liberalism, 261–262

Lincoln, Abraham, 354
Lindbergh, Charles, 417
Liszt, Franz, 280
Literary criticism, 534–535
Literature
  Eighteenth Century, 142–150, 157–165
  England, 48–49
  France, 48–49
  Germany, 48–49
  Nineteenth Century, 280–284, 325–327
  post-colonial, 547–548
  Seventeenth Century, 96–99
  Spain, 48–49
  Twentieth Century, 442–444, 515–516
  World War I, 395–398
Lithuania, 498
Locarno Pact, 408, 411
Locke, John, 16, 74, 76–77, 134, 142
Longfellow, Henry Wadsworth, 310
Lord Acton, 62
Lord Byron, 263, 280, 283–284
Lord Kelvin, 256
Louis Napoleon (France), 264
Louis Phillipe (France), 264
Louis XIII (France), 58, 77, 78
Louis XIV (France), 70, 77–80, 98–99, 137, 138, 153, 214
  art patron, 91
  Baroque art, 91, 92
  legacy of, 83
  wars of, 82–83
Louis XV (France), 134, 138, 174, 228–230
Louis XVI (France), 170, 171, 179, 180, 186, 200
  execution of, in French Revolution, 189
Louis XVIII (France), 170, 200, 259, 263
Lovelace, Richard, 98
Loyola, Ignatius, 28, 56
Luce, Henry R., 416–417
Lucretius, 142
Luddites, 17, 264, 265
Ludendorff, Erich, 385, 398
Luftwaffe, 453, 461, 463
Lully, Jean-Baptiste, 95–96
Luther, Martin, 5, 28, 50–54, 109
Luxembourg
  European Union, 556
  free-trade region, 495
  NATO, 502
Luxemburg, Rosa, 399

MacArthur, General Douglas, 485, 503
Macauley, Thomas, 325

Macedonia, 564
Machiavelli, Niccolo, 11, 28, 46–47
Maginot Line, 453, 460
Mahler, Gustav, 441
Mainwaring, George, 119
Malaspina, Alejandro, 227
Malay peninsula, new imperialism, 335
Mali, 106
Malthus, Thomas, 37, 257, 316
Manchu dynasty, 115, 337, 339, 362,
    364, 556–567
Mandela, Nelson, 511, 553, 566, 576
Mandeville, Bernard, 149
Manet, Edouard, 290, 321
Manhattan Project, 482
Maoism, 557
Marat, Jean-Paul, 146, 204
March Revolution of 1917, 374, 387,
    390, 391
Marconi, Guglielmo, 430
Marcuse, Herbert, 508, 510
Maria Theresa (Austria), 215
Marlborough, Duke of, 214
Marley, Bob, 550
Marlowe, Christopher, 48
Marriage
    age of, 255
    Eighteenth Century, 177
    Great Depression, 433, 435
    Industrial Revolution, 254
    Nineteenth Century, 308
    Renaissance, 35
    Seventeenth Century England, 88–89
    World War II, 482
Marshall Plan, 495–496
Martyn, Thomas J.C., 416–417
Marwick, Arthur, 5
Marx, Karl, 7, 16, 244, 250, 267–269,
    290, 313, 317
Marxism in Russia, 419
Marxist criticism, 535
Marxist-Leninist, 390
Mary (England), 58
Mary Queen of Scots, 58, 85
Masaryk, Thomas, 413
Mass media, 571–575
Matisse, Henri, 436, 439
Matteotti, Giacomo, 418
May, H. Mabel, 396
Maya, 124
Mayer, Arno, 480
Mazarin, Jacques, 78
Mazzini, Giuseppe, 272, 294–295
McCarthy, Joe, 516
McCrae, John, 381, 395
McLuhan, Marshall, 540, 571

McMahon, General Patrice, 301
Medici, 46
Mehmed II (Ottoman), 112
Mehta, Deepa, 552
Meiji Restoration, 335, 542
Mendelssohn, Felix, 280
Mennonites, 54
Mensheviks, 314
Mercantilism, 80
Mercier, L.S., 173
Mesmer, Friedrich Anton, 176
Messerschmitt, 463
Methodists, 142
Metternich. See von Metternich,
    Prince Klemens
Mexico
    independence, 332, 356
    Spanish exploration, 113–114
Michelangelo, 28, 46, 67, 204
Michener, James, 111
Middlemen, 248
Military spending, 376-377
Mill, John Stuart, 256, 290
Miller, Arthur, 515
Millet, Jean-Francois, 320
Milosevic, Slobodan, 565
Mines Act of 1842, 258
Minh, Ho Chi, 545
Mirabeau, 185
Miro, Joan, 439
Mitterand, Francois, 527
Modernization theory, 212
Moghul Empire, 225
    art, 227
Moliere, 98, 99
Monet, Claude, 290, 322
Monk, Thelonious, 533
Monnet, Jean, 556
Monopoly rights, 120
Monroe Doctrine, 358, 558
Monroe, James, 358
Montague, John, 159
Montcalm. See de Montcalm, General
    Louis Joseph, 217
Montenegro, 564
Montesquieu. See de Montesquieu
Montezuma, 120
Montgomery, General Bernard Law,
    473–474, 480
Moral economy, 247
Moravians, 54
More, Thomas, 28, 48
Morelos, Jose Maria, 358
Moro, Aldo, 527
Morroco, 545–546
Mortality in the Renaissance, 37
Mozambique, 336, 547–548

Mozart, Wolfgang Amadeus, 133, 157,
    160–161, 204
Mubarak, Hosni, 562
Multinational corporations, 16, 17
    globalization, 568–569
    imperialism, 568–569
Multiplier effect, 248, 249, 293
Munich Agreement, 450, 454, 455
Musgrave, Thea, 532
Music, 554
    Eighteenth Century, 156–157
    French Revolution, 203–205
    Industrial Revolution, 279
    Millennium, 532–534
    Nineteenth Century, 279–280
    Twentieth Century, 439–442
    World War I, 396
Muslim Brotherhood, 542
Muslims, 224
Mussolini, Benito, 407, 408, 413, 415,
    418, 451, 453, 455, 463, 472
Mutiny of 1857 (India), 340, 359
Mutiny on the Bounty, 231–232
Mwene Mutapa, 106
Mysticism, 50

NAFTA, 14
Naipaul, V.S., 548
Napoleon. See Bonaparte, Napoleon
Napoleon III (France). See Bonaparte,
    Louis Napoleon
Napoleonic Code, 198
Napoleonic government, 196
Napoleonic Wars, 198, 199, 246, 355
Nasser, Gamal Abdel, 544, 561
Nation-state, 291, 295–296
National Assembly of France, 180, 184, 185
National Convention, 203
National Socialist German Workers' Party.
    See Nazis
Nationalism, 261–262, 291, 414
    Africa, 360, 362
    Austria, 305
    England, 304
    Germany, 302, 304, 377
    human rights, 360
    Hungary, 305
    imperialism, 337
    India, 360, 361
    music, 280
    prior to World War I, 362–363
    Russia, 305
NATO, 499, 502
Natural selection, 316
Nazi-Soviet Non-Aggression Pact,
    455–456
Nazis, 408, 497

Germany, 418, 424–426
religion, 427
war crimes trials, 497
women, 429–430
Necker, Jacques, 179
Nehru, Jawaharlal, 542
Nelson, Admiral Lord, 199
Neo-Marxism, 508
Neocolonialism
China, 556–558
Latin America, 558
Netherlands
European Union, 556
free-trade region, 495
NATO, 501
Reformation, 63–64
trade, 64
New Deal, 411
New France, 80
New historicism, 535
New imperialism, 334–337
See also Africa; Asia; Burma; China;
East Indies; India; Indies; Indochina;
Malay peninsula; Singapore
New Poor Law, 244, 258
New wave, 534
New Zealand
beginning of World War I, 381
colonization, 359
prelude to World War II, 456
Newman, John Henry, 325
Newton, Sir Isaac, 72–73, 83
Nicaragua and American intervention,
559–560
Nicholas II (Russia), 313, 377, 379,
387, 419
Nietzsche, Friedrich, 282, 290, 315,
507–508
Nigeria, 336
Night of the Long Knives, 408, 426
Nightingale, Florence, 293
Nijinsky, Vaclav, 397
No-man's-land, 380
Nobel Prize, 290, 377, 411, 555
Normandy Invasion, 473–474
North American Free Trade Agreement
(NAFTA), 569
North Atlantic Treaty Organization.
See NATO
Norway
NATO, 502
Nazi Party, 461
World War II, 458, 459
Novel, 162–163, 444
November Revolution, 390
Nuclear bombs, 483–485
Nuremburg Laws, 408, 427–428

Nuremburg Trials/Tribunal, 481, 497

Oastler, Richard, 253, 258
October Crisis, 566
October Days, 184
Ogoni people, 575, 576
Oil spills, 518
Oil/Energy Crisis, 495, 518, 525–527
Okri, Ben, 548
OPEC, 525, 562
Opera, 157
Operation Barbarossa, 450, 463–466, 480
Operation Dynamo, 459
Operation Husky, 471
Operation Overlord, 450, 471–474
Operation Sea Lion, 461, 463
Opium Wars, 332, 335, 338, 543
Oratorios, 157
Organization for Economic Development
and Cooperation (OECD), 567
Organization of Petroleum Exporting
Countries. See OPEC
Orlando, Vittorio, 399
Ortega, Daniel, 560
Orthodox Church, 225
Orwell, George, 408
Ottoman Empire, 112, 113, 225, 262,
304, 400
agriculture, 225
Greece, 262–263
military, 225
World War I, 378
Owen, Robert, 266
Owen, Wilfred, 395
Oxfam, 555

Paglia, Camille, 530
Palestine, 561
Palestine Liberation Organization (PLO),
540, 561
Pan-African Movement, 360, 361
Pankhurst, Emmeline, 308
Papal bull/order, 51
Paraguay, independence, 332
Pardo, Dr. Arvido, 567
Paris Commune, 301
Paris Peace Conference, 399
Paris Peace Congress, 295
Parliamentary democracy, 499–500
Pascal, Blaise, 49
Patronage, 46–47, 90-91
Patton, General George S., 480
Paul III (pope), 54, 123
Paul V (pope), 71
Peace of Aix-la-Chapelle, 210, 215
Peace of Augsburg, 62
Peace of Nijmegen, 82

Peace of Prague of 1866, 290, 297
Peace of Utrecht, 82, 215
Peace of Westphalia, 63
Peacekeeping, 555
Pearl Harbour, 465, 466, 467, 468
Pearson, Lester B., 555, 561
Peasants' War, 28, 54
Peel, Sir Robert, 265
Perestroika, 528
Perry, Matthew, 542
Peru, independence, 357
Petain, Marshal Philippe, 384, 460
Peter I (Russia), 83
Peter the Great, 83–85
Peterloo Massacre, 244, 265
Philip II (Spain), 57, 58
Philip V (Spain), 215
Philippines, 545–546
Phony War, 458
Phu, Dien Bien, 545
Picasso, Pablo, 437, 441
Pickford, Mary, 431
Pilsudski, Marshal Joseph, 413
Pinochet, General Augusto, 559
Pissarro, Camille, 321
Pius IX (pope), 295, 314
Pius VII (pope), 197, 198
Pius XI (pope), 418
Pizarro, Francisco, 110, 114
Plague, 29, 30
Plains of Abraham, 216–217, 232
Planck, Max, 315
Plato, 41
Plekhanov, George, 387, 389
Plutarch, 7
Pocket boroughs, 265
Poe, Edgar Allan, 310
Pogodin, Mikhail, 84–85
Poincare, Raymond, 413
Pointillism, 323
Poison gas, 385
Poland, 394, 457, 498
communism, 562
invasion of, World War II, 457
prelude to World War II, 454–456
Polo, Marco, 105, 106, 228
Pompidou, Georges, 527
Poor Law Act, 258
Pope, Alexander, 133, 134, 143, 159
Population
England, 249, 251
Europe, 37, 249, 305
France, 249
Germany, 251
urbanization, 251
Poquelin, Jean-Baptiste. See Moliere
Portugal

dictatorship after World War II,   500
  economy after World War II,   506–507
  NATO,   502
Post-colonial era,   8, 9
Post-impressionists,   323
Postmodernism,   7–9, 535
Pot, Pol,   547
Potsdam Conference,   482–484
Pound, Ezra,   443
Poussin, Nicolas,   153
Power loom,   248
Prague Spring,   523
Pratt, Christopher and Mary,   531
Presley, Elvis,   533
Prester John,   109
Primogeniture,   203
Princip, Gavrilo,   305
Principle of utility,   257
Printing press,   43, 139
Prophet Muhammad,   224
Protestantism,   51
Proudhon, Pierre-Joseph,   266
Psychoanalysis,   440
Ptolemy,   105
Public Health Act,   259
Puccini, Giacomo,   290
Punk rock,   534
Purcell, Henry,   97
Purgatory,   33
Puritans,   54

Quadrant,   108
Quadruple Alliance,   260
Quakers,   54, 222
Quebec nationalism,   217
Queen Maria I (Portugal),   137
Queen Victoria (England),   303, 341, 379
Quesnay, Dr. Francois,   137, 228
Quisling, Vidkun,   459, 461
Qur'an,   224

Racism,   415, 478
  Germany,   424–428
Radar,   463
Rajasthani painting,   226–227
Raleigh, Sir Walter,   117
Ramsey, Admiral Bertram,   459
Rap music,   534
Rapallo Agreement,   409
Rape of Nanking,   466
Raphael,   43, 46
Rasputin,   387
Ravel, Maurice,   442
Ray, Satyajit,   552
Raynal, Guillaume-Thomas-Francois,
  222–223
Reagan, Ronald,   505

Realism,   319
Red Army,   419
Red Brigade,   527
Red Cross/Red Crescent,   555
Red October of 1917,   389, 390
Red Shirts,   294–295
Red Terror,   194
Reformation,   11, 27, 50
  demography,   37–38
  Eastern Europe,   64
  England,   58–59
  France,   57–58
  Germany,   62
  Italy,   59–62
  Netherlands,   63–64
  politics,   57–64
  religion,   31–34, 50
  Russia,   64–65
  social control,   57
  social hierarchy,   36
  Spain,   57
  start of,   50–54
  time line,   28
  Turkish Empire,   64–65
Reign of Terror,   134, 148, 170, 190–191
Reinsurance Treaty,   375
Religion,   19
  doctrine of purgatory,   33
  England,   303
  enlightenment,   141
  ethnic tensions in Yugosalvia,   564
  exploration,   123
  Fifteenth Century,   109
  France,   185
  French Revolution,   202, 203
  Germany,   302
  honour code,   34
  India,   339–341
  Japan,   116
  late medieval era,   29
  Nazis,   427
  Nineteenth Century,   314
  providence,   32–34
  purgatory,   33
  Reformation,   31–34, 50
  Renaissance,   36
  salvation,   32–34
  science,   71–73
  slavery,   222
  social community,   33
  social ethic,   33–34
  Victorian Age,   306
Remarque, Erich Maria,   392, 395, 396
Rembrandt,   94–96
Renaissance,   4, 11, 12, 27, 37, 152–153
  art,   42–45, 152–153
  demography,   37–38

family,   35
feudalism,   35–36
firearms,   39–40
fortresses,   39–40
honour code,   34
household,   35
intellectual life,   41–42
Italy,   46–47
justice,   40
marriage,   35
mortality,   37
patronage,   46–47
political bodies,   38–39
property,   35
providence,   32
Rome,   46–47
science,   49
social hierarchy,   35–36, 37
trade,   40
Renaissance Man,   44–45
Renoir, Auguste,   323, 441
Revolutionary Spring (1848),   271
Revolutionary War (U.S.),   5, 173, 179
Rhodes, Cecil,   317, 342
Rhodesia,   336
Ricardo, David,   16, 244, 257
Ricci, Matteo,   228
Richardson, Samuel,   165
Riqueti, Honore Gabriel,   185
Roaring Twenties,   429–430
Robertson, William,   234
Robespierre,   141, 146, 170, 185–187,
  191, 193, 194, 203, 204
Rock and roll,   533
Rococo,   154, 155, 156
Rodin, Auguste,   290, 438–439
Rohm, Ernst,   426
Roland, Madame,   192, 193
Roma,   19–20, 529
Roman Empire,   38
Romania,   498, 563
Romanov dynasty, fall of,   419
Romanticism,   273, 276–277
Rommel, Erwin,   471, 474, 480
Roosevelt, Franklin Delano,   412, 417,
  450, 468, 471–475, 496, 500
Roosevelt, Theodore,   363
Rorem, Ned,   532
Rosetta Stone,   196
Rostow, Walt Whitman,   212, 247
Rotten boroughs,   265
Roundheads,   86
Rousseau, Jean-Jacques,   75, 134, 145,
  146, 171, 176, 203, 280, 356
Royal Adventurers of England,   118
Royal African Company,   118
Royal Air Force,   460, 461

Rubens, Peter Paul,   153
Rubinstein, Nikolay,   278
Rudolf II (Germany),   62
Rushdie, Salman,   548
Russell, Lord John,   265
Russia,   83
    absolutism,   83–85
    agriculture, in 18th Century,   152
    art of the Twentieth Century,   437
    beginning of World War I,   379–380
    civil war,   419
    communism,   419
    democracy,   529
    industrialization,   299, 387
    industry, in 18th Century,   152
    invasion of, during World War II,
    464–465
    Marxism,   419
    military spending,   377
    nationalism,   305
    prior to World War I,   375, 379
    Reformation,   64–65
    revolution of 1905,   314
    socialism,   314–315
    universal male suffrage,   300
    World War I,   386
    World War II,   458, 459, 468–469
Russian Revolution,   386–390
Russo-Japanese War,   332, 361–362, 374,
    378, 387, 542
Russo-Turkish War of 1787-1792,   217
Ruth, Babe,   431

Sack of Rome,   62
Sadat, Anwar,   562
Sadino, Augusto Cesar,   560
Sadler, Michael,   258
Safavid Empire,   225
Sahkarov, Andrei,   522
Saint Augustine,   123
Saint Bartholomew's Massacre,   28, 58
Saint Monday,   253
Salazar, Antonio,   500
Salon,   174
Sandanistas,   560
Saro-Wiwa, Ken,   575, 576
Sartre, Jean Paul,   282, 507–508, 510
Sassoon, Siegfried,   395
Savonarola,   28, 46
Scandinavia, socialism after
    World War II,   500
Schonberg, Arnold,   532
School of Mathematics and Navigation,   84
Schubert, Franz Peter,   157
Schumacher, E.F.,   518, 519
Schumann, Robert,   280
Schutzstaffel,   426

Science,   17, 49, 315–316
Scientific method,   73–74
Scientific Revolution,   41, 71–73
Scopes, John T.,   317
Scorched earth policy,   465
Second Republic,   292
Segregation,   354–355
Senegal, colonization,   359
Sepoys,   340
September Laws,   264
September Massacres,   187
Serbia,   378, 564
    prior to World War I,   379
Servandoni, Giovanni,   158
Seurat, Georges,   323
Seven Years' War,   140, 210, 215–216
Seyss-Inquart, Arthur,   452
Shaka,   359
Shakespeare, William,   36, 42, 48
Shankar, Ravi,   549
Sharon, Ariel,   562
Sharpe, Sam,   350
Shaw, George Bernard,   313, 327, 442
Shelley, Mary,   5
Shelley, Percy Bysshe,   284
Shiro, Azuma,   466
Sholokhov, Mikhail,   515
Shute, Nevil,   515
Sicily,   470–472
Sieyes, Emmanuel Joseph,   180, 182, 223
Simpson, Wallis Warfield,   417
Singapore, new imperialism,   334
Sino-Japanese Wars,   465
Sino-Russian Treaty of 1689,   228
Sitzkreig,   380
Six-Day War,   561
Skepticism,   49
Slavery,   104, 170, 210, 332, 347
    abolished in British Empire,   332
    abolition in France,   210, 223
    abolition of,   220, 222, 349–351
    Africa,   116, 220
    Amerindian,   123, 124
    becoming a slave,   220
    British West Indies,   351–352
    Cape of Good Hope,   221–222
    France,   170, 210
    human rights,   222–223
    Jamaica,   352
    profit from,   221
    religion,   222
    revolt in Haiti,   351–352
    theological basis,   124
    United States,   352–353
    West Indies,   351–353
Slovenia,   564
Smith, Adam,   16, 134, 146–147, 213,

    229, 245, 257, 258
Smith, James,   252
Social Darwinism,   317
Social hierarchy/control/system
    China,   228
    India,   340
    Reformation,   36, 57
    Renaissance,   35–36, 37
Social organization/structure/classes/cul-
    ture,   21
    Africa,   219
    Europe, after World War II,   506–507
    impact of World War II,   483–484
    Nineteenth Century,   306–308
    Seventeenth Century England,   88
    World War II,   483–484
Socialism,   312–315
    See also Communism
    England,   313
    England, after World War II,   500
    France,   313
    Germany,   302, 313
    Italy, after World War II,   500
    Nineteenth Century,   312–315
    origins of,   266
    Russia,   314–315
    utopian,   266
Society of Friends of the Blacks,   148, 223
Society of Jesus,   56
Solzhenitsyn, Alexander,   419, 515, 522
Songhay,   106
Sorel, Georges,   314
South Africa,   336, 349, 350, 359, 362, 381
South East Asia Treaty Organization
    (SEATO),   503
Sovereignty movement (Quebec),   217
Soviet Bloc,   523
Soviet Union
    collapse of,   562–565
    Great Depression,   412
    Great Purge,   422–424
    industrial revolution,   421
    life under Stalin,   422–423
    women,   422
Space program,   516
Spain
    art of the Twentieth Century,   437
    communism after World War II,   500
    constitution,   263
    dictatorship after World War II,   500
    Industrial Revolution,   247
    literature,   48–49
    nationalism,   262
    NATO,   502
    politics,   57
    Reformation,   57
Spanish Armada,   58

Spanish Civil War, 408, 437, 450, 453
Spanish-American War, 332, 355, 361
Speer, Albert, 480
Spencer, Herbert, 317
Spinning jenny, 248
Spitfire, 463
Sprezzatura, 46
Sputnik, 494
Sri Lanka, 547
Stagflation, 526
Stalin, Joseph, 407, 408, 417, 421, 450,
    455, 456, 464, 465, 468, 473, 475, 482,
    494, 495, 500, 519, 522
Star Wars defence system (SDI), 505
Steele, Richard, 164
Stein, S.J., 213
Storm troopers, 424
Stout, William, 88
Strategic Arms Limitation Treaty, 505
Strategic bombing, 472
Stravinsky, Igor, 397
Stresemann, Gustav, 409, 411
Structural Adjustment Programmes, 569
Sturmabteilung, 424
Submarine, 394
Sudan, 336, 359
Sudetenland, 454
Suez, 336
Suez Canal, 332
Suez Crisis, 494, 540, 555, 561
Suffrage. See Universal male suffrage;
    Universal suffrage; Voting
Suffragettes, 312
Suleiman I (Ottoman), 112
Suleiman the Magnificent (Turkey), 64
Sultan Mohammed II, 224
Summit of the Americas, 576
Sun King. See Louis XIV
Suzuki, Kantaro, 484
Sweden, 527
Swift, Jonathan, 133, 134, 143, 159, 163,
    164, 210
Sykes-Picot Agreement, 561
Symbolism, 435

Tacitus, 42
Tainos, 112
Taiping Rebellion, 339, 359
Talon, Jean, 80
Tariffs and the European Economic
    Community (EEC), 496
Tchaikovsky, Pyotr Ilyich, 244, 278
Technology, 17
    Eighteenth Century, 175
    Fifteenth Century, 106, 108
    Industrial Revolution, 245
    music, 279

Nineteenth Century, 307
    science, 175
    society, 248–249
    Twentieth Century, 516–519
    World War II, 457
Teheran Conference, 477
Templars, 140
Tennis Court Oath, 170, 180, 190
Tennyson, Alfred Lord, 325
Tenochtitlan, 113, 114
Terrestrial Paradise, 107
Terror bombing, 457
Terror. *See* Reign of Terror
Terrorism, 16, 540
    roots of, 565–566
    war on, 20–21
Tetzel, Johann, 52
Textile industry
    England, 248–249
    Industrial Revolution, 248–249
Thatcher, Margaret, 527
Theory of relativity, 315
Thermidoreans, 195
Third Reich, 318, 426–428, 461, 477, 480
    life in, 427
    victims of, 428–429
Third Republic (France), 300, 301
Thirty Years War, 58, 62, 69, 70
Thomson, William, 256
Tilak, B.G., 360
Time Magazine, 416–417
Time of Troubles (Russia), 64
Tito, 498, 540, 564
Tojo, Hideki, 466, 467
Total war, 381, 457, 472
Totalitarianism, 423
Toure, Ali Farka, 550
Townsend, Charles, 136
Trade, 25, 567
    Africa, 219, 233–234
    agriculture, 121–122
    America, 233–234
    barriers, reduction, 569
    China, 229–230, 231
    Eighteeneth Century, 233–234
    global, 567
    India, 226
    Netherlands, 64
    reduction of barriers, 569
    Renaissance, 40
    structural reforms, 569
Trade unions, 309–312
Trading companies, 119
Transportation
    Industrial Revolution, 247
    Nineteenth Century, 307–308
    Seventeenth Century, 87

Treaty of Brest-Litovsk, 391
Treaty of Campo Formio, 196
Treaty of Fontainebleau, 200
Treaty of Frankfurt, 298
Treaty of Jassy, 218
Treaty of Karlowitz, 215
Treaty of Kutchuk-Kainardji, 217
Treaty of Lodi (1434), 5
Treaty of London, 381
Treaty of Maastricht, 556
Treaty of Nanking, 332, 338
Treaty of Paris, 210, 217, 259
Treaty of Pressburg, 199
Treaty of Rome, 556
Treaty of Saint-Germain, 400
Treaty of Tordesillas, 104, 118
Treaty of Utrecht, 70, 210
Treaty of Versailles, 374, 399, 401,
    403, 409
Treaty of Westphalia, 69, 465
Tribute system, 121
Tripartite Pact, 463, 465, 467
Triple Alliance, 374, 375, 381
Triple Entente, 374, 375, 381
Trotsky, Leon, 389, 419, 420, 423
Truman, Harry S., 482, 484, 500,
    501, 503
Tull, Jethro, 134, 136
Tunisia, 545–546
Turkey
    human rights, 542
    NATO, 502
Turkish Empire in the Reformation,
    64–65
Turner, Frederick Jackson, 7
Turner, John, 277
Turner, Nat, 353
Two Ocean Naval Expansion Act, 467
Typhus, 29

Uganda, 336, 546
Ukraine, 391
Ulyanov, Alexander Ilich, 386
Ulyanov, Vladimir Ilich. *See* Lenin, V.I.
Underground Railway, 353
Unemployment in the Great
    Depression, 412
Union of Soviet Socialist Republics, 391,
    498–499
    collapse of, 528–529, 562–565
    communism, post-World War II, 519
    ethnic tension after break-up,
    563–565
    freedom in, 519
    secret police, 519
United East India Company, 119
United Fruit Company, 559

United Nations, 494, 496, 542, 553
  founding of, 477
  Security Council, 477, 496
United Nations Children's Fund, 555
United Nations Relief and Rehabilitation
  Agency, 555
United States
  abolition of slavery, 350–351
  constitution, 5, 142
  culture, 514–516
  Eighteenth Century, 247–248
  emancipation, 354–355
  entry into World War II, 468–469
  Great Depression, 412
  intervention in Latin America,
    559–560
  involvement in Vietnam, 504
  Middle East, and the, 559–560
  NATO, 502
  prelude to World War II, 451–456
  slavery, 352–353
  Vietnam War, 504
  World War I, 385–386
Universal Declaration of Human Rights,
  512–513, 540, 543
Universal male suffrage. *See also* Voting
  Austria, 300
  democracy, 300
  England, 265, 300, 303, 309
  France, 292, 300
  Germany, 300
  Russia, 300
Universal suffrage, 261–262
  See also Voting
  England, 265, 309–312
  feminist movements, 308–312
  France, 271
Utilitarianism, 257–258

Valentino, Rudolph, 431
van Beethoven, Ludwig, 157
van Gogh, Vincent, 325
van Mander, Karel, 92
van Rijn, Rembrandt, 94–95
Vancouver, George, 227
Varese, Edgard, 534
Varley, Frederick H., 396
VE Day, 450, 478
Velvet Revolution, 563
Venezuela, independence, 332, 358
Verdun, 381, 384
Versailles, 80–81, 153
  gardens, 81
  Hall of Mirrors, 80
  life at, 82
Vertical integration, 307–308
Vesalius, Andreas, 73

Vichy France, 460
Vico, Giambattista, 11, 12
Victor Emmanuel II (Italy), 295
Victor Emmanuel III (Italy), 415,
  418, 472
Victorian Age, 306
Vienna Treaty, 200
Vietnam
  American involvement in, 503, 504
  American withdrawal, 547
  French occupation, 544–545
Vietnam War, 494
Villa, Pancho, 363
Vimy Ridge, 392–393
VJ Day, 450, 484
Voltaire, 134, 136, 141, 143–144, 149,
  151, 162, 171, 174, 176, 217, 228, 231,
  234, 280, 356
von Beethoven, Ludwig, 161, 170,
  204–205
von Berchtold, Leopold, 378
von Bismarck, Count Otto, 291,
  296–297, 300, 302, 336, 374–376
von Goethe, Wolfgang, 280
von Herder, Johann Gottfried, 148
von Hindenburg, Paul, 425, 426
von Kluge, Field Marshal, 474
von Liebniz, Gottfried, 150, 228
von Metternich, Prince Klemens, 260,
  261, 262
von Moltke, Helmuth, 297
von Papen, Franz, 425
von Ranke, Leopold, 365
von Schiller, Johann, 205
von Schlieffen, General Alfred, 376
von Schuschnigg, Kurt, 451, 452
von Stauffenberg, Colonel, Claus, 474
Voting, 261–262
  democracy, 300
  England, 265, 303, 308
  feminist movements, 308–312
  France, 271, 292
  French Revolution, 186
  Germany, 425

Wagner, Richard, 280, 315
Walcott, Derek, 548
Walesa, Lech, 562
Wallerstein, Immanuel, 118
Walpole, Robert, 157
Walters, Bishop Alexander, 361
War crimes, 565
War Measures Act, 16
War of Devolution, 82
War of the Austrian Succession, 158, 215
War of the First Coalition, 187
War of the Spanish Succession, 82, 155

War on Terrorism, 494
Warhol, Andy, 532
Wars of Religion, 58
Warsaw Pact, 494, 502
Washington, George, 173
Watergate, 494
Watson, James, 518
Watteau, Antoine, 155–156, 230
Weapons of mass destruction, 457
Webb, Sidney and Beatrice, 313
Weber, Max, 49, 290, 318
Weimar Republic, 402, 425, 429
Welfare state
  England, 527
  re-evaluation of, in 1980s, 527
  Sweden, 527
Welfare State (European), 506–507
Wellesley, Arthur, 200
Wellington, Duke of, 200
Wesley, John, 142
West Africa, 359
  colonization, 359
West Indies
  abolition of slavery, 350–353
  slavery, 350–352
White Terror, 194
Wick-Schumann, Clara, 280
Wilhelm I (Germany), 374
Wilhelm I (Prussia), 297, 298
Wilhelm II (Germany), 302, 375,
  379, 398
William IV (England), 265
William of Orange, 64, 70, 86
William the Conqueror, 5
Williams, Henry Sylvester, 360
Wilson, Woodrow, 385, 391, 398,
  399, 400
Winter King, 63
Witte, Sergei, 314, 387
Wolf, Naomi, 530
Wolfe, General James, 216–217
Women, 18
  America, post-World War I, 432–433
  Eighteenth Century, 177
  French Revolution, 192–193
  Great Depression, 433
  Industrial Revolution, 254–255
  Millenium, 530
  Nazis, 429–430
  Nineteenth Century, 308–312
  Soviet Union, 422
  Twentieth Century, 530
  World War I, 393–394
  World War II, 483
Women's Social and Political Union
  (WSPU), 308
Woodstock, 534

Woodsworth, J.S., 456
Woolf, Virginia, 327, 444, 445
Wordsworth, William, 259, 276, 281–282
World Bank, 14, 477, 494, 495, 567, 569
World Health Organization, 555
World music, 548–550
World Population Fund, 555
World Trade Center, 540
World Trade Organization (WTO), 526, 540, 567, 569, 577
World War I, 373, 374
    American entry into, 385
    art, 395–398
    Austria, 378
    beginnings of, 379–384
    causes of, 375
    consequences of, 399–403
    economic system, 393–394, 402–403
    end of, 396–399
    last days of, 392
    leadership, 384–386
    literature, 395–398
    military strategy, 384
    music, 396
    origins, 304
    Ottoman Empire, 378
    outbreak, 378
    results of, 403
    Russia, 386

Russian Revolution, 309
    social impact of, 392–394
    United States, 385–386
    women, 393–394
World War II, 373, 449, 451
    American entry into, 468–469
    birth rate, 482
    D-Day, 473–476
    death toll, 479
    defeat of Germany, 475–476
    Dieppe, 470–471
    dispute regarding strategy, 469–470
    employment, 482
    fall of France, 459
    family, 484
    Finland, 458
    invasion of Sicily, 471–472
    Japan, 482–483
    marriage, 482
    Normandy invasion, 473–475
    nuclear bombs, 482–484
    Operation Overlord, 472–475
    Pacific theatre, 482–483
    phony war, 458
    Russia, 458–459
    social organization, 481–482
    technology, 457
    women, 482
Wycherley, William, 96
Wyeth, Andrew, 531

Xavier, St. Francis, 116

Yalta Agreement, 494, 500
Yalta Conference, 476, 497
Yamamoto, Admiral Isoroku, 467
Yat-sen, Dr. Sun, 364, 557
Yeats, William Butler, 443, 444
Yeltsin, Boris, 494, 529, 530
Yevtushenko, Yevgeny, 522
Yom Kippur War, 540, 562
Young Plan, 411
Young, Owen D., 411
Youth Revolts in France, 510–511
Yugoslavia, prelude to World War II, 454–456, 5648

Zaire, 545–546
Zambia, 336
Zapatista movement, 363
Zedong, Mao, 501, 540, 545, 557, 558
Zhukov, General Georgy, 466
Zimbabwe, 336
Zinsser, Judith, 174
Zola, Emile, 326
Zollverein, 249, 296
Zulus, 359

Credits

Photo Credits

l=left; r=right; t=top; c=centre; b=bottom

2 © David & Peter Turnley/CORBIS/MAGMA; 4 Erich Lessing/Art Resource, NY; 6 Staatliche Museen, Berlin, Germany/Bridgeman Art Library; 8 Ron Chapple/FPG International/Getty Images; 10 © EVERETT COLLECTION/MAGMA; 12 The Granger Collection, New York; 13 Shaney Komulainen/CP Picture Archive; 15 Dario Lopez-Mills/CP Picture Archive; 17 CP Picture Archive; 18 © Wally NcNamee/CORBIS/MAGMA; 20 Paula Bronstein/Stone/Getty Images; 21 © David G. Houser/CORBIS/MAGMA; 24 Scala/Art Resource, NY; 26 Hulton Archive/Getty Images; 29 © Historical Pictures Archive/CORBIS/MAGMA; 30 t Hulton Archive/Getty Images, br © Historical Pictures Archive/CORBIS/MAGMA; 31 © David Lees/CORBIS/MAGMA; 32 Erich Lessing/Art Resource, NY; 33 Museum of Fine Arts, Houston, Texas, USA, Museum purchase with funds from The Brown Foundation, Inc./Bridgeman Art Library; 34 Scala/Art Resource, NY; 37 © Archivo Iconografico, S.A./CORBIS/MAGMA; 39 tl Scala/Art Resource, NY, b © Steve Raymer/CORBIS/MAGMA; 40 Hulton Archive/Getty Images; 42 © David Lees/CORBIS/MAGMA; 43 Art Resource, NY; 44 tl Alinari/Art Resource, NY, br Scala/Art Resource, NY; 45 Art Resource, NY; 47 Alinari/Art Resource, NY; 49 Erich Lessing/Art Resource, NY; 52 Erich Lessing/Art Resource, NY; 55 Scala/Art Resource, NY; 60 Scala/Art Resource, NY; 67 Scala/Art Resource, NY; 68 © Archivo Iconografico, S.A./CORBIS/MAGMA; 69 British Library, London, UK/Bridgeman Art Library; 72 © Bettmann/CORBIS/MAGMA; 74 Hulton Archive/Getty Images; 75 l © Archivo Iconografico, S.A./CORBIS/MAGMA, r © Bettmann/CORBIS/MAGMA; 78 Réunion des Musées Nationaux/Art Resource, NY; 79 © Gianni Dagli Orti/CORBIS/MAGMA; 81 © Archivo Iconografico, S.A./CORBIS/MAGMA; 83 © Archivo Iconografico, S.A./CORBIS/MAGMA; 84 © Steve Raymer/CORBIS/MAGMA; 86 Hulton Archive/Getty Images; 87 Hulton Archive/Getty Images; 89 © CORBIS/MAGMA; 90-91 Scala/Art Resource, NY; 92 Both Alinari/Art Resource, NY; 93-94 Scala/Art Resource, NY; 95 tl Erich Lessing/Art Resource, NY, b Bridgeman Art Library; 97 © Leonard de Selva/CORBIS/MAGMA; 98 © Gianni Dagli Orti/CORBIS/MAGMA; 102 Scala/Art Resource, NY; 105 © Archivo Iconografico, S.A./CORBIS/MAGMA; 106 Giraudon/Art Resource, NY; 107 © CORBIS/MAGMA; 108 © Michael Freeman/CORBIS/MAGMA; 110 © CORBIS/MAGMA; 111 © Archivo Iconografico, S.A./CORBIS/MAGMA; 113 Scala/Art Resource, NY; 115 © CORBIS/MAGMA; 117 © Bettmann/CORBIS/MAGMA; 123 © Bettmann/CORBIS/MAGMA; 125 The Stapleton Collection/Bridgeman Art Library; 127 Giraudon/Art Resource, NY; 130 Victoria and Albert Museum/Art Resource, NY; 132 Giraudon/Art Resource, NY; 135 Erich Lessing/Art Resource, NY; 140 The Pierpont Morgan Library/Art Resource, NY; 142 © Joseph Sohm/ChromoSohm Inc; 143 Scala/Art Resource, NY; 145 Courtesy of Dan Bowyer; 149 Private Collection/Bridgeman Art Library; 152 Scala/Art Resource, NY; 153 l Scala/Art Resource, NY. r Art Resource, NY; 154 Blenheim Palace, Oxfordshire, UK/Bridgeman Art Library; 155 tr Erich Lessing/Art Resource, NY, b Réunion des Musées Nationaux/Art Resource, NY; 156 l Erich Lessing/Art Resource, NY, r Réunion des Musées Nationaux/Art Resource, NY; 158 Hulton Archive/Getty Images; 160 Scala/Art Resource, NY; 164 Philip Mould, Historical Portraits Ltd, London, UK/Bridgeman Art Library; 168 Giraudon/Art Resource, NY; 171 Chris Beetles Ltd. London, UK/Bridgeman Art Library; 172 Giraudon/Art Resource, NY; 175 Louvre, Paris, France/Peter Willi/Bridgeman Art Library; 178 Metropolitan Museum of Art, New York, NY; 181 t Giraudon/Art Resource, NY, bl © CORBIS/MAGMA; 184 Giraudon/Art Resource, NY; 185 Musée de la Ville de Paris, Musée Carnavalet, Paris, France/Bridgeman Art Library; 189 © Bettmann/CORBIS/MAGMA; 190 Musée Carnavalet, Paris, France/Giraudon-Bridgeman Art Library; 191 Giraudon/Art Resource, NY; 192 Private Collection/Bridgeman Art Library; 193 Musée des Beaux-Arts, Quimper, France/Giraudon-Bridgeman Art Library; 198 Erich Lessing/Art Resource, NY; 199 © Bettmann/CORBIS/MAGMA; 200 Giraudon/Art Resource,

NY; 201 © Gianni Dagli Orti/CORBIS/MAGMA; 202 The Granger Collection, New York; 203 Réunion des Musées Nationaux/Art Resource, NY; 204 Réunion des Musées Nationaux/Art Resource, NY; 205 Erich Lessing/Art Resource, NY; 208 Aldo Tutino/Art Resource, NY; 218 The Granger Collection, New York; 220, 223 © Bettmann/CORBIS/MAGMA; 224 tl Art Resource, NY; 225 Werner Forman/Art Resource, NY; 227 tl Art Resource, NY, br Giraudon/Art Resource, NY; 230 Bonhams, London, UK/Bridgeman Art Library; 231-232 Erich Lessing/Art Resource, NY; 240 National Gallery of Scotland, Edinburgh, Scotland/Bridgeman Art Library; 242 The Granger Collection, New York; 251 Hulton Archive/Getty Images; 254, 260, 268, 272 Hulton Archive/Getty Images; 273 Louvre, Paris, France/Bridgeman Art Library; 274-276 The Granger Collection, New York; 277 tl Victoria and Albert Museum/Art Resource, NY, b The Granger Collection, New York; 278 Hulton Archive/Getty Images; 279 Manchester City Art Galleries, UK/Bridgeman Art Library; 281 The Pierpont Morgan Library/Art Resource, NY; 283-284 Hulton Archive/Getty Images; 288 © Leonard de Selva/CORBIS/MAGMA; 294 © Bettmann/CORBIS/MAGMA; 298 © Gianni Dagli Orti/CORBIS/MAGMA; 309 © CORBIS/MAGMA; 310, 312 Hulton Archive/Getty Images; 316 © Stapleton Collection/CORBIS/MAGMA; 319-322 The Granger Collection, New York; 323 tl Musée Marmottan, Paris, France/Giraudon-Bridgeman Art Library, b Private Collection/Bridgeman Art Library; 324 tl Scala/Art Resource, NY, b Musée d'Orsay, Paris, France/Lauros-Giraudon-Bridgeman Art Library; 326 Erich Lessing/Art Resource, NY; 327 Hulton Archive/Getty Images; 329 The Granger Collection, New York; 332 Hermitage, St. Petersburg, Russia/Bridgeman Art Library; 337-338, 340, 342, 345-347, 351, 355, 356 Hulton Archive/Getty Images; 358 Palacio National, Mexico City, Mexico/Index/Bridgeman Art Library; 359, 361, 363, 365 Hulton Archive/Getty Images; 374 Scala/Art Resource, NY; 375 © CORBIS/MAGMA; 376 NAC/C-97752; 381 © Bettmann/CORBIS/MAGMA; 385 William Rider-Rider-D.N.D./NAC/PA-2156; 386 © CORBIS/MAGMA; 388, 392-393 Hulton Archive/Getty Images;394 © CORBIS/MAGMA; 395 © Christel Gerstenberg/CORBIS/MAGMA; 397 Hulton Archive/Getty Images; 398 NAC/PA-1305; 400 l Canadian War Museum/8409, r Canadian War Museum/8911; 401, 410, 413 Hulton Archive/Getty Images; 414 R. Simmons/NAC/C-242; 415 © Bettmann/ CORBIS/MAGMA; 416 © Hulton-Deutsch Collection/CORBIS/MAGMA; 419 Hulton Archive/Getty Images; 420 Time Pix; 421 Time Pix; 422, 422, 429 Hulton Archive/Getty Images; 431 US Holocaust Memorial Museum/86838; 433 © Hulton-Deutsch Collection; 434 Hulton Archive/Getty Images; 435 CP Picture Archive; 437 © Bettmann/CORBIS/MAGMA; 438 Hulton Archive/Getty Images; 439 Erich Lessing/Art Resource, NY; 440 Both Art Resource, NY; 441 tr CNAC/MNAM/Dist. Réunion des Musées Nationaux/Art Resource, NY, b John Bigelow Taylor/Art Resource, NY; 442 Cameraphoto/Art Resource, NY; 443 t Tate Gallery, London/Art Resource, NY, b Scala/Art Resource, NY; 444 CP Picture Archive; 445 bl Erich Lessing/Art Resource, NY; 448 © Hulton-Deutsch Collection/CORBIS/MAGMA; 452 © Bettmann/CORBIS/MAGMA; 455 © Hulton-Deutsch Collection/CORBIS/MAGMA; 456-459, 461 Hulton Archive/Getty Images; 463 NAC/C-87518; 466 © Bettmann/CORBIS/MAGMA; 467 NAC/PA-114781; 471 © Schenectady Museum/Hall of Electrical History Foundation/CORBIS/MAGMA; 473 © CORBIS/MAGMA; 476 Jack H. Smith/NAC/PA163671; 479-480 Hulton Archive/Getty Images; 482 tl Hulton Archive/Getty Images, br CP Picture Archive; 483 CP Picture Archive; 484-485 Hulton Archive/Getty Images; 488 CP Picture Archive; 489 Courtesy of Garfield Newman; 494 © Bill Ross/CORBIS/MAGMA; 496 © David & Peter Turnley/CORBIS/MAGMA; 499, 506 © Bettmann/CORBIS/MAGMA; 507 NAC/PA-114888; 509, 511, 513-514, 518 Hulton Archive/Getty Images; 519 l Hulton Archive/Getty Images, r © EVERETT COLLECTION/MAGMA; 521, 524 Hulton Archive/Getty Images; 525 © Underwood & Underwood/CORBIS/MAGMA; 527, 530 Hulton Archive/Getty Images; 535 tl Giraudon/Art Resource, NY, b CNAC/MNAM/Dist. Réunion des Musées Nationaux/Art Resource, NY; 538 Andrew Medichini/CP Picture Archive; 541 The Andy Warhol Foundation, Inc./Art Resource, NY; 542 Doug Ball/CP Picture Archive; 546 © Paul Almasy/CORBIS/MAGMA; 549 © Steve Raymer/CORBIS/MAGMA; 550-551 Hulton Archive/Getty Images; 552 Robert Wheeler/Stone/Getty Images; 554

Hulton Archive/Getty Images; **555** © EVERETT COLLEC-TION/MAGMA; **557** © David & Peter Turnley/CORBIS/MAGMA; **558** Kevin Frayer/CP Picture Archive; **559** © Liba Taylor/CORBIS/MAGMA; **561** © Bettmann/CORBIS/MAGMA; **562** © Macduff Everton/COR-BIS/MAGMA; **563** CP Picture Archive; **566** Hulton Archive/Getty Images; **568** John Gaps III/CP Picture Archive; **570** Tom Hanson/CP Picture Archive; **572** © Sergio Dorantes/CORBIS/MAGMA; **573** © Liba Taylor/CORBIS/MAGMA; **576** © AFP/CORBIS/MAGMA; **579** CP Picture Archive; **586** © David & Peter Turnley/CORBIS/MAGMA; **590** © CORBIS/MAGMA

Illustration Credits

59 From *The West in the World*, © 2001, McGraw-Hill Limited; **109** *From IMPACT: Western Civilization and the Wider World*, © 1996, McGraw-Hill Ryerson Limited. All Rights Reserved; **122** From *The West in the World*, © 2001, McGraw-Hill Ryerson Limited; **138, 196-197, 211, 214, 219, 221, 224, 245** From *IMPACT: Western Civilization and the Wider World*, © 1996, McGraw-Hill Ryerson Limited. All Rights Reserved; **246** From *Industry and Empire*, by Hobawm, Penguin Books, 1969; **270, 291, 293, 296, 335-336, 357, 359** From *IMPACT: Western Civilization and the Wider World*, © 1996, McGraw-Hill Ryerson Limited. All Rights Reserved; **380** www.go.hrw.com/venus_images/0325MC22.gif; **384, 390, 402, 418, 464** From *IMPACT: Western Civilization and the Wider World*, © 1996, McGraw-Hill Ryerson Limited. All Rights Reserved; **468** *The Penguin Historical Atlas of the Third Reich*, Penguin Books, © 1996; **478** © Bettmann/CORBIS/MAGMA; **502, 528, 567, 574** From *IMPACT: Western Civilization and the Wider World*, © 1996, McGraw-Hill Ryerson Limited. All Rights Reserved

Text Credits

52 www.iclnet.org/pub/resources/text/wittenberg/luther/web/ninetyfive.html; **111** *Caribbean* by James Michener, New York: Fawcett Crest Books, 1989; **147** *Immanuel Kant's Critique of Pure Reason*, translated by Norman Kemp Smith, New York: St. Martin's Press, 1965; **149-150** *Studies on Voltaire: with Some Unpublished Papers of Madame du Chatelet* by O. Wade, Princeton: Princeton University Press, 1947; **152** *A Source Book for Russian History, Vol. 2*, translated by G. Vernadsky, New Haven: Yale University Press, 1972; **171** *The Complete Tales of the Brothers Grimm*, translated by Jack Zipes, New York: Bantam Books, 1987; **174** *A History of Their Own Vol. I.*, by Bonnie Anderson, New York: HarperCollins, 1988; **192-193** *The Memoirs of Madame Roland*, translated and edited by Evelyn Shuckburgh, London: Barrie & Jenkins, 1989; **213, 229** *ReOrient: Global Economy in the Asian Age* by André Gunder Frank, Berkeley: University of California Press, 1998; **367** www.ucl.ac.uk/history/course/europe/weeks/ranke.htm; **399** *All Quiet on the Western Front "Im Westen Nichts Neues,"* by Erich Maria Remarque, Ullstein A.G., 1928; **447** "The Lovesong of J. Alfred Prufrock" in T. S. Eliot, *The Complete Poems and Plays 1909-1950*, New York: Harcourt, Brace & World, 1971; **453** *Dark Soliloquy, Selected Poems of Gertrud Kolmar*, translated by Henry A. Smith, New York, 1975; **470** http://news.bbc.co.uk/hi/english/world/newsid_223000/223038.stm; **491** *Complete Poems* by Randall Jarrell, New York: Farrar, Strauss & Giroux, 1970; **516-517** http://www.un.org/rights/50/decla.htm; **576** *Necessary Illusions: Thought Control in Democratic Societies* by Noam Chomsky, Montréal: CBC Enterprises, 1989; **576-577** *Manufacturing Consent: The Political Economy of the Mass Media*, Edward S. Herman and Noam Chomsky, Mark Achbar, ed, New York: Pantheon Books, 1988.